M000105056

THE FUNDAMENTALS OF
COUNTERTERRORISM LAW

EDITED BY LYNNE ZUSMAN

Defending Liberty
Pursuing Justice

Cover design by Tony Nuccio/ABA Publishing

The materials contained herein represent the opinions and views of the authors and/or the editors, and should not be construed to be the views or opinions of the law firms or companies with whom such persons are in partnership with, associated with, or employed by, nor of the Section of Administrative Law and Regulatory Practice or of the American Bar Association unless adopted pursuant to the bylaws of the Association.

Nothing contained in this book is to be considered as the rendering of legal advice for specific cases, and readers are responsible for obtaining such advice from their own legal counsel. This book and any forms and agreements herein are intended for educational and informational purposes only.

Printed in the United States of America.

Library of Congress Cataloging-in-Publication Data
Fundamentals of counterrorism law / edited by Lynne Zusman.
pages cm
Includes bibliographical references and index.
ISBN 978-1-62722-365-2 (alk. paper)
    1. Terrorism—Prevention—Law and legislation. I. Zusman, Lynne K., editor of compilation.
KZ7220.F86 2014
344.7305'325—dc23   2013044614

Discounts are available for books ordered in bulk. Special consideration is given to state bars, CLE programs, and other bar-related organizations. Inquire at Book Publishing, ABA Publishing, American Bar Association, 321 North Clark Street, Chicago, Illinois 60654.

www.ShopABA.org

Dedication

This book is dedicated to the brave men and women and their families who serve America selflessly so that our liberty and freedom are preserved and those who preceded them in this endeavor.

Acknowledgments

The Editor wishes to acknowledge ABA Publisher Bryan Kay, ABA Head of New Book Content Development Richard Paszkiet, and Editorial Associate Shannon Bridger-Riley for unflagging devotion to this project consisting of both *The Law of Counterterrorism* (ABA 2011) and this book, *Fundamentals of Counterterrorism Law* (ABA 2014).

Thanks as well to the leaders of the ABA Section of Administrative Law and Regulatory Practice for their commitment to excellence in providing legal education concerning important functions of the government, as well as to ABA Executive Director Jack Rives, Holly Cook, and Jim Swanson.

This illustrious team has enabled *Fundamentals of Counterterrorism Law* to become reality and not just "a pipe dream."

Thank you very much.

The Editor
November 2, 2013

Editor's Note

Much of this book deals with international law rules and norms. For some time, the U.S. Department of Defense has been developing a *Law of War/ Law of Armed Conflict Manual,* which encompasses an enduring policy statement of the part of international law that shapes U.S. involvement in armed conflict. As of November 2, 2013, this document has not been issued despite the DoD directive requiring its promulgation. The leadership role of the United States in Rule of Law standards in the international community concerning the conduct of armed conflict is diminished because of this unfortunate situation. And it is particularly distressing in the context of decades of primary participation by the U.S. government in this enormous international effort.

As noted in the Prologue "The Law of Armed Conflict, synonymous with International Humanitarian Law and the Law of War, is the specific portion of international law that regulates and controls the actions of those parties participating in a conflict. . . . This specialized area of international law, which assigns both national and individual obligations, limits the effects of warfare by providing positive and clear rules which, if violated, may result in international sanctions or war crime prosecutions."[1] (Page 4.)

The Editor

---

1. For further information on this subject, please see Edwin Williamson, senior counsel, Sullivan & Cromwell, et al., *Where Is the Law of War Manual?* July 22, 2013, vol.18, no.42, THE WEEKLY STANDARD (http://www.weeklystandard.com). Source URL http//www.weeklystandard.com/articles/where-law-war-manual 7399267.html.

Contents

Prologue

The New Griffin of War*

Shane R. Reeves and Robert E. Barnsby

Famed seventeenth-century jurist Hugo Grotius warned that in warfare belligerents must "not believe that either nothing is allowable, or that everthing is." The latter belief holds that any and all tactics are allowed in warfare, while the former, a largely Christian theological view, holds that warfare is immoral and any resultant actions are therefore prohibited. Grotius understood that unilateral adherence to either of these notions would lead directly to an unworkable paradigm. Rejecting each belief's most extreme position while simultaneously adopting their reconcilable characteristics, Grotius began to develop a feasible legal framework for conducting warfare. Ultimately, as Oxford University's Karma Nabulsi describes in her outstanding work *Traditions of Justice and War,* by seeking the "middle ground" between these two seemingly incompatible views Grotius successfully shaped a conciliatory, realistic model for regulating warfare. The resultant middle ground, which recognized the necessity and legality of "just" wars while proscribing certain aspects of military conduct, solidified Grotius's legacy and, more importantly, set the stage for the profound legal developments—particularly in the 20th century—that would circumscribe subsequent conflicts, including those in which the United States finds itself today.

The Future of Warfare

Reminiscent of the unworkable opposites Grotius encountered, contemporary prognostications concerning the near-term future of armed conflict too often settle into a misleading "either/or" construct. One group of theorists vehemently argues that the future remains one of "asymmetric warfare," which is generally understood as conflict between two unequal adversaries where the weaker opponent uses unconventional or indirect methods to exploit the superior opponent's vulnerabilities. Typically set between a state actor (such as the United States) and either an ideologically motivated non-state armed group (such as Al-Qaeda) or an insurgent group (such as the Taliban in Afghanistan) these conflicts are often labeled as "non-international armed conflicts," "terrorism," or "guerilla warfare," and currently dominate resources and intellectual capital. However, a growing cohort of theorists rejects this asymmetric warfare prediction. This group—warily watching the increasing militarization of Asia, recognizing the sectarian breakdown of the Middle East, and observing the nation-state fragmentation of Africa—contends instead that "conventional warfare" between national armed forces, commonly referred to as "international armed conflict," is the future of warfare.

This ferocious theoretical debate has created a false dichotomy between these competing scholarly predictions. Limiting predictions in this way ignores the reality that contemporary conflicts are both difficult to define and are often an amalgamation of characteristics from traditionally unrelated forms of warfare. For example, state actors regularly use the indirect tactics of asymmetric warfare by blurring the line between combatant and civilian, conducting cyberattacks, and lethally targeting individual actors in order to gain a strategic advantage over their non-state adversaries. Similarly, non-state armed groups and insurgencies do not hesitate to use devices of conventional armed warfare, including traditional weaponry, in conflicts with state actors.

Further confusing attempts to categorize warfare is the often overlapping nature of modem conflicts. For instance, it is not uncommon for battles to simultaneously rage between state adversaries, insurgent groups, and transnational terrorist organizations in the same geographic location. Therefore, in actuality, "asymmetric warfare" and "conventional warfare" are the extreme boundaries on a vast spectrum of warfare possibilities.

Neither purely asymmetric nor purely conventional, modern conflicts are, rather, hybrids that display traits from both forms of warfare. Like the mythological half-eagle, half-lion griffin, which possesses strength far greater than either of its two component animals, the combination of asymmetric and conventional methods of warfare results in particularly potent modern conflicts.

Failure to recognize this new strand of warfare has potentially devastating implications for those nations likely to be involved in future armed conflicts. A nation unable, or perhaps unwilling, to perceive the growing hybrid warfare threat will remain comfortable with outdated and stale military ideas developed from their experiences in previous conventional or asymmetric conflicts. At ease with the status quo, and devoted to obsolete warfare strategies, these nations make misguided budget decisions, generate irrelevant military doctrine, and limit technological innovation. This misallocation of national resources produces a complacent armed force blind to evolutions in contemporary warfare. Therefore, while ready to "fight the last war," these nations, and in particular their armed forces, are woefully unprepared for the novel challenges of a hybrid conflict.

Some nations, such as the United States, have begun to recognize this risk. A document describing the future capabilities required of the United State Army, titled "The Army Capstone Concept Operational Adaptability—Operating Under Conditions of Uncertainty and Complexity in an Era of Persistent Conflict," states that "Army forces must be prepared to defeat what some have described as hybrid enemies: both hostile states and non-state enemies that combine a broad range of weapons capabilities and regular, irregular, and terrorist tactics; and continuously adapt to avoid US strengths and attack what they perceive as weaknesses." While it is encouraging that nations are moving toward addressing the hybridization of warfare in their military doctrine, of greater concern for the global community, and the most dangerous potential development, is the failure of international law—particularly the Law of Armed Conflict—to evolve with the hybridization of war.

Challenges for International Law

The Law of Armed Conflict, synonymous with International Humanitarian Law and the Law of War, is the specific portion of international law that regulates and controls the actions of those parties participating in a conflict. Comprised of both conventional and customary law, this body of law is binding upon all conflict participants in either an international or non-international armed conflict. Intertwining both a humanitarian and functional purpose, the Law of Armed Conflict ensures that those adversely affected by warfare, whether civilians, prisoners of war, or wounded and sick, are protected while simultaneously elucidating the permissible and prohibited activities for conflict participants. This specialized area of international law, which assigns both national and individual obligations, limits the effects of warfare by providing positive and clear rules which, if violated, may result in international sanctions or war crime prosecutions.

However, the continued effectiveness and enforceability of the Law of Armed Conflict is highly dependent on whether the expressed rules remain definitive, understood, and accepted in today's complicated conflicts. Debates concerning indefinite detention at Guantanamo Bay, the use of drone aircraft, the required protections afforded civilian participants in warfare, and various other contentious topics highlight a troubling lack of unanimity in the international community concerning the Law of Armed Conflict. Increasingly, the treaties and customary laws of the past century that comprise the Law of Armed Conflict, while recognized as extremely meaningful, have proven incapable of satisfactorily resolving the myriad of legal issues arising from modern warfare.

The hybridization of warfare only exacerbates these already complicated problems and may ultimately render the Law of Armed Conflict irrelevant. If the trend toward viewing the Law of Armed Conflict as confusing, subjective, and ineffectual continues, conflict participants, as well as much of the international community, may begin to see this area of international law as more of an anachronistic nuisance than a legal imperative. As the law's authority diminishes, traditional legal prohibitions will be violated with impunity and only popular morality will remain to limit actions in war. State and non-state adversaries alike will deem abiding by these long-standing legal norms too significant a disadvantage to continue. Instead, parties in conflict will ignore the obligations embedded in the Law of Armed Conflict under the guise of self-defense or engage in manipulation of the law for strategic reasons by conducting "lawfare."

The term "lawfare," connoting the strategic use of laws as a means of waging war, has rapidly and meaningfully entered the international legal lexicon in recent years. Scholars and practitioners alike are aware of various groups' ability to significantly undermine more powerful nations' traditional methods of waging warfare through the aggressive use of laws—whether treaty-based or customary in nature—arising decades ago in response to very different threats in very different historic contexts. Arguments about detention, targeting, cyber warfare, intelligence law, and related topics characterize lawfare, defined by Harvard Law School's Jack Goldsmith, Texas Law School's Robert Chesney, and the Brookings Institution's Benjamin Wittes in their blog of that name, as the "use of law as a weapon of conflict and, perhaps more importantly, [recognition of] the depressing reality that America remains at war with itself over the law governing its warfare with others."

Whether conflict participants misuse the law as a means of warfare or simply dismiss the law as inconsequential, the international ramifications are potentially catastrophic. As the law diminishes in importance, parties in conflict will most likely emphasize the idea of military necessity—the justification for doing those things in war which are required for securing the complete submission of the enemy—with little concern for their countervailing obligations to prevent unnecessary suffering and protect civilian populations. With the idea of military necessity becoming paramount, a concomitant deterioration of legal incentives to act humanely is inevitable, given the delicate balance between necessity and humanity at which the law has presently arrived. Current legal incentives—the most important of which provides combatant immunity for lawful acts committed by lawful combatants, and includes comprehensive protections for those adversely affected by conflict—create the conditions that enable the equilibrium between necessity and humanity to exist. However, with increasing emphasis placed upon military necessity and the descent of legal incentives to act humanely, even minimal baseline humanitarian behavior by warring groups risks becoming relative. The resultant downward spiral into brutality and savagery would dramatically increase the proliferation of disastrous humanitarian calamities accompanying contemporary conflicts, thereby undercutting any historical efforts to "humanize" warfare.

To preempt the possibility of undermining efforts to humanize warfare, the international community must recognize that questions concerning the effectiveness and practicality of the Law of Armed Conflict are increasing as the hybridization of warfare becomes the new norm. Ignoring this trend, and believing that current legal conditions are sufficient, simply expedites the increasingly ineffectual regulation of contemporary armed conflicts and continues to undermine confidence in the Law of Armed Conflict. Instead, international efforts must be made to push the Law of Armed Conflict into the hybrid warfare age. Whether through treaties or legally obligated customs, the international community must update the Law of Armed Conflict to address the various questions created by hybrid warfare while simultaneously reemphasizing that the comprehensive humanitarian protections afforded under the laws of war remain sacrosanct. Additionally, those participating in the often pernicious act of "lawfare" must be penalized in order to stop their misuse of the law. By taking these positive actions, the international community can begin to reassert the primacy of the law even in the challenging and complex environment of hybrid warfare.

Learning from Grotius

Arguing over whether future conflicts will resemble today's asymmetric fights or the conventional wars of the past assumes that the global community is in warfare stasis. This belief is as dangerous as it is surprising, for history has repeatedly demonstrated that warfare is constantly evolving and adopting less-than-apparent characteristics and traits. Contemporary war theorists must follow Grotius' example, rejecting extreme adherence to either the asymmetric or conventional warfare theories and endeavoring to find a workable "middle ground" paradigm in order to provide truly informed predictions about the future of armed conflict. The importance and urgency of adopting a Grotian approach to this problem cannot be overstated, as the continued relevance of the Law of Armed Conflict is highly dependent upon our willingness to recognize the hybridization of modern warfare.

I

FBI Domestic and Foreign Counterterrorism Operations

Robert M. Blitzer

The FBI Pre-9/11

This chapter's focus is on the Federal Bureau of Investigation's (FBI) counterterrorism intelligence/law enforcement responsibilities and how they have dramatically changed and morphed since September 11, 2001. From the establishment of a formal National Terrorism Program across the FBI *circa* 1982, counterterrorism investigations have often been intertwined with both the collection of National Security information and violations of the laws of the United States. This is the nature of the beast. Although this fact has not changed over the years, the reality of today is that the FBI has had to change the program into an intelligence-driven machine. In other words, intelligence collection and analysis have become more important than arrest and prosecution. Prevention of terrorist attacks is and will remain the main objective of the program. The implementation of intelligence-driven operations was needed for a long time, and September 11 was the catalyst that caused this critical change to actually be implemented. Make no mistake about it: long before September 11, the main focus of the FBI's Counterterrorism Program (CTP) was the prevention of terrorist attacks both here and abroad. However, from 1982 to 2001 the Bureau's program was small but constantly increasing, manpower was underfunded but growing, analysts were scarce, and the tools and technology needed to drive intelligence analysis were rudimentary at best when compared to the present day. It is important for the public to know that from the onset of this national effort FBI personnel were highly committed, worked incredible hours under stressful conditions, and, in spite of gaps in capabilities, the Bureau was highly successful in countering major attacks during almost two decades of fighting against incredible odds. This writer had the honor to have served with these people for more than a decade. It was an amazing experience, to say the least.

Within the FBI's CTP there have been and remain two different kinds of terrorism programs. The first program involves transnational or international groups like the Iranian/Syrian-backed Hezbollah or the Sunni Muslim Al-Qaeda organizations. These groups operate across international borders and have a presence inside the United States and many other countries. As we have seen in a number of instances, "lone wolf" individual sympathizers who self-radicalize because of the influence of extremist Islamic fundamentalists and organizations that operate internationally can also fall under the international terrorism banner. Army Major Nidal Hasan, the Fort Hood shooter, is an example of a self-radicalized international terrorist. Investigation revealed that Hasan was inspired to act by a foreign terrorist leader and organization (Anwar al-Awlaki, who was the head of Al-Qaeda in the Arabian Peninsula). There are certainly "lone wolves" who are domestic or homegrown terrorists, like Timothy McVeigh and Terry Nichols, who bombed the Alfred P. Murrah Federal Building on April 19, 1995, in Oklahoma City, Oklahoma. These people can come from a wide variety of left- and right-wing groups or just be sympathizers who have adopted their ideologies and political beliefs. They are not inspired by any foreign entity.

The second element of the CTP addresses domestic organizations that have developed here at home that are not directly affiliated or directed by foreign organizations or persons. They hold both left-wing and right-wing beliefs. The main difference between the international and domestic groups is that the domestic groups almost always consist of United States persons (citizens-USPERS). For example, in past years violent animal rights and environmental groups have been considered left-wing terrorist organizations. These groups have political agendas that strive to inflict major economic or property damage by freeing animals and/or destroying property through arson or other violent attacks. Additionally, on the right over the years, we have seen several attacks by anti-abortion advocates or by others who believe in the concept of being a "sovereign citizen."

Violent right-wing extremists seeking to stop legal abortion through violence have conducted attacks over the years, and a number of them resulted in significant property damage as well as injuries and death in some instances. Eric Robert Rudolph was such a person. In 1996 Rudolph placed bombs at Centennial Park in downtown Atlanta, Georgia, during the Olympic Games. In 1997 he bombed an abortion clinic in Sandy Springs, Georgia, and the Otherside Lounge, a gay bar, in Atlanta. In early 1998 Rudolph bombed an abortion clinic in Birmingham, Alabama. These crimes resulted in three deaths and injured more than 100 people. All of his attacks were because of his anti-abortion beliefs. After a lengthy hunt by numerous law enforcement agencies, Rudolph was arrested and convicted, and is serving a life sentence for his crimes.

In terms of the definition of terrorism, the FBI has set forth the following in its publications:

> There is no single, universally accepted, definition of terrorism. Terrorism is defined in the Code of Federal Regulations as "the unlawful use of force and violence against persons or property to intimidate or coerce a government, the civilian population, or any segment thereof, in furtherance of political or social objectives" (28 C.F.R. Section 0.85).

The FBI further describes terrorism as either domestic or international, depending on the origin, base, and objectives of the terrorist organization. The FBI uses the following definitions:

> **Domestic terrorism** is the unlawful use, or threatened use, of force or violence by a group or individual based and operating entirely within the United States or Puerto Rico without foreign direction committed against persons or property to intimidate or coerce a government, the civilian population, or any segment thereof in furtherance of political or social objectives.

> **International terrorism** involves violent acts or acts dangerous to human life that are a violation of the criminal laws of the United States or any state, or that would be a criminal violation if committed within the jurisdiction of the United States or any state. These acts appear to be intended to intimidate or coerce a civilian population, influence the policy of a government by intimidation or coercion, or affect the conduct of a government by assassination or kidnapping. International terrorist acts occur outside the United States or transcend national boundaries in terms of the means by which they are accomplished, the persons they appear intended to coerce or intimidate, or the locale in which their perpetrators operate or seek asylum.[1]

Before the events of 9/11, FBI Special Agents assigned to field offices, foreign embassies, and at FBI Headquarters operated according to laws and guidelines formulated and implemented for the most part in the 1970s and early to mid-1980s. For example, President Jimmy Carter signed the Foreign Intelligence Surveillance Act (FISA) into law on October 25, 1978. This law set forth the domestic procedures for both physical and electronic surveillance and collection of foreign intelligence information between foreign powers (e.g., hostile intelligence services, State sponsors of terrorism, terrorist organizations) and their agents operating within the United States.

Prior to the implementation of FISA, Attorney General Edward Levi issued Attorney General Guidelines for FBI Foreign Counterintelligence Investigations in 1976. These guidelines have been amended a number of times by succeeding Attorneys General, the most recent post-9/11 under Attorney General Michael Mukasey in 2008. The guidelines were a result of congressional hearings by the United States Senate Select Committee to Study Governmental Operations. The committee was chaired by Senator Frank Church and was commonly known as the Church Committee. It investigated the domestic collection activities of the intelligence community and found that tighter controls needed to be implemented on several agencies during domestic intelligence operations. These controls included more regulation of FBI activities. The 1976 Levi Guidelines provided the framework for FBI intelligence collection activities within the United States. It also set forth the manner in which counterterrorism intelligence investigations could be conducted. Although amended and now consolidated with other guidelines overall, they have served America well by giving guidance to the FBI that has protected our citizens' civil liberties and privacy. At the same time, the guidelines have provided the FBI with relatively clear guidance on what special agents can and cannot do while collecting intelligence within the United States.

On the criminal investigative side of the house prior to 1984, the FBI had limited jurisdiction to investigate crimes outside U.S. borders that related to terrorist attacks. For many years that jurisdiction involved such areas as "Crime on the High Seas" and "Hijacking or Destruction of Aircraft." However, because of a spate of hijackings abroad, the taking of American hostages in the Middle East and attacks on our diplomatic facilities in a number of countries during the 1970s and 1980s, additional laws were enacted which expanded the FBI's ability to investigate crimes outside our borders. These laws are often referred to as the Extraterritorial Laws or the Long Arm laws, and over the years they have served the United States well.

Before talking more about these statutes, it may be an appropriate place in this chapter to talk briefly about the U.S. government's policy pre-9/11 in terms of preserving our National Security. From the 1970s through 2001, our national policy rested on four main pillars:

(1) *Diplomacy* under the leadership of the Department of State;
(2) *Covert Action* under the operational control of the Central Intelligence Agency (CIA);
(3) *Military Response* under the operational control of the Department of Defense; and
(4) *Law Enforcement* under the leadership of the Department of Justice/FBI (DOJ/FBI).

Notice that the roles of the four agencies were described as either leadership or operational in nature. To be more specific, lead roles were assigned to the State Department for managing terrorist attacks outside the borders of the United States, and management of such attacks inside the borders of the United States fell to the DOJ/FBI. The Defense Department and the CIA, while retaining operational control of their assets, worked closely with the lead agencies in countering and responding as needed to looming terrorist threats. Overall coordination was accomplished through the National Security Council at The White House. As the FBI gained new jurisdiction abroad prior to 9/11, the law enforcement solution was applied and became literally the tip of the spear of the U.S. government's counterterrorism response. There were many large and smaller cases that involved the FBI abroad, such as the downing of PanAm 103 in 1988; the attempted bombing of over a dozen U.S. aircraft transiting Manila, Philippines, in 1995; the bombing of a U.S. military housing complex known as Khobar Towers in Saudi Arabia in June 1996; the bombing of the American Embassies in Kenya and Tanzania in 1998; and the attack on the *USS Cole* in Yemen in 2000.

The extraterritorial statutes mentioned above were key to the international investigations of the above incidents. The first statute was the 1984 Comprehensive Crime Control Act; the second was the 1986 Antiterrorism Omnibus Diplomatic Security and Antiterrorism Act; and the third statute was the Antiterrorism and Effective Death Penalty Act. These three laws gave the law enforcement component of our national counterterrorism policy the teeth needed to go after international terrorist organizations and State sponsors of terrorism who were using surrogate groups to attack U.S. interests around the globe. The following is a brief summary of the key portions of each law.

1984 Comprehensive Crime Control Act—Hostage-Taking Statute

Title 18 Section 1203(a) and (b) contains the key criminal elements that relate to the violation of the Hostage-Taking statute. Responsibility for the enforcement of this law was provided to the Attorney General of the United States. The FBI, in turn, was charged with the responsibility to investigate this crime if the offense occurred either within the United States or abroad. In essence, this new law made it a federal crime for whoever, whether inside or outside the United States, seizes or detains and threatens to kill, to injure, or to continue to detain another person in order to compel a third person or governmental organization to do or abstain from doing any act as an explicit or implicit condition for release of the person detained, or attempts or conspires to do so, shall be punished by imprisonment for any term of years or for life and if death of any person results, shall be punished by death or life imprisonment[2]

With the enactment of this law in October 1984, the FBI began to develop processes and procedures, including training and equipping selected field divisions that would be responsible for deploying abroad in the event that an investigation would need to be conducted. It was clear at the outset that FBI Legal Attachés who are FBI agents posted abroad at a number of embassies across the world would have an enhanced role in coordinating international deployments. Legal Attachés would also need to be fully engaged with Chiefs of Mission either during and/or subsequent to an event to ensure that appropriate clearances and foreign government support were in place before an investigative team would be sent abroad. Lastly, even in the very nascent months of this new responsibility the FBI realized that there needed to be some level of security in order to protect its personnel so that they would be able to conduct effective investigations in foreign lands. It was also recognized that the Legal Attachés would need to help with the logistical needs and with international law enforcement liaison during the course of the investigation. Thus in 1984 the seeds of the FBI's extraterritorial investigative mission were planted and began to grow.

1986 Omnibus Diplomatic Security and Antiterrorism Act—Assault or Murder of a U.S. Citizen Abroad

Title 18 U.S.C. Section 2332(b) continued to expand and define the extraterritorial investigative role of the FBI. While the Hostage-Taking law was aimed at those persons and organizations that were using hostages to extort the United States and other countries, other events such as the 1983 bombings of the Marine barracks and the U.S. Embassy in Beirut, Lebanon, were still fresh in everyone's minds. Although FBI personnel did respond to these attacks, the reality at the time was that we needed a tougher law to go after the terrorists responsible and bring them to justice. The new statute was international in scope because the U.S. government wanted the ability to go anywhere in the world using law enforcement capabilities that for the most part were limited to domestic situations.

In reviewing the language of the statute, the most salient text appears under 2332(b) parts (A) and (B), which says that, "involving conduct transcending national boundaries and in a circumstance described in subsection (b),"[3] whoever:

(A) kills, kidnaps, maims, commits an assault resulting in serious bodily injury, or assaults with a dangerous weapon any person within the United States; or (B) creates a substantial risk of serious bodily injury to any person by destroying or damaging any structure, conveyance, or other real or personal property with the United States or by attempting or conspiring to destroy or damage any structure, conveyance, or other real or personal property within the United States; in violation of the laws of any State, or the United States shall be punished . . . .[4]

The remainder of the statute delineates the kinds of circumstances that the law covers and the penalties and investigative authorities of the Attorney General that were based on previous laws.

The importance of these two laws both then and now cannot be overstated. Together they became the major tools needed to bring the fight directly to individual terrorists, their organizations, and sponsors. As the FBI faced new attacks in the late 1980s and early 1990s, such as PanAm 103, Khobar Towers, and others, these legal tools were in place, and they needed to be so our government would have a broader array of options to use against our enemies.

The Brutal 1990s

With new statutes in place, the FBI entered the 1990s facing an expanded mission with some additional resources, but there was a general belief that the program was behind the curve, and efforts were ongoing to improve the intelligence base throughout the organization. Beginning with the first Persian Gulf conflict (Desert Storm), the FBI's CT and counterintelligence operations increased with the tempo of the conflict and remained intense in the months leading up to combat and for months after combat had ended. The Bureau's role was primarily domestic in nature; however, there were significant intelligence contributions made during both 1990 and 1991 in support of the international effort to oust the Iraqi army from Kuwait.

On February 26, 1993, the World Trade Center in New York was rocked by a massive explosion in the parking garage underneath the Vista Hotel and the North Tower. The blast killed six people and injured more than a thousand. Damage was extensive. After one of the largest criminal investigations in history conducted by the FBI and its partners, Ramzi Ahmed Yousef and several others were arrested, tried, and convicted for this major terrorist attack. Khalid Sheik Mohammad was identified during the investigation as providing funding to the cell that was used to purchase bomb materials. Osama Bin Laden's name also surfaced during the case; however, the intelligence community did not know a lot about him and was unaware of his organization, which was later identified as Al-Qaeda.

Within weeks of the Trade Center attack, the FBI developed intelligence that identified a second cell of terrorists who were planning follow-up bombing of several landmarks in the greater New York area. Among them were the Lincoln and Holland tunnels and the Federal Building housing the FBI and other agencies. This secondary plot had been hatched and was backed by Sheik Omar Abdel-Rahman, also known as the blind sheik, and several of his followers. Rahman, an Egyptian cleric and spiritual leader of a number of Islamic extremist elements around the world, had been in the U.S. for some time and was preaching in a number of mosques located in the greater New York and Northern New Jersey area. He had a large following of radicals throughout the country and he preached violent jihad to them. This plot was foiled through the efforts of the New York Joint Terrorism Task Force, and the sheik and several others were arrested, tried, and convicted for their crimes. All remain in prison.

The Trade Center Bombing and the landmarks plot along with several other events around the world were recognized as major wake-up calls for the United States and its allies. The intelligence community, principally the FBI and the CIA, understood the implications of these events and, along with the National Security Agency, worked even harder to understand the new threats that the country was facing.

On the morning of April 19, 1995, Timothy McVeigh parked a Ryder box truck in front of the Alfred P. Murrah Federal Building in Oklahoma City, Oklahoma, and casually walked away. The truck was filled with explosives and the detonation destroyed the building, killing 168 people and injuring 680 others. A massive FBI-led investigation determined that McVeigh and his close friend Terry Nichols were responsible for the bombing. Both were veterans of the first Gulf conflict and were right-wing "militia" sympathizers. The bombing against a federal facility was done in response to the well-known Waco and Ruby Ridge incidents, where federal law enforcement agencies conducted lengthy sieges against individuals and a so-called religious group called the Branch Davidians. The investigation surrounding the bombing was at that time the largest ever conducted by the FBI. It remains the largest "domestic terrorism" attack ever conducted on U.S. soil. That is an attack perpetrated by homegrown terrorists with no ties to foreign entities.

Immediately following the Oklahoma City bombing, it was clear that the entire terrorism world was undergoing major shifts in both the international and domestic arenas. Beyond the Trade Center and Oklahoma City bombings, there had been other attacks and attempted attacks abroad that further raised the threat level for the nation. With threats from abroad and at home rising, Director Louis Freeh and Attorney General Janet Reno set new requirements for the FBI that included the establishment of substantially larger field and Headquarters elements and the expansion of both the Joint Terrorism Task Forces and Legal Attaché components around the globe. They also went to work with the Congress to develop a package of laws aimed at the threats that we were facing for the foreseeable future. Because of the seriousness of the threat, budgets were examined and recommendations were made to the White House and Congress for additional funding streams to build up FBI capabilities in response to what we were experiencing at home and abroad.

1996 Antiterrorism and Effective Death Penalty Act—Countering Terrorist Infrastructures (Pub. L. 104-132)[5]

The breath, depth, and overall impact of Public Law 104-132 on the U.S. counterterrorism community cannot be overstated. The law was a substantive and aggressive step in bringing the war to the terrorists who were threatening, and continue to threaten, our way of life. Review of the statute is difficult because of the numerous components of government, including the Departments of State, Treasury, Defense, and Justice, to name the most significant players that were affected by the law. It is complex and far-reaching; and when one considers its position in history, it is a precursor to the PATRIOT Act.

For the purpose of this chapter, the major portions of the law that involved the FBI will be summarized. The summarized information has been selected subjectively by the writer, and others may differ with the selections made; however, the intent is merely to highlight key points for the reader to consider in terms of the impact on the Bureau's domestic and international operations. An in-depth analysis of the law is not intended, but the its impact on the FBI was substantial and immediate in terms of increasing and clarifying jurisdictional responsibilities. Increased penalties for violations of new or amended laws gave the law enforcement component of the U.S. government pillars (the four pillars were mentioned above) more tools and teeth to pursue and punish international terrorists. There are nine sections or titles to the law. We will cover five of those titles as follows:

- **Title III—International Terrorism Prohibitions.** A major issue in the war against terrorism from the beginning of the FBI's Counterterrorism Program was the inability of law enforcement and other agencies to develop prosecutable cases against, or to disrupt individual terrorists and/or organizations that were providing material support to, foreign terrorists or terrorist organizations. Pub. L. 104-132 authorized the Secretary of State to designate individuals and organizations as terrorists. Although State had been able to do this in the past, the new law expanded and better defined who and what could be designated. Once they were designated, the Justice and Treasury Departments could go after individuals

15

and groups both here and abroad that were providing material support to terrorists. This was an important change, because historically millions of dollars and other materials had been collected within the United States and sent overseas to support terrorist organizations such as Hamas and Hezbollah. For example, funds were collected from private individuals, religious organizations, and through criminal enterprises. Those dollars could be sent directly overseas to buy goods and services that terrorists needed to survive and operate. Over many years, material support networks had been well established and flourished. Now laws were on the books that could be used to disrupt material support to terrorists and their organizations operating around the world. For example, for many years in the 1990s The Holy Land Foundation, headquartered in Richardson, Texas, was the largest Islamic charity in the United States. Federal prosecutors brought charges against the organization for funding Hamas and other Islamic terrorist organizations based on investigations conducted by the FBI. Its assets were frozen by the European Union and the United States, and it was shut down by the U.S. government following the discovery that it was funding Hamas. The 2008 trial of the charity leaders was thought to be the largest terrorism financing prosecution in American history. In 2009, the founders of the organization were given life sentences. Beyond material support, the new statute made any U.S. person found to be engaging in financial transactions with a State sponsor of terrorism— e.g., Iran—subject to criminal penalties.

- **Title V—Nuclear, Biological, and Chemical Weapons Restrictions.** Over an extended period of time during the 1980s and 1990s, there was concern in government that somehow terrorists would be able to acquire weapons of mass destruction (WMD) capabilities. This threat was perceived to be increasing, and with present-day Iran, a State sponsor of terrorism, moving closer and closer to possessing a nuclear weapon, our fears may soon become our reality. Laws addressing criminal activity involving nuclear, biological, and chemical weapons had been on the books for many years, but given the increasing threat both the U.S. and its Allies were seeing, more needed to be done to add criminal sanctions and penalties to our inventory of WMD laws. The new 1996 Antiterrorism statute strengthened and expanded laws aimed specifically at nuclear, biological, and chemical weapons. For example, unauthorized possession or trafficking in nuclear by-products was inserted into existing law, criminalizing that kind of activity. Dangerous biological agents and the inappropriate handling of them was also a growing concern, and over the years information had been developing indicating that terrorists were trying to

16

experiment with such agents. It was clear that the deployment of an agent such as anthrax or plague virus could have a devastating effect on a military or civilian population. In the new law, rules for housing and transporting such agents were tightened. Additionally, existing statutes were amended to include criminal penalties aimed at unauthorized persons, including international terrorists and others to possess, found to be involved in transferring, or threatening to use such agents as weapons.

Biological weapons remain a concern today and in the future. During the 1990s there were many threats and a few incidents involving Ricin, a deadly biological agent made from the castor bean. A number of domestic cases emerged, but since Ricin is not easily spread, these cases were quickly resolved and prosecutions were successful in each instance. The post-9/11 anthrax attacks certainly were a wake-up call and a confirmation of the concerns that arose in the 1990s about the use of biological weapons. In terms of chemical weapons restrictions, the new law amended Title 18, Section 2332(b) described above. It made it a crime to injure or murder a U.S. citizen by use of a chemical weapon both here and abroad. Penalties included any term in prison up to life, and if a death had occurred, the person(s) responsible could be subject to the death penalty.

- **Title VI—Implementation of Plastic Explosives Convention.** For many years the law enforcement community had been seeking better ways to identify explosives used in both terrorism and criminal matters. After the downing of PanAm 103 in December of 1988 as well as the bombing of other aircraft, attention turned to exploring ways to mark plastic explosives. Marking of explosives allows criminal investigators and forensic examiners to develop leads which ultimately can identify a terrorist organization, a State sponsor of terrorism, a criminal, or a hostile nation as the source of the explosive material.

On March 1, 1991, the Convention on the Marking of Plastic Explosives for the Purpose of Detection was held at Montreal. While the law enforcement community supported implementation, the industry resisted because of the costs of such changes. However, given the bombings that had occurred and the threats facing the country, Congress included language in the 1996 Antiterrorism law that made it a crime not to have markers manufactured into future plastic explosives, thus ending manufacturers' concerns.

Titles VII, VIII, and XI of the law cover changes to criminal procedures that were already on the books, strengthened existing laws, and addressed law enforcement training issues and funding.

Summary

For the FBI and its interagency partners in the law enforcement and intelligence communities, terrorism had become a large and looming concern throughout the 1990s. As the decade came to a close, attacks on the U.S. Embassies in Kenya and Tanzania in the summer of 1998 as well as the 2000 attack on the *USS Cole* in Yemen were painful reminders that the operational tempo of our adversaries was increasing substantially. The FBI remained at the point of the spear in terms of the government's response to terrorist attacks.

Internally, the manpower and organization of the program underwent significant changes with the establishment of a Counterterrorism Division separate and apart from the National Security Division, where it had been housed for several years. "Flyaway teams" to better respond to foreign attacks had been constituted and equipped. Substantial exchanges of personnel with other agencies both at Headquarters and in the field had occurred, and interagency relationships were very good. Intelligence sharing was improving, but there were legal and bureaucratic obstacles that did not allow for a free flow of information both internally and externally with FBI interagency partners.

There had been expansion and new statutory authorities vested in the FBI. The director of the FBI, Louis Freeh, was deeply and fully involved in the expansion of the Bureau's Counterterrorism mission. In fact, he not only worked throughout this period to secure additional funding and resources, but also immersed himself in all of the major investigations that occurred on his watch, providing critical leadership. Traveling extensively abroad and interacting with our ambassadors and foreign allies to widen the FBI's footprint, Director Freeh was successful in establishing new Legat posts in several countries. He also was the first director to develop a long-range strategic plan for the Bureau. As that plan unfolded, the two top priorities were Counterterrorism and Counterintelligence. The writer believes that Director Freeh, given the range and scope of his responsibilities, dedicated the majority of his time and effort into working against the national security threats that had been growing before, during, and after his term.

On September 11, 2001, the tip of the Counterterrorism spear was changed. Diplomacy, Covert Action, and Law Enforcement, while important, would now be dwarfed by the Military Response option. While the four pillars of our strategy remained in place, three of them would now be in support of the military option.

The Post-9/11 FBI

The 9/11 attacks had an immediate and profound impact on the FBI. The loss of life and destruction of critical infrastructure in New York were unprecedented in the history of the nation. It was larger than the Japanese attack on Pearl Harbor, and the lives lost were civilian, not military. Those of us who had lived through the '90s understood immediately what had happened and who had done it. Raymond Kelly, Police Commissioner of the City of New York, wrote Chapter 2 of the previous book in this ABA series, titled *The Law of Counterterrorism*, edited by former Department of Justice Section Chief Lynne K. Zusman. Commissioner Kelly, who has a very distinguished career in both federal and local law enforcement, was appointed to his position in January of 2002. He continues to serve as Commissioner. He recognized that New York was and would remain the most visible target of foreign terrorist organizations and individual international terrorists inspired by foreign groups or individuals. With the support of Mayor Michael Bloomberg, Commissioner Kelly directed that the New York Police Department (NYPD) become more proactive in identifying and thwarting the threats that swirl around his jurisdiction. Under Commissioner Kelly's leadership, the NYPD established a Counterterrorism Bureau and assigned substantial resources to it. He also increased the number of detectives assigned to the FBI's Joint Terrorism Task Force (JTTF) to 120.

The NYPD Counterterrorism Bureau was further staffed with former intelligence community, State Department, and military experts whose mission was to develop and implement policies, procedures, and operations that would protect the city from further calamities such as 9/11. Analysts and linguists were hired, and NYPD even posted detectives in foreign countries, some of whom are imbedded in major foreign police services. Many other initiatives have been adopted, and the city has averted a number of attacks since 9/11 because of the efforts of the NYPD and other agencies around the country and around the world.

During the months following the 9/11 attack, as NYPD was ramping up its counterterrorism operations, the FBI was undergoing immense internal changes under the management of its new director, Robert S. Mueller III. At the time of the attack, Director Mueller had only been on board for a week. A former U.S. Attorney and Assistant Attorney General in the Department of Justice, he came to the FBI with a good understanding of its culture and capabilities. Now he was confronted by an incredible situation, and he clearly recognized that the FBI would be tested as never before.

In the months and years that have followed 9/11, the changes wrought upon the FBI along with the wars in Iraq and Afghanistan have been astounding. Books could be written about the legal, organizational, technological, forensic, and operational changes and improvements that have been developed, tested, and implemented on Director Mueller's watch. Many of the changes have been driven by recommendations of the National Commission on Terrorist Attacks upon the United States as well as changes in laws, guidelines, and Executive Orders. Much of the information relating to these changes is contained in Chapters 7 (Gordon Lederman) and 8 (W. George Jameson) of *The Law of Counterterrorism*, referred to above. This writer encourages the reader to read over those important chapters, because they really set out the important legal issues that continue to support the U.S. government's Counterterrorism Program.

The FBI has been an enormous partner and supporter of both the Department of Defense and the CIA during the conflicts in Iraq and Afghanistan. While the fact is not well known, FBI personnel have been deployed in both theatres of war since 2002 doing what they do best—conducting a wide range of investigations. Using both criminal and intelligence collection techniques, they have provided invaluable information in support of the military and CIA operations. For example, FBI agents have investigated countless crime scenes resulting from bombings, collecting evidence and examining it for fingerprints and DNA, and have been able to reconstruct bombs for attribution purposes. The Bureau has been in the forefront of using biometrics to help the military and the CIA identify and pursue enemy combatants/terrorists. Additionally, the FBI has been on numerous raids of compounds and residences used by terrorists. During these raids, valuable information has been collected and analyzed. Such information is looked at in the context of developing leads that can identify the intentions, plans, and locations of terrorists. Finally, skilled FBI interviewers have been involved in countless interviews of captured individuals, the most famous being Saddam Hussein. In fact, FBI Special Agent George L. Piro, an Arabic speaker, led a debriefing team that gained Hussein's confidence and debriefed him extensively after his capture by U.S. forces near his home town of Tikrit.

Conclusion

This past year has been marked by tremendous upheaval throughout the Middle East. Egypt and Libya have been rocked by changes. Syria is involved in a nasty civil war; Iran is moving quickly toward having a nuclear bomb(s); and Israel is more isolated than it has been in many years. It is difficult to know what major events will emerge during the next months or years, particularly in this volatile part of the world. The four pillars of U.S. counterterrorism policy remain in place and are effective. It seems to this writer that Covert Action may be emerging as the new leading pillar with Diplomacy, Military Action, and Law Enforcement in support for the near term. However, this priority could change in an instant, as it did following 9/11. While the current situation is fluid, the people who support each of these areas remain highly motivated, engaged, and ready to act when needed. As a nation, we are grateful for their dedication, courage, and devotion.

Notes

1. Terrorism 2002-2005, www.fbi.gov.
2. Office of the Law Revision Counsel, U.S. House of Representatives, last modified Jan. 3, 2012, http://uscode.house.gov/uscode-cgi/fastweb.exe?search.
3. http://uscode.house.gov/uscode-cgi/fastweb.exe?search.
4. *Id.*
5. http://books.google.com/books?id=_HxBIRVmN-cC&pg=PA1255&lpg =PA1255&dq=1996+Antiterrorism+and+Effective+Death+Penalty+Act.

II

FBI International Investigations: Benghazi, Libya

Thomas V. Fuentes

The murder of an American citizen outside of the United States is a violation of U.S. law. The FBI has primary jurisdiction in the investigation of such crimes. This applies to all Americans, from tourists, business travelers, and students to government officials. This includes the tragic murder of U.S. Ambassador Christopher Stevens and three other Americans who were killed during a terrorist attack on the U.S. Consulate in Benghazi, Libya, on September 11, 2012.

Such attacks are not new. In August of 1998, the U.S. Embassies in Kenya and Tanzania were bombed, killing 12 and 11 Americans, respectively. Hundreds of FBI special agents and specialized support personnel were dispatched to investigate. The investigation later expanded to other East African countries to as far as South Africa. Many Americans may not be aware that dozens of Al-Qaeda (AQ) members and associates were arrested and successfully prosecuted in the U.S. Southern District of New York. Most are serving sentences of life without parole in U.S. federal prisons.

While all of the above attacks are believed to have been committed by AQ or affiliated groups, there is a critical difference between the Benghazi investigation and the East African investigations; it is the countries where the attacks occurred. The FBI must have permission from the host country and country clearance from the ambassador or current chief of mission. Additionally, the host country must be willing and able to ensure the safety of the investigators.

In 1998, the FBI could immediately deploy investigators because the Kenyan and Tanzanian governments were able to ensure adequate support. This was not limited to the Embassy crime scenes but extended to many other locations within each country. Both countries were also motivated by the fact that hundreds of their own citizens were also killed. The FBI was also able to work with the appropriate counterpart agencies of neighboring countries. Subjects were arrested and transported to New York for trial from as far as South Africa.

The ability of the FBI to work with counterparts throughout the world is not an accident. The bureau follows the philosophy that "in order to have a friend, you must be a friend." The FBI, through its 75 Legal Attaché offices in U.S. Embassies and many Consulates strives to create and enhance mutual trust and cooperation. This program began as a clandestine service during World War II. With passage of the National Security Act of 1947, the FBI's operations overseas became overt and largely confined to criminal matters. This act created the CIA as the U.S. external intelligence-gathering agency. The name "Legal Attaché" is a carryover from the original war-related covert mission.

It is too late to create effective partnerships after the embassy is bombed, or a U.S. airliner is blown out of the sky, or a U.S. Navy ship is attacked in a foreign port or even international waters. The ability of the FBI to conduct successful investigations in East Africa and many other countries throughout the world is the result of years of building trust with host-country counterparts in support of the rule of law.

Regime change in other countries often requires the relationship building, if possible, to begin again. The "Arab Spring" has created such a situation in several countries, including Libya. The revolution in Libya escalated in February 2011, when forces loyal to dictator Muammar Gaddafi fired on protestors in Benghazi. Many were killed, but the revolution spread throughout the nation. Gaddafi was captured and killed in October 2011. A new government is struggling to establish effective services, including law enforcement.

Many militia groups have maintained the ability to wage counterinsurgency by refusing to disarm and/or disband. During the revolution, many countries supplied sophisticated arms and training to the rebels. As an unintended consequence, thousands of Libyans possess and can use a range of weapons, from small arms and rocket-propelled grenades to mortars.

In Libya, the FBI was not afforded immediate access to the Benghazi crime scene because the host country had no qualified law enforcement, intelligence, or military support available. The Libyan government had essentially subcontracted with the local militias to provide basic security services in the region, and members of these groups were suspected of participating in the attack on the U.S. Consulate building.

Many have questioned why the U.S. military was not deployed to provide security for the FBI crime scene investigators. A practical and political calculation had to be made. It was necessary to balance the potential to obtain useful intelligence and criminal evidence against a new attack. While small arms would pose an insignificant threat, what about an attack using mortars? Mortars could be launched from rooftops blocks away using innocent Libyan citizens as human shields. A military response would likely result in the deaths of women and children. Their bodies would be placed in the streets for broadcast by worldwide cable news networks. This potential outcome was deemed too great a price to pay for the immediate processing of the crime scene.

The FBI was able eventually to have secure access to the Benghazi crime scene. In the interim, investigation consisted of extensive debriefings of U.S. Embassy personnel and survivors. Much of this work was conducted in Libya and other countries receiving wounded personnel.

The country of Libya will remain dangerous for the foreseeable future. As long as a significant percentage of the population remains heavily armed and the government and its security institutions remain ineffective, additional violence is likely.

Libya also provides a cautionary tale concerning the ongoing civil war/uprising in Syria. Rebels attempting to oust President Bashar al-Assad are likely receiving arms from other nations. In the aftermath of Syrian regime change, the new government will face many of the same challenges as the Libyans.

In any event, the FBI will seek to establish new partnerships, and is extremely mindful of the role it plays in furtherance of U.S. foreign policy.

III

Terrorism's Threat to Cities Large and Small

Raymond W. Kelly

In the wake of the bombings at the Boston Marathon on April 15, 2013, and the savage killing of a British soldier at a military barracks in Woolwich, southeast of London a month later, much has been written and said in the media about the so-called "new normal," the underlying threat we face from homegrown, smaller-scale, yet still very lethal terrorist attacks. From the standpoint of New York City, there's not much new about the new normal at all. The New York City Police Department (NYPD) has been contending with it for some time and so have others. Nonetheless, the public on both sides of the Atlantic seemed to be taken off guard by both attacks, which were the subject, in part, of the FBI National Executive Institute's Major City Chiefs Conference in Grapevine, Texas, on May 29. The keynote address that I delivered there, "Terrorism's Threat to Cities Large and Small," constituted much of what I had promised to submit to Lynne Zusman's reprise of *The Law of Counterterrorism*, first published under her guidance in 2011 by the ABA's Section of Administrative Law and Regulatory Practice.

Why does the NYPD consider the "new normal" to be not so new? In June 2009, Abdul-Hakim Mujahid Mohammed, formerly known as Carlos Bledsoe, carried out a drive-by shooting on an Army recruiting station in Little Rock, Arkansas, killing two soldiers. He told police that he had intended to kill as many Army personnel as possible. Later that same year, U.S. Army Major Nidal Hissan opened fire at the Fort Hood, Texas, Soldier Readiness Processing Center, killing 12 soldiers and one civilian and wounding more than 30 other people. In the past year and a half alone, 40 or more people have been arrested on terrorism-related charges in the United States and Canada, from New York to Chicago; Tampa; Mobile, Alabama; Aurora, Illinois; Toronto; Broward County, Florida; and Southern California, to name a few.

A big reason for the increase in the tempo of arrests is the outstanding work of the FBI to identify would-be terrorists and apprehend them. In New York, we've benefited tremendously from our partnership with the FBI through the Joint Terrorism Task Force.

New York City has been the subject of at least six terrorist plots since 9/11 targeting everything from subways to synagogues to airports, and iconic locations like Times Square, Wall Street, and the World Trade Center. They've been defeated, thanks to good work by the NYPD, our federal partners, some combination of the two, or just plain luck. However, we are concerned that the success, from a terrorist point of view, of the latest attacks in Boston and London, coupled with the notoriety they've received, could inspire even more attempts in venues beyond major cities. Indeed, less than a week after the British soldier was killed, a French soldier was stabbed outside of Paris last weekend in an attack with terrorist overtones.

In advance of July 4th festivities this year, the Boston Police Department sent a contingent of its officers to the NYPD to see how we protect large gatherings. We also hosted Police Commissioner Edward Flynn at New York City police headquarters to brief representatives from as many as 200 police agencies who are part of the NYPD's Sentry program—police departments with which we share information out of a mutual concern about the continued threat of terrorism. The Boston Marathon was much on our minds as we prepared for our own annual Macy's fireworks display along two miles of Manhattan waterfront on July 4th. Hours in advance of the display, the NYPD conducted multiple sweeps of the areas along the Hudson waterfront where thousands of pedestrians would stand to watch the pyrotechnic displays. When the crowds did arrive, their numbers were augmented by detectives in plain clothes, officers carrying sophisticated radiation detection equipment, and police "explosives wake" dogs whose olfactory prowess is such that they can detect the scent of explosives on the clothing of someone who recently handled bomb-making ingredients. These precautions or some variation of them have become standard operating procedures for the NYPD. However, we also know all too well from experience that one cannot protect against every eventuality. We need good intelligence to stop attacks in their planning stages, and the NYPD Intelligence Division, along with the Joint Terrorism Task Force of the FBI, work hard to get it.

28

As the ABA and the American legal system at large continue to examine how terrorists should be prosecuted once they're captured, three points are relevant: First, the terrorist threat to the U.S. homeland remains severe, complex, and unrelenting. Second, medium-sized cities such as Boston are now in play for terrorism events. Third, the crude and simplistic attacks Al-Qaeda has been encouraging its followers to carry out are now being realized. As we've seen, they're capable of doing tremendous damage.

Let's start with the enduring threat, which we see emanating from three distinct but intertwined sources. One, Al-Qaeda central, is based primarily in the tribal areas of Pakistan. Though diminished greatly by the U.S. military, it still has a functioning leadership as well as an ability to communicate and spread the core ideology that fuels radical Islamists worldwide. Al-Qaeda central still burns with an intense and unrelenting hostility toward America. Its leaders believe they are at war with the United States and that time is on their side. There's no doubt that key leaders, foremost among them Ayman al-Zawahiri, will not give up on the hope of executing another 9/11-scale attack. Their ability to accomplish this at the moment is severely constrained, maybe even negligible, as many in the U.S. intelligence community believe. But it would be a mistake to assume their desire to carry out a mass attack on American soil does not persist to this day. The group's resilience—indeed, its continued existence in the face of the pounding it has absorbed from the United States and our allies for more than a decade—means we cannot assume they will abandon their goal to incur mass casualties.

Next is the spread of Al-Qaeda allies and affiliates throughout Africa and the Middle East. The list of these groups continues to grow. They include: Al-Qaeda of the Arabian Peninsula, based in Yemen and the source of numerous plots against the United States; Al-Qaeda of the Islamic Maghreb, based in Algeria, with a growing capacity to act beyond its base; Al Shabbab, Al-Qaeda's Somalian affiliate, which continues to attract followers from the Somali diaspora here and abroad; Ansar al Sharia in Libya, responsible for the Benghazi attack; and Ansar al Dine, the Al-Qaeda affiliate fueled by weapons and personnel coming from post-Gaddafi Libya. Then there are Al-Qaeda networks in Egypt's Sinai Desert, something rarely seen before the Arab Spring.

Two other Al-Qaeda-linked terrorist organizations stand out in importance today. The first is Al-Qaeda of Iraq, considered defunct as recently as 2008. Its powerful reemergence is a measure of the resilience of such groups. The second is the Al Nusra front in Syria, an Al-Qaeda organization spawned by Al-Qaeda in Iraq. It leads the rebellion against the Assad regime and is fueling the global jihad by attracting personnel from around the world, including North America.

So how do these affiliates overseas pose a threat to us in the United States? For one thing, they send Americans back home to attack us here. In 2009, one of the highest-ranking members of Al-Qaeda central recruited Najibullah Zazi, a native of Queens and a resident of the Denver-Aurora area, to carry out attacks on New York City. Zazi and two associates had traveled to Pakistan hoping to fight U.S. troops in Afghanistan. Instead, they were given training in explosives and sent back to the United States armed with the knowledge to build a bomb. Their plot was subsequently defeated through a joint investigation between the NYPD and the FBI. In 2010, authorities in Chicago arrested Pakistani-American David Headley. Headley had met with leaders of Lashkar-E-Taiba in Pakistan, an Al-Qaeda like-minded group, and conducted surveillance for its November 2008 commando assault on Mumbai. At least 20 young men from Minneapolis, all of Somali descent, joined Al Shabbab in Somalia over the past few years. Our concern: What happens if those who survive return to the United States?

In 2009, Al-Qaeda of the Arabian Peninsula dispatched Umar Abdulmuttallab, the underwear bomber, to blow up an airliner over Detroit. One year later, the same group dropped off two "printer bombs" at UPS and FedEx offices in Yemen addressed to the United States. The aim was to blow up the deadly cargo in planes over the eastern seaboard of the United States. Fortunately, the packages were intercepted in England and Dubai. In 2011, Samir Khan, the intellectual father of Al-Qaeda's on-line magazine, *Inspire*, was killed in a U.S. drone strike. Khan was a resident of Charlotte, North Carolina. Of late, we've seen how the Al Nusra front in Syria is attracting individuals from places such as Illinois to the battlefield there.

Beyond Al-Qaeda's core, its affiliates, allies, and like-minded groups, the danger from homegrown terrorists is a growing feature of the threat landscape we face in the United States and elsewhere. *Inspire* magazine and propaganda like it provide an easy road map for getting involved. The most infamous example of that is the 2010 *Inspire* article "Make a Bomb in the Kitchen of Your Mom," a how-to guide for using readily available household materials to build a bomb. It has now become the go-to manual for terrorists bent on destruction, as was the case in Boston and a number of the plots against New York. Travel to training camps abroad simply isn't necessary, and increasingly it's not part of the profile we uncover when a homegrown terrorist is revealed. The daunting, almost invisible nature of those pursuing "individual *jihad*" transforms the threat by placing mid-sized and even smaller urban centers in the United States in the crosshairs of terrorism. For the individual jihadist, size matters less. You can't get much less complicated then running someone down with a car and then hacking him to death with a meat cleaver and long knives. If terrorism is theater, New York and London will always be in the spotlight. But we learned with the Boston Marathon that all the world's a stage. As horrifying as these events were, Internet chatter among the *jihadi* forums we check regularly shows that many considered its perpetrators in Boston and Woolwich to be heroes. In both cases, we saw that the terrorists were prepared to confront police and die for their cause. Officers in Watertown and Woolwich did heroic jobs, but you can see what we're up against. Unfortunately, one doesn't need much more than a crude explosive device to kill, maim, and capture the world's attention all at once. This means local law enforcement has to be more vigilant than ever.

The challenge with big, complicated terrorism plots is the potential for catastrophic consequences. But they are easier to spot. The challenge with the attacks we saw in Boston and Woolwich and the several that have failed in New York are that they're small and hard to detect. Faisal Shahzad was on no one's radar when he drove his SUV filled with explosives into Times Square in May 2010. We just got lucky in that he elected to use less potent ingredients in the hope of avoiding detection during his acquisition of them. The ease with which terrorists can travel within the United States and beyond also makes inter-agency cooperation a must. For this reason the NYPD created Operation Sentry. This is a dynamic, intelligence-driven partnership among 140 police and law enforcement agencies throughout the Northeast and other parts of the country. Its premise is built on real-world events. For example, the plot to bomb the World Trade Center in 1993 was hatched across the Hudson River, in New Jersey. It was there that the chemicals were mixed, that the truck bomb was assembled and laced with cyanide. The staging area was well outside New York City. In 2005, when suicide bombers struck the London transit system, they did so using explosive-filled backpacks assembled in the city of Leeds, 180 miles north of the target. And Faisal Shahzad constructed his car bomb in Connecticut.

Our partners in Operation Sentry include the Boston Police Department. Immediately after the bombings in Boston, we assigned a lieutenant and two sergeants to the Boston Regional Intelligence Center to gather information. In May, we hosted a group of 20 members of Massachusetts law enforcement to discuss policing major events including July 4th. In the aftermath of the attacks, we also dispatched a lieutenant from our Intelligence Division to Youngstown, Ohio, to meet with executives from Phantom Fireworks. This is the company that unwittingly sold the fireworks to both the Tsarnaev brothers and Faisal Shahzad that they used to construct their bombs. We want Phantom to spread the word to its employees working at 1,200 locations nationwide to be aware that individuals seeking to build explosive devices could exploit their products. We're asking them to deny or flag suspicious purchases and to alert us if they believe there are possible links to terrorism. This is part and parcel of our Operation Nexus program, in which we partner with thousands of business owners in New York, Connecticut, and New Jersey to heighten their awareness of potential terrorist activity. We've also established a program with 11,000 members of the region's private security industry, sharing information and training through an initiative called NYPD Shield.

To defend ourselves, we must also maintain a good working relationship with the FBI and other federal partners through the Joint Terrorism Task Force. Despite the disagreements you've heard about from time to time, the NYPD and the FBI have a strong and essential partnership. It's essential to local law enforcement that intelligence be shared quickly. The only way to catch a lone wolf is through shared intelligence gathering. That's why our efforts to defend against terrorism must be proactive, so that we can find those who are in the earliest stages of planning violent acts and stop them. Oftentimes the use of undercover police officers may be the only effective way to identify homegrown terrorists who are often living here legally and operating alone or with just one or two accomplices. Ideally, through strong partnerships, good intelligence, and expert analysis, we'll identify plots in their earliest stages.

In New York, we're also installing an expanded network of smart cameras and license plate readers which, when tied together, greatly enhance investigations. Smart cameras have the capacity to alert us to the presence of suspicious packages before they detonate, should one be an actual explosive device. Cameras are a very powerful tool for law enforcement. We should all be encouraged by the fact that the public is overwhelmingly supportive of their use. Recent polls show that 80% approve. Although excellent in helping to apprehend suspects after the fact, this technology still amounts to "just in time" prevention. The vast number of targets available to terrorists makes it virtually impossible in all instances to intercept a device after it's been planted. Ideally, we need to disrupt plots long before the backpack is left on the sidewalk.

Good intelligence remains the key to prevention. The threat of terrorism has not diminished. It is here to stay, and we have to face that reality. Intelligence gathering is essential, including the use of undercover officers, to meet the continuing threat of terrorism lawfully and effectively. Technology is a powerful tool, but it has its limitations.

Finally, partnership and information sharing have never been more important in keeping our cities safe. The fight against terrorism is a long haul, one that all of us are in together, including members of the bar. Even with combat thousands of miles away, the front can return to our own backyards at any time. The police must be prepared for that eventuality. The good news is that U.S. law enforcement is better prepared than ever before to meet the threat.

IV

What Is the Mission: Why Is Counterterrorism So Difficult?

Lt. Colonel Tania M. Chacho and
Brig. General (retired) Michael J. Meese

The United States has been engaged in war since September 11, 2001, but the sudden initiation of the conflict and its subsequent evolution in both scale and scope has not been accompanied by a comprehensive examination of the type of war that we are engaged in—its military, political, social, and legal dimensions. The famous strategist Carl von Clausewitz said:

> No one starts a war—or rather, no one in his senses ought to do so—without first being clear in his mind what he intends to achieve by that war and how he intends to conduct it. The former is its political purpose; the latter its operational objectives. This is the governing principle which will set its course, prescribe the scale of means and effort which is required, and make its influence felt throughout down to the smallest operational detail.[1]

In the absence of the American people being "clear in our minds" about what this war is intended to achieve, it is difficult to interpret progress with regard to ends or to evaluate methods used with regards to means.

As a result of this lack of strategic clarity, the American public have difficulty understanding what it means for the war effort when President Bush proclaims "Mission accomplished" from the USS *Abraham Lincoln*, Ambassador Bremer

33

announces that Saddam Hussein is captured, the Pentagon broadcasts that a key Al-Qaeda leader is killed by a drone strike, President Obama announces that Osama bin Laden is killed or says that we have withdrawn from Iraq or are ending combat missions in Afghanistan. Similarly, Americans are confused about the means of war when they hear of the use of drones, enhanced interrogation techniques, special operations, covert operations, or expanding the war to an increasing number of countries.

The purpose of this chapter is to generally explain counterterrorism strategy to help inform the fundamentals of counterterrorism law that constitute the remaining chapters in the book. To adequately address terrorist threats, U.S. policy makers and the public should understand the characteristics of the war that we are in, the characteristics of state-societal relationships, and the legal/organizational framework under which we operate. This chapter will begin by explaining the nature of the war in which we are engaged first from the perspective of military theory and doctrine. Second, recognizing that war is ultimately a human endeavor, the chapter discusses the social terrain on which the war is fought, with particular consideration to the cultural differences between the U.S. and the states in which the war is being fought. Finally, the chapter will explain the practical and legal challenges of executing the war.

The Nature of the Current War

Although most people in the United States would use September 11, 2001, as the start date of the current conflict, leaders of Al-Qaeda would begin much earlier. Osama bin Laden issued a fatwa as his declaration of war against the United States in 1996, explaining that the presence and influence of the United States in the Middle East in general and in Saudi Arabia in particular was intolerable and must be opposed by all means necessary.[2] This declaration was issued after the first World Trade Center attack in 1993 and led to the attacks on the US Embassies in Kenya and Tanzania in 1998 and the attack on the *USS Cole* in 2000. He proceeded to use this approach to inspire followers throughout the Middle East to attack both the "far enemy," which is the United States and the West, as well as the "near enemy," which includes those apostate states in the Middle East. He considered the near enemy to be those "apostate regimes" that are cooperating with the West, moving toward modernizing societies, and not operating in accordance with strict Sharia law.[3]

As Al-Qaeda and the threat to the United States and the West have evolved, they have continued to have several attributes in common. First, they generally are religious-inspired extremists who use extremely narrow interpretations of Islam, which are inconsistent with the views of the vast majority of moderate Muslims, to justify their actions. Second, they tend to reject modernity, including democratic movements, widespread communications, increased participation in government, and enhanced rights for women, workers, and children. Third, they leverage the tactics of asymmetric warfare to pursue their aims, using high-profile and relatively low-cost terrorist weapons and action to influence populations and achieve their ends. Fourth, they believe that they are engaging in a long-term, perhaps eternal, struggle, which is why General John Abizaid, former Commander of U.S. Central Command, coined the term "The Long War" to describe the persistent conflict against religious-inspired extremists.[4] As a result, the United States faces groups motivated by a hostile ideology that is global in scope, ruthless in purpose, insidious in method, and infinite in its duration.[5] It has as its intent to undermine Western power and to eliminate Western influence throughout the Middle East.

To address this threat, the United States has evolved and adapted its strategy to combat terrorism. During the initial phases of the war in Afghanistan and Iraq, there was a belief that the removal of the previous regime and support of alternative local leaders and their military forces would be sufficient impetus for populations to rise up and support the new governments. However, insurgent forces that opposed the U.S. occupation in each country used asymmetric tactics to increase violence against the U.S., the coalition, the Iraq and Afghan governments, and people in each country. In reaction, the U.S. Army and Marine Corps substantially revised their doctrine, eventually publishing a new approach to warfare in FM 3-24, *Counterinsurgency*.[6] Understanding the nature of counterinsurgency is essential to understanding the nature of our current war and the role of counterterrorism.

The counterinsurgency manual captures the nature of the war as described above and is reflected in figure 1. The focus is *not* primarily just killing the enemy, as it is during conventional war; instead, the focus is on population security and "to foster effective governance by a legitimate government."[7] In a counterinsurgency, the enemy is a relatively small part of the population and is competing for influence with the government that is countering the insurgency. In between insurgents and those who support the government is the passive or neutral population, which is primarily concerned for its own welfare. Taking steps to secure and thereby influence the population to be more supportive of the government is the essence of counterinsurgency. The ways to do that include all five lines of operation depicted in the arrows moving from left to right, including conducting combat operations, building up host nation forces, providing essential services, supporting governance, and increasing economic development. Importantly, all of this is in the context of the larger arrow—information operations—so that the local populace understands the actions of the counterinsurgents to defeat the insurgency and therefore will be more likely to support the government.

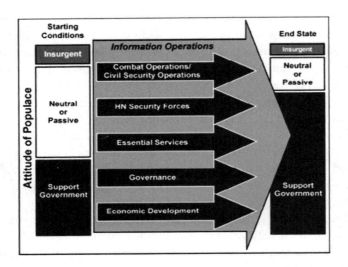

Figure 1-1. Counterinsurgency Lines of Operation[8]

There is often the misperception that counterinsurgency is like peacekeeping operations and consists primarily of stability operations (the bottom three arrows). To be effective, counterinsurgency is much more than just "winning hearts and minds," and must include both offensive and defensive operations in addition to stability operations. Offensive operations concentrate on killing or capturing the enemy to minimize the number of enemy insurgents. However, it is essential that these operations be done in a discriminating way so that offensive actions do not inspire more insurgents than they kill. Defensive operations ensure that friendly forces are protected and minimize casualties, but they must not be so defensive that forces are consolidated on large bases and are precluded from effective partnering with the host nation. During part of the Iraq war in 2005, President Bush explained, "Our strategy can be summed up this way: As the Iraqis stand up, we will stand down."' Understandably, many of the U.S. units, with some notable exceptions, consolidated on large forward operating bases and concentrated on training Iraqi forces instead of spreading out among the population and partnering with Iraqi forces to help them learn to conduct operations.[10] Orchestrating all three aspects of counterinsurgency—offense, defense, and stability operations—reflected in figure 2 is extremely complex and must be done by combatants at all levels.

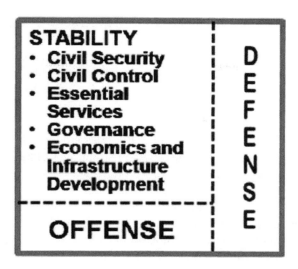

Figure 1-2. Components of Counterinsurgency[11]

With this understanding of counterinsurgency doctrine, we can now discuss the nature of war and the important distinction between counterterrorism (CT) and counterinsurgency (COIN). When viewed at an operational or theater level, such as in Iraq or Afghanistan, counterterrorism generally refers to the offensive part of the counterinsurgency—the kinetic military actions to capture or kill terrorists or insurgents. These offensive operations are sometimes conducted by conventional military units, which are normally assigned as "battle space owners," responsible for a particular area on the ground. CT operations are also often conducted by special operations units, which have specialized intelligence, training, equipment, and personnel to conduct these operations. The success of CT operations is substantially influenced by quality of the existing COIN operation on the ground. The battle space owner's units that provide "boots on the ground" are critical to intelligence, situational awareness, and action after an operation to maximize the success of offensive CT operations. At an operational level, then, counterterrorism is an essential component of effective counterinsurgency and should be integrated with the counterinsurgency campaign to be most effective.

When viewed at a global level, the "nesting" is reversed and counterinsurgency can be part of an overall national counterterrorism strategy. Counterterrorism is defined by the U.S. Department of Defense as "Actions taken directly against terrorist networks and indirectly to influence and render global and regional environments inhospitable to terrorist networks."[12] Counterinsurgency addresses the latter half of that definition by strengthening the ability of a state to control its own territory, thereby indirectly rendering the environment less hospitable to terrorist networks. When policy makers discuss a "CT-only" strategy, they generally mean special operations or other targeting of terrorists *without* a complementary counterinsurgency campaign to support indigenous forces, develop situational awareness, and otherwise leverage offensive military actions. This "CT-only" strategy may entail fewer forces, costs, and risks to troops, but it will likely be less effective because it is only concentrating on offensive operations against an enemy and could exacerbate tensions with the population as a whole.

This relationship between CT and COIN is important to understand because it relates directly to the nature of the war we are fighting. Offensive CT operations are necessary, but they alone are not sufficient. Military offensive operations must be combined with advances in all possible instruments of power to enhance the power of all states to develop legitimate governance and combat terrorism and to render the environment in which terrorists operate as inhospitable as possible. These other elements of power include diplomatic, economic, law enforcement, intelligence, information, and financial efforts that work in a coordinated manner to combat terrorism. While this chapter concentrates primarily on military elements of policy, it is important to recognize that military actions are and should be only one part of the overall U.S. approach to combating terrorists.

In summary, the nature of the war that we have been fighting has been a counterinsurgency campaign with a strong CT component in both Iraq and Afghanistan. In the case of Iraq, the U.S. counterinsurgency campaign helped the Iraqis step back from a civil war in which 3,000 Iraqis were killing each other each month in 2006, and has created a condition in which Iraq is sovereign, secure, and self-reliant, with security forces that are adequate to address the residual (and sometimes significant) violence. While governance remains problematic and political conflicts abound, they are being addressed through Iraqi institutions that, while far from ideal, are generally representative and accountable.[13] Afghanistan is about three years behind Iraq in transitioning with moderately capable Afghan security forces that have taken lead in security throughout Afghanistan.[14] By the end of 2014, the United States, NATO, and the total of 50 nations that constitute the coalition likely will have achieved the objectives stated in President Obama's December 1, 2009, West Point speech:

> Al-Qaeda has been denied a safe haven, the Taliban's momentum has been reversed and it no longer has the capacity to overthrow the Afghan government, and the Afghan security forces and government have been strengthened and are in the lead for their own responsibility.[16]

Outside of Iraq and Afghanistan, special operations forces have conducted operations in Yemen and the Horn of Africa that have largely been CT-only operations that have targeted selected Al-Qaeda cells achieved some success in developing intelligence and then targeting specific individuals.[15] These CT operations are complemented by stability operations conducted by the Combined Joint Task Force-Horn of Africa (CJTF-HOA), which includes approximately 2,000 troops stationed in Djibouti. CJTF-HOA trains security forces in several countries in East Africa in counterterrorism, professionalization, peace operations, humanitarian assistance efforts, and other operations as part of an effort to enhance the long-term stability of the region.[16]

These operations have aimed to capture or kill terrorists who would seek to harm the United States and Western interests as well as to limit the freedom of action of other terrorists, requiring them to divert some of their attention and resources toward their own survival. At the same time, through both comprehensive counterinsurgency campaigns in Iraq and Afghanistan as well as stability operations, such as those conducted by CJTF-HOA, the U.S. has attempted to promote an environment that is less supportive of terrorists. The degree to which these efforts have been successful are partly a function of the complex social terrain in which they are implemented, which is the next part of this chapter.

The Social Terrain

The United States has engaged in a massive war effort since the 9/11 attacks, and a component of this campaign has focused on increasing our understanding of the areas and societies in which Al-Qaeda and other anti-Western terrorists find support. One of the critical realities concerning the current war—both counterinsurgency at an operational level and counterterrorism at a global level— is that "you are not going to kill your way out of this war."[17] Therefore, it is essential to understand the cultural and social aspects in which we are operating so that incorporating non-kinetic and nonmilitary factors becomes an important part of our continued prosecution of the war. Political, economic, and social relationships are so crucial to the functioning of every society. There are significant differences in these relationships when comparing the United States with Iraq, Afghanistan, or other countries, and our ability to comprehend these differences is critical to long-term success. But this understanding does not come quickly, and it also requires a significant commitment of both time and resources. In the long term, to truly reduce the threat of terrorist violence, states need developmental efforts to increase two things: first, their institutional capacity, and second, their civil society. Both efforts provide a means for handling grievances nonviolently and thus offer alternatives to terrorism for promoting change. The U.S. government does have some state-building mechanisms, but often nongovernmental organizations (NGOs) are better equipped to develop the civil society considered so necessary to participatory political systems.

To begin the discussion of the social and political terrain in developing states, it is helpful to first examine the perspective from which we approach it. We tend to view other societies through a lens shaped primarily by our own experiences. American society has a record of addressing grievances through mostly nonviolent means (with several notable historical exceptions), and this has affected U.S. views of political culture and normative behaviors. Despite the birth of the American republic out of an armed uprising, the accepted societal norm has evolved to eschew violence as a viable method of instituting change. Trust runs strong among American citizens that the democratic system offers both alternatives and a means for dissenting voices to be considered, despite recent frustrations with a lack of bipartisanship.[18] Underpinning this trust is faith in a fair and impartial judicial system that enforces laws and metes out punishment to those found in violation.

Despite some notable concerns discussed by Robert Putnam in his famous work, *Bowling Alone,* most scholars view civil society in the United States as generally healthy.[19] Americans participate in a wide variety of civic activities, such as Kiwanis, Little League, and religious organizations. These activities are notable in that they have little to no government interference, and so offer an outlet for interested groups of citizens to share views and activities outside of the control of the state.[20] While Putman found some concerning dips in pre-9/11 levels of American involvement in these activities (such as his often-cited drop in participation in bowling leagues), his post-9/11 follow-up revealed a resurgence in other civic activities, such as volunteerism, particularly among younger Americans.[21] What is notable is that civil society in the United States offers an outlet for social interaction outside of the control of the government, and thus is an important element of American political culture and social terrain.

With such strong institutions and a robust civil society, Americans understandably have a tendency to "mirror image" their political ideas (and ideals) onto foreign countries and societies. The concept behind this is logical: if others can develop the institutions, techniques, and procedures used by Western-style democracies, then they too will turn away from violence as a means of addressing grievances with the state, and terrorism will become less effective and attractive. As Marsha Crenshaw has observed, terrorism is a "collectively rational strategic choice" for grievance redress,[22] so if other options were available and the consequences for terrorist action were unacceptably high, it could reduce the viability of this violent option. Concurrent with conducting counterterrorism operations and supporting the development of host-nation security capacities, the U.S. government counterinsurgency policy seeks to promote the same institutions, techniques, and procedures that have produced stability in Western societies.

Yet the state-societal relationship differs around the world. The Western model offers one arrangement; in non-Western societies, other relationships have developed that determine who obtains power and becomes the political "elites" of the country. In particular, two social structure components play a significant role: the strength of family/ethnic/tribal ties and the fundamental role of religion in the public sphere. These factors become even more important in areas where a legal framework and jurisdiction are not institutionalized; in these situations, informal procedures and relationships tend to dominate.

First, familial and ethnic or tribal ties, and the identity inherent in these, create power arrangements. These relationships determine "who gets what, when, and how," which is a key function of politics and political institutions.[23] If alternate paths exist to making these resource and power allocation determinations, the players and the outcomes can differ greatly. Since counterinsurgency operations depend on understanding who and what holds sway over a population, knowledge of this terrain is critical.

Second, it is important to understand the role of religion in a society: do citizens view it as part of the public or private sphere? Throughout the world, there is a long history of religious involvement in areas beyond the realm of spirituality; for example, Christianity, Judaism, and Islam all have rich histories that contain evidence of their influence on legal, ethical, and intellectual language and thought.[24] In fact, prior to the Treaty of Westphalia and the entry of the state on the political scene, religion defined the language of politics. So while the U.S. Constitution places value on the separation of church and state, many societies emphasize instead the connection between religion and politics. Awareness of this connection is critical in counterinsurgency operations, where mirror-imaging Western concepts regarding the place of religion in the private/spiritual sphere can result in unintended second- and third-order effects.

These elements of social structure also affect the political culture (how individuals view their relationship to politics) within a country. Civil society is often nascent in developing states, which offers little base for development of public activism and participation. While involvement in activities outside of the governmental sphere may not seem a solid springboard for increased political participation, studies have shown that it is exactly these activities that provide citizens with the opportunity to exchange information and ideas that can eventually serve as a counterweight to governmental power.[25] So an absence of clubs, social organizations, or other activities can give rise to movements that advocate violence to create change.

This is particularly true when a government lacks effective institutions that respond to societal needs and demands. Often, developing countries have governmental institutions that suffer from various forms of corruption. Yet this exploitation for personal gain may have a cultural context that increases its validity within the society. For example, in some developing countries, people view "kickbacks" as a valid way to earn money when the opportunity arises. It becomes simply a culturally accepted transaction cost as part of doing business.[26] But this becomes problematic when trying to wage a counterinsurgency and develop economic ties with Western businesses. In Afghanistan and Iraq, for example, U.S. businesses and individuals must adhere to the Foreign Corrupt Practices Act, which prohibits the payment of bribes (both cash and noncash items) to foreign officials. This anti-bribery provision makes it impossible for Americans to distribute any culturally expected payments or gifts that may be necessary to begin a business relationship. The effect is that U.S. companies tend to be reluctant to enter these markets, and so Iraqi and Afghan businesses turn elsewhere for these economic connections, developing ties with other entities.

The U.S. approach favors using state instruments of power (the classic "DIME" formula consisting of diplomatic, informational, military, and economic instruments) to conduct both state-building and counterinsurgency operations. The U.S. has governmental agencies and mechanisms in place to support this approach: for example, the military provides security and infrastructure support, USAID coordinates development aid with the host government, and the State Department conducts diplomacy to coordinate and enhance these efforts. Government policy naturally favors and is organized to implement this type of "top-down" approach. Such approaches appear to support policy coherence, unity of effort, efficient allocation of resources, and coherent division of responsibilities. Yet these approaches have had substantial challenges in promoting effective governance in Iraq and Afghanistan. States with weak institutions, few civil society outlets, and different social structures and political cultures (exacerbated by internal insecurity) simply do not have the mechanisms in place to absorb the "top-down" implementation of either state-building efforts or a counterinsurgency operation. In spite of the lack of success in "top down" approaches, it is unlikely that policy will change toward a more decentralized approach because of the inherent biases within governmental organizations.

A more effective approach could be implemented by nongovernmental organizations (NGOs), which work "bottom-up" and allow social and political development to organically take shape.[27] Their grassroots approach allows change to evolve from existing social structure and political culture, which ultimately strengthens the fabric that connects society to the political institutions that make up the state. NGOs have also achieved success at encouraging the development of civil society, assisting in the creation of outlets for individuals and communities to share thoughts, ideas, and interests.

But despite these successes, the NGO approach to state-building also has drawbacks. The various organizations have different agendas, operate on a much smaller scale, often have longer time horizons, and have fewer resources than the

U.S. government can bring to bear. Perhaps most problematic from a government standpoint is that NGOs operate independently and often as neutral entities, and these organizations are normally not linked to U.S. policy efforts, nor do they want to be linked to such efforts. While NGOs can develop a deep understanding of the social and political terrain and have a long-term focus, their agendas are entirely separate from those of the U.S. government, and most object vehemently to any sort of association with counterinsurgency operations. This creates a dilemma for the government: organizations with perhaps the best understanding of the social and political terrain of developing countries are not within the government, but rather outside of it—and these NGOs want to stay that way. Developing a capacity within the U.S. government to truly understand various societies and political systems takes time, and has unfortunately achieved only limited success in the past.

Policy Development and Implementation

In spite of understanding the nature of the war that the United States is engaged in and attempting to navigate the social terrain in which its forces operate, it is still extremely difficult for the United States to conduct counterterrorism operations effectively for two reasons. First, as discussed above, because the U.S. government is the actor implementing counterterrorism, it is difficult to develop and implement policy in a way that will complement the decentralized, "bottom-up" approach that is most likely to be successful. However, there is a second, more challenging problem than the general preference for a centralized, "top-down" solution. The outcome of the policy process is not even the best one that a centralized government could develop; it is the best one that could be developed considering all of the inherent legal constraints that affect policy implementation. To paraphrase Donald Rumsfeld, "You go to war with the government that you have, not the one that you might want or wish to have."[28] The various authorities of different parts of government are legacies of previous legislation and have not been substantially updated to account for the challenges in the current war. Rather than adjust the law, executive branch agencies develop elaborate and sometimes cumbersome work-arounds to implement policy. While some of these legal distinctions will be discussed in more detail in subsequent chapters, a few examples illustrate some of the challenges.

With regard to legal authorities, agencies of government operate under different titles of the United States Code with different oversight from different congressional committees, as explained in the following table:

Agency	Title of U.S. Code	Congressional Oversight Committee
Department of Defense National Guard	Title 10 Title 32	Armed Services
Department of State	Title 22	Foreign Relations
Intelligence Community	Title 50	Permanent Select Committee on Intelligence
Department of Justice Bureau of Prisons	Title 28 Title 18	Judiciary
Department of Homeland Security Coast Guard	Title 6 Title 14	Various

There was nothing fundamentally wrong with these distinctions when the nature of war kept conflict confined to the Armed Services, overseas development and diplomacy with diplomats, intelligence organizations primarily collecting intelligence, and justice functions limited to the confines of U.S. borders. However, as discussed above, the nature of this war is different.

The problem with these distinctions and the related oversight mechanisms is that with the nature of war that we are engaged in and the social terrain in which it is fought, there can be a misalignment between the part of the U.S. government that has the right capabilities, the right authorities, and the right oversight to best accomplish a particular mission. The most prominent example of this was the raid in Abbottabad, Pakistan, which killed Osama bin Laden. The U.S. Armed Forces (organized under title 10) had the appropriate capability to conduct the mission. The intelligence community (under title 50) had the appropriate authorities and strictly limited reporting requirements to the intelligence committees. So elements of the Joint Special Operations Command were administratively attached to the Director of the CIA for the execution of the operation. With the success of the operation and the understandable deference of the Secretary of Defense to this arrangement, it was not an issue. However, had the operation been a failure, a post-mortem investigation probably would have faulted the convoluted chain of command that was primarily established to work around existing laws.

These capability-authority-oversight misalignments exist in many more mundane areas of security implementation. For example:

- In stopping illegal drug and human trafficking in the vicinity of U.S. territory, for example, the U.S. Navy has the capability, but the U.S. Coast Guard has the legal authority to do so. The services have established a work-around where the Navy flag is lowered and the Coast Guard flag is raised, and temporarily the ship and crew come under the command of the Coast Guard with their authorities and power to arrest criminals.

- In large-scale reconstruction projects in combat zones, the U.S. military has the budget, the troops, and a disproportionately large budget, but the State Department and USAID have the authorities for overseas development. Throughout the last decade, many work-arounds have been tried, such as granting the military funding from the Commanders Emergency Response Program that was sometimes at cross-purposes with USAID development funding. In the most extreme case, the Afghan Infrastructure Fund was developed to address large projects. It required a "dual key" sign-off by the Department of State/USAID and Department of Defense (DoD) for large projects as a compromise between Armed Services and Foreign Relations committees as well as the State and Defense Departments, which found it problematic to cede jurisdiction in support of wartime development efforts.[29]

- In corrections operations, the Department of Justice, and specifically the Bureau of Prisons, have the expertise in the federal government, but again the State Department has the authority for all overseas development assistance. When detention operations in combat zones were identified as a major liability that could impede the mission, DoD had the funding, personnel, and resources to create a detention and corrections joint task force, but had continuous challenges developing Afghan judicial capacity without violating authorities of other agencies. Eventually a month-long senior interagency committee developed a report that supported work-arounds to accomplish the mission, but was particularly convoluted.[30] For example, although the appropriate agency for corrections in Afghanistan under both current law and long-term objectives is the Central Bureau of Prisons under the Afghan Justice Ministry, the prison guards at the U.S.-built detention facility in Parwan had to be assigned and organized under the Afghan Ministry of Defense, because U.S. DoD title 10 authority for the Afghan Security Forces Funds would only allow funding of members of the military, not those in the Justice Department.

- In attempting to enhance U.S. national security, often developing the policing capacity of partner nations is the most effective and efficient approach. The State Department has the authorities for development assistance but does not have significant budget authority and sometimes lacks the expertise. The Justice Department often has the expertise but lacks both the budget and, in most cases, the authority. The Defense Department has the budget, capabilities, and procedures for foreign military sales and training, but title 10 authorities only permit equipment sales or transfers to military units, not the national police forces. Given these legal strictures, the U.S. either forgoes providing equipment and assistance for police forces or requires the nation being assisted to revise its own procedures so that the ministry of defense gets the equipment and either develops the capability or "lends" the equipment to police forces.[31]

By informing the relevant congressional leaders, the executive branch has often been granted wide latitude in national security affairs to implement work-arounds that "dynamically interpret" U.S. law, but each of these exceptions imposes significant challenges on organizations as practices increasingly diverge from the law without formally adjusting authorities to adapt to the new circumstances. In other circumstances, in spite of the importance of the objective to the national security interests of the United States and the capacity of some parts of the government to achieve that objective, legal constraints prevent effective policy from being implemented. In any case, existing legal structures certainly make implementing effective counterterrorism policy more difficult.

Conclusion

While the conduct of war will change, the war that the United States has been fighting for the past 12 years will likely continue into the foreseeable future. It is critical for U.S. policy makers to understand the war that we are in, the social terrain on which it is being fought, and the applicable laws that govern the way in which it is executed. With that understanding, policy can be better informed and implemented to better achieve U.S. objectives. As one continues to examine the fundamentals of counterterrorism law in the remaining chapters of this book, thinking about how to align the law with our current practices can be a significant step forward toward improving the American national security policy.

Notes

1. CARL VON CLAUSEWITZ, ON WAR 579 (Michael Howard & Peter Paret trans. & ed., Princeton Univ. Press, 1976).

2. Osama bin Laden, "Declaration of War against the Americans Occupying the Land of the Two Holy Places," accessed on Feb. 2, 2013, at http://www.pbs.org/newshour/updates/military/july-dec96/fatwa_1996.html.

3. *See, among others,* Will McCants, *Shaykah 'Isa on Near Enemy vs. Far Enemy, in* JIHADICA: DOCUMENTING THE GLOBAL JIHAD, accessed Feb. 8, 2013, at http://www.jihadica.com/shaykh-isa-on-near-enemy-vs-far-enemy/.

4.   Bradley Graham & Josh White, *Abizaid Credited with Popularizing the Term 'Long War,'* WASH. POST, Feb. 3, 2006.

5.   The terms used in this sentence are the same as those used by President Eisenhower to describe the threat to the United States in 1961. The struggle against communism, which involved all elements of power (military and nonmilitary), had to be sustained over time, and eventually prevailed, is an appropriate comparison to the challenges of terrorism today. *See* Dwight D. Eisenhower: Farewell Address to the Nation, Jan. 17, 1961.

6.   COUNTERINSURGENCY, FM 3-34, MCWP 3-33.5 (Wash.: U.S. Army & U.S. Marine Corps, Dec. 15, 2006).

7.   *Id.*, p. 1-21.

8.   *Id.*, p. 5-3.

9.   George W. Bush: War Update, Fort Bragg, N.C., June 28, 2005, accessed on Feb. 12, 2013, at http://www.presidentialrhetoric.com/speeches/06.28.05.html.

10.   For example, during 2005-2006, coalition soldiers were supposed to consolidate from 112 to 50 forward operating bases and "As they stand up we will stand down" is reflected in the fact that the central tenet of General Casey's strategy as the commander in Iraq was "shifting responsibility to the nascent Iraqi Forces." *See* MICHAEL R. GORDON & BERNARD TRAINOR, THE ENDGAME: THE INSIDE STORY OF THE STRUGGLE FOR IRAQ, FROM GEORGE W. BUSH TO BARACK OBAMA 182, 192 (Pantheon Books 2012).

11.   COUNTERINSURGENCY 1–19.

12.   DEPARTMENT OF DEFENSE DICTIONARY OF MILITARY AND ASSOCIATED TERMS 69 (The Joint Staff, Dec. 15, 2012).

13.   *See* GORDON & TRAINOR, *supra* note 11, for the best book on Iraq. Its assessment is especially relevant on pages 685–91.

14.   *See* REPORT ON PROGRESS TOWARD SECURITY AND STABILITY IN AFGHANISTAN (Dep't of Defense, December 2012).

15.   Reporting on these kinds of operations is understandably limited, but was reported in Sean D. Naylor, *The Secret War in Africa*, MILITARY TIMES, October-December 2011. *See also* ERIC SCHMITT & THOM SHANKER, COUNTERSTRIKE: THE UNTOLD STORY OF AMERICA'S SECRET CAMPAIGN AGAINST AL-QAEDA (McMillan 2011).

16.   LAUREN PLOCH, AFRICA COMMAND: U.S. STRATEGIC INTERESTS AND THE ROLE OF THE U.S. MILITARY IN AFRICA, Rep. RL 34003 (Cong. Res. Serv., July 22, 2011), 20–21.

17.   *See* Michael Meese, Testimony before U.S. House of Representatives, Committee on Oversight and Government Reform, Subcommittee on National Security and Foreign Affairs: Innovative Approaches to Defeating Al-Qaeda, Feb. 14, 2008, and Gen. David Petraeus, Distinguished Lecturer in International Affairs, Wheatley Inst., March 25, 2010.

18.   A January 2013 Pew Research Poll showed that Americans generally trust the existing political system but are frustrated with lawmakers. The survey found a majority (56%) agree with the statement, "The political system can work fine, it is the members of Congress that are the problem." *See* Pew Research Center Jan. 9-13 2013 survey, Q23, *available at* http://www.people-press.org/files/2013/01/1-31-13-3.png.

19.   *For example, see* LESTER M. SALAMON, S. WOJCIECH SOKOLOWSKI AND ASSOCS., GLOBAL CIVIL SOCIETY: DIMENSION OF THE NONPROFIT SECTOR, Vol. II (Kumarian Press 2004), which shows the U.S. in the top quarter of the measured components of civil society. *See also* Johns Hopkins Center for Civil Society Studies for additional data published after 2004 (*available at* ccss.jhu.edu.).

20.   For a discussion of the definition of "civil society," the debates surrounding the term, and its relationship to associational life and the public sphere, *see* MICHAEL EDWARDS, CIVIL

SOCIETY (Polity Press 2009). Alan Wolfe offers a succinct definition of civil society adopted here: "Those forms of communal and associational life which are organized neither by the self-interest of the market nor by the coercive potential of the state." Alan Wolfe, *Is Civil Society Obsolete?: Revisiting Predictions of the Decline of Civil Society in "Whose Keeper?"* BROOKINGS, Fall 1997, *available at* http://www.brookings.edu/research/articles/1997/09/fall-civilsociety-wolfe.

21. Putnam outlined his concern about the disintegration of American civic life in his famous work *Bowling Alone*, first published as an article in 1995 and then expanded into a book in 2000. *See* ROBERT PUTNAM, BOWLING ALONE: THE COLLAPSE AND REVIVAL OF AMERICAN COMMUNITY (Simon & Schuster 2001). After the 9/11 attacks, Putnam re-examined the topic and found a surge in civic engagement, particularly among young people; but this study also revealed a growing divide among the classes. *See* Thomas H. Sander & Robert D. Putnam, *Still Bowling Alone?: The Post-9/11 Split*, JOURNAL OF DEMOCRACY, Vol. 21, No. 1, January 2010, at 9–16.

22. *See* Martha Crenshaw, *The Logic of Terrorism: Terrorist Behavior as a Product of Strategic Choice, in* ORIGINS OF TERRORISM: PSYCHOLOGIES, IDEOLOGIES, THEOLOGIES, STATES OF MIND (Walter Reich ed.) (Woodrow Wilson Center Press and Johns Hopkins 1998), pp. 7–24.

23. This description of politics was first coined by Harold Lasswell. *See* HAROLD LASSWELL, POLITICS: WHO GETS WHAT, WHEN, HOW (1936) (Meridian 1958). *See also* ROY C. MACRIDIS & STEVEN L. BURG, INTRODUCTION TO COMPARATIVE POLITICS: REGIMES AND CHANGE (Longman 1991) for a discussion of the power arrangements within individual regimes.

24. *See* Jose Casanova, *Public Religions Revisited, in* RELIGION: BEYOND THE CONCEPT 101–19 (Hent de Vries, ed.) (Fordham Univ. Press 2008). Dr. Nelly Lahoud has also articulated this concept in lectures at the United States Military Academy, West Point.

25. *See* Michael W. Foley & Bob Edwards, *The Paradox of Civil Society*, JOURNAL OF DEMOCRACY, Vol. 7 No. 3 (1996), at 39. Foley and Edwards articulate the "Civil Society II" concept that emphasizes the importance of civil association as a counterweight to the state, as practiced by the Polish resistance movement in the 1980s.

26. *See* Alan Doig & Stephen Riley, *Corruption and Anti-Corruption Strategies: Issues and Case Studies from Developing Countries, in* CORRUPTION AND INTEGRITY IMPROVEMENT INITIATIVES IN DEVELOPING COUNTRIES (United Nations Development Programme 1998), at 45–62, *available at* http://mirror.undp.org/magnet/docs/efa/corruption/Chapter03.pdf.

27. *See* Telmo Rudi Frantz, *The Role of NGOs in the Strengthening of Civil Society*, WORLD DEVELOPMENT, Vol. 15, Supp. 1, Autumn 1987, at 121–27. Interestingly, American history contains many examples of "bottom-up" movements that resulted in political change. Examples include Thomas Paine's *Common Sense*, the Civil Rights movement led by Martin Luther King, and grassroots environmental movements that have led to legislative changes.

28. Then-Secretary of Defense Donald Rumsfeld said to troops in Kuwait on December 8, 2004, "As you know, you go to war with the Army you have. They're not the Army you might want or wish to have at a later time." *See* William Kristol, *The Defense Secretary We Have*, WASH. POST, Dec. 15, 2004, at A33.

29. *See* Office of the Special Inspector General for Afghanistan Reconstruction, *Fiscal Year 2011 Afghanistan Infrastructure Fund Projects Are Behind Schedule and Lack Adequate Sustainment Plans* (SIGAR, July 30, 2012).

30. JTF-435 Interagency Report, February 2010.

31. This dilemma was one of the drawbacks discussed during a training session for officials from the Ministry of Internal Affairs of Georgia, organized by the Jebsen Center for Counter Terrorism Studies at the Fletcher School of Law and Diplomacy, Nov. 28 to Dec. 1, 2005, Tbilisi, Georgia.

V

Lawyers, the Courts,
and Military Commissions

Peter R. Masciola, Christopher L. Kannady,
and Michel D. Paradis

Introduction

The U.S. military has attempted to create a National Security Court for much of
the past decade. It is called the Military Commissions at Guantanamo Bay, Cuba.
It was a bad idea then and remains a bad idea now. The end product has been
overcome by divisive politics that has answered none of the tough national security
questions this country faces.

Few national security issues over the past decades have been as fraught as the
question of what judicial process is due to the detainees at Guantanamo. As the
dust settles, Guantanamo now presents the problem of how to release detainees
who should be released, how a few dozen terrorist suspects should continue to be
detained, and how a handful should be prosecuted, while the cost of keeping the
military commissions continues to grow. Of the 800 men to have passed through
there, only 164 remain at the time of this writing.[1] The number convicted in the

---

Disclaimer: The opinions expressed in this chapter are based entirely on "open source" public
information and are exclusively the personal opinions of the authors. The chapter does not in any
way reflect the opinions, policies, or positions of the Office of the Chief Defense Counsel, the
Department of Defense General Counsel's Office, the Military Commissions, the Military
Services, the Department of Defense, or any part of the United States Government.

Guantanamo Military Commissions totals seven. Five resulted from plea deals in exchange for release and the other two were vacated on appeal.[2] Eight men presently face charges, and the Chief Prosecutor has publicly suggested that no more than 20 detainees, including those already convicted, will ever be criminally charged.[3] These eight men face years of protracted litigation.

We were asked to comment on proposals for a national security court. The first part of this essay identifies our main points of concern, which are in some part legal, but are overwhelmingly pragmatic and rooted in our experiences in Guantanamo. If the Guantanamo experiment has taught us anything, it is that creating a court system from scratch is no small matter. Even if such a novel endeavor were ultimately sustained as constitutional, a conclusion that is by no means obvious, there is little reason to believe that it would avoid repeating the same systemic pitfalls of the Guantanamo Military Commissions.

The second part of this essay endeavors to offer a constructive alternative—a formal national security bar. The essence of this idea is contained in most of the proposals for a national security court. Ours is an attempt to select from the best of everything and propose a streamlined alternative. We suggest that a national security bar be decoupled from the broader proposals because it will not only provide most of the national security benefits national security courts are projected to generate, but will also ensure greater judicial efficiency and due process in a broader range of national security cases.

National Security Courts Are a Bad Idea . . .

Several legal scholars, practitioners, and policy makers have sought to consolidate national security lessons learned since 9/11 into proposals for "national security courts." One of the most prominent of these proposals was presented in a *New York Times* op-ed coauthored by Neal Katyal, who argued *Hamdan v. Rumsfeld*, and Jack Goldsmith, the Office of Legal Counsel head who sought to rescind the infamous "torture memos" after taking office in 2003. Katyal & Goldsmith advocated the creation of "terrorists' courts" as "sensible institutions for the long haul."[4] A far more detailed proposal is presented in a book by Glenn Sulmasy.[5]

While each proposal varies in its details, they generally articulate a pair of common functions for these courts to serve. The first is that national security courts would have the jurisdiction to decide what are, in effect, some combination of Law of Armed Conflict administrative detainee review boards and civil commitment cases. Individuals who have some affiliation with terrorism or pose some kind of national security danger could be brought before these tribunals and held irrespective of whether they have committed a particular crime. Instead, they would be held for alleged noncriminal acts that present a national security threat. The analogy commonly drawn is to the proceedings used to commit the mentally ill and sex offenders, where the first hearing determines commitment and periodic reviews evaluate continued dangerousness.

The second function national security courts are proposed to serve is as an alternative forum for criminal prosecutions in terrorism cases. These courts would dispense with juries and the ordinary procedural rules that would otherwise bar the admission of evidence derived from intelligence collection activities. The paradigm case of such a rule is the creation of a hearsay exception intended to allow the admission of intelligence reports and interrogation summaries, whose sources and authors may be difficult to produce in the context of a criminal trial.

In both classes of case, these courts are imagined to be staffed by expert judges and lawyers. These lawyers and judges would not only have security clearances but, by virtue of being repeat players, would develop institutional knowledge, relationships, and expertise that would facilitate the fairness of the proceedings. The bankruptcy and tax courts are typically cited as the model for specialized courts with specialized participants, and, in the words of Katyal and Goldsmith, "The case here is far more compelling."

Based on our experience with Guantanamo, we are highly dubious about the wisdom of creating a new body of national security courts. Given the lack of legislative momentum in that direction since these proposals were first made five years ago, our view likely reflects an implicit consensus that is no doubt informed by the continued failings of the military commission system. Many learned scholars and policy experts before us have provided detailed critiques of national security courts.[6] These critiques have articulated both legal and policy grounds. Given our particular area of experience, we are going to focus on three areas that intersect and, for us, raise profound doubts about whether any such courts could ultimately become a sustaining credible institution: logistics, precedent, and legitimacy.

Logistics

Perhaps the subtlest problem we see with a national security court is its capacity to deal with the issues that will arise on a day-to-day basis. Partly, that is a financial question. Recently, the annual budgetary commitment for Guantanamo was revealed to be over $450 million.[7] What went little noticed in the reporting, however, was that a quarter of that was simply the cost of supporting the military commissions. A portion of that cost undoubtedly stems from the fact that the commissions are being held in Guantanamo. Travel, lodging, and operating on an island base for any purpose are exorbitantly expensive under the best of circumstances. But even if they were held in the United States, the minimum personnel requirements for the military commissions would be larger than some of the nation's largest corporate law firms.

To administer the military commissions, there has typically been a professional staff of nearly 200 lawyers serving as counsel, advisors, and judges. By and large, their workloads are limited for regulatory reasons to military commission issues, regardless of the actual pace of their workflow. When cases are active, the cost goes up exponentially. Litigation requires experts, investigative travel to hard-to-reach places around the world, and the use of government resources to facilitate the process. On top of that is a vast administrative staff, whose principal responsibility is to maintain the information technology, translation, security, and logistical support. That permanent staff is necessary to keep the commissions able to function at all and must therefore be kept in place regardless of the caseloads at a given period of time.

The value for that investment? No more than two or three cases have been active at any given time since 2009.

The underwhelming output of the military commissions partly reflects the diffuse nature of the terrorist threat. There are just not that many international terrorists—at least, not compared to the number of war criminals in prior conflicts. Assuming the Chief Prosecutor's most optimistic projections are correct, the military commissions will have heard fewer than 20 cases over the course of two decades. Such a sparse caseload raises its own questions about government waste. But the greater concern is how such an underutilized court actually functions.

The ultra-low caseload means there are no successful prosecutions to serve as reliable models. The dribbling trickle of cases hinders the development of precedent and raises the stakes of each individual case. Even cases dealing with allegations of marginal involvement in Al-Qaeda and no allegations of terrorist violence have lasted years and cost millions of dollars. While the personal investment by counsel and the judicial officers alike is admirable, the concentration on a handful of cases has unquestionably perverted many individuals' professional incentives and prevented those involved from developing the ordinary work habits and expectations that are necessary if cases are to proceed justly and efficiently.

The high degree of intensity not only lacks proportionality, it is unsustainable over the long term. Katyal and Goldsmith imagine that an "elite" permanent staff of lawyers and presumably administrative support will flock to work on such a national security court. But it is just as likely that the result will be a court whose capacity so far outstrips its actual needs that seasoned and experienced lawyers will shy away from such an assignment.

Ironically, the most significant danger this poses is not that such a court would gather dust. Bureaucracies being what they are, the class of cases that can be brought under their jurisdiction promises to creep ever wider. As the Constitution Project noted in its critique, the contours of the "war on drugs" and "narco-terrorism" are just as multinational and far more deadly than the political terrorism that motivated the creation of Guantanamo. If the point of these courts is to dispense with juries and give flexibility on the rules of evidence, there is every reason to believe that their very availability would encourage forum shopping in cases where evidence is weak or somehow tainted by government misconduct.

Precedent

Defense lawyers have an ethical duty to mount any non-frivolous challenge to aspects of a system that could put their client's liberty or life at peril. If *everything* about a particular court system is created from scratch, then *every* aspect of a procedural scheme is ripe for fresh reconsideration. There are no longer any shared traditions or working assumptions about how a case should proceed.

Congress's last successful effort at creating a new judicial system with a criminal docket was the Uniform Code of Military Justice (UCMJ) in 1950.[8] But that was no easy task. The court-martial system has been revised constantly over the past 50 years, with substantial revisions to the basic authorities and responsibilities of court-martial participants along the way. The Supreme Court struck many parts of the UCMJ down.[9] It took nearly 25 years and an accumulation of precedent at all levels of the military justice system before courts-martial earned the immunity from interlocutory collateral attacks that is traditionally afforded to other courts, tribunals, and administrative proceedings.[10] And it took yet another 15 years before the Court allowed courts-martial to try service members for crimes that were not directly and provably connected to their military duties.[11]

The court-martial system also had many things working in its favor that a national security court would lack. The court-martial docket is relatively straightforward and routine in terms of the kinds of cases that get heard. Murder cases are rare. Witnesses are typically close at hand. Courts-martial have proven remarkably effective at handling most cases. But their track record on complex and serious crimes is more mixed simply because they do not occur that often. For example, at the time of this writing, the military has not carried out an execution since 1961 because all of the death sentences rendered by courts-martial either have been reversed or are still pending on appeal.[12]

The court-martial system was also not truly created from scratch in 1950. The military had used courts-martial for centuries. While the UCMJ made significant changes to how they were conducted, the military has a deep history of cultural and organizational traditions. That afforded courts-martial a significant degree of continuity in the basic assumptions about their purposes and the personnel serving on them.

The most likely scenario for how a national security court would deal with the problem of precedent is not the UCMJ, but the Guantanamo Military Commissions. And that record is not exemplary. Proceedings before the commissions have regularly descended into chaos and often grind to a halt for months in the face of obstacles that could be handled summarily in established court systems. In 2006, two years into the endeavor, the proceedings had fallen into such a state that a special rule had to be promulgated forbidding the use of sarcasm.[13] Even with the detailed statutory framework put in place by the Military Commissions Act, the military judge formerly presiding over the September 11 trial opined that the military commissions were a "system in which uncertainty is the norm and the rules appear random and indiscriminate."[14]

In dealing with precedent, particularly when confronted by hard legal questions, the presiding judges have frequently been at a loss. Judge Patricia Wald reviewed the decisions of the commissions as part of a project sponsored by the National Institution of Military Justice and found that the military judges demonstrate a disturbing and consistent failure to "explain the bases of their rulings apart from mere citation to the Act or the rules."[15] Given the institutional pressures and chronic uncertainty, the practice at the trial level has been overwhelmingly in favor of summary orders that lack any legal analysis or authority, issued in the knowledge that hard questions can either be resolved on appeal from conviction or mooted by an acquittal.

It is true that proposals for a national security court have generally included judges with a far greater degree of judicial experience and independence than those tasked with the Guantanamo commissions. But the institutional pressures inherent in national security courts will be largely the same as those on the commission system. In the commissions, the defense and prosecution opportunistically argue from a hodgepodge of court-martial, federal, and international legal authorities. The result is rarely the formulation of coherent doctrine. In concluding her review, Judge Wald rightly observed that the "creation of a separate body of constitutional and international common law in a radically different setting and under dramatically different procedures and rules of evidence poses vexing questions for the integrity and consistency of U.S. law which proposals for new hybrid national security courts must confront as well."[16] Guantanamo's history of three major reversals at the Supreme Court over 10 years does not bode well for national security courts that will equally have to grope in the dark to identify their basic standards and governing laws.

Legitimacy

Essentially, national security courts are imagined as operating like an intelligence unit. But instead of evaluating hearsay and other intelligence information for the purpose of battlefield and targeting operations, it would be for the purpose of continued detention and prosecution. The problem is that special courts are by definition not regular, and that irregularity saps them of the legitimacy they need if they are to lay claim to the law's moral authority.

In addition, national security court proposals seem intent on replicating some of the commissions' most controversial aspects. Take the rules of evidence, which, on the surface, appear to mirror the rules for military courts-martial. The rules numbers track the same. But upon deeper inspection, some substantive rules are "reserved" and others are denuded of the substance that ensures fundamental due process in a military trial setting. In the commissions, for example, alleged statements may come in from a detainee via a translator, then through a government agent, and then relayed into a report that yet another witness can rely on in giving testimony with layer after layer of hearsay. Although the reliability of the evidence may be facially challenged, there is no opportunity to challenge the agent or agency that created the document. This opens the door for the selective production and admission of evidence without any of the usual due process and confrontation rigors. While this may help secure convictions that might otherwise be unobtainable, the government and the legal system pays a cost in both fairness and the perception of fairness that taints whatever results are obtained. There is no reason to think, therefore, that the political divisiveness of the commissions would not carry over and prove to be a major obstacle to the legitimacy of national security courts that were similarly flexible with the rules of evidence.

Moreover, national security cases are complex both factually and legally. If Al-Qaeda is the paradigm for the kinds of cases that should go to a national security court, it is important to keep in mind that the nature of that threat is rooted in a rather small and decentralized group of borderless terrorists. Born out of and indeed made possible by the rise of low-cost international networks of communication, travel, and finance, Al-Qaeda rarely constituted much more than a criminal social network of individuals motivated and willing to carry out acts of political violence, big and small, on behalf of a pseudo-religious ideology. The organization's very brand name, "the base," was an ironic inversion of the concept of the traditional headquarters. Consequently, the evidence, witnesses, and events at the center of any terrorism case will depend on subtle relationships between people and events that span multiple continents, languages, and cultures. While the proponents of national security courts point to this complexity as the reason for entirely new rules, it is doubtful that a novel and untested court system will be any better suited to efficiently managing these cases than the established federal courts are. While these borderless terrorist organizations are nontraditional enemies, their violent criminal terrorist acts are anything but new and have been handled effectively in the regular courts for years.

Guantanamo and the Military Commissions were intended to be a laboratory for what rights and process are appropriate for terrorism suspects in a "new" world of borderless terrorism and how the Law of Armed Conflict should evolve. As we have written elsewhere,[17] that experimentation has not been characterized by carefully designed, implemented, and assessed pilot programs. Rather, ad hoc decisions about detention, interrogation, and prosecution were made on the assumption that legal constraints were nonexistent. Along the way, those decisions were tailored to accommodate a begrudging accumulation of rights and procedural protections, which have been added over time to accommodate specific defeats in the courts. While this could optimistically be described as a dialogue between the political branches and the judiciary, the result to date has not been a legal architecture driven by lessons learned, but a chimera of politically driven work-arounds that continues to amble through a thicket of legacy issues that have only become more complicated over time.

Any proposal for even more special courts, therefore, carries a high burden in demonstrating why repeating this kind of experiment will be worthwhile. Our experience convinces us that all of these attempts have watered down the fundamental principal behind our U.S. adversarial justice system: that two sides, prosecution and defense, with equal access to evidence, will fairly litigate the facts and law before an experienced and impartial court, and when the dust settles, the truth will rise and justice will be served.

... But a Dedicated National Security Bar Is a Good One

Proposals for national security courts typically rely on analogies to single-purpose tribunals that adjudicate specialized areas of public law, such as taxes, immigration, and bankruptcy. In many respects, this analogy is apt. These are all areas of law that tend to be unusually complex, often involve detailed fact-finding, and consequently benefit from specialized repeat players who have the expertise to manage legal nuances.

The analogy is inapt, however, insofar as these areas of law tend to operate in a closed legal universe. Bankruptcy courts, for example, only adjudicate questions of bankruptcy law. Indeed, the bankruptcy courts are constitutionally forbidden from hearing anything else.[18] National security cases, by contrast, depend upon courts' general jurisdiction over interlocking areas of criminal law, constitutional law, administrative law, international law, and even 1L favorites such as property, torts, and contracts. All of that is in addition to the specific laws governing classified information and national security issues more generally. National security cases are also generational. While there the courts have a steady diet of bankruptcies and tax complaints, Guantanamo Bay was neither predicted nor comparable to other eras when we were "at war."

The better analogy is to death penalty cases. Capital cases are, at bottom, nothing more than criminal prosecutions. As criminal prosecutions, they implicate a diverse range of factual and legal issues. But because of the unusually serious stakes involved, a complex and specialized body of law has developed to accommodate the heightened need for reliability, due diligence, and public policy deliberation. The response to this specialized complexity has not been to shunt capital cases into special death penalty courts. It has been to cultivate an increasingly formalized death penalty bar of so-called "learned counsel," who, based on training and experience, can be trusted to manage it.[19]

In the same vein, a better solution to the unique problems raised by national security litigation is to establish a national security bar that has the training and experience to handle them. Given that we have spent much of this essay criticizing the details of the military commissions and plans for other national security courts, we will do our best to outline what we think is the best model for such a bar in detail. That includes a proposed regulatory framework, the qualifications of its members, and the uses to which it should be put.

Regulatory Framework

We propose that Title 28 be amended to authorize the creation of a national security bar administered by the Administrative Office of the United States Courts. The conduct of its members will be governed by appropriate criminal laws where necessary as well as a standing committee on professional responsibility with the authority to promulgate rules, adjudicate complaints, and issue advisory opinions.

The bar's membership will be composed of government attorneys, judges, and private lawyers who wish to work on national security cases and have the relevant specialized education and experience. We will endeavor to lay out examples of national security cases in greater detail below, but suffice it to say that this category includes those cases identified by Congress, the government, and the courts as touching on sufficiently serious matters of national defense or involving classified evidence. This would include not only the classes of cases that fall within the proposed jurisdiction of national security courts; it would also include a broader range of civil and criminal matters that warrant the care of specialists. Whatever additional costs such a system would create can be administered through membership dues and the preexisting mechanisms of the Criminal Justice Act,[20] the Equal Access to Justice Act,[21] or the ordinary judicial allocation of costs and fees.

We should say that, to a point, we are not advancing anything novel. There is already a de facto national security bar of attorneys with security clearances working on everything from Guantanamo issues to defense contracting. All we propose is that this de facto bar be formalized in ways that increase its accountability, enhance its effectiveness, and allow the law to rely on its regularity.

The creation of specialized attorney staff is also a component of many proposals for national security courts. A typical model given is the office in which we worked—the Office of the Chief Defense Counsel. This office is a standing agency in the Department of Defense staffed by military and civilian personnel, whose responsibilities are confined to representing those detainees slated for trial by military commissions in Guantanamo. Every attorney in the office has a security clearance. And with the exception of a handful of independent contractors hired as learned counsel in the capital cases, all of the attorneys are either judge advocates or civil servants in the General Service.

While we all have fond memories and the utmost respect for the attorneys in this office (at the time of this writing one of us still works there, another still serves on a case pro bono, and the third led the office for 16 months), it is not a favorable model for a permanent institution. Many of our reasons for saying so mirror our objections to national security courts. There is a substantial risk of government inefficiency and waste as the number of national security cases waxes and wanes. This has happened repeatedly in the Office of the Chief Defense Counsel, where the workflow has been highly unpredictable. Whenever it slows down, the office has concomitant staff reductions. This results in the loss of experienced people. Whenever it speeds up, the available staff and resources prove inadequate, and the learning curve for new hires is substantial. This invariably leads to an uneven quality of representation across cases.

To be sure, there is a virtue to having an in-house staff of government attorneys. As military service members and government employees, the personnel of the Office of the Chief Defense Counsel face serious professional and criminal sanctions for misconduct that go above and beyond their ordinary responsibilities to the bar, especially for issues related to classified information. Those consequences, however, can be easily replicated for members of a national security bar, including criminal penalties and automatic disbarment from all U.S. licensing jurisdictions in particularly egregious situations.

We would also be concerned that the benefits of a dedicated office also do not outweigh the costs of limiting the universe of qualified counsel who are likely to be unwilling or unable to devote their careers to government service. Even today, many of the top national experts on national security litigation work as private attorneys and academics. Bringing them under the umbrella of a national security bar alongside government attorneys is the best way to strengthen the quality and professionalism of counsel in national security cases.

Qualifications

Membership in this bar should be open to anyone who meets the following qualifications. We will first lay out what we see to be the most germane qualifications and then attempt to explain them in greater detail.

1. Active membership in good standing of a State or Territorial Bar;
2. U.S. citizenship;
3. A security clearance approved by the Office of the Director of National Intelligence at the SECRET level or higher;
4. Successful completion of annual training courses on relevant subjects, such as classified information handling, intelligence collection, threat awareness, national security law, etc., as prescribed by:
   i. The Director of National Intelligence;
   ii. The Department of Homeland Security;
   iii. The Department of Defense;
   iv. The Department of Energy;
   v. The Department of Justice; and
   vi. The Administrative Office of the U.S. Courts.
5. Continuing sponsorship by a present member of the national security bar or two active members from an attorney's licensing jurisdiction.

U.S. Bar Membership. This first criterion should be self-evident. The only potential objection to it is that we have not made provision for foreign bar members. It is true that foreign bar members can be and are admitted to certain federal courts, including the Supreme Court. This is often done *pro hac vice*, however, and nothing in our proposal would foreclose foreign bar members from continuing to serve on that basis in national security cases or otherwise. In our experience, foreign bar members add valuable linguistic and cultural expertise, particularly in cases involving events or clients from abroad. If anything, the presence of a national security bar member at the counsel table augurs in favor of greater flexibility in the composition of the remainder of the legal team.

U.S. Citizenship. Various duties and liabilities are unique to U.S. citizens, not the least being restrictions on foreign travel.[22] Additionally, for most security clearances, U.S. citizenship is required anyway.

There is the sound objection that a lawyer's citizenship has nothing to do with his or her qualifications for the bar.[23] Indeed, until the military commissions in Guantanamo prohibited it,[24] a defining feature of war crimes prosecutions was the defendant's ability to be represented by an attorney of his own nationality. This was even true after World War II, when Japanese lawyers and even former Nazis appeared as counsel before the international war crimes tribunals. One could imagine that if the roles were reversed, the United States would have profound objections to its citizens being tried abroad without the benefit of a U.S. attorney at the counsel table.

As with U.S. bar membership, however, the requirement that a member of a legal team be national security–qualified should in no way be understood as requiring *all* members of a legal team to be so qualified. It will typically be the case, as it often is already in federal cases involving classified information, that only one member of a legal team will be appropriately cleared. The presence of such an individual, who faces personal and professional liability for any security breach, should be a basis on which to enhance the choice of other counsel.

Security Clearance. When we speak of national security cases, we are mostly speaking of cases in which there is some testimony, evidence, or subject matter that has in some way been classified against disclosure by the federal government. If you separate out their proposed abrogation of Sixth Amendment rights, the proposals for national security courts largely reduce to creating a forum in which classified evidence can be protected from public disclosure during the course of litigation. This is apparently born out of the concern that present rules in place are inadequate. The Classified Information Procedure Act and its implementing rules presently govern how that evidence is handled in criminal proceedings.[25] A combination of protective orders and the national security privilege regulates the use of classified information in civil proceedings.[26]

The requirement of a security clearance gets to the heart of the concerns motivating a national security bar. The rules for classification and the conferral of security clearances are largely regulatory and presently rooted in Executive Order 13,526.[27] Individuals typically get a standing clearance of SECRET or TOP SECRET, which require renewal every 10 and 5 years, respectively. Those with a TOP SECRET clearance can obtain a further level of clearance for Special Compartmentalized Information (SCI).[28] Someone with a TS/SCI clearance can then be "read on" to various "programs," which are ad hoc categories of information that have been deemed extra-sensitive and can be shared only with other individuals who have been read onto that particular program.

The Director of National Intelligence oversees the security clearance process across the government, but each government agency has its own process for awarding different levels of clearance.[29] Those procedures all involve close scrutiny of an applicant's background, relationships, travel, mental health, finances, and general amenability to blackmail. Government investigators interview a candidate's friends, neighbors, classmates, family members, and co-workers at length about the candidate's loyalty, habits, disposition, and professionalism. All told, the process takes months to complete and for individuals with significant foreign contacts, it has been known to last years. Even after individuals are cleared, they are subject to random audits and must continue to report travel and other relevant activities on a rolling basis.

As one would guess, this process is expensive. Estimates vary and depend in part on the complexity of an individual's background investigation. But the cost of obtaining a clearance regularly runs into the thousands of dollars. Since most clearances are given to government employees, this cost is typically borne by the government. But in cases where private firms and contractors have sought clearances for employees, the government tends to be reimbursed, at least in part, by the contractor.

There is a reasonable question of whether it is appropriate to condition private attorneys' ability to obtain a mandatory license, and as a consequence their client's rights to counsel, on paying such an expense. In short, we think the answer is yes. Ultimately, provision for paying the costs associated with obtaining a clearance in cases of true indigence can be worked out administratively. But as a general proposition, the cost is comparable to other costs associated with litigation and professional certification that are routinely accepted now. Moreover, membership in such a bar would be its own credential, and the expense of obtaining it will ultimately get passed along to clients anyway. Likewise, in criminal cases, rates can be adjusted as appropriate.

Annual Training and Certification. Given the tendency for Continuing Legal Education to devolve into junkets and boondoggles, we are somewhat hesitant to propose additional annual training. But if implemented prudently, the training we propose would serve two important interests.

The first is to ensure that the certification bar membership would carry with it something more than the possession of a security clearance. Even individuals who have long served in government confront a pace of change that is often bewildering. This training would aim to keep individuals up-to-date on best practices in personal and information security, threat assessments, national security law, and classified information handling. It would also provide attorneys with the opportunity to learn about intelligence methods and the relative weight that should be given to information derived from the ever-evolving techniques used in intelligence collection. In short, the training would aim to ensure that an attorney who handles legal matters that touch on national defense is not only trustworthy but also competent in the special demands of the task.

The second is that it provides an opportunity for oversight by all of the relevant stakeholders in the government's national security apparatus. As described above, the security clearance process and the rules governing classified information handling more generally are rather balkanized within the government. A particular agency's rules and practices are adapted to a particular agency's mission requirements and culture. Requiring an individual not only to receive annual training but also to obtain certifications from each of the governmental entities we have listed above ensures that members of a national security bar have the knowledge and experience to work on legal issues that cross departmental boundaries. This would be a significant enhancement to attorney competence and oversight, since that kind of training does not even exist for lawyers in the government at the moment.

Continuing Sponsorship. Sponsorship for admission to bars is already routine. That sponsorship is largely pro forma, and we are aware of no instance where a sponsoring attorney was held liable for subsequent misconduct by an attorney he or she had moved to admit. We therefore use the term "continuing sponsorship" to mean sponsorship in the sense of someone whose reputation remains on the line. In that sense, our notion of what it means to be a sponsor is more akin to how that term is used in the immigration context than in the sense it is presently used for bar admissions.

The key to an effective national security bar is a high degree of trust in its members. That degree of trust is possible only if there are robust systems of accountability in place. We propose that every member of the bar have a sponsor for the full duration of his or her membership. That sponsor should either be another member of the national security bar, or alternatively, two members of the state bar in which the attorney is licensed. Sponsors as well as applicants should undergo a rigorous background investigation before membership is conferred. And if a member of the national security bar is found to have engaged in misconduct, his or her sponsors should be subject to investigation if their sponsorship was undertaken negligently. If it is shown that they failed to exercise a reasonable duty of care in undertaking their sponsorship obligations, they should also be subject to professional sanctions.

At first blush, such a system sounds harsh. But there are two factors that we think mitigate its severity and ultimately make the scheme justifiable on balance.

First, any such system will depend upon adequate checks against abuse. Given the seriousness of misconduct allegations, individuals who make frivolous charges should incur civil and criminal liability for having done so. And the investigation of the sponsor should be limited to cases where actual misconduct has been found against a sponsoree. Liability should not be imposed vicariously, but only for breaches of a reasonable duty of care. That is a vague standard to be sure, but if a sponsor did not actually know an applicant, if money changed hands to gain the sponsorship, or if the sponsor knew the applicant had significant personal issues that went undisclosed, that would fail any reasonable standard of care.

Second, such a system relies on a combination of self-interest and social bonds to deter misconduct that is, in practical effect, akin to the institutional safeguards in place for national security positions within the government. The self-interest arises at the point of sponsorship. Individuals who know that they could face serious professional consequences as a result of another's misconduct will be cautious in undertaking that responsibility in the first place, just as government supervisors expose their own careers when hiring employees to sensitive government positions. Individuals are also more likely to engage in misconduct if the negative consequences will only be felt personally. It is a greater deterrent to know that your own misconduct includes what is, in essence, a betrayal of another's trust. In short, we think the ultimate success of a national security bar will depend on a reputation for atypical professionalism that this kind of collective oversight and accountability should bolster.

The Uses of a National Security Bar

We are not going to attempt an exhaustive list of the kinds of cases to which national security counsel would be well suited. In the main, we imagine that, in lieu of an entirely new court system, Congress could specify particular crimes and causes of action that require both sides to have at least one member of a national security bar at the counsel table. Like capital cases, the judiciary should also have the discretionary authority to require and approve national security counsel in a given case. And there could be either legislation or court rules that permit parties to move to compel the assistance of a national security–qualified attorney if a party feels that it is appropriate to the circumstances of the litigation.

The most obvious candidates for mandatory membership on a national security bar would be attorneys who work in practice areas where a security clearance is effectively mandatory already. This would include attorneys in the National Security Division of the Department of Justice and defense counsel in cases in which the Classified Information Procedures Act has been invoked, as well as certain kinds of courts-martial. These cases do not technically require a security clearance at the moment, but the judges presiding in individual cases have increasingly required it.

The availability of a national security bar could have a salutary effect on a wide class of cases that have become increasingly common and have been negatively affected by competing national security interests. More and more, the courts have struggled to balance national security, particularly the handling of classified evidence, and the equally compelling demands of due process and accountability. To illustrate how a national security bar could ease these tensions, we will briefly focus on three types of cases: detainee *habeas* petitions, proceedings under the Foreign Intelligence Surveillance Act, and civil actions implicating the state secrets privilege.

Habeas petitions. The Guantanamo detainees' long effort to challenge their detention through writs of *habeas corpus* in the federal courts has been well documented.[30] The government captured hundreds of men around the world and brought them to Guantanamo to be indefinitely detained. Detention "for the duration of hostilities" is a well-established incident of the law of war. Indeed, during World War II, hundreds of thousands of German prisoners of war were detained throughout the United States. The difficulty Guantanamo presented arose from the nature of the war.

As we described above, the government sought to utilize its war powers in a conflict against a relatively small group of ideologically organized nonstate actors who hailed from all around the world. The government also claimed the authority to detain individuals whose alleged conduct and capture occurred far from any recognized battlefield in Afghanistan or Pakistan. What the endpoint of that kind of war looks like is at best vague, and what makes a particular individual an "enemy" liable to indefinite detention is vaguer still. The consequence was that detainees sought and ultimately won the right to challenge the government's legal authority to hold them through *habeas corpus*.[31]

The government objected to the federal courts' hearing these *habeas* cases on a variety of jurisdictional and prudential grounds. Its most powerful equitable argument was that litigating these *habeas* petitions would be incredibly difficult. Doing so required the judiciary to wade into novel questions about the legal significance of intelligence activities, the proper handling of classified information, and the relative weight of atypical forms of evidence used in intelligence analysis.

In some respects, these fears have been borne out. An unusual amount of time and attention in the *habeas* litigation is spent not on the merits, but on crafting protective orders for the handling of classified information contained in the government's factual returns. What is more troubling, however, is that there is still a basic lack of sophistication in assessing the relative weight and credibility of intelligence information. Indeed, in one case, the D.C. Circuit reversed a lower court on its belief that the district courts should start applying "conditional probability analysis" in their assessments of different pieces of intelligence.[32] Leaving aside our doubts about lawyers' and judges' knack for advanced statistics, it is clear that this methodology was chosen because it sounded like something intelligence analysts would use. While it is easy to criticize its silliness as well as the results to which it leads, it may be unreasonable to expect trial or appellate court judges to do much better when they are expected to learn the fundamentals of intelligence analytics in the course of litigation from lawyers who have very little knowledge of it themselves.

These are some of the very problems that national security courts are proposed to address. We suggest that many of these problems could have been—and could still be—overcome by a national security bar with the training and experience to litigate these matters intelligently. It would have mitigated the uncertainty over the proper handling of classified information that postponed judicial review for so long.

And it would have ensured that the judges and lawyers had more than a Wikipedia-level understanding of the kind of evidence they were litigating. In other words, it would not only have brought a swifter and ultimately fairer resolution to many of these cases, it would also have prevented the creation of a lot of bad law.

FISA Proceedings. The Foreign Intelligence Surveillance Act (FISA) was passed in the 1978 to regulate the government's interception of communications.[33] As part of that regulatory scheme, FISA created the Foreign Intelligence Surveillance Court (FISC) as an adjunct to the federal courts.[34] It is composed of a pool of 11 active federal judges, who serve seven-year terms and approve applications by the government to conduct certain kinds of electronic surveillance.

The applications to conduct surveillance against a particular target are made in secret and *ex parte*. The resulting orders and judicial opinions from the FISC are secret as well. The targets of FISA orders generally are unaware that they are being subject to any surveillance. And the only nongovernmental litigants who have the right to challenge an order are those individuals and companies, such as telecommunications firms, who have been ordered to turn over information about a particular target.[35] Even then, their participation is ordinarily kept secret and is limited to the assertion of their particular corporate equities rather than the privacy interests the putative target would likely assert. Between the court's creation in 1978 and 2012, the FISC rejected only 11 out of almost 34,000 requests.[36]

Historically, the FISC's orders were limited to applications to intercept the communications of specific targets. In 2008, the jurisdiction of the FISC was broadened to authorize the review and approval of programmatic requests.[37] In effect, judges on the FISC now have an obligation to issue advisory opinions on the facial legality of dragnet electronic surveillance programs that are not directed at any particular target.

The FISC recently incurred fresh scrutiny after a series of leaks showed that it had approved the large-scale interception of Internet and telephony data.[38] The legal rationales for this were apparently based on a secret body of common law that it had developed in the course of interpreting FISA over the past decade. These revelations led to calls to make the FISC's deliberations more transparent, or at least more adversarial. Judge James Robertson, a former judge on the FISC, lamented that while federal judges are very practiced at weighing competing claims of legality, their reliability breaks down when legal issues are argued *ex parte*. In particular, he expressed concern over the fact that the FISC is now in the business of approving entire intelligence programs, not simply discrete surveillance targets. Federal judges, he suggested, are not equipped to evaluate the relative merits and implications of the highly technical questions these broader approvals require.

There have accordingly been proposals for a FISC ombudsman or a "devil's advocate" to serve, in effect, as the loyal opposition to FISA applications. The Obama Administration recently embraced this proposal.[39] Judge Robertson even suggested these attorneys could work in a separate legal office within the government modeled on the Office of the Chief Defense Counsel.[40] Opponents of these proposals object to expanding the class of people who have access to highly classified information as well as the extent to which adding more participants will slow the FISA application process down.[41]

We share some of the critic's concerns about the efficiency costs of having opposing counsel on the other side of every FISA application. Ordinary search warrants and subpoenas are obtained *ex parte*. To be sure, search warrants and subpoenas are often subject to some degree of adversarial litigation on the back end—i.e., when the fruits of a search are used against a litigant at trial. But we are skeptical about the ultimate value of adding another participant, because doing so would risk changing the nature of the approval process in counterproductive ways.

For all of its real and perceived flaws, the general view of individuals who have worked within the FISC is that both the judges and government counsel behave with diligence and candor. Adding a devil's advocate could create a perverse incentive for government attorneys to adopt litigation positions that press the outer boundaries of reasonableness as a trial tactic. And for many of the same reasons we think a national security court is a bad idea, we question the wisdom of creating an entirely new governmental office of devil's advocates.

That said, injecting some degree of adversarial process into the FISC is a good idea and, if implemented sensibly, one that the government should welcome. Rather than a devil's advocate on the other side of every FISA application, we suggest that it could be prudently handled through the mechanisms of a standing national security bar on an as-needed basis. Federal judges generally know when they are dealing with issues at the margins of their competence. The practice of appointing *amicus curiae* to argue certified issues in federal courts, most notably the Supreme Court, is well established and often effective at helping to clarify complex issues. We propose that FISC judges should have the same discretion to draw *amicus* from members of a national security bar when the issues presented by a particular application would benefit from more rigorous scrutiny. There also could be standing court rules that compel the appointment of an *amicus* when the government makes programmatic requests or seeks to utilize new surveillance methods.

In order to make such a process efficient, one could imagine that members of a national security bar could sign up for a standing "pool" of available counsel in the same way that attorneys can sign up for CJA pools across the country. And just as FISA requires a certain percentage of the FISC judges to be local,[42] there is no reason why membership in such a pool could not equally be conditioned on an individual's reasonable proximity to the Prettyman Courthouse in D.C., where the FISC sits. Indeed, the availability of such *amicus* is likely to speed up the FISA approval process, insofar as the relevant deliberations and research will not fall exclusively on the shoulders of the judge. Such an option therefore presents one of the few occasions where adversarial litigation will bolster not only the fairness and credibility of legal proceedings, but also their efficiency.

State Secrets Privilege. The state secrets privilege is, at its core, an evidentiary privilege. The Supreme Court has recognized that the government is entitled to refuse to disclose classified information in court proceedings.[43] In the criminal context, this led to the passage of Classified Infromation Procedures Act (CIPA) and its implementing rules, which allow the government to withhold relevant classified discovery in circumstances where the defense would not be compromised.[44]

As this doctrine developed, however, the rule has become that any civil action that touches on subject matters or evidence that are classified will be dismissed outright. All that is generally required is a certification from an appropriately senior government officer that the information is closely held by the government and its disclosure would be detrimental to national security—the very definition of classified information. In relatively short order, therefore, an evidentiary privilege evolved into a new breed of substantive immunity from suit.[45]

There is an increasing variety of disturbing cases that have been dismissed under the state secrets privilege. Indeed, it is fair to say that the state secrets privilege has become the crown jewel of a "national security canon" that has prevented meaningful judicial review of often-important governmental policies.[46] Cases dismissed on the basis of the privilege have involved credible allegations of civil rights abuses,[47] torture,[48] and even the targeted killing of U.S. citizens.[49] On a more mundane level, there are cases in which the government has arguably exploited the privilege to get out of its contracts.[50]

Many commentators who have analyzed the development of this doctrine have been critical of it.[51] Despite the proliferation of its use over the past decade, the Supreme Court has yet to pass upon its modern development. When the Court last ratified the use of the state secrets privilege in the 1950s, the quantity of classified information was much smaller.[52] Over the past decade, the use of classification at all levels of government has proliferated and with it, the invocation of the state secrets privilege. The sheer extent to which facially important and meritorious cases have been getting dismissed will inevitably lead to either congressional action or a fresh look by the Supreme Court.[53]

We would submit that the state secrets privilege is another area in which a national security bar would aid sensible reforms. The government's interests in preventing any and all disclosure of classified information will be protected by the involvement of lawyers and judges who not only have security clearances but also invested in a rigorous process to demonstrate their bona fides in the handling of sensitive national security information.

The existence of a national security bar can also be taken into account in legislation or court rules, such as those used to implement CIPA. One of the most controversial aspects of CIPA cases is the government's ability to make *ex parte* presentations to the court in order to withhold the production of classified information. A notorious instance of this occurred in the case of the vice president's former aide, Scooter Libby, where the accused was barred from reviewing relevant memoranda and documents that he himself had written whilst in government. To accommodate nondisclosure, CIPA allows for the preparation of substitutions and summaries of evidence whose adequacy defense counsel can only guess. Allowing appropriately cleared counsel to participate in this process would go a long way toward diminishing the prejudicial effect CIPA sometimes has on a criminal accused's ability to prepare a meaningful defense.

In both civil and criminal cases, one could also imagine that the rules could give litigants who voluntarily submitted to bench trials conducted by members of such a bar even more leeway in reviewing the full range of relevant evidence. This may result in certain court closures, which in the criminal context could raise significant concerns about public trial rights. But, all told, the presence of a national security bar in these kinds of cases would allow the law to adapt in ways that give the government the confidence to defend the legality of its policies on the merits, whilst retaining control over its legitimate secrets.

Conclusion

A national security court is a bad idea. The fact that the proposal has been in serious circulation for over five years without movement suggests that there is little stomach for creating another experimental court system. But some of the most significant problems the proposals for a national security court aimed to address cannot be lightly dismissed. National security issues are important and crop up in the least-expected places, as the recent Boston Marathon bombings and NSA surveillance leaks demonstrate.

The United States has too many secrets, to be sure. The thicket of secrecy that has grown up around the national security state over the past decade has many roots. Some are as petty as how effective classification is in protecting bureaucratic turf and evading oversight. But much of the government's growing portfolio of secrets was filled by new technological sources and methods that have unleashed a torrent of information into the government's analytical machine. It is therefore too facile to condemn the government's bias toward overclassification without articulating robust ways of sorting out those secrets the government has every right to keep.

When national security policies conflict with the law or seek to utilize the law to some end, there is an inevitable clash of interests. Good-faith legal proceedings depend on a comprehensive and reliable search for the truth. There is a strong tradition in the United States that the credibility of this truth-finding process is safeguarded by active public scrutiny. Government secrecy, by its very nature, aims to conceal the truth, most especially from public scrutiny.

Our objections to a national security court are primarily pragmatic and based on our experiences with the Guantanamo Military Commissions. In short, we think such an institution would be wasteful, inefficient, and would be mired in years of quagmire litigation searching for precedent, just like Guantanamo. Imposing and then finding new uses for a national security court is heavy-handed and rigid. It will ossify specific choices about the proper balance between judicial transparency and government secrecy that may very well prove to be wrong or unwise over time. Our years of litigation experience fuels our strong belief that a new national security court will also lead to the watering down of the fair adversarial process that is the heart and soul of U.S. jurisprudence.

Our proposal for a national security bar, by contrast, is not driven by a judgment about what the proper balance should be. It is rooted in the conviction that it is far wiser to put content-neutral tools in place that are designed to empower trusted specialists to negotiate that balance over time. A professional bar of national security counsel could enable national security law to remain flexible as new facts, expectations, threats, and opportunities emerge.

Notes

1.   *See* The Guantanamo Docket, *available at* http://projects.nytimes.com/guantanamo.

2.   Hamdan v. United States, 696 F.3d 1238 (D.C. Cir. 2012); Al Bahlul v. United States, 2013 WL 297726 (D.C. Cir. 2013) (rehearing en banc pending).

3.   Jane Sutton, *US Scales Back Plans for Guantanamo Prosecutions*, REUTERS, June 11, 2013.

4.   Jack Goldsmith & Neal Katyal, *The Terrorists Court*, N.Y. TIMES, July 11, 2007. In a similar vein, Katyal recently proposed a "Drone Court" within the executive branch to provide an adversarial process before an individual is targeted by a drone. Neal Katyal, *An Executive Branch "Drone Court,"* N.Y. TIMES, Feb. 20, 2013.

5.   GLENN SULMASY, THE NATIONAL SECURITY COURT SYSTEM: A NATURAL EVOLUTION OF JUSTICE IN AN AGE OF TERROR (Oxford 2009).

6.   *See, e.g.*, Constitution Project, A Critique of "National Security Courts" (June 23, 2008), *available at* http://www.constitutionproject.org/pdf/Critique_of_the_National_Security_Courts.pdf.

7. Carol Rosenberg, *Total U.S. tab tops $5B for Guantánamo prison*, MIAMI HERALD, July 30, 2013) (reporting $2.7 million/prisoner in total annual costs); Carol Rosenberg, *Guantanamo: The Most Expensive Prison on Earth*, MIAMI HERALD, Nov. 21, 2011 (reporting $800k/prisoner in annual operating costs).

8. 10 U.S.C. §§ 801, *et seq.*

9. Kinsella v. United States *ex rel.* Singleton, 361 U.S. 234 (1960); Reid v. Covert, 354 U.S. 1 (1957) (plurality op.); United States *ex rel.* Toth v. Quarles, 350 U.S. 11 (1955).

10. Schlesinger v. Councilman, 420 U.S. 738 (1975).

11. Solorio v. United States, 483 U.S. 435 (1987).

12. *See* Dwight Sullivan, *A Matter of Life and Death: Examining the Military Death Penalty's Fairness*, FED. LAWYER (June 1998); *see also* DEATH PENALTY INFO. CENTER, THE U.S. MILITARY DEATH PENALTY, *available at* http://www.deathpenaltyinfo.org/us-military-death-penalty.

13. Presiding Officers Memorandum (POM) #16, Rules of Commission Trial Practice Concerning Decorum of Commission Personnel, Parties, and Witnesses (Feb. 16, 2006).

14. United States v. Mohammed, et al., Order (July 13, 2009).

15. Hon. Patricia M. Wald, *Foreword to the Military Commission Reporter*, 12 Green Bag 2D 449, 454 (2009).

16. Hon. Patricia M. Wald, *Foreword to the Military Commission Reporter*, 12 Green Bag 2D 449, 456 (2009).

17. Christopher Kanady, Peter Masciola & Michel Paradis, *The 'Push-Pull' of the Law of War: The Rule of Law and Military Commissions*, in COUNTER-TERRORISM: INTERNATIONAL LAW AND PRACTICE (Oxford 2012).

18. *See* Northern Pipeline v. Marathon Pipe Line, 458 U.S. 50 (1982).

19. ABA, *Guidelines for the Appointment and Performance of Defense Counsel in Death Penalty Cases*, 31 HOFSTRA L. REV. 914 (2003); *see also* 10 U.S.C. § 949a(b)(2)(C)(ii) (affording learned counsel in military commissions).

20. 18 U.S.C. § 3006A.

21. 28 U.S.C. § 2412.

22. *See, e.g.*, Haig v. Agee, 453 U.S. 280 (1981).

23. *See In re* Griffiths, 413 U.S. 717 (1973).

24. 10 U.S.C. § 949c(b)(3)(A) (2009).

25. 18 U.S.C. App. III. §§ 1–16.

26. *See generally* Todd Garvey & Edward Liu, *The State Secrets Privilege: Preventing the Disclosure of Sensitive National Security Information During Civil Litigation*, CRS-R41741 (Aug. 16, 2011).

27. E.O. 13,526, 75 Fed. Reg. 707 (Jan. 5, 2010); 32 C.F.R. pt. 2001; *see generally* Jennifer Elsea, *The Protection of Classified Information: The Legal Framework*, CRS-RS21900 (Jan. 10, 2013).

28. Office of the Director of National Intelligence, Intelligence Community Directive 704, *Personnel Security Standards and Procedures Governing Eligibility for Access to Sensitive Compartmented Information and Other Controlled Access Program Information* (Oct. 1, 2008).

29. *See* Office of the Director of National Intelligence, Intelligence Community Directive 703, *Protection of Classified National Intelligence, Including Sensitive Compartmented Information* (June 21, 2013); E.O. 13,526, at § 4.1.

30. *See, e.g.*, Jonathan Hafetz, *Calling the Government to Account: Habeas Corpus in the Aftermath of* Boumediene, 57 WAYNE L. REV. 99 (2011); Gerald Neuman, *The Habeas Corpus Suspension Clause after* Boumediene v. Bush, 110 COLUM. L. REV. 537 (2010).

31. Boumediene v. Bush, 553 U.S. 723 (2008).

32.   Al-Adahi v. Obama, 613 F.3d 1102 (D.C. Cir. 2010).

33.   The Foreign Intelligence Surveillance Act of 1978, 92 Stat. 1783 (codified as amended at 50 U.S.C. ch. 36).

34.   50 U.S.C. § 1803.

35.   50 U.S.C. § 1861(f).

36.   Electronic Information Privacy Center (EPIC), Foreign Intelligence Surveillance Act Court Orders 1979-2012, *available at* http://epic.org/privacy/wiretap/stats/fisa_stats.html (last visited Aug. 14, 2013).

37.   50 U.S.C. § 1881a.

38.   *See, e.g.*, Glenn Greenwald, NSA collecting phone records of millions of Verizon customers, THE GUARDIAN (June 6, 2013); Claire Cain Miller, *Tech Companies Concede to Surveillance Program*, N.Y. TIMES (June 7, 2013).

39.   Remarks by the President in a Press Conference (Aug. 9, 2013).

40.   Privacy & Civil Liberties Oversight Board, *Workshop Regarding Surveillance Programs Operated Pursuant to Section 215 of the USA PATRIOT Act and Section 702 of the Foreign Intelligence Surveillance Act* (July 9, 2013), at 91 (statement of Judge James Robertson).

41.   *Id.* at 267 (statement of James Baker).

42.   50 U.S.C. § 1803(a)(1).

43.   United States v. Reynolds, 345 U.S. 1, 7–8 (1953).

44.   18 U.S.C. App. III §§ 1–16.

45.   *See, e.g.*, Robert Chesney, *State Secrets and the Limits of National Security Litigation*, 75 GEO. WASH. L. REV. 1249 (2007) (collecting cases from the 1950s until 2006); Lindsay Windsor, *Is the State Secrets Privilege in the Constitution?*, 43 GEO. J. INT'L L. 897 (2012) (Note).

46.   Stephen Vladeck, *The New National Security Canon*, 61 AM. U. L. REV. 1295 (2012).

47.   *See, e.g.*, Mohamed v. Jeppesen Dataplan, Inc., 614 F.3d 1070, 1077–80 (9th Cir. 2010) (en banc) (warrantless surveillance); El-Masri v. United States, 479 F.3d 296, 299–300 (4th Cir. 2007) (kidnapping).

48.   *See, e.g.*, Arar v. Ashcroft, 585 F.3d 559, 580–81 (2d Cir. 2009) (en banc) (rendition to Syria).

49.   Al-Aulaqi v. Obama, 727 F. Supp. 2d 1, 52 (D.D.C. 2010).

50.   Gen. Dynamics Corp. v. United States, 131 S. Ct. 1900 (2011).

51.   *See, e.g.*, Jameel Jaffer, *Known Unkowns*, 48 HARV. C.R.-C.L. L. REV. 457 (2013).

52.   United States v. Reynolds, 345 U.S. 1 (1953).

53.   *See, e.g.*, Robert Chesney, *Legislative Reform of the State Secrets Privilege*, 13 ROGER WILLIAMS U. L. REV. 443 (2008); Jeremy Telman, *Our Very Privileged Executive: Why the Courts Can (and Should) Fix the State Secrets Privilege*, 80 TEMP. L. REV. 499 (2007).

VI

Military Commissions: A National Security and Justice Institution for Our Time

Mark S. Martins and Edward S. White*

In "Leave the Courts, Take the Lawyers," our military commissions colleagues Peter Masciola, Michel Paradis, and Christopher Kannady argue that modern military commissions have been a failure and that they serve as an object lesson in why any attempt to create a specialized national security court is doomed. They organize their criticism—based largely on their own experiences as defense counsel in military commissions—around three concepts: logistics, precedent, and legitimacy. In this response, we will attempt to provide a different perspective born of our experiences with military commissions.

While others have debated the pros and cons of creating a system of specialized national security courts, and the Guantanamo Bay defense bar has done its best to attack military commissions from every vantage in defense of their clients, reformed military commissions under the Military Commissions Act of 2009[1] have, in fact, become a mature national security and justice institution for our time—a court that, consistent with our values and traditions, fills a narrow, important, and properly empowered and constrained role within our government. Certainly *not* the secret, exclusive, and separate terror trial chamber that some have sought[2] and others have feared,[3] reformed military commissions are complementary to other instruments authorized by law during genuine hostilities and are fully part of our constitutional and democratic government.

73

Wartime tribunals of ancient pedigree,[4] military commissions do not try common crimes committed by ordinary civilians. Rather, military commissions try violations of the law of war, committed in the context of and associated with hostilities, by enemy belligerents.

Military commissions trace their American roots to the boards of officers convened by General George Washington during the Revolutionary War[5] and to the councils of war convened by General Winfield Scott during the Mexican-American War in the first half of the nineteenth century.[6] General Washington used military tribunals to try spies. General Scott used his authority and responsibility as a commander in the field to adapt military commissions, as he used them to deal with guerrilla attacks on his supply lines and other lawless conduct in Mexico. By the time of the American Civil War, military commissions were an established forum of military justice for punishing violations of the law of war,[7] and they were routinely used to punish both spying and unprivileged belligerency by guerrillas, as well as illegitimate attacks on civilian persons and property. Military commissions continued to be used during the Philippine Insurrection in the early twentieth century[8] and both during and following the Second World War.[9]

In Al-Qaeda and its associated forces, the United States continues to face a dangerous, organized, transnational armed group intent on attacking the United States, its people, and its allies for political purposes. As amply demonstrated by the attacks of September 11, 2001, Al-Qaeda and its associates are capable of horrendous violence. And should increasingly available biological, chemical, nuclear, or cyber weapons of mass destruction fall into their hands, the consequences are difficult to fathom. Such organized, transnational, politically motivated violence is substantially different from the private criminality of individuals and groups adjudicated as common crime by ordinary civilian courts, and all three branches of the U.S. government (including two presidents of different political parties and two different Congresses) have recognized that the United States is, in fact, at war with Al-Qaeda and its associated forces.[10] Meanwhile, Al-Qaeda's mode of fighting tempts even peaceful peoples to respond outside the law, a dynamic that can hand costly victories to our enemies in the form of fundamental changes in our way of life and departures from our values. One test of our national security and justice institutions is whether they enable effective responses within the space defined by our law and our values, decreasing the horrific losses that can stem from cycles of complacency, attack, and misdirected excess in response.

Despite the domestic American consensus that we are at war, the United States faces in Al-Qaeda and its associated forces a type of warfare that has, admittedly, strained the ability of our society and institutions to respond. Some of the hostile acts of Al-Qaeda and its members violate both the civilian criminal law and the law of war, giving rise to debate over whether such acts should be adjudicated in civilian or military courts. Al-Qaeda operates in the shadows, attempting to shield its activities behind innocent civilians and within states where the usual institutions of international order have broken down. In this conflict, the United States must use all of the legitimate instruments of its power and authority—from diplomacy to economic means, to law enforcement, to intelligence, to military force, if and as necessary. While serving justice, which is an end in itself and not capable of being described as a mere "tool," military commissions nevertheless are also available to serve the very functional objective of deterring and punishing violations of the law of war.

Undoubtedly, as our leaders again turned to military commissions in the wake of the September 11, 2001, attacks, it was a mistake to assume this military institution could simply be revived, after more than 50 years, without taking into account the revolutions in international law, U.S. constitutional criminal procedure, and U.S. military justice in the years since the end of the Second World War.[11] As a result, early missteps left military commissions open to legitimate criticism, but also to improvement. The Presidential Military Order,[12] which initially authorized military commissions in 2001 on the President's authority alone, was substantially recast, following the Supreme Court's 2006 decision in *Hamdan v. Rumsfeld*,[13] by the Military Commissions Act of 2006. That act, for the first time in American history, provided detailed congressional authority for, and procedural guidance to, military commissions. That act was further substantially reformed by the Military Commissions Act of 2009, which addressed a number of serious criticisms leveled by opponents of the 2006 Act.

Most important, the 2009 Act flatly prohibits the use of statements obtained by either torture or cruel, inhuman, or degrading treatment.[14] Further, with one narrow exception for statements made incident to lawful conduct during military operations at the point of capture, or closely related active combat engagement, all statements of an accused admitted as evidence must have been voluntary.[15] Likewise, statements of others offered as evidence must be evaluated by the judge to determine whether the will of the declarant was overborne.[16] Significantly, however, there is no requirement that *Miranda* or similar warnings be given.[17]

The admission of hearsay as evidence is governed by the rules of evidence applicable in general courts-martial (which are essentially the same as the Federal Rules of Evidence),[18] with one additional "residual" hearsay exception for situations when "direct testimony from the witness is not available as a practical matter, taking into consideration the physical location of the witness, the unique circumstances of military and intelligence operations during hostilities, and the adverse impacts on military or intelligence operations that would likely result from the production of the witness."[19] Thus, as in international war crimes courts, a narrow category of lawfully obtained, probative, reliable hearsay, uttered by witnesses who are now genuinely unavailable, as established by the offering party, may be admitted by the judge if in the interests of justice.

The accused may not be compelled to be a witness against himself at trial. He has the right to discovery of the evidence against him, as well as to discovery of potentially exculpatory and mitigating evidence and information that tends to impeach prosecution evidence. He has a right to obtain witnesses and evidence comparable to that available to criminal defendants in the federal civilian courts, as well as the right to compulsory process. He can call witnesses and cross-examine the prosecution's witnesses. An accused may seek to suppress evidence that is not reliable or probative, or if the probative value is substantially outweighed by the danger of unfair prejudice, confusion of the issues or jurors, or that is unduly cumulative.

The accused may be represented by civilian counsel, and he is provided military defense counsel free of charge. In capital cases, the accused also has a right to a defense counsel learned in death penalty jurisprudence—a right not available to U.S. servicemembers facing capital courts-martial. The accused also has the right to defend himself without counsel if he so chooses.

With the narrow differences relating to admissibility of statements of the accused (no *Miranda*) and hearsay (a slightly broader aperture justified by operational factors in the context of hostilities), the rules of evidence and procedure are nearly identical to the rules of evidence and procedure applicable in courts-martial under the Uniform Code of Military Justice (UCMJ),[20] including the rules governing discovery. Also, under the 2009 Military Commissions Act, genuine and justifiable national secrets are protected under classified information procedures developed and refined since 1980 in U.S. federal civilian court criminal trials. Obviously, the handling of classified information is a major concern in cases of the type brought before military commissions. In any war, especially one against an enemy such as Al-Qaeda, the ability to safeguard sources, methods, and activities of intelligence is critical. By the same token, classified information must be available to the defense where relevant and necessary.

The 2009 Act and implementing rules provide a variety of procedures to protect classified information, while providing the defense the use of the information it needs to make its case. On rare occasions, the judge may close the proceedings to the public. Under the act, however, the proceedings may only be closed once the judge has determined it is necessary to do so to "protect information the disclosure of which could reasonably be expected to cause damage to the national security, including intelligence or law enforcement sources, methods, or activities" or to "ensure the physical safety of individuals."[21] This standard essentially codifies the requirements for closure set out by the U.S. Supreme Court in *Press-Enterprise Co. v. Superior Court* and related cases.[22]

In practice, only one hour and 55 minutes out of 201 total hours of pretrial sessions to date[23] in the heavily litigated cases of *United States v. Mohammad, et al.* and *United States v. al Nashiri* have been closed to the public. In each instance, a fully verbatim record was made for appellate review, and an unclassified, redacted transcript of the closed proceedings was made public within days of the hearing. With the public release of those unclassified, redacted transcripts, less than one percent of the proceedings have not been made public.

In addition, unofficial transcripts of all public sessions of the military commissions are posted on the military commissions' website within one business day of the court session, and all public filings are available online once cleared for public release. While Guantanamo is admittedly inaccessible to the broader public, more than 60 news media organizations and 30 nongovernmental organizations send representatives to view the proceedings, and anyone with photo identification who can get to the Washington, D.C. area can view the proceedings via closed circuit video transmission, a level of access identical to or surpassing that in U.S. federal civilian court criminal trials or courts-martial. Indeed, the Center for Constitutional Rights—no fan of military commissions—favorably compared the transparency of military commissions with the public availability of information in the general court-martial of Private Bradley Manning.[24]

As should be clear from the above, a well-developed body of laws, rules, and regulations, as well as a rich historical record of precedent, govern military commissions tried under the 2009 Act. Our friends on the other side of the debate argue that military commissions are lawless tribunals where judges and the parties opportunistically cherry-pick arguments from a variety of sources and authorities. All litigation in our adversarial system, however, involves contending parties drawing on a variety of sources for precedent, arguments, and analogies. Counsel and judges in courts-martial under the UCMJ routinely cite and argue by analogy from federal civilian court precedents. Likewise, our civilian courts routinely look to the laws and judicial decisions of other jurisdictions, including to international law and foreign laws. As in every other American court or court-martial, in military commissions the parties zealously and methodically litigate the issues that need to be resolved, and the judges professionally and diligently apply their best legal reasoning to the issues before them. That they have to reconcile various principles of law from diverse areas of the law is completely unremarkable and, in fact, is fully consistent with the fair administration of justice.

It is true that the detention of military commissions–accused persons in Guantanamo Bay, Cuba, imposes certain logistic costs that would not be present if the trials were held in a location that was already equipped with the infrastructure necessary to conduct these trials—say, the Southern District of New York. For example, the Office of Military Commissions operates flights from Andrews Air Force Base to the U.S. Naval Station, Guantanamo Bay, for trial participants and support staff and provides for their lodging and transportation on the base. Likewise, the U.S. government has constructed two courtrooms and work spaces in Guantanamo.

Two points should be made about those expenses. First, while there are ongoing operational expenses (such as the flights, space and vehicle maintenance, lodging costs), significant sums have already been invested in constructing a state-of-the-art military commissions courtroom and other infrastructure in Guantanamo. Those facilities now constitute a capital asset, going forward. Second, the ongoing expenses associated with conducting trials in Guantanamo result from Congress's decision that those detainees should not be brought into the United States. Those expenses should be conceptually separated from the expenses arising out of the operation of military commissions at Guantanamo, as they do not result from operating a separate system, but rather from the congressional policy determination that these trials, if there are to be trials, should occur in Guantanamo.

Moreover, our friends on the other side of the debate overstate the logistical obstacles involved in military commissions. Many of the same logistical requirements and expenses would exist even if these cases were held in a federal district court in the United States. For example, regardless of location, these trials require the infrastructure necessary to handle and store classified information, as well as to communicate over highly secure networks. They require—regardless of forum—lawyers, paralegals, judges, courtroom staff, security experts, investigators, and translators. Apart from travel to and from Guantanamo for hearings, much of the other travel related to investigating and preparing these cases—such as travel to interview witnesses or view evidence—would be necessary regardless of the forum.

And do not forget that, were trials such as that of the 9/11 conspirators to take place in a federal district court, it would not simply be business as usual in the civilian courthouse where the trial would be held. There would undoubtedly be extraordinary expenses beyond those involved in the normal operations of those courts. In January 2010, when it appeared the 9/11 conspirators would be tried in southern Manhattan, the security costs of holding the trial were estimated to be "hundreds of millions of dollars a year."[25]

The point here is simply that any discussion of the high cost of military commissions must consider the nature of the various types of expenses involved, which of those expenses would exist in any forum, and what extraordinary expenses would the ordinary civilian courts incur if they were to try these cases.

As our colleagues point out, there are many legal professionals employed in military commissions. Surely, over time, the staffing has not always matched the workload. In part, that was the result of obstacles and interruptions that arose as this institution was updated for the current time and conflict. Zealous and capable defense counsel challenged the military commissions convened under the Presidential Military Order, ultimately resulting in a Supreme Court decision that now guides our actions. That decision resulted in a hiatus while the political branches worked on what became the Military Commissions Act of 2006. Subsequently, after the 2008 presidential election, President Obama suspended military commissions for many months in 2009 while he and his Administration thoroughly reviewed military commissions and sought reforms, which ultimately resulted in the Military Commissions Act of 2009. These periods of interruption in the forward progress of military commission trials undoubtedly left certain elements of the Office of Military Commissions with more staff than necessary for a time. In the Office of the Chief Prosecutor, we managed staffing issues by allowing personnel who could be spared to deploy with operational units or return temporarily to their parent Service during the slow times.

Since early 2012, however, military commissions have been methodically involved in trying six defendants in two capital cases. Charges have been sworn against three others that await referral decisions by the Convening Authority. We have actively pursued appeals in two other cases. At present, at least in the Office of the Chief Prosecutor, our staff is fully employed in important work advancing the cause of justice in war. These massive, complex capital cases would require similar staffing even if tried in federal district court. The individuals involved might be different, to some extent, but it is difficult to imagine these cases could be tried with significantly less total man-hours, whatever the forum.

So, the past is prologue. Looking forward, military commissions have been reformed and updated. Despite their growing pains, they have become a national security and justice institution adapted to our time and current challenges. We submit that, if given a fresh look, reformed military commissions will persuade our fellow citizens and reasonable people of good faith around the world that they are legitimate and effective, and that they can and should be used if and when necessary. We further believe that time and experience will demonstrate that reformed military commission trials are also consistent with our values and best traditions.

Notes

1. 10 U.S.C. § 948a *et seq.* (2009).

2. Andrew C. McCarthy, *A Case for a National Security Court*, 57 WAYNE L. REV. 275 (2011); GLENN SULMASY, THE NATIONAL SECURITY COURT SYSTEM: A NATURAL EVOLUTION OF JUSTICE IN AN AGE OF TERROR (2009); Kevin E. Lunday & Harvey Rishikof, *Due Process Is a Strategic Choice: Legitimacy and the Establishment of an Article III National Security Court*, 39 CAL. W. INT'L L.J. 87 (2008).

3. Mark R. Shulman, *National Security Courts: Specialized Justice or Star Chambers?*, 15 ILSA J. INT'L & COMP. L. 533 (2009); Stephen I. Vladeck, *The Case Against National Security Courts*, 45 WILLAMETTE L. REV. 505 (2009); LIBERTY AND SECURITY COMM. & COALITION TO DEFEND CHECKS AND BALANCES, THE CONSTITUTION PROJECT, A CRITIQUE OF "NATIONAL SECURITY COURTS" (June 23, 2008).

4. Hamdan v. Rumsfeld, 548 U.S. 557, 590–91 (2006); A. Wigfall Green, *The Military Commission*, 42 AM. J. INT'L L. 832 (1948).

5. *See, e.g.*, Proceedings of a Board of General Officers, Held by Order of His Excellency, the Commander in Chief, at General Knox's Quarters, Valley Forge (June 2, 1778), *in* 15 THE PAPERS OF GEORGE WASHINGTON: REVOLUTIONARY WAR SERIES 297 (Edward G. Lengel ed., 2006) (proceedings in the case of Thomas Shanks, former Ensign in the Tenth Pennsylvania Regiment, charged with being a spy); PROCEEDINGS OF A BOARD OF GENERAL OFFICERS, HELD BY ORDER OF HIS EXCELLENCY GEN. WASHINGTON, COMMANDER IN CHIEF OF THE ARMY OF THE UNITED STATES OF AMERICA, RESPECTING MAJOR JOHN ANDRÉ, ADJUTANT GENERAL OF THE BRITISH ARMY (Phila., Francis Bailey 1780) (proceedings in the case of Major John André, Adjutant General of the British Army, charged with being a spy).

6. WILLIAM WINTHROP, MILITARY LAW AND PRECEDENTS 832–33 (rev. 2d ed. 1920).

7. *Id.* at 831, 839–40.

8. Lester Nurick & Roger W. Barrett, *Legality of Guerrilla Forces Under the Laws of War*, 40 AM. J. INT'L L. 563 (1946).

9. FRANK M. BUSCHER, THE U.S. WAR CRIMES TRIAL PROGRAM IN GERMANY, 1946-1955 (1989); PHILIP R. PICCIGALLO, THE JAPANESE ON TRIAL: ALLIED WAR CRIMES OPERATIONS IN THE EAST, 1945-1951 (1979). In addition to military commissions, the United States tried German war criminals by military tribunals at Nuremberg under the authority of Control Council Law No. 10. *See generally* TELFORD TAYLOR, FINAL REPORT TO THE SECRETARY OF THE ARMY ON THE NUREMBERG WAR CRIMES TRIALS UNDER CONTROL COUNCIL LAW NO. 10 (1949).

10. *See, e.g.*, Authorization for Use of Military Force, Pub. L. No. 107-40, 115 Stat. 224 (2001); Military Commissions Act of 2006, Pub. L. No. 109-366, 120 Stat. 2600; Military Commissions Act of 2009, Pub. L. No. 111-84, div. A, tit. XVIII, 123 Stat. 2574 (codified at 10 U.S.C. §§ 948a *et seq.*); President Barack Obama, Remarks at the National Archives and Records Administration, 1 Pub. Papers 689, 691 (May 21, 2009); Hamdan v. Rumsfeld, 548 U.S. 557, 628–32 (2006); Hamdan v. United States, 696 F.3d 1238, 1240 (D.C. Cir. 2012).

11. Of course, it is equally a mistake to ignore or reject the long and effective history of military commissions.

12. President George W. Bush, Mil. Order, 66 Fed. Reg. 57,833 (Nov. 13, 2001).

13. 548 U.S. 557 (2006).

14. 10 U.S.C. § 948r(a) (2009).

15. *Id.* § 948r(c). For a statement to be admitted pursuant to the point of capture exception, the military judge must find that the totality of the circumstances renders the statement reliable, that the statement possesses sufficient probative value, and that the interests

of justice would best be served by admitting the statement into evidence. *Id.* The narrow exception relating to point-of-capture statements has been analogized to the public safety exception to *Miranda* recognized in federal criminal courts. *Cf.* New York v. Quarles, 467 U.S. 649 (1984).

16.   10 U.S.C. § 949a(b)(3)(D) (2009).

17.   *Id.* § 948b(B) (2009) (stating that the warning provision of Article 31 of the Uniform Code of Military Justice is in applicable to military commissions).

18.   *Id.*

19.   *Id.*

20.   *Compare* Manual for Military Commissions (2012), *with* Manual for Courts-Martial (2012) (as amended by Exec. Order No. 13,643, 78 Fed. Reg. 29,559 (May 15, 2013)).

21.   10 U.S.C. § 949d(c) (2009).

22.   478 U.S. 1 (1986).

23.   Sept. 20, 2013.

24.   Writ-Appeal Pet. for Review of Army Ct. of Criminal Appeals Decision on Appeal for Extraordinary Relief and Supporting Mem. of Law at 26–27, *Center for Constitutional Rights v. United States*, No. 20120514 (C.A.A.F. June 26, 2012), *available at* http://ccrjustice.org/files/Writ-Appeal-Petition-for-Review-of-ACCA-Decision-on-Appl-for-Extraordinary-Relief-C-A-A-F-June-26-2012.pdf.

25.   Scott Shane & Benjamin Weiser, *U.S. Drops Plan for a 9/11 Trial in New York City*, N.Y. Times, Jan. 29, 2010, *available at* http://www.nytimes.com/2010/01/30/nyregion/30trial.html.

VII

Pulling the Purse Strings Tight: Use of Funding Restrictions to Limit Executive Prerogatives Regarding the Guantanamo Bay Detention Facility

Mark Toole

Introduction

On May 23, 2013, President Obama, in a major foreign policy speech delivered at the National Defense University, recommitted his administration to the process of closing the detention facility at Guantanamo Bay, Cuba.[1] In so doing, he was renewing a pledge he had made when he originally ran for President in 2008 and which he pursued after he was elected. On January 22, 2009, two days after his first inauguration, President Obama issued Executive Order 13,493.[2] The order called for the closing of the Guantanamo Bay detention facility no later than January 22, 2010. Specifically, in section 3, the President directed that the facility would be closed as soon as practicable, but not later than one year from the date of the order.[3] Regarding the disposition of detainees still held at Guantanamo at the time of the closure, the order provided that they would be returned to their home country, released, transferred to a third country, or transferred to another United States detention facility in a manner consistent with the law and the national security and foreign policy interests of the United States.[4]

In some important respects, progress has been made in accomplishing the transfer aspect of the January 2009 order, and a number of detainees have been released or transferred from the facility to either their home country or a third country. There were about 245 detainees at Guantanamo when President Obama took office, and by May 23, 2013, there were 166.[5] Still, by that date, the crux of the order—that is, the closing of Guantanamo—had not been realized. The primary reason for the lack of success in efforts to close the facility has been a determination by Congress that federal dollars would not be appropriated for that purpose. Consequently, through exercise of its control over the purse, Congress has been able to inhibit a legitimate exercise of executive power—one that was arguably an important aspect of the President's agenda.

Separation of Powers Principles

Implicit in the Constitution is the recognition that branches of government will compete for power. Recognizing that political reality, the Framers sought to diffuse power through reliance on the principle of separation of powers. A great strength of the U.S. Constitution has proven to be the Montesquieu-influenced division of power between the executive, legislative, and judicial branches of government. The purpose of the separation of powers was to ensure that one branch of government was unable to accumulate too much power and thereby threaten liberty. The Framers saw the threat to liberty as an obvious and not improbable consequence of the accrual of unrestrained power. As James Madison noted in *Federalist 47*, the accumulation of all power in the same hands could "justly be pronounced the very definition of tyranny."[6] Accordingly, the legislature was afforded the power to make laws, the executive the power to execute the laws, and the judicial branch the power to interpret the law.

Endeavoring to keep the delegated powers of government from threatening liberty, the Framers introduced into the constitutional scheme doctrines and provisions that enabled one branch of government to effectively check a legitimate exercise of power by another branch of government. Another scheme designed to limit an aggrandizement of power is the constitutional principle of checks and balances. These relate to constitutional powers granted to each branch of government to prevent one branch from dominating the others.

The veto power outlined in Art. 1, § 7, cl. 2 of the Constitution is the most commonly understood example of a constitutional check. Through use of veto power, the Executive can nullify an effort by Congress to pass a law. The veto power permits the Executive to effectively restrain the legislature from exercising its constitutionally delegated authority.

The "countercheck" to the veto is outlined in Art. I, § 7, cl. 2 of the Constitution. It allows the legislature to reconsider the vetoed bill and, if two-thirds of both Houses of Congress vote to enact it, to override the President's veto. If the veto is overridden, the bill becomes law.[7] While the veto is the most commonly understood check, there are other explicit and inherent checks outlined in the Constitution.[8] However, with a relatively evenly divided and sometimes highly partisan Congress, the requisite two-thirds in both houses becomes very difficult to attain, resulting in the executive veto potentially being a very powerful check on legislative actions.

The principles of separation of powers and checks and balances, while designed to limit and channel governmental power, can inherently cause clashes or struggles between the branches of government. The Framers must have expected that, as it was never the idea that the powers of the respective branches be completely separate and distinct. In *Federalist No. 48*, Madison pointed out that the principle of separation of powers does not mean that the branches are "wholly unconnected with each other."[9] Madison wrote that the branches had to be connected and blended to give each a "constitutional control" over the others. At the same time, none of the branches should possess, "directly or indirectly, an overruling influence over the others in the administration of their respective powers."[10]

Those circumstances, however, in which one branch of government may, in the exercise of an enumerated or implied power, violate some other constitutional provision or doctrine, such as the doctrine of separation of powers, and thus inappropriately constrain the legitimate exercise of power by another branch are not clearly defined. Essentially, the question arises as to whether the Constitution's structural principle of separation of powers can limit a particular branch's exercise of an enumerated or implied power. This issue could arise in a number of contexts, but most commonly seems to arise in the area of legislative appropriations as a potential interference on the legitimate exercise of executive power in the area of foreign affairs.

The Power to Appropriate

Spending power is one of the most fundamental powers of government. Article I, § 8, Cl. 1 of the Constitution provides that Congress shall have the power to pay the debts and provide for the common defense and general welfare of the United States. Through use of this "Spending Clause" power, Congress has been able to accomplish many legislative objectives, for some of which it may have lacked either the enumerated or implied power to carry out through nonfiscal legislative means.

While at the Constitutional Convention there was some debate over where "money bills" should originate, there was consensus that the power of the purse should be placed with the legislature. The debate over where money bills should originate was not over in which branch they should originate, but in which House of the legislature.[11] As Louis Fisher has noted, the Framers, conscious of history and knowledgeable that divisions over sources of revenue for military expeditions had drawn England into a civil war, sought to avoid that calamity by vesting the power of the purse in Congress.[12] The importance of the power of the purse was recognized by Madison in *Federalist No. 58*. He stated, "[t]he power over the purse may, in fact, be regarded as the most complete and effectual weapon with which any constitution can arm the immediate representatives of the people, for obtaining a redress of grievance, and for carrying into effect every just and salutary measure."[13]

The parameters of Congress's Spending Clause power were outlined by the Supreme Court in *United States v. Butler*.[14] In *Butler*, the Court weighed the constitutionality of the Agricultural Adjustment Act of 1933. The act imposed an excise tax on processors and packagers of certain agricultural products. The proceeds from the tax were used to pay farmers in return for a promise not to grow certain crops. The intent was to stabilize the price of those affected agricultural products. In a majority opinion written by Justice Owen Roberts, the Court adopted the Hamiltonian view of the scope of the Tax and Spend Clause and held that that power is not limited to taxing and spending in the enumerated legislative fields.[15] Rather, the clause confers a power separate and distinct from the enumerated powers, and its exercise is not restricted by them.[16] Consequently, Congress has the substantive power to tax and to appropriate. The power is limited by the requirement that it be exercised to provide for the general welfare of the United States and that it not violate any independent constitutional bar.[17] In *Butler*, the Court found that, in fact, while the tax and appropriation scheme may have been for the general welfare, it was unconstitutional because it was used to enforce a regulation of matters of state concern with respect to which Congress had no right to interfere. Accordingly, there was a Tenth Amendment bar to the exercise of the Agricultural Adjustment Act's regulatory scheme.

In *South Dakota v. Dole*, the Supreme Court again considered the parameters of Congress's Spending Clause power.[18] The Court's opinion focused on Congress's ability to make conditional appropriations to affect the actions of a state. Specifically, the Court considered the constitutionality of attaching conditions to the receipt of federal moneys upon a state's compliance with federal statutory and administrative directives.[19] In *South Dakota v. Dole*, the federal provision at issue allowed the secretary of transportation to withhold a percentage of appropriated highway transportation funds from states that failed to prohibit persons under the age of 21 from purchasing alcoholic beverages. Effectively, the federal government was conditioning appropriations on a state's changing its state law.

South Dakota had argued that the conditional appropriation violated the Twenty-first Amendment and inappropriately invaded the state's Tenth Amendment prerogatives. While those provisions might bar Congress from directly mandating that states raise their drinking age, since Congress was acting indirectly under its spending power to encourage uniformity in the states' drinking ages, the legislative effort was within constitutional bounds even if Congress may not regulate drinking ages directly.[20]

The question became whether those provisions posed the type of "independent constitutional bar" limitation described by the Court in *Butler*. The Court determined that the "independent constitutional bar" limitation on the spending power is not a prohibition on the indirect achievement of objectives that Congress is not empowered to achieve directly, but rather it "stands for the unexceptionable proposition that the power may not be used to induce the States to engage in activities that would themselves be unconstitutional."[21] Accordingly, the "independent constitutional bar" limitation would prevent a grant of federal funds from being conditioned on invidiously discriminatory state action or the infliction of cruel and unusual punishment.[22]

While recognizing that attaching conditions on the receipt of federal moneys was an incident of Spending Clause power, the Court made clear that the exercise of that power was subject to several general restrictions.[23] Those restrictions include the requirement that the expenditure be made for the general welfare; that the condition on the state's receipt of federal funds be unambiguous; that the condition be related to the particular national project or program; and, finally, the condition must not be so coercive as to amount to compulsion. Finding that the conditional appropriation of highway transportation funds met the stated criteria, the act was constitutional.

To Fund or Not to Fund

The Supreme Court's Spending Clause cases established that Congress, when acting for the general welfare and absent an independent constitutional bar, can achieve a broad range of objectives through spending and conditional spending. The power to spend carries with it the concomitant power to decide not to spend. It follows that the withholding of federal funding can likewise be a constitutionally appropriate means to achieve legislative objectives. One objective may be the blocking of an executive action that Congress finds obnoxious. Congress has used its power of the purse to inhibit executive prerogatives. It used that power to halt military operations in Southeast Asia in 1973[24] and prohibited all assistance for conducting military or paramilitary operations in Angola in 1976.[25] Perhaps the most well-known incident of Congress using the power to keep the purse closed involved the Boland Amendments. The Boland Amendments were a series of legislative restrictions on federal funding for the Contras in Nicaragua. Secret efforts by the Reagan Administration to bypass these restrictions and fund the Contras with resources secured by alternative means led to the Iran-Contra scandal. The most restrictive of the Amendments was enacted in 1984. It provided that:

> [N]o funds available to the Central Intelligence Agency, the Department of Defense or any other agency or entity of the United States involved in

intelligence activities may be obligated or expended for the purpose or which would have the effect of supporting, directly or indirectly, military or paramilitary operations in Nicaragua by any nation, group, organization, movement or individual.[26]

The Reagan Administration engaged in efforts to fund the Contras covertly through profits from arms sales to Iran, private donations, and with donations from foreign countries. When the efforts became public and Congress initiated hearings into the matter, the administration argued that if the Amendment applied to the President and the National Security Council, it was an unconstitutional usurpation of the President's power to conduct foreign policy.[27] Bruce Fein argued that the Boland Amendments gratuitously intruded on the President's authority to enforce international law and to deter or repel aggression threatening national security.[28]

Twenty-five years later, when congressional funding restrictions again tied the hands of a President in his pursuit of foreign affairs and national security objectives, a similar argument was forwarded. In signing into law the National Defense Authorization Act for Fiscal Year 2011, an act containing provisions restricting the use of funds appropriated to the Department of Defense from being used to transfer Guantanamo detainees into the United States or using such funds to assist in the transfers, President Obama stated that the provisions represented a "dangerous and unprecedented challenge to the critical executive branch authority to determine when and where to prosecute Guantanamo detainees."[29] Provisions barring use of appropriated funds to transfer Guantanamo detainees into the United States were also in the National Defense Authorization Acts for Fiscal Years 2012 and 2013. In signing the 2013 act into law, President Obama again indicated his opposition to those provisions and stated that under some circumstances they violated constitutional separation of powers principles.[30]

There seems little doubt as to the constitutionality of the President's order to close Guantanamo either as a valid exercise of his commander-in-chief power or consistent with his inherent authority coupled with a delegation of authority from Congress in the Authorization for Use of Military Forces (AUMF). In passing the AUMF shortly after 9/11, Congress authorized the President to "use all necessary and appropriate force against nations, organizations, or persons he determines planned, authorized, committed, or aided the terrorist attacks that occurred on September 11, 2001, or harbored such organizations or persons, in order to prevent any future acts of international terrorism against the United States by such nations, organization or persons."[31] Acting pursuant to the AUMF, President George W. Bush sent troops to Afghanistan to wage a campaign against Al-Qaeda and the Taliban regime. During the fight, enemy personnel were captured in Afghanistan and elsewhere, and were sent to Guantanamo for detention and potential prosecution. Detention operations were arguably a consequence of the AUMF.

The Supreme Court explicitly recognized the broad nature of executive power in the area of foreign affairs in *United States v. Curtiss-Wright*. Weighing the constitutionality of a presidential proclamation that prohibited the sale of arms to the warring countries of Bolivia and Paraguay, Justice Sutherland, writing for the Court and differentiating between the scope of constitutional authority afforded federal power that relates to internal (domestic) and external (foreign) affairs, characterized the President as "the sole organ of the federal government in the field of international relations."[32] Accordingly, the constitutional scope of the Executive's power in the area of foreign affairs was so broad that the President's act in prohibiting an American company from selling to a potential foreign customer would have been deemed constitutional even without a basis for its exercise and act of Congress.[33]

In *Dames & Moore v. Regan*, however, the Court acknowledged that consideration of congressional action was relevant in a determination of the constitutionality of executive action in the field of foreign affairs. The Court outlined the applicability Justice Jackson's three-tier analysis outlined in his concurring opinion in *Youngtown Sheet & Tube Company v. Sawyer*.[34] In *Dames & Moore*, the Court considered the constitutionality of certain actions taken by President Carter to secure the release of American hostages.

In upholding President Carter's authority to nullify judicial attachments, transfer frozen Iranian assets, and send private commercial claims against Iran to a special tribunal for resolution, as part of an executive agreement with Iran, the Court considered evidence of congressional authorization for the President's action.

Justice Rehnquist, writing for the majority, found that the nullification of attachments and the transfer of assets were taken pursuant to specific congressional authorization in the International Emergency Economic Powers Act (IEEPA).[35] However, apparently affording some deference to the scope of executive power in the area of foreign affairs while finding no specific legislative authority for the suspension of private claims, Justice Rehnquist did determine that IEEPA and the Hostage Act indicated congressional acceptance of a broad scope of executive action in circumstances such as those presented by the hostage crisis.[36]

Additionally, a long history of congressional acquiescence to the settling of claims by U.S. nationals against foreign countries by executive agreements, without the advice or consent of the Senate, indicates Congress's implicit approval of this practice.[37] Accordingly, inaction by Congress, coupled with a history of acquiescence to a particular executive practice, will put the President's action into the top tier of Justice Jackson's three-tier analytical scheme. The opinion furthers the Court's view of the broad scope of executive power in the area of foreign affairs but emphasizes the impact of congressional authorization, even implicit authorization, in weighing the constitutionality of the President's actions. Consequently, while the President's authority in the realm of foreign affairs is broad, it is not necessarily free of the restraining influence of Congress.

Should a challenge to Congress's unwillingness to fund an executive action find its way to the Court, it seems unlikely the challenge would be heard.

The doctrine of justiciability relates to the appropriateness of a case or issue for judicial decision. A justiciable complaint is one that can be adequately resolved by a court. One justiciability doctrine that can lead to the dismissal of a complaint is the political question doctrine. A case may be dismissed under the political question doctrine if the issues presented appear to have a textually demonstrable constitutional commitment to a coordinate political department.[38] In a challenge brought by the executive branch over a legislative determination not to appropriate federal funds to an Executive-initiated effort, the judiciary would have to acknowledge that in Article I, § 8, cl. 1 the Constitution specifically commits spending determinations to Congress. While the political question doctrine would not prohibit a court from addressing the controversy, it allows the court to essentially abjure and defer to its coordinate branches and the political process to work as a constraint on those elected branches of government. In *Goldwater v. Carter*, Senator Barry Goldwater challenged President Carter's termination of a treaty with Taiwan without the approval of the Senate.[39] A plurality of the Court saw the President's abrogation of the treaty as a question that was political, "and therefore nonjusticiable because it involves the authority of the President in the conduct of our country's foreign relations and the extent to which the Senate or the Congress is authorized to negate the action of the President."[40]

However, if the Court did consider a challenge to Congress's determination to withhold federal funding from efforts related to closing the Guantanamo detention facility, the issue would be whether the prohibition on appropriations violates separation of powers principles. The question can be presented as whether under separation of powers principles the President's efforts to close the Guantanamo detention facility is an exercise of executive power that would be free from constraint by the other two branches of government. As Louis Fisher has pointed out, while broad, the congressional power of the purse is not unlimited, as Congress cannot use appropriations bills to enact bills of attainder, to restrict the President's pardon power, or to establish a national religion.[41] Additionally, it would be unconstitutional for Congress to reduce the salaries of the President or federal judges.[42] Nonetheless, as Madison observed in *Federalist 58*, Congress holds the purse, "that powerful instrument," which, experience had shown, allowed the reduction of the "overgrown prerogatives of the other branches of government."[43]

The President is vested with executive powers outlined in Article II. The establishment of a detention facility at the Guantanamo Bay naval facility was an exercise executive power. It was, however, an exercise of executive power executed in coordination with congressional enactment of the Authorization to Use Military Force. An executive effort to close the Guantanamo detention facility may be an exercise of executive power in the area of foreign affairs, but it also an act with significant domestic impact, particularly if detainees are brought to the United States for prosecution and/or detention. Additionally, the closure and transfer are not aspects an of executive act occurring in the midst of a crisis. which, as The Prize Cases indicated, might legitimize an otherwise questionable exercise of executive power.[44] And, as the Supreme Court's Guantanamo precedent has shown, issues related to the detainees and the detention facility are subject to constitutional restraints.[45] Nonetheless, the President may not need congressional approval to close the facility. Arguably, the President inherently, or pursuant to the AUMF, has the authority to determine the facility is no longer necessary.

Congress may, through its control of the purse, however, prevent the President from accomplishing his intent. A defense authorization act that specifically prohibits use of federal funds for an executive initiative is, of course, the opposite of evidence of acquiescence. While an argument can be made that legislative prohibitions on what specific nations the President can or cannot negotiate with regarding the transfer of detainees may be inconsistent with the Court's holdings in *United States v. Curtiss-Wright* and *Dames & Moore v. Regan*, and, consequently, violate separation of powers doctrine, a legislatively enacted prohibition on the use of federal funds to transfer detainees into the U.S. evidences a lack of congressional concurrence, which could put the action into Justice Jackson's lowest tier of executive authority. Moreover, a decision by Congress not to fund is one that is justified as an express power within the "spending power." The question remains whether a legislative prohibition that restrains an executive action taken to keep the nation safe violates separation of powers principles.

As Louis Henkin observed, it is difficult to accept that the President should command a power expressly conferred upon Congress.[46] Henkin argues, however, that while Congress is constitutionally free to spend or not to spend for the common defense or general welfare, it is required to appropriate funds for the activities of the other branches of government that are within their independent constitutional authority. Accordingly, some have pointed out that "Congress would overstep its boundaries it if refused to appropriate funds for the President to receive foreign ambassadors or make treaties."[47] However, decisions relating to the Guantanamo detention facility are not necessarily within the independent constitutional authority of the Executive if, just from the standpoint of determining who can be admitted into the country, Congress has the constitutional authority to set immigration policy. The Guantanamo detention facility is arguably the product of cooperation between the President and Congress. It seems unlikely, under a violation of separation of powers theory, that a court would essentially direct Congress to appropriate funds to facilitate its closure and the transfer of detainees into the United States.

Conclusion

The Framers understood that separation of powers doctrine, together with the concept of checks and balances, would prevent the aggrandizement of power in any particular branch of government, which they saw as a dire threat to liberty. The consequent friction between the branches caused by the constitutional scheme is illustrated in the President's determination to close the Guantanamo detention facility in the face of congressional refusal to commit funds to support the effort. Still, President Obama is not the first chief executive to have his initiatives frustrated by a Congress tight with the purse. Whether Congress, acting within the scope of its express powers, can inhibit the President acting within the scope of his authority, violates separation of powers principles may be seen by a court as a political question and, accordingly, nonjusticiable. It may be a matter best left to the two political branches for resolution through coordination and compromise. While the President takes the lead in terms of setting the nation's foreign policy, both Congress and the Executive have responsibilities in the areas of foreign affairs, national security, and military matters. Two-thirds of the Senate must approve of a treaty before it becomes binding.[48] Ambassadors can be appointed only with the advice and consent of the Senate.[49] The President serves as Commander-in-Chief, but among its enumerated powers Congress can declare war; raise and support the Army; provide and maintain a Navy; and make rules and regulations for the governance of the military.[50] While the responsibilities may overlap, each branch operates within its own sphere of authority. Prohibiting the use of federal funding for a particular presidential objective as a part of an appropriations bill invites a veto by the Executive. While it would be politically difficult to veto a defense appropriations bill, it is a legitimate constitutional option. With a closely divided Congress, it would be very difficult to override any veto. Limiting the Executive's foreign policy options is a natural consequence of the separation of the sword and the purse. President Obama's signing statement of January 3, 2011, may have recognized this reality with his pledge to work with Congress to lift the prohibition through legislation.[51] That may be the resolution envisioned by the Framers.

Notes

1.   President Barack Obama, Remarks at the National Defense University (May 23, 2013), *available at* http://www.whitehouse.gov/the-press-office/2013/05/23/remarks-president-national-defense-university.

2.   74 Fed. Reg., no. 16, Jan. 27, 2009.

3.   *Id.*

4.   *Id.*

5.   Brad Knickerboker, *Obama Renews Push to Close Guantanamo Military Prison*, CHRISTIAN SCIENCE MONITOR, May 23, 2013, *available at* http://www.csmonitor.com/USA/Justice/2013/0523/Obama-renews-push-to-close-Guantanamo-military-prison.

6.   THE FEDERALIST No. 47, at 269 (Madison) (Clinton Rossiter ed., 1961).

7.   U.S. CONST. art. I, § 7, cl. 2.

8.   U.S. CONST. art. II, § 2, cl. 2, requires concurrence of two-thirds of the Senate before a treaty is ratified, and provides that certain presidential appointments require the advice and consent of the Senate.

9.   THE FEDERALIST No. 48, at 276 (Madison) (Clinton Rossiter ed., 1961).

10.   *Id.*

11.   That controversy was resolved with Art. I, § 7, cl. 2, which provides that all bills for raising revenue shall originate in the House of Representatives, but the Senate may propose or concur with amendments on as other bills.

12.   Louis Fisher, *How Tightly Can Congress Draw the Purse Strings?* AM. J. INT'L L., Vol. 83, No. 4; *The United States Constitution in Its Third Century*, FOREIGN AFFAIRS (Oct. 1989), 758, 761.

13.   FEDERALIST No. 58 at 327 (Madison) (Clinton Rossiter ed., 1961).

14.   United States v. Butler, 297 U.S. 1 (1936).

15.   James Madison asserted that the power amounted to no more than a reference to the other powers enumerated in the subsequent clauses of Article I, § 8, and, consequently, the grant of power to tax and spend for the general national welfare must be confined to the enumerated legislative fields committed to the legislature.

16.   *Butler, supra* n. 14, at 65

17.   *Id.* at 65, 66.

18.   South Dakota v. Dole, 483 U.S. 203 (1987).

19.   *Id.* at 207.

20.   *Id.* at 206.

21.   *Id.* at 210.

22.   *Id.*

23.   *Id., citing* Fullilove v. Klutznick, 448 U.S. 448, 474 (1980) (opinion by Burger, C.J.). See Lau v. Nichols, 414 U.S. 563, 569 (1974); Ivanhoe Irrigation Dist. v. McCracken, 357 U.S. 275, 295 (1958); Okla. v. Civil Service Comm'n, 330 U.S. 127, 143–44 (1947); Steward Machine Co. v. Davis, 301 U.S. 548 (1937).

24.   Second Supp. Appropriations Act, 1973, Pub. L. No. 93-50, § 307, 87 Stat. 99, 129; continuing Appropriations for FY 1974, Pub. L. No. 93-52, § 108, 87 Stat. 130, 134 (1973). *supra* n.12, 763.

25.   Int'l Security Assistance and Arms Export Control Act of 1976, Pub. L. No. 94-329, § 404, 90 Stat. 729, 757.

26.   Joint Resolution of Oct 12, 1984, Pub. L. No. 98-483, §8066(a), 98 Stat. 1837, 1935 (1984).

27. Anthony Ricci, *The Iran-Contra Affair and the Boland Amendment: President Reagan Claims He Is Above the Law*, 12 SUFFOLK TRANSNAT'L L.J. 135, 137 (1988–1989).

28. Bruce Fein, *The Constitution and Covert Action*, 11 HOUS. J. INT'L 53 (1988).

29. White House Office of the Press Secretary, statement by the President on H.R. 6523, Jan. 7, 2011, *available at* http://www.whitehouse.gov/the-press-office/2011/01/07/statement-president-hr-6523.

30. White House Office of the Press Secretary, statement by the President on H.R. 4310, Jan. 3, 2013, *available at* http://www.whitehouse.gov/the-press-office/2013/01/03/statement-president-hr-4310.

31. Authorization for Use of Military Force, Pub. L. 107-40, §§ 1 & 2, 115 Stat. 224.

32. United States v. Curtiss-Wright, 299 U.S. 304 (1936).

33. *Id.*

34. Youngtown Sheet & Tube Co. v. Sawyer, 343 U.S. 579 (1952). Pertinently, Justice Rehnquist noted for the Court that:

> Justice Jackson's concurring opinion elaborated in a general way the consequence of different types of interaction between the two democratic branches in assessing Presidential authority to act in any given case. When the President acts pursuant to an express or implied authorization from Congress, he exercises not only his powers but those delegated by Congress. In such a case, the executive action would be supported by the strongest of presumptions and the widest latitude of judicial interpretation, and the burden of persuasion would rest heavily upon any who might attack it. . . . When the President acts in the absence of congressional authorization, he may enter 'a zone of twilight in which he and Congress may have concurrent authority, or in which its distribution is uncertain.' . . . In such a case, the analysis becomes more complicated, and the validity of the President's action, at least so far as separations powers principles are concerned, hinges on a consideration of all the circumstances, which might shed light on the views of the Legislative Branch toward such action, including 'congressional inertia, indifference, or quiescence.' . . . Finally, when the President acts in contravention of the will of Congress, 'his power is at its lowest ebb,' and the Court can sustain his actions 'only by disabling the Congress from acting upon the subject.'

35. Dames & Moore v. Regan, 453 U.S. 654, 674 (1981).

36. *Id.* at 678.

37. *Id.* at 680. *See* HAROLD KOH, NATIONAL SECURITY CONSTITUTION 131–46 (1990).

38. Baker v. Carr, 369 U.S. 186, 217 (1962). *See* LAWRENCE TRIBE, AMERICAN CONSTITUTIONAL LAW 366–85 (3d ed. 2000).

39. Goldwater v. Carter, 444 U.S. 996 (1979).

40. *Id.*

41. L. Fisher, *supra* n. 12, at 762.

42. U.S. CONST. art. II, § 1, cl. 6, and art. III, § 1.

43. FEDERALIST 58 (Madison) (C. Rossiter ed., 1961) at 327.

44. *See The Prize Cases*, 67 U.S. 635 (1863). President Lincoln's blockade of southern ports at the onset of the Civil War was found constitutional in the absence of a congressional declaration of war. The Court acknowledged the importance of deference to the executive in a time of crisis.

45. *See* Hamdi v. Rumsfeld, 542 U.S. 547 (2004); Rasul v, Bush, 542 U.S. 466 (2004); and Hamdan v. Rumsfeld, 548 U.S. 557 (2006).

46. LOUIS HENKIN, FOREIGN AFFAIRS AND THE U.S. CONSTITUTION 114 (2d ed. 2002).
47. L. Fisher, *supra* n. 12, at 762.
48. Art. II, § 2, cl. 2.
49. *Id.*
50. Art. I, § 8, cls. 11–14.
51. President Barack Obama, *supra* n. 29.

VIII

Presidential Usurpation or Congressional Abdication: An Alternative View of Legislative-Executive Relations and the Power to Go to War*

Paul S. Rundquist

Congress may be The First Branch identified in the American Constitution, but as government has evolved, Congress is no longer the central branch in the American government. The evolution of American political processes, both formal and informal, has tended to enhance the visibility of the president as the principal source of authority and direction in the American government, despite attempts by Congress to change that trend.

Most scholars recognize that it did not have to be that way. The first independent American government, the Articles of Confederation, was a flawed system, but was one that was making strides toward assuming a more functional role. Congress, under the Articles, was seemingly on its way to evolving into a parliamentary system. The Congress had begun to designate outsiders to serve, during the pleasure of the Congress, as the American equivalent of Cabinet ministers. Some may observe that there did not appear to be a "first minister" among these newly selected "commissioners." However, it is also true that the post of Prime Minister was itself rather late to appear in British practice. Whether

* An earlier version of this chapter appeared in *Assertive Multilateralism and Preventive War: Die Aussen—und Weltordnungspolitik der USA von Clinton zu Obama aus theoretischer Sicht*, Jochen Hils, Jurgen Wilzewski, and Reinhard Wolf, editors; Nomos Verlag, Baden-Baden, 2012. The author expresses his gratitude to the editors and publisher for their permission to reprint the chapter material in this volume.

the Congress of the Articles of Confederation would have evolved into a functional parliament, we shall never know. The plan to provide for amendments to the Articles to make the government sufficiently strong never came about. Instead, the convention, called to propose amendments to the Articles of Confederation, secretly abandoned its mandate and, by what might be seen as a sophisticated legislative coup, sought to overturn the Articles of Confederation with a constitution and a republican form of government to be created over the head of the established national legislature.

The original constitution gave the Congress a decisive role in government. Most framers of the Constitution, along with most of their fellow citizens, assumed that the office of President was to be George Washington's for so long as he cared to have it. However, thereafter, most people expected that no single national unifying figure would be present on the political stage. Consequently, the chance that one candidate would come to dominate the votes in the Constitution's Electoral College was so small that most assumed that the election would, in most instances, fall to the House of Representatives. Few dispute that the Congress was the more important branch in these early decades. "The rise of legislative parties as gatekeepers for the presidency, together with the expectation that elections would often be decided in the House of Representatives (as they were in two of the four open-seat presidential elections from 1800 to 1824), meant that Congress played a major role in selecting the President. As a result, the American government effectively operated for much of its first forty years with a congressionally dominated fusion of legislative and executive powers. [1]

Although the House did not remain the presidential kingmaker that most expected in the early 18th Century, congressional leaders played an influential role in the nominating caucuses. These party meetings were the key feature of early 19th Century presidential elections, and later, congressional leaders played key roles as power brokers at presidential nominating conventions. On matters of foreign policy, Congress played an influential role. The War of 1812 was largely a Congress-made war, representing the policy goals of western agrarian interests embodied by House Speaker Henry Clay. Tariff legislation was a subject in which Congress's role was so strongly entrenched that presidents until Franklin Roosevelt largely deferred to the wishes of their party leaders in the House and Senate.

So influential was the Congress in setting the national agenda that a leading scholar of the late 19th Century called the Speaker of the House the American equivalent of a "Premier."[2] Most of the presidents of the 19th Century viewed their job as being primarily administrative in character, with congressional leaders pushing for the enactment of party convention platforms with the aid of a presidential cabinet often dominated by former Senators and Representatives who thought it likely they would return to serve in Congress again.[3]

In the face of this general congressional dominance, there were periods when presidents successfully exercised strong political influence and increased the power of the executive branch. Even Washington, that most meticulous of Presidents who sought to adhere to the spirit of the framers, moved to increase presidential autonomy. Initially seeking to consult personally with the Senate on the ratification of treaties, Washington stopped meeting in person with the Senate on such matters, and instead, allowed his Secretary of State and other diplomats to negotiate agreements with foreign states, and then submitted treaties to the Senate by written message for ratification, but not for further consultation. Jefferson, Madison, Jackson, Lincoln, and Cleveland are lauded by historians as "Great" or "Near Great" presidents,[4] and each shares a common characteristic in desiring to expand the reach of presidential power.

The history has been substantially different in the 20th Century, with the rise of presidential power under two Roosevelts, Wilson, Truman, Johnson, and Reagan. Authors such as Fisher,[5] Sundquist[6] among others have reviewed, in fuller detail, the 20th Century shift of power from Congress to the President, and the post–World War II attempts by Congress to reassert, with mixed success, some of the powers it had given to the executive or allowed the executive to assume. The attitude of American citizens and, it should be noted, most of its politicians is that the primary responsibility for leadership lies with the American president.

No President—-at least, no President since William Howard Taft[7]—wished to preside over an executive branch of government over which the president's authority had declined. Rarely do presidents, when they seek a precedent for contemporary actions, refer to a president widely assumed by scholars and the public to be weak, incompetent, or both. It is difficult to find an occasion when James Buchanan has been cited as a role model for seeking bipartisan compromise on contentious national issues. Instead, presidents who acted to expand presidential authority are held up as precedent setters—Lincoln for the use of commander-in-chief powers in time of emergency and Theodore Roosevelt for unilateral unauthorized use of troops outside the US, to cite but two. Advocates of strong executive power, including advocates of the "unitary executive" such as John Yoo,[8] point to specific presidents such as Jefferson[9] who utilized power in this twilight zone of presidential authority, while ignoring or minimizing the role of presidents who refrained from such action.[10]

The litany of post–World War II congressional reform efforts is indeed long. Reform commission recommendations, studies by standing committees, both bicameral and unicameral undertakings, all began with the best of intentions and some actually achieved significant successes. Nevertheless, the complexities of the interaction between the President and Congress are a continuing source of tension between the branches and a source of continuing calls for change in how the two branches deal with each other. While it is important to consider whether the shift in power between the branches came about either by presidential usurpation or by congressional abdication, this should not deter scholars or practitioners from focusing on possible future changes in presidential and congressional actions and practices.

1. Some Thoughts on Reforming Legislative-Executive Relations

In the past half century, the US Congress has been acutely aware of institutional shortcomings, so much so that the pressure for reform—or, at least, for studies of reform options—come around on an average of once per decade. Thus, the House and Senate set up the Joint Committee on the Organization of Congress to consider changes that would be necessary for Congress to handle increased responsibilities in the post–World War II world. From it, came the Legislative Reorganization Act of 1946, with attempts to restructure the congressional committee system, to regulate lobbying, and to establish a new congressional budget process. After two decades of mixed success, Congress tried again with a second joint committee, and after five years of work, a Legislative Reorganization Act of 1970. Thereafter, the pace accelerated. The House passed a "Subcommittee Bill of Rights" in 1973 that institutionalized the decentralization of authority in the modern house, along with the House Committee Reform Amendments of 1974. Both chambers acted to pass the Congressional Budget and Impoundment Control Act of 1974, and both acted on internal administrative reforms in 1976 (Senate) and 1977 (House). Recodification of the unwieldy House Rules was undertaken with support from both parties in 1986, but was not successfully completed until 1997. Studies of a third Joint Committee on the Organization of Congress (1993) were followed by the Republican Revolution of 1995.

In reforming itself, Congress owns a rather slim track record of success in areas where presidents claim a dominant role, such as budget and management, foreign and defense issues, and most of all, national security broadly defined. When major requests from the president on national security crises come to the Congress, "the Congress remains reluctant to deny a president his foreign policy requests or to pass policies of their own. Even when Congress succeeds in putting into law its preferences in US foreign policy, the results are often less than meets the eye."[11] One such example must clearly be in the commitment of troops to combat. "Although it was capable of passing the War Powers Resolution, Congress has never been able to enforce its provisions."[12] Even Bill Clinton, on the verge of an impeachment by the House of Representatives, was able to begin bombing of suspected WMD targets in Iraq. As another analyst observed, "The bottom line is that the weakest president at his worst hour is far more powerful than any Senator or member of the House."[13]

100

The long-standing disputes over war powers issues tend to obscure the fact that Congress, in passing the War Powers Resolution, gave the President legal authority to send troops into combat for at least sixty days before needing the consent of Congress. If the War Powers Resolution was indeed such a statutory success, how does one explain the decision of Senator Thomas Eagleton, an original sponsor of the measure, to vote against the passage of the final version that came out of the House-Senate conference committee?[14] In a further example of limited reform success, the Budget Act explicitly acknowledged the presidential right of impoundment that Congress had so strongly denied earlier. In general, attempts by Congress to regain authority often include at least some acknowledgement by Congress of presidential discretionary power, in foreign policy and in other areas as well.

2. Who Matters Most and What Matters Most and When Does It Matter?

Whether presidents dominate policy because they successfully usurp congressional powers, or whether presidential power grows because Congress allows it to happen is not the only important issue. Other issues need to be examined as well.

What are the broad categories of national security activities with which government officials in the legislative and executive branches must be concerned? James Lindsay has developed a three-fold categorization of security policy. The most visible, high-saliency category, according to Lindsay, is crisis policy that carries with it the perception of an immediate threat to US national interests, and typically involves the potential use of force. Lindsay claims that crisis policy "is the least common type of foreign policy." Second is strategic policy, covering the goals and tactics of foreign and defense policy. Third is structural policy focusing on the resources that are provided for security policy.[15]

Realistically, Congress routinely exercises the most influence on the allocation of resources. The fact that equipment procurement and base location decisions are the most politically significant security policy matters for representatives and senators should not surprise any knowledgeable observer. However, crisis policy has the greatest long-term national consequences and is the factor that, in Lindsay's view, the Congress is least capable of influencing. In this view, Congress may not be capable of influencing such global, macro-level decisions as authorizing military force in Afghanistan and Iraq have cost, in the aggregate, more than $1.5 trillion. That view also claims to explain that Congress can, for example, repeatedly challenge the president and the military over nearly two decades to insist on funding the V22 Osprey aircraft (over the objections of presidential budget staff from both parties and by many military strategists) because such decisions involve far lower political and economic costs.

Under what circumstances can congressional involvement in crisis policy increase or decrease? Various studies have suggested various factors. Unified government comes in for a substantial degree of criticism. The War on Terrorism era, post 9/11 has, in the view of some, seen little substantial influence from Congress.

> Here again, however, the Madisonian vision founders on the realities of partisan political competition. Especially when government is unified by party, we should not expect Congress to resist executive power in the way that courts and commentators take for granted. . . . An important part of the explanation for congressional passivity in the post-9/11 period is the fact of unified government. For Congress to respond to executive initiatives is to give the opposition party an opportunity to call into question, criticize, or potentially embarrass the President. If a partisan majority in Congress generally shares the President's ideological and policy goals, abdication might further the party's interest in uniting behind the President. Why run the risk that unpleasant facts will be revealed in congressional deliberations or that blame for failures will fall on the party as a whole?[16]

Although this argument may be generally persuasive for the 2001-2007 period, it is not entirely so. The Senate was, theoretically, under Democratic control at the time of the 9/11 attack, and the Bush administration initially opposed the plan of Senator Joseph Liebermann (then a Democrat) to establish a department of homeland security. Nevertheless, the Senate Democratic majority ultimately supported the Bush administration's revised position calling for a larger Department of Homeland Security than even the Liebermann bill called for, and there was little objection to massive support for military action against those responsible for the 9/11 attacks. Moreover, the Levinson and Pildes view that a strong congressional opposition party is essential to rein-in presidential power ignores the facts of Senate procedures whereby a relatively weak minority party (so long as it has at least 40% of Senate voting strength) can prevent any action by a strong Senate majority—even a presidential majority. Their analysis cannot account for the circumstances of the Senate vote on the Iraq war in 2002. The action came when the Democrats theoretically held a one-seat majority in the Senate at a time when the Bush administration was using the Iraq war resolution as a mid-term election campaign issue. Democratic leader Daschle, according to Fisher,[17] "could have used his position as majority leader to delay a vote until after the election." But, he allowed a vote to take place so that, as he said in an interview, because "the bottom line is . . . we want to move on" to a debate over economic conditions which would favor Democratic candidates in the November election[18]. In any event, only 21 Democratic Senators and two Republicans voted against the measure in the Senate, and lengthy delay would not have been possible once Daschle decided to bring the measure up for debate.[19]

In their study of the War Powers Act, David Auerswald and Peter Cowhey[20] argue that Congress regularly places upon presidents obligations (reporting requirements, budgetary limitations, accounting procedures) that Auerwald and Cowhey claim can prove quite burdensome to the executive in carrying out an overseas military activity. Be that as it may. Regardless of the constraints, however burdensome these constraints or reporting requirements might be, the President has won and the troops have been committed.

Still another factor to consider is whether the action contemplated is unilateral or multilateral. Analysis of this issue is becoming more complex. How broad does the involvement of the international community need to be for a foreign policy action to be considered multilateral? Does the United States need or merely seek multilateral partnerships in military intervention? It appears that the United States wishes to form multilateral coalitions when possible, but does not wish to formally renounce unilateral action if necessary. Some scholars[21] suggest that a trend toward a more multipolar world might conversely increase US unilateralism as the US finds it more difficult to form successfully the consensus positions needed in organs such as the UN Security Council.

3. Reforming Congress and Foreign Policy

Reforming Congress is an uncertain business. As a long-ago Speaker of the House, Thomas B. Reed, once observed, "Reform is an indefinable something to be done, at a time nobody knows when, that will achieve nobody knows what.[22]" Congress has devoted enormous amounts of time over the past sixty years in efforts to strengthen its infrastructure, reform its rules, and enhance its powers, all for little clear or permanent success.

In issues of legislative-executive relations, one must expect Congress to recognize its own power to remake itself. If the Constitution gives Congress the authority to be the "judge of its own proceedings," then the authority to remake itself into something more effective and efficient largely lies in its own hands. Whether Congress, or either of its chambers, sees fit to exercise such authority is an entirely different matter.

Encouraging Uncertainty in the House. The contemporary House of Representatives has seen a rise in the influence of party leaders and a commensurate reduction in the ability of individual members or small groups within either or both parties to force agenda items to the floor. The contemporary House's centralization comes as a reaction to the decentralization and democratization of the House that characterized the reform period of the late 1960s and 1970s. The question in legislative-executive relations is whether an increase in uncertainty might not be beneficial for the policy-making process. Two particular changes in House rules and practices deserve note here, specifically with regard to spending legislation: the virtual end of the Holman Rule and the use of restrictive rules on appropriations bills.

The Holman Rule and related provisions in House rules allowed the House, when it was so inclined, to control spending in creative fashions for more than a century. In general, an appropriations bill is required to fund programs and government activities which have previously been authorized in law. But, Congress, acting as a transformative legislature, has always believed that it is not required to provide all that may have been required for authorized governmental purposes. As a result, the "proviso" to an appropriations bill has been an important historical part of congressional authority. The term derives from the typical language of such items (*"Provided,* that none of the funds in this or any other law may be used for [certain specified purposes]").

The Wilmot Proviso, for example, was a major legislative initiative of the congressional opponents to slavery during the Mexican War. Wilmot's amendment sought to forbid the use of appropriated funds to permit the introduction of slavery into lands acquired by the United States during the Mexican War of 1846-1848. The limitation amendment has been an important weapon in the Congress's arsenal against executive power and also as a weapon available to backbench and dissident House members against the power of congressional party and committee leaders.

Related to the limitation amendment is the so-called Holman Rule, named for William S. Holman, a fiscal conservative Democratic congressman of the 19th century who proposed to modify the historic ban in House Rules against including changes to permanent law in an appropriations bill. Holman's Rule allowed amendments in appropriations bills to change permanent law if the change saved money. Limitation amendments and Holman Rule amendments have been a key source of policy changes in the United States. The legal ban on the use of Federal government funds to finance abortions began as a limitation amendment, as did the proposal to end US military involvement in Southeast Asia and the ban on US government assistance to the Contra forces in Nicaragua.

Holman Rule and limitation amendments were made virtually unusable by rank-and-file House members when, in 1997, House Rules were amended to prevent the offering of any limitation amendments on the floor of the House until all money amendments had been previously disposed of and until the House had first had the opportunity to vote to stop the offering of limitation amendments entirely.[23] The end result was a shift in power to the majority members of the Appropriations Committee (which could control the inclusion of limitation language in the bill the committee drafted) and to the majority party leadership (which could claim priority recognition to offer the motion to block the offering of limitation amendments).

The declining power of the minority party and of rank-and-file members of both parties began in the mid-1980s as party leaders sought to limit policy and parliamentary surprise during House floor action on major bills. Increasingly, the "open rule" environment which characterized the "reformed" House of the early 1970s—with no limitation on the number of amendments that could be offered in the House to major bills—was replaced by the contemporary House Rules Committee which, through "restrictive" or "closed" rules, sought to limit or prevent amendments to be offered to bills on the House floor. As a leading student of the House Rules Committee, Donald Wolfensberger of Washington's Woodrow Wilson Center observed,

> When we combine our observations about the increasing importance of special rules, the increasing powers of party leaders, and the declining role and powers of committees, we begin to see the picture of a much different Congress than the old "text book" version in which legislation underwent a very orderly and deliberative scrutiny through the subcommittee, full committee, and floor stages. Today, with party unity and discipline so central to the future control of both the House and Senate, deliberation and thorough committee consideration are subordinated to producing favorable legislative results for the majority party. Members are now content to delegate to their party leaders the responsibility for putting together the party's program and seeing it through to passage—whatever it takes.[24]

The Senate and Tennis: Play and Debate Must Be Continuous. The informal evolution of the American Senate has resulted in a chamber which has become a parody of itself as a deliberative body. As all know, the Senate operated reasonably well without a rule to end debate until 1917. Then, Senate Rule XXII was amended to permit a supermajority of Senators to vote to impose a limit on further debate on a pending matter. Rules changes adopted by the Senate from the 1950s through the 1970s increased the number of issues on which debate could be limited, reduced the size of the required supermajority, or both.[25]

The growing inability of the Senate to bring a matter to a vote is not related to Rule XXII, but rather to changes in the degree to which the Senate enforces its own rules. Senate Rule XIX states that no Senator shall speak more than twice upon any one question in debate on the same legislative day without leave of the Senate. Thus, even if the Senate could not achieve the supermajority vote required to end debate, debate could indirectly be limited if all opposing Senators had already spoken twice on the controversial matter in question. However, the Senate decided in 1980 that a strict interpretation of the two-speech rule would not be enforced against a "minor" speech. Moreover, the Senate in 1977, determined that the presiding officer, after cloture under Rule XXII, could take steps on his or her own initiative to prevent further delay (for example, by seeking a quorum call when no legislative business had transpired after cloture had been invoked) while refraining from giving the chair such authority under ordinary Senate business. However, the presiding officer was expressly prohibited from exercising such powers under normal Senate proceedings.[26]

The Senate could be made a more efficient body by enforcing the two-speech rule, and by ending dilatory calls for the appearance of a quorum. Greater efficiency would mean that Senators seeking to delay a vote on a controversial matter could still bring the Senate to a halt by speaking at length and, in fact, speaking at length twice. However, Senators could not bring the Senate to a halt by sitting in their offices and threatening via text message to leaders to speak at length. To achieve that purpose, they would have to come to the Senate chamber to speak and to be accountable to the public for their actions. In 2011, several junior Senate Democrats planned to force a rules change under the claim that a majority had the right to change the rules at the beginning of a new Congress. Senior Democrats opposed this move, and hoped to preserve the core of filibuster rights because they feared the Democrats could lose control of the Senate in 2012. (That did not happen, but the 2014 election may be equally threatening to Democrats. Of the 34 Senate seats at stake in 2014, 20 are held now by Democrats. However, in the 2012 presidential election, President Obama lost 7 of the 20 states represented by those Democratic Senators.) Vague promises of fair play between majority and minority leaders and pledges of greater openness about holds and a ban on forced reading of preprinted floor amendments overcame the demand by juniors for more serious reforms.[27]

4. Reforming the Presidency

The Presidency is in need of reform as well. The history of the 20th Century presidency shows the continual expansion of presidential and executive branch authority in times of war or other national crisis. The presidency of the 21st Century has been no different.

Problems in legislative-executive relations do not lie exclusively with the Congress. The imperial presidency has been allowed to function because the Congress defers to the President in large number of policy matters.[28] However, the imperial presidency also exists in part because the president acts in an imperial manner and accepts recommendations that he act imperially. Presidents are criticized for being out of touch or isolated in the White House cocoon because of the circumstances of contemporary political life. Terrorist attacks, assassination attempts and other hazardous situations have brought pressure on presidential security services and on presidential advisors to keep the president safe at all costs — including the cost of isolating the president from the citizenry and from other essential political actors. The fleet of presidential aircraft and million dollar armored limousines known by such nicknames as "the beast" reinforce the isolation of the president. Political and policy advisors, in turn, limit presidential visits generally to audiences that are both friendly and can be assembled in easily secured environments. Presidents who appear only on television from the White House, or at speeches at military bases (à la Bush) or at university basketball arenas or union-shop factories (à la Obama) contribute to the impression, real or imagined, that presidents are isolating themselves from the public they ostensibly represent.

Consult When Consultation Is Not Necessary. President Obama began his administration with a rare personal appearance with question-and-answer period at both party organizations in both houses of Congress. That salutary collaborative approach did not become a regular part of Obama administration interaction with Congress. When major compromises were needed over health care reform legislation and other matters, negotiations were more difficult because no existing relationship had developed between the president and most members of Congress.

With rare exceptions (Lyndon Johnson and Gerald Ford come to mind), presidents do not normally come into office having extensive relationships with members of Congress. Unless presidents take steps to develop close relationships with Congress, including at least minimally acceptable contacts with opposition party leaders, the ability to forge a consensus or a compromise on major policies will be hampered. However, such interaction takes time and presidents don't have the time to cultivate collaborative networks within Congress. Even regular meetings with congressional leaders cannot guarantee smooth working relationships with the rank-and-file in Congress, as shown by problems with moderate House Democrats and issue-outlier Democratic Senators during the health care reform debate.

The President's Room is a room set aside in the Capitol Building for the president that has largely fallen into disuse over the past century, except for brief presidential visits on Inauguration Day and on the evening of State of the Union addresses. Its earlier purpose—to provide a place in the Capitol for presidential meetings with small groups of congressmen—has largely been abandoned since the 1920s. When presidential and congressional terms both ended on March 3 before the passage of the 20th Amendment to the Constitution, presidents would typically come to the Capitol on the last day of a congressional term to sign legislation passed at the last minute. In addition, presidents such as Wilson made regular use of the room, and even today the president could return regularly to the Capitol, so long as the Secret Service resisted the urge to close off all

Washington street traffic in order to transport the president less than a mile across town to the Capitol.

Use the Veto, Don't Just Threaten It. The Constitution assumes that each branch of government has sufficient power to defend its prerogatives against encroachment by the other branches. However, when government actors rely on informal channels and indirect uses of power, the relationship between Congress and President becomes less precise. Presidents from Washington onward viewed the veto as an essential presidential power and many presidents were aggressive users of such veto authorities. However, in recent administrations, the absolute and relative number of vetoes (compared to legislative enactments) has declined greatly. In part, this is a result of the expanded congressional relations operation in the White House along with the expanded role of the Office of Management and Budget in monitoring congressional action on the president's legislative agenda. Presidential staff, meeting informally with congressional committee leaders, and threaten a presidential veto unless certain changes in legislation are made.

An alternative view of vetoes suggests that a formal veto announces clear presidential policy preferences and gives Congress clear instructions as to what policies will elicit presidential support. Half of all formal presidential vetoes were cast by only three presidents (Cleveland, Franklin Roosevelt, and Truman), and over the 28 years of White House service by those three presidents, there was opposition party control in Congress for only six years. Moreover, presidents have shown a marked aversion to vetoing appropriations bills. Bill Clinton is the modern record-holder for vetoing appropriations bills (14 during his term), but a greater attention to aggressive use of the veto power could help to clarify the roles of the president and the Congress, and also clarify the policy preferences of the White House and the congressional majority.[29]

A discussion of presidential vetoes inevitably raises the question of presidential signing statements. The occasion at which a president formally signs a bill into law has become part of the political theatre surrounding the policy process in the US. Although President George W. Bush was particularly visible in using signing statements to indicate his opposition to certain portions of a law or to signal his unwillingness to enforce a law or parts of it enthusiastically, signing statements date back to President Madison and the most extensive use of signing statements was evident to some scholars in the Clinton administration. Signing statements allow presidents to side-step difficult issues and to submit such difficult issues to a clear and quick resolution through veto override attempts.[30] As Lawrence Tribe[31] as noted, signing statements are "informative and constitutionally unobjectionable," but that signing statements also permit Presidents to avoid "fac(ing) the political music by issuing a veto and subjecting that veto to the possibility of an override in Congress." Even presidents who complained about the Bush administrations use of signing statements have found signing statements useful. On New Year's Eve 2011, President Obama issued a signing statement announcing his intention not to follow a number of significant provisions in the Defense Authorization Act.[32]

Keep the Sherpas at the Base Camp. The creative application of the English language has caused the name of the Mount Everest guides to evolve into a description of the senior staff who prepare for summit meetings of major governmental leaders. In this context, presidents have increasingly devolved too much authority upon staff advisors and, in turn, the size of the advisory bureaucracy within the Executive Office of the President has grown to an unmanageably large size. The greater the number of advisors to the president the more difficult it is to say who actually does speak for the president when efforts are underway to reach a compromise between the branches.

Ever since Theodore Roosevelt undertook the construction of the West Wing of the White House, the size of the presidential establishment has grown, as has that of the Congress—in what the late Senator Daniel Patrick Moynihan labeled as an example of the "Iron Law of Emulation."[33] Times change and occasionally the size of the establishment fluctuates up or down, but staff levels rarely decline substantially or permanently.

The ability of the formal political actors to meet, confer, and deliberate has become more difficult with the increasing role and visibility of staff aides both in the executive and in the legislative branches. With the systematic increase of personal and committee staff in Congress a generation ago, the current growth area is in party leadership staff, especially staff specializing in public affairs and press relations. Within the White House, especially the Obama White House, staffing growth has been enormous at the level of special coordinators for major policy domains, otherwise known as czars. This practice dates from the Nixon administration with the emergence of domestic policy advisors and other policy coordinators. The Obama administration has expanded upon recent practice with greater use of policy czars in areas such as health, environment, Guantanamo and other terrorist-receiving jails, among nearly three dozen such posts. Senator Robert C. Byrd[34] was critical of the Obama administration's use of White House policy coordinators. Too often in the past such staff had "an unfortunate history of assuming too much power," creating a situation in which "too often I have seen lines of authority and responsibility become tangled and blurred, sometimes purposely to shield information and to obscure the decision-making process." This view was shared by scholar Mark Rozell who observed that the policy czars "aren't people who are going through confirmation hearings; they're not heading departments and agencies over which Congress does direct oversight." In Rozell's view, "cabinet secretaries (then) begin to play a lesser role in the system. I think it leads to less accountability in the process."[35]

The greater the number of people who claim to speak on behalf of the president or on behalf of executive entities and the greater the number of similar people working on behalf of congressional leaders, committees, or influential members of Congress, the less likely it is that a policy compromise can be reached quickly or understandably. The resources of the American president have grown beyond anything comprehended by those experts in public administration who first called out in alarm that "the President needs help." The size of the White House and the executive branch staffs have grown to the point that the president needs help supervising the help. Moreover, the complexity of staff relations has grown: gone are the days of long service as White House chief of staff (and the concomitant development of policy rapport and personal comfort between the President and the staff chief). President Obama has the doubtful distinction of having three chiefs of staff and one acting chief of staff in a little over three years. The increasing bureaucratization of the chief of staff's office is also apparent, with the designation of a formal deputy during George W. Bush's administration and the division of the deputy's job into two posts under Obama.

5. Final Thoughts as America Considers Still More Military Engagements

Governmental institutions are established by human beings for the benefit of human beings in such a manner that an intermediate set of human beings can decide on broad issues affecting the great mass of people who inhabit a state. As a human creation run by humans, institutions are fallible and this applies to all branches of a multi-branch government, regardless of the intentions of those who comprise these institutions now.

Such fallibility was evident in March 2011, the military establishment of the United States, France, Great Britain, Canada, Denmark, and the Netherlands, among others, began military operations in Libya. Two days before, the United Nations Security Council authorized UN member countries to take "all necessary means" to protect civilian populations in Libya from violence. The decision marked an enormous success for the Obama administration (and in particular, for the U.S. ambassador to the United Nations, Susan Rice) in forging a consensus among Security Council members to support the resolution. The doctrine of liberal interventionism seemed to be a complete success, and marked a major step in the UN implementing its announced (but difficult to enforce) doctrine of a "responsibility to protect" civilians in hostile zones.[36]

What was missing, of course, was a formal authorization from the American Congress for US military involvement in enforcement of the Libya resolution.[37] On the same day that the Security Council voted, the US House of Representatives instead of debating the merits of starting military activities in yet another country, rejected by a vote of 90-321 a proposal supported only by far-left Democrats to force the withdrawal of American troops from Afghanistan. At 5:55 p.m. on March 17, the House of Representatives adjourned until March 29, and the Senate adjourned at 6:40 p.m. until March 28.

At 2 p.m. on Friday, March 18, President Obama met with a group of House and Senate party and committee leaders (although the Speaker of the House and the Senate Republican Leader participated by telephone conference call because they had already departed Washington). At 10:15 p.m. that evening, President Obama and his family left Washington to begin a five-day trip to Latin America. The next evening, March 19, air attacks on Libyan air defense installations commenced. Thus, America began its third major foreign military operation in ten years at a time when the President was out of the country and neither House of Congress in session, and few politicians and few citizens seemed to mind.

When the Congress adjourned for its brief vacation (officially a "Constituency Work Period"), the adjournment resolution gave leaders in both houses the authority to summon Congress back into session early if circumstances required. Apparently, the leaders of the majority party in both chambers did not think that the beginning of a war required Congress to be in Washington.

On April 1, 2011, the White House released a memorandum prepared in the Department of Justice by a deputy to the Attorney General. In the author's view, the provisions of the War Powers Resolution had not been triggered because of the limited duration and scope of US involvement in the Libyan campaign.

> (T)he historical practice of presidential military action without congressional approval precludes any suggestion that Congress's authority to declare war covers every military engagement, however limited, that the President initiates. In our view, determining whether a particular planned engagement constitutes a "war" for constitutional purposes instead requires a fact-specific assessment of the "anticipated nature, scope, and duration" of the planned military operations. This standard generally will be satisfied only by prolonged and substantial military engagements, typically involving exposure of U.S. military personnel to significant risk over a substantial period. Again, Congress's own key enactment on the subject reflects this understanding. By allowing United States involvement in hostilities to continue for 60 or 90 days, Congress signaled in the WPR that it considers congressional authorization most critical for "major, prolonged conflicts such as the wars in Vietnam and Korea," not more limited engagements.[38]

In effect, the Obama administration claimed that the War Powers clock had not been triggered because of the narrow scope of American involvement in the military action and because American forces were not in direct military engagement with combatants. Thus, the presence of American aircraft carriers far enough off the coast of Libya to avoid direct attack by Libyan forces (regardless of their allegiance), the use of drone aircraft by American forces, and the presence of fighter planes operated by British and French aviators mitigated against the need for congressional approval of the operation.

One knowledgeable observer, Robert Chesney of the Brookings Institution, questioned many portions of this memorandum. He was careful to note that an American admiral was commanding the NATO operation. Under terms of the War Powers Resolution, such command structure was cause for triggering the required congressional approval, regardless of the small number of American troops that might be involved, or whether they were actually coming under military attack from Libyan forces.[39]

Time moved forward, but no immediate congressional action related to the War Powers Resolution was immediately undertaken.

On June 3, the House of Representatives tried to have its way on both sides of the issue. First, the House rejected a resolution, introduced by Rep. Dennis Kucinich (D-Ohio) contemplated by the War Powers Act directing the president to withdraw forces from Libya. The resolution was defeated 148-265. And, later on the same day, it debated and passed a non-binding resolution proposed by Speaker John Boehner (R-Ohio) expressing the opinion of the House that ground troops should not be introduced into Libya, and requiring the president to report to the House within 14 days on the state of American engagement. The Boehner resolution passed 268-145.

On June 24, 2011, two measures came before the House of Representatives, as a result of action taken by the Rules Committee to schedule them for debate. The first, H.J. Res. 68, sponsored by Democrat Alcee Hastings of Florida, proposed to authorize the US mission to Libya for up to one year, and would have required periodic reports from the administration to Congress on the state of the mission there. Hastings explained his somewhat conflicted position on his own measure:

> If I had my way, Mr. Speaker—and I don't—we wouldn't be in Libya at all. But I don't have my way, and here we are, and the solution now is not to cut off all funding and suddenly walk out. We have a responsibility to our allies. As long as we are continuing to supply logistics, materiel, and critical intelligence and operational capabilities—and no boots on the ground—we must support our allies who are carrying out the direct combat operations. We must stand with NATO. [40]

The House did not share his concerns and the time-limited authorization measure was defeated by a vote of 123-295.

Later that same day, the House took up a measure (H.R. 2278) sponsored by a third-term Republican member, Tom Rooney (Florida), who sought a vote to limit (without time) the use of funds for the Libya campaign to costs that were associated with off-shore activities, goals that were quite different from those of his colleague Hastings.

After 90 days and the President has not ceased activity or hostilities in Libya, the time has come and gone and we've sent our indication over to the administration time and time again that we disapprove. But, because the War Powers resolution, by some either Republican or Democrat or in the House or the Senate, is questionable whether or not they consider it constitutional or not, the President has operated in what we now know is called the zone of twilight as to whether or not he even needs our approval.[41]

The constitutional balance between branches was the strong focus of remarks by Rep. Tom McCaul (R-Texas), a third-term House Member.

In applying the War Powers Act to the facts here in this case, it is clear that the President failed to comply with the requirements to get congressional approval; and when we examine the merits of the case for involvement in Libya, this administration has wholly failed to define a clear national interest, mission, or goal.[42]

This measure, as well, was defeated, by a vote of 180-238.

In July 2011, the House debated a limitation amendment that the Rules Committee made in order to the defense appropriations bill. The sponsor of the permitted amendment, Dennis Kucinich (D-Ohio), compressed his proposal into the simplest possible language:

Sec. __. None of the funds in this Act may be used for military operations in or against Libya except under a declaration of war against Libya pursuant to clause 11 in section 8 of article I of the Constitution.

(This amendment) recognizes Congress' power to appropriate and links it, in this case, to Congress' ability to declare war and enables this House to definitively—definitively—make a statement that it is our prerogative, our Constitutional right, to determine whether or not this Nation goes to war, and we are not going to see any war funded absent a declaration of war by this Congress. (...) This amendment (...) gives the House one last opportunity within this bill to speak very clearly about article I, section 8, clause 11 and to do it in the context of an appropriations bill which says that we will not permit any funds to be spent unless this Congress moves forward with a declaration of war.[43]

The principal statement against the Kucinich amendment came from Kucinich's own party—from the ranking Democrat on the Appropriations Committee, Norman Dicks of Washington.

(T)he President has made a very strong case for our military action in Libya. I think, as Commander in Chief, he has the authority. We had a U.N. resolution, the NATO allies were involved and so was the Arab League. The idea that we're going to pull out of this unilaterally and undermine the NATO alliance I think is a terrible mistake. There is another option. The other option is the War Powers Act. And I hope at some point the President will ask for congressional support of his initiative in Libya.

After Kucinich's amendment was defeated, the House turned its attention from matters of life and death to celebrate the 85th birthday of Rep. John Dingell (D-MI), who was then in his 56th year of House service. On the Kucinich amendment, Dingell voted "No." Nine months later, Kucinich was defeated re-nomination in the Ohio Democratic primary by Rep. Marcy Kaptur. Kaptur had voted in favor of the Kucinich amendment. Such are the unpredictable divisions within parties and within ideological groups in Congress on the subject of legislative-executive relations, particularly within the realm of foreign policy.

In short, a majority of the president's party avoided an institutionally-based showdown with the head of their party. At the same time, the majority Republican party sought to avoid a position for or against the Libyan action to preserve its options for future doubts about the policy. And, ultimately, the authorization for entering into the Libyan conflict came from the United Nations Security Council, the Arab League, and the North Atlantic Treaty Organization, and not from the legislative branch of the American government, although the Congress continued to pay the bills it had taken no steps to authorize.

The result is that a president who criticized his predecessor for acting in a way that challenges constitutional principles may now have gone even farther in challenging those same principles.

Yale Professor Bruce Ackerman was troubled by yet another unfortunate precedent in the use of expansive presidential powers:

It's open for Obama to assert that his power as commander in chief allows him to wage war without Congress, despite the Constitution's insistence to the contrary. Many modern presidents have made such claims, and Harry Truman acted upon this assertion in Korea. But it's surprising to find Obama on the verge of ratifying such precedents. He was elected in reaction to the unilateralist assertions of John Yoo and other apologists for George W. Bush-era illegalities. Yet he is now moving onto ground that even Bush did not occupy. After a lot of talk about his inherent powers, Bush did get Congress to authorize his wars in Afghanistan and Iraq. Now, Obama is putting Bush-era talk into action in Libya—without congressional authorization.[44]

A year after the start of the Libyan engagement, the old regime there has been toppled but no new stable regime has yet emerged in the face of separatist tribal elements. New crisis points have emerged. Syria has shown itself to be a new humanitarian danger point, but this time the Obama administration hesitates to get involved. Meanwhile, Republican presidential candidates call strongly for military intervention in Iran, which calls the president has labeled reckless. The president—earlier a critic of creative legal arguments that justified broad expansions of Bush administration presidential power—now is served by an Attorney General who claims for the President the authority to order the killing of American citizens suspected of terrorist connections. As Attorney General Holder stated before an audience at Northwestern Law School in Chicago:

> Some have argued that the President is required to get permission from a federal court before taking action against a United States citizen who is a senior operational leader of al Qaeda or associated forces. This is simply not accurate. "Due process" and "judicial process" are not one and the same, particularly when it comes to national security. The Constitution guarantees due process, not judicial process (. . . The Constitution's guarantee of due process is ironclad, and it is essential—but, as a recent court decision makes clear, it does not require judicial approval before the President may use force abroad against a senior operational leader of a foreign terrorist organization with which the United States is at war—even if that individual happens to be a U.S. citizen.[45]

Legal critics, even many normal supporters of the Obama administration, were quick to respond negatively that the administration's legal justification smacked of the thinly justified arguments of the Bush administration.[46] Legal critic Jonathan Turley, who has written consistently against expansive presidential power, has seen enough of an emergent imperial presidency in the Obama administration.

The president's insistence that his Libyan campaign is limited in its purposes and duration is no excuse. These are precisely the issues that he should have defined in collaboration with Congress. Now that he claims inherent power, why can't he redefine U.S. objectives on his own? No less important, what is to stop some future president from using Obama's precedent to justify even more aggressively unilateral actions?[47]

The buck stops on Capitol Hill, and even officials with long service in Congress are more interested in finding a multinational solution to military intervention than focusing on the role of Congress in authorizing foreign military engagements. In an extended exchange in early March 2012 between Sen. Jeff Sessions (R-Alabama) and Defense Secretary Leon Panetta, who earlier served 16 years in Congress, Panetta refused to say explicitly that congressional authorization was necessary for US military involvement in Syria, while repeatedly stressing the importance to obtain support from multinational organizations for such actions.[48] Changing the culture of deference requires consistent congressional action, regardless of the election timetable. As we have seen, however, party interests and elections often outweigh institutional concerns when presidential actions threaten Congress's role.[49]

A generation ago, Nelson Polsby identified the American Congress as the only truly "transformative" legislature, one that had the ability to determine its own agenda or to alter in fundamental ways the lawmaking proposals with which it was faced. However, some have suggested that the Congress in the past generation has declined into the category of an "arena legislature." Polsby defined arena legislatures as those where the dominant parties ratify decisions made elsewhere, in the executive or in the parties or in interest organizations.[50] Although the U.S. Information Agency has ceased to exist, the *Outline of American Government* that USIA published in 1989[51] remains available on line. It notes in passing that, "the people get the kind of government they deserve." Perhaps that assessment is also correct.

References

Ackermann, Bruce (2011): Obama's Unconstitutional War, in: Foreign Policy (electronic edition), 24 March 2011. (http://www.foreignpolicy.com/articles/2011/03/24/obama's_unconstitutional_war; visited March 9, 2012).

Argersinger, Peter (1992): No Rights on This Floor: Third Parties and the Institutionalization of Congress, in: Journal of Interdisciplinary History, 22, 4 (Spring 1992), pp. 655-690.

Auerswald, David and Peter H. Cowhey (1997): Ballotbox Diplomacy: The War Powers Resolution and the Use of Force, in: International Studies Quarterly, 41, 3 (September 1997), pp. 505-528.

Bach, Stanley and Steven S. Smith (1988): *Managing Uncertainty in the House of Representatives*, Washington, D.C.

Bazelon, Emily (2012): Eric Holder says the United States can kill American citizens overseas and he doesn't think he should explain why, in: Slate Magazine (electronic edition) 6 March 2012. http://www.slate.com/articles/

news_and_politics/jurisprudence/2012/03/eric_holder_s_speech_on_targeted_killings_was_incredibly_unsatisfying_.html

Beth, Richard S. (2003): Filibusters and Cloture in the Senate, *CRS Report to Congress* (Report RL30360, March 28, 2003 (electronic version, www.opencrs.com, visited March 1, 2011).

Binder, Sarah and Steven S. Smith (1998):. Political Goals and Procedural Choice in the Senate, in: Journal of Politics, 60, 2, pp. 398-416.

Brown, Chris. (2011): Recent actions in Libya show that 'liberal interventionism' to support the human rights of civilians is not exempt from politics, blog entry, April 15, London School of Economics. http://blogs.lse.ac.uk/politicsandpolicy/2011/04/11/libya-intervention/?pfstyle=w p

Byrd, Robert C. (2009): Letter to The Honorable Barack Obama. Feb. 23, 2009. (electronic version at: http://www.eenews.net/public/25/9865/features/documents/2009/02/25/document_gw_02.pdf.

Carr, Thomas P. (2011): Suspension of the Rules in the House of Representatives, CRS Report to Congress (electronic version), Report RL34274, February 1, 2005 (www.opencrs.com, visited March 1, 2011).

Chesney, Robert M. (2012): A Primer on the Libya/War Powers Resolution Compliance Debate," Brookings Institution Governance Studies, March 11, 2012 (http://www.brookings.edu/opinions/2011/0617_war_powers_chesney.aspx).

Davis, Christopher M. (2008): House Floor Activity: The Daily Flow of Business, Congressional Research Service Report to Congress (electronic version), Report RS20233, April 16, 2008 (www.opencrs.com visited March 1, 2011).

Fisher, Louis (1985): *Constitutional Conflicts Between Congress and the President.*, 5th edition. Lawrence, Kansas, 2007 (First edition, Princeton, New Jersey 1985)

Fisher, Louis (2003): Deciding on War Against Iraq: Institutional Failures, in: Presidential Studies Quarterly, 118, 3, pp. 389-410.

Fisher, Louis and David Adler (1998):. The War Powers Resolution: Time to Say Goodbye, in: Political Science Quarterly, 113, 1, pp.1-20.

Foyle, Douglas (2004): .Leading the Public to War: The Influence of American Public Opinion on the Bush Administration's Decision to Go to War in Iraq, in: International Journal of Public Opinion Research; 16, 3, pp. 269-291.

Grimmett, Richard F. (2010): The War Powers Resolution: After Thirty-Six Years (Congressional Research Service Report R41199), April 22, 2010. http://assets.opencrs.com/rpts/R41199_20100422.pdf

Hart, A(lbert) B(ushnell) (1891), The Speaker as Premier, in: Atlantic Monthly, LXVII, March 1891, pp. 380-386.

Henning, Charles (1989): The Wit and Wisdom of Politics. Golden, Colorado.

Holder, Eric (2012): Text of the Attorney General's National Security Speech (http://www.lawfareblog.com/2012/03/text-of-the-attorney-generals-national-security-speech/)

Hulse, Carl. (2011): Senate Approves Changes Intended to Ease Gridlock, in: New York Times (electronic edition), January 27, 2011.

Huntington, Samuel P.(1984):. Congressional Responses to the 20th Century, in: Thomas Ferguson and Joel Rogers, The Political Economy, Armonk, New York, pp. 180-202 (reprinted from David Truman, *Congress and America's Future,* 1973).

Jones, Charles O. (1968): Joseph G. Cannon and Howard W. Smith: An Essay on the Limits of Leadership in the House of Representatives, in: Journal of Politics, 30, pp. 617-646.

Kosar, Kevin (2010): Regular Vetoes and Pocket Vetoes: An Overview, CRS Report for Congress (electronic version), Report RS22188, October18, 2010 (www.opencrs.com, visited March 1, 2011.)

Krass, Caroline. (2011): Authority to Use Military Force in Libya: Memorandum for the Attorney General. April 1, 2011 (http://www.justice.gov/olc/2011/authority-military-use-in-libya.pdf)

Kreps, Sarah E. (2008): Multilateral Military Interventions: Theory and Practice, in: Political Science Quarterly, 123, 4, pp. 573-605.

Lake, Eli M. (2012): Obama Embraces Signing Statements After Knocking Bush for Using Them, in: *The Daily Beast,* January 4, 2012 (http://www.thedailybeast.com/articles/2012/01/04/obama-embraces-signing-statements-after-knocking-bush-for-using-them.html)

Levinson, Daryl L and Richard N. Pildes (2006): Separation of Parties, Not Powers in: Harvard Law Review, 119, no. 8, June 2006, pp. 2312-2386.

Lindsay, James M. 1994. Congress, Foreign Policy, and the New Institutionalism, *in:* International Studies Quarterly, 38, June 1994, pp. 281-304.

Lindsay, James M. and Randall Ripley (1993): How Congress Influences Foreign and Defense Policy," in: Lindsay, James M. and Randall Ripley (Ed.): Congress Resurgent: Foreign and Domestic Policy on Capitol Hill. Ann Arbor 1993.

Marshall, William P. (2008): Eleven Reasons Why Presidential Power Inevitably Expands and Why It Matters, in: *Boston University Law Review,* 88, pp. 505-522.

Moynihan, Daniel (1978): Imperial Government, in: Commentary Magazine, June 1978, p. 65.

Oleszek, Walter J. (2003): The House Corrections Calendar, CRS Report for Congress (electronic version). Report 97-301, Dec. 4, 2003.

Ostrogorski, M(oise). (1899): The Rise and Fall of the Nominating Caucus, Legislative and Congressional, in: *The American Historical Review*, 5, 2, December 1899, pp. 253-283.

Rich, Frank. (2002): It's The War, Stupid!, in: *New York Times*, October 12.

Schlesinger, Arthur M. Jr. (1997): Rating the Presidents: Washington to Clinton, in: *Political Science Quarterly*, 112, 2 (Summer 1997).

Schroeder, Richard C. and Nathan Glick. (1989): An Outline of American Government. Washington: U.S. Information Agency (http://usinfo.org/facts/gov/oagtoc.htm, visited March 1, 2011).

Sinclair, Barbara (1993): Congressional Party Leaders in the Foreign and Defense Policy Arena, in: Lindsay, James M. and Randall Ripley (Ed.): Congress Resurgent: Foreign and Domestic Policy on Capitol Hill. Ann Arbor 1993.

Straub, Noelle (2009): Sen. Byrd Questions Obama's Use of Policy Czars, in: New York Times, (electronic edition) February 25, 2009.

Sundquist, James L. (1982): The Decline and Resurgence of Congress. Washington, D.C.

Taft, William Howard (1915): Our Chief Magistrate and His Powers, New York (Electronic Text) http://www.archive.org/stream/ourchiefmagistra00taftuoft/ourchiefmagistra00taftuoft_djvu.txt

Talev, Margaret (2009): White House Aides Have Too Much Power, Byrd Says, in: McClatchy Newspapers (electronic edition), February 25, 2009 (site visited March 1, 2011).

Tribe, Laurence (2006): Signing Statements Are a Phantom Target, in: Boston Globe (electronic edition), August 6, 2006 (visited March 1, 2011).

Turley, Jonathan (2012): Obama's Kill Doctrine, in: Foreign Policy (electronic version), March 6, 2012. http://www.foreignpolicy.com/articles/2012/03/06/obama_s_kill_doctrine).

U.S. Congress, House (2009): Constitution, Jefferson's Manual, and the Rules of the House of Representatives for the 111th Congress, House Document 110-162, Washington, D.C.

U.S. Congress, Senate, Committee on Rules and Administration (1985): Senate Cloture Rule, Committee Print, no. 99–95. 99th Cong., 1st session, Washington, D.C.

U.S. Senate (1985): U.S. Congress. Senate. Committee on Rules and Administration. Senate Cloture Rule. Committee Print, no. 99–95. 99th Cong., 1st sess.

Whiteman, David. (1983): A Theory of Congressional Organization: Committee Size in the House of Representatives, in: American Politics Research, 11, 1, January 1983, pp. 49-70.

Wilzewski, Jürgen (2012): Suspending the Imperial Presidency? Obama und das Verhältnis zwischen Exekutive und Legislative, in: Florian Böller/Jürgen

Wilzewski (Ed.): Weltmacht im Wandel. Die USA in der Ära Obama, Trier, pp. 57-87

Wilzewski, Jürgen (2010): Testing the Constitutional System. Die Bush-Doktrin und die Rückkehr der imperialen Präsidentschaft, in: Söhnke Schreyer/Jürgen Wilzewski (Ed.): Weltmacht in der Krise. Die USA am Ende der Ära George W. Bush, Trier, pp. 49-74.

Woolley, John and Gerhard Peters (2011):.American Presidency Project: Presidential Signing Statements (http://www.presidency.ucsb.edu/signingstatements. php#ixzz1H3fUtTGK; site visited March 1, 2011.)

Wolfensberger, Donald M. (2007): Rules, Rules Rules: Congress Relies on Them, remarks at symposium "Congress in the Classroom," Dirksen Center for Congressional Studies, July 31, 2007 (electronic version: www.dirksencenter.org/Rules-Rules-Dirksen-rmks-drw.doc site visited March 1, 2011).

Yoo, John (2008): Jefferson and Executive Power, in: Boston University Law Review, 88, pp. 101-37.

Notes

1. Levinson and Pildes 2006: 2320-2322.
2. Hart 1891; Ostrogorski 1899.
3. In the 30 years after the Civil War, nearly 40 percent of all cabinet secretaries were former Members of Congress. By the middle decades of the 20th Century, the percentage had declined to 15 percent. Huntington 1984: 186.
4. Schlesinger 1997.
5. 1985, 2007.
6. 1982.
7. Taft's lectures on the presidency in 1915 at Columbia University contain the famous maxim on limited presidential power. "The true view of the executive functions is, as I conceive it, that the president can exercise no power which cannot be fairly and reasonably traced to some specific grant of power or justly implied and included within such express grant as proper and necessary to its exercise." The full text of the lectures is now available on line. http://www.archive.org/stream/ourchiefmagistra00taftuoft/ourchiefmagistra00taftuoft_djvu.txt
8. Yoo 2008.
9. Yoo 2008, in this article, note 108, quotes from a letter by Jefferson to Tom Paine, the radical intellectual hero of the American Revolution, discussing the doubtful legality of Jefferson's purchase of the Louisiana Territory. In the letter, Jefferson states, "I infer that the less we say about the constitutional difficulties respecting Louisiana the better, and that what is necessary for surmounting them must be done *sub-silentio.*"
10. Marshall, 511.
11. Lindsay 1994: 281.
12. Sinclair, 225.
13. Marshall, 507.
14. Fisher and Adler 1998: 5.
15. Lindsay and Ripley, 19.

16. Levinson and Pildes, 2351-2.
17. 2003: 398.
18. Rich 2002, A21.
19. A detailed summary of military interventions and the use of the War Powers Resolution or similar procedures in Congress can be found in Grimmett 2010.
20. 1997: 523.
21. Kreps 2008.
22. Quoted in Henning, 1989, 233.
23. U.S. Congress, House 2009: sec. 1038, 1054, 1064.
24. Wolfensberger 2007: 11.
25. Under the original 1917 cloture rule, debate could only be limited on a bill or resolution. Subsequent changes in the period noted allowed cloture to be invoked on any debatable matter, including motions to take up a matter, nominations, and conference reports on bills. The margin to invoke cloture changed from 2/3 of the full Senate, to 2/3 of those present and voting, to 3/5 of the full Senate. See Beth 2003; see in addition, U.S. Senate 1985.
26. Binder and Smith 1998.
27. Hulse 2011.
28. Wilzewski 2012; 2010.
29. Kosar 2011.
30. Woolley and Peters 2011.
31. Tribe 2006.
32. Lake 2012.
33. Moynihan 1978: 65.
34. Byrd 2009.
35. Straub 2009.
36. Brown, 2011.
37. Wilzewski 2012: 77-82.
38. Krass 2011: pp. 8-9 Internal footnotes in quoted text omitted.
39. Chesney 2011.
40. Hastings, *Congressional Record*, June 24, 2011: H4542.
41. Rooney, *Congressional Record*, June 24, 2011, p. H4551.
42. McCaul, *Congressional Record*, June 24, 2011, H4553.
43. *Congressional Record*, electronic version, July 8, 2011, H4765.
44. Ackerman 2011.
45. Holder 2012.
46. Bazelon, 2012.
47. Turley, 2012.
48. An unofficial transcript of the exchange between Senator Sessions, Secretary Panetta, and General Martin Dempsey can be found at http://www.maggiesnotebook.com/2012/03/congress-impotent-at-calling-war-nato-un-only-approval-criteria-for-panetta/ . By comparison, *The New York Times* did not mention the exchange in its news report. Elizabeth Bumiller, "U.S. Defense Officials Say Obama Reviewing Military Options in Syria," http://www.nytimes.com/2012/03/08/world/middleeast/united-states-defense-officials-stress-nonmilitary-options-on-syria.html?_r=1&scp=11&sq=leon%20panetta&st=cse. *The Washington Post* mentioned the Sessions-Panetta exchange only in passing, several days after the event. Karen DeYoung, "Talk of military aid rises as hopes fade for peaceful Syria solution," http://www.washingtonpost.com/world/national-security/talk-of-military-aid-rises-as-hopes-fade-for-peaceful-syria-solution/2012/03/10/gIQAzis83R_story.html

49.   As this chapter is reviewed for publication, the Obama administration has delivered to the congressional intelligence committees a memorandum from Justice Department legal counsel justifying the use of drone strikes to kill American citizens viewed as imminent terrorist threats. The administration acted after reports in *Time* magazine and elsewhere about such policies. Several Senate Democrats and Republicans voiced concerns over the legal theory of the memorandum (during Intelligence Committee hearings on the appointment of John Brennan to be Director of Central Intelligence), but most members of Congress have been denied access to the memorandum. Under House and Senate Rules, a member of either intelligence committee may offer a motion to release classified information in the possession of the intelligence committee. If the committee, by majority vote, decides that it wants to disclose such information, a convoluted process may follow ultimately leading to a vote in the full House or Senate to disclose such classified information. Although the provisions have been part of House and Senate procedure for four decades, they are rarely invoked. This provides further proof of a culture of congressional deference to the executive.

50.   Argersinger 1992: 103.

51.   Schroeder and Glick 1989.

IX

A Legal Ethics Primer
for National Security Lawyers

Michael Noone

"Of course it's a violation of international law; that's why it's a covert action."[1]

This chapter is dedicated to two friends and former colleagues: the late Mary C. Lawton, Department of Justice Counsel for Intelligence and Head of the Office of Intelligence Policy and Review, and Colonel Mary Perry USAF (ret.), whose last active-duty assignment was as a legal advisor for intelligence matters in the Secretary of Defense's Office of General Counsel.

Sir Hersch Lauterpacht's aphorism that "if international law is at the vanishing point of the law, then the law of war is at the vanishing point of international law"[2] could appropriately be applied to professional responsibility standards when applied to government lawyers engaged in the practice of national security law. Legal ethics norms for lawyers in private practice were first articulated in the nineteenth century.[3] Subsequently they were applied, by extension, to lawyers in government practice.[4] The recent controversy over the application of those norms to the lawyers who participated in writing the "Torture Memos"[5] evidences the fact that we are at the vanishing point of professional responsibility law. This chapter will suggest why that is the case.

The diagnosis is not necessarily terminal. After all, the law of war has expanded since 1952 when Sir Hersch wrote his comment: three additional Protocols to the Geneva Conventions and numerous national and international instruments have been added in an attempt to clarify what has come to be known as International Humanitarian Law. The ethical norms applicable to the peculiar problems faced by national security lawyers are yet to be fully developed. The goals of this chapter are to explain who national security lawyers are; the peculiar ethical issues they confront; and to offer suggestions for an approach that may aid them in resolving those issues.

The American Bar Association's publication *Red Flags: A Lawyer's Handbook on Legal Ethics*[6] offers a helpful summary of the ethical problems private practitioners may face. The problems arise in the context of the four fiduciary duties private lawyers owe their clients: communication, competence, confidentiality, and loyalty. The book's only references to government lawyers relate to the ethical problems that may occur when a former government lawyer returns to private practice. A student Note, "Rethinking the Professional Responsibilities of Federal Agency Lawyers,"[7] claims that there are two traditional models of professional responsibility for private practitioners; ". . . both models start from the assumption that the client's interests are fully formed and fixed, prior to the start of the lawyer's representation. . . . both models attempt to make predictable, categorical judgments about the ethical valence of certain actions . . . both models seek to establish trans-substantive ethical principles, ostensibly in an effort to provide predictability in application of the ethical codes . . . ."[8] The author asserts that many of the same values and goals underlie the models relied on for government lawyers, one based on agency loyalty, the other focused on the public interest. The author offers an alternative "critical" model intended to ensure "that all relevant perspectives are brought to bear on the question,"[9] with a significant caveat: "With the possible exception of national security issues, such actions by the government lawyer are fully consistent with values of democratic accountability and transparent government."[10] The author doesn't explain how "the critical model" can be applied to government lawyers engaged in offering advice on national security matters.[11]

Legal ethics rules are based on norms defining the duties a lawyer owes to his clients; to the courts that will be called upon to adjudicate claims brought on behalf of the client; to the public; and to other members of the bar. The duties lawyers in private practice owe their clients are straightforward: don't lie, cheat, or steal from your clients; don't have sex with them; keep them informed of what you're doing on their behalf; and do whatever you told them you were going to do for the agreed price. Duties to the courts? Don't lie or mislead them, and appear when you're told to. Duties to the public? Try not, by word or deed, to give additional ammunition to critics of our legal system. Duties to other members of the bar? Don't lie to or about them; don't interfere with their relationship with their clients. The principles are clear and their application in a particular situation will be clear as well.

The reciprocal duties owed by a client to his lawyer are opaque: what can a lawyer do when a client has breached his contractual duty to the lawyer by, for example, refusing to pay fees or cooperate in maintenance of the case? And, how does a lawyer reconcile duty to the client with duty to the courts and public when the client engages in behavior that the lawyer knows is illegal or anti-social?

The problems posed by "reciprocal duties" owed by the client to the lawyer are palpable, but many—if not most—of them can't arise when the government lawyer's client is the United States, particularly when the issue arises in the context of litigation. Government litigators, trial attorneys, and judges are bound by the same norms as their civilian counterparts. The preamble to the American Bar Association's *Model Rules of Professional Conduct* identifies various representational functions a lawyer may perform on behalf of his or her clients: advisor of the client's legal rights and obligations; advocate, asserting the client's position under the rules of the adversary system; negotiator, seeking a result advantageous to the client but consistent with the requirements of honest dealing; and evaluator, examining the client's legal affairs and reporting about them to the client or to others.[12] The government lawyer's role as litigator is bound by conventional norms. What of the roles of advisor, negotiator, and evaluator in the context of national security law?

Many government lawyers can claim to be engaged in national security work. "National security" is a portmanteau term, simply indicating that the work is of national importance and implicitly claiming that unless it is carried out by expert professionals, the safety and tranquility of the nation will be at risk. Thus, SEC lawyers engaged in regulating the market and Postal Service lawyers involved in ensuring that goods and services are delivered promptly and efficiently are engaged in national security concerns, albeit in a less immediate fashion than the Department of Justice (DoJ) lawyers in the Office of Legal Counsel (OLC) charged with drafting guidance for investigators interrogating Al-Qaeda suspects. In order to shrink the universe of national security lawyers to a manageable size and highlight the issues that, for example, inspired the DoJ memos on enhanced interrogation techniques, I will use the term "national security lawyer" to refer only to those lawyers who have been granted security clearances and access to Sensitive Compartmented Information (SCI), often in conjunction with a Special Access Program (SAP).[13] Most—but not all[14]—of those lawyers are employees of the executive branch. Information within the executive branch is designated as "classified" pursuant to the provisions of a statute or Executive Order. Presently

Executive Order E.O. 13,526 maintains the three long-standing classification levels, or classification markings, of top secret, secret, and confidential.[15] Sensitive Compartmented Intelligence and Special Operations activities require a special background investigation (SBI) which ". . . involves a more intrusive scrutiny into the attorney's private life than for other government positions, and certainly far more than what would ordinarily be considered acceptable in the private sector. . . . At some point near the end of the SBI, a polygraph examination is administered and the attorney is asked to corroborate the truthfulness of his application and comment on any inconsistencies found during the course of the SBI."[16] These matters have, since 2004, been handled according to standards and procedures set by the Director of National Intelligence.[17] SCI is divided into categories called control systems (e.g., "Special Intelligence" refers to communications intelligence), and compartments and subcompartments designated by a code word. The code words that have been declassified appear to have been based on the degree of protection afforded the information.[18] Thus, a national security lawyer must not only have a security clearance at the requisite classification level but also have been granted explicit permission to access a compartment or subcompartment. The compartment or subcompartment may refer to a Special Access Program, established by an authorized, typically high-ranking person in the executive branch.[19]

National security lawyers don't create compartments; they're called on to advise and evaluate the formulation and implementation of policies relating to a particular code-worded program. Historically, they were not called on during the formulation process because program managers didn't see that an activity had a legal dimension or were reluctant to face a lawyer's searching scrutiny of a proposal. This attitude has, I understand, melted away, and lawyers' opinions are routinely sought to justify any SCI/SAO operation. A national security lawyer told me recently, "They (action officers and supervisors) won't leave the building without clearing it with us first." What kind of executive actions might the national security lawyer be called on to evaluate? The lawyer will be called upon to evaluate intelligence, a term that has various meanings: ". . . the process by which specific types of information important to national security are requested, collected, analyzed and provided to policymakers; the products of that process; the safeguarding of these processes and this information by counterintelligence activities; and the carrying out of operations as requested by lawful authorities."[20]

Intelligence can be thought of as a product, as an organization, or as a process. The focus of this chapter is the role of lawyers in the process ". . . the means by which certain types of information are required and requested, collected, analyzed, and disseminated, and ... the way in which certain types of covert action are conceived and conducted."[21] Note that the process, as described, has two facets:

the first reflects the "intelligence cycle" model originally formulated by the CIA: planning and direction, collection, processing, analysis and production, dissemination, and formulation of requirements.[22] The second facet focuses on covert action, "an activity or activities . . . to influence political, economic or military conditions abroad, where it is intended that the role of the United States will not be apparent or acknowledged publicly."[23] The process, as described, fails to make two important distinctions. First, spatially: the CIA's intelligence cycle description doesn't distinguish between domestic and foreign intelligence. The CIA cannot conduct intelligence within the United States or on U.S. citizens.[24] This chapter will focus on ethics challenges for national security lawyers engaged in the formulation and implementation of overseas programs. National security lawyers have been called upon to participate as negotiators, seeking to resolve jurisdictional disputes over whether particular intelligence activities were foreign or domestic (e.g., recruitment of foreigners in the U.S. for overseas use: FBI or CIA?). Ethical issues arising from these kinds of interagency jurisdictional disputes will not be covered here. The second distinction is legislative:[25] the statutory requirement that requires the executive branch to notify Congress of covert actions. The statute provides four exceptions to the requirement:

(1) Activities the primary purpose of which is to acquire intelligence, traditional counterintelligence activities, traditional activities to improve or maintain the operational security of U.S. Government programs, or administrative activities;

(2) Traditional diplomatic or military activities or routine support to such activities;

(3) Traditional law enforcement activities conducted by U.S. Government law enforcement agencies or routine support to such activities; or

(4) Activities to provide routine support to the overt activities (other than activities described in paragraph (1), (2), or (3) of other U.S. Government agencies abroad.

There will be instances when an agency will conclude that the operation falls within one of the exceptions and need not be reported to Congress, although agency lawyers may acknowledge that an alternative reading of the relevant statutory provision would call for reporting. Ethical issues arising from these kinds of intrabranch disputes will not be covered. If this chapter is not concerned with litigation issues, nor with interagency and intrabranch disputes, what ethical issues remain?

The *Shorter Oxford English Dictionary*[26] provides several definitions of the term "ethics"; one is "the rules of conduct recognized in certain limited departments of human life." The *Rules of Professional Responsibility* promulgated by the American Bar Association and various state bar associations would satisfy that definition. But how can the duties derived from Professional Responsibility Rules and articulated in the ABA's *Red Flags*[27] for private lawyers—communication, confidentiality, loyalty, and competence—be applied to a national security lawyer when there is no equivalent lawyer/client relationship? The duty to communicate his opinions will be satisfied by communicating with his supervisor and the project officer who sought his advice, surrogates for the private client. They will set the norms for timely and comprehensive reporting. Failure to satisfy those norms will be sanctioned, not by a bar association but within the civil service.[28] The duty of confidentiality is subsumed by the security classification system: the national security lawyer is obliged to reveal official information that has come into his possession to anyone with the proper clearances who has established a need to know. Breach of that duty may be sanctioned, not only by the civil service system but also by the criminal justice system. The duty of loyalty that a lawyer in private practice owes his client and former clients has no parallel in national security legal relationships. The lawyer in private practice must ensure that his representation of a particular client and the loyalty he owes that client do not conflict with the duty of loyalty he owes other clients, present and past. The national security lawyer owes no equivalent duty to his surrogate "clients"—supervisors, project officers, others with a need to know—because their interests, in an institutional sense, cannot conflict. The final duty of competence can be articulated in a national security setting.

The American Bar Association's *Model Rules of Professional Conduct* dictate: "A lawyer shall provide competent representation to a client. Competent representation requires the legal knowledge, skill, thoroughness and preparation reasonably necessary for the representation."[29] If one accepts that "the client" is the designated agency representative to whom the attorney's advice is directed, what constitutes competent representation? In an April 2012 speech at Harvard Law School, Stephen W. Preston, general counsel of the Central Intelligence Agency, offered a protocol for national security lawyers.[30] His example derives from an application of the "Covert Action" statute, 50 U.S.C.A. § 413b, but the protocol could as well be applied to intelligence collection activities. Its application raises several ethical issues. He asks:

- **Is the activity authorized by U.S. law?**
  In his "use of force" scenario, Preston points to the President's Article II responsibilities to protect the country from imminent attack. Arguably, the "Congressional Authorization to Use Armed Forces against those responsible for the recent attacks launched against the United States"[31]

would reinforce the authority of the executive branch to engage in activities calling for the use of force. The authorized activities could fall within two legal regimes: Title 18 (Department of Defense) or Title 50 (War and National Defense).[32] The Covert Action statute imposes *ex post facto* reporting requirements on the Executive[33] and requires the President to make a "Finding" before the action can be initiated. A competent national security lawyer would be expected to identify the legal authority relied on, the decision level required to authorize the action, and what statutory restrictions—e.g., the need for a Presidential Finding—applied. The national security lawyer's fundamental obligation is to ensure that the proposed activity is not *ultra vires* under domestic (U.S.) law. Clandestine operations relying on a U.S. cover identity could—but have not—raised ethical issues. CIA lawyers must have been engaged in two historical espionage activities: Project Azorian, the recovery of a Soviet Golf Class submarine,[34] and Air America, an airline secretly owned and operated by the CIA.[35] Both involved corporate filings, including false statements of ownership, which were intended to deceive third parties.[36] In both cases, sufficient time had passed for the agency to admit its deceptions and, implicitly, violations of state laws requiring declarations of ownership, assets, etc.

- **Is the proposed action in conformity with International Law principles?** In his use of force scenario, Preston relies on the inherent right to self-defense confirmed in Article 51 of the U.N. Charter. What if the proposed action involves the clandestine collection of intelligence from a target country that poses no threat to the United States? In a provocative article, "The Unresolved Equation of Espionage and International Law,"[37] John Radsan, formerly an assistant general counsel at the Central Intelligence Agency, offers no legal justification for the practice, pointing out that neither customary international law nor treaty law addresses peacetime espionage. His own experience is illustrative: "As a lawyer in the CIA, I helped the agency and its officers to keep their operations, abroad and at home, consistent with the U.S. Constitution, relevant executive orders, and internal regulations. To remain in compliance with U.S. law, CIA lawyers must master various legal subfields. . . . These lawyers, however, do not need to develop any expertise in the domestic laws of other countries; the CIA takes for granted that its operations will violate an array of foreign laws."[38] If a national security lawyer were called upon to review an espionage program and to respond to Mr. Preston's "compliance with international law" checklist question, apparently it would be ethical of him to say, "I'm certain this violates the target country's laws." Of what relevance is the case of Thomas K. Scanlan, a Minnesota lawyer disciplined for his conviction in Canada for overseeing the production of a stock prospectus that violated Canadian securities law? The Supreme Court of Minnesota held that its Disciplinary Rule 1-02 extended beyond political and geographic boundaries.[39] In order for the Minnesota court's reasoning to apply to a U.S. national security lawyer who had participated in approving a covert violation of a friendly nation's (i.e., Canada's) laws, he would have to have been convicted by a national court of criminal behavior associated with the operation. Bar authorities would have to decide whether approval of a U.S. government-authorized operation which violated another nation's sovereignty evidenced disqualifying behavior warranting discipline. I think that bar authorities would create a national security exception, excusing lawyers who participated in conspiring to violate another nation's laws, particularly in cases where a civil law jurisdiction permitted convictions in absentia, as was the case of CIA agents engaged in the kidnaping/extraordinary rendition of Abu Omar from Italy. [40]

- **Compliance in execution.**
  Under U.S. law, Mr. Preston's protocol is based on a hypothetical covert action and calls for the national security lawyer first to comply with the terms dictated by the President in the applicable Finding. He cites the provision of the National Security Act of 1947 that "[a] Finding that may not authorize any action that would violate the Constitution or any statute of the United States."[41] The proposed covert action must fall within the authority granted by the Presidential Finding or it will be *ultra vires*, arguably exposing the operators to both criminal and civil liability. Mr. Preston's checklist question asks, "Is the Finding being implemented in accordance with U.S. law?" His earlier question was "Is the activity authorized by U.S. law?" Both call for a straightforward "yes" or "no" answer to the question "Is it legal?" The Preston checklist does not ask, "Is it a good idea?" The ABA's *Model Rules of Professional Responsibility* suggests a more expansive approach:

  > In representing a client a lawyer shall exercise independent professional judgment and render candid advice. In rendering advice a lawyer may refer not only to the law but to other considerations such as moral, economic, and social factors that may be relevant to the client's situation.[42]

If a national security lawyer follows Mr. Preston's protocol, and the proposal and its implementation are *infra vires*, then the lawyer can ethically approve them. If they are not, he can't. When called upon to decide whether a proposed action is within the scope of a Presidential Finding, should the national security lawyer act as an impartial evaluator of the proposal? That's the role envisioned by Professor Bruff for the Department of Justice Office of Legal Counsel in *Bad Advice*.[43] I think intelligence community counsel and their superiors see the national security lawyer's role differently: as a team player committed to helping his team achieve the Finding's desired goal, if necessary modifying the methods employed, etc. The Preston Protocol assumes a Title 50 operation, but it would apply as well to Title 18 actions. Military lawyers are routinely asked to coordinate (review and comment on) proposals with legal implications. The implicit question: "Is what's been proposed legal?" Commanders expect a response that assesses the legality not only of the proposal but of its implementation as well. Most don't expect a discussion of the ABA Model Rules' "other considerations," etc.

National security lawyers must often be solicited for answers that would apparently violate legal norms. "Under what circumstances could the U.S. justify the intentional peacetime invasion of a sovereign's air or water space without seeking consent of the sovereign?" "May U.S. embassy guards be armed with jacketed hollow-point bullets although these bullets are contrary to local law?" The questions call for careful legal research, exemplary casuistry, and superior expository skills. Typically the answers will be scenario-dependent. We don't know whether legal advice was sought before the Clinton White House "War Council" established Operation Infinite Reach in 1998, which authorized Cruise missile intrusions in Sudanese airspace when the al Shifa pharmaceutical plant was bombed, and similar intrusions into Afghan airspace attacking suspected Al-Qaeda training camps.

The national security lawyer's product (the articulation of his legal opinion) will depend on agency practice. Simply initialing the "coordination" block on a proposal may be sufficient to indicate legal review and approval.[44] In other situations, agencies may call for a full-blown "review for legal sufficiency," exemplified in the Department of Justice Office of Legal Counsel "Torture Memos."[45] Extended legal reviews are the government equivalent of opinions of counsel, routinely used in commerce and designed to establish "due diligence" in, for example, a merger or acquisition (M&A). These Opinion Letters serve to validate the legality of the transaction if it were to be challenged by third parties, e.g., disaffected shareholders or some supervisory entity. The *Restatement of the Law Governing Lawyers*[46] states that the M&A lawyer's liability to these nonclients is based on a negligence standard, which, presumably, would be the standard applied by bar disciplinary committees. The *Restatement*'s standard is derived from tort law—whether the opinion deviated from an accepted standard of care, whether the nonclient had been invited by the client to rely on the opinion, had done so, and the nonclient is not too remote from the lawyer to seek the law's protection. Duty, Breach, Cause in Fact, Proximate Cause, and (presumably) Damages—all familiar concepts to any lawyer trained in the common-law tradition.

Opinions of counsel are sought—and granted— to protect, for example, buyers and sellers from liability claims and to guarantee the creditworthiness of the transaction. The Enhanced Interrogation (Torture) Memos were apparently fashioned for the same purpose: to protect operators and decision makers from liability: criminal, civil, and (possibly) political. It certainly isn't unethical for a lawyer, in public or private practice, to issue an opinion letter as long as the proposed action is not illegal on its face, the opinion is issued in good faith, and the advice rendered falls within accepted notions of legal competency. Opinions of counsel letters would not, in my opinion, appropriately reflect on "moral, economic and social factors that may be relevant to the client's situation."[47] They are intended to memorialize, if necessary, for possible public view the legal rationale which justifies a proposed transaction. If, in his opinion, the transaction can't be legally justified, the ethical lawyer will have explained that to his client and, with the client's permission, to the lawyers representing the other parties to the transaction.

Opinions of counsel in the public sector are intended for the same purpose. The CIA sought DoJ guidance in order to assure CIA operatives and their superiors that reliance on "enhanced interrogation techniques," however defined, would not expose them to legal liability. Under a new chief executive, DoJ's withdrawal of the Torture Memos, after their contents became known and controversial, simply evidenced a change in policy. However, the new Administration's Office of Professional Responsibility (OPR) recommended that the two senior authors of the memos be referred to their state bars for possible disciplinary action because they failed to provide "thorough, candid, and objective" analysis in their memoranda regarding interrogation of detained terrorist suspects. This was, I believe, the first time that advice rendered in good faith by government lawyers was treated as the potential basis for disciplinary action, i.e., professional malpractice charges. The recommendation was not accepted.[48] The memorandum rejecting the recommendation is more than 50 pages long and focused on perceived procedural and substantive errors made by the OPR. Since national security lawyers' professional advice has, for the first time, been subject to scrutiny as a professional misconduct offense, the incident serves to remind the national security lawyer that his advice should be rendered with the thought that a new administration, or even a change in office leadership from one political appointee to another, may lead to second-guessing.

I suggest that the national security lawyer prepare a "Memo for the Record" in which he explains the legal reasoning on which his opinion was based and, perhaps, the circumstances surrounding the inquiry that generated it. Memos for the record serve two useful purposes: to detail the national security lawyer's legal reasoning (if it's subsequently challenged) and to memorialize the circumstances when information was delivered or the legal opinion sought. Other parties to the exchange may have different recollections, or claim no recollection at all. Memos for the Record (M/Rs) are the hallmark of an ethical and careful lawyer. Office practices differ: Does the M/R need to be classified? Where and how should M/Rs be stored?

National security lawyers in the executive branch have been the focus of this essay and the literature on which it is based. There are national security lawyers, i.e., individuals with security clearances and Special Compartment Information access, serving in the legislative branch as well: certainly on the staff of the House and Senate Intelligence and Appropriation committees, probably on the staff of the Armed Services, Homeland Security, and Energy committees. There may be others as well. These committees have two fundamental responsibilities: oversight and legislation.[49] The appropriation committees legislate by allocating revenues; the others authorize expenditures. They all engage in oversight.

Who are the committee lawyers' clients? The chairmen of their committees? Possibly one or more may be detailed to the chair of the minority party. Their functions? Much as those listed in the ABA's Model Rules:[50] advisor, advocate (rarely, and in cooperation with the Department of Justice), negotiator, and evaluator. Their fiduciary duties? Quite like those of lawyers in private practice: communication, competence, confidentiality, and loyalty. I don't know of any case in which a congressional national security lawyer faced bar discipline for breach of their official fiduciary duties. Nor, because of the relative clarity of those duties, compared with those of lawyers in the executive branch,[51] does their peculiar status as national security lawyers create special problems. Of course, like any private practitioner, their clients may create problems: Senator Patrick Leahy, a member of the Senate Select Committee on Intelligence, delivered a yet-to-be-classified staff memo on the Iran-Contra Affairs to a journalist.[52] Representative Robert Toricelli, a member of the House Intelligence Committee, breached committee rules by disclosing classified information.[53] Staff members were not involved in either case. In 2009 Representative Nancy Pelosi, House Speaker and former chair of the House Intelligence Committee, denied that she had been briefed on the use of "enhanced interrogation techniques" utilized to gain information from terrorism suspects.[54] The senior lawyer on the committee staff subsequently resigned.[55] Had she lost confidence in him, or he in her? No known bar disciplinary action was undertaken.

"Professional responsibility" poses a problem for national security because it is based on the lawyer/client dyad. The dyad was challenged by the development of depersonalized business models. To whom did the lawyer for a corporation or partnership owe ethical duties of confidentiality or loyalty? The normative response was that these duties were owed to the so-called "control group," not to the shareholders at large. Is there an equivalent control group in the executive branch? Full disclosure is the essence of the lawyer/client relationship: each must be open and honest with the other. How does that transfer to a relationship based on "need to know?" In *The Terror Presidency*,[56] Professor Jack Goldsmith, subsequent head of the Office of Legal Counsel (OLC), argues forcefully and persuasively that State and Defense Department lawyers should have been involved in answering the "enhanced interrogation technique" questions posed by the CIA.[57] Presumably that authority was at some level higher than OLC: the attorney general? Or the Office of the President, represented by the vice president, who had already decided that those entities would not be asked? The national security lawyer has to temper his notions of professional responsibility, conditioned by his concepts of confidentiality and professional collegiality, with the iron law of secrecy.

The professional norm that regulated lawyers' behavior both in and out of government was described as legal ethics. Now the accepted term is "professional responsibility." "Ethics" suggests a norm that strives toward virtue; "professional responsibility" suggests a passive norm that, if met, avoids punishment. This move, from internal (ethics) to external (responsibility) reflected a fundamental change in American character, described in David Riesman's *The Lonely Crowd*.[58] Riesman, a lawyer[59] turned sociologist, doesn't speak of professional standards and argues for individual autonomy, but his analysis suggests that when one speaks of the "professional responsibility" of national security lawyers in the executive branch, there are or should be a set of agreed-upon norms by which their behavior can be judged by others. There are not, and perhaps there can't be. Jack Goldsmith's description[60] of Lincoln and Roosevelt's responses to national security crises suggests that there may be exceptional occasions when the President must take action inconsistent with the law. If he acts contrary to his lawyers' legal advice, they're insulated from disciplinary action. If they agree with him, what defense do they have to charges that they have acted unprofessionally? Simply by saying, "I agreed that violating the law in those exceptional circumstances was the right thing to do." Would you rather be thought of as an ethical national security lawyer or as one who's professionally responsible? Inner-directed or Other-directed?[61]

Notes

1. RICHARD A. CLARKE, AGAINST ALL ENEMIES: INSIDE AMERICA'S WAR ON TERROR 144 (Free Press 2004), quoting former Vice President Al Gore.

2. *The Problem of the Revision of the Law of War*, 29 BRIT YB INT'L 3760 at 382 (1952), 952.

3. GEORGE SHARSWOOD, AN ESSAY IN PROFESSIONAL ETHICS 72 (Fred B. Rothman & Co., 5th ed 1993) (1854).

4. MODEL RULES OF PROFESSIONAL CONDUCT FOR FEDERAL LAWYERS (Fed. Bar Ass'n 1990).

5. Lawyers in the Department of Justice Office of Legal Counsel sought, at the CIA's request, to distinguish enhanced interrogation techniques from the word "torture" defined in 18 U.S.C. § 2340-2340A. The legal and policy controversy is summarized in Gregory Huckabee & Michael Davidson, *Application of the Advice of Counsel in Controversial Cases*, THE LAW OF COUNTERTERRORISM, Lynn K. Zusman ed. (ABA 2011), at 69, 71-42; *see also* HAROLD H. BRUFF, BAD ADVICE: BUSH'S LAWYERS IN THE WAR ON TERROR (Univ. Press of Kan. 2009).

6. ALI/ABA 2005, supplemented in 2009.

7. 115 HARV. L. REV. No. 4, 1192 (2002).

8. *Id.* 1172.

9. *Id.* 1189.

10. *Id.* 1191.

11. Nor do the MODEL RULES OF PROFESSIONAL CONDUCT FOR FEDERAL LAWYERS (Federal Bar Ass'n 1990), which focuses on "the identity of the client and where counsel's loyalties belong" and "the question of client confidentiality" (p. 1).

12. *Preamble*, A LAWYER'S RESPONSIBILITIES, p.1 (2011).

13. Major General Charles Dunlap, USAF (ret.), casts a wider net in *Ethical Issues of the Practice of National Security Law: Some Observations*, 38 OHIO N.U. L. REV. 1057–95 (2011-2012); his application of the *ABA Model Rules of Professional Conduct* to government lawyers makes no distinction between the level of access granted. In his comprehensive article, *Sed Quis Custodiet Ipsos Custodes: The CIA's Office of General Counsel?* 2 J.NAT'L SEC. L. & Pol'y, 201–55 (2006-2008), John Radsan, a former assistant general counsel at the Central Intelligence Agency mentions SCI access but doesn't discuss legal ethics issues. Nor does George C. Harris, *The Rule of Law and The War on Terror: The Professional Responsibilities of Executive Branch Lawyers in the Wake of 911*, 1 NAT'L SEC. L & POL'Y, 409–53 (2005) speak of the particular problems posed by SCI material.

14. *See* text accompanying notes 49 to 55, *infra*.

15. CLASSIFIED INFORMATION POLICY AND EXECUTIVE ORDER 13526, Cong. Res. Serv. pub. 7-5700 (Dec. 10, 2010).

16. Dorian D. Greene, *Ethical Dilemmas Confronting Intelligence Agency Counsel*, 2 TULSA J. COMP. & INT'L L. at 97 (Fall 1994).

17. Intelligence Reform and Terrorism Protection Act of 2004, P. L. 108-458, 118 Stat. 3638.

18. *See Critique of the Codeword Compartment in the CIA*, March 1977, *available at* http://www.fas.org./sgp/ othergov/codeword.html.

19. E.O. 13,526, section 6.1 (oo) (2009).

20. MARK M. LOWENTHAL, INTELLIGENCE FROM SECRETS TO POLICY 9 (Sage/CQ Press, 5th ed. 2012).

21. *Id.*

22. Hans Born & Aidan Mills, Beyond the Oxymoron: Exploring Ethics through the Intelligence Cycle, Ethics of Spying, Jan Goldman ed. (Scarecrow Press, 2d ed. 2010), 34, 42.
23. 50 U.S.C. § 413b(e).
24. The Covert Action Statute, 50 U.S.C. § 413b.
25. Note 14, *supra.*
26. Clarendon Press, 3d ed. 1972.
27. Note 6, *supra.*
28. Civilian attorney positions are within the excepted service, 5 U.S.C. § 2103, i.e., not in the competitive service, nor in the Senior Executive Services, but within the civil service system.
29. Rule 1.1.
30. *See* https://www.cia.gov/news-information/speeches-testimony/2012-speeches-testimony.
31. Joint Resolution of Sept. 14, 2001 (Pub. L. 107-40).
32. In *Military Intelligence Convergence and the Law of Title 10/Title 50 Debate*, 5 J. Nat'l Sec. L. & Pol'y 539–629 (2012), Professor Robert Chesney points out "disaggregating issues (based on these statutory distinctions) that have bedeviled government lawyers behind closed doors for some time" and suggests useful changes. Until those changes are made the National Security lawyer must ask, as a preliminary question: "Title 18 or Title 50?"
33. 50 U.S.C. § 413b(b).
34. [Author excised] *Project Azorian—The Story of the Hughes Glomar Explorer*, Studies in Intelligence, Fall 1985. *See* www.gwu.edu (~nsarchiv/nukevault/ebb305/doc01).
35. William M. Leary, CIA Air Operations in Laos, 1955-1974, supporting the "Secret War," www.cia.gov /library/center-for-the-study-of intelligence/csipublications/csi-studies/winter99.
36. Air America employees' subsequent legal efforts to seek civil service coverage are summarized in *DNI Support Request for Air America Retirement Benefits Legislation*, www.air-america.org/news/docu ments/gary_bisson_letters. As to the Glomar Explorer, *see* United States v. County of Los Angeles, 588 F.2d 308 (9th Cir. 1979).
37. Ethics of Spying, A Reader for the Intelligence Professional, Vol. 2, Jan Goldman ed. (Scarecrow Press, 2010), 144–71.
38. *Id.* at 162.
39. In the Matter of Application for the Discipline of Thomas K. Scanlan, 260 N.W.2d 834 (Minn. 1978.
40. *See* www.NYTIMES.COM…/Italian court convicts 2 Americans in kidnaping (Feb. 1, 2013).
41. 50 U.S.C. § 413b(a)(5).
42. ABA Model Rules of Prof'l Conduct R. 2.1, Advisor. The "other considerations" provision is permissive, not mandatory.
43. Note 5, *supra.*
44. *See, e.g.*, Figure 7. "Marking on a Staff Summary Sheet," DOD M5200.01, Feb. 4, 2012.
45. Note 5, *supra.*
46. Chapter 4, § 73.
47. ABA Model Rule 2.1, note 42, *supra.*
48. January 5, 2010 Memorandum for the Attorney General, From: David Margolis, Associate Deputy Attorney General, Subject: Memorandum of Decision Regarding the Objections to the Findings of Professional Misconduct in the Office of Professional Responsibility's

[OPR's] Report of Investigation into the Office of Legal Counsel's Memoranda Concerning Issues relating to the Central Intelligence Agency's Use of "Enhanced Interrogation Techniques" on Suspected Terrorists," www.judiciary house .gov/hearings/pdf/DAGMargolisMemo100105.

49.   Richard Posner, in *Uncertain Shield: the U.S. Intelligence System in the Throes of Reform* (Rowman & Littlefield 2006) devotes Chapters 7 and 8 to Congress's role in Intelligence.

50.   Note 12, *supra.*

51.   See my comments on the "Preston Protocol" text accompanying notes 30 to 42, *supra.*

52.   *See* www.NewYorkTimesArchives.July29,1987.

53.   *See* www.fas.[FederationofAmericanScientists]org./sgp/bulletin/sec47/(1995).

54.   *See* www.USAToday30.USAToday.com/News/…/2009-05-14-Pelosi-WaterBoarding. index.html.

55.   *See* www.DemocraticLeader.gov>Newsroom.>press.relethso[MikeSheehyRetires].

56.   LAW AND JUDGMENT INSIDE THE BUSH ADMINISTRATION (W.W. Norton, 2007).

57.   *Id.* at 166–67.

58.   Yale Univ. Press, 1950.

59.   Harvard Law School, clerk for Supreme Court Justice Louis Brandeis.

60.   THE TERROR PRESIDENCY, *Administration*, note 5, *supra* at 191–92.

61.   Keith Petty, *Professional Responsibility Compliance and National Security Attorneys: Adopting the Normative Framework in Internalized Legal Ethics*, 2011 UTAH L. REV. 1563–1628. Analysis is congruent with Riesman's, which he doesn't cite.

X

A Broad Overview of the Law of Armed Conflict in the Age of Terror

Shane R. Reeves and David Lai

Introduction

Applying and enforcing the laws that regulate warfare is increasingly difficult in today's armed conflicts. Escaping traditional conflict classifications, not limited by geography, and an "amalgamation of asymmetric and conventional tactics," modern warfare strains the traditional Law of Armed Conflict paradigm.[1] The advent of terrorism, which is fought by a "blend of military and law enforcement models" and regulated by a mixture of the Law of Armed Conflict, human rights law, and domestic criminal law, only exacerbates the legal uncertainty permeating contemporary warfare.[2] As this ambiguity becomes the norm rather than the exception in warfare—particularly in conflicts between state actors and non-state ideologically motivated terrorist groups[3]—understanding the fundamentals of the Law of Armed Conflict is imperative for effective regulation of these broadly scoped conflicts.[4]

As a preliminary matter, it is important to note that when the Law of Armed Conflict is triggered, "the obligations created by international humanitarian law apply not just to states but to individuals and non-state actors."[5] Terrorist organizations often ignore these universal legal obligations and view the Law of Armed Conflict "as an asymmetric warfare asset that may be leveraged in order to gain an advantage against" state actor adversaries.[6] As "non-state armed groups cannot survive direct and conventional conflicts" with superior state opponents,[7] they often "avoid mirroring Western military organizations and approaches to war" while operating "well outside the moral framework" that traditionally regulates hostilities.[8] Yet, despite the practical reasons for non-state armed groups' moral relativism, the Law of Armed Conflict encompasses "universal norms of behavior"[9] that cannot be deviated from regardless of the context of the conflict. The Law of Armed Conflict "seek[s], for humanitarian reasons, to limit the effects" of war,[10] and it is primarily for this reason that all conflict participants, including terrorist organizations, are ultimately legally responsible for their actions.

This chapter is a broad overview of the Law of Armed Conflict. It discusses the distinction between *jus ad bellum* and *jus in bello*, the legal sources of the Law of Armed Conflict; the classification of armed conflicts; the delineation of individual battlefield status; and the core principles that regulate warfare. These concepts are at the foundation of the Law of Armed Conflict, and understanding these basic tenets is critical for any individual who is interested in discussing the legality of terrorist activity.

What Is the Law of Armed Conflict?

At the most fundamental level, law and war are seemingly irreconcilable terms. "Law" implies an orderly polity where human relations and behaviors are governed usually by plentiful and inescapable rules, whereas the term "war" connotes an abandonment of restraint of rules by substituting in their place brutal force.[11] For the greater part of recorded history, the relationship between the imposed obligations of law and the violence of war was best understood as described by Cicero, the famous Roman philosopher, when he stated "*inter arma leges silent*" – in times of war the laws are silent.[12] However, despite an absence of formal legal obligations,[13] belligerents made some efforts to limit the brutality of warfare, particularly when men began to fight as organized groups, through informal rules and customs.[14] Seventeenth-century jurist Hugo Grotius, recognizing these customary obligations while simultaneously understanding the savagery of hostilities, noted that in warfare, belligerents must "not believe that either nothing is allowable, or that everything is."[15]

This philosophy articulated what was already understood: the violence in warfare, though a necessity, should be restricted in some manner.[16] Needing to limit the violence of war thus was the genesis for the Law of Armed Conflict and the delicate balance between military necessity and humanity, which remains the theoretical underpinnings of this specialized area of international law. The Law of Armed Conflict, though at times criticized as "holding together on paper better than in practice,"[17] remains the primary means of the international community to regulate that most horrific of human conditions—war.

Jus Ad Bellum versus Jus in Bello

The international law that broadly regulates warfare comprises two distinct strands known as *jus ad bellum* and *jus in bello*. *Jus ad bellum*, which lays the framework for when a state actor may resort to war, is "governed by an important, but distinct, part of the international law set out in the United Nations Charter,"[18] and allows for the use of force only in cases of self-defense or if condoned by the collective judgment of the international community.[19] *Jus in bello*, on the other hand, governs the actions of those participating in a conflict by establishing a delicate balance between military necessity—"the wartime necessity of killing and destroying military objectives"—and humanity—"the wartime requirement of preventing unnecessary suffering and protecting the civilian population."[20] The International Committee of the Red Cross (ICRC), in describing the differences between these areas of international law, states that "*[j]us ad bellum* refers to the conditions under which one may resort to war or to force in general; *jus in bello* governs the conduct of belligerents during a war, and in a broader sense comprises the rights and obligations of neutral parties as well."[21]

Maintaining the bifurcation between *jus ad bellum* and *jus in bello* is extraordinarily important, and while the two applications can, and often do, run parallel to one another, each must be determined independently.[22] As *jus ad bellum* only governs states' rights to use force and *jus in bello* aims to regulate conduct of conflict participants, "the politics of deciding who has breached that law [in using force] should not have a bearing on the protections of war victims."[23] Conflating these bodies of law creates moral ambiguity for those participating in a perceived "illegal war," and conversely, if a state enters into a "legal war," it can equally undermine its legitimacy through unlawful conduct in that conflict.[24] In other words, "[i]t is perfectly possible for a just war to be fought unjustly and for an unjust war to be fought in strict accordance with the rules."[25]

Often in asymmetric struggles between a conventionally superior state actor and an ideologically motivated terrorist group, the separation between *jus ad bellum* and *jus in bello* collapses.[26] The state actor may claim that the terrorists' "unjust" or illegal acts justify an equally "unjust" response and therefore as a group they are not entitled to rights and privileges under *jus in bello*.[27] Conversely, terrorist organizations typically assert extralegal legitimacy to justify their illegal violence by proclaiming "moral or religious motives for waging war."[28] Both approaches are troubling and dangerous, as they allow the conflict participants "to justify their violations by reference to the 'justness' of their cause" and "to excuse their disregard" for well-defined legal obligations.[29] As long as either party "makes application of *jus in bello* contingent on the validity" of their adversaries' "*jus ad*

141

bellum case, the result will be a reciprocal failure to ensure respect" for humanitarian considerations.[30]

Questions concerning a state's *jus ad bellum* justifications for using military force are often political decisions that are controversial and irresolvable.[31] However, violations or breaches of *jus in bello*[32] "cannot be justified on the ground that the enemy is responsible for commencing the hostilities in flagrant breach of the *jus ad bellum*."[33] *Jus in bello* "is predicated on the postulate of equal application of its legal norms to all Parties to the conflict"[34] and thus once a state is in a "period of war, international armed conflict, or occupation,"[35] regardless of *jus ad bellum* disputes, responsibilities become universally obligatory. Once triggered, these nonderogable *jus in bello* obligations supplant other bodies of law, such as domestic law or general human rights law—*lex specialis derogat legi generali*[36]—and are called the Law of Armed Conflict.

Sources of the Law of Armed Conflict

The Law of Armed Conflict, synonymous with the "law of war" or "international humanitarian law," is a "set of rules which . . . protects persons who are not or are no longer participating in the hostilities and restrict the means and methods of warfare."[37] There are two principal sources of the Law of Armed Conflict: the Geneva tradition and the Hague tradition. The Geneva tradition seeks to ensure humane treatment of those adversely affected by warfare by assigning the wounded and sick in the field,[38] the shipwrecked at sea,[39] prisoners of war,[40] and civilians[41] certain legal protections. The Hague tradition,[42] or the "targeting method," regulates the means and methods of warfare by setting forth limitations on the conduct of those participating in the conflict.[43] Updating both of these traditions, and subsequently acting as a point of convergence for these two distinct bodies of law, are the 1977 Additional Protocols I and II that supplement the Geneva Conventions and the Hague Regulations.[44] Various other treaties[45] and customary practices[46] supplement the Law of Armed Conflict and provide specific guidance on particular aspects of warfare. Informed by both "the customary and treaty law applicable to the conduct of warfare,"[47] the Law of Armed Conflict thus is an amalgamation of conventional treaty law and customary practices which continues to evolve in response to the changes of modern warfare.[48]

When Is the Law of Armed Conflict Applicable?

Classifying a conflict is a necessity for determining whether the Law of Armed Conflict is applicable and, if so, the scope of that application.[49] Article 2 of the 1949 Geneva Conventions, often called "Common Article 2" as it is repeated verbatim in all four of the Conventions,[50] states that in "all cases of declared war or of any other armed conflict which may arise between two or more of the High

Contracting Parties, even if the state of war is not recognized by one of them," the Conventions apply.[51] In hopes of regulating as many conflicts as possible, the drafters of the Geneva Conventions used the broad term "armed conflict" in lieu of the more restrictive term "war" noting that "the occurrence of de facto hostilities is sufficient" to satisfy the conditions established in Common Article 2.[52] Thus, when "force is directed by one state against another irrespective of duration or intensity,"[53] a conflict is deemed international,[54] and all the conventional and customary law that composes the Law of Armed Conflict becomes applicable.[55]

For those armed conflicts "not of an international character occurring in the territory of a state," such as an internal civil war between a state and a non-state armed group,[56] the applicable law is described in the four Geneva Conventions Common Article 3.[57] Called a "convention in miniature" Common Article 3, along with binding customary law,[58] is the only applicable international law[59] in an internal armed conflict.[60] As one scholar noted, "legally . . . the Parties to the conflict are bound to observe Article 3 and may ignore all other Articles [of the Geneva Convention]."[61] Determining when a non-international armed conflict exists versus a mere "internal disturbance" such as riots or "isolated and sporadic acts of violence" is often difficult.[62] Similar to international armed conflicts, the drafters of the Geneva Conventions wanted the scope of application for non-international armed conflicts to "be as wide as possible" to ensure "respect for certain rules" that are "essential in all civilized countries."[63] As a result, there are no universally accepted conditions to objectively distinguish between an internal disturbance and a non-international armed conflict, though there are a number of criteria that may indicate the difference between a domestic police action and a civil war.[64] In those situations where an armed disturbance does not reach the level of a "conflict," domestic law applies and the Law of Armed Conflict is irrelevant.[65]

Recent conflicts in Afghanistan and Iraq illustrate the distinctions between an international and non-international armed conflict while simultaneously highlighting how conflict classification is at times a fluid exercise. The U.S.-led military campaign against the de facto government of Afghanistan—the Taliban—began on October 7, 2011, and clearly was an international armed conflict to which the entirety of the Law of Armed Conflict applied.[66] By June 19, 2002, with the establishment of a new Afghan Transitional Administration, *Loya Jirga*, and a newly elected leader, Hamid Karzai, the conflict between the Afghan government and the remnants of the Taliban evolved into a non-international armed conflict in which the U.S. and allies were participants solely by invitation.[67] Similarly, the United States' invasion of Iraq on March 20, 2003, qualified as an international armed conflict, as it involved two "High Contracting Parties," thus triggering the complete Law of Armed Conflict.[68] During the U.S. occupation of

Iraq, the Law of Armed Conflict remained the applicable regulatory legal body.[69] However, when the new Iraqi government formed on June 28, 2004, the "United States remain[ed] present in Iraq ostensibly to aid and assist Iraq in its fight against its insurgents—a common Article 3 conflict in which Iraqi law [was] paramount; aside from common Article 3, the Geneva Conventions and Protocol I no longer appl[ied]."[70]

Categorizing conflicts, like those in Afghanistan and Iraq, is not an easy exercise and is often a debate that is resolved only in retrospect.[71] Yet the applicability of the Law of Armed Conflict, and whether it may regulate conduct, is contingent upon whether a conflict is deemed international or non-international.[72] The importance of conflict classification therefore cannot be overstated, as this determination establishes the rules governing hostilities.

Who Is Affected by the Law of Armed Conflict?

When the Law of Armed Conflict is applicable, the triggering conflict also helps establish the individual status of those involved in the hostilities. The current trend toward increased civilian participation in warfare has made this determination very difficult.[73] However, "on a battlefield no one is without some status,"[74] and this "battlefield status" determines the associated rights, duties, and responsibilities of both warfare participants and other persons not engaged in the hostilities.[75] Thus, identifying a person's status, though often difficult in contemporary warfare, is a necessity as an individual's "role in the armed conflict" determines "their associated legal protections."[76]

In international armed conflicts, the Law of Armed Conflict broadly divides individual's into two classifications, combatants and civilians, with consideration of noncombatants in subset categories.[77] However, in modern-day asymmetric wars involving terrorism, the traditional state-to-state conflict is rare and non-international armed conflicts are the norm. As such, the so-called unlawful combatant, or unprivileged belligerent, is increasingly more prominent as a de facto individual status.[78] While an unprivileged belligerent is not technically an additional category of battlefield status, it is effectively "a shorthand expression . . . describing those civilians who take up arms without being authorized to do so by international law."[79] As an individual's status during hostilities—whether combatant, civilian, non-combatant, or unprivileged belligerent—will determine the extent of his protections and immunities, it is important to briefly define each specific categorization.

Combatants

Combatants are defined generally as "[m]embers of the armed forces of a Party to a conflict" that "have the right to participate directly in hostilities."[80] "While for the purposes of the principle of distinction members of State armed forces may be considered combatants in both international and non-international armed conflicts," combatant status only exists "in international armed conflicts."[81] The Law of Armed Conflict includes as combatants: the regular armed forces of a State Party to the conflict; members of militia, volunteer corps, and organized resistance movements that are under responsible command, have a fixed, distinctive sign recognizable at a distance, carry their arms openly, and conduct their operations in accordance with the laws of war; members of a regular armed force who profess their allegiance to a government or authority not recognized by the detaining power; and those inhabitants of a non-occupied territory that form a *levee en masse*.[82] All members of the armed forces, save those with protected status such as medical and religious personnel,[83] are considered combatants even if they do not participate in hostilities, as the status is only concerned with the legal right to participate and not actual conduct during hostilities. As a result, an individual deemed a combatant may "immediately be targeted without any specific conduct"[84] on his or her part unless "out of combat" through surrender, capture, or *hor de combat*.[85]

If captured by the enemy, a combatant is entitled to the status of prisoner of war "subject to the *conditio sine quo non*" that he is operating in accordance with the obligations required to attain combatant status.[86] As a prisoner of war, the individual enjoys assimilation rights[87] and can assert combatant privilege from prosecution.[88] This privilege, oftentimes called "combatant immunity," shields a prisoner of war from any "criminal responsibility for killing or injuring enemy military personnel or civilians taking an active part in hostilities, or for causing damage or destruction to property," provided their actions complied with the Law of Armed Conflict.[89] Captured combatants are therefore "not regarded as criminals or convicts . . . [but] guarded as a measure of security and not of punishment."[90]

Noncombatants

"Noncombatant" is a broad term that covers a myriad of individuals involved, though not actively participating, in either an international or non-international armed conflict. Military medical and religious personnel, prisoners of war, and those who are *hor de combat*—"out of combat"—are all considered noncombatants.[91] Some general protections are provided to those with a noncombatant status, including an absolute prohibition on being attacked[92] and a requirement for humane treatment.[93] However, noncombatants also may have other specific protections dependent upon the type of armed conflict and their particular situation. For example, a combatant captured by the enemy during an international armed conflict will have the enumerated protections described in Geneva Convention III, whereas during a non-international armed conflict a captured fighter will be protected only by Common Article 3 and other applicable customary international law.

Though both may be considered a "noncombatant" upon capture, the prisoner of war "must be released and repatriated without delay after the end of hostilities,"[94] while insurgent fighters may be "prosecuted for their unlawful acts, either by a military court or under the domestic law of the capturing state."[95] Thus, unlike combatant status, which exclusively applies in international armed conflict and confers express obligations and rights, noncombatant status is an overarching battlefield categorization that provides universal general protections to a variety of uniquely situated individual battlefield participants.

Civilians

Despite the obvious significance of distinguishing between combatants and civilians in warfare, the Law of Armed Conflict does not define the term "civilians."[96] However, the commentary to Additional Protocol I states that "the principle protection of the civilian population is inseparable from the principle of distinction which should be made between military and civilian persons," and therefore "it is essential to have a clear definition of each of these categories."[97] As a result, a civilian is defined as "any person who does not belong to one of the categories referred to in Article 4(A)(1), (2), (3) and (6) of the Third Geneva Convention and in Article 43 of this Protocol."[98] Those listed in Article 4(4) and (5)—examples include journalist and others that accompany the armed force—maintain their civilian status but are afforded the special status as a prisoner of war if captured.[99] As the "protection of civilians is one of the main goals" of the Law of Armed Conflict,[100] a civilian is guaranteed "not only his life, health and dignity . . . but even his personal liberty."[101] However, this status is not absolute, as a civilian only "enjoy[s] the protections afforded" by the Law of Armed Conflict "unless and for such time as they take a direct part in hostilities."[102] Thus, if an enemy civilian takes up arms "or participate[s] actively in hostilities," the benefits of civilian status are forfeited.[103]

Unprivileged Belligerents

The term "unprivileged belligerent," also sometimes referred to as unlawful combatant, is not a distinct individual battlefield status[104] and does "not appear in the Geneva Conventions, Additional Protocols, or any other LOAC treaty, convention or protocol."[105] The term is instead descriptive for those who unlawfully engage in combat activities by taking a part in hostilities "without being entitled to do so."[106] Unprivileged belligerents may include spies and saboteurs,[107] mercenaries,[108] members of a state armed force who violate the Law of Armed Conflict,[109] members of a non-state armed group,[110] or civilians who "directly participate in hostilities."[111]

There are a number of adverse consequences associated with being labeled an unprivileged belligerent or unlawful combatant. Similar to a combatant, an unprivileged belligerent remains a lawful target regardless of his location or activities.[112] However, if captured, an unprivileged belligerent is not afforded prisoner of war protections or any combatant privileges.[113] Without immunity, unprivileged belligerents "may be prosecuted and punished to the extent that their activities, their membership, or the harm caused by them is penalized under national law"[114] even if "these acts do not constitute war crimes under international law."[115] For example, "[A]l Qaeda fighters who directly participate in hostilities" are considered unprivileged belligerents as they cannot gain combatant status.[116] As a result, they may be "targeted as combatants" but if captured are not entitled to prisoner of war status but rather may "be interned and tried in domestic or military courts for acts they committed that rendered them unlawful combatants."[117] The harsh penalties of unprivileged belligerency are intended to "simultaneously reward soldiers for being readily identifiable and deter civilians from entering the fray, thereby keeping the line between combatants and civilians as discernible as possible and maximizing civilian safety."[118]

What Are the Basic Rules of Conduct in Warfare?

The Meta-Principles: Military Necessity and Humanity

The Law of Armed Conflict "is predicated on a subtle equilibrium between two diametrically opposed impulses: military necessity and humanitarian considerations."[119] The balance between these countervailing concepts "permeates throughout the entirety of the law ensuring that force is applied on the battlefield in a manner that allows for the accomplishment of the mission while simultaneously taking appropriate humanitarian considerations into account."[120] Military necessity, which is the recognition that during warfare peacetime norms are relaxed,[121] cannot be left unchecked or warfare is defined by "brutality and savagery."[122] Conversely, "if benevolent humanitarianism were the only beacon to guide the path of armed forces, war would have entailed no bloodshed, no destruction and no human suffering; in short, war would not have been war."[123] The challenge underscoring all Law of Armed Conflict norms is therefore to "fix 'the technical limits at which the necessities of war ought to yield to the requirements of humanity'"[124] and to ensure that neither principle gains primacy. The Law of Armed Conflict, and all subordinate positive law, is built upon the basic premise that human suffering should be minimized without "undermining the effectiveness of military operations."[125] Thus, considerations of military necessity and humanity "constitute guiding principles for the interpretation of the rights and duties of belligerents within the parameters" established within the specific provisions of the Law of Armed Conflict.[126]

Basic Principles of the Law of Armed Conflict

The legality of a conflict participant's conduct during armed conflict is examined "in the light of the core concepts, the four of which are closely intertwined."[127] These four core concepts—military necessity, distinction, proportionality, and unnecessary suffering—are at the foundation of the Law of Armed Conflict and generally govern the conduct of hostilities. A summary of each principle helps identify legal and illegal actions in warfare.

Military Necessity

Military necessity is generally considered one of the four basic principles of the Law of Armed Conflict.[128] However, as noted above, military necessity is best understood not as a stand-alone principle but rather as a broad "attempt to realize the purpose of armed conflict, gaining military advantage," which is counterbalanced by the humanitarian consideration of "minimizing human suffering and physical destruction" in warfare.[129] Defined in contemporary doctrine as "those measures not forbidden by international law which are indispensable for securing the complete submission of the enemy as soon as possible,"[130] the principle "proscribes, indirectly, what might otherwise constitute lawful acts of warfare."[131] Military necessity is thus a "meta-principle" with general applicability that permeates throughout the entirety of the Law of Armed Conflict, which is continually addressed in subsidiary positive law.[132] More specifically, military necessity is "discounted in the rules" that comprise the Law of Armed Conflict, with the particular provisions of the law either allowing for violence and destruction or forbidding such conduct out of deference to humanitarian considerations.[133]

For example, Hague Regulation IV Article 23(g) makes it forbidden "to destroy or seize the enemy's property, unless such destruction or seizure be imperatively demanded by the necessities of war."[134] In contrast, Hague Regulation IV Article 28 states, "The pillage of a town or place, even when taken by assault, is prohibited."[135] While Article 23(g) makes allowances for military necessity, Article 28 absolutely forbids consideration of the principle.[136] Further, in those circumstances where the positive law does not establish a specific standard, military necessity remains accounted for through a "blend of positive requirements" and "prohibitions."[137] Thus, for practical purposes, referencing the "self-contained nature of the individual rules" is more useful for determining when military necessity applies than alluding to the overarching principle.[138] "[I]t can be stated categorically that no part" of the Law of Armed Conflict "overlooks military requirements, just as no part . . . loses sight of humanitarian considerations," as every legal norm is crafted with these two principles in mind.[139]

Distinction

Distinction, or discrimination, considered a "fundamental and 'intransgressible'"[140] principle, is a historical practice that is universally recognized in both customary practice and treaty law as inviolable.[141] The principle of distinction, "[i]n order to ensure respect for and protection of the civilian population and objects," requires "the Parties to the conflict" to "at all times distinguish between the civilian population and combatants and between civilian objects and military objectives and accordingly . . . direct their operations only against military objectives."[142] Distinction is the most significant of the core principles, as "[i]t is the foundation on which the codification of the laws and customs of war rests."[143]

The principle of distinction legally obligates conflict participants to target only military objectives[144] and combatants[145] while simultaneously distinguishing themselves from the civilian population.[146] Embedded within this obligation is an absolute prohibition on the intentional targeting of civilians or indiscriminate attacks.[147] However, civilian casualties or injuries do not necessarily indicate a violation of the distinction principle, as incidental loss of civilian life may lawfully occur during military operations.[148] To ensure that "the clearest possible distinction between combatants and civilians"[149] exists, belligerents have an affirmative duty to "distinguish themselves from the civilian population so as not to place the civilian population at undue risk."[150] This duty includes "not only physical separation of military forces and other military objectives from civilian objects . . . but also other actions, such as wearing uniforms."[151] Though the modern shift toward asymmetric warfare has increasingly blurred the traditional lines demarcating combatant from civilian,[152] conflict participants remain responsible for determining "how . . . the principle of distinction should be implemented in the challenging and complex circumstances of contemporary warfare."[153]

Proportionality

The principle of proportionality requires conflict participants to balance the necessity of a military action with the protection of civilians and their property during military operations.[154] The proportionality principle holds that an attack "which may be expected to cause incidental loss of civilian life, injury to civilians, damage to civilian objects, or a combination thereof which would be excessive in relation to the concrete and direct military advantage anticipated" is considered indiscriminate and a Law of Armed Conflict violation.[155] However, while the Law of Armed Conflict strictly prohibits the intentional targeting of civilians and civilian objects,[156] it does "recognize the inevitability of collateral civilian casualties."[157] The principle therefore carefully uses the term "incidental"[158] to distinguish the resultant loss of civilian life or property from illegal intentional targeting of the civilian population.[159]

A violation of the principle of proportionality is thus dependent upon what constitutes an "excessive" loss of civilian life or property. As "no rule can foresee every potential application,"[160] a determination whether the incidental loss of civilian life or damage to civilian objects is "excessive" is driven by the specific facts and circumstances surrounding the decision.[161] The principle of proportionality judges whether "a reasonable well-informed person in the circumstances . . . making reasonable use of the information available to him or her, could have expected excessive casualties to result from the attack,"[162] and therefore "to violate proportionality, the discrepancy between loss of civilian life and destruction of civilian objects must be clearly disproportionate to the direct military advantage anticipated."[163] At times, the injury to civilians and damage to their property "can be exceedingly extensive without being excessive, simply because the military advantage anticipated is of paramount importance."[164] As such, this limiting principle had awkwardly proven to have tremendous tolerance for even significant afflictions on the civilian population yet, "notwithstanding, there is still widespread agreement that in times of armed conflict a better, equally realistic alternative simply does not exist."[165]

Unnecessary Suffering

Unlike the broader meta-principle of humanity, which informs the entire body of the Law of Armed Conflict, the principle of unnecessary suffering is singularly focused on the interaction between combatants.[166] As a general rule the "right of belligerents to adopt means of injuring the enemy is not unlimited"[167] and thus "[i]t is prohibited to employ weapons, projectiles and material and methods of warfare of a nature to cause superfluous injury or unnecessary suffering."[168] This principle therefore regulates the development and use of weapons by prohibiting military personnel from using arms "per se calculated to cause unnecessary suffering" or using otherwise lawful weapons "in a manner calculated to cause unnecessary suffering."[169]

Unnecessary suffering is left undefined within the Law of Armed Conflict. However, "the prohibition of unnecessary suffering constitutes acknowledgement that necessary suffering to combatants is lawful,"[170] and therefore a weapon is not banned "merely because it causes 'great' or even 'horrendous' suffering or injury."[171] Instead, a weapon must "increase suffering without really increasing military advantage,"[172] and "[t]hus in principle it is necessary to weigh up the nature of the injury or the intensity of suffering" against "the 'military necessity' before deciding whether there is a case of superfluous injury or unnecessary suffering."[173]

In practicality it is difficult to assess whether a weapon, or how it is used, violates the principle of unnecessary suffering, as "in the eyes of the victim all suffering is superfluous and any injury is unnecessary."[174] Interpretations of what constitutes unnecessary suffering are inconsistent, and no coherent test exists which objectively weighs a weapon's "effect on the victim" against "military necessity."[175] For this reason, enforcement of the principle of unnecessary suffering is dependent upon either "the practice of States or on their express agreement to prohibitions or restrictions on the use" of a particular weapon.[176]

Conclusion

This chapter provides a general framework for analyzing Law of Armed Conflict issues and is by no means a detailed or comprehensive study of this extensive body of international law. However, a basic understanding of conflict classification, individual battlefield status, and the general principles that regulate conflicts helps clarify "the rights and protections afforded a fighter . . . as well as the prohibitions that may apply to his/her conduct."[177] Upon this foundation all additional analysis and application of the Law of Armed Conflict follows and informs the more specific rules that regulate warfare. Perhaps more important, it is through this prism that the legality of all contemporary warfare challenges—whether it is the use of a drone to kill a terrorist operative, detention of a member of Al-Qaeda, or a cyber-attack by a state actor—is initially viewed and scrutinized. As non-state armed groups, faced with tremendous disparity in military strength and capabilities, continue to feign protected status, mingle "combatants and military objectives with the civilian population and civilian objects," and use "civilians as human shields"[178] it is imperative that interested parties realize that this conduct is unequivocally prohibited by the law. This understanding can only begin by gaining a working knowledge of the basic tenets of the Law of Armed Conflict.

Notes

1. *See* David Wallace & Shane R. Reeves, *The Law of Armed Conflict's "Wicked" Problem: Levee en Masse in Cyber Warfare*, 89 INT'L L. STUD. 646 (2013); U.S. DEP'T OF DEF. QUADRENNIAL DEFENSE REVIEW REPORT 8, February 2010 [hereinafter QDR] (discussing the difficulty in categorizing contemporary conflicts).

2. GARY SOLIS, THE LAW OF ARMED CONFLICT: INTERNATIONAL HUMANITARIAN LAW IN WAR 239 (2010).

3. *See* U.S. DEP'T OF ARMY, TRADOC PAM. 525-3-1, THE UNITED STATES ARMY OPERATING CONCEPT 2016-2028 [hereinafter CAPSTONE CONCEPT], ¶ 2–2(a) (Aug. 19, 2010).

4. *See* Robert Gates, U.S. Sec'y of Defense, Remarks at Maxwell Air Force Base, Ala. (Apr. 15, 2009), *at* http://www. defense.gov/transcripts/transcript.aspx?transcriptid=4403 (discussing how modern conflicts encompass a broad spectrum of operations and lethality).

5. SOLIS, *supra* note 2, at 157 (quoting Christopher Greenwood, *Scope of Application of Humanitarian Law*, *in* THE HANDBOOK OF HUMANITARIAN LAW IN ARMED CONFLICT 45, 74 (Dieter Fleck ed., Oxford Press 2d ed. 2007)).

6.   David Wallace & Shane Reeves, *Non-State Armed Groups and Technology: The Humanitarian Tragedy at Our Doorstep?*, 3 U. MIAMI NAT. SEC. & LAW OF ARMED CONFLICT J. 1, 15 (forthcoming summer 2013).

7.   *Id.*

8.   *See* Kenneth F. McKenzie Jr., *The Rise of Asymmetric Threats: Priorities for Defense Planning, in* NAT'L DEF. UNIV., QDR 2001 STRATEGY-DRIVEN CHOICES FOR AMERICA'S SECURITY 75, 88 (Michele A Flournoy ed., 2001).

9.   *Id.*

10.   INT'L COMM. OF THE RED CROSS, ADVISORY SERVICE ON INTERNATIONAL HUMANITARIAN LAW, *What is International Humanitarian Law?* (2004), *at* http://www.icrc.org/eng/assets/files/ other/ what_is_ihl.pdf (last visited May 3, 2013) [hereinafter ICRC IHL].

11.   *See* MORRIS GREENSPAN, THE MODERN LAW OF LAND WARFARE 62 (1959).

12.   *See* SOLIS, *supra* note 2, at 1.

13.   *See* ROBERT KOLB & RICHARD HYDE, AN INTRODUCTION TO INTERNATIONAL LAW OF ARMED CONFLICT 37 2008) (discussing how warfare was traditionally harsh, with few rules limiting the conduct of participants).

14.   *See* JOHN KEEGAN, WAR AND OUR WORLD 26 (2001) (stating, "[w]ar may have got worse with the passage of time, but the ethic of restraint has rarely been wholly absent from its practice . . . Even in the age of total warfare . . . there remained taboos."); SOLIS, *supra* note 2, at 3.

15.   HUGO GROTIUS, ON THE LAW OF WAR AND PEACE 9 (Stephen C. Neff ed., 2012).

16.   *See* Brian J. Bill, *The Rendulic "Rule": Military Necessity, Commander's Knowledge, and Methods of Warfare, in* 12 YEARBOOK OF INTERNATIONAL HUMANITARIAN LAW 119 (2009).

17.   GEOFFREY BEST, WAR & LAW SINCE 1945 5 (2002).

18.   *Id.*

19.   The United Nations Charter prohibits the threat or use of force by state actors. *See* U.N. Charter art. 2, para. 4 ("All members shall refrain in their international relations from the threat or use of force against the territorial integrity or political independence of any state."). There are two generally recognized exceptions to this broad legal prohibition: actions authorized by the U.N. Security Council, *see id.* art. 39, or when a state is acting under its "inherent right of individual or collective self-defense." *See id.* art 51. When can a state justifiably exercise its right of self-defense is debatable and outside the scope of this chapter. For a more detailed discussion, *see generally* INT'L & OPERATIONAL LAW DEP'T, THE JUDGE ADVOCATE GENERAL'S LEGAL CTR. & SCH., U.S. ARMY, LAW OF ARMED CONFLICT DESKBOOK 29–35 (2010) [hereinafter DESKBOOK] (discussing the various views on the inherent right of self-defense in *jus ad bellum*).

20.   Major Shane R. Reeves & Lt. Col. Jeremy Marsh, *Bin Laden and Awlaki: Lawful Targets*, HARV. INT'L REV., web perspectives, Oct. 26, 2011, *available at* http://hir.harvard.edu/ bin-laden-and-awlaki-lawful-targets (last visited June 4, 2013).

21.   Robert Kolb, *Origin of the Twin Terms Jus Ad Bellum/Jus In Bello*, 320 INT'L REV. RED CROSS 553, 553 n.1 (Oct. 31, 1997), *available at* http://www.icrc.org/eng/resources/documents/ misc/57jnuu.htm (last visited June 22, 2013).

22.   *See* Jasmine Moussa, *Can the Jus ad Bellum Override the Jus in Bello? Reaffirming the Separation of the Two Bodies of Law*, 90 INT'L REV. OF THE RED CROSS 963, 965 (Dec. 2008).

23.   Andrew J. Carswell, *Classifying the Conflict: A Soldier's Dilemma*, 91 INT'L REV. RED CROSS 143, 152 (Mar. 2009), *available at* http://www.icrc.org/eng/resources/documents/article/ review/review-873-p143.htm (last visited May 22, 2013).

24.   *See* Moussa, *supra* note 22, at 968 (quoting MICHAEL WALZER, JUST AND UNJUST WAR. A MORAL ARGUMENT WITH HISTORICAL ILLUSTRATIONS 21 (2d ed. 1997)).

25. *Id.*

26.   Asymmetric warfare is defined as "leveraging inferior tactical or operational strength against the vulnerabilities of a superior opponent to achieve a disproportionate effect with the aim of undermining the opponent's will in order to achieve the asymmetric actor's strategic objectives." McKenzie, *supra* note 8, at 76.

27.   Moussa, *supra* note 22, at 988 (citing Theodore P. Seto, *The Morality of Terrorism*, 35 Loy. L.A. L. Rev. 1227, 1227 (2002)).

28.   Toni Pfanner, *Asymmetrical Warfare from the Perspective of Humanitarian Law and Humanitarian Action*, 87 Int'l Rev. Red Cross 149, 159 (2005), *available at* http://www.icrc.org/ Web/eng/siteeng0.nsf/htmlall/review-857-p149/ile/irrc_857_Pfanner.pdf (noting that that "concepts of 'crusade' and '*jihad*' are increasingly used" by non-state groups to justify violence).

29.   Moussa, *supra* note 22, at 988.

30.   *Id.*

31.   *Compare* Sean D. Murphy, *Assessing the Legality of Invading Iraq*, 92 Geo. L.J. 173 (2004) (asserting that the U.S. lacked a legitimate basis for using force against Iraq) *with* U.S. Dep't of Justice, Office of Legal Counsel: Mem. Op. for the Counsel to the President (Nov. 8 2002), *at* http://www.usdoj.gov/olc/2002/iraq-unscr-final.pdf (last visited June 5, 2013) (arguing the legality of the use of force against Iraq).

32.   When a state may respond in self-defense against a non-state-armed group located inside a passive state host is an unresolved issue. *See, e.g.,* Ashley S. Deeks, *Pakistan's Sovereignty and the Killing of Osama Bin Laden*, Am. Soc'y of Int'l Law Insights, *at* http://www. asil.org / insights110505.cfm (last visited June 7, 2013) ("the most controversial aspect . . . is the U.S. argument that this conflict can and does extend beyond the 'hot battlefield' of Afghanistan to wherever members of al Qaeda are found"). Many scholars "base the legality of cross-border attacks against non-state actors on whether the 'host' State is unwilling or unable to deal with the non-state actors who are launching armed attacks from within the territory." Deskbook, *supra* note 19, at 35 (referencing Yoram Dinstein, War, Aggression and Self-Defence 244–46 (4th ed. 2005)). *See also* Michael Schmitt, *Responding to Transnational Terrorism under the Jus Ad Bellum: A Normative Framework*, 56 Naval L. Rev. 1 (2009) (discussing the extra responsibilities of a state crossing borders to engage a terrorist organization in a host nation).

33.   Yoram Dinstein, The Conduct of Hostilities under the Law of International Armed Conflict 4–5 (2d ed., 2010).

34.   *Id.* at 4.

35.   Capt. (U.S. Navy) Brian J. Bill, *Human Rights: Time for Greater Judge Advocate Understanding*, The Army Lawyer 54, 58 (June 2010).

36.   "Special law prevails over general law." *Id.*

37.   ICRC IHL, *supra* note 10; *see also* U.S. Dep't of Def., Directive 2311.01E: DoD Law of War Program, ¶ 3.1 (2006), *available at* http://www.dtic.mil/whs/directives/corres/pdf/ 231101e.pdf [hereinafter DoD LoW Program] (defining the law of war as the part of international law that regulates the "conduct of armed hostilities" and is often called "the law of armed conflict"). The law of war, the law of armed conflict, and international humanitarian law are interchangeable. For the remainder of this chapter, we will use the term "law of armed conflict."

38.   *See generally* Geneva Convention for the Amelioration of the Condition of the Wounded and Sick in Armed Forces in the Field, Aug. 12, 1949, 6 U.S.T. 3114, 75 U.N.T.S. 31 [hereinafter GC I].

39.   *See generally* Geneva Convention for the Amelioration of the Condition of Wounded, Sick and Shipwrecked Members of Armed Forces at Sea, Aug. 12, 1949, 6 U.S.T. 3217, 75 U.N.T.S. 85 [hereinafter GC II].

40.   *See generally* Geneva Convention Relative to the Treatment of Prisoners of War, Aug. 12, 1949, 6 U.S.T. 3316, 75 U.N.T.S. 135 [hereinafter GC III].

41.   *See generally* Geneva Convention Relative to the Protection of Civilian Persons in Time of War, Aug. 12, 1949, 6 U.S.T. 3516, 75 U.N.T.S. 287 [hereinafter GC IV].

42.   *See generally* Hague Convention No. IV, Respecting the Laws and Customs of War on Land, Oct. 18, 1907, 36 Stat. 2227, and Annex, 36 Stat. 2295 [hereinafter Hague Regulation IV]; Hague Convention No. V, Respecting the Rights and Duties of Neutral Powers and Persons in Case of War on Land, Oct. 18, 1907, 36 Stat. 2310; and Hague Convention No. IX, Respecting Bombardment by Naval Forces in Time of War, Oct. 18, 1907, 36 Stat. 2351.

43.   The rules "relating to the methods and means of warfare are primarily derived from articles 22 through 41" of Hague IV. INT'L & OPERATIONAL LAW DEP'T, THE JUDGE ADVOCATE GENERAL'S LEGAL CTR. & SCH., U.S. ARMY, OPERATIONAL LAW HANDBOOK 14 (2012) [hereinafter HANDBOOK]. *See also* Derek Jinks, *Protective Parity and the Laws of War,* 79 NOTRE DAME L. REV. 1493, 1494 (2004) ("This is not to say that Geneva Law includes no rules governing means and methods of warfare, or that Hague law includes no rules governing the treatment of war victims … [but this] terminology, although conceptually imprecise, emphasizes the distinction between the two kinds of regimes—one governing the treatment of person subject to the enemy's authority (Geneva law), the other governing the treatment of person subject to the enemy's lethality (Hague law).").

44.   In 1977 Additional Protocol I and Protocol II were drafted to supplement the 1949 Geneva Conventions under the belief that neither the "Geneva Tradition" nor the "Hague Tradition" sufficiently covered areas of warfare and, as a result, "represent a mix of both" traditions. DESKBOOK, *supra* note 19, at 19. It is important to note that, unlike the Hague and Geneva Conventions, the United States has not ratified AP I or AP II, but finds many portions of the protocol customary international law. *See generally* Michael J. Matheson, *Remarks on the United States Position on the Relation of Customary International Law to the 1977 Protocols Additional to the 1949 Geneva Conventions,* 2 AM. U.J. INT'L L. & POL'Y 419 (1987).

45.   *See, e.g.,* Convention on Prohibitions or Restrictions on the Use of Certain Conventional Weapons Which May Be Deemed to Be Excessively Injurious or to Have Indiscriminate Effects, Oct. 10, 1980, 1342 U.N.T.S. 137 [hereinafter CCW]; 1954 Hague Convention on Cultural Property, May 14, 1954, 249 U.N.T.S. 240.

46.   *See* ICRC IHL, *supra* note 10 ("Many provisions of international humanitarian law are now accepted as customary law—that is, as general rules by which all States are bound.").

47.   U.S. DEP'T OF THE ARMY, FIELD MANUAL 27-10, THE LAW OF LAND WARFARE 3 (Change 1, 1976) [hereinafter FM 27-10].

48.   *Compare* SOLIS, *supra* note 2, at 14 (noting that, despite a dramatic increase in the number of treaties since World War II, customary international law remains the basis for much of the Law of Armed Conflict) *with* Bill, *supra* note 16, at 131 (stating "[t]he law of war has become, and will continue to develop as, a set of positive rules, displacing customary notions of conduct.").

49.   *See* ICRC IHL, *supra* note 10 (stating "international humanitarian law applies only to [international or non-international] armed conflict; it does not cover internal tensions or disturbances such as isolated acts of violence. The law applies only once a conflict has begun, and then equally to all sides regardless of who started the fighting.").

50.   *See* DESKBOOK, *supra* note 19, at 39 ("All four Geneva Conventions of 1949 have 'common articles' which are verbatim in each.").

51.   GC I, *supra* note 38, art. 2. The 1977 Additional Protocol I, which supplements the Geneva Conventions, also applies "in the situation referred to in Article 2" as well as in those "armed

conflicts which peoples are fighting against colonial domination and alien occupation and against racist regimes in the exercise of their right of self-determination." Protocol Additional to the Geneva Conventions of 12 August 1949, and Relating to the Protection of Victims of International Armed Conflict (Protocol I) art. 1(3)–(4), June 8, 1977, 1125 U.N.T.S. 3 [hereinafter AP I]. This controversial expansion of the term "armed conflict" is one of the reasons the U.S. has not ratified the treaty. *See* DESKBOOK, *supra* note 19, at 21. However, the U.S. finds much of Additional Protocol I and II as customary international law and is therefore obligated to follow those specific provisions when an armed conflict is triggered. *See generally* Matheson, *supra* note 44.

52. INT'L COMM. OF THE RED CROSS COMMENTARY, III GENEVA CONVENTION RELATIVE TO THE TREATMENT OF PRISONERS OF WAR 23 (Jean S. Pictet et al. ed., 1960) [hereinafter COMMENTARY, GC III].

53. HELEN DUFFY, THE "WAR ON TERROR" AND THE FRAMEWORK OF INTERNATIONAL LAW 219 (2005) (The Geneva Convention Common Article 2 "shall apply to all cases of declared war or of any other armed conflict which may arise between two or more of the High Contracting Parties, even if the state of war is not recognized by one of them.") .

54. *See* COMMENTARY, GC III, *supra* note 52, at 23 ("Any difference arising between two States and leading to the intervention of members of the armed forces is an armed conflict within the meaning of Article 2, even if one of the Parties denies the existence of a state of war.").

55. *See* DESKBOOK, *supra* note 19, at 18–20 (noting that the entirety of the Law of Armed Conflict applies in an international armed conflict). It is important to note that the Law of Armed Conflict is also the applicable law in cases of "partial or total occupation." GC I, *supra* note 38, art. 2.

56. "Armed conflict not of an international character occurring in the territory of the High Contracting Parties" is defined as a non-international armed conflict. *See, e.g.,* GC I, *supra* note 38, art. 3. "Non-international armed conflict generally arises, as the ICTY noted, 'within a state,' although the conflict need not unfold, at least entirely, within one state's geographic borders." DUFFY, *supra* note 53, at 222.

57. "Whereas the existence of an international armed conflict triggers the entire body of the law of war, the existence of an internal armed conflict only triggers application of Common Article 3's" protections. *See* DESKBOOK, *supra* note 19, at 22.

58. Additional Protocol II supplements "Article 3 common to the Geneva Conventions" but limits the applicability of the law to only those situations where "dissident armed forces or other organized armed groups" which are "under responsible command" and exercise "control over a part" of a state. *See* Protocol Additional to the Geneva Conventions of August 1949, and Relating to the Protection of Victims of Non-International Armed Conflict (Protocol II) art. 1, June 8, 1977, 1125 U.N.T.S. 609 [hereinafter AP II]. These formal conditions for applicability are in contrast to the more vague and nonbinding criteria established in the commentary to the Geneva Conventions and are another objection the U.S. has to the additional protocols. *See infra* note 64 and accompanying text (discussing the distinction between internal disturbance and non-international armed conflict).

59. Due to the internal nature of these conflicts, domestic law will still apply and, "unlike combatants during international armed conflict, guerrillas do not receive immunity for their war-like acts." *See* DESKBOOK, *supra* note 19, at 22.

60. *See* COMMENTARY, GC III, *supra* note 52, at 34 ("Article 3 is like a 'Convention in miniature.' It applies to non-international conflicts only, and will be the only Article applicable" to the conflict participants).

61. SOLIS, *supra* note 2, at 153–54.

62. *See* AP II, *supra* note 58, art. 1(2).

63. *See* COMMENTARY, GC III, *supra* note 52, at 36–37 ("No Government can object to observing, in its dealings with enemies, whatever the nature of the conflict between it and them, a few essential rules. . . .").

64. The commentaries to the Geneva Conventions give a list of nonbinding criteria that include: the non-state armed group is an organized military force, under responsible command, with control of territory, respects the Law of Armed Conflict, and the state actor responds with their regular armed forces. *See* COMMENTARY, GC III, *supra* note 52, at 36. The International Criminal Court describes a non-international armed conflict as one that takes place in the territory of a State when there is protracted armed conflict between government authorities and organized armed groups or between such groups. Rome Statute of the International Criminal Court, art. 8(2)(f), July 17, 1998, U.N.T.S. 90.

65. ICRC IHL, *supra* note 10 (stating, "International humanitarian law applies only to [international or non-international] armed conflict; it does not cover internal tensions or disturbances such as isolated acts of violence. The law applies only once a conflict has begun, and then equally to all sides regardless of who started the fighting.").

66. *See* Robin Geiss & Michael Siegrist, *Has the Armed Conflict in Afghanistan Affected the Rules on the Conduct of Hostilities?*, 93 INT'L REV. RED CROSS 11 (2011).

67. *Id.*

68. *See* GC I, *supra* note 38, art. 2.

69. *See id.* The Law of Armed Conflict remains the applicable body of law during a partial or total occupation of a territory. *Id.*

70. SOLIS, *supra* note 2, at 154.

71. *See* Carswell, *supra* note 23, at 151 ("[T]he law is asking commanders to make an *ex post facto* determination regarding a series of events that has yet to occur."). The U.S., in recognition of the ambiguity of the contemporary battlefield, mandates that all military members "comply with the law of war during all armed conflicts, however such conflicts are characterized, and in all other military operations." DoD LoW PROGRAM, *supra* note 37, para.1.

72. SOLIS, *supra* note 2, at 149–86.

73. *See* INT'L COMM. OF THE RED CROSS, INTERPRETIVE GUIDANCE ON THE NOTION OF DIRECT PARTICIPATION IN HOSTILITIES UNDER INTERNATIONAL HUMANITARIAN LAW 7 (Nils Melzer ed., 2009), *available at* http://www.icrc.org/ eng/assets /files/other/icrc-002-0990.pdf [hereinafter ICRC INTERPRETIVE GUIDANCE].

74. SOLIS, *supra* note 2, at 187.

75. Sean Watts, *The Notion of Combatancy in Cyber Warfare*, 4th Int'l Conference on Cyber Conflict, NATO Cooperative Cyber Defence Centre of Excellence 4 (2012). Professor Watts's conference paper updates concepts and ideas developed previously, and in great depth, in his article *Combatant Status and Computer Network Attack*, 50 VA. J. INT'L L. 392–449 (2009).

76. *See* DESKBOOK, *supra* note 19, at 40.

77. *See* DINSTEIN, *supra* note 33, at 27 (noting that the Law of Armed Conflict "posits a fundamental principle of distinction between combatants and civilians.").

78. *See id.* at 29 ("A person is not allowed to wear simultaneously two caps: the hat of a civilian and the helmet of a soldier. A person who engages in military raids by night, while purporting to be an innocent civilian by day, is neither a civilian nor a lawful combatant. He is an unlawful combatant.").

79. SOLIS, *supra* note 2, at 208.

80. AP I, *supra* note 51, art. 43(2). *See also* HANDBOOK, *supra* note 43, at 16 ("Combatants are military personnel lawfully engaging in hostilities in an armed conflict on behalf of a party to

the conflict. . . . [They] are also *privileged* belligerent, i.e., authorized to use force against the enemy on behalf of the state.").

81.   JEAN-MARIE HENCKAERTS & LOUISE DOSWALD-BECK, CUSTOMARY INTERNATIONAL HUMANITARIAN LAW: RULES (2005) [hereinafter RULES] Rule 3 (definition of combatant).

82.   GC I, *supra* note 38, art. 13; GC III, *supra* note 42, art. 4. AP I, article 44(3) allows a belligerent to attain combatant status by carrying his arms openly during each military engagement and when visible to an adversary while deploying for an attack. AP I, *supra* note 51, art. 44(3). "The Additional Protocol standard lowers the threshold for obtaining combatant status . . . by eliminating the classic requirement for 'having a fixed distinctive sign recognizable at a distance' . . . ." Jinks, *supra* note 43, at 1498. The U.S., concerned that the elimination of this requirement undercuts the principle of distinction, rejects AP I, art. 44(3) as customary law and maintains the traditional combatant requirements outlined in the Geneva Conventions. HANDBOOK, *supra* note 43, at 17.

83.   Medical and religious personnel, though members of the armed forces, are considered noncombatants. SOLIS, *supra* note 2, at 191–94.

84.   DESKBOOK, *supra* note 19, at 134. *See also* SOLIS, *supra* note 2, at 188 ("[I]f a combatant is home on leave and in uniform, far from the combat zone, and is somehow targeted by an opposing combatant, she remains a legitimate target and may be killed—just as the opposing combatant, if discovered outside the combat zone, may be killed by his enemy.").

85.   *See* LESLIE C. GREEN, THE CONTEMPORARY LAW OF ARMED CONFLICT 124 (2d ed. 2000) (stating that combatants are lawful targets who are continuously a "legitimate object of attack, but only as long as they are capable of fighting, willing to fight or resist capture.").

86.   DINSTEIN, *supra* note 33, at 29.

87.   "POWs are assimilated, for protective purposes, into the armed forces of the detaining state. As such, they are entitled to trial before the same courts, and according to the same procedures as member of the regular armed forces of the detaining state." Jinks, *supra* note 43, at 1506.

88.   "[T]hey bear no criminal responsibility for killing or injuring enemy military personnel or civilians taking an active part in hostilities, or for causing damage or destruction to property, provided their acts comply with the LOAC." HANDBOOK, *supra* note 43, at 16.

89.   *Id.*

90.   U.S. DEP'T OF THE ARMY, FIELD MANUAL 27-10, THE LAW OF LAND WARFARE 27 (1914). It is "especially forbidden" to "declare that no quarter will be given," to kill or wound "treacherously" an adversary's armed forces or those who have surrendered. Hague Regulation IV, *supra* note 42, art. 23.

91.   For a detailed list of all groups considered "noncombatants" *see* DESKBOOK, *supra* note 19, at 135–37.

92.   *Id.*

93.   *See, e.g.,* JEAN-MARIE HENCKAERTS & LOUISE DOSWALD-BECK, CUSTOMARY INTERNATIONAL HUMANITARIAN LAW: PRACTICE, 19872024-50 (§ 1–§ 354) (2005) [hereinafter PRACTICE] (discussing the fundamental guarantee of humane treatment for wounded and sick and persons deprived of their liberty); AP II, *supra* note 58, at Art. 4 ("All persons who do not take a direct part or who have ceased to take part in hostilities . . . shall in all circumstances be treated humanely, without any adverse distinction.").

94.   INT'L COMM. OF THE RED CROSS, PRISONERS OF WAR AND DETAINEES PROTECTED UNDER INTERNATIONAL HUMANITARIAN LAW, *at* http://www.icrc.org/eng/war-and-law/protected-persons/prisoners-war/overview-detainees-protected-persons.htm (last visited May 3, 2013).

95.   SOLIS, *supra* note 2, at 191.

96. *See, e.g.,* Derek Jinks, *The Declining Significance of POW Status,* 45 HARV. INT'L L.J. 367, 381 (2004) (noting that the Geneva Conventions do not define who falls within the category of "civilian.").

97. INT'L COMM. OF THE RED CROSS, COMMENTARY ON THE ADDITIONAL PROTOCOLS OF 8 JUNE 1977 TO THE GENEVA CONVENTIONS OF 12 AUGUST 1949, 610 (Yves Sandoz et al. eds., 1987) [hereinafter AP I COMMENTARY].

98. AP I, *supra* note 51, art. 50(1).

99. *See generally* GC III, *supra* note 40, art. 4(A)(4)(5).

100. ICRC INTERPRETIVE GUIDANCE, *supra* note 73, at 1.

101. DINSTEIN, *supra* note 33, at 29.

102. AP I, *supra* note 51, art. 51(3).

103. DINSTEIN, *supra* note 33, at 29–30.

104. *See* HCJ 769/02 Pub. Comm. Against Torture in Israel v. Gov't of Israel [2005], *at* http://elyon1.court.gov.il/ files_eng/02/690/007/e16/02007690.e16.htm (noting that according to the state of current international law there is no separate category for unprivileged belligerents).

105. SOLIS, *supra* note 2, at 206–08 (quoting CrimA 6659/06, Anonymous v. State of Israel [2008] *at* http://elyon1. court.gov.il/files_eng/06/590/066/n04/06066590.n04.htm).

106. Knut Dormann, *The Legal Situation of "Unlawful/Unprivileged Combatants,"* 85 INT'L REV. RED CROSS 45 (2003), *available at* http://www.icrc.org/Web/eng/siteeng0.nsf/htmlall/ 5LPHBV/.

107. *See* Hague Reg. IV, *supra* note 42, art. 2931; AP I, *supra* note 51, art. 46.

108. *See* AP I, *supra* note 51, art. 47 (stating "a mercenary shall not have the right to be a combatant or a prisoner of war.").

109. *See* DINSTEIN, *supra* note 33, at 29 ("[U]nder customary international law, a sanction (deprivation of the privileges of a prisoner of war) is imposed on any combatant masquerading as a civilian in order to mislead the enemy and avoid detection."); DESKBOOK, *supra* note 19, at 134 ("An unlawful combatant can be . . . a member of the armed forces who violates the laws of war.")

110. *See* ICRC INTERPRETIVE GUIDANCE, *supra* note 73, at 32–34. Individuals who are components of organized non-state armed groups are unlawful combatants due to their functional membership through their "continuous combat function" for the group. "Membership must depend on whether the continuous function assumed by an individual corresponds to that collectively exercised by the group as a whole, namely conduct of hostilities on behalf of a non-State party to the conflict." *Id.* at 31. Members of non-state armed groups do not have the privileges affiliated with combatant status. *Id.*

111. AP I, *supra* note 51, art. 51.3. There is much debate concerning what constitutes "a direct part in hostilities." *Compare* ICRC INTERPRETIVE GUIDANCE, *supra* note 73, at 5–6 ("The Interpretive Guidance provides a legal reading of the notion of 'direct participation in hostilities' with a view to strengthening the implementation of the principle distinction.") *with* Kenneth Watkin, *Opportunity Lost: Organized Armed Groups and the ICRC 'Direct Participation in Hostilities' Interpretive Guidance,* 42 N.Y.U. J. INT'L L. & POL'Y 641 (No. 3, 2010) *and* Michael N. Schmitt, *The Interpretive Guidance on the Notion of Direct Participation in Hostilities: A Critical Analysis,* 1 HARV. NAT. SEC. J. 1, 5 (May 2010) (criticizing the Interpretive Guidance recommendations). However, there is agreement that once a civilian directly participates in hostilities, his civilian status and protections are suspended and consequently "may be attacked in the same manner as identified members of an opposing armed force." HANDBOOK, *supra* note 43, at 20.

112. *See* DESKBOOK, *supra* note 19, at 134.

113.　*See Ex parte* Quirin, 317 U.S. 1, 30–31 (1942) ("Lawful combatants are subject to capture and detention as prisoners of war" while "[u]nlawful combatants are likewise subject to capture and detention, but in addition they are subject to trial and punishment . . . .").

114.　ICRC Interpretive Guidance, *supra* note 73, at 84.

115.　Dinstein, *supra* note 33, at 30–31 (*citing* Allan Rosas, The Legal Status of Prisoners of War: A Study in International Humanitarian Law Applicable in Armed Conflicts, 82 (1976)) ("Unlawful combatants 'may be punished under the internal criminal legislation of the adversary for having committed hostile acts in violation of its provisions (e.g., for murder), even if these acts do not constitute war crimes under international law.").

116.　Solis, *supra* note 2, at 219

117.　*Id.*

118.　Michael Byers, War Law: Understanding International Law and Armed Conflict 118 (2005).

119.　Dinstein, *supra* note 33, at 16.

120.　Shane R. Reeves & Jeff S. Thurhner, *Are We Reaching a Tipping Point? How Contemporary Challenges Are Affecting the Military Necessity-Humanity Balance,* Harv. Nat. Sec. J. Features Online 1 (2013).

121.　Bill, *supra* note 16, at 119 ("The concept of military necessity is a recognition that, at its most core level, war is different than peace. In war, actions are permitted which would not be permitted in peace.").

122.　Rob McLauglin, *The Law of Armed Conflict and International Human Rights Law: Some Paradigmatic Differences and Operational Implications, in* Yearbook of International Humanitarian Law 222 (Michael N. Schmitt ed., 2010) (citing United Kingdom Ministry of Defence, The Manual on the Law of Armed Conflict, 2004, ¶ 1.8.).

123.　Dinstein, *supra* note 33, at 16.

124.　*Id.* (citing *Declaration Renouncing the Use, in Time of War, of Explosive Projectiles Under 400 Grammes Weight* preamble, Nov. 29, 1868, 18 Martens Nouveau Recueil (ser. 1) 474). "The 1868 St. Petersburg Declaration, for example, explicitly recognized the need to strike such a balance." Michael N. Schmitt, *Military Necessity and Humanity in International Humanitarian Law: Preserving the Delicate Balance,* 50 Va. J.Int'l L., 795, 799 (2010).

125.　Dinstein, *supra* note 33, at 17.

126.　ICRC Interpretive Guidance, *supra* note 73, at 78–79.

127.　Solis, *supra* note 2, at 251.

128.　*See* Deskbook, *supra* note 19, at 131.

129.　Solis, *supra* note 2, at 260.

130.　FM 27-10, *supra* note 47, ¶ 3.a.

131.　Moussa, *supra* note 22, at 981.

132.　*See* Bill, *supra* note 16, at 131 ("Military necessity is a meta-principle of the law of war . . . in the sense that it justifies destruction in war. It permeates all subsidiary rules.").

133.　*Id.* at 129.

134.　Hague Reg. IV, *supra* note 42, art. 23(g). *See generally* Bill, *supra* note 16, at 129 n.49 (listing other examples of specific Law of Armed Conflict rules that allow for military necessity).

135.　Hague Reg. IV, *supra* note 42, art. 28.

136.　The concept of "military necessity" has also been used as an affirmative defense to war crimes. *See* Bill, *supra* note 16, at 132. This is most "associated with the German defendants tried after World War II" where the defendants asserted the maxim *"Kriegsraison geht vor Kriegmanier,"* or "the necessities of war go before the rules of war." *Id.* It is important to note that the German defendants did not claim "that military necessity as contained within a particular rule relieved them of culpability, but rather that military necessity excused them from following *any* rule, whether it contained a military necessity exception or not." *Id.* This defense was rejected, as "it has been repeatedly affirmed that this principle cannot be invoked to justify violations of international humanitarian law." Moussa, *supra* note 22, at 980–81.

137. Bill, *supra* note 16, at 132.

138. *Id.*

139. DINSTEIN, *supra* note 33, at 17.

140. Adv. Op., Legality of the Threat or Use of Nuclear Weapons, 1996 I.C.J. 226, 257 (July 8).

141. SOLIS, *supra* note 2, at 251–52.

142. AP I, *supra* note 51, art. 48.

143. AP I COMMENTARY, *supra* note 97, at 598.

144. "[M]ilitary objectives are limited to those objects which by their nature, location, purpose or use make an effective contribution to military action and whose total or partial destruction, capture or neutralization, in the circumstances ruling at the time, offers a definite military advantage." AP I, *supra* note 51, art. 52(2).

145. *See* RULES, *supra* note 81, at 3 (stating that hostilities "may only be directed against combatants . . . [but] must not be directed against civilians").

146. AP I, *supra* note 51, art. 51(2) ("[t]he civilian population as such, as well as individual civilians, shall not be the object of attack."); AP II, *supra* note 58, art. 13(1) ("[t]he civilian population and individual civilians shall enjoy general protections against the dangers arising from military operations.").

147. *See* AP I, *supra* note 51, art. 51(4)–(5).

148. *See id.* art. 51(5)(b). Civilians may also forfeit their protection from attack, as noted *infra* section IV.d., by directly participating in hostilities or acting as voluntary human shields. *See id.* art. 51(7).

149. BYERS, *supra* note 118, at 118.

150. W. Hays Park, *Special Forces' Wear of Non-Standard Uniforms*, 4 CHI. J. INT'L L. 493, 514 (2003).

151. *Id.*

152. Nils Melzer, *Foreword to Keeping the Balance Between Military Necessity and Humanity: A Response to Four Critiques of the ICRC's Interpretive Guidance on the Notion of Direct Participation in Hostilities*, 42 N.Y.U. J. INT'L L. & POL. 831, 833 (2010) (discussing the difficulties in contemporary armed conflicts due to the "blurring of the traditional distinctions and categories upon which the normative edifice of IHL has been built. . . .").

153. ICRC INTERPRETIVE GUIDANCE, *supra* note 73, at 7.

154. *See* HANDBOOK, *supra* note 43, at 12.

155. AP I, *supra* note 51, art. 51(5)(b); Art. 57(2)(b) (similarly directs that "an attack shall be cancelled or suspended if it becomes apparent that the objective is not a military one or . . . that the attack may be expected to cause incidental loss of human life, injury to civilians, damage to civilian objects, or a combination thereof, which would be excessive in relation to the concrete and direct military advantage anticipated."). *See also* FM 27-10, *supra* note 47, at ¶ 41.

156. *See* AP I, *supra* note 51, art. 51(2)–(3).

157. W. Hays Parks, *Rolling Thunder and the Law of War*, 33 AIR U. REV. 2 (Jan.-Feb. 1982) *at* http://www.airpower.au.af. mil/airchronicles/aureview/1982/jan-feb/parks.html (last visited June 20, 2013).

158.   Another common term used for "incidental" civilian casualties and damage to civilian objects is "collateral damage." *See* U.S. Dep't of Navy, Naval Warfare Pub. 1-14M, The Commander's Handbook on the Law of Military Operations ¶¶. 8.1; 8.3 (July 2007).

159.   Parks, *supra* note 157 ("what is prohibited is the intentional attack of the civilian population per se or individual civilians not taking part in the conflict . . .").

160.   Solis, *supra* note 2, at 286.

161.   *See, e.g.,* Human Rights Council, *Human Rights in Palestine and Other Occupied Arab Territories: Report of the United Nations Fact Finding Mission on the Gaza Conflict* 5, U.N.Doc. A/HRC/12/48 173 (Sept. 15, 2009), *available at* http://www2.ohchr.org/english/bodies/hrcouncil/specialsession/9/docs/UNFFMGC_Report.pdf (last visited June 20, 2013) (stating that the threat to "several hundred civilian lives and . . . civilian property" was disproportionate in comparison to the "advantage gained from using white phosphorous to screen Israeli armed forces' tanks from anti-tank fire from armed opposition groups" and therefore violated the principle of proportionality). *But see* State of Israel, *Gaza Operations Investigations: An Update* 32 (Jan. 2010), *available at* http://www.mfa.gov.il/mfa/foreignpolicy/terrorism/pages/gaza_operation_investigations_update_jan_2010.aspx (last visited June 20, 2013) ("With respect to exploding munitions containing white phosphorous, the Military Advocate General concluded that the use of this weapon in the operation was consistent with Israel's obligations under international law.").

162.   Prosecutor v. Galiæ, Case No. IT-98-29-T, Judgment, p.58 (Dec. 5, 2003).

163.   Solis, *supra* note 2, at 274 (citing ICC Statute, Art.8(2)(b)(iv)).

164.   Yorman Dinstein, *Discussion: Reasonable Military Commanders and Reasonable Civilians,* 78 Int'l L. Stud. 211, 215 (2002); Parks, *supra* note 150 (stating that "excessive" collateral civilian casualties is a high threshold that requires a number of casualties so vast that it "shock[s] the conscience of the world" and only "acts so blatant as to be tantamount to a total disregard for the safety of the civilian population" are condemned).

165.   Geiss, *supra* note 66, at 30.

166.   AP I Commentary, *supra* note 97, at 400 (noting the importance of "avoiding any injury or suffering of combatants in excess of that necessary to put the enemy *hors de combat*").

167.   Hague Reg. IV, *supra* note 42, art. 22.

168.   AP I, *supra* note 51, art. 35; Hague Reg. IV, *supra* note 42, art. 23(e) (forbidding the employment of "arms, projectiles, or material calculated to cause unnecessary suffering").

169.   Handbook, *supra* note 43, at 12.

170.   *Id.*

171.   Dinstein, *supra* note 33, at 59.

172.   *Id.* (citing B.M. Carnahan, *Unnecessary Suffering, the Red Cross and Tactical Laser Weapons,* 18 LLAICLJ 705, 713 (1995–1996)).

173.   AP I Commentary, *supra* note 97, at 408.

174.   *Id.* at 407.

175.   *Id.* at 409.

176.   *Id.* at 406. *See, e.g.,* CCW, *supra* note 45 (prohibiting or restricting various weapons).

177.   Solis, *supra* note 2, at 186.

178.   Geiss, *supra* note 66, at 21 (citing The Islamic Emirate of Afghanistan: the Liaha [code of conduct] for Mujahids, art. 81).

XI

Privatizing the War on Terror: The Legal and Policy Challenges of Outsourcing America's Counterterrorism Fight to Private Military, Security, and Intelligence Contractors

Colonel David Wallace*

"How is it in our nation's interest to have civilian contractors rather than military personnel performing vital national security functions . . . in a war zone?"

U.S. Senator Carl Levin[1]

"There are two ways to look at this activity: as a grim attempt to turn public anxiety into a business opportunity or—the viewpoint naturally favored by those in the industry—as a chance to fight the good fight while upholding sound capitalist principles."

Los Angeles Times
Columnist Michael Hiltzik[2]

Introduction

On September 11, 2001, the so-called war on terror[3] began out of the blue with the murderous attacks by Al-Qaeda operatives, which killed more than 3,000 Americans and citizens of other countries at the World Trade Center, the Pentagon, and in a field near Shanksville, Pennsylvania.[4] To put that unforgettable fall morning into context:

---

*   The opinions expressed in this chapter are those of the author and are not intended to represent the official positions of the U.S. Military Academy of the U.S. Army.

163

[t]he September 11 attacks killed more Americans than were killed at Pearl Harbor, and unlike Pearl Harbor, almost all of those killed on September 11 were civilians. In ten years of fighting in Vietnam, the United States lost 58,209 citizens; on the single day of September 11, the United States lost more than five percent of that number. It was the greatest loss of American life resulting from hostilities in a single day since the Civil War.[5]

Global terrorism had come of age for the United States in the form of a counterterrorism fight against the forces of militant Islam.[6] September 11 represented the start of a new kind of armed conflict in which the pathways of globalization were the means through which power was channeled.[7]

In the aftermath of September 11, the United States pursued a dual policy. On the one hand, America, orchestrating and implementing all of its instruments of its national power, aggressively pursued and sought to punish and defeat those to blame for the violence inflicted upon our homeland and people. On the other hand, the country increased its security and intelligence resources and capabilities to prevent another strike.[8] Against this backdrop, a tectonic shift occurred in the United States and around the world concerning the realization and conceptualization of military, security and intelligence services, i.e., the privatization or, more accurately, the corporatization of warfare. Author Keric Clanahan perceptively captured the essence of this privatization trend by noting that the "reliance on contractors has increased dramatically, but nowhere has this dependence manifested itself more significantly than in the first post-Millennium decade of conflict in Iraq and Afghanistan where contractors frequently outnumbered troops . . . ."[9]

To begin with, it is necessary to understand and appreciate what is meant by private military, security, and intelligence contractors.[10] Such firms and their employees have been the object of great interest, debate, and scrutiny among and between public officials, scholars, military leaders, industry representatives, reporters, and others.[11] Private military, security, and intelligence contractors are, irrespective of how they describe themselves, private enterprises hired by states, corporations, international and nongovernmental organizations, and others to provide a wide range of services.[12] Like other corporations, most private military, security, and intelligence companies are registered bodies with legal personalities, hierarchical structures, websites, and public relations operations.[13] Such firms draw on the same support as all business entities: financial, legal, marketing, and administrative.[14]

Although it has been estimated that 70% of the companies comprising the industry are located in the United States or Great Britain,[15] the pool of labor for the industry is indeed global, often hiring ex-military, law enforcement, and intelligence personnel. In many instances, employees from private military, security, and intelligence companies have taken over the duties and functions that have been traditionally performed by a state's armed forces and intelligence services: security, logistics, technical support, training, intelligence gathering and analysis, participation in combat, and the interrogation of prisoners, among other things.[16] Firms in the industry vary considerably depending upon capitalization, number of personnel, corporate interrelationships, and geographical location, as well as other characteristics. The unifying factor, however, is that all the firms offer services within the military domain.[17]

This chapter will explore the fundamental paradigm shift that resulted in the outsourcing of America's counterterrorism fight to private contractors through both a legal and policy lens. After providing contextual background information related to the privatization phenomenon, the chapter will hone in on a couple of important legal questions central to the use of private actors in the war on terror. Finally, the chapter will conclude with a brief discussion of the policy implications associated with the trend.

Privatization of Warfare: Background and Typology

Neither private contractors on a battlefield[18] nor hiring outsiders to fight one's wars is a new phenomenon. Private actors serving in combat zones have been a fixture of armed conflict throughout history.[19] The United States has a long history of using private contractors to augment regular military forces in support of its national foreign policy and security needs.[20] The Continental army, for example, employed contractors for transportation, carpentry, engineering, food, and medical services.[21] Likewise, the British used Hessian troops-for-hire in the same conflict.[22]

Similarly, it is well known that privateers—private ships authorized by a government to engage in warfare—helped win the American Revolution and the War of 1812.[23] In the American Civil War, the Union Army retained the services of British and Canadian individuals along with a range of immigrants who were motivated by a desire for citizenship.[24] Both world wars also saw the use of private actors in support of our national war effort. Of note, on December 24, 1941, more than 1,100 American civilian contractors accompanying the U.S. armed forces were constructing airfield facilities at Wake Island. They were captured by invading Japanese forces. Reportedly, more than 60 of the civilians actually directly engaged in combat against Japanese forces.[25] In the Vietnam conflict, approximately 80,000 contractors supported America's wartime effort.[26] All in all, the use of private contractors in direct or indirect support of national security and defense has a long historical trajectory in the United States.[27]

The end of the Cold War, however, marked a dramatic change in the number of private military, security, and intelligence contractors participating in armed conflicts around the world as well as a significant expansion in the nature and scope of their activities and functions. According to P. W. Singer, perhaps the world's foremost expert on the privatization of warfare, the emergence of the worldwide private military and security industry was "distinctly representative of the changed global security and business environments at the start of the twenty-first century."[28] While done with little fanfare or public notice, the extent of the shift toward the privatization of military, security, and intelligence services has been breathtaking.[29]

More specifically, the private sector has increasingly become a major supplier of military, security, and intelligence services in America's so-called war on terror,[30] marking a fundamental change in the national security infrastructure of the United States. Some estimate the value of annual contracts for the industry to be as high as $100 billion.[31]

To fully understand and appreciate this phenomenon, it is essential to consider the confluence of forces at the end of the Cold War that sparked this trend. It is widely acknowledged that the 50 years of the Cold War fueled a period of hypermilitarization among the Soviet Union, the United States, and associated satellite states. Both sides constructed large and well-funded military-industrial complexes.[32] When the Cold War ended in the early 1990s, nations around the world downsized their armed forces in an effort to cut costs and to reap a so-called "peace dividend."[33] By way of illustration, in the three years after the end of the Cold War, worldwide military force structure declined by 7 million.[34] The United States, for example, reduced its armed forces by 35% and cut costs by $100 billion.[35] Not surprisingly, these large-scale military demobilizations created a robust, globally accessible, well-trained labor market of ex-military personnel ready for private industry to exploit.[36]

Additionally, the predictability, stability, and structure of the bi-polar world ended with the end of the Cold War. For 50 years, America and the Soviet Union were able to control other nations within their respective spheres of influence, thereby keeping a lid on long-simmering conflicts.[37]

Once the lid came off, so-called "release conflicts" soon erupted in the Balkans, Sierra Leone, the Congo, and elsewhere. The number of armed conflicts involving Western countries during the Cold War has already been surpassed in the three decades since it ended.[38]

In addition to the reduction of military force structure, weapons—large and small—and other armaments of war became readily available on the open market as countries sold off their arms stocks in garage-style fashion[39] and reoriented defense industries.[40] Moreover, the increased technological advancements in weapons, munitions, and other instruments of war resulted in nations becoming more reliant on military contractors for their expertise.[41] Finally, the changes outlined above occurred within the context of a broader neo-liberal movement, which began in earnest in Great Britain under Margret Thatcher[42] but spread to the United States under President Ronald Reagan.[43] Generally speaking, this neo-liberalism as a politico-economic theory favors, among other things, greater privatization of governmental services.

By contrast, some commentators contend that the significant push to outsource military activities in the United States began as early as 1966 with the release of revised Office of Management and Budget (OMB) Circular A-76.[44] Those who put the mid-1960s as the starting point for the phenomenon note that private contractors played a significant role in the nation-building efforts of South Vietnam, and their numbers have grown in the decades that followed.[45]

Regardless of the precise starting point of the phenomenon, there has been an impressive expansion in the employment of private military, security, and intelligence contractors since the September 11, 2001, attacks on the United States.

The use of private contractors by multiple stakeholders has been one of the defining features of the armed conflicts in Iraq, Afghanistan, and elsewhere in the war on terror.[46] Many consider private contractors a de facto part of U.S. military force structure.[47] According to the Commission on Wartime Contracting in Iraq and Afghanistan, an independent and bipartisan panel created by Congress in 2008 to examine waste, fraud, abuse, accountability, and other issues in contingency contracting, the United States can no longer conduct large or sustained military operations or respond to major disasters without heavy support from contractors.[48]

The private sector has also become a major supplier of tools and brainpower to America's intelligence community.[49] Hence, a quiet revolution has occurred in our intelligence organizations toward significant outsourcing of functions to corporations. This trend departs from the long-established practice of keeping operations in U.S. government hands.[50] To illustrate this point, since September 11, the Central Intelligence Agency (CIA) has been spending over one-half of its budget on for-profit contractors per year. The number of contractor employees at the CIA exceeds the agency's full workforce.[51] One of the world's leading authorities on the privatization phenomenon, Simon Chesterman, observed:

> [t]hough it lags behind the privatization of military services, the privatization of intelligence has expanded dramatically with the growth in intelligence activities following the 11 September attacks on the United States. In a report published three days after those attacks, the Senate Select Committee on Intelligence encouraged a symbiotic relationship between the Intelligence Community and the private sector.[52]

It is hard to overstate the important role private contractors play in support of America's counterterrorism efforts. Critical intelligence functions of U.S.

intelligence agencies are now run by private corporations.[53] In sum, "[w]e can't spy . . . if we can't buy."[54]

In addition to the CIA and the U.S. military, the Department of State has, in recent years, also relied heavily on private security to protect its personnel and property overseas. The infamous shooting at Nisour Square in September 2007 in which Blackwater Worldwide employees killed 17 innocent Iraqis occurred in performance of a State Department contract.[55] This incident is discussed in greater detail below. Additionally, since the U.S. military left Iraq, a small army of contractors has been employed to fill the void—many of them working for the State Department.[56] Another well-known incident involving private security contractors working for the State Department involved the attack on the U.S. Consulate in Benghazi, Libya, on September 11, 2012. Although the facts and circumstances surrounding the incident are still being investigated as of this writing, it appears that militants overwhelmed the guards and set fire to the structure before the occupants could escape. Ambassador Christopher Stevens and three others were killed in the night of violence.[57] Two of the four individuals killed were former U.S. Navy Seals serving as part of a security contractor force.[58]

There have been various efforts to classify or categorize the private military and security industry. Different commentators have sought to develop an accurate, workable typology for the industry. For example, such companies and their employees have been characterized as "combat versus non-combat," "active versus passive," "offensive versus defensive," or "armed versus unarmed" in their operations or in a similar fashion.[59] P. W. Singer offered the most widely known and accepted typology for the industry. In a brilliant simple and straightforward way, Singer uses a spear analogy. That is, Singer notionally separates the private military and security industry into three groups based on the type of services the firms offer. His categories are military provider firms, military consulting firms, and military support firms.[60]

Military provider firms are at the tip of the spear. Provider firms operate at the tactical level of the battle space, with the natural and probable consequence that they engage in combat. The most often-cited examples of military provider firms are the now-defunct South African firm Executive Outcomes and the British company Sandline International.[61] In a well-known episode, the besieged government of the West African country of Sierra Leone hired Executive Outcomes in 1995 to repel and defeat the Revolutionary United Front (RUF) and end one of the most vicious civil wars in history.[62] At one point in the conflict, circumstances appeared hopeless for the government as the RUF forces approached within 20 kilometers of the Sierra Leone capital of Freetown.[63] A well-armed, expertly trained, combined-arms Executive Outcomes task force using highly effective and novel military tactics routed the RUF rebels in a mere two weeks.[64]

In terms of the war on terror, there are various examples of companies that may, in some cases, be accurately characterized as being provider firms. Such firms have performed, among other things, the following tasks in Afghanistan and Iraq: (1) guarding static sites to include military objectives like forward operating bases; (2) personal security details for diplomats and other persons requiring special protection (to include military personnel); and (3) convoy security for movement of personnel and goods.[65] Needless to say, it can be extraordinarily difficult to distinguish between offensive and defensive combat, particularly in a low-intensity conflict with no positional front lines,[66] such as Afghanistan and Iraq. Author Hannah Tonkin insightfully notes that armed security personnel working in and amongst the most hostile parts of a conflict can make it extremely difficult to distinguish between national troops and armed security guards.[67]

The second category in Singer's typology is military consulting firms. These firms provide advisory or training services for their clients on everything from restructuring military forces to purchasing equipment for operational planning. For example, Virginia-based private contractor Military Professional Resources Incorporated (MPRI) is staffed by a significant number of former U.S. military personnel. By way of illustration, MPRI has worked closely with the Afghan National Army for years providing expert advice on critical aspects of their structure and operations. In Singer's typology, military consulting firms like MPRI and others are the shaft of the spear.[68]

Lastly, military support firms specialize in providing nonlethal aid, including intelligence, logistical, and technical support, to their clients. In many instances, military support firms relieve soldiers of doing many mundane but necessary tasks, such as kitchen police (KP) duty, laundry, and latrine cleaning. Brown & Root, Inc., for example, provided U.S. forces in the Balkans with services ranging from water purification to repatriating dead bodies. These types of firms are ubiquitous in the theater of operations and are, by analogy, the handle of the spear.[69]

Given Singer's typology, where would intelligence services fit into his paradigm? Depending on the specific service provided, intelligence contractors could be suitably placed into any of the categories. Most notably, intelligence contractors are reportedly serving as military provider firms in some respects. In one particular case in point, *The New York Times* reported that the CIA hired contractors in 2004 to locate and kill senior Al-Qaeda operatives.[70] Additionally, the CIA covert drone program purportedly uses civilian contractors for a variety of tasks, such as flying the drones and maintaining and loading Hellfire missiles.[71] The CIA also has reportedly used private contractors to participate in paramilitary operations—i.e., covert actions involving combat with enemy forces.[72] As a symbolic depiction of the often dangerous and heroic roles played by civilian intelligence contractors, there are a number of stars carved into the CIA's memorial *wall of heroes* at its headquarters in Langley, Virginia, representing contractors killed in the line of duty.[73]

With an understanding of the background of the private military, security, and intelligence contractors from various perspectives, the next step is to explore some of the legal issues and concerns associated with the privatization of warfare particularly in the context of America's counterterrorism fight in the war on terror.

Legal Issues and Concerns with the Privatization of Warfare

The use of private military, security, and intelligence contractors has raised, and continues to raise, a variety of challenging legal issues. Included among the many issues are questions such as: What is the battlefield status of such corporate warriors under international humanitarian law? Are private contractors, in fact, a new class of corporate mercenaries for the twenty-first century? What are the best mechanisms for regulating such contractors and holding them accountable both individually and corporately? Should business interests and market forces—rather than international humanitarian and human rights law—regulate the use and conduct of private military, security, and intelligence contractors?[74] Are there fissures in the national and international regulatory frameworks governing such actors? Does the emergence of the private military, security, and intelligence industry and its current growth trajectory constitute a threat to traditional notions of states' monopoly on violence during armed conflicts? The answers to these questions and many others are crucial to understanding and appreciating the phenomenon of private military, security, and intelligence contractors.

In the remainder of this section of the chapter, I will briefly address two of the primary legal issues or areas of concern regarding the use of private contractors: accountability/responsibility and inherently governmental functions. It is, however, important to note that the synopsis of these two issues is, by necessity, an overview.

Discussions about the privatization trend in warfare inevitably lead to assertions that private contractors routinely operate without meaningful accountability, responsibility, and impunity.[75] Such claims are not without merit. Private military, security, and intelligence contractors have been implicated in a range of international humanitarian law violations, human rights abuses, and other serious criminal misconduct during the war on terror.[76] In Iraq, Afghanistan, and elsewhere, private contractors have been accused of participating in torture and rape and inflicting unprovoked acts of violence on civilian populations, with a remarkable few being held accountable for their actions.[77] Author Hannah Tonkin accurately notes that "[S]tates often fail to take the same measures to control PMSC[78] personnel that they would ordinarily take to control national soldiers, and many of the accountability mechanisms that exist for the national armed forces are weak or absent in the case of PMSCs."[79] This disparity in the treatment between national troops and contractors is illustrated well with the infamous detainee abuse scandal at Abu Ghraib. Although the facts of the scandal are generally known and the horrific images from the photographs are seared into our collective memory, the role of contractors in the case is a more obscure point.

In late 2003, early 2004 at the Abu Ghraib prison complex just west of Baghdad's city center, contractor-employees from two U.S.-based companies, CACI International and Titan Corp., allegedly encouraged and participated in manifestly illegal and blatantly sadistic torture and abuse of Iraqi prisoners.[80] A number of soldiers involved in the same or similar pattern of abuse were identified, investigated, tried, and punished for their misconduct. By contrast, the civilian contractor personnel involved in the incident have not been held accountable for their actions. Discussing the role of aggressive interrogation techniques used by private contractors at the prison, former commander of the 800th Military Police, Colonel (ret.) Janice Karpinski commented:

> [w]hen you take those same techniques and put them in the hands of irresponsible and non-accountable people like these civilian contractors were, you are combining lethal ingredients. You get civilian contractors who have a playground, and they get out of control.[81]

Another infamous incident involving private contractors occurred on September 16, 2007, in Nisour Square in Baghdad. A convoy of U.S. Department of State vehicles carrying diplomats to a meeting in western Baghdad was guarded by a heavily armed Blackwater corporate personal security detail. Believing that they had been ambushed or were otherwise under attack, the Blackwater guards began firing recklessly into the crowds. Although the underlying facts of the episode are not entirely clear regarding how the shooting started, the consequences of the slaughter have echoed around the world: 17 Iraqi citizens slain, including innocent women and children.[82] The United States did, in fact, charge several guards with manslaughter (and attempted manslaughter) as well as weapons violations. After much legal wrangling, a federal district court judge dismissed the criminal charges pending against the contractor employees, citing the misuse of compelled statements from the accused contractor employees.[83] In April 2011, a federal appellate court determined that the federal district court incorrectly interpreted the law in the case. The appeals judges returned the case to the lower court to determine "as to each defendant, what evidence—if any—the government presented against him that was tainted as to him."[84]

In light of the above incidents as well as others, there have been efforts, both internationally and domestically in the United States, to create better accountability mechanisms over private contractors. One notable effort occurred when Congress amended the Uniform Code of Military Justice (UCMJ) to provide jurisdiction over contractors during declared wars or contingency operations.[85] This small but important change had the effect of potentially applying the UCMJ to significant numbers of contractor personnel accompanying U.S armed forces in Iraq, Afghanistan, and elsewhere in the war on terror.[86] To date, however, very few contractors have been prosecuted under the UCMJ.

Beyond the issue of holding private contractors accountable, another important legal issue involves the boundaries governing the nature and type of services private military, security, and intelligence contractors can provide and the policy implications that flow from the decision to use such corporate warriors. As one might reasonably expect, the use of private contractors in military, security, and intelligence operations raises many issues regarding the appropriateness of entrusting private contractors with duties and responsibilities that have been customarily reserved for military and civilian federal personnel in national security matters.[87] Viewed in a broader context, determining what functions belong inherently to the government is part of a larger debate about the proper role of the federal government *vis-à-vis* the private sector.[88] In the final report of the U.S. Commission on Wartime Contractors, it notes, in part, the following:

> Ten years of war in Iraq and Afghanistan have seen the United States using too many contractors for too many functions with too little forethought and control. Even if every instance of contracting has satisfied the legal restrictions on contractor performance of "inherently governmental functions"—a dubious proposition at best—the Commission believes far too little attention has been devoted to the question whether all of that contracting was appropriate for contingency operations.[89]

Federal guidance on the concept of inherently governmental functions appears in a number of sources, including the Federal Activities Inventory Reform (FAIR) Act of 1998,[90] the Office of Management and Budget Circular A-76, and the Federal Acquisition Regulation (FAR). At its essence, the concept of inherently governmental functions under federal statute, regulations, and policy is intended to be a barrier to ensure that only government personnel perform certain critical functions, such as waging war, conducting diplomacy, or making commitments that bind the government.[91] Hence, an inherently governmental function is too intimately related to the public interest to require performance by federal government employees.[92]

In general, there are a number of factors agencies have used to determine whether a function is inherently governmental. Those factors include, but are not limited to: (1) whether there are statutory restrictions defining the activity as inherently governmental; (2) whether there is official discretion (and how much) in the performance of the function; (3) whether the individual had authority to take action that will significantly and directly affect life, liberty, or the property of the public; (4) whether there are special agency authorities, such as the power to deputize private persons; (5) whether the activity is already being performed by the agency; and (6) whether certain actions are taken regarding the adjudication of claims or entitlements.[93]

While the concept of an inherently governmental function appears to be clear-cut, multiple and/or inconsistent definitions of the term "inherently governmental" have caused significant ambiguity and uncertainty regarding the boundaries of privatization in the war on terror.[94] For over a decade in Iraq, Afghanistan, and elsewhere in the war on terror, there have been numerous instances when private military, security, and intelligence contractors have performed functions that could reasonably be interpreted as inherently governmental.

One particularly timely case in point involves private contractors and the use of unmanned aircraft vehicles (UAV),[95] often referred to as drones. As has been reported in the popular media, drones can range in size from devices barely bigger than a paper plane to formidable missile-sized systems.[96]

The most well-known drone is the Predator. It looks like a baby plane—27 feet long and powered by a pusher propeller in the back weighing 1,130 pounds— and costs approximately $4.5 million.[97] The United States has enthusiastically embraced drone technology, believing that it amounts to a safer, cheaper, and more effective way to wage warfare in the U.S.'s fight against terrorism.[98] Personnel engaged in drone operations may work far from, and at times closer to, battlefields. There are dozens of drone command centers operating across the globe at such places as the CIA's Langley, Virginia, headquarters and Nevada's Creech and Nellis Air Force Bases near Las Vegas.[99] In the period from 2002 until 2011, the United States increased its inventory of drones from 167 to over 7,000 in all branches of the armed forces.[100]

Drone strikes were used somewhat sparingly during the early years of the war on terror.[101] President Obama, however, has relied heavily on covert drone strikes as the centerpiece in his prosecution of the war on terror. According to CNN's Peter Bergen, President Obama has authorized 283 strikes in Pakistan alone, amounting to six times more than the number during President George W. Bush's eight years in office. The estimated number of deaths from drone attacks during the Obama Administration is *more than four times what it was during the Bush Administration*—somewhere between 1,494 and 2,618.[102]

So what functions are private contractors performing in the drone operations? Working alongside military and federal civilian personnel, such contractors maintain and repair drones and related sensors and communication systems.[103] Additionally, there are purportedly contractor personnel employed in drone operations providing significant brainpower in intelligence processing, exploitation, and dissemination.[104]

In one reported instance in 2010, a U.S. airstrike mistakenly killed 15 Afghans. The investigation of the incident discovered that an American civilian contractor played a key role in analyzing the feeds from the Predator drone. That is, "[t]he contractor had overseen other analysts at Air Force Special Operations Command at Hurlburt Field in Florida as the drone tracked suspected insurgents near a small unit of U.S. soldiers in rugged hills of central Afghanistan. Based partly on her analysis, an Army captain ordered an airstrike on a convoy that turned out to be carrying innocent men, women, and children."[105]

Finally, contractor personnel are participating in various degrees in aircraft, sensor, and weapons operations. According to author Keric Clanahan:

> Small tactical UAS operations seems to be the only Air Force UAS mission that existed recently (and may still exist) where military members are not always in operational control of a military aircraft. The Air Force currently employs three types of small tactical UAS: the Scan Eagle, RQ-11B Raven, and Wash III. These drones are remotely piloted by individuals on the ground who are in receipt of direct camera feeds. . . . Although the Air Force owns these aircraft, which are utilized by troops in theater, contractor personnel have operated such drones.[106]

As mentioned previously, the predator drones in the CIA program are flown by civilians, both intelligence officers and private contractors. The contractors operating CIA drones are, in many cases, considered to be seasoned professionals, often retired military and intelligence officials.[107]

Another example of a private contractor arguably engaging in inherently governmental functions involves the widespread use of private security contractors in the war on terror, particularly in Afghanistan and Iraq. The term "private security contractors" refers to those actors who perform a wide range of security-related tasks that include protecting people (including military personnel, State Department officials, and other high-value targets); guarding facilities; escorting convoys (considered to be among the most dangerous jobs in Iraq); staffing checkpoints; and training and advising security forces.[108] By way of illustration, "The protection of the US embassy in Iraq, together with the associated multitude of diplomats and US personnel travelling through the Green Zone following the 2003 invasion, required a particularly large armed force, which was comprised almost exclusively of contractors from Blackwater, DynCorps, and Triple Canopy."[109]

The American public became acutely aware of the presence of private security contractors in Iraq in March 2004 when media reports, including graphic photographs, showed a frenzied mob killing four Blackwater security contractors in Fallujah. The four contractors were on a mission to pick up kitchen equipment. The victims were viciously attacked. They were shot and their vehicles were burned. Their dismembered bodies were hung from a bridge.[110] The unforgettable images of Iraqis celebrating the sight of charred corpses were disturbing.[111] Public awareness and scrutiny continued to mount as more news reports chronicled multiple events involving private security contractors, including the infamous cases of abuse at Abu Ghraib prison and Bagram Airfield as well as numerous shooting incidents in Afghanistan and Iraq.

In sum, there has been and continues to be significant discussion and debate about the appropriate and lawful boundaries defining the nature and scope of the functions performed by military, security and intelligence contractors during armed conflicts. According to P. W. Singer, we are now starting to see a debate within the U.S. armed forces whether outsourcing of some roles and functions have gone too far and a rollback is needed.[112]

Policy and Practical Implications for Using Private Military, Security, and Intelligence Contractors

In addition to the legal issues and concerns outlined above, there are significant policy implications that flow from the use of private military, security, and intelligence contractors. Below is a sampling of some of these concerns. It should be noted that it is beyond the scope of this chapter to analyze any of the specific policy matters in depth. Rather, it is important to recognize and appreciate the profound and complex policy concerns raised by a decision to employ such contractors.

The first issue involves the potential impact of the private sector siphoning off highly skilled members of the armed forces and intelligences services. Given the difference in salaries between the public and private sectors as well as greater work flexibility, it is easy to see how, after receiving extensive and expensive training and experience in the military and intelligence services, talented individuals could be lured away to private firms. Again, P. W. Singer captured the essence of the problem when he wrote: "While soldiers have always had competing job options in the civilian marketplace, such as Air Force pilots leaving to fly airliners, the private military firm industry is significantly different. Private military firms keep the individuals within the military and thus the public sphere. More important, the private military industry is directly competitive with the public military. It not only draws its employees from the military, it does so to fill military roles, thus shrinking the military's purview."[113]

A second, and related, point is the confusion and tensions associated with the placement of private contractors within military structures.[114] Unlike their uniformed counterpart, private contractors can walk away from inconvenient or dangerous missions or circumstances. Put in a slightly different manner, "[w]hen American life and liberty are on the line, financial incentives alone cannot inspire selfless and courageous action. Contractors thus introduce into any military operation a degree of uncertainty that is not present when soldiers perform the same or similar critical tasks."[115] As private contractors, "[t]heir duty, as explained to them by their superiors before they ship out, is to make as much money for their companies as they possibly can."[116] Even if such contractors are patriotic Americans, their ultimate duty is to their corporate shareholders or company bottom lines, not to the U.S. Constitution, as is the case with uniformed members of the armed forces or civilian public servants.[117] As such, their incentives and interests can be dissimilar from those of the members of the armed forces they are serving with or near.

A third issue is that the "bar to entry" into an armed conflict or other situation involving violence is arguably lower because there is less public concern, interest, or scrutiny into the health and safety of contractors versus members of the nation's military forces or intelligence services. In a recent article, Steven Schooner and Colin Swan noted that as of June 2010, more than 2,008 contractors have been killed in Iraq and Afghanistan. Additionally, more than 44,000 contractors have been injured, of which more than 16,000 were seriously wounded.[118]

Fourth, an overarching question has been and continues to be whether it is more cost-effective to use private contractors than members of the armed forces. According to the Commission on Wartime Contracting in its August 2011 Final Report to Congress, the short answer is, "it depends."[119] More specifically, it depends on a wide range of factors, many of which are not under direct government control.[120] The commission specifically recommended that considerations of costs cannot be a driving factor in determining whether and what to contract.[121]

Moreover, the commission wisely noted that national security is not a business decision, and considerations of costs in matters of sustained combat and arduous diplomatic actions overseas are far less important than mission accomplishment.[122] In a related point, private military, security, and intelligence companies provide countries like the United States with flexibility in terms of force structure and ability to organize tasks. Again, the above policy concerns are simply a representative list that just scratches the surface. There are many others that must be considered.

Conclusion

The emergence and exponential growth in the number of private military, security, and intelligence contractors as well as the ever-widening scope of their activities is most certainly one of the most noteworthy developments in the war on terror. In parallel with this expansion, but particularly in the context of the prolonged armed conflicts in Iraq and Afghanistan,[123] there has been and continues to be significant interest and focus on various legal and policy implications associated with using such private contractors.

The contours and conceptions of these legal and policy issues associated with the fundamental paradigm shift toward privatization in American's counterterrorism efforts discussed in this chapter are hardly fixed. Whether it involves the legally appropriate boundaries of the nature, type, and scope of services that should be outsourced, the regulation and accountability of these corporate actors, or the policy/practical implications that flow from these questions and many more, much work still needs to be done to address and understand this fundamental shift in warfare in the twenty-first century.

Notes

1. Deborah Avant, *Think Again: Mercenaries*, 134 FOREIGN POLICY 20 (July/August 2004), 20–28.

2. TIM SHORROCK, SPIES FOR HIRE: THE SECRET WORLD OF INTELLIGENCE OUTSOURCING 356, Simon & Schuster (2008). Michael Hiltzik was writing about Paladin Capital Group, a private equity fund created after 9/11 to focus exclusively on the homeland and security and intelligence markets.

3. Begun in 2001, the War on Terror has also been known as the Global War on Terror and the War on Terrorism. Under the Obama Administration, the War of Terror has been characterized as the Overseas Contingency Operation.

4. RICHARD M. PIOUS, THE WAR ON TERRORISM AND THE RULE OF LAW 1, Roxbury Publishing Co. (2006).

5. DAN CALDWELL & ROBERT E. WILLIAMS, JR., SEEKING SECURITY IN AN INSECURE WORLD 170, Rowman & Littlefield Publishers, Inc. (2006).

6. JACKSON NYAMUYA MAOGTO, BATTLING TERRORISM: LEGAL PERSPECTIVES ON THE USE OF FORCE AND THE WAR ON TERRORISM 111, Ashgate Publishing Ltd. (2005).

7. SEAN KAY, GLOBAL SECURITY IN THE TWENTY-FIRST CENTURY: THE QUEST FOR POWER AND THE SEARCH FOR PEACE 2, Rowman & Littlefield Publishers, Inc. (2006).

8. NORMAN FRIEDMAN, TERRORISM, AFGHANISTAN AND AMERICA'S NEW WAY OF WAR 23, Naval Inst. Press (2003).

9. Keric D. Clanahan, *Drone-Sourcing? United States Air Force Unmanned Aircraft Systems, Inherently Governmental Functions and the Role of Contractors*, FED. CIR. BAR J., May 4, 2012. *Available at* SSRN: http://ssrn.com/abstract=2051154.

10. Throughout the paper, the term "private military, security, and intelligence contractors" will mean not only the corporations, but also their staff and employees unless otherwise noted. Other terms like private soldiers, for-profit soldiers, corporate warriors may be used throughout the paper and are meant to be synonymous with private military, security, and intelligence contractors. In much of the burgeoning scholarship related to the privatization of warfare, intelligence contractors are generally not grouped with military and security contractors. Given that intelligence contractors have been absolutely indispensible in America's counterterrorism fight since 9/11, they have been put together with military and intelligence contractors for analysis and consideration in this chapter.

11. KATERI CARMOLA, PRIVATE SECURITY CONTRACTORS AND NEW WARS: RISK, LAW AND ETHICS 9.

12. Montreux Document on pertinent international legal obligations and good practices for States related to operations of private military and security companies during armed conflicts,

p.9, *available at* http://www.icrc.org/eng/resources/documents/misc/montreux-document-170908.htm.

13.   Hannah Tonkin, State Control over Private Military and Security Companies in Armed Conflicts 36, Cambridge Univ. Press (2011).

14.   Christopher Kinsey, Corporate Soldiers and International Security: The Rise of Private Military Companies 14, Routledge (2006).

15.   Nils Rosemann, *Code of Conduct: Tool for Self-Regulation for Private Military and Security Companies*, Geneva Center for Democratic Control of the Armed Forces, Occasional Paper No. 15, p.9 (2008).

16.   Anicee Van Engeland, Civilian or Combatant?: A Challenge for the 21st Century 127, Oxford Univ. Press (2011).

17.   P. W. Singer, Corporate Warriors, The Rise of the Privatized Military Industry 88, Cornell Univ. Press (2008). In the context of the war on terror, the United States has pursued a war paradigm in which private military, security, and intelligence contractors have supported that effort. Many of these firms have provided security or intelligence services outside of an armed conflict. An example would contractors from Blackwater providing security in New Orleans in the aftermath of Hurricane Katrina.

18.   The Third Geneva Convention, Article 4(A) 4 specifically accounts for contractors on the battlefield. It identifies supply contractors as "[p]ersons who accompany the armed forces without being members thereof . . . ." The Third Geneva Convention entitles such contractors to prisoner-of-war status upon capture.

19.   Laura A. Dickinson, Outsourcing War & Peace: Preserving Public Values in a World of Privatized Foreign Affairs p. 3, Yale Univ. Press (2011).

20.   Deborah C. Kidwell, *Public War, Private Fight: The United States and Private Military Companies*, p.vii, Global War on Terrorism Occasional Paper 12, Combat Studies Inst. Press (2005).

21.   Industrial College of the Armed Forces, National Defense University, Privatized Military Operations—Final Report, industry study (Spring 2006), p.2 (on file with the author).

22.   Allison Stranger, One Nation Under Contract—The Outsourcing of American Power and the Future of Foreign Policies 84, Yale Univ. Press (2009).

23.   Tyler Cowen, *To Know Contractors, Know Government*, N.Y. Times, Oct. 28, 2007, *available at* http://www.nytimes.com/2007/10/28/business/28view.html?_r=0 (last visited Dec. 4, 2012).

24.   Allison Stranger, *supra* note 22.

25.   Gary D. Solis, The Law of Armed Conflict—International Humanitarian Law in War 200, Cambridge Univ. Press (2010).

26.   Allison Stranger, *supra* note 22.

27.   Molly Dunigan, Victory for Hire: Private Security Companies' Impact on Military Effectiveness 125, Stanford Univ. Press, Stanford Security Studies (2011).

28.   P. W. Singer, Corporate Warriors, The Rise of the Privatized Military Industry 49, Cornell Univ. Press (2008).

29.   Laura A. Dickinson, Outsourcing War & Peace: Preserving Public Values in a World of Privatized Foreign Affairs 3, Yale Univ. Press (2011).

30.   The War on Terror (also known as the Global War on Terror and War on Terrorism) is a term commonly applied to an international military campaign led by the United States and the United Kingdom with the support of other NATO as well as non-NATO countries. Originally, the campaign was waged against Al-Qaeda and other militant organizations with the purpose of

eliminating them. The ongoing conflict has more recently been characterized as Overseas Contingency Operations.

31.   *Private Military Companies*, 88 Int'l Rev. of the Red Cross 445 (September 2006).

32.   Ken Silverstein, Private Warriors viii, Verso (2000); P. W. Singer, Corporate Warriors, the Rise of the Privatized Military Industry 53, Cornell Univ. Press (2008).

33.   Silverstein at viii.

34.   Sheehy, Maogot & Newell, Legal Control of the Private Military Corporation 13.

35.   Scott M. Sullivan, *Private Force/Public Goods*, Connecticut Law Review at 881.

36.   P. W. Singer, Corporate Warriors, the Rise of the Privatized Military Industry 49-50, Cornell Univ. Press (2008).

37.   David Isenberg, *A Government in Search of Cover, Private Security Companies in Iraq*, in Chesterman & Lehnardt, From Mercenaries to Market 83, Oxford Univ. Press (2007).

38.   Sullivan, *supra* note 35 at 881.

39.   Singer *supra* note 36 at 53–55.

40.   Kateri Carmola, Private Security Contractors and New Wars: Risk Law and Ethics 42, Routledge (2011).

41.   Isenberg, *supra* note 37, at 82.

42.   Devan R. Desal, *Have Your Cake and Eat it Too: A Proposal For a Layered Approach to Regulating Private Military Companies*, U.S.F. L. Rev., Summer 2005, p. 833. In the United States, the push for outsourcing of public functions to the private sector can be traced back to 1996, when the Office of Management and Budget release a revised Circular A-76.

43.   Singer, *supra* note 36, at 67.

44.   David Isenberg, *A Government in Search of Cover, Private Security Companies in Iraq*, in Chesterman & Lehnardt, From Mercenaries to Market 83, Oxford Univ. Press (2007), *citing* Defense Outsourcing: The OMB Circular A-76 Policy, Cong. Res. Serv. 2005, RL 30392, April 21, 2005 (fn. 1, p.82).

45.   David Isenberg, *supra* note 37.

46.   Human Rights First Written Testimony for the Commission on Wartime Contracting in Iraq and Afghanistan, Hearing on "Are Private Security Contractors Performing Inherently Governmental Functions?" p. 1. www.humanrightsfirst.com. The Commission on Wartime Contracting is an independent, bipartisan commission established by Congress to study wartime contracting practice in Afghanistan and Iraq. Congress authorized the commission in Section 841 of the National Defense Authorization Act of 2008. The so-called "Truman Committee" served as a model for the commission. Led by Sen. Harry Truman, the Truman Committee investigated covernment fraud and waste during and after World War II. www.wartimecontracting.gov.

47.   Deane-Peter Baker, Just Warriors, Inc. 1, Continuum Int'l Publishing Group (2011).

48.   Commission on Wartime Contracting, Final Report to Congress, Transforming Wartime Contracting: Controlling Costs, Reducing Risks (August 2011) p.13, *available at* http://www.wartimecontracting.gov/docs/CWC_FinalReport-lowres.pdf (last visited Oct. 15, 2012).

49.   Tim Shorrock, Spies for Hire: The Secret World of Intelligence Outsourcing 11, Simon & Schuster (2008).

50.   R.J. Hillhouse, *Intelligence Outsourcing*, The Nation, July 30, 2007, *available at* http://www.thenation.com/article/outsourcing-intelligence# (last visited Oct. 16, 2012).

51.   Tim Shorrock, *supra* note 49.

52. Simon Chesterman, *Intelligence Services*, p.184, *in* PRIVATE SECURITY, PUBLIC ORDER: THE OUTSOURCING OF PUBLIC SERVICES AND ITS LIMITS, Oxford Univ. Press (2009).

53. R.J. Hillhouse, *supra* note 50.

54. Simon Chesterman, *supra* note 52.

55. Tanya Roth, *Court Dismisses Nisour Square Charges Against Blackwater Employees*, FindLaw, Jan. 4, 2010, *available at* http://blogs.findlaw.com/decided/2010/01/court-dismisses-nisour-square-charges-against-blackwater-employees.html (last visited Dec. 6, 2012).

56. Michael R. Gordon, *Civilians to Take U.S. Lead as Military Leaves Iraq*, N.Y. TIMES, Aug. 18, 2010, *available at* http://www.nytimes.com/2010/08/19/world/middleeast/19withdrawal.html?pagewanted=all (last visited Dec. 6, 2012).

57. *How the Benghazi Attack Unfolded*, WALL ST. J., Sept. 21, 2012, *available at* http://online.wsj.com/article/SB10000872396390444620104578008922056244096.html (last visited Dec. 6, 2012).

58. Fran Townsend, "Former Navy SEALs died after coming to the aid of others," CNN, Sept. 23, 2012, *available at* http://www.cnn.com/2012/09/21/world/africa/libya-consulate-attack/index.html (last visited Dec. 6, 2012).

59. Sarah Percy, *Morality and Regulation, in* SIMON CHESTERMAN & CHIA LEHNARDT, FROM MERCENARIES TO MARKET, p.12, Oxford Univ. Press (2007).

60. P. W. SINGER, CORPORATE WARRIORS: THE RISE OF THE PRIVATIZED MILITARY INDUSTRY, Cornell Univ. Press (2008) 91–148.

61. Sarah Percy, *supra* note 59 at 12–15.

62. P. W. SINGER, *supra* note 60 at 3.

63. *Id.* at 3–4.

64. *Id.* at 4.

65. Commission on Wartime Contracting in Iraq and Afghanistan, Final Report: Transforming Wartime Contracting: Controlling Costs, Reducing Risks, p. 52, *available at* http://www.wartimecontracting.gov/docs/CWC_FinalReport-Ch2-lowres.pdf.

66. HANNAH TONKIN, STATE CONTROL OVER PRIVATE MILITARY AND SECURITY COMPANIES IN ARMED CONFLICT 40, Cambridge Univ. Press (2011).

67. *Id.* at 50.

68. P. W. SINGER, *supra* note 60 at 119–35.

69. *Id.* at 136–48.

70. HANNAH TONKIN, *supra* note 66 at 41.

71. Jane Mayer, *The Predator War: What are the risks of the C.I.A.'s covert drone program?* THE NEW YORKER, Oct. 26, 2009, *available at* http://www.newyorker.com/reporting/2009/10/26/091026fa_fact_mayer (last visited March 2, 2013). Read more: http://www.newyorker.com/reporting/2009/10/26/091026fa_fact_mayer#ixzz2MOP3v9BD.

72. Tim Shorrock, *supra* note 50 at 373. In Bob Woodward's book, *Obama's Wars*, he reports of the existence of a CA

73. Dana Priest, *America's Security Overload*, THE DAILY BEAST, Sept. 21, 2011, *at* http://www.thedailybeast.com/articles/2011/09/21/government-private-contractors-hinder-fight-on-terrorism.html (last visited March 2, 2013).

74. SIMON CHESTERMAN & CHIA LEHNARDT, FROM MERCENARIES TO MARKET 2, Oxford Univ. Press (2007).

75. Angelina Fisher, *Accountability to whom?" in* PRIVATE SECURITY, PUBLIC ORDER: THE OUTSOURCING OF PUBLIC SERVICES AND ITS LIMITS, p. 46, Oxford Univ. Press (2009).

76. Human Rights First, Written Testimony for the Commission on Wartime Contracting in Iraq and Afghanistan, Hearing on "Are Private Security Contractors Performing Inherently

Governmental Functions?" June 18, 2010, p.1. *Available at* http://www.humanrightsfirst.org/wp-content/uploads/pdf/CWC-Hearing_Written_Testimony.pdf (accessed Nov. 26, 2010).

77.   Human Rights First, How to End Impunity for Private Security and Other Contractors, A Blueprint for the Next Administration (released November 2008, updated December 2009), p.1. *Available at* http://www.humanrightsfirst.org/wp-content/uploads/pdf/PSC-081118-end-cont-impun-blueprint.pdf (accessed Nov. 26, 2011); JAMES COCKAYNE & EMILY SPEERS MEARS, PRIVATE MILITARY AND SECURITY COMPANIES: A FRAMEWORK FOR REGULATION, Int'l Peace Inst., March 2009, p.2, *available at* http://www.ipacademy.org/media/pdf/publications/pmsc_epub.pdf (accessed Nov. 26, 2011).

78.   PMSC is an often-used abbreviation for private military and security contractors.

79.   HANNAH TONKIN, *supra* note 66 at 2.

80.   A.M. Taguba, Article 15-6 Investigation of the 800th Military Police Brigade (2004), *at* www.npr.org/iraq/2004/prison_abuse_report.pdf.

81.   BENEDICT SHEEHY, JACKSON MAOGOTO & VIRGINIA NEWELL, LEGAL CONTROL OF THE PRIVATE MILITARY CORPORATIONS 123, *citing* M. Cohn, Interview with Janis Karpinski: Abu Ghraib General Lambastes Bush Administration (2005). Retrieved from http://www.truthout.org/docs_2005/082405Z.shtml.

82.   P. W. Singer, *Can't Win with 'Em, Can't Go to War without 'Em: Private Military Contractors and Counterinsurgency,* Foreign Policy at Brookings Policy Paper 4 (September 2007) at 1; Charles Savage, *Judge Drops Charges from Blackwater Deaths in Iraq,* N.Y. TIMES, Dec. 31, 2009, *available at* http://www.nytimes.com/2010/01/01/us/01blackwater.html (accessed Jan. 5, 2010).

83.   Mem. Dec. of Op., *available at* http://media.washingtonpost.com/wp-srv/politics/documents/Blackwater (accessed Aug. 22, 2010).

84.   James Risen, *Ex-Blackwater Guards Face Renewed Charges,* N.Y. TIMES, Apr.il 22, 2011, *available at* http://www.nytimes.com/2011/04/23/us/23blackwater.html 9 (accessed Nov 26, 2011).

85.   10 U.S.C. § 802(a)(1) (2007).

86.   David C. Hammond, Crowell & Moring LLP, *The First Prosecution of a Contractor Under the UCMJ: Lessons for Service Contractors,* SERVICE CONTRACTOR, p.33 (Fall 2008), *available at* http://www.crowell.com/documents/The-First-Prosecution-of-a-Contractor-Under-the-UCMJ.pdf (last visited Feb. 22, 2013).

87.   Jennifer K. Elsea, Moshe Schwartz& Kennon H. Nakamura, *Private Security Contractors in Iraq: Background, Legal Status and Other Issues,* CRS Report for Congress, updated Sept. 29, 2008, p.31, *available at* http://assets.opencrs.com/rpts/RL32419_20080929.pdf (last visited Nov. 29, 2012).

88.   JOHN R. LUCKEY, VALERIE BAILEY GRASSO & KATE M. MANUEL, INHERENTLY GOVERNMENTAL FUNCTIONS AND THE DEPARTMENT OF DEFENSE OPERATIONS: BACKGROUND, ISSUES, AND OPTIONS FOR CONGRESS, Cong. Res. Serv.. p.1, June 15, 2009, *available at* http://www.fas.org/sgp/crs/misc/R40641.pdf (last visited Nov. 30, 2012).

89.   Commission on Wartime Contracting in Iraq and Afghanistan, Final Report: Transforming Wartime Contracting: Controlling costs, reducing risks, p. 38, *available at* http://www.wartimecontracting.gov/docs/CWC_FinalReport-Ch2-lowres.pdf.

90.   31 U.S.C. § 501 (2012).

91.   Final Report, *supra* note 89 at 41.

92.   U.S. Congress, Federal Activities Inventory Reform Act of 1998, Pub.L. 105-270, codified at 31 U.S.C. § 501 (1998), Section 5.

93.   John R. Luckey et al, *supra* note 88 at 46, Appendix B.

94.   John R. Luckey et al., *supra* note 88.

95.   WILLIAM H. BOOTHBY, WEAPONS AND THE LAW OF ARMED CONFLICT 229–33, Oxford Univ. Press (2009). It is important to note that some authors distinguish between Unmanned Aerial Vehicles (UAVs) and Unmanned Combat Vehicles (UCVs). In this distinction, UAVs are vehicles that are used for any purpose other than the delivery of kinetic force against enemy personnel and objects. By contrast, UCVs are platforms that carry, deliver, or direct forces. For the purpose of this chapter, the term UAV or drone describes both classes of vehicles.

96.   Barry Neild, "Not just for military use, drones turn civilian," CNN, July 12, 2012, *available at* http://www.cnn.com/2012/07/12/world/europe/civilian-drones-farnborough/ index.html.

97.   P. W. SINGER, WIRED FOR WAR 32–33, Penguin Press (2009).

98.   Brianna Lee, "5 Things You Need to Know about Drones," PBS, Sept. 13, 2012, *available at* http://www.pbs.org/wnet/need-to-know/five-things/drones/12659/ (last visited Dec. 1, 2012).

99.   Stephen Lendman, *America's Drone Command Centers: Remote Warriors Operate Computer Keyboards and Joysticks*, GLOBAL RESEARCH, Apr. 29, 2012, *available at* http:// www.globalresearch.ca/america-s-drone-command-centers-remote-warriors-operate-computer-keyboards-and-joysticks/30590.

100.   Keric D. Clanahan, *Drone-Sourcing? United States Air Forces Unmanned Aircraft Systems, Inherently Governmental Functions, and the Role of Contractors*, 22 FED. CIRC. B. J., May 12, 2012, at p.8.

101.   PATRICK B. JOHNSTON & ANOOP SARBAHI, THE IMPACT OF U.S. DRONE STRIKES ON TERRORISM IN PAKISTAN, p.2, Feb. 25, 2012, *at* http://patrickjohnston.info/materials/drones.pdf.

102.   Peter Bergen, "Drone is Obama's weapon of choice," CNN, Sept. 19, 2012, *available at* http://www.cnn.com/2012/09/05/opinion/bergen-obama-drone/index.html.

103.   Keric D. Clanahan, *supra* note 100 at p.23.

104.   *Id.* at p.27.

105.   David S. Cloud, *Civilian contractors playing key roles in U.S. drone operations*, L.A. TIMES, Dec. 29, 2011, *available at* http://articles.latimes.com/2011/dec/29/world/la-fg-drones-civilians-20111230 (last visited Dec. 2, 2012).

106.   Keric D. Clanahan, *supra* note 100 at p.31–32.

107.   Jane Mayer, *The Predator War*, THE NEW YORKER, Oct. 26, 2009, *available at* http:// www.newyorker.com/reporting/2009/10/26/091026fa_fact_mayer.

108.   David A. Wallace, *The Future Use of Corporate Warriors with the U.S. Armed Forces: Legal, Policy, and Practical Considerations*, DEFENSE ACQUIS. REV. J., Defense Acquisition Univ., July 2009, p.127, *available at* http://www.dau.mil/pubscats/Pages/Defense%20ARJ.aspx (last visited Dec. 2, 2012).

109.   HANNAH TONKIN, STATE CONTROL OVER PRIVATE MILITARY AND SECURITY COMPANIES IN ARMED CONFLICT 49, Cambridge Univ. Press (2011).

110.   BBC News, March 31, 2004, "Bodies mutilated in Iraq attack," *available at* http:// news.bbc.co.uk/2/hi/middle_east/3585765.stm.

111.   David Barstow, *The struggle for Iraq: The Contractors: Security Firm Says Its Workers Were Lured Into Iraqi Ambush*, N.Y. TIMES, Apr. 9, 2004, *available at* http://www.nytimes.com/ 2004/04/09/world/struggle-for-iraq-contractors-security-firm-says-its-workers-were-lured-into.html?pagewanted=all&src=pm (last visited Dec. 2, 2012).

112.   P. W. SINGER, CORPORATE WARRIORS: THE RISE OF THE PRIVATIZED MILITARY INDUSTRY 258, Cornell Univ. Press (2008).

113.   *Id.* at 257.

114. KATERI CARMOLA, PRIVATE SECURITY CONTRACTORS AND NEW WARS: RISK, LAW, AND ETHICS 86, Routledge (2010).

115. ALLISON STRANGER, ONE NATION UNDER CONTRACT: THE OUTSOURCING OF AMERICAN POWER AND THE FUTURE OF FOREIGN POLICY 90, Yale Univ. Press (2009).

116. DINA RASON & ROBERT BAUMAN, BETRAYING OUR TROOPS: THE DESTRUCTIVE RESULTS OF PRIVATIZING WAR, Foreword by Jonathan Alter, p.xi, Palgrave MacMillan (2007).

117. HUMAN RIGHTS FIRST, HOW TO END IMPUNITY FOR PRIVATE SECURITY AND OTHER CONTRACTORS: BLUEPRINT FOR THE NEXT ADMINISTRATION 1, *available at*

118. Steven L. Schooner & Collin D. Swan, *Contractors and the Ultimate Sacrifice*, SERVICE CONTRACTOR MAGAZINE (September 2010), p.16, *available at* http://graphics8.nytimes.com/packages/pdf/world/2010/contractor-casualties-gw-paper.pdf (last visited March 6, 2012).

119. Commission on Wartime Contracting in Iraq and Afghanistan, Final Report: Transforming Wartime Contracting: Controlling costs, reducing risks, pp.39–40, *available at* http://www.wartimecontracting.gov/docs/CWC_FinalReport-Ch2-lowres.pdf (last visited March 12, 2013).

120. *Id.* at 40.

121. *Id.* at 40.

122. *Id.* at 40.

123. Francesco Francioni & Natalino Ronzitti, *Introduction*, p.1 *in* WAR BY CONTRACT: HUMAN RIGHTS, HUMANITARIAN LAW, AND PRIVATE CONTRACTORS, Francesco Francioni & Natalino Ronzitti eds., Oxford Univ. Press (2011).

XII

"A Game of Drones"— Unmanned Aerial Vehicles (UAVs) and Unsettled Legal Questions

Maritza S. Ryan

On November 4th, 2002, Qaed Salim Sinan al-Harethi (a.k.a. Abu Ali)—considered the top Al-Qaeda operative in the country of Yemen and a major player in the *U.S.S. Cole* attack—climbed into a white SUV with several other men. Unbeknownst to Al-Harethi and his companions, at that moment a pilotless drone circled silently above them at an altitude of 10,000 feet. The $5 million Predator,[1] a UAV (Unmanned Aerial Vehicle)[2] equipped with the latest in hi-tech video, infrared, and radar cameras and armed with two missiles,[3] had been relaying full-motion video of the suspected terrorist's movements to a ground control station 150 miles away in the country of Djibouti. As al-Harethi's SUV turned onto a deserted road in the Yemeni countryside, the remote-controlled drone launched a Hellfire missile at its target. In an instant, the vehicle and its occupants were incinerated.[4] His passengers burned beyond recognition, little was left of al-Harethi: he had to be identified by a mark on his leg, which had been blown clear in the blast.[5] For the first time, the United States had personally targeted and killed an Al-Qaeda member outside the borders of a war zone, in a country with which we were not at war.[6] Although not individually targeted, an American citizen, Ahmed Hijazi, happened to be a passenger in al-Harethi's vehicle and also died in the blast.

In the immediate aftermath of the lethal Predator strike on al-Harethi, President George W. Bush and the Central Intelligence Agency (CIA)—named by unidentified government officials as having been behind the operation—declined to comment publicly. Deputy Secretary of Defense Paul Wolfowitz later generally confirmed the strike in an interview on CNN, designating it "a very successful tactical operation."[7] Richard Boucher, a spokesman for the Department of State who, as late as March 2002, had condemned Israel's openly stated policy of conducting "targeted killings" in the occupied Palestinian territories, also refused to talk specifically about the Yemen strike, while still steadfastly maintaining that "[o]ur policy on targeted killings in the Israeli-Palestinian context has not changed."[8] According to media reports, as early as the fall of 2001, President Bush had already issued a classified "finding" authorizing the use of covert, lethal action against specifically listed "high-value targets," to include Osama bin Laden and approximately two dozen other individually named Al Qaeda operatives.[9]

While the Bush administration remained officially silent, the report of the successful UAV strike in Yemen unleashed a torrent of controversy regarding both the legality of targeted strikes and the ultimate effectiveness of their use as a strategy. The strike on a suspected Al-Qaeda terrorist in a nominally friendly country seemed to signal a new level of aggressiveness in the "Global War on Terror," even as the strategic and domestic ramifications of this escalation remained unclear.

Though the UAV technology he used was cutting-edge, President Bush was not the first chief executive to order such a targeted strike against suspected terrorists. President William J. Clinton had signed several highly classified orders "authorizing the CIA to use lethal force to apprehend bin Laden"[10] after intelligence had linked Al-Qaeda to several U.S. embassy bombings throughout Africa that killed over 200 people. In 1998, President Clinton issued the command to unleash Cruise missile strikes against the Al-Qaeda leader, who at the time was believed to be visiting one of his training camps in Afghanistan. The missiles failed to hit bin Laden, but the Clinton White House struggled with defining a legal basis for the bold attempt to kill him, well before the 9/11 attacks and the commencement of the "Global War on Terror," arguing that bin Laden "was, in effect, a piece of terrorist 'infrastructure' to be 'degraded.'"[11] The Bush administration defended its own successful 2004 Yemen strike against al-Harethi on the basis that "the U.S. was engaged in a war, and . . . was dealing with enemy combatants."[12]

Early in President Barack Obama's first term, the new administration announced an end to the use of the phrase "Global War on Terror," signaling its rejection of the Bush-era view of the entire world as the battlefield for an armed conflict without any foreseeable end.[13] President Obama once again made the capture or death of Osama bin Laden the top priority for the nation's intelligence and military services. On May 2, 2011, he authorized Operation Neptune Spear, a high-risk special operations raid into Pakistan which successfully engaged its target, isolated in a private compound located less than a kilometer away from a Pakistani military academy.[14] The killing by SEAL Team 6 of Osama bin Laden, who had been listed as the FBI's #1 "most wanted" since 1999,[15] was met with almost universal acclaim, frequently tinged with relief.[16]

While still basking in the glow of the successful Operation Neptune's Spear, President Obama authorized another operation that garnered a markedly more contentious response, abroad and even domestically. In September of 2011, the President authorized a lethal strike against an American citizen, Anwar Al-Awlaki, who had been known as the "Osama bin Laden of the Internet."[17] Along with fellow American citizen and suspected Al-Qaeda colleague Samir Khan, Al-Awlaki perished in much the same way that al-Harethi had a decade earlier, struck and killed by a direct hit delivered by a Reaper drone,[18] also in Yemen, as his convoy paused on its way to a new hiding place.[19]

The Obama Administration's intentional targeting of an American citizen as a suspected terrorist was a significant milestone in the continuing campaign against Al-Qaeda and associated terrorist groups.[20] Moreover, it came within the context of a pronounced shift toward the use of remotely piloted "drone" weaponry, even as U.S. troops began their withdrawal from Iraq and Afghanistan. According to open media sources, during only his first two years in office, President Obama authorized nearly four times the number of lethal UAV strikes as President Bush had in eight years.[21] As of April 2012, the Obama administration has executed an estimated 295 strikes, killing somewhere between 1,489 and 2,297 suspected militants and an unknown number of civilians.[22]

Just as the strikes by ever more technically sophisticated drones have proliferated, however, so have the vigorous debates regarding their legality.[23] This chapter aims to examine the legal arguments regarding the remote targeting and killing of suspected terrorist operatives: Is the proper legal framework that of the law of armed conflict, international law, domestic law, or perhaps a combination of some or all of them? Does it matter whether the person at the computer toggle switch, controlling the UAV and activating its weapons system from perhaps thousands of miles away, wears a military uniform or civilian clothes? President Obama, acting as Commander-in-Chief—and, per critics alarmed by his drone policy, also a "constitutional lawyer . . . playing prosecutor, judge, jury and executioner all at once"[24]—has included American citizens suspected of terrorist activities on a constantly updated target list, and has demonstrated no hesitancy in authorizing lethal strikes against them.[25] Is a designated target's American citizenship—or, for that matter, his or her location on the globe—relevant? How does the perceived lawfulness of drone strikes under international law shape their effectiveness as a leading component of our overall national strategy? This chapter will explore these and other critical questions arising in the ongoing debate over the United States' use of weaponized UAVs in its efforts to eradicate the threat of terrorism in a post-9/11 world.

UAV Strikes vs. Assassinations

Many euphemisms for targeted strikes are often used interchangeably, reflecting both the confusion and the clash of opinions regarding their legality. The terms used cannot help but be loaded with meaning, and include "assassinations," "targeted killings," "summary executions," and "extra-judicial killings." For our purposes in examining specifically the use of drones, a "targeted strike" refers to the use of UAVs to target an individual with lethal force.[26] It is a tactic, a method—albeit with important strategic implications—born of unprecedented advances in intelligence gathering, surveillance, and precision-guided missile technology. As it has for every weapons system ever developed, its legality—and effectiveness—depend wholly on when, where, and against whom it is used.[27]

Although some commentators and government officials around the world have referred to the use of UAVs to kill suspected terrorists as assassinations, these strikes can be clearly distinguished. The United States does maintain an official policy against assassinations dating back to the 1970s. After congressional hearings led by Senator Frank Church exposed a covert CIA program designed to kill certain heads of state during peacetime—notably Fidel Castro in Cuba, Rafael Trujillo of the Dominican Republic, and Vietnam's Ngo Dinh Diem[28]—President Gerald Ford issued Executive Order 11,905, Section 5 of which provides:

> (g) Prohibition of Assassination. No employee of the United States Government shall engage in, or conspire to engage in, political assassination.[29]

Both Presidents Jimmy Carter and Ronald Reagan issued their own executive orders upholding the ban on assassination, the latest of which, President Reagan's E.O. 12,333, has never been revoked. None of them specifically defined the word "assassination," however, and the Carter and Reagan versions leave out the word "political," but the general thrust of the orders has been interpreted as prohibiting the intentional killing of an individual "for political purposes"[30] during peacetime. President Bush's White House spokesman, Ari Fleischer, confirmed this view immediately following the Yemen strike, stating that "[t]here's an executive order that prohibits the assassination of foreign leaders, and that remains in place."[31]

Even Osama bin Laden himself, as the head of a dispersed network of terrorist cells we refer to as Al-Qaeda, never qualified as a foreign leader, nor was he targeted for political reasons. His status as chief of a stateless, transnational terrorist organization actively involved in planning attacks around the world, and not as a leader of any government, by definition placed him outside both the letter and the intent of Executive Order 12,333. It follows, then, that the killing of a subordinate terrorist chief or other operative within his organization similarly cannot constitute an assassination.

In distinguishing between the 2004 Yemen strike and unlawful assassinations, however, National Security Adviser Condoleezza Rice went further, indicating that Al-Qaeda operatives were "enemy combatants" operating all around the world. "We're in a new kind of war," said Dr. Rice, six days after the Yemen strike, "and we've made it very clear that this new kind of war [will] be fought on different battlefields."[32] Immediately after American citizen Anwar al-Awlaki's killing by drone, President Obama was more circumspect, acknowledging his death but declining to comment directly on U.S. involvement.[33]

The Department of Justice's "White Paper"

In February of 2013, the NBC news organization obtained a "leaked" White Paper produced by the Department of Justice (DoJ) dated November 8, 2011, titled "Lawfulness of a Lethal Operation Directed Against a U.S. Citizen Who Is a Senior Operational Leader of Al-Qaeda or an Associated Force."[34] In seeking to establish the lawfulness of lethal drone strikes, the white paper—which was officially released days later[35]—wrestled with identifying the proper legal framework applicable to the lethal targeting of suspected Al-Qaeda terrorists, citizen and non-citizen, whether located on a "hot" battlefield in the midst of active hostilities or driving down a desert road, thousands of miles away from a combat zone. Rather than quell legal qualms, the DoJ White Paper has, at least initially, seemed to inflame them.[36] Nevertheless, the leaked document provides important insights into the Obama Administration's evolving thinking on its drone policy, while at the same time helping frame the debate regarding their use.[37] The paper explored two legal bases justifying the targeted killing of certain individuals, to include those with U.S. citizenship: (I) "the existence of an armed conflict with Al-Qaeda" and (II) the inherent right national self-defense.[38]

The Law of Armed Conflict

"The United States is in an armed conflict with Al-Qaeda and its associated forces . . ."[39]

"Given the degree of violence in [the attacks of 9/11], and the nature and scope of the organization necessary to carry them out," casting our efforts against Al-Qaeda terrorists and any nations harboring them as a "war" was a natural response.[40] Three days after the attacks on the World Trade Center and the Pentagon, Congress passed a joint resolution, Authorization for Use of Military Force (AUMF),[41] signed by George W. Bush on September 18, 2001. The AUMF authorized the President

> to use all necessary and appropriate force against those nations, organizations, or persons he determines planned, authorized, committed, or aided the terrorist attacks that occurred on September 11, 2001, or harbored such organizations or persons, in order to prevent any future acts of international terrorism against the United States by such nations, organizations or persons.

In so doing, the United States invoked the terms of that *lex specialis*[42] known as the Law of Armed Conflict (LOAC, also called International Humanitarian Law, or IHL) during which the normal rules of international law are held in abeyance. The LOAC is embodied in both treaty (prominently, the four Geneva Conventions, the Hague Convention, and Additional Protocols I and II to the Geneva Conventions) as well as customary law (often as codified in the two Protocols). The four basic principles underlying all of LOAC are understood to be Distinction, Military Necessity, Proportionality, and Unnecessary Suffering. Distinction—also known by the terms Discrimination and Humanity—is the primary tenet running through the whole of the Law of Armed Conflict. The principle of Distinction requires that any act of targeting people or objects must distinguish between the proscribed and the permissible. For example, civilians are non-combatants who may normally not be targeted; so also protected are their livestock, homes, vehicles, and other property. On the other hand, it is lawfully permissible for military forces to target combatants and military objectives, defined as "those objects which by their nature, location, purpose or use, make an effective contribution to military action and whose total or partial destruction, capture or neutralization, in the circumstances ruling at the time, offers a definite military advantage."[43]

Military Necessity permits those actions that further the mission of defeating the enemy, so long as they are not otherwise contrary to the laws, customs, and usages of war.

The principle of Proportionality recognizes that executing a military mission may cause unintentional harm to civilians and or their property, but requires that commanders make a considered determination whether such anticipated collateral damage is "proportional and not excessive in relation to the concrete and direct military advantage to be gained."[44]

Finally, the fourth principle of the Law of Armed Conflict forbids the employment of "arms, projectiles, or material calculated to cause unnecessary suffering."[45] "The only legitimate object" of war being "to weaken the military forces of the enemy," the principle of Unnecessary Suffering prohibits the use of weaponry or ammunition that would uselessly aggravate the sufferings of disabled soldiers or render their treatment or recovery impossible.[46]

International Armed Conflicts

According to Common Article 2 of the Geneva Conventions, the Law of Armed Conflict applies in "cases of declared war or of any other armed conflict which may arise between two or more of the High Contracting Parties, even if the state of war is not recognized by one of them."[47] Under international law, nation-states alone enjoy "a monopoly on violence."[48] That is, only states may grant persons "combatant status," which authorizes them "to take part in hostilities against other states" and "carry out acts that would otherwise be unlawful, without sanction."[49] In international armed conflicts, combatants may legally target their enemy's combatants and other legitimate military targets on sight. If captured, combatants become prisoners of war, but they may not be prosecuted for acts of war that are not otherwise unlawful under the Law of Armed Conflict (for example, they may be tried and punished for targeting civilians, who are "protected persons," but not for carrying out attacks on valid military targets such as Army supply convoys).

Osama bin Laden purported to declare war—on terms that clearly rejected LOAC principles, particularly that of distinction—when he issued a 1998 "World Islamic Front Statement" relayed as a self-styled *fatwah*[50] to his followers: "The ruling to kill the Americans and their allies—*civilians and military*—is an individual duty for every Muslim who can do it, in any country in which it is possible to do it. . . ."[51] Nevertheless, as noted earlier, bin Laden was never a national leader, and, whatever else Al-Qaeda may be, it is a non-state actor and therefore cannot, according to traditional interpretations of LOAC, grant combatant status to any of its members.

Once a state of armed conflict existed between the United States and its allies and the nation of Afghanistan, those Al-Qaeda elements that joined forces with the sitting Taliban government to repel a military invasion could, under its auspices, have attained combatant status.[52] Of course, any combatant could still be held liable for conduct, such as acts of terror, that is contrary to the law of armed conflict.[53] That part of our campaign against Al-Qaeda, from the opening salvoes of the war in Afghanistan until the point that a new government took control, qualified as an international armed conflict. The same analysis would apply to the 2004 invasion of Iraq. Under the Geneva Conventions, both conflicts were, at their inception, international in nature. Al-Qaeda operatives fighting in concert with or in support of the Taliban government in Kabul—and, likewise, those individuals supporting Saddam Hussein in the field after commencement of U.S.

and allied operations there—could correctly have been categorized as combatants, and as such could be directly targeted according to the LOAC.

Common Article 3 Armed Conflicts

Despite the continued presence of U.S. and allied troops for an extended period of time in both Afghanistan and Iraq, however, once the mission of those foreign troops shifted to supporting the new governments established there, combat operations in each nation ceased to be international in nature. As the Supreme Court recognized in *Hamdan vs. Rumsfeld*[54] in 2006, the LOAC continues to apply to the continuing armed conflict, specifically under Common Article 3. The Geneva Conventions' Common Article 3 provides that, as a conflict ceases to be one between nation-states, it may enter into a second category, that of Non-International Armed Conflicts (NIAC). NIAC are defined simply as those conflicts "not of an international character occurring in the territory of one of the High Contracting parties."[55] Former members of the armed forces of Afghanistan, associated Taliban insurgents, civilians who sporadically engaged in violence against government troops, or Al-Qaeda terrorists: under the NIAC legal regime, all of these players on the battlefield become "unprivileged belligerents." Unprivileged (or unlawful) belligerents is a term used more or less interchangeably with unlawful combatants, but is arguably the more precise label, as it presumptively excludes such fighters (i.e., belligerents lacking membership in the regular armed forces of any nation) from the category of combatants, which are *a priori* state-sanctioned and lawful.[56]

Unlike opposing sides in an international armed conflict, which pits one nation's combatants against those of another, only the government's armed forces (and any foreign troops acting in concert with them) enjoy combatant immunity in a NIAC. The four major principles underlying the LOAC continue to apply. For instance, under the principle of distinction, government troops may not target civilians unless, and only while, they take a direct part in hostilities. Once identified as having done so, these civilians can also later be apprehended and prosecuted for any acts of violence or offenses committed against either civilian or military targets under both domestic and international law.[57]

Al-Qaeda as an "Organized Armed Group"

Although NIAC never grants combatant status to any non-state fighters, it nevertheless accounts for the existence of "nonstate organized armed groups."[58] Accordingly, the DoJ White Paper argues that "Al-Qaeda and associated forces," as referenced in the September 2001 Authorization to Use Military Force (AUMF),[59] would qualify as such a group given that, collectively, they are a nonstate actor, organized, and armed.[60] In accordance with the ICRC interpretation, upon joining and throughout their membership in Al-Qaeda, individuals assuming a "continuous combat function"[61] no longer qualify as civilians and may be targeted based only on their membership status, and regardless of their actual activities at any given moment. Per this paradigm, the United States and its allies could lawfully target Al-Qaeda fighters at any time, whether close-up and personal through the sights of an M-16 rifle, or via a computer screen observed by a UAV operator thousands of miles away.[62] Moreover, Al-Qaeda is not merely a non-state actor, but also a transnational one whose activities span any number of countries.[63] Per the white paper, its members—assuming that they are performing a "continuous combat function"—could therefore be lethally targeted wherever they might happen to be, so long as the traditional principles underlying the LOAC are followed.

Pushing the NIAC Paradigm

That a sort of NIAC "cloud" follows Al-Qaeda members as they travel around the globe—perhaps far away from any "hot" battlefield—which permits their direct targeting is still a highly controversial concept.[64] Scholars and commentators are likewise divided as to a number of related issues: can a NIAC transcend the territory of one state, i.e., become a transnational armed conflict, and still fall within the meaning of Common Article 3?[65] As the armed conflicts within Iraq and Afghanistan continue to wind down, what is the necessary level of intensity of armed conflict in order for a NIAC to be extant? Does Al-Qaeda, ever more dispersed and decentralized, actually possess the requisite features to qualify as an "organized" armed group fighting against a nation-state or alliance of nation-states? If status as a member of a non-state-sponsored, transnational, organized armed group is sufficient to permit lawful lethal targeting under the laws of war, does this mean that an armed conflict exists everywhere on the globe and continues until the last member of Al-Qaeda—or of its "associated forces"—is killed?

On a more granular level, what kind of activity on the part of a suspected Al-Qaeda member constitutes a "continuous combat function?" At what point do their activities become so attenuated as to prohibit the use of lethal force in a wartime scenario? The late Anwar al-Awlaki, for example, had become well known as a highly effective propagandist for Al-Qaeda via his sermons and teachings on the Internet; his colleague, Samir Khan, who was killed in the same airstrike, similarly was the editor of *Inspire*, a web-based *jihadist* magazine which frequently called on followers to attack Americans and the West. Roles involving public affairs, financing, or recruiting functions are not sufficient to constitute taking a direct part in combat and therefore fail to satisfy the "continuous combat function" requirement. Consequently, the U.S. government has alleged that al-Awlaki had "gone operational" and had been acting as a chief within the "Al Qaeda in the Arabian Peninsula" organization at the time of his death.[66] The fact that he was an American might have made him more effective as a propagandist, but did not make him any less targetable as an individual fulfilling a "continuous combat function" for the group.

Distinction and Proportionality

Our use of drones in targeting suspected members of armed groups also raises issues regarding at least two of the four principles underlying the Law of Armed Conflict, specifically Distinction and Proportionality. The term "signature strikes," for example, refers to the practice of deploying drones not against a specific, positively identified target, but rather based on "a pattern of behavior—young men of military age test-firing mortars at a training camp in South Waziristan, say, or riding under arms in a truck toward the Afghan border."[67] The farther they are from an active battlefield, the greater the possibility that these types of "signature strikes" might be prone to error[68] and fall short of the primary duty to *distinguish* between lawful targets. The use of a technologically advanced weapons system at a stand-off distance of half the globe may complicate but does not relieve the legal responsibility to distinguish, for example, between a "member of a non-state organized armed force" or a "civilian currently taking a direct part in the hostilities of such a force"—each of whom may lawfully be targeted—and a civilian who, even though she may be indirectly supporting those hostilities in some way, nevertheless remains protected from attack.[69]

Moreover, the current administration's alleged method of calculating "collateral damage"—i.e., unintentional harm to civilians, to include causing their deaths— is unfortunately reminiscent of the use of designated "Free Fire Zones" during the Vietnam era.[70] "In an area of known militant activity, all military-age males were considered to be enemy fighters," and "[t]herefore, anyone who was killed in a drone strike there was categorized as a combatant."[71] Such formulations would preclude meaningful application of the Proportionality principle, which requires that collateral damage not be excessive in relation to the definitive military advantage to be gained.[72]

National Self-Defense against Imminent Attack

"Targeting a member of an enemy force who poses an imminent threat of violent attack to the United States is . . . a lawful act of national self-defense."[73]

The White Paper also cites as a legal basis for its use of drones, in addition to the authority vested by Congress by its AUMF, "the President's constitutional responsibility to protect the nation and the inherent right to national self-defense recognized in international law," noting Article 51 of the United Nations Charter.[74] A fundamental *raison d'être* of the United Nations is the concept that, in the interest of establishing and maintaining international peace and security, all signatories agree to repose within this multinational institution—and specifically, in the Security Council—the authority to wage war.[75] The UN Charter does not foreclose a signatory's use of military force in all circumstances, leaving open the possibility that states may still resort to force during exigent circumstances before the Security Council can reasonably act. Article 51 notes, "Nothing in the present Charter shall impair the inherent right of individual or collective self-defence if an armed attack occurs against a Member of the United Nations."[76]

Logically, if a right to self-defense exists once an attack has already occurred, would there not also be a concomitant right to anticipatory self-defense, a right to act after a potential attack is detected but *before* it is launched? As the events of 9/11 painfully demonstrate, a small number of highly motivated terrorists can—given effective leadership, some training, modest resources, and a plan—kill or injure thousands of innocent people and do tremendous amounts of damage to our infrastructure, economy, and national psyche in a very short period of time. *Ergo,* the White Paper's emphasis on a crucial prerequisite: that an individual targeted for a lethal drone strike pose an "imminent threat of violent attack" against the United States or its interests. As noted earlier, such a prerequisite is not required under the LOAC/IHL legal regime. Combatants and members of armed groups—even while they are sleeping, or eating lunch in a mess tent—as well as civilians who are taking a direct part in hostilities (e.g., carrying ammunition for fighters)—may be attacked with lethal force based on their status alone, and regardless of any actual threat of attack they might pose in return. Absent the backdrop of an ongoing armed conflict of some type, any right to anticipatory national self-defense turns on the existence of an imminent threat emanating from the individual being targeted.

How imminent must imminent be? Per the White Paper, the United States need not have "clear evidence that a specific attack on U.S. persons and interests will take place in the immediate future"[77] before striking. Rather, the very nature of the threat posed by Al-Qaeda operatives and their associates "demands a broader concept of imminence."[78] Once intelligence has determined that individuals—particularly "high-ranking ones serving in leadership positions—or groups are engaged in a continuous cycle of planning terror attacks, argues the White Paper, time is of the essence. The ongoing nature of the threat requires that the United States act while there is still a meaningful opportunity to disrupt the planning cycle, at whatever stage of development a particular attack might have reached.

Since the U.S. is wielding lethal force, albeit in a preemptive fashion, the White Paper accepts "the premise that any such lethal operation . . . would [necessarily] comply with the four fundamental law-of-war principles governing the use of force: necessity, distinction, proportionality, and humanity (the avoidance of unnecessary suffering)."[79]

Arguably, "because of past attacks and the ongoing threat of future Al-Qaeda attacks, the United States' use of self-defensive force is permissible under Article 51 of the U.N. Charter, and satisfies the necessity and proportionality requirements of *jus ad bellum*."[80] In terms of necessity, which permits those actions that contribute to the successful conclusion of the mission that are otherwise lawful, it seems that technology tips the scales. A remotely piloted UAV can, for remarkably extended periods and nearly undetectably, seek, find, and kill a targeted individual—even one hiding in a remote, inaccessible, and possibly lawless corner of the world— and it can do so without exposing military personnel to risk of injury or death. Capturing instead of simply killing terrorist operatives could allow invaluable access to their personal effects, including cell phones, laptops, passports, and other papers, and would still effectively disrupt any attack being led or conducted by the captured individual. Moreover, such intelligence windfalls could foil many other plots and expose other co-conspirators and their methods. Yet, the same factors that make drones so attractive—UAVs are unfazed by the remoteness and inaccessibility of the terrain and the inability (or unwillingness) of a local government to exert control there—make capture operations difficult, dangerous, and perhaps impossible for military personnel with boots on the ground. "Feasibility," as a close cousin to necessity, "would be a highly fact-specific and potentially time-sensitive inquiry"[81] in each and every instance. The infeasibility of capture also coincides with proportionality considerations. Unlike a capture operation, a drone can capitalize on extremely narrow windows of opportunity. It is capable of striking in the instant of time and space in which the targeted individual is most exposed and away from the civilian population that might otherwise become collateral damage. As in the highly publicized cases of both Al-Harethi and Al-Awlaki, those windows of opportunity often occur when the individuals are traveling across open, unpopulated areas. UAVs, because of their superior surveillance and targeting ability, may in such instances offer a reduced risk of causing collateral damage (that is, harm to civilians) as well as reducing risk to U.S. military personnel. [82]

Limits to Anticipatory Self-Defense

International law does recognize an anticipatory or preemptive right to self-defense, but one that appears to be much more limited than the White Paper's "broader concept of imminence" would suggest. Self-defense envisions "the right to use force against a real and imminent threat when 'the necessity of that self-defence is instant, overwhelming, and leaving no choice of means, and no moment of deliberation.'"[83] Moreover, per a less-oft-quoted phrase in Article 51 of the UN Charter, the right to self-defense is also time-limited: it exists only "until the

Security Council has taken measures necessary to maintain international peace and security."[84]

How these factors—the actual imminence of the threat and permissible duration of the defensive response—may reasonably be defined remain controversial. The White Paper's definition of imminence, allege critics, "is so broad as to be almost meaningless."[85] The only real criterion seems to be "membership in a group continually plotting against the United States—even if that plot has not reached its end-stage."[86] Moreover, in contrast to the breadth and depth of the 9/11 attacks, the potential terrorist threat now is more of the sporadic, low-intensity type that we can expect for the foreseeable future: none of these disparate terrorist acts qualifies as an "armed attack" envisioned in Article 51. In contrast, the White Paper argues that the threat of terror is inherently one of many separate acts of violence, but each instance of which poses a very "imminent and real" threat.[87] Forcing the United States to delay acting until the individuals planning to cause harm to Americans and their interests reached "some theoretical end stage of the planning for a particular plot," argues the paper, would pose an unacceptable risk of failure.[88]

Even commentators who remain skeptical of the U.S.'s drone program recognize that "[i]nternational law permits the use of lethal force in self-defence in response to an 'armed attack' as long as that force is necessary and proportionate."[89] In determining the legality of an initial resort to force (*jus ad bellum*), such as in the case of self-defense, however, they argue that the principles of Necessity and Proportionality apply in a more restrictive way than they would in an ongoing armed conflict (*jus in bello*). Necessity under self-defense "requires a State to assess whether it has means to defend itself other than through armed force," not just whether the military action contemplated will further attainment of the mission while otherwise complying with the laws of war.[90] Likewise, in evaluating the legality of self-defense, Proportionality "requires States to use force only defensively and to the extent necessary to meet defensive objectives," rather than merely balance possible collateral damage against the military advantage expected to be gained.[91] Though not prohibiting all targeted strikes per se, the principles as applied in a self-defense scenario tend to reinforce Article 51's self-limiting qualities and require evaluation on a case-by-case basis. The White Paper does not disagree, though it rejects critics' contentions that such an analysis would not support a lengthy drone campaign as a whole.

Law Enforcement and the "Public Authority Exception"

"Our systematic effort to dismantle terrorist organizations must continue. But this war, like all wars, must end."[92]

Accustomed as we are to working within the constraints of Posse Comitatus, it is commonly understood that the military may not participate actively in law enforcement. [93] Domestically, this is a valid view, but abroad, the constraints of the Posse Comitatus Act do not apply. The phenomenon that is Al-Qaeda, as the most successful purveyor of transnational terrorism the world has ever known, has posed a threat lurking somewhere on the continuum between law enforcement and conventional armed conflict. As the ICRC has noted:

> The defining feature of any act legally classified as "terrorist" under either international or domestic law is that it is always penalized as criminal: no act of violence legally designated "terrorist" is, or can be, exempt from prosecution.[94]

The controversy over drones demonstrates that a criminal organization devoted to carrying out terrorist acts while possessing the proven capability to launch military-style, devastating attacks—e.g., Al-Qaeda—will constantly challenge the traditional categories and outlines of the law of armed conflict. Though greatly decimated in the last dozen years, allegedly by the ongoing drone campaign that is the subject of this chapter,[95] Al-Qaeda and its ideologically motivated adherents will remain highly dangerous for the foreseeable future.[96] Some have argued that, as it flattens and morphs into more loosely linked or even disarticulated organization—with lone wolves, inspired by Al-Qaeda leaders long dead, stepping up to fill the void[97]—the loose terrorist alliance may become even more dangerous and unpredictable. At the same time, as the U.S. and its allies withdraw its conventional troops from active combat zones, the Non-International Armed Conflict/Transnational Armed Group paradigm will increasingly lose its applicability. Likewise, the argument for national self-defense framework may become less salient as the threat posed by Al-Qaeda becomes even more sporadic, subtle, and individualized.

Though not fully explored in depth by the White Paper as an alternative, stand-alone legal justification for targeted strikes, the law enforcement paradigm is raised in the context of discussing domestic statutes and whether they would prohibit lethal targeting, particularly in the case of U.S. citizens. "Even in domestic law enforcement operations," notes the White Paper, a police officer may use deadly force against a particularly dangerous individual as a last resort, such as when "it is necessary to prevent escape" and "the officer has probable cause to believe that [a] suspect poses a threat of serious physical harm, either to the officer or to others."[98] The "public authority exception" allows that a death resulting from police officers' lawful use of lethal force while in the course of performing their duties is not murder.

In dealing with an international criminal, the same analogy could apply. Admittedly, in the case of officers attempting an apprehension which must at some point be aborted, there is, at least theoretically, a moment when a warning might be given that allows the suspect to surrender. That opportunity is logically foreclosed in the case of lethal force administered by drone. Therefore, under human rights law (i.e., outside the framework of the law of armed conflict), a drone strike executed "by law enforcement officials cannot be legal because, unlike in armed conflict, it is never permissible for killing to be the *sole objective* of an operation."[99]

Nevertheless, it is also true that "lethal force under human rights law is legal if it is strictly and directly necessary to save life."[100] For example, in cases where arrest is not feasible, and only the use of lethal force will minimize or avoid death or serious injury to civilians—both judgment calls which must be made in the spur of the moment—police officers may resort to lethal force.[101] Similarly, the argument can be made that in certain cases—for example, one in which a high-ranking Al-Qaeda operative is actively orchestrating further criminal operations, and his capture is either impossible or too dangerous to effect—a targeted strike could be considered a reasonable option of last resort. In the case of Mr. al-Harethi, for example, an earlier attempt to apprehend him in the lawless, remote area in which he and his heavily-armed followers had been hiding encountered stiff resistance and resulted in the deaths of 18 Yemeni troops.[102] Additional attempts to capture the man considered to be the highest-ranking Al-Qaeda member in Yemen would likely have been just as futile. Thus, it could be argued that the use of lethal force prevented further loss of innocent life while ensuring that the suspected mastermind behind the *U.S.S. Cole* bombing did not continue to escape arrest indefinitely, free to plan and execute further crimes.

Blended Parameters for Targeted Strikes

The White Paper's conclusion as to the parameters for permitting targeted strikes against an individual outside of the traditional battleground seems to factor in all three legal paradigms—national self-defense, law enforcement, and non-international armed conflict:

> Here the Department of Justice concludes only that where the following three conditions are met, a U.S. operation using lethal force in a foreign country against a U.S. citizen who is a senior operational leader of Al-Qaeda or an associated force would be lawful:
>
> (1) an informed, high-level official of the U.S. government has determined that the targeted individual poses an imminent threat of violent attack against the United States *[National Self Defense]*;

(2) capture is infeasible, and the United States continues to monitor whether capture becomes feasible *[Law Enforcement]*; and

(3) the operation would be conducted in a manner consistent with applicable law of war principles *[Law of Armed Conflict]*.[103]

The Question of American Citizenship

Moreover, the White Paper posited that any person, regardless of nation of citizenship, could be lawfully targeted under the criteria so delineated. On March 6, 2013, Senator Rand Paul (R-Ky.) "filibustered" the nomination of John Brennan, the main architect of the Obama Administration's drone program, to be the head of the CIA. Senator Paul spoke for a near-record 13 hours. "I wanted to sound an alarm bell from coast to coast," he later wrote. "I wanted everybody to know that our Constitution is precious and that no American should be without first being charged with a crime."[104]

Senator Rand Paul's alarm about the U.S. drone program echoed across the domestic political spectrum. Could the United States use drones to lethally target its own citizens? As the White Paper concluded, and the President confirmed in remarks made at the National Defense University in May of 2013, the answer is yes. Whether under the Law of Armed Conflict/IHL Regime or under the rubric of national self-defense, "the U.S. citizenship of a leader of Al-Qaeda or its associated forces," noted the White Paper, "does not give that person constitutional immunity from attack."[105] Likewise, the President rejected the idea that American citizenship should "serve as a shield" against drone strikes for those who "go[] abroad to wage war against America" and are "actively plotting to kill U.S. citizens" in instances where preemption by capture is not possible.[106]

> "[T]he high threshold that we've set for taking lethal action," noted Obama, "applies to all potential terrorist targets, regardless of whether or not they are American citizens."[107] "And," the President added, "before any strike is taken, there must be near-certainty that no civilians will be killed or injured—the highest standard we can set."[108]

Domestic Accountability and International Reaction

"President Obama's aggressive campaign of drone strikes has generated controversy overseas and among terrorism experts," but, according to recent polls, the "American public has few qualms with drone strikes."[109] A new Monitor/TIPP poll finds that a firm majority of Americans—57 percent—support the current level of drone strikes targeting "Al Qaeda targets and other terrorists in foreign countries."[110] Similarly, a Gallup poll taken in April found that 65% of Americans support drone attacks on terrorists abroad, though the percentage approving the use of such airstrikes against U.S. citizens who are suspected terrorists drops to 41%. In reaction to the April 15, 2013, Boston Marathon bombings—an attack planned and executed by two American naturalized citizens[111]—even Senator Paul suggested that using drones to help find and possibly strike the two suspected terrorists on U.S. soil could be acceptable under a law enforcement paradigm. "I have never argued against any technology being used against having an imminent threat, an act of crime going on," Senator Paul said.[112]

International attitudes toward the U.S. program stand in stark contrast to Americans' general acceptance of drone strikes. A June 2012 poll conducted by the Pew Research Center in 20 countries, including allies such as Germany and Mexico, revealed that a majority were opposed to the American drone campaign. "In US-friendly Muslim nations such as Egypt, Jordan, and Turkey, the disapproval rates were enormous, ranging from 81 to 89 percent."[113] In Pakistan, "only 17% back American drone strikes against leaders of extremist groups"—which themselves are highly unpopular—"even if they are conducted in conjunction with the Pakistani government"; most ominously, nearly 3/4 of the Pakistani population consider the United States "an enemy."[114]

The Future in Drones?

"The government announced a successful UAV strike against a high-level transnational terrorist suspected of masterminding riots and attacks against both civilians and local police forces. A skilled propagandist and self-styled spiritual guru, the splittist agitator had been avoiding capture for many years by hiding in the mountainous northern tribal regions. As a senior-level leader of a dispersed network, he was suspected of promoting passive and active resistance to local government officials and inciting a campaign of terrorist acts, namely, a series of horrific suicides by self-immolation."

The preceding paragraph is notional only—this targeted strike never occurred—but what if "the government" were China, and the "splittist agitator" the Dalai Lama?[115] This thought problem features a chilling scenario we would hope never to see, but one that is based on unprecedented developments in UAV and rapid proliferation of the technology that are occurring now. "There's been a period when the United States had a monopoly" on drone technology; "[t]hat is over."[116]

"In an apparent bid to catch up with the U.S. and Israel in developing [the UAV] technology that is considered the future of military aviation," China has been ramping up drone production: "Western defense officials and experts were surprised to see more than 25 different . . . models" of UAVs displayed at a Chinese air show in 2010.[117] According to a July 2012 Report by the Government

Accountability Office (GAO), the number of nations possessing some type of UAV system in their arsenals "nearly doubled from about 40 to more than 75" since 2005.[118] The "countries of proliferation concern," which include China, Iran, Pakistan, and Russia, "developed and fielded increasingly more sophisticated systems" with "new UAV capabilities, including armed and miniature UAVs," effectively "increase[ing] the number of military applications for this technology."[119] Less sophisticated UAVs can also be dangerous: "such drones can be equipped with chemical or biological weapons or be used to provide intelligence about the location of American forces."[120] Because UAVs are more economical to deploy than jets and trained pilots, even countries impacted by austerity measures, including members of the EU, are pouring resources into research and development and purchases of new drone weaponry.[121] Widespread proliferation highlights the critical importance of developing a legal framework for the use of UAVs that will matter well beyond the United States' current program in combating terrorism. Such a legal regime will need to be one, notes the UN Special Rapporteur on Counterterrorism and Human Rights, Ben Emmerson, "that we can live with if it is being used by Iran against Iranian dissidents hiding inside the territory of Turkey or Syria or Iraq," and that "we'd be prepared to see China use against dissident groups from Tibet."[122] "When it comes to lethal drone strikes against foreign targets, America's government and Congress should be aware," warned John Bellinger, former legal adviser for the U.S. Department of State and the National Security Council during the George W. Bush Administration, that "'what is sauce for the goose is sauce for the gander.'"[123]

The Obama administration's targeted strike policy should, therefore, help set "clear, internationally accepted rules" based on a common understanding of international law and respect for its fundamental principles.[124] The United States, as the current leader in advanced UAV technology, is only now beginning to engage the global community in an ongoing dialog about the legality and morality of employing drones. In his remarks at the National Defense University on May 23, 2012, President Obama "described new rules intended to bind both his government and successive presidents," hoping to set "norms for other countries" as they acquire ever more advanced UAV technology, norms that might develop into customary international law over time.[125] Moreover, noting the dearth of "substantive public discussion about drone attacks among policymakers at the international level," some have called for negotiation of a formal international treaty governing UAVs:

> The time has come for some kind of international convention on the legal framework surrounding the uses of such weapons, which promise

to shape the warfare of the future as much as tanks and bombers did during the 20th century.[126]

As Ben Emmerson, the UN Special Rapporteur currently conducting a major investigation into civilian drone deaths put it, "Drones are here to stay. Their military logic is undeniable."[127] For the foreseeable future, the unprecedented capabilities—and unsettled legal issues—that UAVs represent will continue to be, in President Obama's words,

> "something that you have to struggle with . . . if you don't, then it's very easy to slip into a situation in which you end up bending rules thinking that the ends always justify the means. That's not been our tradition. That's not who we are as a country."[128]

The Obama administration's recent inclination toward seeking more transparency and public engagement at home and abroad is both fully consistent with America's professed values and absolutely indispensable to our strategic, long-term interests in securing a more peaceful and just world.

Notes

1.   *See* Eric Schmitt, *U.S. Drones Crowding Skies Over Iraq and Afghanistan*, N.Y. TIMES, April 5, 2005, p. A-1.

2.   Even the proper term for UAVs is controversial: the Air Force favors RPA (Remotely Piloted Aircraft), and eschews the term "drone" altogether. Aram Roston, *The 'D' Word: What To Call a UAV: A drone? Not according to Air Force officers*, C4ISR JOURNAL, March 26, 2013, at http://www.defensenews.com/article/20130326/C4ISR02/303260023/The-8216-D-8217-Word-What-Call-UAV.

3.   USAF Factsheet, http://www.af.mil/news/factsheets/RQ_1_Predator_Unmanned_Aerial.html.

4.   Ian Urbina, *On the Road with Murder, Inc.*, ASIA TIMES, Jan. 26, 2003, p.3.

5.   James Risen, *CIA Seeks and Kills al-Qaeda Chief*, Nov. 6, 2002, N.Y. TIMES, at http://www.smh.com.au/articles/2002/11/05/1036308313504.html?oneclick=true.

6.   Pamela Hess, *Experts: Yemen Strike Not Assassination*, UPI, Nov. 8, 2002, at www.upi.com/view.cfm?StoryID=20021107-042725-6586r.

7.   "U.S. missile strike kills al Qaeda chief; CIA drone launched missile Tuesday," CNN, Nov. 5, 2002, at http://www.cnn.com/2002/WORLD/meast/11/05/yemen.blast/.

8.   Max Boot, *Retaliation for Me, But Not for Thee: A foolish inconsistency is the hobgoblin of the State Department*, WEEKLY STANDARD, Vol. 008, No. 10, Nov. 18, 2002, at http://www.weeklystandard.com/Content/Public/Articles/000/000/001/883gplpc.asp?pg=2.

9.   James Risen & David Johnston, *Bush Has Widened Authority of CIA to Kill Terrorists*, N.Y. TIMES, Dec. 15, 2002, at www.globalpolicy.org/wtc/targets/2002/1215cia.htm.

10.   BILL CLINTON, MY LIFE (Alfred A. Knopf, 2004), at 804.

11.   Richard Lowry, *A View to a Kill: Assassination in war and peace*, NATIONAL REVIEW, March 11, 2002, at http://www.findarticles.com/p/articles/mi_m1282/is_4_54/ai_83117148, p.4.

12.   "US 'still opposes' targeted killings," BBC NEWS, Nov. 6, 2002, at http://news.bbc.co.uk/2/low/middle_east/2408031.stm.

13.   Toby Harnden, *Barack Obama adviser rejects 'global war on terror'*: "President Barack Obama's top counter-terrorism adviser has rejected the notion of a "global war on terror," arguing that it led to an obsessive focus on a tactic and suggested America was at war with the world," THE TELEGRAPH, Aug. 7, 2009, at http://www.telegraph.co.uk/news/worldnews/barackobama/ 5990566/Barack-Obama-adviser-rejects-global-war-on-terror.html.

14.   Peter Baker, Helene Cooper & Mark Mazzetti, *Bin Laden Is Dead, Obama Says*, N.Y. TIMES, May 1, 2011, at http://www.nytimes.com/2011/05/02/world/asia/osama-bin-laden-is-killed.html?pagewanted=all&_r=0; also, Philip Sherwell, *Osama bin Laden killed: Behind the scenes of the deadly raid*, THE TELEGRAPH, May 7, 2011, at http://www.telegraph.co.uk/news/ worldnews/al-qaeda/8500431/Osama-bin-Laden-killed-Behind-the-scenes-of-the-deadly-raid.html.

15.   FBI Ten Most Wanted Fugitives, for Murder of U.S. Nationals Outside the United States; Conspiracy to Murder U.S. Nationals Outside the United States; Attack on a Federal Facility Resulting in Death: USAMA BIN LADEN, Deceased, at http://www.fbi.gov/wanted/ topten/usama-bin-laden.

16.   Larisa Epatko, "World Reaction to Bin Laden Death Ranges From Caution to Glee," PBS NewsHour, May 2, 2011, at http://www.pbs.org/newshour/rundown/2011/05/bin-laden-world-reacts.html.

17.   Aamer Madhani, *Cleric al-Awlaki dubbed 'bin Laden of the Internet,'* USA TODAY, Aug. 24, 2010, at http://usatoday30.usatoday.com/news/nation/2010-08-25-1A_Awlaki25_ CV_N.htm

18.   MARK MAZZETTI, THE WAY OF THE KNIFE: THE CIA, A SECRET ARMY, AND A WAR AT THE ENDS OF THE EARTH (Penguin Press, 2013) at 310.

19.   BBC News, Middle East, "Islamist cleric Anwar al-Awlaki killed in Yemen," Sept. 30, 2011. According to local leaders, al-Awlaki had been "moving around within Yemen in recent weeks to evade capture." http://www.bbc.co.uk/news/world-middle-east-15121879.

20.   FoxNews.com, *Obama Administration Acknowledges Drone Strikes Killed 4 Americans Since 2009*, May 22, 2013, at http://www.foxnews.com/politics/2013/05/22/four-americans-killed-since-200-in-drone-strikes-holder-says/#ixzz2X5Y2F6rG.

21.   JONATHAN MASTERS, TARGETED KILLINGS, Council on Foreign Relations, February 2012, at http://www.cfr.org/counterterrorism/targeted-killings/p9627.

22.   These numbers are in dispute, though all sources agree that the use of drones in targeted strikes ramped up during the Obama administration. *See* Columbia Univ. School of Law, Human Rights Clinic, *Counting Drone Strike Deaths*, October 2012, at http:// web.law.columbia.edu/sites/default/files/microsites/human-rights-institute/ COLUMBIACountingDronesFinalNotEmbargo.pdf.

23.   *Experts Challenge Legality of U.S. Drone Strikes in Pakistan*, NATIONAL SECURITY LAW BRIEF, Am. Univ. Wash. Coll. of Law, Oct 23, 2010, at http://nationalsecuritylawbrief.com/ 2010/10/23/experts-challenge-legality-of-u-s-drone-strikes-in-pakistan.

24.   Medea Benjamin, *as quoted by* Courtney Hanson, *Medea Benjamin Discusses US Drones during Atlanta Visit*, ATLANTA PROGRESSIVE NEWS, Sept. 20, 2012, at http:// www.atlantaprogressivenews.com/interspire/news/2012/09/20/medea-benjamin-discusses-us-drones-during-atlanta-visit.html.

25.   Per a May 22, 2013, letter from U.S. Att'y Gen. Eric Holder to Sen. Patrick Leahy, since 2009, four American citizens—including Samir Khan, the editor of *Inspire*, Al-Qaeda's English language Internet magazine, and Abdulrahman, Anwar al-Awlaki's teenage son—were killed in drone strikes, but the senior al-Awlaki was the only one specifically targeted. Holder Letter on Counterterror Strikes Against U.S. Citizens Holder Letter on Counterterror Strikes

Against U.S. Citizens *Holder Letter on Counterterror Strikes Against U.S. Citizens*, N.Y. TIMES, May 22, 2013, http://www.nytimes.com/interactive/2013/05/23/us/politics/23holder-drone-lettter.html.

26.　According to UN Special Rapporteur Philip Alston, there is no accepted definition of "targeted killing" under international law; the technique we are examining in this chapter, that of using weaponized drones, is but one among many different possible means. "The common element in all these contexts is that lethal force is intentionally and deliberately used," notes Alston, "with a degree of pre-meditation, against an individual or individuals specifically identified in advance by the perpetrator." Philip Alston, Report of the Special Rapporteur on extrajudicial, summary or arbitrary executions, Addendum, Study on targeted killings, May 28, 2010, p.5, at http://www2.ohchr.org/english/bodies/hrcouncil/docs/14session/A.HRC.14.24.Add6.pdf (hereinafter Alston Report).

27.　As is explored by Petra Ochmannova in *Unmanned Aerial Vehicles and Law of Armed Conflict Implications*, CYIL 2 (2011), UAVs or drones may represent a technical revolution in the manner of waging war, but are otherwise lawful weapons and subject to the same legal considerations under LOAC as manned jets or long-range artillery.

28.　The Church Committee, Interim Report: Alleged Assassination Plots Involving Foreign Leaders, 1975, at http://aarclibrary.com/archive/contents/church/contents_church_reports_ir.htm.

29.　Executive Order 13,095, at http://www.archives.gov/federal_register/executive_orders/print_friendly.html?page=1998_content.html&title=NARA%20%7C%20Federal%20Register%20%7C%20Executive%20Orders.

30.　Elizabeth B. Bazan, Assassination Ban and E.O. 12333: A Brief Summary, CRS Report for Congress, Order Code RS21037, updated Jan. 4, 2002.

31.　"Valid Target? Policy Forbids Killing Foreign Leaders; Should that Mean Saddam, al Qaeda?" ABCNEWS.com, Washington, March 16, 2004, accessed at http://www.ftlcomm.com/ensign/currentEvents/iraqWarII/fair/targetABC.pdf or http://more.abcnews.go.com/sections/nightline/World/iraq_assassination03. As is well known, a key aspect of the "Shock and Awe" war plans for Operation Iraqi Liberation was the "decapitation" of Iraqi military command and control, specifically targeting Saddam Hussein himself. In the context of this armed conflict between the U.S.-led coalition nations and Iraq, the argument can properly be made that the Iraqi president—who wore a uniform and personally directed military operations—was a combatant and, therefore, a valid military target. When captured, Hussein became a prisoner of war.

32.　ANTHONY DWORKIN, THE YEMEN STRIKE: THE WAR ON TERRORISM GOES GLOBAL, Global Policy Forum, Nov. 14, 2002, at http://www.globalpolicy.org/wtc/targets/2002/1114crimes.htm.

33.　David Cole, *President Obama, did or did you not kill Anwar al-Awlaki?* WASH. POST, Feb. 8, 2013, at http://articles.washingtonpost.com/2013-02-08/opinions/36984141_1_habeas-corpus-union-troops-disappearances

34.　Dep't of Justice White Paper, Lawfulness of a Lethal Operation Directed Against a U.S. Citizen Who Is a Senior Operational Leader of Al-Qaeda or An Associated Force, *available at* http://msnbcmedia.msn.com/i/msnbc/sections/news/020413_DOJ_White_Paper.pdf (hereinafter White Paper).

35.　Steve Aftergood, *DoJ White Paper Released as a Matter of Discretion*, FAS Project on Government Secrecy, Feb. 11, 2013, at http://blogs.fas.org/secrecy/2013/02/doj_discretion/.

36.　Deborah Pearlstein, *Targeted Killings Can Be Legal: But the Obama administration's white paper fails to explain why*, SLATE, Feb. 8, 2013, at http://www.slate.com/articles/news_and_politics/jurisprudence/2013/02/white_paper_on_drones_targeted_killings_can_be_legal_but_the_obama_administration.html

37. Charlie Savage & Scott Shane, *Memo Cites Legal Basis for Killing U.S. Citizens in Al Qaeda*, N.Y. TIMES, Feb. 5, 2013, at http://www.nytimes.com/2013/02/05/us/politics/us-memo-details-views-on-killing-citizens-in-al-qaeda.html?_r=0.

38. White Paper, p.3.

39. White Paper, p.2.

40. ABA, Task Force on Treatment of Enemy Combatants—Preliminary Report, Aug. 8, 2002, at http://www.abanet.org/leadership/enemy_combatants.pdf.

41. The text of the AUMF, 115 Stat. 224, Pub. L. 107-40, Sept. 18, 2001, is *available at* http://www.gpo.gov/fdsys/pkg/PLAW-107publ40/pdf/PLAW-107publ40.pdf.

42. Meaning "Specific Law"—the Law of Armed Conflict is a subset of International Law as a whole.

43. Article 52(2) of Additional Protocol I.

44. Article 51(5)(b) of Additional Protocol I.

45. The principle that weapons causing unnecessary suffering must be avoided is set forth in the Hague Regulations, Art. 23, sub-para. (e).

46. Preamble of the St. Petersburg Declaration to the Effect of Prohibiting the Use of Certain Projectiles in Wartime (Nov. 29/Dec. 11, 1868).

47. Common Art. 2, 1949 Geneva Conventions.

48. Charles Garraway, *Interoperability and the Atlantic Divide—A Bridge Over Troubled Waters*, 34 ISRAEL YEARBOOK ON HUMAN RIGHTS 105 (Martinus Nijhoff, 2004), at 107.

49. Garraway, at 108.

50. Per the Islamic Supreme Council of America, at http://www.islamicsupremecouncil.org/understanding-islam/legal-rulings/44-what-is-a-fatwa.html, a *fatwâ* is an Islamic legal pronouncement issued by a scholar expert in religious law (a mufti): "To issue a new *fatwâ* as an unqualified and unauthorized individual is impermissible and forbidden in Islam. . . . The *fatwâs* of unqualified individuals are considered 'null and void.'" Osama bin Laden was not a mufti and would not have been qualified to issue a *fatwa*.

51. World Islamic Front for Jihad Against Jews and Crusaders: Initial "Fatwa" Statement, Fed'n of Am. Scientists, at http://www.fas.org/irp/world/para/docs/980223-fatwa.htm.

52. Article 43(1) of Additional Protocol I notes that combatant status turns on whether the fighters are considered part of the "regular armed forces" of a nation: "*The armed forces of a party to the conflict consist of all organized armed forces, groups and units which are under a command responsible to that party for the conduct of its subordinates.*" Rule 4 of the ICRC's 2005 Customary International Law Study also states: "The armed forces of a party to the conflict consist of all organized armed forces, groups, and units which are under a command responsible to that party for the conduct of its subordinates."

53. Report prepared by the International Committee of the Red Cross: International Humanitarian Law and the challenges of contemporary armed conflicts, 31st Int'l Conf. of the Red Cross and Red Crescent, Geneva, Switzerland, Nov. 28–Dec. 1, 2011, at p.48.

54. Hamdan v. Rumsfeld, 548 U.S. 557 (2006).

55. Common Article 3.

56. *See* Michael H. Hoffman, *Terrorists Are Unlawful Belligerents, Not Unlawful Combatants: A Distinction with Implications for the Future of International Humanitarian Law*, 34 CASE W. RES. J. INT'L L. 227 (2002).

57. Nils Melzer, Int'l Comm. of the Red Cross [ICRC], Interpretive Guidance on the Notion of Direct Participation in Hostilities under International Humanitarian Law (May 2009)

[hereinafter Interpretive Guidance], at http://www.icrc.org/Web/eng/siteeng0.nsf/htmlall/direct-participation-report_res/$File/direct-participation-guidance-2009-icrc.pdf.

> Civilians lose protection against direct attack for the duration of each specific act amounting to direct participation in hostilities, whereas members of organized armed groups belonging to a non-State party to an armed conflict cease to be civilians . . . and lose protection against direct attack, for as long as they assume their continuous combat function.

Note 41 at p. 40.

58. Interpretive Guidance, at http://www.icrc.org/Web/eng/siteeng0.nsf/htmlall/direct-participation-report_res/$File/direct-participation-guidance-2009-icrc.pdf.

59. Specifically, the resolution authorized the President to use "all necessary and appropriate force against those nations, organizations, or persons *he determines* planned, authorized, committed, or aided" (emphasis mine) in the 9/11 terrorist attacks, or "in order to prevent *any future* acts of international terrorism against the United States" by these nations, organizations, or persons (emphasis mine).

60. Interpretive Guidance, at http://www.icrc.org/Web/eng/siteeng0.nsf/htmlall/direct-participation-report_res/$File/direct-participation-guidance-2009-icrc.pdf, at page 31:

> Nevertheless, it is widely recognised that a non-state party to a NIAC means an armed group with a certain level of organization. International jurisprudence has developed indicative factors on the basis of which the 'organization' criterion may be assessed. They include the existence of a command structure and disciplinary rules and mechanisms within the armed group, the existence of headquarters, the ability to procure, transport and distribute arms, the group's ability to plan, coordinate and carry out military operations, including troop movements and logistics, its ability to negotiate and conclude agreements such as cease-fire or peace accords, etc. Differently stated, even though the level of violence in a given situation may be very high (in a situation of mass riots for example), unless there is an organised armed group on the other side, one cannot speak of a NIAC.

61. *Id.* at http://www.icrc.org/Web/eng/siteeng0.nsf/htmlall/direct-participation-report_res/$File/direct-participation-guidance-2009-icrc.pdf, at page 31:

> Continuous combat function requires lasting integration into an organized armed group acting as the armed forces of a non-State party to an armed conflict. Thus, individuals whose continuous function involves the preparation, execution, or command of acts or operations amounting to direct participation in hostilities are assuming a continuous combat function. An individual recruited, trained and equipped by such a group to continuously and directly participate in hostilities on its behalf can be considered to assume a continuous combat function even before he or she first carries out a hostile act.

62. David A. Wallace, *Operation Neptune's Spear: The Lawful Killing of Bin Laden*, Israel L. Rev. (2012) 367–77.

63. Peter Margulies, *Networks in Non-International Armed Conflicts: Crossing Borders and Defining 'Organized Armed Group*,*'* 89 Int'l L. Stud. 54 (2013).

64. Per Jelena Pejic, the ICRC's position is that the NIAC does not follow the suspected terrorist. The ICRC does not subscribe to the concept that a global, transnational, non-international armed conflict exists between the U.S. and Al-Qaeda. *See* Simon Schorno, ICRC-led discussion

on typology of armed conflicts and related issues, Mar. 19, 2013, at http://intercrossblog.icrc.org/blog/ihl-and-challenges-contemporary-armed-conflicts-typology-conflicts-part-i

65. John C. Dehn & Kevin Jon Heller, *Debate: Targeted Killing: The Case of Anwar Al-Awlaqi*, 159 U. Pa. L. Rev. 175 (2011).

66. Charlie Savage, *Secret U.S. Memo Made Legal Case to Kill a Citizen*, N.Y. Times, Oct. 8, 2011, at http://www.nytimes.com/2011/10/09/world/middleeast/secret-us-memo-made-legal-case-to-kill-a-citizen.html?pagewanted=all. Al-Awlaki was suspected of helping to recruit the Detroit flight "underwear bomber" and plotting two other unsuccessful attacks against airplanes, all "part of a pattern of activities that counterterrorism officials have said showed that he had evolved from merely being a propagandist—in sermons justifying violence by Muslims against the United States—to playing an operational role in Al Qaeda in the Arabian Peninsula's continuing efforts to carry out terrorist attacks."

67. Steve Coll, *Remote Control: Our Drone Delusion*, The New Yorker, May 6, 2013, at www.newyorker.com/arts/critics/books/2013/05/06/130506crbo_books_coll.

68. Richard Engel & Robert Windrem, "CIA didn't always know who it was killing in drone strikes," classified documents show, NBC News Investigations, June 5, 2013, at http://openchannel.nbcnews.com/_news/2013/06/05/18781930-exclusive-cia-didnt-always-know-who-it-was-killing-in-drone-strikes-classified-documents-show?lite.

69. John C. Dehn & Kevin Jon Heller, Debate: *Targeted Killing: The Case of Anwar Al-Alwaki*, 159 U. Pa. L. Rev. PENNumbra 175 (2011), at pp.192–93.

70. Lewis M. Simons, *Free Fire Zones*, Crimes of War Project, at http://www.crimesofwar. rg/a-z-guide/free-fire-zones/.

71. "It was something of a trick of logic." Michael Mazzetti, *as quoted by* Steve Coll, in *Remote Control: Our Drone Delusion*, The New Yorker, May 6, 2013, at www.newyorker.com/arts/critics/books/2013/05/06/130506crbo_books_coll.

72. Art. 51(5)(b) of Additional Protocol I.

73. White Paper, p.1.

74. *Id.*, p.2.

75. Under Article 1, The Purposes of the United Nations, the purpose listed first is:

> To maintain international peace and security, and to that end: to take effective collective measures for the prevention and removal of threats to the peace, and for the suppression of acts of aggression or other breaches of the peace, and to bring about by peaceful means, and in conformity with the principles of justice and international law, adjustment or settlement of international disputes or situations which might lead to a breach of the peace.

Per Art. 2, § 4, "All Members shall refrain in their international relations from the threat or use of force against the territorial integrity or political independence of any state. . . ." Article 39 further states that "[t]he Security Council shall determine the existence of any threat to the peace, breach of the peace, or act of aggression and shall make recommendations, or decide what measures shall be taken . . . to maintain or restore international peace and security."

76. UN Charter, *available at* http://www.un.org/en/documents/charter/chapter4.shtml.

77. White Paper, p.7.

78. *Id.*

79. *Id.*, p.8.

80. Andrew C. Orr, *Unmanned, Unprecedented, and Unresolved: The Status of American Drone Strikes in Pakistan Under International Law*, 44 Cornell Int'l L.J. 729 (2011), p.732. The term *jus ad bellum* refers to "the reasons for or legality of resorting to force," while the related

term *jus in bello* "is the law that governs the way in which warfare is conducted." ICRC, *IHL and other legal regimes—jus ad bellum and jus in bello, available at* http://www.icrc.org/eng/war-and-law/ihl-other-legal-regmies/jus-in-bello-jus-ad-bellum/overview-jus-ad-bellum-jus-in-bello.htm.

81. White Paper, p. 8.

82. *Id.*

83. Alston Report, p.15, *citing* R.Y. Jennings, *The Caroline and McLeod Cases*, 32 Am. J. Int'l L. 82, 92 (1938).

84. Art. 51, UN Charter.

85. Elias Groll, *Has Obama already violated his new and improved drone policy?* Foreign Policy, May 29, 2013, *available at* http://blog.foreignpolicy.com/posts/2013/05/29/has_obama_already_violated_his_new_drone_policy_wali_ur_rehman_pakistan.

86. *Id.*

87. White Paper, p.7.

88. *Id.*

89. Alston Report, p. 12.

90. *Id.*, p.14.

91. *Id.*, p.14.

92. Remarks by the President at the National Defense University (NDU), Fort McNair, Wash., D.C, May 23, 2013, *available at* http://www.whitehouse.gov/the-press-office/2013/05/23/remarks-president-national-defense-university (hereinafter NDU).

93. The Posse Comitatus Act (PCA), tit. 18, U.S.C. § 1385.

94. Report prepared by the International Committee of the Red Cross, International Humanitarian Law and the challenges of contemporary armed conflicts, 31st Int'l Conference of the Red Cross and Red Crescent, Geneva, Switzerland, Nov. 28–Dec. 1, 2011, at p.48.

95. Daniel Klaidman, Kill or Capture: The War on Terror and the Soul of the Obama Presidency 118 (Houghton Mifflin Harcourt, 2012).

96. Andrew Liepman, *Al Qaeda Is Weak and Bungling—But Still Dangerous*, US News & World Report, Feb. 25, 2013, *available at* http://www.usnews.com/opinion/blogs/world-report/2013/02/25/al-qaedas-current-status-inept-weakened-but-dangerous.

97. Devlin Barrett & Jennifer Levitz, *Boston Suspects Inspired by Muslim Cleric: Tsarnaev Brothers Allegedly Planned to Originally Strike on July 4, After Watching Online Videos by Anwar al-Awlaki*, Wall St. J., May 2, 2013, *available at* http://online.wsj.com/article/SB10001424127887324582004578459574033933556.html.

98. White Paper, p. 9, *citing* Tennessee v. Garner, 471 U.S. 1, 11 (1985). In *Tennessee v. Garner*, 105 S. Ct. 1694, 85 L. Ed. 2d 1 (1985), the Supreme Court found that police who shot and killed an unarmed suspect not known to be violent while trying to prevent his escape violated the Fourth Amendment. The decision held that lethal force can only be used when "necessary to prevent the escape and the officer has probable cause to believe that the suspect poses a significant threat of death or serious physical injury to the officer or others."

99. Alston Report, p.11.

100. *Id.*

101. As noted by Kenneth Roth, Executive Director of Human Rights Watch, "The relevant standards governing such actions come from the UN Basic Principles on Use of Force and Firearms by Law Enforcement Officials, issued in 1990, which is not a treaty, but a set of principles . . . widely regarded as stating the relevant law." Kenneth Roth, *What Rules Should Govern US Drone Attacks?* N.Y. Rev. of Books, April 4, 2013, *available at* http://

www.nybooks.com/articles/archives/2013/apr/04/what-rules-should-govern-us-drone-attacks/
?pagination=false&printpage=true.

102.   Ori Nir, *Bush Seeks Israeli Advice on "Targeted Killings,"* THE FORWARD, Feb. 7, at
www.forward.com/issues/2003/03.02.07/news5.html. The U.S. Predator strike was conducted
with the permission of the Yemeni government, which was also instrumental in providing the
necessary intelligence to identify and track al-Harethi.

103.   White Paper, pp.5, 16.

104.   Sen. Rand Paul, *My filibuster was just the beginning*, WASH. POST, March 8, 2013,
available at http://articles.washingtonpost.com/2013-03-08/opinions/37557027_1_senate-floor-
filibuster-majority-leader-harry-reid.

105.   White Paper, p.5.

106.   NDU, *supra* note 92.

107.   *Id.*

108.   *Id.*

109.   Howard LaFranchi, *American public has few qualms with drone strikes, poll finds*,
CHRISTIAN SCIENCE MONITOR, June 3, 2013, *available at* http://www.csmonitor.com/USA/
Military/2013/0603/American-public-has-few-qualms-with-drone-strikes-poll-finds.

110.   *Id.*

111.   Chelsea J. Carter & Greg Botelho, "CAPTURED!!! Boston police announce Marathon
bombing suspect in custody," CNN, April 19, 2013, *available at* http://www.cnn.com/2013/04/
19/us/boston-area-violence.

112.   Justin Sink, *Rand Paul would have supported drone use in hunt for marathon bomber*,
THE HILL, Apr. 23, 2013, http://thehill.com/blogs/blog-briefing-room/news/295509-rand-paul-
would-have-supported-drone-use-in-hunt-for-marathon-bomber#ixzz2WiYzu9I1. Sen. Paul
is quoted as saying, "If someone comes out of a liquor store with a weapon and $50 in cash, I don't
care if a drone kills him or a policeman kills him." On the other end of the political spectrum,
Sen. Al Franken also agreed that drones could have been useful in tracking and targeting the
Tsarnaev brothers. Jason Koebler, *Boston Bombing Changes Lawmakers' Views on Drone Killings of
Americans on U.S. Soil: After Boston, lawmakers see case for use of drones to kill Americans*, US NEWS
& WORLD REPORT, Apr. 23, 2013, *available at* http://www.usnews.com/news/articles/2013/04/
23/boston-bombing-changes-lawmakers-views-on-drone-killings-of-americans-on-us-soil.

113.   MEDEA BENJAMIN, DRONE WARFARE: KILLING BY REMOTE CONTROL 9 (Verso, 2013).

114.   Pew Research Global Attitudes Project, *Pakistani Public Opinion Ever More Critical of
U.S.: 74% Call America an Enemy*, June 27, 2012, available at http://www.pewglobal.org/2012/
06/27/pakistani-public-opinion-ever-more-critical-of-u-s/.

115.   The hypothetical draws from actual allegations made against the exiled Tibetan spiritual
leader and Nobel Peace Prize Winner, the Dalai Lama, by the People's Republic of China. *See*
Andrew Jacobs, *China Attacks Dalai Lama in Online Burst*, N.Y. TIMES, March 24, 2012, *available
at* http://www.nytimes.com/2012/03/25/world/asia/china-attacks-dalai-lama-in-online-
burst.html?_r=0; also, "China blames Dalai Lama for Tibetan self-immolation," AP/FoxNews,
March 27, 2012, *available at* http://www.foxnews.com/world/2012/03/27/china-blames-dalai-
lama-for-tibetan-self-immolation/#ixzz2XJ736gxC

116.   Shaun Waterman, *U.N. official: U.S. claim for using drones viewed as invalid*, WASH.
TIMES, May 14, 2013, *available at* http://www.washingtontimes.com/news/2013/may/14/un-
official-us-claim-for-using-drones-viewed-as-in/#ixzz2XBiSPs7d, *quoting* Ben Emmerson, the
U.N. Special Rapporteur on Counterterrorism and Human Rights.

117.   Jeremy Page, *China's New Drones Raise Eyebrows*, WALL ST. J., Nov. 18, 2010, *available
at* http://online.wsj.com/article/SB10001424052748703374304575622350604500556.html.

118. United States Government Accountability Office (GAO) Report, NONPROLIFERATION: Agencies Could Improve Information Sharing and End-Use Monitoring on Unmanned Aerial Vehicle Exports, July 2012, GAO-12-536.

119. U.S. Gov't Accountability Office (GAO) Report, *Nonproliferation: Agencies Could Improve Information Sharing and End-Use Monitoring on Unmanned Aerial Vehicle Exports*, July 2012, GAO-12-536.

120. *Experts: Drones basis for new global arms race: The success of U.S. drones has triggered a global arms race, military experts say*, USATODAY, Jan. 9, 2013, available at http://www.usatoday.com/story/news/world/2013/01/08/experts-drones-basis-for-new-global-arms-race/1819091/.

121. *See* David Cenciotti, *First European experimental stealth combat drone rolled out: the nEUROn UCAV almost ready for flight*, THE AVIATIONIST, Jan. 20, 2012, *available at* http://theaviationist.com/2012/01/20/neuron-roll-out/#.Ucny5zrD-GY; also, Daniel Solon, *Drone Sales Flourish in a Time of Austerity*, N.Y. TIMES, June 16, 2013, *available at* http://www.nytimes.com/2013/06/17/business/global/drone-sales-flourish-in-a-time-of-austerity.html?pagewanted=all.

122. Shaun Waterman, *U.N. official: U.S. claim for using drones viewed as invalid*, WASH. TIMES, May 14, 2013, *available at* http://www.washingtontimes.com/news/2013/may/14/un-official-us-claim-for-using-drones-viewed-as-in/#ixzz2XBiSPs7d.

123. *Out of the shadows: Barack Obama's rules for drones could shape the new global laws of war*, THE ECONOMIST, June 1, 2013, http://www.economist.com/news/united-states/21578689-barack-obamas-rules-drones-could-shape-new-global-laws-war-out-shadows

124. *Id.*

125. *Id.*

126. Peter Bergen & Jennifer Rowland, "A dangerous new world of drones," CNN, Oct. 8, 2012, *available at* http://www.cnn.com/2012/10/01/opinion/bergen-world-of-drones; *see also* Matthew Bolton, *Time to Ban Killer Robots? Considering an International Convention on Robotic Weapons*, GLOBAL POLICY, Oct. 2, 2012, *available at* http://www.globalpolicyjournal.com/blog/02/10/2012/time-ban-killer-robots-considering-international-convention-robotic-weapons.

127. Shaun Waterman, *supra* note 122.

128. Jessica Yellin, "Drone Program Something You 'Struggle With,' Obama Says," CNN, Sept. 10, 2012, *available at* http://politicalticker.blogs.cnn.com/2012/09/10/drone-program-something-you-struggle-with-obama-says.

XIII

Counterterrorism Operations, International Law, and the Debate over the Use of Lethal Force

James W. Zirkle[*]

Direct American military involvement in the war in Afghanistan is winding down. The leadership of Al-Qaeda has been decimated. But the threat to American interests and regional stability posed by jihadist terrorist groups operating in the Middle East and Africa is spreading and remains a major international concern. Terrorist groups continue to plot deadly attacks against the United States and other countries. No longer is this conflict confined primarily to Afghanistan and the tribal areas of Pakistan. In the Middle East and Africa, jihadist groups are attempting to establish control of territory in states that have weak or no effective governments, or where a government such as Syria is preoccupied with civil war. The debates, both policy and legal, involved in the "global war on terror" will continue and likely increase after the withdrawal of American and allied combat forces from Afghanistan. The threat of international terrorism has obviously not gone away, but it has been mitigated by both military and law enforcement action. This chapter will provide a brief overview of some of the more significant legal issues presented by these threats, including the use of drones for the targeted killings of terrorist leaders, including one American.[1]

* The author wishes to acknowledge the excellent work of former research assistant, Molly Masenga, Georgetown University Law Center Class of 2012, in the preparation of this chapter.

There is currently much debate in the press and scholarly publications concerning the legality of some aspects of the war on terror. There is not even agreement on the use of the term "war on terror." Language, as all lawyers know, is imprecise. It does not have the precision of mathematics. The word "war" can have many meanings. Perhaps it is preferable to speak in terms of "armed conflict," a phrase, however, not without its own ambiguities. Two of the more significant areas of disagreement arise from the fact that the armed conflicts of today are primarily non-international armed conflicts (NIACs). The battlefields of today more frequently do not involve traditional forces arrayed against each other in pitched battles. Instead, civilians affiliated with terrorist groups take up arms and deliver murderous attacks across international boundaries with no regard for human life, much less state sovereignty.[2] Because these conflicts are not state against state, the boundaries of the "battlefield" can be more difficult to ascertain.[3] Because of the nature of NIACs, the battleground is often not neatly contained within defined state borders. This can lead to a second point of disagreement. When lethal force is employed, should it be pursuant to International Humanitarian Law (IHL), essentially the Law of Armed Conflict (LOAC), or should International Human Rights Law (HRL) be applied?

Human Rights Law or International Humanitarian Law?

In some respects Human Rights Law can be viewed as the peacetime analog to International Humanitarian Law. In terms of constraining a government's use of force, it is similar to U.S. law governing the exercise of police power. Human Rights Law, rightly understood, goes well beyond International Humanitarian Law or the exercise of police power, for example, in nondiscrimination on the basis of various characteristics, or due process requirements, or in providing remedies, or prescribing representative government. There are important distinctions. One of the most important concerns the use of deadly force. Under International Humanitarian Law, military forces in an armed conflict can lawfully target enemy combatants with lethal force as a first option. Human Rights Law, by contrast, like domestic law, generally permits the use of lethal force only as a last resort to avert death or serious injury.

There is disagreement regarding the extent to which HRL applies on the battlefield.[4] In the event of a conflict between IHL and HRL, the U.S. has traditionally taken the view that IHL prevails in an International Armed Conflict (IAC).[5] The determining factor is the presence (or absence) of an armed conflict. It makes no sense to say that all human rights apply on the battlefield. It's silly to contend that armed hostilities have to be conducted according to due process and nondiscrimination. During armed conflict, IHL applies as *lex specialis*.

Military personnel in certain circumstances can be subject to HRL, just as police in appropriate circumstances can employ lethal force. An example of the former is found in the *McCann* case. British soldiers on active duty, members of the Special Air Service (SAS) in civilian clothes, were acquitted of alleged human rights violations in an incident involving the killing of three Irish Republican Army (IRA) members in a counterterrorism operation in Gibraltar. The case was brought alleging that the use of lethal force in a NIAC violated Article 2 of the European Convention on Human Rights.[6] The European Court of Human Rights found that the SAS solders acted appropriately in employing lethal force in circumstances where they reasonably believed that the terrorists were about to detonate explosives.[7]

Every person on a battle field has an individual status—for example, civilian or military, belligerent or nonbelligerent, privileged combatant or unprivileged combatant. At the risk of oversimplification, in an armed conflict "lawful combatants" (to use yet another term) have the "combatant's privilege" i.e., the right under international law to, inter alia, employ lethal force against the enemy. A "lawful combatant" is a member of the armed forces of a Party to a conflict (other than, for example, medical personnel and chaplains) and as such has the right to participate directly in hostilities.[8] An "unlawful combatant" is an individual taking a direct part in hostilities who is not a member of the armed forces of a Party to the conflict. An unlawful combatant does not enjoy the combatant's privilege, is not entitled to POW status if captured, and may be prosecuted, as noted above, for violations of international or domestic law.[9] A POW can only be tried for war crimes.

Under LOAC and IHL, terrorists who are civilians may be targeted with lethal force when taking a direct part in hostilities, i.e., as long as they are acting as combatants. Those who are making bombs, planting improvised explosive devices (IEDs), or otherwise engaging in hostile activities would be lawful targets, not subject to the protections generally afforded civilians. Managing terrorist organizations such as Al-Qaeda could be viewed as a 24/7 job, a continuous combat function, making the leadership targetable at all times. These individuals are all lawful targets under the law of war and may be targeted with lethal force. Such killings are incidents of war and should not be viewed as assassinations.

There is broad agreement that the word "assassination" could apply in a case of murder for a political purpose. This could involve the killing of a political figure, such as a U.S. President or foreign leader, e.g., Archduke Ferdinand. Where an armed conflict exists, however, one should not conflate the term "targeted killing" with "assassination." The targeting in WW II by the allies of Admiral Yamamoto, the architect of the Japanese attack on Pearl Harbor, was not an assassination because the admiral was a lawful combatant. The fact that he was individually targeted was irrelevant as a matter of law. Similarly, the targeting of civilians actively engaged in hostilities in an armed conflict does not constitute an assassination.[10]

The face of the terrorist threat has morphed somewhat with the decimation of the top leadership of Al-Qaeda. Terrorists have moved into other regions of the Middle East and Africa. The threat continues and spreads. This migration presents a number of legitimate questions. For example, what are the boundaries of the battlefield? When can hostilities be viewed as having ended? In an international armed conflict, hostilities cease when one side surrenders or an armistice is reached. An NIAC presents a different situation. Current international law does not perfectly fit the situation posed by international terrorism. Under the law of war, for instance, combatants may be held until the cessation of hostilities. Unlawful combatant detainees may be tried and sentenced for criminal acts or must be released (along with POWs) at the end of hostilities. The threat of international terrorism, however, will continue for the foreseeable future, given the number of states that cannot or will not control terrorist attacks against other states originating from their own territory. In regard to current detainees it seems both unrealistic and unjust to hold detainees indefinitely without trial at Guantanamo Bay.[11] Without minimizing the fact that Congress has been less than helpful and repatriation, even of those cleared for release, presents substantial difficulties, it is becoming increasingly apparent that the present situation is not sustainable and must be reexamined.[12]

Military force may be employed, as discussed below, when authorized by the Security Council, with the permission of a host state, or in self-defense when faced with an armed attack, pending Security Council approval. Covert actions may or may not have the acquiescence of a foreign state.[13] Realistically, law enforcement activities are an option only where a foreign state both consents and maintains sufficient control of its own territory to facilitate such cooperation. The U.S., with minor exceptions, exercises no law enforcement authority abroad. There is close law enforcement cooperation between the U.S. and western states. But it is difficult to see law enforcement as a realistic option in states with little or no control over their own territory, where the threat is most acute.

The international community, when drafting the Geneva Conventions after WW II, understandably focused on the use of force by one state against another— an international armed conflict (IAC). They did not fully anticipate the rise of well-funded and organized groups such as Al-Qaeda, capable of launching devastating armed attacks against sovereign states, whether from complicit states or from weak or failed states. International law requires that states not allow their territory to be used to launch attacks against innocent neighboring states. When such attacks occur, questions are presented regarding the right to employ armed attacks in self-defense.

U.S. law in this area, although subject to ambiguity, is relatively straightforward. Following the 9/11 attacks, the Congress, through the Authorization for the Use of Military Force (AUMF), authorized the President to undertake military action against those responsible for those attacks: Al-Qaeda, a non-state actor, and the Taliban, which permitted Al-Qaeda to operate in and from Afghanistan.[14] The UN also authorized the use of force. As affiliates and groups inspired by Al-Qaeda have established an operational presence in other Middle-Eastern and African states, the potential theater of military operations appears to be expanding, and there is a concern that at some point the original congressional authorization, the AUMF, may no longer be adequate to fully authorize this broader armed conflict. It must be noted that Congress can also authorize through appropriations. President Obama has indicated that he will not seek an expansion of the AUMF.[15]

What is the more appropriate response to the continuing threat of international terrorism? Depending on the circumstances, it could be by the employment of military force, which can involve direct affronts to state sovereignty, covert actions that also can involve such affronts (although less publicly), or the response could be left to law enforcement. Terrorism *not* on the battlefield can be dealt with criminally. Terrorism on the battlefield might or might not. That said, the question of whether to bring terrorists captured abroad to the U.S. for trial is difficult and complex, and in some instances may not be possible—or a good idea.[16] Part of the answer lies in where the criminal conduct arises. In a stable country with reliable law enforcement capabilities and the will to pursue terrorists, the law enforcement option may be not only the preferred but also the only option. But every foreign country is not a Great Britain or a Canada. Countries with weak police or judiciaries may not be capable, or willing, to take on an investigation and prosecution. With the ending of the armed conflict in Iraq and the soon-to-be-concluded direct U.S. participation in armed conflict in Afghanistan, the President has indicated that in the future the preference will not be large-scale military operations.[17] This may suggest an increased reliance on special operations and covert actions as well as law enforcement.

Drones and Targeted Killing

As one scholar has observed: "Targeted killing using armed drones has raised profound anxieties in legal, policy, and advocacy communities in the United States and abroad . . . [o]thers are equally adamant that targeted killing using drone technology is a significant step toward making conflict less harmful to civilians and more discriminating in its objectives."[18] The use of drones as weapons platforms presents interesting issues. From a legal perspective, an armed drone is basically no different than an F-16. Both are weapons platforms capable of delivering lethal kinetic strikes. But as weapon systems they have very different characteristics. Drones are capable of maintaining a lengthy time over target. They were originally developed for reconnaissance purposes, and their ability to remain aloft for extended periods of time, *vis-à-vis* manned aircraft, allows them to more carefully select and attack their target, characteristics consistent with the legal requirements of proportionality and distinction. With no onboard pilot, the risk to U.S. personnel is negated, and they are reportedly less costly than manned aircraft. In fact, they are not like "drones" in the entomological sense. Given their capabilities, they are more accurately referred to as Remotely Piloted Aircraft or Unmanned Aerial Vehicles. Their capabilities are impressive and will only increase, making them even more attractive to other states as a weapons platform.

The anxiety, to use Professor Anderson's term, arising from the use of this weapon seemingly has more to do with how and when it is employed than the characteristics of the weapon itself. As the terrorist threat has migrated to other weak states, drones present a capability to launch very precise kinetic strikes inside that state, raising questions of the geography, or boundaries, of the battlefield, as well as sovereignty. The ability to track and target individuals seems to some to raise humanitarian concerns: is lethal force bad when the target is not anonymous?

This anxiety becomes most acute when the target is a U.S. citizen.[19] Questions are raised regarding whether such targeting, absent some degree of due process, is consistent with constitutional due process. It is well established that Americans carry their constitutional rights *vis-à-vis* the U.S. with them when they go abroad. The answer lies in which body of law applies—whether the individual is a lawful battlefield target as a belligerent in an armed conflict. Under the Law of Armed Conflict, combatants may be targeted for lethal force without regard to their country of citizenship. On a battlefield one does not ask the enemy for his passport. Only one American, Anwar al-Awlaki, has been the target of a drone strike.[20] In the case of al-Awlaki, the analysis should focus on whether he was a combatant on a battlefield in an armed conflict. If so, he was a lawful target. Under such circumstances there is no constitutional right to due process.[21]

Covert Action

Prior to 9/11, international terrorism, with some exceptions, was viewed as a matter for law enforcement.[22] After the 9/11 attacks, Congress authorized, and the UN approved, the use of military force against those responsible.[23] The President also has authority under Article II of the Constitution to defend the United States from armed attack. According to many news reports, the United States has also engaged in covert actions targeting these international terrorists.

What is a covert action?[24] How does it differ from a military special operation? A covert action is a classified activity undertaken abroad to affect activities or outcomes where the involvement of the United States will not be acknowledged, hence the term "covert."[25] Covert action is defined in both Title 50 of the United States Code and Executive Order 12,333.[26] It must be approved in advance by the President in a classified written "finding" that the approved activity is necessary to support identifiable foreign policy objectives and is important to the national security of the United States.[27] There are specific statutory congressional notification requirements.[28] Covert actions are usually the responsibility of the Central Intelligence Agency, or the Armed Services in time of war as directed by the President.[29] But the President retains the authority to direct other departments or agencies to undertake covert actions, again subject to a finding and in compliance with congressional reporting requirements. As far as is known, no such third-agency covert actions have ever been undertaken.

The military, however, under Title 10 authority can undertake operational activities that may be very similar to covert actions. Special operations forces undertake classified focused strikes that can range from rescue to kill/capture missions.[30] These are not covert actions. While secret, they are not "covert" in the sense of maintaining deniability of U.S. involvement. They do not require a formal presidential finding and are not required to be reported to the congressional intelligence committees. The Department of Defense (DoD) also has broad authority to conduct foreign intelligence and counterintelligence activities, including but not limited to "battlefield preparation" in support of military action. The intelligence collected tends to support tactical considerations, such as the nature and strength of the defenses that may be encountered. In counterterrorism operations; however, there appears to be a convergence in tactics and methods between CIA covert actions and DoD special operations and other military tactics.[31] Neither the President nor the CIA has either confirmed or denied the involvement of the CIA in specific covert operations, which have been widely reported, accurately or not, in the press. The President has, however, acknowledged the U.S. drone program.[32] And it has been officially acknowledged that the military operation that killed Osama bin Laden was carried out by U.S. combatants under CIA authority. This does not appear to have been a typical covert action given the direct involvement of the military and its quick public acknowledgment.[33]

International Law and Limitations on the Use of Force

Article 2(4) of the UN Charter prohibits the threat or use of force by member states in their international relations.[34] Article 51, however, recognizes that states have a limited right of self-defense if subject to an armed attack.[35] So what is the test for an armed attack or conflict?[36] It is relatively easy to identify the presence of an armed conflict when two or more states are engaged in extended military operations against each other. In this circumstance the law of war (*jus in bello*), also referred to as the Law of Armed Conflict (LOAC) or international humanitarian law, will apply, as noted above. The combatants will enjoy the "combatants' privilege," i.e., the right to kill enemy military forces, and the full protections of the 1949 Geneva Conventions will apply.[37]

In general, when considering a non-international conflict, i.e., a conflict not state-on-state, the usual test for whether it is an armed conflict under international law has been to consider the intensity and duration of the conflict. For example, localized riots of limited duration, common criminal activities, or limited terrorist activities would likely not constitute an armed conflict in terms of international law. Domestic law would apply. By contrast, if military engagements such as those in a civil war are ongoing, an armed conflict would exist under international law, and Common Article 3 of the 1949 Geneva Conventions alone would apply. Common Article 3 in general terms requires that the parties to the conflict treat humanely those not taking part in the conflict, including civilians, those who are detained or who have laid down their arms, and the sick and wounded.[38]

International terrorist groups such as Al-Qaeda, non-state actors who sponsor and engage in armed attacks across international boundaries, are a relatively new threat not anticipated in the international structure and laws that have evolved over the past four centuries. The Peace of Westphalia, which ended the 30 Years' War in 1648, established a new world order, composed of individual sovereign states with the authority to exercise complete control (with narrow exceptions) within their respective territories. The law that evolved generally focused on the rights of states *vis-à-vis* other states. States enjoyed an inherent right of self-defense against armed attacks, enforced *inter alia* by the right (and available resources) to take military action. Armed attacks were usually attributable to the state from whence they originated.

A frequently cited articulation of this inherent right of self-defense is found in the correspondence that followed in the wake of the famous "Caroline Affair" involving the United States and Canada, then part of the British Empire.[39] The diplomatic resolution of this 1837 dispute has become the classic statement of a state's inherent right of self-defense. Briefly stated, within the context of a Canadian insurrection and cross-border attacks originating in the United States, Canadian militia, with support from the British, entered a New York port to destroy the *SS Caroline*, a small steamer that was being used by American sympathizers to supply armed Canadian insurgents encamped on Navy Island, an island belonging to Canada in the Niagara River. The insurgents were well armed. On December 29, 1837, the *Caroline* left its Buffalo, New York, port to ferry men and supplies to the Island. After several trips, the ship tied up in Schlosser, New York. During that evening, Canadian soldiers, backed by the British, attacked the ship, then set her on fire and adrift to go over Niagara Falls. One person was killed.

Following the destruction of the vessel, the British government claimed that the United States was not enforcing its laws along that stretch of the river and that the attack was an act of necessary self-defense. In an exchange of diplomatic notes between Secretary of State Daniel Webster and Lord Ashburton, his British counterpart, Webster emphasized that the attack on the *Caroline* was "an offense to the sovereignty and the dignity of the United States." He also stressed that while the "right to self-defense always attaches to nations, as well as to individuals," that right is limited to "clear and absolute necessity," and he placed the burden on the British government "to show a necessity of [self-defense], instant, overwhelming, leaving no choice of means, and no moment for deliberation." Webster went on to state that even when justified by such necessity, the means employed must be reasonable and not excessive.

In the end the American and British governments agreed on the legal principles set forth by Secretary Webster while disagreeing on their application to the incident at hand. The right of a state to respond with military force to an armed attack by a non-state entity, while not universally accepted, is rapidly evolving post-9/11 in reaction to major and continuing attacks upon states by groups such as Al-Qaeda.[40] Article 51 of the UN Charter, while not by its terms limiting the inherent right of self-defense to situations involving attacks on states by other states, does require any state exercising this right to make an immediate report to the Security Council.

While force may be employed in self-defense in response to an armed attack, its intensity and duration is limited to what is necessary to repel the attack (or imminent continuing threat). As Webster noted, there must be no reasonable alternative to the use of force. And the force employed must be reasonable and not excessive. The Security Council can authorize the use of force when other measures, such as economic sanctions, would not be effective in resolving the threat.[41]

There is considerable discussion within the academic community regarding the availability and scope of the right of self-defense. Professor Mary Ellen O'Connell provides a useful analysis in comparing the decision by the United States to launch its attack on Afghanistan following 9/11 and (at the time of her analysis) a possible decision to attack Iraq, concluding that the former was in accord with the international law of self-defense and the latter, assuming Iraq did not attack the United States, would not be.[42]

The question of how much force can lawfully be employed in self-defense is also a point of disagreement. Is the use of force limited to that which is necessary to repel an attack?[43] If a victim state, in employing force to defend itself, continues the armed conflict beyond the point of repelling the actual act of aggression, should the head of state be subject to prosecution in the International Criminal Court?[44] In December of 1941, if the U.S. had been aware that the Japanese battle fleet was steaming to the Hawaiian Islands to attack Pearl Harbor, could the U.S., under the law that exists today, have lawfully launched a "preemptive strike" against the Japanese fleet? If so, how close would the fleet have had to be to its target? Would that even be a factor? When Israel launched its preemptive strike against Egypt and Syria in the 1967 Six-Day War, it was widely condemned by the international community.

Preemptive and Anticipatory Self-Defense

The wording of Article 51 speaks in terms of ". . . the inherent right of self-defense *if an armed attack occurs* against a Member of the United Nations . . . ." [Emphasis added.] The article clearly recognizes a right of self-defense following an armed attack. It does not limit that right of self-defense to international armed conflicts, i.e., a state on state attack. It also does not directly address the lawfulness of a preemptive use of force in the face of an imminent armed attack. There is disagreement within the academic community regarding whether a state may use force to repel or eliminate a threat of force. Professor O'Connell, along with the sources that she cites, concludes that there are only two exceptions to the prohibition in Article 2(4) to the use of force. Those exceptions are (1) the use of force authorized by Article 51 in defense of an ongoing armed attack and (2) when otherwise authorized by the Security Council.[45]

Others have argued that the "inherent" right of self-defense includes the right of a state to use force in the face of an imminent armed attack.[46] A concise statement of this view is put forward by Blank and Noone:

> Immediacy, the final requirement for lawful self-defense, will generally not be relevant in the case of a response to an ongoing attack, given the need to respond to repel or deter the attack. Immediacy considerations do arise when a state uses force in self-defense in advance of an attack or long after an attack is over. In the latter case, a forceful response long after an attack will no longer serve defensive purposes, but will be retaliatory, and therefore unlawful. The first scenario is often termed "anticipatory self-defense"—the use of force to prevent an imminent attack and the death and damage it will cause. A state need not wait until it is the victim of aggression to act in self-defense. Although the precise contours of the delineation between an imminent threat triggering the lawful use of force in self-defense and actions not so justified are not entirely clear, the *Caroline* requirement that an imminent attack be "instant, overwhelming, [and] leaving no moment for deliberation " continues to provide the basic framework.[47]

This is far from a theoretical issue. As referenced above, in June 1967 Israel, following an escalating series of clashes between Israeli units and its Arab neighbors—primarily Syria—and an Egyptian military buildup in the Sinai, launched a surprise attack on Egyptian airfields in what became known as the Six-Day War.[48] In a matter of hours the Egyptian Air Force, the most immediate threat to Israel, was destroyed. When the conflict ended on June 10, 1967, Israel had won a decisive war and captured the Gaza Strip, the Sinai Peninsula, the West Bank, East Jerusalem, and the Golan Heights. Israel was widely condemned by the international community for launching a preemptive strike.[49] But by not waiting for Egypt to strike first, Israel almost certainly avoided more extensive Israeli casualties and battle damage.[50] Is it realistic to expect a state to remain passive when confronted with an imminent attack? States can usually be expected to act in their own self-interest in such situations.

The Israeli Strikes on the Iraqi Nuclear Facilities

On Sunday, June 7, 1981, F-15s and F-16s of the Israeli Air Force launched an attack against Iraq's Osiraq nuclear research reactor, built with French assistance, at the Al-Tuwaitha Nuclear Center near Baghdad, destroying the reactor.[51] Saddam Hussein's purpose was to build a nuclear weapon. In 1981, estimates regarding Iraq's ability to build such a weapon varied greatly, ranging from one to two years to five to 10 years. The International Atomic Energy Agency had inspected the Iraqi installations in January 1981 and stated that it found no evidence that the reactor would be used to produce nuclear weapons.[52] Israel's Prime Minister Begin invoked the doctrine of self-defense, describing the operation as an act of "supreme, legitimate self-defense," while acknowledging in a later radio interview that ". . . we were in mortal danger—not immediately but eventually." This statement helped fuel contentions that Israel's actions were illegal under Article 2(4) and the anticipatory self-defense model from the Caroline Incident ("instant, overwhelming, leaving no choice of means and no moment for deliberation").[53] The UN Security Council unanimously condemned the bombing as a "clear violation of the Charter of the United Nations and the norms of international conduct," but came just short of calling it an act of aggression or imposing sanctions.[54]

In retrospect, the raid alleviated a serious if somewhat distant problem: the prospect of a nuclear-armed Iraq. It created the more immediate (and more manageable) problem of tension in the region. In light of the difficulties in dealing with Saddam Hussein in later years, international assessment of the Osiraq raid has been somewhat kinder. In an article by Nicholas Kristof in *The New York Times* in 2002 he writes:

In retrospect, the condemnations were completely wrong . . . . Thank God that Menachem Begin overrode his own intelligence agency, which worried that the attack would affect the peace process with Egypt, and ordered the reactor destroyed. Otherwise Iraq would have gained nuclear weapons in the 1980s. . . . So pre-emption sometimes works, and even doves tend to favor cross-border intervention to prevent genocide in the Rwandas of the world.[55]

The Attack on the Syrian Nuclear Facilities

In early September 2007, 16 years after the bombing of the Iraqi reactor, an Israeli air attack destroyed a covert nuclear reactor in a remote area of eastern Syria near the town of al-Kibar. This reactor had been built with the assistance of North Korea. Unlike the reaction to the destruction of the Osiraq reactor, the international reaction was muted, probably due in part to the adamant denial by Syria that a nuclear reactor had been destroyed, but also perhaps due to an increased recognition of the risks involved should a nuclear arms race develop in the Middle East. In a background briefing by senior U.S. officials on April 24, 2008, the following observation was made regarding Israeli involvement: ". . . Israel considered a Syrian nuclear capability to be an existential threat to the state of Israel. . . . We understand the Israeli action. We believe this clandestine reactor was a threat to regional peace and security, and we have stated before that we cannot allow the world's most dangerous regimes to acquire the world's most dangerous weapons."[56] More recently, in the course of the Syrian civil war, Israel has launched strikes inside Syria targeting munitions allegedly destined for Hezbollah.

The Nuclear Threat Posed by Iran

The threat posed by the development of a nuclear capability by a state such as Iran that advocates the destruction of Israel and actively supports international terrorism obviously extends beyond a direct threat to Israel. Such a capability could lead to a nuclear arms race in the Middle East. And the prospect of a well-organized terrorist group possessing highly radioactive material is a chilling one. But at what stage, if any, in the course of such a development does a threat become sufficiently imminent to justify an armed attack pursuant to Article 51?[57] Once a nuclear reactor goes on-line, any such attack could spread radioactive material across a broad area, posing a substantial risk to surrounding populations. There have been many reports in the press of offensive targeting of the Iranian nuclear program.[58] Successful targeting can slow the development of a nuclear capability. And diplomatic negotiations remain the preferred policy approach. But in the context of the Iranian nuclear program, the question remains whether an anticipatory military strike similar to the Israeli strikes against the Iraqi and Syrian reactors would be permissible under Article 51. If past practice is an indicator, the recognition of a right to initiate such a strike seems highly unlikely. It probably does not matter. A more realistic guide to interpreting the right of self-defense acknowledged in Article 51 may be found in the diplomatic correspondence following the *Caroline* incident, i.e., a state has a right to self-defense using military force when faced with a clear, otherwise unavoidable and imminent threat.[59] Diplomatic protestations aside, the expectations of the international community in this regard will be found in the more substantive reactions, if any, to any such an anticipatory strike.

Conclusion

Every state has the inherent right to defend itself, and every state has an obligation not to allow its territory to be used by a third party for the purpose of attacking another state. Terrorism threatens the fabric of international society, not just the interests of the specific country where the terrorism attack occurs or against which the attack is directed. It is a global problem and deserves a global response and coordination. It is usually preferable to meet armed attacks (actual or contemplated) jointly with others, or at least in an internationally agreed framework, such as, for example, with the approval of the UN Security Council or the relevant regional organization or body.

The international law governing counterterrorism operations and the use of force is complex. Discussion of these subjects by the public is sometimes hindered by a failure to appreciate the distinctions between International Humanitarian Law and Human Rights Law. Lawyers can play an important role by helping to guide the discussion within the appropriate legal framework.

Professor John Fabian Witt in *Lincoln's Code* describes how President Lincoln in the midst of the Civil War promulgated a code of conduct governing the conduct of the war.[60] The Lieber Code, among other things, required that civilians and prisoners of war, both North and South, be treated humanely. As he elegantly describes in his book, the United States has always been at the forefront in the development of humanitarian rules for the conduct of war—from the American Revolution to the 1949 Geneva Conventions. Law evolves. Today the world is faced with a toxic cocktail of failing states and international terrorist organizations that, with state backing, are intent on acquiring territory to control with their perverted ideology and from which to launch future attacks. States will always defend themselves from such attacks. The law of war is complicated and sometimes difficult to apply. Technology evolves. And scholars, who play a major role in the development of international law, remain divided regarding when and how military force should be used. It will all get worked out, of course, over time. Meanwhile, a lot of important work remains for policy makers and, not least, lawyers.

Notes

1. The Attorney General, in a letter dated May 22, 2013, to the Senate Judiciary Committee, acknowledged that four Americans have been killed by drone strikes. One, Anwar al-Awlaki, was targeted; the other three, including his son, were not.

2. These terrorists may be referred to as "illegal combatants" or "unprivileged belligerents." Not being part of an organized armed force that observes the law of war, they are a criminal enterprise and do not enjoy the combatant's privilege that permits the use of deadly force. If captured, they are not eligible for prisoner of war (POW) status and can be prosecuted as common criminals.

3. *See generally* John O. Brennan, "Strengthening Our Security by Adhering to Our Values and Laws," Remarks delivered at the Harvard Law School on Sept. 16, 2011, available on Lawfare.

4. *See* DYCUS ET AL., NATIONAL SECURITY LAW, 5th ed. 385–86, Wolters Kluwer Law & Business (2011).

5. *Id.* An IAC is a state-on-state conflict.

6. Convention for the Protection of Human Rights and Fundamental Freedoms, 213 U.N.T.S. 222, Nov. 4, 1950.

7. McCann v. United Kingdom, European Court of Human Rights, 21 E.H.R.R. 97 (1996). *See generally* DYCUS ET AL., *supra* n.4.

8. *See* 1977 Additional Protocol I, Article 43.2, and GARY D. SOLIS, THE LAW OF ARMED CONFLICT: INTERNATIONAL HUMANITARIAN LAW IN WAR 186–202, Cambridge Univ. Press (2010).

9. A POW is privileged and may only be prosecuted for war crimes. A person who accompanies an armed force may also qualify for POW status. *See generally* SOLIS, *supra* n.8, at 198. A CIA officer engaged in hostilities would likely not be entitled to POW status if captured unless accompanying the armed forces.

10. For a more detailed analysis of what is and is not an assassination, *see* W. HAYS PARKS, MEMORANDUM OF LAW: EXECUTIVE ORDER 12333 AND ASSASSINATION, Dep't of the Army Pamphlet 27-50-204, *available at* www.hks.harvard.edu./, *reprinted in* ARMY LAWYER 4 (Dec. 1989). *See also* DYCUS ET AL., *supra* n. 4, at 403–10.

11. There are no POWs at Guantanamo. Under the 1949 Geneva Conventions, the detainees do not qualify for that status.

12. President Obama, in a speech delivered at the National Defense University (NDU) on May 23, 2013, reiterated the need in his view to close the prison at Guantanamo Bay. He also provided wide-ranging comments on the terrorist threat, including the need to end the war on terror in its present form.

13. There have been many reports in the press suggesting that some drone strikes in the tribal areas of Pakistan were tolerated if not approved by that government. There has been no comment on this by the U.S.

14. Following the 9/11 attacks Congress, by joint resolution in the Authorization for the Use of Military Force (AUMF), authorized the President to ". . . use all necessary and appropriate force against those nations, organizations, or persons he determines planned, authorized, committed, or aided the terrorist attacks that occurred on September 11, 2001, or harbored such organizations, or persons, in order to prevent any future acts of international terrorism against the United States by such nations, organizations or persons." Pub. L. No. 107.40, § 2(a), 115 Stat. 224 (2001). *See also* the Anti-Terrorism and Effective Death Penalty Act of 1996 (Pub. L. 104-

132), providing additional authority to employ covert action and military force to combat international terrorism.

15. *See generally* NDU speech, *supra* n.12.

16. The issue of whether non-POWs detained on the battlefield should be tried by military tribunals or federal courts is beyond the scope of this chapter. The answer will depend on the circumstances.

17. *See generally* NDU speech, *supra* n.12.

18. Kenneth Anderson, "Targeted Killing and Drone Warfare: How We Came to Debate Whether There is a 'Legal Geography of War,'" Hoover Institution Online Volume Essay, "Future Challenges" (working paper version), April 26, 2011; *see also* "Lawful Use of Combat drones," comments of Mary Ellen O'Connell before the Subcommittee on National Security and Foreign Affairs of the House of Representatives, April 28, 2010. *See also* Lewis & Vitkowsky, *The Use of Drones and Targeted Killing in Counterterrorism*, 12 ENGAGE: J. FEDERALIST SOC'Y PRAC. GROUPS 73 (2011).

19. The only U.S. citizen specifically targeted was Anwar al-Awlaki. His son, who was subsequently killed in another drone strike, was not a target. AG Holder, *supra* n.1. *See* Delahunty & Motz, Killing Al-Awlaki: The Domestic Legal Issues, Univ. of St. Thomas School of Law Legal Studies Research Paper No. 11-38 (2012).

20. Att'y Gen. Holder, *supra* n.1.

21. *But see* Benjamin McKelvey, *Due Process Rights and the Targeted Killing of Suspected Terrorists: The . Unconstitutional Scope of Executive Killing Power*, 44 VAND. J. TRANSNAT'L L. 1353 (2011).

22. Such exceptions, for example, would include the military strikes against Libya ordered by President Reagan.

23. NDU speech, supra, n. 12.

24. For an interesting debate on the constitutionality of covert war, see Jules Lobel, *Covert War and the Constitution*, 5 J. NAT'L SECURITY L. & POL'Y 393 (2012) and Robert F. Turner, *A Response*, p. 409.

25. By comparison, the clandestine collection of foreign intelligence abroad, although a classified activity not usually publicly attributable to the United States, is not considered a covert action because intelligence gathering is not undertaken to directly affect activities or conditions abroad.

26. The statutory authority of the CIA to conduct covert actions is found in 50 U.S.C. § 403, which gives the agency authority to ". . . perform such other functions and duties related to intelligence affecting the national security as the President or Director of National Intelligence may direct." A statutory definition of covert action is found in the FY 1991 Intelligence Authorization Act. "As used in this title, the term 'covert action' means an activity or activities of the United States Government to influence political, economic, or military conditions abroad, where it is intended that the role of the United States Government will not be apparent or acknowledged publicly . . . ". Pub. L. No. 102-88, §§ 601–603, 105 Stat. 429, 441–45 (1991), *as amended*. It is also codified in Title 50 in the National Security Act of 1947, *as amended*. A similar definition is found in § 3.5(b) of Executive Order 12,333, *as amended*, 73 Fed. Reg. 45,325 (July 30, 2008*)*. For a discussion of the legal authorities of the CIA and Intelligence Community, *see* Jameson, *Intelligence and the Law: "Introduction to the Legal and Policy Framework Governing Intelligence Community Counterterrorism Efforts,"* THE LAW OF COUNTERTERRORISM (Lynne Zusman ed.), A.B.A. (2011). For views on the legality of counterterrorism covert actions, *see* Harold H. Koh, "The Obama Administration and International Law," speech before the annual meeting of the Am. Soc'y of Int'l Law, Wash. D.C. (March 25, 2010); *see also* Stephen

W. Preston, *CIA and the Rule of Law*, 6 J. NAT'L SEC. L. & POL'Y 1 (2012); Jack Goldsmith, *Fire When Ready*, www.foreignpolicy.com/articles/2012/03/19/. For a contrary view, *see* Philip Alston, *The CIA and Targeted Killings Beyond Borders*, 2 HARV. NAT'L SEC. J. 283 (2011).

27.   *See* FY 1991 Intelligence Authorization Act, *supra* n.26.

28.   *Id.*

29.   EO 12,333, § 1.7(a)(4).

30.   *See generally* WILLIAM H. MCRAVEN, SPEC OPS: CASE STUDIES IN SPECIAL OPERATIONS WARFARE: THEORY AND PRACTICE, Ballantine Books (1996).

31.   Robert Chesney, *Military-Intelligence Convergence and the Law of the Title 10/Title 50 Debate*, 5 J. OF NAT'L SEC. L & POL'Y 539 (2012). *See also* Andru E. Wall, *Demystifying the Title 10-Title 50 Debate: Distinguishing Military Operations, Intelligence Activities & Covert Action*, 3 HARV. NAT'L SEC. J. 85 (2011).

32.   NDU speech, *supra* n.13.

33.   Acknowledging classified intelligence activities can have adverse diplomatic consequences. Although not a covert action, when U-2 pilot Francis Gary Powers was shot deep inside Soviet territory on a collection mission and put on trial by the Soviet Union, President Eisenhower had little choice but to acknowledge that the U.S. had been making secret reconnaissance flights in Soviet airspace. The Soviets had been well aware of the flights, tracking them on radar. Once the secret was out, the USSR felt compelled to take action. They cancelled a summit meeting with the U.S. and bilateral relations were significantly chilled.

34.   "All Members shall refrain in their international relations from the threat or use of force against the territorial integrity or political independence of any state, or in any other manner inconsistent with the Purposes of the United Nations." Art. 2(4). In addition, Art. 2(3) provided that "All Members shall settle their international disputes by peaceful means . . . ."

35.   "Nothing in the present Charter shall impair the inherent right of individual or collective self-defence if an armed attack occurs against a Member of the United Nations, until the Security Council has taken measures necessary to maintain international peace and security . . ." Art. 51. Chapter VII of the Charter defines actions to be taken by the Security Council regarding threats to the peace, breaches of the peace, and acts of aggression.

36.   The International Committee of the Red Cross (ICRC) proposes the following definitions, finding that they reflect the prevailing international law:

(1) **International armed conflicts** exist whenever there is *resort to armed force between two or more States.*

(2) **Non-international armed conflicts** *are protracted armed confrontations* occurring between governmental armed forces and the forces of one or more armed groups, or between such groups arising on the territory of a State [party to the Geneva Conventions]. The armed confrontation must reach a *minimum level of intensity* and the parties involved in the conflict must show a *minimum of organization.* [Emphasis in the original].

"How is the Term 'Armed Conflict' Defined in International Humanitarian Law?" ICRC Opinion Paper, March 2008.

37.   Conventions I, II, III, and IV, and Common Article 2.

38.   For an excellent analysis and discussion of these issues, *see* SOLIS, *supra* n. 8.

39.   The full texts of the diplomatic exchange between Webster and Lord Ashburton can be found at the Avalon Project of the Yale Law School, *available at* http://avalon.law.yale.edu/.

40.   Following the 9/11 attacks, both the UN Security Council and NATO recognized that the United States had a right of self-defense permitting it to use force respond to the armed attacks. S.C. Res. 1368, 1, U.N. Doc. S/RES/1368 (Sept. 12, 2001); Press Release, NATO,

Statement by the North Atlantic Council (Sept. 12, 2001). *See generally* BLANK & NOONE, INTERNATIONAL LAW AND ARMED CONFLICT 16–20, Wolters Kluwer (2013) and SOLIS, *supra* n. 9, p. 164. There is considerable scholarly discussion in this area.

41. *See* Art. 42 of the UN Charter.

42. Mary Ellen O'Connell, *The Myth of Preemptive Self-Defense*, Am. Soc'y of Int'l Law Task Force on Terrorism, August 2002.

43. *See* Jeremy Rabkin, *Even Republics Must Sometimes Strike Back*, 7 FIU L. REV. 87 (2011).

44. *See* Robinson & Haque, *Advantaging Aggressors: Justice & Deterrence in International Law*, 3 HARV. NAT'L SEC. J. 143 (2011).

45. Att'y Gen. Holder, *supra*, n. 1. *But see* Rabkin, *supra* n. 43.

46. *See* Kenneth Anderson, *Targeted Killing and Drone Warfare: How We Came to Debate Whether There Is a 'Legal Geography of War,'* Hoover Inst. Online Vol. Essay, "Future Challenges" (forthcoming 2011), pp. 7–8.

47. BLANK & NOONE, *supra* n. 40.

48. Also known as the 1967 War and the 1967 Arab-Israeli War, among other terms, depending on one's observational standpoint. For an excellent account of the war, at least from an Israeli perspective, *see* MICHAEL B. OREN, SIX DAYS OF WAR: JUNE 1967 AND THE MAKING OF THE MODERN MIDDLE EAST, Oxford Univ. Press (2002).

49. It should be remembered that this conflict occurred during the height of the Cold War. There were concerns that the U.S., a supporter of Israel and the Soviet Union, an ally of the Arab states, might inadvertently be drawn into the conflict.

50. On October 6, 1973, Arab armies launched a surprise attack on Israel in what is known as the Yom Kippur War. Against impressive initial successes, Egypt and Syria and their allies eventually suffered a military defeat. But Israel had been taken by surprise and was no longer viewed as invulnerable.

51. For an account of the daring military strike, *see* RODGER W. CLAIRE, RAID ON THE SUN, Broadway Books (Random House) (2004).

52. Iraq is a party to the Treaty on the Non-Proliferation of Nuclear Weapons. Article II of the Treaty requires non-nuclear-weapon State Parties ". . . not to manufacture or otherwise acquire nuclear weapons or other nuclear explosive devices."

53. While the raid was widely condemned in the American press, the criticism was not quite unanimous. *The Wall Street Journal* observed: ". . . whatever else might be said about the Israeli attack on the Osiraq nuclear reactor near Baghdad, we now know that there is at least one effective anti-proliferation policy in the world."

54. The U.S., while joining in the unanimous Security Council resolution "strongly" condemning Israel, privately made it known that the U.S. would veto any article calling for sanctions against Israel.

55. Nicholas Kristof, *The Osiraq Operation*, N.Y. TIMES, Nov. 15, 2002.

56. ODNI-provided transcript, *available at* www.cfr.org/syria/background-briefing-senior-us-officials-syrias-covert-nuclear-reactor/.

57. Iran continues to develop a nuclear weapons program despite UN efforts to dissuade it, including sanctions.

58. For example, the insertion of the Stuxnet worm to destroy centrifuges used to refine Iranian nuclear material has been widely reported and commented on.

59. It bears recalling, however, that Canada had already suffered incursions when it undertook the action that destroyed the *Caroline*.

60. JOHN FABIAN WITT, LINCOLN'S CODE, Free Press, 2012.

XIV

The Advent of Preventive War in Counterterrorism—Are We Playing by New International Law Rules?

Michael J. Davidson and Gregory M. Huckabee

Introduction—Times Change

On January 30, 2013, Israeli aircraft destroyed a convoy of trucks in Syria that were transporting advanced weaponry to the Hezbollah, a militant group based in Lebanon and committed to Israel's destruction.[1] Although Hezbollah's possession of the weaponry would not present an imminent threat, Israel viewed the future military threat as sufficiently compelling to launch an attack. One Israeli commentator explained Israeli's dilemma was whether to attack now and risk an escalation of hostilities or wait and confront a greater threat in the future.[2] Further, the decision to attack similar arms transfers, including chemical weapons, would be predicated on "reliable intelligence."[3]

If Clausewitz is correct that "[w]ar is merely an extension of politics," are we seeing in the 21st century a transition from ideological-based political notions of "freedom, democracy, property rights, religion . . ." to a concept of "Realpolitik"— politics or diplomacy based primarily on power and on practical and material factors and considerations devoid of ideology or law? What happened to the principle of self-defense in international law and relations when potential enemies now include rogue nations and transnational organizations with access to increasingly lethal weaponry? Has the war on terror legitimized the controversial concept of preventive wars and lesser military actions short of war? Can preventive military action still be "just" and/or a legitimate act of self-defense when terrorist activity merely portends worse things yet to come? What if the underlying facts upon which the military action is taken eventually are discovered to be erroneous? What follows is a discussion of the historical development of the concept of self-defense (both moral and legal) and how that concept is evolving based on counterterrorism considerations.

How We Arrived Here

Development of the Notion of a Just War and Its Impact on International Law

The Just War Doctrine originated with Augustine (354–430 A.D.), bishop of Hippo, in what is now Algeria. No longer a pacifist, fringe religion, Christianity had been embraced by the Roman Empire, and Christians were an integral part of the empire's government. When the Roman General Boniface announced his intention to abandon the military and become a monk, as the Vandals invaded Northern Africa, Augustine was compelled to develop a reasoned argument that permitted Christian warriors to kill, and Christian leaders to reconcile their Christian beliefs with their civic wartime duties. Augustine's embryonic "Just War" theory included a duty to defend others, undertake war in response to certain evils (e.g., lust for power, cruelty) and only in response to lawful authority, to enter a war with the intent of restoring peace, and to love one's enemies.[4]

Theologians continued to refine the Just War theory. In the thirteenth century, Thomas Aquinas added requirements of proportionality and discrimination and recognized self-defense as justification for the use of lethal force.[5] Also, Aquinas added three conditions for a just war: (1) legitimate/constitutional authority must make the decision to go to war, (2) war must be waged for a just cause, and (3) the national leadership must resort to war with the right intention.[6]

During the sixteenth and seventeenth centuries, Francisco de Vitoria and Francisco Suarez influenced Just War thought to add three additional conditions: (1) the evils associated with war (e.g., human casualties) must be proportionate to the injustice precipitating military action, (2) peaceful means must first be exhausted, and (3) the war must have a reasonable chance of success.[7] De Vitoria and Suarez also began to draw distinctions between *jus ad bellum* (the decision to wage war) and *jus in bello* (just conduct in war).[8] The modern-day Just War criteria contain six basic tenets: (1) a just cause (e.g., self-defense), (2) initiated by a legitimate/competent authority; (3) military force is used for a right (just) intention; (4) there exists a reasonable probability of success; (5) proportionality, i.e., the good to be achieved by military force outweighs the harm expected to be inflicted; and (6) war is a last resort; all reasonable peaceful alternatives must first be exhausted.[9]

Without question, the Just War tradition and its theorists directly influenced the development of international law, which reflects it. Although Augustine was the first to formalize a just war doctrine, international law and its incorporation of the concept of *jus ad bellum* (right to war), initiating a war that could be either right or wrong in nature, can be traced back to the Greeks.[10] Dutch jurist Hugo Grotius incorporated Just War Doctrine in founding the modern discipline of the law of nations in 1625 with his classic work, *The Law of War and Peace*.[11] English philosopher Jeremy Bentham emerged in 1789 and renamed Grotius's law of nations with a new term surviving to the present—"international law."[12] From there international law developed rapidly, especially in the nineteenth century, as nations not only sought to develop the laws of war, but also to restrain the use of arms.[13]

Principles from the *Just War Doctrine* found their way into specific conventions, treaties, and international agreements, becoming "international law." For example, in 1863 President Abraham Lincoln issued General Orders 100, prepared by Columbia College Professor Francis Lieber, that has become a foundational document for the modern law of war.[14] "It distinguished between guerilla forces acting under a government warrant—the historic 'right authority'—and private armed bands, the latter commonly referred to today as armed non-State actors."[15]

Besides conventions, treaties, and international agreements, nation-states created international organizations to enforce international law. The conflagration of the "Great War to End All Wars," also known as World War I (1914–1918), followed only 21 years later by World War II (1939–1945), convinced the U.S. and its allies that the ineffectual League of Nations desperately needed a more forceful successor.[16] The United Nations became the conceptual model for enforcing international law.

International Law: Art. 51, UN Charter—Framework for Self-Defense as It Impacts Counterterrorism

While the preamble of the Charter of the United Nations states, "We the peoples of the United Nations determined to save succeeding generations from the scourge of war, which twice in our lifetime has brought untold sorrow to mankind . . . ," Art. I of the Charter affirms the following as a UN purpose:

> [T]o maintain international peace and security, and to that end: to take effective collective measures for the prevention and removal of threats to peace, and for the suppression of acts of aggression or other breaches of the peace, and to bring about by peaceful means, and in conformity with the principles of justice and international law, adjustment or settlement of international disputes or situations which might lead to a breach of the peace.[17]

Unwilling to surrender national sovereignty in view of the hapless League of Nations predecessor, drafters provided in Article 51 that the Charter preserves the "[I]nherent right of individual or collective self-defense if an armed attack occurs against a Member of the United Nations, until the Security Council has taken the measures necessary to maintain international peace and security. . . ."[18] The Charter's concept of self-defense balanced developed legal and moral concepts with practical concerns of nations living in a very violent world.

The question naturally arises whether self-defense is only permitted when a member state suffers "an armed attack" precluding anticipatory self-defense. Even if the United States knew in advance the 9/11 hijackers were coming from Afghanistan to take over and use commercial aircraft as weapons against U.S. targets, does Article 51 preclude the U.S. from taking action in advance against Al-Qaeda abroad? If so, then is U.S. counterterrorism action limited to American shores? Although a literal reading of the Charter's language may suggest such a restrictive use of force in self-defense, subsequent legal interpretation and practical application of the concept of self-defense have broadened the parameters of permissible legal action.

Further, supplementing this agreement is the 1977 Additional Protocol I to the Geneva Conventions of 1949. Article 51(2) states in part: "Acts or threats of violence for the primary purpose of which is to spread terror among the civilian population are prohibited." While only 173 nations have ratified or accessed this Protocol (not including the United States), many scholars would argue that the principle of customary international law makes it applicable to the world community of nation-states.[19]

Anticipatory Self-Defense: Responding to the Imminent Threat

The concept of anticipatory (or preemptive) self-defense is relatively straightforward. When an adversary has its fist cocked and is ready to strike, the intended victim does not need to wait until being hit before defending himself. The legitimacy of anticipatory self-defense has been recognized by Just War theorists[20] and other scholars.[21]

Anticipatory self-defense is well grounded in international law, dating back to at least 1837, when British militia crossed into New York and destroyed the *Caroline*, a U.S. ship providing support to Canadian rebels.[22] The U.S. government had been unable or unwilling to stop the use of the ship, men, and supplies to the Canadian rebels.[23] In one of the first articulations of the standard for anticipatory self-defense, Secretary of State Daniel Webster wrote in 1842 that such use of force was justified "only when the necessity for action is 'instant, overwhelming, and leaving no choice of means and no moment of deliberation.'"[24] Since that time, scholars have confirmed a right to anticipatory self-defense, but using a standard less restrictive than that articulated by Webster.[25] What is clear, however, is that customary international law recognized the legality of anticipatory self-defense against an imminent threat long before the adoption of the UN Charter.[26]

The oft-cited example of a legitimate exercise of anticipatory self-defense is the June 5, 1967, Israeli attack on a menacing Arab coalition.[27] In May 1967, Egypt and Syria closed the Strait of Tiran. Egypt began to mass its forces in the Sinai, ordered UN forces out of the area, threatened to destroy Israel in the event of war (as did Syria), and formed an alliance with Syria, Jordan, and Iraq.[28] Israeli diplomatic efforts were unsuccessful.[29]

The military threat to Israel was significant. Within immediate striking distance of Israel, Arab forces possessed 240,000 troops, 1,700 tanks, and 1,300 artillery and mortars; and that force could have doubled over time.[30] By itself, Egypt deployed in the Sinai "approximately 100,000 combat troops supported by 900 battle tanks, 200 assault guns and 900 field guns, heavy mortars and howitzers."[31] Of great concern to Israel were the 385 Egyptian combat aircraft, which could strike Israeli bases in 7 to 15 minutes from Egyptian forward airbases, effectively precluding Israeli interception.[32] For the Israelis, the first five minutes of the war would be decisive.[33]

While the combined military forces of Egypt, Syria, and Jordan failed on the battlefield against Israel, at a subsequent conference on September 1, 1967, Arab policy was formally established that future attacks against Israel would be carried on through other means. "These included sponsorship of transnational terrorism by armed non-State groups."[34]

One of the most notorious subsequent transnational terrorist acts was the pro-Palestinian group Black September's attack on the XX Summer Olympic Village in Munich on September 5 and 6 of 1972, resulting in the death of 11 members of the Israeli Olympic team. While the world looked on in horror and collective shock, this incident, more than any other "led many nations to create dedicated specially trained counterterrorist forces and military or civilian law enforcement mechanisms to address the trans-national terrorist threat."[35] As pointed out by one of the most experienced U.S. Department of Defense legal counsel responsible for advising military and political leaders, W. Hays Parks, "Typical of that time, responses to terrorist attacks were primarily reactive rather than proactive."[36]

The principle of anticipatory self-defense is invoked in modern times in the context of an active terrorist threat located in a country that is unable, or unwilling, to employ its own military or law enforcement assets against the terrorists. As one commentator recently noted, "If we know a freelance jihadist cell in Yemen is actively plotting an attack, we don't have to wait until after the fact. Elementary self-defense justifies attacking first."[37]

But what about UN Article 51, which only authorizes self-defense after an "armed attack"? This provision is read not as an exclusive circumstance warranting self-defense, but one among others. The Charter's literal language leaves open the question whether preemptive or anticipatory defense is permitted, as the term "inherent" implies.[38] History and an emerging legal consensus, however, suggest that question may be answered in the affirmative.

Preventive War: When Reacting to an Imminent Threat Is Too Late

Although the terms are sometimes used interchangeably, preventive self-defense differs from anticipatory self-defense in that there is no imminent threat of attack. The rationale for preventive military action is that if you wait until the threat is imminent, then you have waited too long. Preventive war has been referred to as a "war of discretion"; the attacker chooses to take military action "because of its fears for the future should it fail to act now."[39] It is the military option of "shooting on suspicion."[40]

In the nuclear context, Israel has twice launched preventive attacks to stop potential enemies from obtaining nuclear weapons. First, in 1981, Israeli aircraft destroyed an Iraqi nuclear facility still under construction as an act of self-defense. Israel posited that the nuclear facility represented a threat to Israel because Iraq intended to use it to build nuclear weapons to be used against Israel.[41] Clearly, Iraq had been a long-standing enemy of Israel, refusing to recognize Israel's existence and having participated in every war between Israel and the Arab nations.[42] Israel argued that it had attempted peaceful means to resolve the situation but felt compelled to act before the facility became operational.[43] Significantly, the Iraqi nuclear facility posed no imminent threat to Israel.

The Israeli attack was uniformly condemned, not only by the Arab and communist countries but by the West and the United States as well.[44] Indeed, in a unanimous decision, the United Nations Security Council issued a resolution condemning the Israeli attack "as a clear violation of the charter of the United Nations and the norms of international conduct."[45]

On September 6, 2007, Israel again destroyed a nuclear facility under construction, this time in Syria. The Syrian claim that the facility was intended for missile storage and maintenance was refuted by a 2011 International Atomic Energy Agency (IAEA) report, which concluded that Syria was "'very likely' . . . building a secret nuclear reactor in 2007 . . . ."[46] The IAEA report also supported allegations by the United States and its allies that the purpose of the facility was to make fuel for nuclear weapons.[47] In stark contrast to the attack on Iraq, criticism of the Israeli attack on the Syrian facility was relatively nonexistent.

The obvious problems with a preventive war theory are that (1) it may be applied prematurely and unnecessarily, and (2) a preventive war rationale for the use of military force is too easily subject to abuse. The United States could have launched a preventive attack on the Soviet Union. Indeed, although the United States never adopted preventive war as part of its official doctrine, instead renouncing a first strike, early in the Cold War various military and civilian leaders argued for a preventive nuclear war.[48] One rationale advanced for a preventive attack against the Soviet Union was "that because of the changed nature of war, 'an overt act of war has been committed by an enemy when that enemy builds a military force intended for our eventual destruction, and that destruction of that force before it can be launched or employed is defensive and not aggression.'"[49] As history has shown, the Cold War ended peacefully. Had the United States actually launched a preventive war against the Soviet Union, the response would likely have resulted in an unnecessary WW III, complete with nuclear exchanges and widespread destruction on a horrific scale.

In addition, preventive war triggers both Just War and international legal concerns about exhausting diplomatic options before taking military action. The Just War doctrine contemplates that military action will be taken only as a last resort, after reasonable (not all) diplomatic efforts have failed. The UN Charter admonishes its members to settle disputes by peaceful means and to refrain from the threat or use of force unless force is authorized by the Security Council or constitutes a bona fide act of self-defense. A preventive military attack risks unreasonably truncating a potentially successful diplomatic effort.

Any preventive war theory must distinguish between preventive war as a legitimate form of self-defense and as a pretext for an act of illegal aggression (aka crime against peace). Most military action can be rationalized, at least in part, as including some preventive component. Clearly, not all military action designed to prevent a potential adversary from gaining a future military advantage, which might ripen into an imminent threat, should be considered legal or just.

Although the term suffers from definitional problems, a war of aggression is illegal under international law, a point emphasized by the International War Crimes Tribunal at Nuremberg.[50] Based on the prosecutions of the international military tribunals at Tokyo and Nuremberg, the crime of aggression is recognized in customary international law, and is a crime within the jurisdiction of the International Criminal Court.[51] Generally, aggression is viewed as a "crime of state," with individual responsibility "confined to persons who 'exercise control over or direct the political or military action of a State.'"[52]

In 2010, the Assembly of State Parties to the International Criminal Court drafted a definition for the crime of aggression. While this is not yet law, it is proposed to go into effect in 2017 after a vote of the parties. The crime of aggression was defined as "the planning, preparation, initiation or execution, by a person in a position effectively to exercise control over or to direct the political or military action of a State, of an act of aggression which, by its character, gravity and scale, constitutes a manifest violation of the Charter of the United Nations."[53]

Unfortunately, the proposed definition does not adequately address the rise of terrorist organizations, instead focusing on state actors to the exclusion of non-state terrorist organizations. As one commentator criticized, were this definition applied today, Al-Qaeda would escape prosecution for attacks like those launched on 9/11.[54]

Similarly, the current international legal model does not adequately address the modern terrorist threat, particularly in the context of what constitutes self-defense. The UN Charter was written following a traditional war characterized by national armies fighting other national armies. On the State-to-State level, most nations plan to use weapons of mass destruction as a last option, and deterrence has been largely effective. Even a nation like North Korea presumably modifies its behavior to avoid military retaliation. This responsive threat will likely keep North Korea in check despite its recent 2012-2013 war-pitched rhetoric and withdrawal from the 1953 Armistice Agreement.[55]

The Bush Administration argued persuasively that terrorism has altered the traditional paradigm. Terrorists and their sponsoring nations view WMD as a "weapon of choice" that allows them to intimidate their neighbors, facilitate their own military aggression, overcome the conventional military superiority of the United States, and attack us using a weapon capable of inflicting significant harm to our civilian population and military forces, but which is also "easily concealed, delivered covertly, and used without warning."[56] Under such circumstances, the concept of an "imminent" threat must adapt to the capabilities and objectives of terrorists.[57]

The adequacy of an "imminent" threat as the minimum threshold for permissible military action is being reconsidered in light of Iran's perceived quest to develop nuclear weapons. Former Israeli Ambassador to the United Nations Dore Gold (1997–1999) observes that an Iran with nuclear weapons poses a far greater problem to the U.S. and its allies than it did previously with the Taliban in Afghanistan.[58] "Along Israel's borders, a nuclear Iran would undoubtedly embolden Iranian surrogates like Hezbollah and Hamas to use greater military force without fearing Israeli military retaliation . . . which would make them more prone to take risks and make their terrorist operations—and Israel's self-defense response—into a hairline trigger for a wider regional war."[59]

Especially at the nation-state level, articulated nuclear threats must be taken seriously. On December 14, 2001, the Iranian president, Ali Akbar Rafsanjani, stated, "The use of an atomic bomb against Israel would totally destroy Israel, while the same against the Islamic world would only cause damage. Such a scenario is not inconceivable."[60] For a nation's leader to make such a statement, should this not cause adversaries to at least pause? Would the pause legitimately escalate to possible military action if it were reinforced?

At a September 15, 2005, meeting with French Foreign Minister Philippe Douste-Blazy and two other European Union foreign ministers in New York, Iranian president Mahmoud Ahmadinejad asked them, "Do you know why we would wish for chaos at any price? Because after chaos, we see the greatness of Allah."[61] Can one imagine British Prime Minister David Cameron, or German Chancellor Angela Merkel, or even President Obama making either of these statements? One has to ask, for what purpose did Iranian leaders make them? Forebodingly, what if they believe them? Is this what an imminent threat might look like, at least from Israel's point of view? What about the United States? A veteran of all too many attacks, invasions, and unforeseen wars, Winston Churchill observed of the human condition and warfare: "Madness is however an affliction which in war carries with it the advantage of surprise."[62]

Words, words—do they mean anything of significance in terms of imminent threat to anyone but Israel and the United States? From a just war/international law analysis, probably not, but what happens when Iranian war-threatening rhetoric is combined with menacing action? The International Atomic Energy Agency (IAEA), the UN watchdog responsible for policing the 1968 Nuclear Non-Proliferation Treaty, found traces of weapons-grade uranium in samples taken by its inspectors that have no function in a civilian non-military nuclear program.[63] Furthermore, it found that some Iranian nuclear activities were taking place on military bases.[64] Britain, France, and Germany (EU-3) had tried to negotiate a cessation of nuclear weapons development by Iran. Their collective effort culminated in a final admission statement of "Iran's documented record of concealment and deception" followed by a February 4, 2006, IAEA referral of the case of Iran to the UN Security Council.[65] Despite UN Security Council Resolution 1696, adopted July 31, 2006, requiring Iran to suspend its enrichment and reprocessing efforts, Iran failed to respond. This was followed by Resolution 1737, sponsored by France, Germany, and the United Kingdom, which imposed sanctions against Iran for failing to stop its uranium enrichment program following Resolution 1696. It banned the supply of nuclear-related technology and materials and froze the assets of key individuals and companies related to the enrichment program. It was unanimously passed December 23, 2006. Both resolutions referred to Chapter VII of the UN Charter, which addressed cases of aggression and threats to international peace. In all, the Security Council would adopt a total of five resolutions attempting to stop Iran's nuclear weapons development activity to no avail.[66]

Individual nations have taken action as well in the face of Iranian actions and Iran's perceived commitment to the development of nuclear weapons. On July 18, 1994, a Hezbollah suicide bomber targeted a Jewish community center (AMIA) in Buenos Aires, Argentina. The attack resulted in 85 dead and 151 injured.[67] While it took until October 25, 2006, to complete the investigation, Argentine Attorney General Dr. Alberto Nisman released an 800-page report finding that the decision to conduct the attack was adopted by a consensus of the higher representatives of the Iranian government at the time.[68]

Argentina elected to terminate the contract of an Argentinian company called INVAP. This company had previously taken over a contract from the U.S. to assist in conversion of a facility so it could use uranium, enriched to 20 percent U-235 (in significant excess of normal enrichment levels used for civilian purposes). The official reason cited in Nisman's report for contract cessation was "the statements made by President Rafsanjani, who maintained that Iran had a right to make nuclear weapons and that it would never be deterred from this aim." Thereafter, "Argentina decided to discontinue relations with Iran in terms of nuclear technology transfer."[69] Does this and other evidence cumulatively give rise to, and provide adequate justification for, self-defensive action to defeat an impending imminent threat?

When combined with President Ahmadinejad's remarks at a conference in Tehran on October 26, 2005, that "Israel must be wiped off the face of the map," does Israel have cause for concern?[70] When pictures are added to such messages in the form of televised images on September 22, 2003, of trucks in Tehran carrying Shahab-3 missiles draped with banners which read "Israel must be uprooted and wiped off [the pages of] history," does this combination rise to being an "imminent threat" justifying a preventive strike of its nuclear weapons development facilities?[71]

Dennis B. Ross, a senior-level U.S. diplomat, brings an interesting long-view perspective to this conversation. An old hand at Middle-East intrigue based on his extensive background, judging President Ahmadinejad, Ross observes, "With an Iranian president who sees himself as an instrument for accelerating the coming of the twelfth Imam—which is preceded by the equivalent Armageddon—one should not take comfort in thinking that Iran will act responsibly."[72]

In 2004, Spanish Prime Minister José Maria Aznar related an earlier conversation he had with Iran's supreme ruler Ayatollah Ali Khamenei that not only was the republic waiting for the return of the Hidden Imam expecting the destruction of Israel and the U.S., he explicitly spoke about "setting Israel on fire."[73] Even an Iranian military leader, Mohammad Ali Jafari, commander of the Revolutionary Guards, wrote in 2008: "In the near future, we will witness the destruction of the cancerous microbe Israel by the strong capable hands of the nation of Hezbollah."[74] With national leaders espousing such sentiment, can they be trusted with the penultimate weapon of human destruction? Furthermore, given this background, must Israel and the United States wait until Iran develops nuclear weapons, thus ripening the threat into an "imminent" one, before legitimate military action can be taken?

Modern Application

The Bush Doctrine (of Preventive War)

The Bush Administration included the ability to wage preventive war as part of its national security strategy. In September 2002, the Bush Administration issued the National Security Strategy of the United States of America.[75] Emphasizing that it was fighting a global war against terrorism, the administration warned that it would hold nations accountable that harbored terrorists and that it would deny terrorists sanctuary in such countries.[76] Further, President Bush stated that the United States would not permit terrorists to obtain weapons of mass destruction: "as a matter of common sense and self-defense, America will act against such emerging threats before they are fully formed."[77] For President Bush, "[t]he lesson of 9/11 was that if we waited for a danger to fully materialize, we would have waited too long."[78]

Operation Iraqi Freedom was widely viewed as the Bush Administration's first manifestation of its preventive war strategy: the United States was not responding to an imminent threat; rather it was taking military action to prevent a future threat.[79] Indeed, President Bush characterized the Iraqi threat not as imminent, but rather as "grave and gathering."[80]

Citing the Just War Doctrine and other moral precepts, religious groups both attacked and supported the pending, then actual, military invasion. Opponents claimed that Iraq failed to present an imminent threat and was not clearly linked to the terrorist attacks of 9/11; military action was not viewed as purely defensive; innocent lives would be lost; and nonviolent avenues of resolving the crisis had not been exhausted.[81] In contrast, supporters argued that the invasion was a defensive war, pointing to Saddam Hussein's attacks on neighboring countries, use of WMD against his own people, the likely future human costs of inaction, and support to Al-Qaeda, which had attacked the United States.[82]

Israeli Airstrikes on Nuclear Facilities in Iraq, Syria, and Iran (?)

As noted earlier, Israel has twice launched preventive strikes to stop adversaries developing nuclear weapons. Israel (and to a lesser extent the United States) now faces a similar situation with respect to the suspected development of nuclear weapons by an openly hostile Iran. Although the development of Iranian nuclear weapons may not pose an imminent threat by itself, Israel could view the development of an Iranian nuclear weapon as an unacceptable security risk and launch a preventive strike against suspected nuclear weapon facilities.

As far back as January 2002, the CIA issued a report finding that Iran was "one of the most active countries seeking to acquire (weapons of mass destruction) technology from abroad."[83] What makes such studied intelligence more worrisome are reports that the Iranians are farther ahead with nuclear weapons development than thought.[84]

During President Obama's March 2013 trip to Israel, the groundwork was laid for defining what the basis for a preventive strike might look like. The President observed on Israeli television that "[R]ight now, we think it will take a little bit over a year for Iran to possess a nuclear weapon, but obviously we do not want to cut it too close."[85]

The U.S. Director of National Intelligence, James Clapper, provided context for the President's statement one day earlier in a threat assessment. Clapper said that while Iran has "the scientific, technical and industrial capacity to eventually produce nuclear weapons . . . the central issue is its political will to do so." He went on to state that the U.S. intelligence community's assessment is that Iran could not produce sufficient weapons-grade material for a nuclear bomb "before this activity is discovered."[86] Remembering that this is the same intelligence community that inaccurately assessed the Iraqi Weapons of Mass Destruction (WMD) threat, observers have every right to be skeptical.

On what legitimate factual basis can Israel reasonably claim a threat of future nuclear attack justifying a self-defensive, preventive strike? Israel's imminent fear of an Iranian nuclear strike is based not only on ". . .Iran's extreme anti-Israeli rhetoric mixed with Holocaust denial," but it has also

> . . . [f]ed fears in Europe, Israel, and the U.S. that the Islamic Republic is a reincarnation of Nazi Germany and that its very existence threatens the survival of Israel. This anxiety has become especially strong since Ahmadinejad became president of Iran in 2005 and began repeating earlier statements from Khomeini about how Israel should be erased from the pages of time.[87] It is not implausible, as the Foreign Policy Association suggests, that "[g]iven Israel's history and the manner of its founding, such statements have created anxiety that Israel is facing a threat to its very existence from a group of irrational and fanatical leaders in Tehran determined to develop nuclear weapons.[88]

The Iranian public view is that its nuclear program is not a technical or legal issue, "but rather political and psychological—matters of national pride, respect, and sovereignty."[89] In support of this, arguments are made questioning whether an Iranian nuclear weapon is any more dangerous than a Pakistani nuclear arsenal, especially in view of its record of military and intelligence services supporting dangerous groups and individuals, like Osama Bin Laden.[90]

President Obama is on record stating as U.S. policy "that it is 'unacceptable' for Iran to possess a nuclear weapon."[91] It would appear at a minimum that "possession of a nuclear weapon by Iran," coupled with its bellicose rhetoric and behavior, would constitute an "imminent threat" unacceptable to the United States. Prime Minister Benjamin Netanyahu argues, however, that a "red line" must be drawn in that Iran cannot be permitted to have the capacity to build a nuclear weapon.[92] That "capacity to build" red line appears to constitute the requisite threat for Israel, legitimizing self-defense in the form of a preventive strike. At a greater distance from Iran, the U.S. has reportedly already engaged in a form of preventive war strike through cyberwar measures against Iran's nuclear program and computer networks that have proven successful in setting back its development.[93] Israeli participation in this endeavor is less transparent.

Distance between the U.S. interpretation of Iran's imminent threat as being in "possession of a nuclear weapon" and Israel's definition of an actionable threat as the "capacity to build" a nuclear weapon clearly exists. Yet President Obama stated during his March visit to Israel that "there is not a lot of daylight" between Israel and the U.S. on assessments of the status of Iran's nuclear program.[94]

Regardless, the U.S. recognizes Israel's inherent right to self-defense determinations. At a joint news conference during President Obama's visit, he said, "Each country has to make its own decisions when it comes to the awesome decision to engage in any kind of military action. And Israel is differently situated than the United States."[95] Prime Minister Netanyahu responded by stating, "Thank you for unequivocally affirming Israel's sovereign right to defend itself by itself against any threat."[96] Taken together with President Obama's airport arrival statement that "it's in our fundamental security interest to stand with Israel,"[97] it would seem the U.S. security interest is lashed to the Israeli red line, preventive self-defense threat determination.

Preventive War and a Mistake of Fact Defense?

It is well established in the United States that a mistake or ignorance of fact may excuse what otherwise would be a criminal act.[98] The "mistake of fact" defense is contained in the Model Penal Code[99] and continues to be recognized by U.S. federal, military, and state law.[100] Additionally, the defense is recognized by international judicial bodies, such as the International Criminal Court and the International Tribunal for Rwanda.[101] American military law articulates the defense as follows:

> It is a defense to an offense that the accused held, as a result of ignorance or mistake, an incorrect belief of the true circumstances such that, if the circumstances were as the accused believed them, the accused would not be guilty of the offense. If the ignorance or mistake goes to an element requiring premeditation, specific intent, willfulness, or knowledge of a

particular fact, the ignorance or mistake need only have existed in the mind of the accused. If the ignorance or mistake goes to any other element requiring only general intent or knowledge, the ignorance or mistake must have existed in the mind of the accused and must have been reasonable under all the circumstances. However, if the accused's knowledge or intent is immaterial as to an element, then ignorance or mistake is not a defense.[102]

A basic premise behind the defense is that the government should not prosecute those "who are not morally culpable."[103]

The defense should have application both as a moral and legal defense to preventive military actions that ultimately turn out to be premised on erroneous factual beliefs. Clearly, one of the major driving forces behind the decision to launch Operation Iraqi Freedom was the Bush Administration's concern that Iraq had weapons of mass destruction (WMD).[104] Indeed, some commentators have referred to WMD as the *casus belli* for the invasion.[105] Although a thorough analysis of the war is far beyond the scope of this chapter, the Bush Administration's preventive war justification does provide a modern vehicle to discuss this defense.

On the eve of the war, both U.S. and foreign intelligence sources believed Iraq possessed chemical and biological weapons.[106] Indeed, on February 5, 2003, then-Secretary of State Colin Powell brought "solid intelligence" to the UN Security Council that Iraq possessed and was concealing WMD.[107] As it planned the Iraqi invasion, the American military, mindful that Saddam had used WMDs in the past, planned the invasion assuming that Iraq had, and would use, WMDs against coalition forces.[108] When WMD were not located in the immediate wake of the invasion, many believed that Iraq had simply moved the weapons out of the country or destroyed them immediately prior to the invasion.[109] Regardless, coalition forces located little WMD in Iraq.[110]

Preventive military action assumes that time is not on the side of the attacker, and that it must take military action before a threat ripens into an imminent one. Accordingly, intelligence relied upon will not be perfect given time constraints and other operational handicaps, such as the ability to obtain intelligence and the further ability to gauge its accuracy. Operation Iraqi Freedom serves as an example of a preventive military operation based, in part, on faulty intelligence. Although the collective judgment of the international intelligence community was that Iraq possessed WMD, they were incorrect. Further, the United States lacked a well-developed human intelligence infrastructure in Iraq, and Saddam had ejected UN weapons inspectors from Iraq in 1998.[111] As with anticipatory self-defense, preventive military action should be judged "by what was known and reasonably believed at the time the action was taken, not by what was later learned or even what was 'objectively' true."[112]

Motive is important when judging the legitimacy of preventive military action. The Just War doctrine requires a right intention, that military force was motivated solely for a just cause. Similarly, criminal law judges behavior in the context of *mens rea*. The crime of aggression appears to require a specific intent to participate in aggressive military action.[113] Evidence that the high-level policy official participated in planning and implementing a military action knowing that it is intended as an aggressive action also establishes the requisite *mens rea*.[114]

If the senior policy-level members of the Bush Administration had knowingly relied on faulty intelligence and had deliberately misled Congress and the American people in order to justify the invasion, then the legality and justness of the war would be seriously in doubt, despite the many alternative justifications subsequently offered for the invasion. Indeed, some have alleged that the invasion's justification was indeed fraudulent.[115]

In contrast, if the Bush Administration was simply mistaken, honestly and reasonably relying on faulty intelligence that Iraq had continued to develop WMD and posed a continuing threat, then a strong argument remains that the invasion was neither illegal nor unjust. It is worth noting that President Bush and others in his Administration appeared to have been legitimately caught off-guard by the failure to locate WMD in Iraq.[116] Since the invasion, it has become apparent that faulty intelligence was relied on to justify the invasion, but it also appears that doubts about the accuracy of the intelligence were not elevated to President Bush and many of his senior staff.[117] Further, senior Bush Administration officials adamantly deny knowing that the evidence of WMD was false,[118] and postwar investigations refute the allegation that CIA intelligence analysts skewed their judgments based on political pressure.[119]

Even U.S. state law recognizes a right to self-defense based on reasonable appearance of danger. Virginia's law concerning self-defense generally provides a workable standard for preventive warfare. In *McGhee v. Commonwealth,* the Virginia Supreme Court, articulating what it perceived as "ancient and well-established" law, stated:

> It is not essential to the right of self-defense that the danger should in fact exist. If it reasonably appears to a defendant that the danger exists, he has the right to defend himself against it to the same extent, and under the same rules, as would obtain in case the danger is real. A defendant may always act upon reasonable appearance of danger, and whether the danger is reasonably apparent is always to be determined from the viewpoint of the defendant at the time he acted.[120]

To say that preventive military action is neither illegal nor unjust because it was premised on a reasonably held but mistaken set of facts seems incomplete.

Under such circumstances, the preventive action should not warrant receiving a moral stamp of approval and being characterized as "just." Perhaps such military activity should simply be relegated to the moral no-man's land and called by some lesser characterization, such as "not unjust."

Conclusion

Modern-day terrorism has altered the legal and moral landscape when discussing the contours of permissible self-defense. Historically, on the State-to-State level, most nations were deterred from using weapons of mass destruction by the threat of retaliation, and to a lesser extent by sanctions. The United States based its military strategy in large part on that assumption during the Cold War. The rise of terrorism and its non-State and State-supported actors require a different counterterrorism strategy. Deterrence does not enjoy the same prophylactic effect when applied to terrorists.

The civilized community of nations cannot permit terrorists to have access to weapons of mass destruction. The body of legal and moral precepts that guides their actions should accommodate the need to head off military threats before they mature. The possession of WMD by non-State but State-supported groups like Hezbollah and Al-Qaeda give rise to a fear and risk of unparalleled scope and breadth. At a nation/State level, lawless governments represented by North Korea and Iran require a new counterterrorist strategy that includes the right of preventive self-defense. While anticipatory self-defense is included within the definition of inherent self-defense and recognized in international law and Article 51 of the UN Charter, the nature of the danger posed to millions of innocents necessitates a new and more elastic legal approach to counterterrorism efforts individually and collectively. Preventive military action may be justifiably predicated on reasonably perceived danger at the time taken. Hence, ill-considered, provocative statements, coupled with preparatory action at a nation/State level involving WMD, may give rise to a limited right of self-defense.

New international law rules are evolving to meet the advent of terrorism. The "practice of nations" is changing to meet the unprecedented danger posed by the cataclysmic possession of WMD in the hands of those who would bring darkness to an enlightened civilization. The concept of anticipatory self-defense, and its imminent-threat trigger, has gained legitimacy in both legal and Just War calculus. In the wake of 9/11, with the recognition of the large-scale damage terrorists are capable of inflicting, the notion of preventive military action as a form of legitimate self-defense is also gaining recognition. In the counterterrorism context, waiting until a threat is imminent is waiting too long.

Notes

1. Joel Greenberg & Babak Dehghanpisheh, *Israeli Strike in Syria May Be Start of Stepped-Up Plan,* WASH. POST, Feb. 10, 2013, at A11; Ben Hubbard, *Israeli Airstrike Hits Truck Convoy in Syria,* WASH. EXAMINER, Jan. 31, 2013, at 20.

2. Greenberg & Dehghanpisheh, *supra* note 1, at A11.

3. *Id.*

4. The initial development of the Just War theory was paraphrased from Michael J. Davidson, *War and the Doubtful Soldier,* 19 NOTRE DAME J. OF LAW, ETHICS & PUB. POL'Y 91, 102–04 (2005).

5. RICHARD J. REGAN, JUST WAR: PRINCIPLES AND CASES 17 (1996); Davidson, *supra* note 4, at 104.

6. REGAN, *supra* note 5, at 17.

7. *Id.* at 17–18.

8. *Id.* at 18.

9. *Philosophers Agree on Criteria for Justifiable War,* WASH. POST, Feb. 2, 1991, at G1; Davidson, *supra* note 4, at 105. Some authorities also require comparative justice; that is, the injustice suffered by the "just" side must outweigh any comparative injustice by the other side. Davidson, *supra* note 4, at 105.

10. M. JANIS, AN INTRODUCTION TO INTERNATIONAL LAW 168–69 (1999).

11. *Id.* at 1.

12. JEREMY BENTHAM, AN INTRODUCTION TO THE PRINCIPLES OF MORALS AND LEGISLATION 296 (1970).

13. JANIS, *supra* note 10, at 170.

14. General Orders No. 100 was preceded by Dr. Lieber's essay, *Guerilla Parties Considered with Reference to the Law and Usages of War,* contained in R.S. HARTIGAN, LIEBER'S CODE AND THE LAW OF WAR 31–44 (1983).

15. W. Hays Parks, *Perspective and the Importance of History,* YEARBOOK OF INT'L HUMANITARIAN LAW 2011, Vol. 14, at 367 (2011).

16. LESLIE C. GREEN, THE CONTEMPORARY LAW OF ARMED CONFLICT 8–9 (2000).

17. U.N. Charter, 1 UNTS XVI, 1–3 (Oct. 24, 1945).

18. *Id.*

19. Parks, *supra* note 15, at 377. "The determination of customary international law is based in part on the 'practice of nations,' a synonym for history."

20. *See, e.g.,* REGAN, *supra* note 5, at 51; MICHAEL WALZER, JUST AND UNJUST WARS 74 (2d ed. 1977).

21. *See, e.g.,* Captain Sean M. Condron, *Justification for Unilateral Action in Response to the Iraqi Threat: A Critical Analysis of Operation Desert Fox,* 161 MIL. L. REV. 115, 129–34 (1999); Lt. Col. Uri Shoham, *The Israeli Aerial Raid upon the Iraqi Nuclear Reactor and the Right of Self-Defense,* 109 MIL. L. REV. 191, 195–97 (1985); COLIN S. GRAY, THE IMPLICATIONS OF PREEMPTIVE AND PREVENTIVE WAR DOCTRINES: A RECONSIDERATION v. (2007) ("not controversial; legally, morally, or strategically").

22. Shoham, *supra* note 21, at 197.

23. *Id.*

24. PHILIP C. JESSUP, A MODERN LAW OF NATIONS 163–64 (1959); *see also* Sholom, *supra* note 21, at 196.

25. Shoham, *supra* note 21, at 196 ("those requirements may be too restrictive for modern times").

26. Condron, *supra* note 21, at 129–30.

27. WALZER, *supra* note 20, at 85 ("clear case of legitimate anticipation"); ALAN A. DERSHOWITZ, PREEMPTION 83 (2006) ("lawful instance of anticipatory self-defense").

28. Davidson, *supra* note 4, at 110; WALZER, *supra* note 20, at 83; DERSHOWITZ, *supra* note 27, at 80; *see* EDWARD LUTTWAK & DAN HOROWITZ, THE ISRAELI ARMY 224 (1975) ("Arabs were proclaiming the imminence of a war of extermination").

29. WALZER, *supra* note 20, at 84; LUTTWAK & HOROWITZ, *supra* note 28, at 224.

30. LUTTWAK & HOROWITZ, *supra* note 28, at 222.

31. *Id.*

32. *Id.*

33. DERSHOWITZ, *supra* note 27, at 81.

34. Parks, *supra* note 15, at 362.

35. *Id.* at 363.

36. *Id.* at 365.

37. Charles Krauthammer, *In Defense of Obama's Drone War,* WASH. POST, Feb. 15, 2013, at A19.

38. Green, *supra* note 16, at 340; *also see* Operation El Dorado Canyon (1986 strike against Libya) and the 1998 missile attack against certain terrorist elements in Sudan and Afghanistan—AIR FORCE OPERATIONS AND THE LAW, A GUIDE FOR AIR, SPACE, AND CYBER FORCES (2d ed.), U.S. Air Force, at 7 (2009).

39. GRAY, *supra* note 21, at v.

40. *Id.* at vi.

41. Shoham, *supra* note 21, at 191.

42. *Id.* at 206–07. Iraq had previously stated, on multiple occasions, its intent to eliminate Israel. *Id.* at 223.

43. *Id.* at 191. A later attack would expose Iraqi civilians to radiation. *Id.*

44. *Id.* at 191–92.

45. *Id.* at 192 (citation omitted).

46. Joby Warrick, *IAEA Connects Syria to Secret Nuclear Program,* WASH. POST, May 25, 2011, at A11.

47. *Id.*

48. Gian P. Gentile, *Planning for Preventive War, 1945-1950,* JOINT FORCES Q. 68 (Spring 2000).

49. *Id.* at 71 (the argument characterizes an offensive action as defensive; "[w]ar is won by preventing, not deterring, an enemy from striking first").

50. WILLIAM A. SCHABAS, THE INTERNATIONAL CRIMINAL COURT: A COMMENTARY ON THE ROME STATUTE 109 (2010).

51. *Id.* at 101, 109.

52. *Id.* at 113; *see also* Davidson, *supra* note 4, at 123–24 ("The crime of aggression is committed only by high-level policy makers and not by soldiers and their commanders.").

53. Steve Beytenbrod, *Defining Aggression: An Opportunity to Curtail the Criminal Activities of Non-State Actors,* 36 BROOK. J. INT'L L. 647, 649 (2011).

54. *Id.* at 649.

55. Anne Gearan, Chico Harlan, *U.S. Officials Warn N. Korea After It Scraps Armistice,* WASH. POST (Mar. 11, 2013).

56. GEORGE W. BUSH, THE NATIONAL SECURITY STRATEGY OF THE UNITED STATES 15 (President of the U.S. September 2002), *originally available at* http://www.whitehouse.gov/nsc/nss.pdf [on file with the authors].

57. *Id.*

58. DORE GOLD, THE RISE OF NUCLEAR IRAN 288 (2006).

59. *Id.*

60. Islamic Republic News Agency, Dec. 14, 2001; *also cited in* Michael Rubin, *Can Iran Be Trusted?* MIDDLE EASTERN OUTLOOK, Sept. 2006, American Enterprise Inst.

61. Paper: French FM in Memoir—Ahmadinejad Tells European FMs in 2005 Meeting, "After Chaos We Can See the Greatness of Allah," The MEMRI Blog, Feb. 2, 2007; *also cited in* DORE GOLD, THE RISE OF NUCLEAR IRAN 29 (2009).

62. CHURCHILL AND ROOSEVELT: THE COMPLETE CORRESPONDENCE, VOL. I at 257, Warren F. Kimball ed. (1984); *see also* WINSTON S. CHURCHILL, THE SECOND WORLD WAR, VOL. 3, at 603 (1983).

63. As of July 2011, 189 States are recognized as signatories to the treaty. Among them are the United States, Great Britain, China, and Russia. Israel is not a signatory. 21 U.S.T. 483, 729 U.N.T.S. 161.

64. STEVEN R. WARD, IMMORTAL: A MILITARY HISTORY OF IRAN AND ITS ARMED FORCES 320, Georgetown Univ. Press (2009).

65. *Europe: Our Discussions with Iran Have Reached an Impasse*, MIDDLE EAST Q. 65–66 (Spring 2006).

66. GOLD, *supra* note 58, 49–50.

67. *Id.* at 132.

68. *Id.* at 132–33.

69. ALBERTO NISMAN & MARCELO MARTINEZ BURGOS, REPORT: REQUEST FOR ARRESTS 147–50 (2006).

70. Nazila Fathi, *Wipe Israel 'off the map,' Iranian says*, N.Y. TIMES, Oct. 27, 2005. The literal translation of Ahmadinejad's comment (originally in Persian) was "Our dear Imam ordered that this Jerusalem-occupying regime must be erased from the page of time." JOSHUA TEITELBAUM, WHAT IRANIAN LEADERS REALLY SAY ABOUT DOING AWAY WITH ISRAEL: A REFUTATION OF THE CAMPAIGN TO EXCUSE AHMADINEJAD'S INCITEMENT TO GENOCIDE, Jerusalem Center for Public Affairs (2008).

71. *Id.*

72. Dennis Ross, *A New Strategy on Iran*, WASH. POST, May 1, 2006. During the Carter Administration, he served under Deputy Assistant Secretary of Defense Paul Wolfowitz working Middle-Eastern affairs; during the Reagan Administration he served as Director of Near East and South Asian affairs in the National Security Council and Deputy Director of the Pentagon's Office of Net Assessment; during the H.W. Bush administration he was Director of the State Department's Policy Planning Staff; President Bill Clinton subsequently named Ross a Middle East envoy during his administration; and under President Obama, Ross was appointed Special Advisor for the Persian Gulf and Southwest Asia to Secretary of State Hillary Clinton, and later the White House announced that Ross was joining the National Security Council staff as a special assistant to the President and Senior Director for the Central Region (Middle East).

73. AMIR TAHERI, THE PERSIAN NIGHT 310; *see also* Yossi Verter, *Anzat: Khamenei Said in 2001 Iran Aimed 'To Set Israel Alight,'* HAARETZ, Mar. 15, 2006.

74. JOSHUA TEITELBAM, *supra* note 70 at 17 (2008).

75. GEORGE W. BUSH, THE NATIONAL SECURITY STRATEGY OF THE UNITED STATES (President of the U.S., September 2002), *originally available at* http://www.whitehouse.gov/nsc/nss.pdf. [on file with the authors].

76. *Id.* at iv–v, 5.

77.   *Id.* at v; *see id.* at 14 (". . . prepared to stop rogue states and their terrorist clients before they are able to threaten or use weapons of mass destruction against the United States and our allies and friends").

78.   GEORGE W. BUSH, DECISION POINTS 229 (2010).

79.   Miriam Sapiro, *War To Prevent War*, LEGAL TIMES, April 7, 2003, at 42, 43; *see* Joseph S. Nye, *Before War*, WASH. POST, Mar. 13, 2003, at A27 ("Iraq is the first test of the new Bush doctrine of preventive war").

80.   Charles Krauthammer, *Ted Kennedy, Losing It*, WASH. POST, Sept. 26, 2003, at A27.

81.   Alan Cooperman, *Iraq War Not Justified, Church Leaders Say*, WASH. POST, Oct. 12, 2002, at A14 (no imminent threat); Bill Broadway, *Religious Leaders' Voices Rise on Iraq*, WASH. POST, Sept. 28, 2002, at B11; *Bishops, Ethicists Urge Bush to Avoid War*, WASH. POST, Sept. 11, 2002, at B9.

82.   Cooperman, *supra* note 81, at A14; *Baptists, Methodists at Odds Over Iraq Strike*, WASH. TIMES, Sept. 11, 2002, at A6,

83.   George Gedda, *U.S. Says Iran Making Headway on Nuclear Weapons Program*, ASSOCIATED PRESS, Feb. 11, 2002.

84.   KENNETH M. POLLACK, THE PERSIAN PUZZLE: THE CONFLICT BETWEEN IRAN AND AMERICA 351 (2004).

85.   *Obama and Netanyahu Inch Closer on Iran, but Is It Too Late?*, USA TODAY, Mar. 21, 2013, at 7A.

86.   *Id.*

87.   FOREIGN POLICY ASSOC., GREAT DECISIONS, IRAN AND OBAMA: POETRY, GREETINGS AND MUTUAL RESPECT 80 (2013).

88.   *Id.*

89.   *Id.* at 81.

90.   *Id.*

91.   *Id.*

92.   *Id.*

93.   *Id.* at 72.

94.   *In Israel, two leaders pledge allegiance and hope for peace*, USA TODAY, Mar. 21, 2013, at 7A.

95.   *Id.*

96.   *Id.*

97.   *Id.*

98.   ROLLIN M. PERKINS & RONALD N. BOYCE, CRIMINAL LAW 1044 (3d ed. 1982) (citing cases dating to the mid 1800s).

99.   RONALD N. BOYCE, DONALD A. DRIPPS, ROLLIN M. PERKINS, CRIMINAL LAW 819 (11th ed. 2010) (Section 2.04).

100.   *See, e.g.,* United States v. Mardirosian, 602 F.3d 1, 8 (1st Cir. 2010); United States v. McMonagle, 38 M.J. 53 (C.O.M.A. 1993); State v. Kurrus, 49 A.3d 260, 265 (Conn. App. Ct. 2012) ("Mistake of fact is a legally permissible defense . . . ."); Price v. State, 712 S.E.2d 828 (Ga. 2011); State v. Landry, 15 So. 3d 138, 151 (La. Ct. App. 2009); State v. Pecora, 622 N.E.2d 1142, 1144 (Ohio Ct. App. 1993).

101.   WILLIAM A. SCHABAS, THE INTERNATIONAL CRIMINAL COURT: A COMMENTARY ON THE ROME STATUTE 499–502 (2010) ("only if it negates the mental element required by the crime"); C. SCHELTEMA & W. VAN DER WOLF, THE INTERNATIONAL TRIBUNAL FOR RWANDA: FACTS, CASES, DOCUMENTS 273 (1999) ("The Commission wishes to note that it considers the defenses

of duress and mistake of fact as possible defenses to individual allegations of serious human rights violations.").

102.   MANUAL FOR COURTS-MARTIAL, UNITED STATES, *Rule for Courts-Martial 916(j)* (2012 ed.)

103.   *Mardirosian*, 602 F.3d at 9.

104.   Raymond W. Copson, *Iraq War: Background and Issues Overview*, Cong. Res. Serv. 19 (Apr. 22, 2003) ("Iraq's chemical, biological, and nuclear weapons programs, along with its long-range missile development and alleged support for terrorism, were the justifications put forth for forcibly disarming Iraq.").

105.   Stephanie Gaskell, *After 10 Years, Jury Still Out on Invasion of Iraq*, POLITICO, Mar. 20, 2013).

106.   GEORGE W. BUSH, DECISION POINTS 229 (2010) ("virtually every major intelligence agency in the world had reached the same conclusion"); Stephen J. Hadley, *Six Takeaways for America*, WASH. POST, Mar. 22, 2013, at A15 ("all the world's major intelligence services").

107.   Glenn Kessler & Walter Pincus, *A Flawed Argument in the Case for War*, WASH. POST, Feb. 1, 2004, at A1, A26.

108.   GEN. TOMMY FRANKS, AMERICAN SOLDIER 353, 355 (2004).

109.   Rowan Scarborough, *Retired General Confident Iraqi Weapons Will Be Found*, WASH. TIMES, June 16, 2003, at A12; Bill Gertz, *Spy Chief Says Iraq Moved Weapons*, WASH. POST, Oct. 29, 2003, at A3 (destroyed or moved to Syria weeks before the war).

110.   Coalition forces found 500 artillery projectiles containing downgraded mustard gas or sarin nerve agents. *Chemical Arms Found in Iraq, Report Reveals*, WASH. TIMES, June 22, 2006, at A12.

111.   FRANKS, *supra* note 108, at 197, 353.

112.   DERSHOWITZ, *supra* note 28, at 83

113.   DONJA DE RUITER, AGGRESSION AND INTERNATIONAL CRIMINAL LAW 20 (2011)

114.   *Id.*

115.   Steve LeBlanc, *Kennedy Says Case for War Built on 'Fraud,'* WASH. POST, Sept. 19, 2003, at A2 ("administration officials relied on 'distortion, misrepresentation, a selection of intelligence' to make their case for war"); *see What the Road to War Really Looked Like*, WASH. EXAMINER, Dec. 7, 2005, at 15 (Bush critics allege he deliberately exaggerated the Iraqi threat and withheld intelligence casting doubt on Iraq's WMD program).

116.   Dana Milbank, *Bush Was Surprised at Lack of Iraqi Arms*, WASH. POST, Feb. 9, 2004, at A1.

117.   *Powell: White House Not Told of Pre-War Intelligence Doubts*, WASH. EXAMINER, Dec. 19, 2005, at 12.

118.   *Still Fighting Over a Flawed Case for War*, WASH. POST, Feb. 3, 2013, at B3. In his memoirs, General Franks notes that not only did he believe the intelligence at the time, but he thought President Bush, Secretary Powell, and CIA Director Tennant did as well. FRANKS, *supra* note 108, at 563.

119.   Dana Priest, *No CIA Slanted Iraq Data*, WASH. POST, Jan. 31, 2004, at A1 (Congressional and CIA investigations).

120.   248 S.E.2d 808, 810 (Va., Nov. 22, 1978).

XV

Cyberterrorism

Professor Thomas A. Marks and Rodney S. Azama

Introduction

Cyberterrorism is the convergence of terrorism and cyberspace. It is generally understood to mean unlawful attacks and threats of attack against computers, networks, and the information stored therein when done to intimidate or coerce a government or its people in furtherance of political or social objectives. Further, to qualify as cyberterrorism, an attack should result in violence against persons or property, or at least enough harm to generate fear. Attacks that lead to death or bodily injury, explosions, plane crashes, water contamination, or severe economic loss would be examples. Serious attacks against critical infrastructures could be acts of cyberterrorism, depending on their impact. Attacks that disrupt nonessential services or that are mainly a costly nuisance would not.
—*Dorothy E. Denning* (Georgetown University)[1]

Emergence of Cyberterrorism

Cyberterrorism[2] is a post–Cold War phenomenon. Today, it is often forgotten that in the mid-1980s, the Internet as we recognize it was a military tool and that even the CIA existed primarily in a "hard copy" world. During the Vietnam War, a letter sent from nearly anywhere in the war zone could be delivered and a response received in "just" five days, which was considered extraordinary. Today, we would expect the end of the world if any computer communication function took so much as five seconds.

So revolutionary has been the compression of time and space that all facets of life—certainly warfare—have been affected.[3] Most particularly, the salience of framing and narrative, both intangible qualities that exist symbiotically with speed of dissemination of images and rationalizations, have impacted upon warfare at the strategic level to the extent that we can speak of "new war" as distinct from traditional "war."[4] Indeed, the traditional domains of warfare—air, land, sea, and space—have been joined in doctrine by a fifth, cyber (sometimes called "virtual terrain").[5]

If fusion of the tangible and intangible may be seen as a defining characteristic of the post–Cold War world, it can readily be discerned that terrorism acting in the cyber domain will fall into two principal categories: tactical actions or even campaigns that utilize the tools provided by the "world of the net," and strategic leveraging of the new global context created by the fusion of tangible and intangible worlds. The widespread use of the Internet by terrorist groups instrumentally for attacks, communication, and recruiting would be examples of the first,[6] with construction of campaigns occurring when the resultant "bundles" of tactical efforts become linked efforts in time and space.[7] An example of the second would be a terrorist threat group consciously structuring its strategic approach so that it exists in the two worlds of tangible and intangible space.[8]

It is the first area, the tactical, which draws most attention, particularly the concern that now-routine cyberhacking and cyberwarfare attacks will be executed by terrorist groups in the same manner that traditional violence (e.g., bombs) is used to target the innocent, with the ultimate being a "WMD-like" cyberattack in its consequences (e.g., as portrayed in the film *The Net*[9]). Significantly, the actual instances of such attacks are reported to be few and thus far of a particular quality, denial of service.[10] In contrast, states have engaged in more destructive behavior, notably Russia in its dealing with those countries of the former Soviet Union that have attracted Moscow's ire, notably Estonia and Georgia, and, more recently (apparently), American and Israeli attempts using the "Stuxnet" cyberworm to slow Iranian nuclear weapons development.[11]

In the second area, the strategic, much less has been discussed, but the results are far more profound. The exploitation of the intangible dimension, using electronic images and narrative—by Hezbollah and Hamas, for instance—has been so adroit as to mobilize tangible capacity, which threatens not only Israel's strategic war-fighting efforts but, by calling into question its legitimacy as a state, its very existence.[12] In similar fashion, Liberation Tigers of Tamil Eelam (LTTE) remnants have shifted from emphasis upon tangible action (i.e., kinetics), where the group was decisively defeated in the final May 2009 fighting, to lawfare,[13] enabled by an intangible effort conducted almost exclusively in the virtual world. This shift has not only allowed the Tamil self-defined liberation struggle to continue but has estranged Sri Lanka from its traditional Western supporters and increasingly isolated it on the world stage.[14]

These cases thrust forth a final point in considering cyberterrorism, the reality—often lost in general discussions on terrorism but integral to Western doctrinal publications—that terrorism itself has two forms when seen from a war-fighting perspective: terrorism as a logic and terrorism as a method (the terminology is that of Wieviorka[15]). The latter is terrorism as but one tool utilized by the mass mobilization effort of an insurgency, while the former is what the literature once termed "pure terrorism," that which structurally is estranged from the social base it purports to represent.

The implications for the discussion above are substantial. Utilized by an insurgency, cyberterrorism will manifest itself at all three levels of war, from the tactical through the campaign (i.e., operational art) to the strategic. The insurgent effort will operate in both tangible and intangible dimensions and will unfold along lines of effort that implement a strategic approach. In contrast, cyber actions by a pure terrorist group must necessarily unfold tactically and to an extent in campaigns, with the focus an effort to translate kinetic damage into message and, thus, influence.

Analytical Considerations

Distinctions in Defining Cyberterrorism

As noted in the discussion above, cyberterrorism, in its plain face meaning, is terrorism that occurs in the so-called cyber domain. which some sources claim is a corruption of the proper use of "cyber." Regardless, the definition that introduced the chapter falls well within common understanding and usage. It can readily be seen, however, that such definition pushes forward a number of distinctions that must be made: that between cyberterrorism and cyberwarfare; that between terrorism and cyberterrorism; and that between cyberterrorism and criminality "of the cyber sort." Each of these will be considered in turn.

Considering the first: Cyberwarfare, as normally considered in the literature, has to do with the actions of states.[16] In contrast, terrorism of any type has to do with sub-state actors. Cyberterrorism, therefore, as discussed above, can be delimited as either tactical/campaign—the use of cyber-tools in the same manner as any other means available to a terrorist group (e.g., for communications, defenses, attacks)—or as a more strategic approach to war-fighting that leverages the realities and potentialities of the cyber domain.

Two observed realities of the new age of globalization increase the salience of these observations. The first, as most prominently discussed by Rupert Smith in his *The Utility of Force: The Art of War in the Modern World*,[17] highlights that changes in global realities, from settlement patterns to linkages, result in a situation wherein conflict invariably must be waged as "war amongst the people" (with its numerous legal implications). Simultaneously, this "war," as per the "Fourth Generation" theorists, notably William S. Lind in a series of articles,[18] will be characterized by its conflation of state and non-state actors, with any number of the latter emerging with concentrations of power superior to those of actual states. A logical outgrowth of this has been the official adoption by militaries of the notion that conflicts will more often than not be "hybrid," involving a variety of martial forms, one of which will be terrorism.[19]

Not stated but manifest is that Chinese and Vietnamese theorists,[20] in their extensive conceptualization and incorporation into doctrine of, respectively, "political warfare" and "the war of interlocking," were in some cases at least half a century in advance of such Western discussion. Though the cyber world was not yet in existence, little that is in the Chinese or Vietnamese works requires such specificity. Indeed, applied to the cyber domain, their fusion of tangible and intangible merely becomes more potent.

Terrorism and Cyberterrorism

Chinese and Vietnamese theorists thus emphasized half a century ago what for the West emerged as a seminal shift only at the end of the Cold War, the centrality of "human terrain" to all warfare. Any consideration of terrorism has long been more than a little aware of this reality. Terrorism, regardless of permutations—occasioned overwhelmingly by newly emerging states' historic determination not to be constrained or condemned in wars of national liberation—is today essentially considered to be violence perpetrated against the innocent [persons and property protected by the laws of war] by sub-state actors for the purpose of political communication. Even "religious" terrorism is but a version of this, since the ultimate aims of religious actors are political (i.e., to determine the societal rules of the game, which is a political goal).[21]

All terrorist actions are attempts to shape facets of the human domain. Tactical cyberterrorism, discussed above, focuses on individuals and property, while the strategic effort extends to the far more profound business evident in the Hezbollah and Hamas efforts: the actual altering of perception to the extent that no state counter can gain traction, much like coating a road with oil. Orwell's masterpiece, *1984*, comes quickly to mind here, but he was discussing state action, while we are considering sub-state actors.

It is important to reiterate that here we are focusing upon much more than the communication of messages,[22] as is normally associated with terrorism as "propaganda by the deed." Rather, we endeavor to call attention to the intangible restructuring of reality to elicit favorable tangible reaction. The critical importance of framing and narrative stems directly from this reality. Put perhaps offhandedly but accurately, seeing is no longer believing; believing determines what one sees. In the present-world context, terrorists, as armed politicians, have grasped this point as well as any "normal" politicians.[23]

Such conceptualization brings to the fore the very issue that has mired state policy makers today when dealing with rivals: when can an attack be said to have taken place? If there is an inability to answer definitively such a straightforward question with respect, say, to a well-documented case, such as the recent penetration of numerous political and economic targets by Chinese PLA cyber-units,[24] how much greater is the incapacity to discern attacks by non-state actors?[25] Noteworthy in this respect are the recent attacks by the "Syrian Electronic Army." It remains unknown to what extent its attacks, which have attempted to do tangible damage (e.g., attack on the computers of the Haifa water system),[26] have been the work of (a) the Syrian government, (b) sympathizers, or (c) sponsored sympathizers—that is, a mix of (a) and (b).[27]

Taken one step further, how can actual attacks, such as that on Haifa (assuming the perpetrator is a non-state actor), be separated from more indirect efforts, such as those associated with altering the very context from which perception is derived? Such efforts, associated historically with the propaganda tactics and campaigns of fascism, are used to alter the mind (chronicled masterfully, in the case of Hitler and Germany, by Leni Riefenstahl in *Triumph of the Will*, 1935[28]). Already, the use of cyberweapons to shape frames and narratives is held by many to be merely one facet of democratic discourse.

Europe, for example, perpetuates the artificial boundary between the tangible and the intangible by claiming that Hezbollah consists of separate military (kinetic) and political (nonkinetic) "wings."[29] Not only could nothing be further from reality, but this obscures the actions in the intangible dimension that mold minds so that they are of the same quality as committed fascists. Ironically, while extensive academic (and, at one point in time, operational) work has been done on fascist and communist efforts in this area, little has been done beyond the tactical aspects where terrorist groups are concerned, the most prominent area of research being, of course, the numerous studies dealing with the impact of the Internet upon self-radicalization.[30] This misses the far more important area of strategic "perception management."[31]

Cybercrimes, Hacktivism, and Cyberespionage

The final distinction that must be made is between cyberterrorism and other forms of cybercriminality. This is particularly important, because a central element of a globalized world is what the appropriate literature has termed the "terror-crime nexus." Therein, one finds much the same divisions of analysis that have been highlighted above concerning terrorism itself. At the tactical level, there exist the money-laundering mechanisms which have provided sensational scandals for the media of late, with prominent banks implicated in activities involving terrorist funds (transactions that largely involve use of the Internet). At the strategic level, there is the fusion of criminal fundraising with the very essence of a terrorist organization that one associates with FARC and ELN in Colombia, but increasingly with Hezbollah and those of the Mexican cartels; the latter can be judged to be possibly proto-political even as they remain essentially criminal.[32] The point is that it is not only analytically fruitless but dangerous to separate the cyber elements from any other in such nexus. Wire-transferring illicit funds to be laundered, for example, cannot artificially be separated from more the traditional lugging of bags of cash, even if the tactical means are distinct. Hence cybercrimes, while not "terrorism" per se, are invariably today part and parcel of terrorist group activity, especially financing and resourcing.[33]

More intriguing are the political and proto-political aspects of "Hacktivism." As well covered in myriad discussions, there are the purely criminal aspects of hacking. Of more interest to us here, at what point do the anarchist sentiments underlying much recent hacker activity assume such political salience that they should be treated as terrorism under the definitional terms of reference, especially the inclusion of property under the key "innocent" term? Certainly the actions of individuals as portrayed in *We Are Legion: The Story of the Hacktivists*[34] rise to the level of political as seen in ecoterrorists or animal rights terrorists.[35] And the lack of cohesive group structure or even common ideological platform does not in any way obviate the reality of terrorism should all elements of the definition be present.[36]

Still, it is the noble sentiments of all three, but especially the hacktivists, that have led to considerable ambiguity, with the Orwell tie-in explicit in the film *V for Vendetta* (from the 1990 graphic novel).[37] The plot of *V for Vendetta*, with a lone-wolf "terrorist" engaged in a struggle against a "fascist" world, summons forth a facet of academic work on terrorism that considers the difficulty of using established terminology and analytical constructs in a context lacking or even devoid of legitimacy. In other words, in a situation that borders on genocide, such as created by the Russians in Chechnya,[38] or the Chinese in Tibet and Xinxiang,[39] or the Britain of *V for Vendetta*,[40] who or what qualifies as "innocent"? If no such category exists—i.e., the state and all who are involved with it are "guilty"—then how does one identify any actor as a terrorist, cyber or otherwise?[41]

Matters are much clearer for this analysis where cyberespionage is concerned. Certainly, spying or its reverse (counterintelligence) can be attached to the actions of terrorists,[42] but normally espionage is thought to be within the purview of states, with similar action by non-state actors simply one more aspect of their criminality.

As noted above, it is in fact cyberespionage as opposed to cyberterrorism which thus far has proved of greatest concern to the present world order and its states.

Cyberterrorism Trends

Globalization, Technology, and the Cyber Environment

Globalization, though not negating basic parameters or terminology for the analysis of terrorism, has created a "new terrorism," as oft noted by commentators. In particular, it has turned the effort to communicate politically through the use of violence into a truly worldwide effort, with the targeting of potential and intended audiences rivaling—possibly for the first time in history—the approaches and mechanics of commercial advertising and branding. This, as noted previously, has allowed framing and narrative to emerge as such potent components of any political violence involving or labeled terrorism. On the one hand, threat groups, using the astonishing capabilities inherent to cybercommunications, can theoretically reach a universe of potential sympathizers, supporters, and recruits. On the other hand, they can leverage intangible images and tales of injustice and suffering as any kinetic effort would deploy tangible weapons systems.

The neutralization of Israeli kinetic power during the 2006 Lebanon incursion (discussed previously) is normally held up as the paradigmatic case in this regard, but to this can be added the less effective but nonetheless potent Hamas effort in 2008,[43] as well as the unsuccessful but troubling LTTE tactical effort commencing in 2009 which, in effect, has prevented Sri Lanka strategically from reaping the fruits of a kinetic knockout after nearly three decades of conflict.

In all of these cases, technology was leveraged as weapons system, with intangible "rounds" fired not merely as harassing fire but rather at predetermined targets where they would have maximum tangible impact. The resulting demonstrations and demands for tangible action against Israel and Sri Lanka reached the point, in the latter case, of strategic demands for "humanitarian intervention"— that is, invasion by the international community, as happened in the Balkans (the Kosovo case). In the present, in March 2013, the cyber-dissemination of powerful images of alleged atrocity from the 2009 *denouement* was used to spearhead a successful United Nations effort at condemning Sri Lanka. Simultaneously, the ruling coalition in India found itself threatened when the same images provoked the withdrawal of a Tamil Nadu partner in the face of New Delhi unwillingness to join the most extreme anti-Colombo positions.[44]

Such efforts have been increasingly enabled by cyber-technological advances which have made the likes of the film *Kony 2012* possible.[45] Analysts have long followed similar, far more sinister efforts orchestrated by terrorist rather than advocacy groups, especially their ability to manipulate digital images before disseminating the product via the Internet (e.g., *YouTube*). These are of far greater immediate impact and concern than the much more widely publicized but still hypothetical direct attacks upon critical infrastructure.

Indeed, as maturation of globalization continues, with concurrent leaps in cyberenvironment salience, actions and trends such as this are sure to grow more pronounced.[46] Of most concern is the difficulty of timely, adequate response to well-planned cyber-manipulation that is inherent to the architecture and processes of the cyber world. Sri Lanka again provides a powerful lesson, as the quite successful traditional military blockade of the battle area—a portion of an island, after all—proved incapable of creating a cyberblockade, which allowed LTTE to deliver images on-target and provoke the consequences discussed above. The same may be said of Israel's effort in Hamas, where it also was able to seal off the battle area in a traditional sense but could not shut down cyberweapons and their consequent tactical and strategic effects.

Actors, Usage, Methodologies

It can readily be seen that several consequences flow from the points just made. First, in an increasingly globalized context, would-be violent political actors can make contact with like-minded individuals. This was well-illustrated by the effort of Anwar al-Awlaki of Al-Qaeda on the Arabian Peninsula, which ultimately involved an astonishing array of actors self-radicalized through, initially, al-Awlaki messages disseminated by the Internet, but later through direct contact.[47] Second, this highlights the extent to which the entire globe now functions in the same manner as the more traditional nation-state area of operations once did. Third, of much greater significance, whereas the state in a traditional counterterrorism or counterinsurgency effort (which necessarily included a counterterrorism campaign) always had to be concerned at the growth of internal challenge and possible external intervention, cyber-enabled processes now can achieve such salience and momentum that they threaten the state itself, as in the Israeli and Sri Lankan cases. This means that any terrorist group with even a modicum of situational awareness will construct its strategic approach informed with just such realities in mind. It is the evidence that this was done in Lebanon 2006 and Gaza 2008 that makes (respectively) the Hezbollah and Hamas cases of such interest.

On the negative side, an interesting consequence of these variable trends is that would-be mass mobilization efforts by insurgents appear to be as yet incapable of escaping the same consequences that have often been noted as resulting from social media—many casual acquaintances but few actual friends.[48] In similar fashion, divorcing the recruitment and sustainment processes of mass mobilization from an actual social base that can achieve critical mass in geographic and temporal spaces can result in isolated, spectacular acts—as seen in the cases of al-Awlaki recruits such as Umar Farouk Abdulmutallab (the "Underwear Bomber," convicted in February 2012) or Major Nidal Malik Hasan (the convicted perpetrator in the November 5, 2009, Ft. Hood terrorist shooting)[49]—but thus far has not achieved actual mass mobilization. The impact of social media upon the uprisings that are collectively known as the "Arab Spring" is often held up as showcasing the potential for such action; however, not only has such action eluded the strategies and implementation of terrorists, but the role of cyber acts therein remain contested and not completely understood.[50] The result is that use of the cyber domain for mobilization efforts has paradoxically reinforced the very structural estrangement from the intended social base that is the essence of "terrorism as logic" as distinguished from the mass mobilization of insurgency that is engendered by "terrorism as method."

Thus, the greatest threat is posed by those groups that can leverage the cyber domain in such manner as to enable strategic approaches that call for use of intangible framing and narrative to mobilize tangible efforts against their foes,[51] normally states. In constructing counters, states are impacted by the usual constraints one associates with any unwieldy bureaucracy: inability not only of timely, appropriate response but of recognition of the challenge that is at hand. Assuming the latter takes place, the challenge is meshing of instruments of national power in such manner as to respond. Depending on the structure and characteristics of the threat group, this is the age-old battle of primary-group dexterity versus secondary-group inertia.

Notes

1. Testimony before the Special Oversight Panel on Terrorism, Committee on Armed Services, U.S. House of Representatives, May 23, 2000.

2. Denning's definition above is sufficient for our purposes with the critical addition that "terrorism" is executed by sub-state actors, as is presently accepted by all save a minority within academic and policy communities determined to apply the same criteria to states—which is considered by most as so expanding the category as to make it useless for analysis. Our usage therefore is in a sense derivative: cyberterrorism is the use of the cyber domain *by terrorists*. For further discussion, *see* Dimitar Kostadinov, *Cyberterrorism Defined (as distinct from 'Cybercrime')*, INFOSEC Institute Resources, *available at* http://resources.infosecinstitute.com/cyberterrorism-distinct-from-cybercrime/.

3. For an engaging discussion, *see* Ch. 5, *The Future of Terrorism, in* ERIC SCHMIDT & JARED COHEN, THE NEW DIGITAL AGE: RESHAPING THE FUTURE OF PEOPLE, NATIONS AND BUSINESS 151–82 (Alfred A. Knopf, 2013)

4. Our usage here moves beyond the discussion which presently absorbs those concerned with the term directly (i.e., "new war") or its various permutations (e.g., Fourth Generation Warfare, compound war, hybrid war). Their focus is overwhelmingly on the role of the state or on a synergy of actors and actions (e.g., the use of cyberwarfare in conjunction with state-sponsored irregular warfare). In contrast, we speak to the duality occasioned by warfare that is fought simultaneously in the tangible and intangible worlds—in other words, "on the ground" and "in the

mind." Ironically, it was Taiwan, following the loss of the mainland, which best responded to this new reality. *See* THOMAS A. MARKS, COUNTERREVOLUTION IN CHINA: WANG SHENG AND THE KUOMINTANG (Frank Cass, 1998), *passim*.

5.   Predictably, terminology remains in a state of flux. U.S. military publications increasingly discuss the "electromagnetic spectrum and cyberspace" or "the EM-Cyber Environment," even while noting the merging that is taking place. For a particularly useful discussion, *see* JONATHAN W. GREENERT, IMMINENT DOMAIN, NAVAL INST. PROCEEDINGS 138 (December 2012), 16–21 (Admiral Greenert is the Chief of Naval Operations), *available at* http://www.usni.org/magazines/proceedings/2012-12/imminent-domain.

6.   For useful discussion, *see* John J. Kane, *Virtual Terrain, Lethal Potential: Toward Achieving Security in an Ungoverned Domain*, Ch. 3.6 *in* TOWARD A GRAND STRATEGY AGAINST TERRORISM 252–81.

7.   *E.g.*, a strategic communications campaign, which self-evidently is executed through a series of discrete acts that are linked in time and space to form one component of a larger strategic effort.

8.   Though Al-Qaeda is perhaps the best-known example, certainly the most effective is LTTE, or the Liberation Tigers of Tamil Eelam (see text below).

9.   Columbia Pictures (1995; re-released in a special edition, 2003), available commercially at (among others) Amazon.

10.   Useful discussion may be found at *Cyber-warfare: Hype and Fear*, THE ECONOMIST, December 8, 2012, 62–63, *available at* http://www.economist.com/news/international/21567886-america-leading-way-developing-doctrines-cyber-warfare-other-countries-may, and Peter W. Singer, *The Cyber Terror Bogeyman*, ARMED FORCES J., November 2012, 12–15, *available at* http://www.brookings.edu/research/articles/2012/11/cyber-terror-singer. It should be noted, however, in light of episodes that have occurred since publication, that both appear to have underestimated the potential threat.

11.   For the Russian case considered within a legal framework, *see* ENEKEN TIKK, KADRI KASKA & LIIS VIHUL, INTERNATIONAL CYBER INCIDENTS: LEGAL CONSIDERATIONS (Cooperative Cyber Defence Centre of Excellence [CCD COE], 2010), *available at* http://www.ccdcoe.org/231.html. For strategic implications of the same case, *see* Stephen Blank, *Web War I: Is Europe's First Information War a New Kind of War?*, 27 COMPARATIVE STRATEGY, no. 3 (2008), 227–47; *available at* http://www.tandfonline.com/doi/pdf/10.1080/01495930802185312. For strategic implications of the Iranian case, *see* James P. Farwell & Rafal Rohozinski, *Stuxnet and the Future of Cyber War*, 53 SURVIVAL, no. 1 (Feb.-Mar. 2011), 23–40, available at http://www.iiss.org/en/publications/survival/sections/2011-2760/survival—global-politics-and-strategy-february-march-2011-f7f0/53-1-05-farwell-and-rohozinski-f587; the authors build upon this discussion with *The New Reality of Cyber War*, 54 SURVIVAL, no. 4 (Aug.-Sept. 2012), 107–20, *available at* http://www.tandfonline.com/doi/abs/10.1080/00396338.2012.709391?journalCode=tsur20.

12.   *See esp.* David A. Acosta, *The Makara of Hizballah: Deception in the 2006 Summer War*, Master's thesis completed at Naval Postgraduate School (Monterey, Cal.), June 2007, *available at* http://webscience.blogs.usj.edu.lb/files/2011/07/poster.pdf. A fascinating one-page "poster," Asymmetric Cyber-warfare Between Israel and Hezbollah: The Web as a New Strategic Battlefield, is useful not only for its display but for the references in an inset box (lower-right corner); *available at* http://webscience.blogs.usj.edu.lb/files/2011/07/poster.pdf; a slightly different URL leads to the base document (with the same title) from which the poster is derived: Sabrine Saad, Stephane B. Bazan & Christophe Varin (no further source data); *available at* http://www.websci11.org/fileadmin/websci/Posters/96_paper.pdf.

13.   Numerous sources are now available on this term. For a succinct discussion, *see* Thomas A. Marks, *Lawfare's Role in Irregular Conflict, in* Focus Quarterly 4 (Special Issue: Counterterrorism), no. 2 (Summer 2010), 12–14, *available at* http://www.jewishpolicycenter.org/1740/lawfare-irregular-conflict.

14.   To our knowledge, there is no single reference on this ongoing LTTE effort; it is discussed briefly in *id.*

15.   Michel Wieviorka, *Terrorism in the Context of Academic Research, in* Terrorism in Context, Martha Crenshaw ed. (Pa. State Univ. Press, 1995), 597–606. For application to theory and practice, *see* Thomas A. Marks, Robert Sharp & Sebastian Gorka, *Getting the Next War Right: Beyond Population-Centric Warfare*, 1 Prism, no. 3 (June 2010), 79–98, *available at* http://www.ndu.edu/press/lib/images/prism1-3/Prism_79-98_Marks_Gorka_Sharp.pdf.

16.   *See, e.g.,* the discussion of China in Michael Joseph Gross, *Enter the Cyber-Dragon*, Vanity Fair (September 2011), 220–34, *available at* http://www.vanityfair.com/culture/features/2011/09/chinese-hacking-201109.

17.   Vantage, 2007.

18.   *See especially* William S. Lind, *Understanding Fourth Generation War*, Military Review, Sept.-Oct. 2004, 12–16, *available at* http://www.au.af.mil/au/awc/awcgate/milreview/lind.pdf.

19.   *See, e.g.,* the testy but illuminating exchange between proponents of "compound" and "hybrid" warfare in *Letters to the Editor*, 77 Journal of Military History, no. 2 (April 2013), 790–96; for further reference, Frank G. Hoffman, *Hybrid Warfare and Challenges*, Joint Force Q., no. 52 (1st quarter 2009), 34–39. Regardless of terminology, the extent to which the same "hybridization" challenges any assessment of the intangible domain can be found in Alex Michael, Cyber Probing: The Politicisation of Virtual Attack, special series (Defence Acad. of the UK, Dec. 2010), *available at* http://www.isn.ethz.ch/isn/Digital-Library/Publications/Detail/?id=121405&lng=en.

20.   *See* Marks, *supra* note 4; therein, the Vietnamese theorists are also discussed, though briefly.

21.   For definition and discussion, *see* Thomas A. Marks, *Counterinsurgency in an Age of Globalism*, 27 Journal of Conflict Studies, no. 1 (Summer 2007), 22–29, *available at* http://journals.hil.unb.ca/index.php/JCS/article/view/5936/6985.

22.   This facet of the subject is discussed well in Gabriel Weimann, Terror on the Internet: The New Arena, the New Challenges (U.S. Inst. for Peace, 2006).

23.   A detailed effort to grapple with this point, which perhaps leans too heavily on particular aspects of communications theory but is superb nonetheless, is provided by Jonathan Matusitz in *Terrorism and Communication: A Critical Introduction* (Sage, 2013).

24.   Among the numerous sources available, *see especially* William Wan & Ellen Nakashima, *Report Ties Cyberattacks on U.S. Computers to Chinese Military, in* Wash. Post, Feb. 19, 2013, *available at* http://articles.washingtonpost.com/2013-02-19/world/37166888_1_chinese-cyber-attacks-extensive-cyber-espionage-chinese-military-unit, as well as the linked posts by Max Fisher. The original article contains the URL link to the Mandiant security firm report, which was as close to a smoking gun as one is likely to see in the cyberworld. Report *available at* http://intelreport.mandiant.com/. *See also* the extensive article: David E. Sanger, David Barboza & Nicole Perlroth, *Chinese Army Unit Is Seen as Tied to Hacking Against U.S.*, N.Y. Times, Feb. 18, 2013, *available at* http://www.nytimes.com/2013/02/19/technology/chinas-army-is-seen-as-tied-to-hacking-against-us.html?pagewanted=all&_r=0. More generally, consult William C. Hannas, James Mulvenon & Anna B. Puglisi, Chinese Industrial Espionage: Technology Acquisition and Military Modernisation (Routledge, 2013).

263

25.   A point made by Mark Bowden in *Worm: The First Digital World War* (Atlantic Monthly Press, 2011), which deals with the "Conficker" cyberworm which appeared in November 2008.

26.   *Israel Says It Foiled Syrian Cyber Attack on Water System in Haifa*, ASSOCIATED PRESS, May 25, 2013, *available at* http://www.huffingtonpost.com/2013/05/25/israel-syria-cyber-attack_n_3336670.html.

27.   *See* Helmi Noman, *The Emergence of Open and Organized Pro-Government Cyber Attacks in the Middle East: The Case of the Syrian Electronic Army*, OPENNET INITIATIVE, undated but accessed May 27, 2013, *available at* https://opennet.net/emergence-open-and-organized-pro-government-cyber-attacks-middle-east-case-syrian-electronic-army, and Information Warfare Monitor (InfoWar Monitor), *Disrupted Attacks and Hyped Targets*, OPENNET INITIATIVE, undated but accessed May 27, 2013, *available at* https://opennet.net/syrian-electronic-army-disruptive-attacks-and-hyped-targets.

28.   Synapse Films (2006) has produced an excellent DVD transfer, available commercially at (among others) Amazon.

29.   Nicholas Kulish, *Despite Alarm by U.S., Europe Lets Hezbollah Operate Openly*, N.Y. TIMES, Aug. 15, 2012, online edition (accessed May 27, 2013), *available at* http://www.nytimes.com/2012/08/16/world/europe/hezbollah-banned-in-us-operates-in-europes-public-eye.html?pagewanted=all&_r=0.

30.   Useful on this topic is Catherine Bott et al., *The Internet as a Terrorist Tool for Recruitment and Radicalization of Youth*, White Paper prepared for U.S. Dep't of Homeland Security (Science and Technology Directorate) by Analytic Services Inc., April 24, 2009, *available at* http://www.homelandsecurity.org/docs/reports/Internet_Radicalization.pdf. Similar material but from the perspective of counter may be found at TIM STEVENS & PETER R. NEUMANN, COUNTERING ONLINE RADICALISATION: A STRATEGY FOR ACTION (Int'l Centre for the Study of Radicalisation and Political Violence, King's College, Jan. 2009), *available at* http://icsr.info/wp-content/uploads/2012/10/1236768491ICSROnlineRadicalisationReport.pdf. For a perceptive discussion on the interface between larger terrorism context and self-radicalization, as illustrated by the April 2013 Boston Marathon bombers, *see* Richard Barrett, *Did Tamerlan 'Self-Radicalize'?*, DAILY BEAST, April 25, 2013, *available at* http://www.thedailybeast.com/articles/2013/04/25/did-tamerlan-self-radicalize.html.

31.   *See, e.g.*, SUSAN L. CARUTHERS, WINNING HEARTS AND MINDS: BRITISH GOVERNMENTS, THE MEDIA AND COLONIAL COUNTER-INSURGENCY 1944-1960 (Leicester Univ. Press, 1995); or, more recently (though examining a particular facet of the subject), CLIFFORD BOB, THE MARKETING OF REBELLION: INSURGENTS, MEDIA, AND INTERNATIONAL ACTIVISM (Cambridge Univ. Press, 2005). Likewise, there is ample material on both sides of the tactical and even operational use of cyberwarfare to further terrorist efforts. On the larger subject of strategic perception management, though, there appears to be as yet no benchmark work. Touching upon the issue in part is BRIGITTE L. NACOS, MASS-MEDIATED TERRORISM: THE CENTRAL ROLE OF THE MEDIA IN TERRORISM AND COUNTERTERRORISM (Rowman & Littlefield, 2007); *see especially* 113–41.

32.   For a detailed discussion, *see* JOHN ROLLINS & LIANA SUN WYLER, TERRORISM AND TRANSNATIONAL CRIME: FOREIGN POLICY ISSUES FOR CONGRESS (Cong. Res. Serv., Oct. 19, 2012), *available at* http://www.fas.org/sgp/crs/terror/R41004.pdf.

33.   For an extensive discussion of this larger issue, to which cyber-criminality is now symbiotically linked, *see* JODI VITTORI, TERRORIST FINANCING AND RESOURCING (Palgrave Macmillan, 2011).

34.   Luminant Media (2012), available commercially at (among others) Amazon.

35.   At least one excellent review finds so little political in the Anonymous posture that it would no doubt disagree with this conclusion; *see* Sue Halpern, *Are Hackers Heroes?*, N.Y. REVIEW

OF BOOKS (Sept. 2012), 42–45, *available at* http://www.nybooks.com/articles/archives/2012/sep/27/are-hackers-heroes/?pagination=false. Halpern's position, though, would seem at odds with the emerging literature, a perusal of which would perhaps find even the use of "proto" as inadequate in describing the political agenda of at least some hackers. *See, e.g.*, one of the books she reviews: PARMY OLSON, WE ARE ANONYMOUS: INSIDE THE HACKER WORLD OF LULZSEC, ANONYMOUS, AND THE GLOBAL CYBER INSURGENCY (Little, Brown, 2012); and three she does not: HEATHER BROOKE, THE REVOLUTION WILL BE DIGITISED: DISPATCHES FROM THE INFORMATION WAR (William Heinemann, 2011); REBECCA MACKINNON, CONSENT OF THE NETWORKED: THE WORLDWIDE STRUGGLE FOR INTERNET FREEDOM (Basic Books, 2012); and ANDRY GREENBERG, THIS MACHINE KILLS SECRETS: HOW WIKILEAKERS, CYBERPUNKS, AND HACKTIVISTS AIM TO FREE THE WORLD'S INFORMATION (Dutton, Sept. 2012).

36.   For a useful discussion, *see* GEORGE MICHAEL, LONE WOLF TERROR AND THE RISE OF LEADERLESS RESISTANCE (Vanderbilt Univ. Press, 2012).

37.   Film released by Warner (2006); graphic novel is Alan Moore (Warner Books, 1990); both available commercially at (among others) Amazon.

38.   For the point under discussion, *see* JAMES HUGHES, CHECHNYA: FROM NATIONALISM TO JIHAD (Univ. of Pa. Press, 2007), especially Ch. 5, *Chechnya and the Meaning of Terrorism*, 128–61.

39.   Tibet is perhaps the more glaring case, where, over a period of time, violence has systematically eliminated a way of life; *see* WANG LIXIONG & TSERING SHAKYA, THE STRUGGLE FOR TIBET (Verso, 2009); also useful, despite its having been passed by events in some respects, is RONALD D. SCHWARTZ, CIRCLE OF PROTEST: POLITICAL RITUAL IN THE TIBETAN UPRISING (Columbia Univ. Press, 1994). For Xinxiang, of a number of possibilities, an older text is revealing; *see* DRU C. GLADNEY, DISLOCATING CHINA: MUSLIMS, MINORITIES, AND OTHER SUBALTERN SUBJECTS (Univ. of Chicago Press, 2004).

40.   SPENCER LAMM, V FOR VENDETTA: FROM SCRIPT TO FILM (Universe, 2006). In the story, Britain, following a nuclear war, is ruled by a fascist party (Norsefire), which uses a brutal police state to cow the remnants who have not previously been outright purged. Thus the scenario dovetails well with the cases under discussion.

41.   This is certainly the logic of both ecoterrorism and animal rights terrorists, though individuals so labeled would vehemently deny that they fall within the designation "terrorists." For an overview, *see* DONALD R. LIDDICK, ECO-TERRORISM: RADICAL ENVIRONMENTAL AND ANIMAL LIBERATION MOVEMENTS (Praeger, 2006); for an alternative position, *see* WILL POTTER, GREEN IS THE NEW RED: AN INSIDER'S ACCOUNT OF A SOCIAL MOVEMENT UNDER SIEGE (City Lights Publishers, 2011).

42.   For one aspect of this subject, *see, e.g.*, BLAKE W. MOBLEY, TERRORISM AND COUNTERINTELLIGENCE: HOW TERRORIST GROUPS ELUDE DETECTION (Columbia Univ. Press, 2012).

43.   *See especially* the "SOCAL Connected" video program (approx. 20 minutes), "Israel and Hamas Use Twitter, Social Media as New Theater of War," KCET (Burbank, Cal.), *available at* http://www.kcet.org/shows/socal_connected/content/science-and-technology/israel-and-hamas-use-twitter-social-media-as-new-theater-of-war.html.

44.   For a succinct summary of the issues, *see* Sruthi Gottipati & Hari Kumar, *Allegations of War Crimes in Sri Lanka Shake Indian Government*, N.Y. TIMES, Mar. 19, 2013, online edition *available at* http://india.blogs.nytimes.com/2013/03/19/allegations-of-war-crimes-in-sri-lanka-shake-indian-government/, which can be supplemented by accessing the various files at Channel 4's pursuit of the issue: http://www.channel4.com/news/sri-lanka-civil-war. This can be augmented

by "Sri Lanka 'War Crimes': Main Allegations," *BBC*, June 17, 2011, *available at* http://www.bbc.co.uk/news/world-south-asia-13158916.

45. The video and commentary are *available at* http://invisiblechildren.com/kony/. Released in March 2012, the film called for the apprehension and trial of indicted war criminal Joseph Kony (originally in Uganda) and rapidly became "the most viral video of all time" [according to *Time*]. *See* http://en.wikipedia.org/wiki/Kony_2012.

46. A particularly good discussion is Dorothy E. Denning, *Terror's Web: How the Internet is Transforming Terrorism, in* HANDBOOK ON INTERNET CRIME, Yvonne Jewkes & Majid Yar eds. (Willan Pub'ng, 2009), 194–213; typescript *available at* http://faculty.nps.edu/dedennin/publications/Denning-TerrorsWeb.pdf.

47. Published before Al-Awlaki's death is JACK BARCLAY, CHALLENGING THE INFLUENCE OF ANWAR AL-AWLAKI (Int'l Centre for the Study of Radicalisation and Political Violence, King's College, Sept. 2010), *available at* http://icsr.info/wp-content/uploads/2012/10/1283965345ICSR_ChallengingtheInfluenceofAnwarAlAwlaki.pdf. For discussion following his death, *see* TimesCast video clip, "Al-Awlaki's Influence," N.Y. TIMES (2:41 minutes), *available at* http://www.nytimes.com/video/2011/09/30/world/middleeast/100000001084038/timescast—al-awlakis-influence.html. More recently, *see* Margaret Coker, *Cleric Cited by Tsarnaev Lives On—Online*, WALL ST. J., May 5, 2013, *available at* http://online.wsj.com/article/SB10001424127887323687604578465023366949366.html.

48. This reality has been so widely demonstrated that analysis has moved on to the more intriguing area of the precise nature of individual interface with mobilization efforts enabled by technology. *See, e.g.*, BRUCE BIMBER, ANDREW FLANAGIN & CYNTHIA STOHL, COLLECTIVE ACTION IN ORGANIZATIONS: INTERACTION AND ENGAGEMENT IN AN ERA OF TECHNOLOGICAL CHANGE (Cambridge Univ. Press, 2012).

49. *The New York Times* archive for Al-Awlaki is *available at* http://topics.nytimes.com/topics/reference/timestopics/people/a/anwar_al_awlaki/index.html.

50. *See, e.g.*, Marc Lynch, *Twitter Devolutions: How Social Media Is Hurting the Arab Spring*, FOREIGN POLICY, Feb. 7, 2013, *available at* http://www.foreignpolicy.com/articles/2013/02/07/twitter_devolutions_arab_spring_social_media.

51. It is perhaps noteworthy that in Shirow Masamune's 1989 *manga* series, *The Ghost in the Shell*, English trans. (Dark Horse Comics, 2009), the terrorist villain(s) operates by infiltrating the minds of his targets (humans with cyber-brains) and planting alternative worlds therein to lead them into second- and third-order terroristic actions as a consequence of what, in reality, are virtual "memories." The animated film of the same name was released in the U.S. in 1998 (Palm Pictures); it is available commercially at (among others) Amazon.

XVI

Demystifying Terrorist Financing

Jeff Breinholt

Terrorist financing is how terrorist groups and individuals obtain things of value to allow them to maintain their operations and perpetrate violence. Countering terrorist financing involves the process of looking beyond the terrorists themselves to those who somehow help them financially. The term has gained widespread currency after 2001. The 9/11 Commission devoted a monograph to the issue,[1] and the Paris-based Financial Action Task Force (FATF) has moved beyond money laundering to include terrorist financing within its remit. The FBI created a special headquarters-based section to disrupt terrorist financing operations. The Treasury Department's Office of Foreign Assets Control (OFAC) has grown exponentially.

The most important tool in countering terrorist financing involves the maintenance of lists of people and groups who are involved in the terrorist-financing enterprise. The U.N. Security Council maintains one such list. Stateside, there are two U.S.-maintained lists that have a very similar function. Under the Immigration and Nationality Act, the State Department runs a list of Foreign Terrorist Organizations (FTOs). If a group is included on the list, it becomes a crime for anyone, anywhere in the world, to knowingly provide anything of value to the group. 18 U.S.C. § 2339B. Meanwhile, the Treasury Department frequently updates its list of Specially Designated Global Terrorists (SDGTs), created by Executive Order 13,224, the so-called global terrorism sanctions list. It is a crime under the International Emergency Economic Powers Act (IEEPA) for anyone subject to U.S. jurisdiction to willfully engage in financial transactions with groups and individuals who are SDGTs. 50 U.S.C. § 1701 *et seq.* Of the two U.S. lists, Treasury's

SDGT list is far more expansive, as it includes groups and individuals, both foreign and domestic. Every FTO (and there are currently 53) is an SDGT, but not every SDGT—some 500 plus—is an FTO.

As a matter of effective statecraft, it is not unreasonable to ask why the U.S. maintains multiple terrorism lists for countering terrorist financing, as each seemingly accomplishes largely the same purpose. This chapter seeks to demystify the American system for countering terrorist financing by answering that question through a bit of legal history that got its start in the early 1980s.

The Strange Case of Eugene Tafoya

In 1980, there were some 10,000 Libyans living in the United States. Many of them did not like living under the tyrannical rule of the Libyan strongman, Col. Moammar Gaddafi. Gaddafi would keep close tabs on them from overseas.

Meanwhile, Eugene Tafoya needed a job. He had been honorably discharged from the Army's Green Berets and was living in New Mexico. One thing led to another, and Tafoya found himself working for Gaddafi.

On October 14, 1980, Tafoya, posing as an IBM recruiter, visited dissident Faisal Zagallai's home in Ft. Collins, Colorado, and tried to kill him in his living room, leaving Zagallai blind in one eye. Tafoya escaped through a window.

A few months later, two boys playing in an irrigation ditch near Zagallai's home found a pistol. The serial numbers were traced back to a North Carolina pawn shop near Fort Bragg and a person who sold the weapon to Tafoya. Using credit card and rental car receipts, authorities tracked Tafoya down in New Mexico, where a search uncovered a hit list that targeted American citizens. As it turned out, Tafoya was linked to rogue CIA operatives Edwin Wilson and Frank Terpil. Wilson was eventually convicted of various crimes in U.S. courts.[2]

The Colorado prosecution of Tafoya for the attempt on Zagallai's life did not include the Gaddafi evidence, and, although he was convicted on January 5, 1982, he received only a two-year sentence.[3]

At that point, two creative prosecutors from the U.S. Department of Justice's Criminal Division stepped in and obtained a tax indictment against Tafoya.[4] Their theory: Tafoya committed a crime by filing 1980 and 1981 federal income tax returns that omitted his assassination fees. The jury convicted him. The Fifth Circuit, affirming Tafoya's conviction, rejected his argument that the prosecution had unfairly transformed his murder prosecution into a tax case and that he never received income from his activities, only expense money.[5]

Growing Tafoya Out: The Concept of "Actionable Intelligence"

Now *Tafoya* is a terrorist financing case only in the broadest sense: the culprit, an American-trained sharpshooter, sought to give a terrorist—in this case Moammar

Gaddafi—something of value. In this case it was not money; rather, it was murder services, sometimes referred to as "wet work." Expanding *Tafoya* into an explanation of why the U.S. currently maintains overlapping and duplicative sets of terrorist financing lists requires an understanding of the term "actionable intelligence."

Actionable intelligence is the holy grail of the intelligence cycle, which consists, broadly speaking, of two main components: "collectors" and "consumers." "Collectors" are those people in charge of monitoring a certain type of stream of information. They are judged by how effectively they interact with their consumers—those persons who have the authority to unleash a certain official action on a target.[6]

What constitutes actionable intelligence depends on the traditions of the consumer. It is information that meets certain standards of timeliness and reliability, which, according to the traditions of the consumer, justifies some official action. Good collectors understand these traditions.

In the prosecution world, the proxy for actionable intelligence is "admissible evidence": information that has been put into a form that, according to the applicable rules of evidence, can be introduced into a judicial proceeding. Note that the type of exactitude required for criminal trials is arguably greater than what would constitute actionable intelligence for some other purpose—say, a military strike or a diplomatic overture. After all, neither the Pentagon nor the State Department justifies all of its findings and targeting decisions on its receipt of something as exacting as admissible evidence. That is simply not their tradition. That is not to say they are cavalier about what facts they credit in choosing their responses to international mischief. They have no more incentive to get it wrong than do we prosecutors.

So collectors and consumers represent a symbiotic relationship in the intelligence cycle. They each yearn to disseminate/receive information that qualifies as "actionable intelligence." When this happens, we know the collectors are doing their job well, and the consumers are empowered to act on the basis of good information.

To illustrate this concept further, we might ask, Was Eugene Tafoya's association with Gaddafi actionable? How about in the state court proceeding? The fact that Tafoya tried to kill Faisal Zagallai was all the prosecutors were required to prove, not his motivation. Of course, armed with information about who put Tafoya up to the job, the prosecutor could have tried to make the jury hate him more, but that was not an element of the crime of attempted murder. The impetus for the hit was irrelevant. The fact of the association was not actionable.

What about the federal prosecution? There, the prosecutors' working theory was that Tafoya and Gaddafi had some sort of cognizable association. Specifically, it was an employer-employee relationship, giving rise to a promise of payment (i.e., taxable income) for service rendered, which payment was ultimately omitted on Tafoya's tax return. So the Tafoya-Gaddafi association was indeed relevant in the federal tax fraud case. It was actionable.

What about the fact that Gaddafi was obnoxious, and that the nature of their association was illegal—a murder-for-hire scheme? Was that actionable? In the federal tax prosecution, the answer is no. What Tafoya and Gaddafi had was an actionable relationship that did not depend on whether it was legal or not. After all, Tafoya could have been doing lawful work for Gaddafi's enterprise and he would have been just as guilty, assuming he made the decision to omit his Gaddafi income from his tax return.

For criminologists, terrorist financing experts, and legislators, the question becomes how to make Gaddafi's relative obnoxiousness actionable. Can we make it a crime to engage financially with obnoxious people? More precisely, can we make it a crime for anyone to knowingly engage in a financial transaction with people the United States officially designates as obnoxious?

That is exactly what has been done, through the lists published by the State and Treasury Departments. They serve the function of defining who, exactly, legally qualifies as obnoxious, and making this designation actionable through legal prohibitions.

The Efficacy of Lists in Counterterrorism

Terrorist financing lists are a form of economic embargo: the U.S. tells the world who is embargoed, and prosecutors prosecute people who violate it. Any financial transaction qualifies; no dirty money is required.

The power of this terrorist financing list-making approach is illustrated by the arguments that would be made by persons ensnared in the crime. If Gaddafi were on a list of designated obnoxious people and financially associating with him was a crime, what arguments could Eugene Tafoya make if he was arrested minutes after making a deal with Gaddafi to serve as his hitman?

Let's look at the example of Hamas, the Palestinian terrorist organization that also doubles as a charity. This makes it a slightly harder First Amendment case than *Tafoya*.

Consider the following figure:

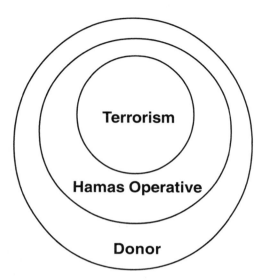

In an effort to prevent mischief represented by the center circle, a prosecutor obtains indictments against three different persons: (1) the Hamas leader within the smallest circle; (2) the Hamas operative in the middle circle; and (3) in the outer circle , the person in the United States who knowingly provided funds to the Hamas operative.

The third of these defendants, indicted for violating the embargo, might make the following argument in his motion to dismiss:

> I am charged with doing something that is not inherently dangerous—providing funds to the charity of my choice. In making this donation to Hamas, I intended my funds to be used for philanthropic goals, never violence. The United States government, if anything, should encourage charitable gift-giving. My decision to give to Hamas is protected by my First Amendment rights to express myself however I want and to associate with whomever I choose. Moreover, people looking at what you are doing to me will naturally be deterred from giving funds to Hamas, and their First Amendment-protected activities will be chilled.

The prosecutor responds:

> The terrorist financing embargo represents Congress's clear intent to dry up American sources of funds for international terrorists. Under this statute,

the United States identifies the groups it views as designated foreign terrorist organizations. That action brands groups that use violence to achieve their political goals, and the fact that they may also engage in philanthropy does not change the terrorist nature of that organization. As a person within the United States, the defendant is prohibited by the embargo from providing any funds to certain groups, including Hamas, no matter how the defendant intends Hamas to use his donations. This is a reasonably tailored prohibition, supported by clear legislative history, which comports with First Amendment jurisprudence, just as the laws that prohibit United States citizens from purchasing items produced with embargoed countries have been affirmed. In addition, the statutory scheme has been upheld when challenged on these same grounds by persons who are alleged to have engaged in the same type of conduct as the defendant.[7]

Note that this prosecutor's argument responds to the arguments of the defendant situated in the outermost ring, the one furthest removed from the violent activity depicted in the inner circle. With regard to the constitutionality of the embargo, as applied to particular facts, the conduct of the other two defendants is an even easier argument. That is, these two defendants would have a more difficult time arguing that their alleged conduct is protected by the First Amendment.[8]

There we go. By making a list, we have maximized the chances of law enforcement putting their arms on the future Eugene Tafoyas of the world before they pull the trigger. Through lists, it was a crime to promise Gaddafi, a designated obnoxious person, anything of value.[9]

Signaling Function

There is another reason lists are effective. Through naming and shaming obnoxious people and groups, we put the scrupulous players—especially those in the financial community, those who serve as gatekeepers—on notice that there are certain players who are off-limits. This serves as a deterrence; merely by listing obnoxious people, we drive a wedge between them and the financial community, who know very well that they can be held liable for aiding in the violation of the embargo. By publishing lists of obnoxious people, the banks can take action, particularly when they have other information that their customers are in cahoots with them.

As noted, terrorism lists proliferate. What are their specifics?

The State Department List

The State Department's FTO list was congressionally mandated in April 1996 with the enactment of the Antiterrorism and Effective Death Penalty Act

(AEDPA).[10] That same act created the crime of knowingly providing material support to designated FTOs (18 U.S.C. § 2339B).

To be designated as an FTO, an organization must meet the following statutory criteria:

(i)   It must be a foreign organization;
(ii) It must engage in terrorist activity as defined by statute; and
(iii) The terrorist activity or terrorism must threaten the security of U.S. nationals or the national security (national defense, foreign relations, or economic interests) of the United States.

Designation results in certain consequences. For example, any person in the United States or subject to the jurisdiction of the United States is prohibited from providing "material support or resources" (as defined in the statute) to a designated FTO under 18 U.S.C. § 2339B.

Section 2339B was specifically designed to obviate the thorny proof problems that existed with the terrorist financing offense in existence up to that time (especially 18 U.S.C. § 2339A, enacted two years earlier). Section 2339B makes it unnecessary to follow money through foreign bank accounts. The section also eliminates a person's anticipated defense that he or she did not intend the donation to be used to buy weapons. It is now a crime to provide anything of value to any designated FTO, even if the donor intends his or her support to be applied for benevolent purposes. For prosecutors, this puts to rest any defense claim that these groups are freedom fighters. Once an FTO is designated, financial transactions only need to be proved as flowing in. In many ways, this is simpler than proving money laundering.

FTO designations are effective for a five-year period and are renewable. The first FTO designation list, containing 29 groups, was published October 8, 1997. The list is compiled every five years by the State Department's Counterterrorism Bureau, though some FTOs are announced in the middle of the term. There are currently 53 FTOs.

It is difficult to overestimate the effect of the State Department's FTO list on law enforcement counterterrorism operations. More than 300 people have been charged with material support offense, most of them after 9/11, especially after the USA PATRIOT Act tore down the wall that separated FBI law enforcement and intelligence operations.[11] I estimate that about half of all new terrorism indictments announced these days involve the crime of material support. It is an astounding trajectory.

The Treasury Lists

Under the International Emergency Economic Powers Act (IEEPA), 50 U.S.C. §§ 1701–1706, persons can be prosecuted for violating executive branch orders that prohibit financial transactions with individuals and groups that have been identified as threatening U.S. national security.[12] The IEEPA is a relatively recent addition to this country's arsenal of sanctions to be used against hostile states and organizations in times of national emergency. For much of the twentieth century, the U.S. sanctions programs were governed by the Trading with the Enemy Act (TWEA) enacted in 1917.[13]

The language of IEEPA vests the President with the power to prescribe regulations to regulate, direct and compel, nullify, void, prevent, or prohibit any acquisition, holding, withholding, use, transfer, withdrawal, transportation, importation or exportation of, or dealing in, or exercising any right, power, or privilege with respect to, or transactions involving, any property in which any foreign country or a national thereof has any interest by any person (50 U.S.C. § 1792(a)(1)(B)).

Mechanically, the IEEPA terrorism provisions are accomplished by lists promulgated and regularly updated by the Treasury Department.

In January 1995, President Clinton, exercising his IEEPA authority, issued Executive Order 12,947, declaring a national emergency to deal with the extraordinary threat posed by foreign terrorists who disrupt the Middle-East peace process. (See 60 Fed. Reg. 5079 (1995).) In Section 1 of that order, the President prohibited "any transaction or dealing by United States persons . . . in property or interests in property of the persons designated in or pursuant to this order . . . , including the making or receiving of any contribution of funds, goods, or services to or for the benefit of such persons." (60 Fed. Reg. 5079.) And Section 4 of the order empowered the Secretary of the Treasury "to take such actions, including the promulgation of rules and regulations, and to employ all powers granted to [the President] by IEEPA as may be necessary to carry out the purposes" of the Order. (60 Fed. Reg. 5080.) Thereafter, the Treasury Department, via the Office of Foreign Assets Control (OFAC), promulgated, inter alia, 31 C.F.R. § 595.204, which, in relevant part, repeated the mandate of Executive Order 12,947 regarding the prohibition on "the making or receiving of any contribution of funds, goods, or services" to or for the benefit of terrorists designated in, or pursuant to, the Executive Order. (31 C.F.R. § 595.204.) OFAC also promulgated a regulation prohibiting conspiracy to commit such an act. (See 31 C.F.R. § 595.205.) Then, in August 1998, President Clinton added Al-Qaeda to the list of terrorists subject to sanctions under the order. (See Executive Order 13,099, 63 Fed. Reg. 45,167 (1998).)

In July 1999, again drawing upon his IEEPA authority, President Clinton issued Executive Order 13,129, declaring a national emergency to deal with the threat posed by the Taliban. Specifically, the President found that the actions of the Taliban in Afghanistan in allowing territory there to be used as a safe haven and base of operations for Osama bin Laden and Al- Qaeda constituted an unusual and extraordinary threat to the national security and Foreign policy of the United States. (See 64 Fed. Reg. 36,759 (1999).) Presidents Clinton and Bush subsequently determined, in June 2000 and in June 2001, that the national emergency with respect to the Taliban would continue. (See 65 Fed. Reg. 41,549 (2000); 66 Fed. Reg. 35,363 (2001).) In Section 2 of Executive Order 13,129, President Clinton prohibited "any transaction or dealing by United States persons . . . in property or interests in property blocked pursuant to this order, . . . including the making or receiving of any contribution of funds, goods, or services to or for the benefit of the Taliban." (64 Fed. Reg. 36,759.[14])

Then came 9/11, by which time George W. Bush was president. Two weeks after the attacks, on September 23, 2001, President Bush signed Executive Order No. 13,224 the IEEPA list of designated terrorists has expanded to global terrorism, and designee were known as Specially Designated Global Terrorists (SDGTs). The President named SDGTs in the annex to the September 2001 Executive Order, and this list has regularly expanded ever since. The Secretary of the Treasury, in consultation with the Secretary of State and Attorney General, determines persons and groups "owned or controlled or to act on behalf of SDGTs" and persons who "assist, sponsor, provide support, or are otherwise associated with SDGTs," for purposes of administrative blocking actions. Any transaction or dealing in blocked property, including any contribution of funds, goods, or services to or for the benefit of SDGTs, is a federal felony.

The SDGT list now numbers more than 500 groups and individuals; it includes all of the organizations on the State Department's list of designated FTOs. Thus, there is a potential IEEPA violation in some § 2339B investigations. However, unlike the list of designated FTOs, the IEEPA list of designated entities is not limited to foreign groups. The Texas-based Holy Land Foundation for Relief and Development (HLFRD), for example, was designated under IEEPA on December 7, 2001, prior to its indictment. The list is also not limited to organizations, as it includes Osama bin Laden himself, as well as the leaders of various terrorist organizations, such as Hamas leader Mousa Abu Marzook.

Harmonizing the Two Sets of Lists: A Prosecutor's Tool versus Signaling

Whether by design or by happenstance, the various U.S. terrorist financing lists serve different functions, which might make their duplication easier to understand. To appreciate this fully, we might go back to our old friend Eugene Tafoya.

What is served by announcing a list of obnoxious people, like Moammar Gaddafi, and prohibiting financial transactions with them? On the one hand, we want to widen the scope of people we can prosecute beyond the front-line terrorists. That way, law enforcement can have a real shot at putting their hands on the Tafoyas of the world before they pull the trigger (or, as in his case, fail to report their assassination fees on their income tax returns). Under the "designated obnoxious people" system, the crime occurs as soon as the financial arrangement is concluded.[15] Violence, while perhaps contemplated, has not yet occurred. Terrorist financiers can nevertheless be incapacitated at an early stage. I refer to this effect as a prosecutor's tool.

On the other hand, there is a prophylactic function: signaling to the more scrupulous members of society exactly what is expected of them, so they can conform their activities accordingly. In this scenario, Gaddafi would be deprived of any relationship with U.S. financial institutions because banks would know that he was designated. I refer to this effect as a signaling tool.

In national security parlance, although both 2339B and IEEPA represent economic embargoes, the term "sanctions" typically is reserved for the latter. This undoubtedly reflects that the government entity administering the program— Treasury's OFAC—is in the economic sanctions business, whereas the State Department is less so. Thus, when people refer to terrorism sanctions, they are typically not referring to the § 2339B process. Instead, they are referring to the OFAC list of SDGTs.

If there have been approximately 300 people prosecuted under § 2339B, where there are around 50 FTOs, how many IEEPA prosecutions have there been involving the more than 500 OFAC-designated SDGTs? Doing the arithmetic, one would expect around 3,000 terrorism-related IEEPA prosecutions. However, in reality, since 9/11 there have been only 30 or so persons convicted of illegal transactions with SDGTs. Many of these are § 2339B cases in which the IEEPA charge was thrown in as a complementary charge.[16] The remainder were stand-alone IEEPA prosecutions.[17]

Part of this discrepancy between the number of 2339B and IEEPA prosecutions involves the nature of the substantive crime. Section 2339B is more prosecutor-friendly: the mens rea element is "knowingly," as opposed to the IEEPA willfulness requirement, and the 2004 changes to the 2339B statute gave the statute clear extraterritorial reach, whereas IEEPA jurisdiction is limited to the U.S. Moreover, the IEEPA criminal penalties often require references to regulations, which are not contained in the U.S. Criminal Code and are complicated to grasp. Apart from these differences, the criminal penalties between the two statutes are largely the same.

Another explanation for the disparity involves the term "sanctions" and its relation to the signaling function described above. Perhaps the reason there are not more criminal charges involving SDGTs is because the Treasury Department views the SDGT designation process as an end in itself, rather than an intermediate step on the way to prosecution. Under this reasoning, the mere designation of an SDGT sends an immediate (and strong) signal to the financial community that they are to do their part in stopping all dealings in SDGT property. Criminal prosecutions, if they are to happen, are an afterthought.

This theory is a big advance to the task of harmonizing the two main U.S. government lists of terrorist financiers. The goal of the FTO/2339B is criminal prosecution, based on the expediencies described above. Meanwhile, IEEPA/SDGT is geared more toward signaling banks and other guardians of the U.S. financial system, to deter rather than punish people who would otherwise deal in terrorist monies.

This hypothesis has support from a recent book by Treasury insider Juan Zarate, who devotes extensive space to discussing the signaling function of the Treasury terrorist sanctions.[18] He notes, for example, that:

> [In] Treasury we realized that the private-sector—most importantly the banks—could drive the isolation of rogue behavior better than government—based on their own interests and desires to avoid unnecessary business and reputational risk. . . . The strategies that resulted focused squarely on protecting the broader international financial system and tending to and leveraging the environment so legitimate financial institutions would reject dealings with rogue and illicit financial actors.[19]

Later, he posits:

> When a counter-terror finance effort is successful, it ostracizes known financiers from the formal financial and commercial worlds and deters fundraisers, donors and sympathizers from giving support and money to terrorist groups[20] . . . It was a preventative tool—not a prosecution—and we were targeting networks, not just criminals.[21]

Conclusion

This chapter seeks to demystify terrorist financing.

Those who follow developments in terrorist financing may be puzzled as to why the U.S. maintains two overlapping lists of terrorist organizations and individuals. As noted, there are currently over 50 Foreign Terrorist Organizations (FTOs) on the list maintained by the State Department and some 500-plus Specially Designated Global Terrorists (SDGTs) on the list maintained by the

Treasury Department. The legal consequences of the two lists—the prosecution of those who engage in financial transactions with listed entities/individuals and the freezing of assets—are largely the same. Why the duplication?

To answer this question, we can go back to the concept of actionable intelligence, which I described as the holy grail of the intelligence cycle for both collectors and consumers. What separates actionable intelligence from raw intelligence is the traditions of the consumers—what they require in order to take some action. If my theory about the two terrorist lists is correct, what we are talking about can be explained in terms of different consumers.

For the State Department FTO list, the consumer is American law enforcement. Prosecutors and cops can use the FTO list to determine who should be investigated and prosecuted under § 2339B.

The consumer of the Treasury SDGT list, on the other hand, is banks, which must decide whether to take some action when faced with a proposed transaction involving an SDGT. Is it a fair supposition to describe banks as intelligence consumers and, therefore, part of the U.S. intelligence community? There is no question that, with the Bank Secrecy Act (BSA), financial institutions are required to be the eyes and ears of the U.S. government in ferreting out crimes that are being committed by their customers. The actions of banks when faced with this problem vary, from filing a Suspicious Activity Report (SAR) to cutting off its relationship with the client. In terrorist financing, their big tool is the SDGT list.

Notes

1. *Available at* http://govinfo.library.unt.edu/911/staff_statements/911_TerrFin_Monograph.pdf.

2. *See* United States v. Wilson, 750 F.2d 7 (2d Cir. 1984) (upholding Wilson's conviction for obstruction of justice and attempted murder of prosecutors and witnesses in the U.S. District Court for the Southern District of New York); United States v. Wilson, 732 F.2d 404 (5th Cir. 1984) (affirming Wilson's conviction for illegal shipment of plastic explosives in the U.S. District Court for the Southern District of Texas); United States v. Wilson, 721 F.2d 967 (4th Cir. 1983) (sustaining Wilson's conviction for illegal export of an M-16 rifle and four revolvers in the U.S. District Court for the Eastern District of Virginia). Wilson's conviction in Texas was later vacated because of a knowingly false affidavit used to support the government's case at trial. United States v. Wilson, 289 F. Supp. 2d 801 (S.D. Tex. 2003). *See also* Murray Waas, *The Terpil Transcripts: Dinner with Idi and Other Tales*, THE NATION, Nov. 28, 1981, at 568 (reporting that Tafoya was just one element of a multipart operation of Libyan-recruited and -trained hit men connected to the murder and maiming of a dozen opponents of Gaddafi's regime exiled throughout Europe and the United States). *See also* Agnus Deming, *Kaddafi's U.S. Connection*, NEWSWEEK, July 20, 1981, at 44.

3. *See Ex-Green Beret Gets 2-Year Term*, N.Y. TIMES, Jan. 6, 1982, at A12; *see also* People v. Tafoya, 703 P.2d 663 (Colo. Ct. App. 1985) (disagreeing with Tafoya's assertion that the trial court erred in denying his motion to suppress evidence and affirming his conviction).

4. The prosecutors were Karen Morrissette and Dan Fromstein. Both are now retired.

5. United States v. Tafoya, 757 F.2d 1522 (5th Cir. 1985).

6. One can get a good idea of who the consumers are by considering the various types of tools the U.S. relies on in counterterrorism: diplomacy, economic sanctions, law enforcement, intelligence, and military.

7. There is long-standing Supreme Court precedent upholding the government's authority to place restrictions or outright bans on dealings with foreign entities that have acted against United States interests. Such restrictions and bans have long been upheld by the Supreme Court against constitutional attacks. In *Regan v. Wald*, 468 U.S. 222, 104 S. Ct. 3026, 82 L. Ed. 2d 171 (1984), the Supreme Court upheld a prohibition on dealings with Cuba. Years earlier, in *Zemel v. Rusk*, 381 U.S. 1, 85 S. Ct. 1271, 14 L. Ed. 2d 179 (1965), the Supreme Court recognized the Fifth Amendment right to travel, but nonetheless upheld the Secretary of State's refusal to validate an American citizen's passport for a journey to Cuba. Lower courts have likewise rejected arguments that restrictions on dealings with hostile foreign nations—designed to deprive such regimes of resources—violate First Amendment rights. *See* Freedom to Travel Campaign v. Newcomb, 82 F.3d 1431 (9th Cir. 1996) (upholding Cuban travel ban against First and Fifth Amendment attacks, noting that "[t]he purpose of the travel ban is the same now as it has been since the ban was imposed almost 35 years ago—to restrict the flow of hard currency into Cuba"); Walsh v. Brady, 927 F.2d 1229 (D.C. Cir. 1991) (denying First Amendment challenge to prohibition against payments to Cuba); *Veterans and Reservists for Peace in Vietnam v. Reg'l Comm'r of Customs*, 459 F.2d 676 (3d Cir. 1972) (upholding Trading with the Enemy Act and Foreign Assets Control Regulations against First Amendment attack); Farrakhan v. Reagan, 669 F. Supp. 506 (D.D.C. 1987) (rejecting a First Amendment claim by an organization wishing to transfer funds to Libya in violation of economic sanctions regulations), *aff'd without opin.*, 851 F.2d 1500 (D.C. Cir. 1988).

8. Note that Eugene Tafoya, because he was demonstrably involved in actual violence, would probably be closer to the center of the circles. That is, his conduct would not merely be providing money to terrorists.

9. The mere promise would suffice to establish a crime because the terrorist-financing laws include attempt and conspiracy within their terms. Moreover, as a matter of accounting, the promise to kill people would be represented by a liability journal entry (an account payable), with the quid pro quo of payments representing an asset (account receivable).

10. Pub. L. No. 104-132, 110 Stat. 1214 (1996), and codified in 8 U.S.C. § 1189.

11. Uniting and Strengthening America by Providing Appropriate Tools Required to Intercept and Obstruct Terrorism Act of 2001, Pub. L. No. 107-56, 115 Stat. 272 (2001), §§ 218, 504.

12. Section 1705(b) of Title 50, part of IEEPA, provides that whoever "willfully violates, or willfully attempts to violate, any license, order, or regulation issued under this chapter" commits a felony.

13. *See* 50 U.S.C. app. §§ 1–44. As amended in 1933, TWEA granted the President broad authority "to investigate, regulate, . . . prevent or prohibit . . . transactions" in times of war or declared national emergencies. *See* 50 U.S.C. app. § 5(b); Congress changed this statutory scheme in 1977 to limit TWEA's application to periods of declared wars, but created IEEPA to provide the President similar authority for use during other times of national emergency. *See* S. Rep. No. 95–466 at 2, *reprinted in* 1977 U.S.C.C.A.N. 4540, 4541; *see also* Regan v. Wald, 468 U.S. 222, 227–28, 104 S. Ct. 3026, 82 L. Ed. 2d 171 (1984); United States v. Arch Trading Co., 987 F.2d 1087, 1093 (4th Cir. 1993) ("IEEPA . . . was drawn from and constitutes an extension of the [TWEA].").

14. Executive Order No. 13,129 was revoked on Sept. 23, 2001, by E.O. 13,268, after the President determined that the success of the U.S. military campaign in Afghanistan significantly

altered the threat posed by the Taliban. E.O. 13,224 was amended to cover those individuals previously designated under the Taliban Executive Order. Approximately $254 million of Taliban funds and assets have been blocked under the order, of which $1.7 million is blocked offshore.

15.　*See* note 10.

16.　This makes a certain amount of sense, because as mentioned all FTOS are also SDGTs. The classic examples of cases involving complementary 2339B and IEEPA charges after 9/11 involve the Holy Land Foundation for Relief and Development (Hamas) and John Walker Lindh (Al-Qaida): United States v. El-Mezain, 664 F.3d 467 (5th Cir. 2011); United States v. Lindh, 212 F. Supp. 2d 541 (E.D. Va. 2002). For other cases in which 2339B charges were joined with IEEPA counts, *see* United States v. Hashmi, 2009 WL 4042841 (S.D.N.Y. 2009); United States. v. Paracha, 2006 WL 12768 (S.D.N.Y. 2006).

17.　For the relatively rare stand-alone IEEP prosecutions (where such charges are not joined with 2339B), *see* United States v. Islamic American Relief Agency, 2009 WL 4016478 (W.D. Mo. 2009); United States v. Mirza, 454 Fed. Appx. 249 (5th Cir. 2011); United States v. Benkahla, 2006 WL 2871234 (E.D. Va. 2000); United States v. Elashyi, 554 F.3d 480 (5th Cir. 2008); United States v. Elashi, 440 F. Supp. 2d 536 (N.D. Tex. 2006); United States v. Dhafir, 461 F.3d 211 (2d Cir. 2006).

18.　J. ZARATE, TREASURY'S WAR: HOW BANKERS AND OPERATIVES UNLEASHED A NEW ERA OF FINANCIAL WARFARE (Public Affairs, 2013)

19.　*Id.*, p.10–11.

20.　*Id.*, p.29

21.　*Id.*, p.35. This ethos at Treasury is undoubtedly due in part to the fact that, with the creation of the Department of Homeland Security, Treasury lost most of its law enforcement assets, making it more of a traditional Ministry of Finance. As Zarate notes:

[T]he enforcement element of Treasury was traditionally seen as the little brother to the 800-pound gorilla of federal law enforcement, the FBI, and the Department of Justice, whose primary mission was to enforce the law. "Enforcement," as the office and its "guns and badges" had been known for decades, always seemed an odd fit at the Treasury Department. . . . Most wondered what Treasury was doing mixed up in the law enforcement world. The guns and badges of the Treasury had a long, storied history, but in the modern era, they seemed to play second fiddle to the Department of Justice. *Id.*, p.129.

XVII

On the Front Lines of the Home Front: The Intersection of Domestic Counterterrorism Operations and Drone Legislation

Colonel Dawn M.K. Zoldi*

I. Introduction

Find. Fix. Finish. Doctrinally, the targeting cycle remains the same, whether the target is located abroad or at home.[1] Yet operations to prevent, counter, or respond to domestic terrorism are different from those overseas in many respects. State and federal law enforcement agencies, not the Department of Defense (DoD), will be the country's first line of defense for domestic counterterrorism (CT) operations.[2] Even so, the DoD may be called upon to support law enforcement agencies. What if any one of these agencies planned to use a drone in support of its CT efforts at home?[3] For some, this very idea raises the specter of illicit government surveillance—or even more controversial, the extrajudicial killing—of Americans on United States soil.

To allay fears related to privacy and due process, 43 states have proposed 86 drone bills to "protect citizens' privacy" or free them from "unwarranted" surveillance.[4] Eight states have already passed such legislation.[5] Of these state proposals, 90% apply to state and local government actors, primarily to law enforcement agencies.[6] Forty-one percent also extend their applicability to U.S. or

---

* The views contained herein are those of the author and should not be attributed to the Department of Defense, the U.S. Air Force, or Air Combat Command.

federal government employees.[7] Twelve percent of state bills directly address the U.S. military, but many more could also apply.[8] Federal drone legislation has also been introduced.[9] These proposals largely track state initiatives and apply to both state and federal actors. In addition, while DoD drone policies apply directly to DoD personnel, they also have indirect effects on the civilian agencies they support. Thus, drone legislation and policies will impact conduct across the range of governmental actors during all operations, but in particular domestic CT operations.

The underlying assumption of this chapter is that states and the Congress will continue to revisit the subject of domestic drone use in relation to privacy and due process until laws are passed. The purpose of this article is to review these legislative drone proposals and policies, explore their potential impact on domestic CT operations and identify best practices that allow drones to be used to their full operational potential in CT operations, while protecting privacy and liberty.

II. Find and Fix

Finding a target means detecting it.[10] Fixing the target means determining its positional location.[11] Drones perform both of these functions well.[12] To the extent that proposed drone laws and existing drone policies address using these assets to collect information or evidence about a person, they have implications for "finding and fixing" terrorists domestically. Below is an overview of state and federal drone bills and DoD policies relevant to the "find and fix" aspects of domestic CT operations.

A. State Legislation—Information Collection

Almost universally, state drone legislation prohibits the use of drones to collect information or evidence.[13] There are, however, exceptions, the most common being where law enforcement obtains a judicial warrant or court order.[14]

Highly relevant to a domestic CT scenario, 22% of proposed state drone bills permit drone use without a warrant in relation to a terrorist attack. All the state bills that contain a "terrorist attack" exception use similar language: "To counter a high risk of a terrorist attack by a specific individual or organization if the United States Secretary of Homeland Security . . . determines that credible intelligence indicates that there is such a risk."[15] Although the bills do not define "counter," the language appears to be preventive in nature, to thwart a likely future or imminent terror attack. The bills also do not define "terrorist attack." A scan of publicly available DHS documents does not provide an obvious definition of "terrorist attack."[16] Because the exception always requires a predicate determination by the Secretary of Homeland Security that a high risk of a terrorist attack exists before it can be invoked, the secretary's interpretation as to what acts rise to the level of a domestic terror attack would be determinative.

Along similar lines, Arkansas, Hawaii, Maine, and Michigan would allow state or federal agencies to use drones for emergencies involving "conspiratorial activities threatening the national security interest."[17] Like the terror attack exception, the national security interest conspiracy exception contains significant terms that remain undefined, such as "conspiratorial activity" and "national security interest." As such, these state provisions would be subject to individual interpretation.[18]

Most terror attack scenarios would invoke the potential of immediate danger of death, serious physical injury, or significant property damage. All but 14 states have proposed drone bills to permit their use in a proactive manner to save lives in emergency situations.[19] These provisions are most commonly styled as an "imminent danger to life" exception.[20] Most of these same provisions also permit drone use to prevent property damage.[21]

Other CT-relevant exceptions include provisions that would permit drone use on or over public lands or to monitor borders.[22] Depending on the facts of a particular CT event, state drone legislative exceptions, such as those permitting drones to pursue fleeing suspects, to prevent the destruction of evidence, or to be used in situations tantamount to "judicially recognized exceptions to the warrant requirement," might also apply.[23] Less relevant in the CT arena, but worth mentioning, fewer than a quarter of drone bills surveyed permit their use where the target or property owner has consented.[24]

Some state drone bills also contain exceptions that would allow drones to be used to mitigate the effects of a domestic terrorist event, including provisions for disaster response and search and rescue (SAR).[25] Other provisions that might be employed after a terror attack include those from Illinois, Oregon, and Texas, which allow drones to assess crime scenes.[26]

In addition to when a drone may be used, many state bills address how they may be used by including time, place, and manner restrictions. These operational restrictions and procedural requirements would impact all operations, including CT. One of the most common time restrictions on drone use is a 48-hour mission execution window.[27] Place restrictions focus primarily on the home and areas surrounding it, farms and agricultural areas, and places of worship.[28] Manner restrictions generally require users to collect information only on the target and to avoid or minimize collection on other individuals or property.[29] For example, Massachusetts, North Dakota, and West Virginia do not allow drone surveillance of citizens exercising their constitutional rights relating to freedom of speech and freedom of assembly.[30]

Many states also restrict how the information collected is used, disseminated, or retained. A number of bills reviewed prohibit use of facial recognition or other biometric matching technology on drone-collected information, primarily involving non-targets.[31] The Maine bill would not permit use of biometrics even on data related to the target of the collection.[32] Very few bills address dissemination of information beyond the collecting agency.[33] That said, some states require dissemination, in the form of notice, to the subject of the drone monitoring.[34]

On the other hand, the majority of bills address retention. The primary theme in retention is to delete information collected unlawfully or on non-targets within 24 hours of collecting it.[35] Other states have retention limits on information lawfully collected on a target of surveillance, unless it is necessary to maintain it for a criminal investigation or prosecution.[36]

A majority of bills contain extensive documentation, oversight, and reporting requirements.[37] A handful of states require public notice of drone operations, images, and government agency drone reports filed.[38] California and Michigan contain a unique requirement to distinctively mark the body of a drone in some manner.[39]

Finally, state drone proposals contain a wide range of ramifications for violating their provisions, from exclusion of evidence to personal liability. The threat of personal liability, whether civil or criminal, has the potential to impact an operator's decision-making process during CT operations and merits discussion. More than half of the state bills create civil liability for violators.[40] Many include civil equitable relief, including injunctions, to preclude drone use in advance of employment or to prevent the use of information collected.[41] Bills contain a wide spectrum of potential civil penalties that include actual damages, punitive damages, and even treble damages.[42] Several states create criminal liability, ranging from a simple misdemeanor to felonies.[43] A few bills also provide for administrative discipline.[44] Exclusionary rules will be discussed further in "Section II—Finish."

B. Federal Legislation—Information Collection

Against this backdrop of state legislative activity, federal legislators have also introduced drone proposals. To a great extent, these mimic state requirements with regards to prohibitions, exceptions, operational restrictions, and violation ramifications.[45]

The *Preserving Freedom from Unwarranted Surveillance Act of 2013* is short and simple, similar to several of the state bills. While it would apply to persons or entities "acting under the authority of the United States," the focus appears to be on law enforcement.[46] As with the majority of state bills, it prohibits the use of a drone "to gather evidence or other information" with the additional caveat "pertaining to criminal conduct or conduct in violation of a regulation." Also like many state bills, this Act contains a warrant exception, exceptions allowing for patrol of borders, "exigent circumstances," danger to life, pursuit of fleeing felons, to prevent destruction of evidence, and to thwart imminent terrorist attack.[47] It also allows for civil liability and injunction in the same terms used by most states, "to obtain all appropriate relief to prevent or remedy a violation of this Act."[48]

Two virtually identical acts, both titled *The Drone Aircraft Privacy and Transparency Act of 2013 (DAPTA)*, have been proposed that would also amend the *FAA Modernization and Reform Act of 2012*.[49] Both *DAPTA* bills target specific federal agencies and law enforcement, but their information collection provisions are much broader and apply to "any person or entity."[50] An expansion on the common provision found in many states, the *DAPTAs* would specifically require a warrant for drone use *for intelligence purposes* as well as for law enforcement surveillance—with danger to life and terrorist attack exceptions.[51] Procedurally, the *DAPTAs* require filing of the justification for such emergency use with the Secretary of Transportation (SecTrans) within seven days post-flight and the destruction of incidentally collected information.[52]

With regard to specific agency requirements, the *DAPTAs* direct SecTrans, in consultation with several other agency heads, to carry out a privacy study, adopt rules to protect privacy, and require data collection and minimization statements from drone users.[53] These bills also require the FAA to post approved certificates of drone use on a public website.[54]

Of all state and federal bills reviewed, the *DAPTAs* contain one of the most far-reaching ramification schemes. In addition to private civil causes of action against individuals and the government, the *DAPTAs* allow state governments to bring suit on behalf of their residents to enjoin, enforce, seek damages, or obtain other relief.[55] They also contain an exclusionary rule applicable to "any trial, hearing or other proceeding," including before state courts.[56] The bills also create a new enforcement mechanism pursuant to the Federal Trade Commission (FTC) Act. In cases where drones are not operated consistent with the data collection statement submitted, the FTC may treat this as an unfair or deceptive act or practice.[57] In addition, the *DAPTAs* require mandatory license revocation for noncompliance with data collection statements.[58]

Whereas the *DAPTAs* contain an extensive ramification scheme, of all the federal legislative proposals, the *Preserving American Privacy Act of 2013 (PAPA)* contains the most extensive overall regulatory schemes. It would apply to U.S. departments or agencies as well as to states.[59] The *PAPA* takes a nuanced approach regarding the information covered by it as "information that is reasonably likely to enable identification of an individual" or "information about an individual's property that is 'not in plain view.'"[60]

Similar to the majority of state laws, the *PAPA* would prohibit operation of a drone to collect or disclose information "for a law enforcement purpose" with the following exceptions: pursuant to a warrant or judicial order; to patrol or secure the border; with consent from the individual about whom the information would be collected; and in emergency situations, defined as "immediate danger of death or serious physical injury to any person; conspiratorial activities threatening the national security interest or conspiratorial activities characteristic of organized crime."[61]

The *PAPA* also contains a host of operational and procedural restrictions similar to state bills reviewed. Federal agencies must obtain a warrant no later than 48 hours after an "exigent circumstances" operation begins.[62] Drone collection pursuant to a court order is limited to a 48-hour execution window, renewable for up to 30 days, and with a 10-day post-operational notice to the subject or a 48-hour pre-operational notice to the public.[63] The Act also contains a 10-day notice requirement to the subject of the collection unless doing so would jeopardize an ongoing investigation.[64] It also contains extensive reporting, in terms similar to state bills, from the Administrative Office of the U.S. Courts and the Attorney General (AG) to Congress.[65] One unique twist to the *PAPA* is that any collection of covered information requires drone operators to minimize collecting information on non-targets, as well as the filing of a "data collection statement" with the AG, which will ultimately be filed on a publicly available website, along with any federal licenses granted to operate the drone.[66]

The *PAPA* includes the full gambit of ramifications found in state bills for violating its provisions, including administrative discipline for intentional violations.[67]

Finally, the *PAPA* states that it should not be construed to "preempt any state law regarding use of unmanned aircraft systems exclusively within the borders of that state."[68] Thus, if passed, government operators would have to comply with both the PAPA and applicable state law(s).

C. DoD Support of Law Enforcement and Information Collection Policies

As mentioned, although civilian law enforcement agencies will take lead in domestic CT operations, DoD may be called upon to provide support. DoD support to law enforcement agencies is limited by law, including the Posse Comitatus Act (PCA), for fear of military encroachment on civil authority and domestic governance. The PCA restricts direct military assistance for law enforcement purposes except as authorized by the Constitution or Congress. It states:

> Whoever, except in cases and under circumstances expressly authorized by the Constitution or Act of Congress, willfully uses any part of the Army or the Air Force as a posse comitatus or otherwise to execute the laws shall be fined not more than $10,000, imprisoned not more than two years, or both.[69]

For this reason, the DoD has implemented policies pertaining to the provision of support to civilian agencies, including DoDD 3025.18, *Defense Support to Civil*

Authorities (DSCA). It governs DoD's provision of temporary support to U.S. civilian agencies for domestic emergencies and law enforcement support.[70] Most activities or missions involving a drone outside of DoD-controlled airspace require approval from the Secretary of Defense (SecDef) or his delegee, with limited exceptions.[71] SecDef approval for drone use is explicitly required for DSCA, including support to law enforcement agencies.[72]

SecDef has concurrently delegated seven specific authorities to the four-star General Officer or Flag Officer commanders of U.S. Northern Command (CDRUSNORTHCOM) and U.S. Pacific Command (CDRUSPACOM) in the Chairman of the Joint Chiefs of Staff (CJCS) DSCA Execute Order (EXORD).[73] The CJCS DSCA EXORD permits USNORTHCOM and USPACOM to request traditional intelligence resources, such as intelligence, surveillance, and reconnaissance (ISR) platforms that include drones, to conduct DSCA missions. The EXORD applies to domestic incidents, including "actual or potential . . . terrorist attacks."[74] SecDef approval authorizes the use of these capabilities for non-intelligence purposes. Once SecDef validates the mission from the primary agency in charge of the incident (e.g., Department of Homeland Security or Federal Emergency Management Agency for domestic terrorism), USNORTHCOM and USPACOM are authorized to provide Incident Awareness and Assessment (IAA)[75] for situational awareness, damage assessment, evacuation monitoring, and Search and Rescue (SAR); chemical, biological, radiological, and nuclear (CBRN) assessment; hydrographic survey; and dynamic ground coordination.[76] Should a CT incident occur, several of these authorized purposes would be useful for drone operations, once SecDef approves the mission.

DoD Instruction (DoDI) 3025.21, *Defense Support of Civilian Law Enforcement Agencies,* must be read in tandem with the DSCA regulation and CJCS EXORD, as it provides additional guidance for DoD support to law enforcement agencies, including sharing information collected during military operations; the use of military equipment and facilities; training; funding; and reporting mechanisms for such support.[77] The DoDI outlines legal and policy restrictions on DoD support to law enforcement agencies and prohibits the military from interdicting vehicles, conducting searches and seizures, arrests, and similar activities (apprehension, stop and frisk) for law enforcement agencies, as well as engaging in questioning of potential witnesses, using force or threats to do so except in self-defense or defense of others, collecting evidence, forensic testing, and *surveillance or pursuit of individuals* or vehicles (emphasis added).[78]

Despite the general prohibition on surveillance, the DoDI specifically authorizes domestic terrorist incident support, upon SecDef approval.[79] Enclosure 3 to the DoDI states that DoD personnel may be made available to a federal law enforcement agency to operate or assist in operating equipment, to the extent the equipment is used in a supporting role, with respect to a domestic CT operation, including support of FBI Joint Terrorism Task Forces.[80] This provision implements 10 U.S.C. § 374, which states that SecDef may provide DoD personnel to operate equipment for federal law enforcement agencies with respect to domestic CT operations for purposes of, among other things, "aerial reconnaissance."[81] Although the Act itself does not elaborate, the DoD defines reconnaissance (or RECON) as "[A] mission undertaken to obtain, *by visual observation* or other detection methods, *information about the activities and resources of an enemy or adversary*, or to secure data concerning the meteorological, hydrographic, or geographic characteristics of a particular area." (Emphasis added.)[82]

In addition to these DSCA and law enforcement-related rules, DoD has an additional set of policies that directly relate to intelligence capabilities' collection of information on U.S. persons (USPER) that also apply to drone operations.[83] Executive Order (EO) 12,333, *United States Intelligence Activities*, as amended, and its implementing directives and instructions, guides the conduct of intelligence activities within a strict intelligence oversight (IO) framework that balances the need for effective intelligence with the "protection of constitutional rights" through collection, retention, dissemination, and oversight processes.[84] Under this framework, when conducting an authorized mission, drones can only collect information on USPER that:

- is obtained with the individual's consent
- is publicly available
- constitutes foreign intelligence or counterintelligence (FI/CI)[85]
- concerns potential intelligence sources or agents
- is needed to protect intelligence sources or methods
- is related to threats to or to protect the physical security of IC-affiliated persons, installations
- is needed to protect intelligence and CI methods, sources, activities from disclosure
- is required for personnel security or communications security investigations
- is obtained during the course of a lawful FI/CI or international narcotics or terrorism investigation
- is necessary for administrative purposes
- is acquired by overhead reconnaissance not directed at USPER and is incidentally obtained that may indicate involvement in activities that may violate federal, state, local or foreign laws.[86]

Under DoD policy, collection of USPER information by intelligence assets "shall be accomplished by the least intrusive means."[87] This means, generally, to the "extent feasible" that information should be collected from publicly available sources or with the consent of the person concerned.[88] Should publicly available information or consent not be feasible or sufficient, other means of obtaining the information include collection from cooperating sources, through the use of other lawful investigative techniques that do not require a warrant or approval of the AG, or by obtaining a judicial warrant.[89]

Under these IO rules, the approval authority to collect permissible USPER information varies depending on any special collection procedures to be used.[90] Intelligence capability cooperation with law enforcement agencies is addressed in DoD 5240.1-R under Procedure 12, which permits DoD to provide specialized equipment and personnel to federal law enforcement authorities when lives are endangered.[91] As mentioned earlier, SecDef approval is required to use a drone in support of law enforcement agencies, and the type of support DoD can provide does not include "surveillance" in the law enforcement sense.[92] In an intelligence context, physical surveillance is a term of art. It is a specific means of intelligence collection defined as "a systematic and deliberate observation of a person by any means on a continuing basis. . . ." This collection method is authorized only for CI and FI purposes relating to USPER who are present or former employees of the intelligence component, present or former contractors of such components or their present or former employees, applicants for such employment, or contracting or military persons.[93] However, as mentioned earlier, drones can be used under the CJCS DSCA EXORD for IAA and, per 10 U.S.C. § 374, for aerial reconnaissance in support of federal law enforcement agencies.[94]

DoD policy also contains specific guidance on retaining information retrievable by reference to a USPER's name or other identifying data. If properly collected, USPER data may be retained. Otherwise, with limited exception, USPER information "acquired incidentally" will be retained only temporarily, for no more than 90 days, "solely for the purpose of determining whether that information may be permanently retained under" the DoD procedures.[95] One notable exception is where incidentally acquired USPER information "may indicate involvement in activities that may violate federal, state, local, or foreign law."[96]

Once properly collected and retained, USPER information may be disseminated only to limited government recipients for the "performance of a lawful governmental function," including DoD employees and contractors, federal, state or local law enforcement (if the information involves activities that may violate the laws for which they are responsible to enforce), intelligence agencies and authorized Federal Government agencies or foreign governments when pursuant to an agreement with them."[97] Any other dissemination requires approval of the DoD component's legal office after consultation with the Department of Justice and the DoD General Counsel.[98]

III. Finish

In targeting, "finish" equates to "engage." The means of engagement depends upon the desired effect on the target and could include either a lethal strike or nonlethal means of incapacitation, such as capture, detention (or incarceration), and, ultimately, prosecution.[99] In the domestic arena, proposed drone legislation addresses both of these means of engagement through provisions that address "weaponized" drones and that exclude data obtained by drones from court. DoD has its own policies on domestic use of weaponized drones.

A. State Armed Drone and Exclusionary Rule Provisions

Most states restrict operators from carrying weapons, or employing weapons from drones, and limit CT target engagement to other means. Almost a third of the proposals specifically preclude equipping a drone with weapons.[100] Of these, several forbid equipping drones with nonlethal weapons.[101] For example, West Virginia contains a unique provision prohibiting the use of drones armed with, "pepper spray, bean bag guns, mace and sound-based weapons."[102] Oregon is the only state that specifically bans drone operators from "directing a laser."[103]

Proposed state drone bills impact nonlethal engagement options as well by creating exclusionary rules for violating their provisions. More than half of the state bills contain a criminal exclusionary rule.[104] Slightly more than a third of the bills contain provisions excluding information gathered by drones from civil or administrative hearings.[105] Several contain a "fruit of the poisonous tree" exclusionary rule, which prohibits use of information or evidence derived from information gathered by drones.[106] Montana and Oregon expressly ban the government from including information acquired by drones in an affidavit to obtain a warrant.[107]

B. Federal Armed Drone and Exclusionary Rule Provisions

In the federal arena, one bill has been proposed solely for the purpose of prohibiting SecTrans, responsible for the Federal Aviation Administration (FAA), from authorizing "a person to operate an unmanned aircraft system in the national airspace system for the purpose, in whole or in part, of using the unmanned aircraft system as a weapon or to deliver a weapon against a person or property."[108] The *No Armed Drones Act of 2013 (NADA)*, as its name suggests, would amend the *FAA Modernization and Reform Act of 2012* to do this. The *PAPA*, discussed above, also forbids use of weaponized drones.[109]

Three other bills have been introduced to prohibit the use of drones to use lethal force against a person in the U.S. However, all include a significant and CT-relevant exception that allows lethal force to be used if the person poses a threat to life. The *Life, Liberty, and Justice for All Americans Act* prohibits the

President from using "lethal *military* force against a citizen of the United States who is in the United States," including the use of a drone, unless the President determines that:

(1) the individual poses an imminent threat of death or serious bodily injury to another individual; and

(2) using such force will prevent or minimize such deaths or serious bodily injuries.[110]

Senate Bill 505 (S.505), a bill to prohibit use of drones to kill U.S. citizens in the United States, prohibits "the Federal Government" from using a drone "to kill a citizen of the United States who is located in the United States" unless the individual "poses an imminent threat of death or serious bodily injury to another individual."[111] There is no additional requirement that the use of force will prevent or minimize such deaths or injuries. *House of Representatives Bill 1242* contains verbatim language of S.505.[112]

Whereas the draft bills would allow drones to employ lethal force against a U.S. citizen so long as that person poses an imminent bodily threat, the Obama Administration has stated that the President does not have the authority "to use a weaponized drone to kill an American not engaged in combat on American soil."[113] Thus, unless federal law is passed to affirmatively provide that authority, under current policy, a USPER would only be engaged with a weaponized drone domestically if he was considered to be engaged "in combat."

With regard to nonlethal engagement, several federal bills copy state efforts to exclude drone-collected data if obtained in violation of outlined restrictions. The *DAPTA* bills include an exclusionary rule applicable to any court or hearing—criminal, civil, administrative—regarding information obtained, or information derived from that obtained, in violation of their provisions.[114] The *PAPA* includes a blanket exclusionary rule, like many states, to prohibit use of information unlawfully collected, "in any trial, hearing, or other proceeding in or before any court, grand jury, department, officer, agency, regulatory body, legislative committee, or other authority of the United States, a State, or a political subdivision thereof. . . ."[115]

C. Department of Defense (DoD) Armed Drone Policy

Department of Defense Directive 3025.18, *Defense Support of Civil Authorities (DSCA)*, which includes support to law enforcement agencies, states, "Use of armed drones for DSCA operations is not authorized.[116] Additionally, the 2006 DepSecDef Memo, *Interim Guidance for Use of Unmanned Aircraft Systems*, states, "Use of armed UAS for domestic HD (homeland defense) or DSCA operations is not authorized." As mentioned above, unless an individual is engaged in combat on U.S. soil, the Obama Administration's stated position is that the President lacks the authority to lethally target him.[117] This policy would apply to DoD personnel, as well as other federal officers.

DoD policy does not contain provisions for excluding evidence improperly collected or received from hearings.[118] Instead, violating DoD IO policies or otherwise engaging in "questionable intelligence activity" which may violate the law, or any such executive order, presidential directive, or applicable DoD policy triggers special notification, investigation, and reporting requirements outside of the Service, to SecDef and, ultimately, to Congress.[119]

IV. Find-Fix-Finish: Domestic Drone Rules as Applied

To illustrate how this tapestry of state, federal, and DoD drone rules would impact domestic CT operations, consider the following hypothetical situation based on the 2013 Boston Marathon bombings.

A. The Facts

During a renowned running event in X state involving thousands of participants and spectators, two suspects of unknown nationality were identified placing homemade bombs in two different locations. These bombs were made from pressure cookers and contained ball bearings. They exploded 12 seconds apart near the finish line, wounding 180 people. Ten were killed. Civilian witnesses reported sightings of the suspects at different locations in the city. The suspects are considered armed and dangerous. In response, the local law enforcement agency, which possesses a drone, employs it to locate the suspects and to engage them, if necessary. While monitoring the area, the drone's sensors, which include full-motion video (FMV) capability, detect and capture footage of a robbery in progress, unrelated to the bombing. Given the sheer number of people in the area, the FMV footage also captures images of private citizens as they either try to leave the area or assist in response efforts. The drone eventually locates the suspects running on foot several miles from the scene. Its FMV capability is used to videotape the subsequent law enforcement engagement. The suspects engage in a firefight with law enforcement agencies. The drone is equipped with lethal weaponry, and this capability is used to kill one suspect in defense of other law enforcement personnel on the ground. The other suspect is injured and ultimately prosecuted in state court.

- Was the drone use lawful?
- Could federal or military personnel or assets have assisted?
- Is the evidence obtained against the surviving suspect admissible in a criminal court?

- Can video of the robbers and related testimony be used against them in a criminal trial?
- What should be done with the video containing incidental images of other USPER?

B.   State Legislation Analysis

Because Florida, Idaho, Illinois, Montana, Oregon, Tennessee, Texas, and Virginia have all passed drone legislation, testing the hypothetical domestic CT scenario against their provisions provides a realistic illustration of how drone legislation would impact CT operations. Because they are different in so many respects, reviewing each individually demonstrates the type of analysis that would need to be done for any intrastate CT operation. Interstate issues would require analysis of several states' laws.

1.   Florida

The *Florida Freedom from Unwarranted Surveillance Act* applies only to state or local law enforcement agencies.[120] Although it prohibits local law enforcement from using drones to gather evidence or information, it contains exceptions that allow such use with a warrant, to counter a high risk of a terror attack, to prevent imminent danger to life or serious damage to property, and to forestall the imminent escape of a suspect or the destruction of evidence.[121] It contains a criminal exclusionary rule for evidence obtained in violation its terms.[122] It is silent on the issue of weaponized drones, evidentiary exclusion, and dissemination and retention of information collected.

Under the facts presented, the local law enforcement agency's use of the drone to find, fix, and lethally engage the target is lawful. Tracking and imaging the suspects without a warrant would qualify as necessary to forestall the suspects' imminent escape or prevent imminent danger to life. These bases are more reliable than "countering" a high risk of a terrorist attack in this scenario, particularly because the attack has already occurred, and there are no indications the U.S. Secretary of Homeland Security has determined that credible intelligence indicates there is risk of a second attack. With regard to the use of force against one of the suspects, the law does not prohibit the use of weaponized drones. Assuming the use of force in defense of others was otherwise appropriate, the law enforcement agency's firing bullets from a drone and killing one of the suspects would be justifiable—just as if a police sniper had taken the shot from his rife while in a helicopter. The law does not impact federal or military actors, and their assistance would be subject to their own authorities and approval procedures.

Because Florida law does not contain a criminal exclusionary rule, even if the drone's use to collect evidence was somehow deemed unlawful, it does not preclude the admission of the videotaped pursuit and arrest in criminal court or the testimony of the person who was monitoring. As the language is also silent on information incidentally collected, such as the videotaped robbery, Florida drone law would not preclude its use in court. Finally, because Florida law does not speak to retention of data captured, video containing images of other USPER would likely be handled under Florida's other privacy or records retention laws.

2. Idaho

The Idaho law adds a new section to Chapter 2, Title 21 of the Idaho Code, Section 21-213, *Restrictions on Use of Unmanned Aircraft Systems*.[123] It prohibits use of a drone "to intentionally conduct surveillance of, gather evidence or collect information about . . . specifically targeted persons" absent a warrant and except for emergency response for safety, SAR, or controlled substance investigations.[124] It applies not only to state agencies, but also to "persons" and "entities."[125] Like the Florida law, the Idaho law is silent on the issue of weaponized drones, evidentiary exclusion, and dissemination and retention of information collected.

Whether or not the law enforcement agency's use of a drone in this situation was lawful would depend on the interpretation of the term "emergency response for safety," which is not defined. However, a manhunt of armed and dangerous fleeing suspects who have just detonated a bomb targeting civilians should reasonably qualify as an "emergency response for safety." Because the law is broadly written to include "persons" and "entities," it would apply to federal and military personnel. Their ability to assist local law enforcement agencies would also hinge on the interpretation of "emergency response for safety," in addition to their internal authorities and permissions.

Assuming the use of force was otherwise valid, the use of lethal force would be considered lawful, given that the law is silent on the issue of weaponized drones.

Because the law does not contain a criminal exclusionary rule, all other things being equal, the video of the arrest, and related testimony, would be admissible. Likewise, because there is no discussion of incidentally collected information, the video would also be admissible as against the robbers. Given the lack of provisions on retention, other Idaho laws might apply to handling the video that contains incidental images of USPER.

3. Illinois

Analysis of the same fact pattern in Illinois would yield results similar to those of Idaho and Florida, with minimal deviation. The applicability of Illinois' *Freedom from Drone Surveillance Act* is limited to local law enforcement agencies.[126] The law prohibits them from using a "drone to gather information."[127] However, it contains a long list of exceptions: to counter a high risk of a terrorist attack, pursuant to a search warrant, if there is a reasonable suspicion that swift action is needed to prevent imminent harm to life, or to forestall the imminent escape of a suspect or the destruction of evidence, for SAR unconnected to a criminal investigation, for crime scene photography, and of private property with consent.[128] Like Idaho and Florida, the Illinois law is silent on the issue of weaponized drones. However, it addresses evidentiary exclusion and retention and dissemination of information collected.[129]

In these particular circumstances, exceptions for imminent harm to life or to forestall the imminent escape of a suspect would justify law enforcement agencies' use of a drone. Again, because the attack has already occurred and there are no facts indicating that the Secretary of Homeland Security has made a determination of continuing risk, the terrorist attack exception would ironically not seem to apply. This law also does not prohibit the use of weaponized drones, so lethal action against one of the suspects with a drone would be lawful if it meets other legal criteria for law enforcement's use of force. The law does not apply directly to federal or military actors or inhibit their ability to assist.

Although the Illinois drone law contains an exclusionary rule, it would not preclude admissibility under these circumstances because the information was not gathered unlawfully.[130] Under its retention provisions, law enforcement agencies must destroy all information gathered within 30 days unless there is reasonable suspicion that the information contains evidence of criminal activity or information relevant to an ongoing investigation or pending criminal trial.[131] Under the latter part of this clause, information pertaining to the bombing suspect and the robbers could both be retained beyond 30 days for use in criminal court. The incidentally collected USPER information, however, would need to be destroyed within 30 days.

4. *Montana*

The Montana law simply prohibits the admissibility of information obtained from a drone "in any prosecution or proceeding within the state" unless obtained pursuant to a warrant or a judicially recognized exception to the warrant requirement.[132] The law also prohibits use of information obtained by a drone in an affidavit to obtain a warrant unless it was collected pursuant to its own warrant; it would otherwise qualify under a judicially recognized exception to the warrant requirement; or is obtained through the monitoring of public lands or international borders.[133] There are no other provisions.

As discussed in the context of the Florida, Idaho, and Illinois laws, a good case may be made for the application of the imminent danger to life and fleeing felon exceptions. Admissibility of the evidence, whether in the case of the surviving suspect or the robbers, would hinge on such an analysis. Because the law focuses on the activity, not the actors, it appears to broadly apply to all operators and local law enforcement agencies, federal and military alike.[134] However, the same exceptions to the warrant requirement would apply equally for all of these actors.

The law does not address weaponized drones and thus does not preclude the lethal action taken in this case. Retention of information is also not discussed. USPER information incidentally collected would need to be addressed by resorting to other privacy laws.

5. Oregon

Oregon House Bill 2710, *Use of Drones by Law Enforcement Agencies*, applies to local law enforcement agencies and prohibits them from operating a drone, acquiring information through the operation of a drone, or disclosing information acquired through the operation of a drone.[135] Exceptions to these prohibitions include obtaining a warrant, exigent circumstances (person committed a crime, is committing a crime, or is about to commit a crime), written consent, SAR, in emergencies where there is an imminent threat to life and safety, during a governor-declared state of emergency, crime scene reconstruction, and for training purposes.[136] The law specifically exempts the U.S. Armed Forces from its provisions and is silent on the issue of federal actors.[137] The law prohibits "public bodies" from operating a drone capable of "firing a bullet or other projectile, directing a laser or otherwise being used as a weapon."[138] Among other things, the law contains a broad exclusionary rule for evidence collected, and evidence derived therefrom, in violation of its provisions.[139] It does not contain provisions on incidentally collected information.

In the instant case, the law enforcement agency's "finding and fixing" the terrorist suspects was lawful under the exigent circumstances and imminent threat to life and safety provisions because there is reasonable belief that the suspects committed a crime and may be about to commit more. For this reason, the evidence would be admissible against the surviving suspect. However, given the weaponized drone provision in the law, the agency's lethal action in this case was not sanctioned.

The law does not apply to federal actors and specifically exempts the U.S. Armed Forces from its provisions. Even though it generally prohibits law enforcement agencies from acquiring information from the operation of a drone, acquisition or receipt is allowed under exigent circumstances or where there is an imminent threat to life or safety.[140] Thus, federal and military actors could share information collected with local law enforcement agencies unhampered.

In the absence of a prohibition on using information incidentally collected, video of the robbers would be used against them in a criminal trial if otherwise admissible. USPER information incidentally collected would also be addressed by resorting to other privacy laws.

6. *Tennessee*

Tennessee's *Freedom from Unwarranted Surveillance Act* also only applies to local or state law enforcement agencies.[141] It prohibits them from using a drone except to counter a high risk of a terror attack, after obtaining a search warrant, to prevent imminent danger to life, in searching for a fugitive or escapee, to monitor a hostage situation, and for SAR.[142] The law also states that use of a drone to gather evidence or information constitutes a search under the U.S. and Tennessee Constitutions, and, absent a warrant or judicially recognized exception to that requirement, evidence obtained in violation shall not be admissible in a criminal prosecution.[143] The law also contains a section on retention. Non-target data must be deleted within 24 hours after collection.[144] The law is silent on weaponized drones.

Applying the Tennessee law to these facts, all activities of law enforcement agencies were appropriate. Use of the drone is justified as preventing imminent danger to life and in searching for a "fugitive."[145] Because preventing imminent danger to life is an exception to the constitutional requirement for a warrant, the video obtained would be admissible against the surviving suspect. Federal and military personnel or drone assets could have assisted, if approved, as the law applies only to local law enforcement agencies.

With regard to the decedent, the law does not prohibit the use of lethal force. In this case, assuming such force was appropriate to defend the lives of law enforcement personnel on the ground, it was lawful.

Unlike the other laws discussed before it, Tennessee law addresses incidentally collected information. Because it requires that data collected on non-targets be deleted no later than 24 hours after collection, videos of both the robbers and other USPER would have to be destroyed. Ironically, in addressing retention, Tennessee has severely limited the use of collected information for what otherwise would be lawful purposes, such as in a criminal investigation or for prosecution of persons other than the target.

7. *Texas*

The *Texas Privacy Act* is organized differently form the other laws. It contains a large "nonapplicability" section that outlines lawful uses for drones.[146] While it is too lengthy to describe all the nonapplicable drone uses here, several CT-related provisions include: consent; search or arrest warrant; immediate pursuit of a suspect (who may have committed an offense greater than a misdemeanor); documenting a crime scene; "for the purpose of conducting a high-risk tactical operation that poses a threat to human life"; on public real property or a person on that property; and as part of an "operation, exercise or mission of any branch of the United States military."[147] Otherwise, the law is applicable to any person.[148] Such a person commits an offense if he uses a drone to image an individual or private property with "intent to conduct surveillance."[149] Images illegally obtained as well as those incidentally collected during lawful operations cannot be used in any proceeding or otherwise disclosed.[150] Civil action against violators is also available.[151] The law does not address retention and contains no weaponized drone provision.

Texas law provides multiple bases to use a drone to monitor suspects, including pursuit and high-risk tactical operations exceptions. These exceptions would apply to local and federal law enforcement agencies. The military, on the other hand, would have even more leeway, as the law specifically exempts their missions and operations. As the law contains no prohibitions on the use of weaponized drones, assuming the use of lethal force was otherwise justifiable, it is lawful.

Assuming the initial collection was lawful, the evidence against the surviving suspect would be admissible. However, incidentally collected images of the robbers or other USPER could not be used in trial or otherwise disclosed. As the law does not address retention, presumably other records-retention rules would apply.

8. *Virginia*

The Virginia law is somewhat unique in that it prohibits local law enforcement agencies' use of drones before July 1, 2015, unless in support of Amber and similar missing person alerts, for SAR situations involving an immediate danger to the missing person, and to train for those purposes.[152] The law also exempts the Virginia National Guard as well as higher education and research institutions engaging in research and development.[153]

Under Virginia law, finding, fixing, and finishing the suspects is a nonstarter for local law enforcement agencies. Federal and military assets may have been able to employ drones, however. Admissibility of evidence as against both the surviving suspect and the robbers would turn on a Fourth Amendment analysis. Likewise, other privacy laws would regulate the disposition of the video containing incidental images of other USPER.

C. Federal Legislation Analysis

While some federal drone bills closely track state proposals, others contain specific provisions pertaining only to use of force. All apply to federal actors, but some extend their application to states as well. Applying the facts of the hypothetical scenario to these bills yields a wide range of results.

1. *The Preserving Freedom from Unwarranted Surveillance Act of 2013*

This Act applies only to "persons or entities acting under the authority of the United States" and not to state law enforcement agencies.[154] Under its provisions, federal actors, including the DoD, in this case would be able to gather evidence or other information with a drone under its "exigent circumstances," danger to life, and "fleeing felon" (forestall imminent escape of a suspect) exceptions.[155] It does not contain a criminal exclusionary rule or address weaponized drones or incidental collection.[156] Thus, this bill would not inhibit federal employees from lawfully collecting information and admitting it into court or using a drone to conduct lethal operations. In fact, for DoD, it would provide affirmative authority to use drones in a surveillance-type role, where current authorities otherwise do not. USPER information incidentally collected would be handled according to other laws and policies.

2. *The Drone Aircraft Privacy and Transparency Acts of 2013 (DAPTAs)*

The *DAPTAs'* collection provisions apply to "any person or entity" and thus to federal, DoD, and state actors.[157] Although the bills generally require a warrant for surveillance, in this case their danger to life exception would apply.[158] As a practical matter, the collecting agency, including law enforcement agencies, would have to file the justification for its emergency use with the SecTrans within seven days after flight.[159] The *DAPTAs* do not address weaponized drones. While the bills include an exclusionary rule applicable to any court or hearing for information obtained in violation of their provisions, these would not apply because the instant collection was lawful.[160] Under the *DAPTAs*, information pertaining to the robbers could be retained for use in a criminal prosecution. However, law enforcement agencies would need to destroy incidentally collected USPER information.

3. *The Preserving American Privacy Act of 2013 (PAPA)*

The *PAPA* applies to departments or agencies of the U.S. as well as to states, and thus to local law enforcement agencies.[161] Because the Act is not to be construed as preempting state law, all agency operators would have to comply with both the *PAPA* and applicable state law(s).[162]

Because the *PAPA* forbids use of weaponized drones, lethal action would not be authorized.[163] Although the *PAPA* would prohibit operation of a drone to collect or disclose information for a law enforcement purpose, its exceptions for emergency situations include "immediate danger of death or serious physical injury to any person" and "conspiratorial activities threatening the national security interest."[164] Both of these bases would provide justification to use a drone to pursue the two fleeing terrorists. Before the mission could occur, however, law enforcement agencies would have to file a "data collection statement" with the Attorney General (AG) and FAA for approval to operate the drone.[165] Law enforcement agencies would have to implement complimentary procedures. After the event, the *PAPA* would require the agencies to obtain a warrant within 48 hours and provide notice to the subject within 10 days.[166] While these requirements may be consistent with federal law enforcement agency procedures, they do not readily translate into current DoD practice. Assuming all of the above procedures were correctly followed, the *PAPA*'s blanket exclusionary rule applicable to federal and state courts would not apply.[167]

Even though the *PAPA* requires drone users to minimize collection of non-target information such as that collected on the robbers in our scenario, it can be retained for criminal prosecution. Other USPER information, however, would have to be destroyed if reasonably likely to enable identification of an individual.[168]

4. *The No Armed Drones Act of 2013 (NADA)*

This bill would prohibit the FAA from issuing approval to operate a drone in the national airspace system for the purpose, in whole or in part, of using it as a weapon or to deliver a weapon against a person or property.[169] It would impact the scenario insofar as no agency would be able to obtain FAA authorization to use a weaponized drone.

5. *The Life, Liberty, and Justice for All Americans Act, Senate Bill 505, and House of Representatives Bill 1242, Bill to prohibit use of drones to kill US citizens in U.S.*

The *Life, Liberty, and Justice for All Americans Act*, which affects only the DoD, allows the President to authorize a *military* drone to lethally target an American in the United States, but only if that individual poses an imminent threat of death or serious bodily injury to another and using force will prevent or minimize the risk. S.505 and H.B.1242 are identical to the *Life, Liberty, and Justice for All Americans Act*, with two exceptions: (1) they apply to the federal government (more broadly than just the military) and (2) do not contain the requirement that the use of force will prevent or minimize deaths or injuries.[170] The facts in this case fairly raise the issue of imminent threat and, despite current DoD policy to the contrary, this Act would permit use of lethal force against terror suspects.[171] They would impact the hypothetical case insofar as they would provide affirmative authority for the federal government to employ lethal drones in limited circumstances.

D. DoD Policy Analysis

In the hypothetical scenario, the local law enforcement agency asks for DoD drone support to track fleeing terrorist suspects. Would DoD be able to do this? Under current DoD policy, a request from law enforcement to assist with a drone would be considered DSCA, in particular support to law enforcement agencies, and would require SecDef approval. DoD drones cannot conduct "surveillance" for local law enforcement agencies.[172] However, as a SecDef approved NORTHCOM mission, drones could be used in a limited manner to assist with dynamic ground coordination and provide situational awareness, subject to IO policies on collection, retention, dissemination, and oversight pursuant to the CJCS DSCA EXORD.[173] Short of this, only if federal law enforcement agencies became involved and requested DoD specialized assistance could SecDef approve drone use for aerial reconnaissance under 10 U.S.C. 374. Admittedly, neither one of these authorities is a perfect fit for this scenario.

With regard to information collected, SecDef would likely require that IO policies apply to the law enforcement agencies' support operation. Pursuant to DoD 5240.1-R, DoD drones could be used in support of a federal CT effort, and information pertaining to the person targeted could be retained permanently. Incidentally collected information, such as that on the robber, could be retained temporarily, up to 90 days, and disseminated to local law enforcement for use in a prosecution.

Use of armed drones for DSCA is not authorized.[174] Even if it were, as mentioned above, unless an individual engaged in combat on U.S. soil, the current Administration's position is that the President lacks the authority to lethally target him.[175] Specific statutory authority such as passage of the *DAPTAs* or *PAPA*—or the reality of another catastrophic event like 9/11—might change this policy position.

E. The Key Take-Aways

Applying the facts to a Boston Marathon bomber-like scenario demonstrates that state and federal proposals facilitate drone use for the "find and fix" phases of domestic CT operations more so than the "finish" phase. The application also provides several other key take-aways.

1. Find and Fix—Define the Exceptions, Add "IO-Like" Protections, Codify DoD Support

Virtually all state and federal bills reviewed apply to government actors, primarily to law enforcement, and prohibit the use of drones to gather information or evidence absent a warrant or court order, with exceptions.[176] While on the surface these procedures appear to provide new privacy protections, they merely codify Fourth Amendment concepts that already exist.[177] The most common exception found in drone bills is the warrant requirement, yet to require law enforcement to obtain a warrant before searching for evidence is already well established black-letter law. As illustrated by our hypothetical scenario, during a fast-moving, real-world terror attack it may not be practical to obtain a warrant when time is of the essence. Clearly defining and codifying appropriate exceptions to the warrant requirement will avoid ambiguity and confusion during time-sensitive operations.

a. Define the Exceptions

Most bills permit drone use without a warrant in emergency circumstances to save lives.[178] This is critical in the CT context, as any terror attack would invoke the potential of immediate danger of death, serious physical injury, or significant property damage. As demonstrated by the hypothetical scenario, these common state exigent circumstances and imminent danger to life exceptions, as well as those in the federal *Preserving Freedom from Unwarranted Surveillance Act of 2013*, the *DAPTAs*, and the *PAPA* proposals, prove very useful in a domestic CT context.[179] The 14 state bills that currently fail to include an imminent danger exception should reconsider their position on this critical emergency response issue— particularly because the Supreme Court has already endorsed the concept of "exigent circumstances."[180]

Although phrased differently, the "fleeing felon" exceptions found in Florida, Illinois, Tennessee, and Texas, and the federal *Preserving Freedom from Unwarranted Surveillance Act of 2013* assisted law enforcement agencies to "find and fix" at-large terrorist suspects.[181] Despite the prevalence of this exception in bills actually passed and reviewed here, only 16 bills of the 102 surveyed contain this CT-friendly language.[182] Of those, the only "fleeing felon" language that would not assist CT operations is Wisconsin's bill, which is phrased as "to locate an escaped prisoner."[183] Legislators should seriously consider adding this exception to their bills, given its utility in a domestic CT setting.

Also related to terminology, as demonstrated by application of the Florida, Illinois, and federal *PAPA* bills to our hypothetical fact pattern, the "terror attack" and "national security conspiracy" exceptions would benefit from clarification.[184] With regard to the former, all the terror attack exceptions are worded the same: "To counter a high risk of a terrorist attack by a specific individual or organization if the United States Secretary of Homeland Security . . . determines that credible intelligence indicates that there is such a risk." Application of this exception proved difficult in our scenario because the key term "countering," which seems reactive in nature, has been coupled with the phrase "high risk of a terrorist attack," which appears prospective. How does one counter what has yet to happen?

A reasonable interpretation is that this exception is preventive. If this is the case, the terror attack exception provides little value where an attack has already occurred. Additionally, in our hypothetical the predicate finding was not present because it was not clear that the U.S. Secretary of Homeland Security determined by credible intelligence that risk of terror attack existed. The lack of such a finding would be the case in a lone- or two-wolf scenario where the problem might be considered local, as opposed to a national one (like 9/11) requiring the full engagement of the National Security apparatus.

Similarly, with regard to the "national security conspiracy" exception, Arkansas, Hawaii, Maine, Michigan, and the federal *PAPA* all allow state or federal agencies to use drones for emergencies involving "conspiratorial activities threatening the national security interest."[185] Yet significant terms remain undefined, such as "conspiratorial activity" and "national security interest." In our hypothetical involving two suspects, basic criminal conspiracy theory might apply. However, at what point does a domestic terror incident become a national security event—a lone-wolf actor involved in a single episode and having limited impact, multiple simultaneous events, or only in a catastrophic 9/11-type attack? Until these terms are defined, even if only by criteria to apply, these terror-related exceptions will continue to miss the mark.

With regard to facilitating CT operations, very few state or federal bills carve out exceptions that would facilitate post-attack recovery, including search and rescue operations, disaster response, or damage assessment.[186] In fairness, these activities should be fairly embraced by an "imminent danger to life" exception, but a better practice would be to provide for these operations explicitly.

b.   Add "IO-Like" Protections (Where Needed)

Transitioning from information collection to information handling, most drone proposals fail to address the issues that most directly impact privacy: use, dissemination, and retention. To the extent that current state privacy laws are insufficient to address how law enforcement agencies handles information it collects—regardless of the means of collection—such issues are important to address. Of the eight state bills analyzed in our hypothetical exercise, only two addressed incidentally collected information. The *Texas Privacy Act* would forbid use or disclosure of incidentally collected information in any proceeding.[187] The Tennessee law goes one step further and requires such be deleted no later than 24 hours after collection, without exception.[188] Both of these laws unduly restrict information that would otherwise be legally available to prosecutors. The drafters of the Illinois law, as well as those for the federal *DAPTA* and *PAPA* bills, recognize this by permitting non-target information to be retained if necessary to a criminal investigation or prosecution.[189] These bills track the DoD's incidental collection rules, which also allow retention and dissemination of incidentally collected information relating to criminal acts and are worth repeating.[190]

While not addressed by the state laws reviewed in our hypothetical scenario, as discussed earlier, many bills prohibit use of facial recognition or other biometric matching technology on non-target information.[191] If the non-target has committed a crime, such as our robber in the bombing scenario, prohibiting law enforcement agencies from using this valuable identification tool seems unduly restrictive.

c.   Codify DoD Support

While DoD IO and drone policies prove useful for protecting privacy in the CT context, for a number of reasons, DoD could benefit from legislation that provides direct statutory authority for drone use in CT operations. DoD's role in domestic CT is one of support to LEA and is limited by the Posse Comitatus Act (PCA).[192] However, the PCA allows the military to enforce the laws "in cases and under circumstances expressly authorized by the Constitution or Act of Congress." While the President could use the military in a domestic CT event under his Article II powers, he acts at the zenith of those powers when there is congressional authorization for the action.[193]

Although current policies allow DoD to use drones domestically for IAA and limited aerial reconnaissance, neither one of these bases is the perfect solution for DoD-enabled CT operations in the U.S.[194] Codifying the ability for DoD to employ drones in support of state and local law enforcement agencies' CT efforts, particularly in situations where local resources are overwhelmed, would alleviate ambiguity and pave the way for partnering more fully, particularly in catastrophic events. Also, given the Obama Administration's stated position that the President lacks authority to use military force on U.S. non-combatants on U.S. soil, such codification would provide DoD affirmative authority to use drones for CT where none currently exists.

2.   *Finish—Reconsider Prohibitions*

Prohibitions on weaponized drones and excluding evidence where the Fourth Amendment otherwise would not require it has a direct impact on domestic CT operations, as well as significant second- and third-order effects.

Of the eight state drone bills used in the hypothetical scenario, only one addresses weaponization of drones. The Oregon law prohibits "public bodies" from operating a drone capable of "firing a bullet or other projectile, directing a laser or otherwise being used as a weapon."[195] The federal *PAPA* and *NADA* proposals would likewise forbid weaponized drones.[196] The *Life, Liberty, and Justice for All Americans Act,* Senate Bill 505 and House Bill 1242, acknowledge this by including an exception that would allow lethal drone action where there is an imminent threat to life or limb.[197]

Other state and federal bills should follow suit. A drone may very well be the best asset for a particular situation, particularly high-risk tactical situations. The drone can perform the same task as a police helicopter with a sniper on board, but without risking the lives of law enforcement personnel.

Prohibitions on the use of weaponized drones also impact critical training for the military and its partners. For example, in California, Senate Bill 15, which is currently under advisement, states that "an unmanned aircraft system may not be equipped with a weapon." Doing so is punishable by a fine and imprisonment.[198] Federal preemption aside, the proposal contains no military exemption, yet California is home to military ranges, bases, and test sites for the Active, Reserve, and Guard components of virtually all the military Services.[199] Other states, such as Oregon, on the other hand, contain a military exception for all of its provisions, including the weaponized drone provision.[200] Given the Armed Forces' statutory duty to organize, train, and equip (OT&E) combat-ready forces, an explicit military exemption like that in the Oregon bill is worth replicating (at a minimum, to avoid unnecessary conflict and litigation).[201]

The majority of state and federal bills surveyed would also exclude evidence obtained in violation of their drone-related procedures at hearings.[202] These provisions are problematic on several levels. Aside from being arguably unconstitutional, bills that fail to include the full spectrum of Fourth Amendment exceptions create unnecessary windfalls for criminal suspects. This windfall is not just limited to criminal suspects. States that preclude admission of drone information from civil and administrative hearings extend otherwise inapplicable Fourth Amendment warrant requirements to civil cases.[203]

Several state and federal drone bills also create civil, criminal, or administrative liability against law enforcement agencies or individual officers for failing to abide by their requirements.[204] These provisions may very well have a chilling effect on CT operators who will now have to make life-and-death decisions under the added threat of personal liability.

V. Conclusion

Current state, federal and DoD drone proposals and policies facilitate drone use for the "find and fix" phases of domestic CT operations more so than the "finish" phase, across the continuum of potential terror attacks. Regarding the "find and fix" phase, while most drone proposals prohibit information collection, they contain multiple exceptions useful in the CT context, including imminent danger to life and exigent circumstances. Ironically, the two main attempts to statutorily relate drone use directly to domestic CT operations—the "terror attack" and "national security conspiracy" exceptions—generally miss their mark due to lack of definitional meaning and lack of relevance for localized state attacks not rising to the national level. Although the majority of the state and federal drone bills were introduced to protect privacy, many fail to address critical privacy-related issues, such as dissemination and retention. To the extent that existing privacy laws that already pertain to law enforcement agency–collected information are inadequate, the DoD IO regime bears emulating. On the other hand, the DoD could benefit from legislation that provides affirmative and unambiguous statutory authority for drone use in domestic CT operations to allay Posse Comitatus concerns, among others.

Finally, with regard to the "finish" phase of domestic CT operations, policy makers need to seriously reconsider prohibitions on weaponized drones and rules that require deletion of drone-acquired data, prohibit the use of biometrics, and require exclusion of drone evidence where the Fourth Amendment otherwise would not. Doing so will allow drones to be used to their full operational potential while protecting our security and privacy.

Notes

1. "Find, fix and finish" is shorthand for the F2T2EA process: find, fix, track, target, engage, and assess. *See* Joint Publication 3-60, Joint Targeting, Jan. 31, 2013, https://jdeis.js.mil/jdeis/index.jsp?pindex=27&pubId=537 (also available publicly at http://www.fas.org/irp//doddir/dod/jp3_60.pdf). DoD joint targeting doctrine applies to the U.S. military. However, these concepts provide a useful analogy to the rules for the use of force in a domestic law enforcement context.

2. Joint Publication 1-02, Department of Defense Dictionary of Military and Associated Terms, defines counterterrorism as "actions taken directly against terrorist networks and indirectly to influence and render global and regional environments inhospitable to terrorist networks." JP 1-02, p.17, http://www.dtic.mil/doctrine/new_pubs/jp1_02.pdf. As a matter of policy, the Obama Administration rejects "the use of military force where well-established law enforcement authorities in this country provide the best means for incapacitating a terrorist threat." Letter, Att'y Gen. Eric Holder to Sen. Rand Paul, March 4, 2013, http://www.paul.senate.gov/files/documents/BrennanHolderResponse.pdf. From a federal standpoint, the Department of Justice (DoJ) is the primary federal agency for domestic CT operations. Joint Publication 3-26, Counterterrorism, Nov. 13, 2009, p.IV-2, http://www.dtic.mil/doctrine/new_pubs/jp3_26.pdf.

3. In the robotics industry and within the DoD, drones are typically referred to as "unmanned aerial vehicles" (UAV) or "unmanned aerial systems" (UAS). In 2010, the U.S. Air Force changed the term UAV to "remotely piloted aircraft" (RPA) by institutionalizing RPA pilot training and designating RPA pilots as rated officers (career aviation status). *Air Force officials announce remotely piloted aircraft pilot training pipeline*, Air Force News, http://www.af.mil/news/story.asp?id=123208561; AFI 11-402, *Aviation and Parachutist Service, Aeronautical Ratings and Aviation Badges*, Dec. 13, 2010, ¶ 2.2. This change in terminology is significant in that it recognizes that these vehicles are not "unmanned," but rather are piloted, albeit remotely, by trained and rated officers. However, in everyday parlance, people commonly refer to RPAs as "drones." For the sake of simplicity, the term "drone" is used throughout this chapter. For an

overview of the various types of drones, from military to commercial off-the-shelf products, the Association for Unmanned Vehicle Systems International (AUVSI) has a searchable database of drone airborne platforms at http://robotdirectory.auvsi.org/UnmannedSystemsandRobotics Directory/Home/ (*no endorsement intended or implied).

    4.   Appendix A outlines pending state drone legislation. Drone legislation and policy is a dynamic issue. Some of these bills have already died in committee, and by the time of publication, more bills will have been introduced. The usefulness of reviewing all bills is to glean trends.

    5.   FL, ID, IL, MT, OR, TN, TX, and VA have all passed drone legislation. Twenty-four states have introduced two or more bills simultaneously, including AK, AZ, AR, CA, GA, IL, IN, IA, KY, MA MI, MN, NJ, NY, NC, OK, OR, PA, RI, SC, TN, VA, WA, and WV. *See* Appendix A. CO, CT, DE, LA, MS, SD, and UT have not introduced drone legislation.

    6.   There are few outliers. The New Hampshire bill was specifically drafted so as "not to impair or limit otherwise lawful activities of law enforcement personnel . . . ." NH HB 619, § 2. One of two Arkansas bills would exempt law enforcement officers and emergency responders operating drones as part of their official job duties. AR SB 1109, § 1, 5-60-3(b)(1)(A)–(B). Michigan and North Carolina would allow drone use if not for an intelligence or law enforcement purpose. MI HB 4455 § 5, ¶ (e) and NC HB 312, § 2(b). Iowa, Pennsylvania, and Virginia prohibit drone use prior to July 1, 2015, with exceptions. IA SF 276, 80C.1., PA SB 875, § 3, and VA HB 2012, 1. § 1.

    7.   Bills that apply, either directly or by implication, to federal or U.S. government employees tend to use broad terms such as "all persons" or "agents." *See* AL SB 317, § 1(2) (applies to "any municipal, county, state, or federal agency the personnel of which have (sic) the power of arrest and perform a law enforcement function); AK HB 159a, § 13(b) ("government employee or agent"); AR SB 1109, § 1., 5-60-106(b)(1)(A)–(B) (would apply to a federal agency, unless acting at the request of a state law enforcement officer or emergency responder); AZ HB 2574, § 13-3007.B. ("unlawful for a person to use drones to monitor . . ."); CA SB No. 15, § 2(a)–(b), *amending* § 1708.8 of the Civil Code ("A person is liable . . ."); GA SB 200, § 4(1); *see also* GA HB 560, § 2, *amending* Art. 2 of Ch. 5 of tit. 17, GA. CODE ANN. as 17-5-33(1) and (2) (extends provisions to "a law enforcement officer of any department or agency of the United States who is regularly employed and paid by the United States, this state or any such political subdivision . . ."); HI SB 783, § 2563B-2(b) ("an agent of the state or any political subdivision thereof, or an individual . . ."); ID SB 1134, § 1(2)(a) ("no person"); IN SB 20, § 4(a) ("a person"); KY 14 RS BR 1, § 1(1)(c) ("Agent of any prohibited agency"); MA SB 1664, § 1(c) and HB 1357, § 1(c) (apply to "government entities" or "government officials," without further definition); MI HB 4455, § 1, ¶ (an "individual acting or purporting to act for or on behalf of this (sic) State or local unit of government"); MN HF 990, § 3, Subd. 1(b) ("Person," defined as any individual); MO HB 46, § 305.637.2. ("No person, entity or state agency"); NJ AB 3929 ("state, local, or interstate law enforcement agency"); NY AO 8091, § 1, ¶ 5 ("he or she"); NY AO 6244, § 1, ¶ 1. (applies to persons or entities acting "under color of the authority of any State, county, municipal or local governmental entity or authority, or "acting on behalf of any such entity or authority"); NY AO 4537AO 6370, ¶ 5(C). (includes any "agent of" State or local law enforcement agencies); NY AO 6541, § 66-A(2) ("agent of the state or any political subdivision thereof"); NC HB 312, § 2(a)(2) ("Person—any employee or agent of the United States or any state"); OH HB 207, § 4651.50(A) ("any person acting on behalf of a law enforcement agency"); OK HB 1556, § 3(B)(6), OR SB 853, § 1(2) and MN HF 1620/ 1706, § 3, Subd. 1.(c). (apply, in some manner, to "federal agenc(ies)"); OR HB 2710, § 1(1)(b) (police officers are defined to include DoJ criminal investigators); OR SB 71, throughout ("a person") and OR SB 853, § 2(2)("a person"); RI Gen. Assembly Jan. 2013, *amending* tit. 12 of GEN. LAWS, Ch. 5.3, 12-5.3.-1.

("'person' means any individual, partnership, association, joint stock company, trust or corporation, whether or not any of the foregoing is an officer, agent or employee of the United States, a state, or a political subdivision of a state"); and 12-5.3.-2. ("It shall be unlawful for a municipal law enforcement agency, or any individual or entity on such agency's behalf, to operate an unmanned aerial vehicle, or to disclose or receive information acquired through the operation of an unmanned aerial vehicle."); SC HB 3415, *amending* Ch. 13, tit. 17 of 1976 Code as 17-13-180(A)(2); TX HB 912, Ch. 423, § 423.003(a) ("a person") and Ch. 423, § 423.002(8) (". . . a person who is otherwise acting under the direction or on behalf of a law enforcement authority"); WV HB 2732, Art. 7, § 1-7-2 ("law enforcement agency means a lawfully established federal, state or local public agency that is responsible for the prevention and detection of crime. . . ."); WY HB 0242, 7-3-1002(a)(ii) (include "federal agency" in their definition of the term "law enforcement agency"); WA HB 1771, § 6 and WA SB 5782, § 2(6) ("'Person' includes any individual . . ."); WI AB 203/SB 196, § 3(2) ("whoever").

8. KY 14 RS BR 1, § 1(4)(b) (permits the "U.S. Armed Forces" stationed in the State to "use drones for purposes of training"); OK HB 1556, § 5.C. and § 4.A ("United States military" permitted to operate "weaponized" drones over public land for purposes of testing and training; "incidental over flight" of private lands allowed while in transit to or from "its destination or base of operation," if the flight was otherwise compliant with FAA regulations); NJ Assembly No. 3157, ¶ 5 (exempts "any member of the Armed Forces of the United States or member of the National Guard while on duty or traveling to or from an authorized place of duty" from disorderly persons offense for purchasing, owning, or possessing a drone); MO HB 46 § 305.639(2) (permits higher education institutes to conduct educational, research, or training programs in collaboration with the DoD); OR SB 853, § 12(1) (excludes "the Armed Forces of the United States . . . or any component of the Oregon National Guard from using drones during a drill, training exercise or disaster response"); OR HB 2710, § 16 (*passed) (exempts the "Armed Forces of the United States" from its provisions); PA SB 875, § 5(1)–(3) (exempts its National Guard "during training required to maintain readiness for its federal mission, when facilitating training for other United States Department of Defense units, or when such systems are utilized for the Commonwealth for purposes other than law enforcement, including damage assessment, traffic assessment, flood stages, and wildfire assessment . . ."); TX HB 912, Ch. 423, § 423.002 ("non-applicability" section excludes drone use that is "part of an operation, exercise, or mission of any branch of the United States military"); and VA HB 2012, ¶ 1 § 1 (*passed) (exempts its National Guard from prohibitions in words *verbatim* of PA bill above). State bills that broadly apply to any "person" or "entity," extend their reach to "agents" of State law enforcement, or purport to apply to those acting under State authority would also apply to DoD officials, employees, or personnel.

9. Appendix B lists drone bills introduced during the 113th Session of Congress (2013).

10. JP 6-30, p. II-21, ¶ (4)(a)(1).

11. *Id.*, at p. II-25.

12. Drones do not operate without input from a host of professionals, including pilots, sensor operators, and intelligence analysts acting in concert. While a gross oversimplification of a complex system and process, this article uses the same language found in proposed legislation ("drones collect" etc.) with full acknowledgment that it is inaccurate from both a technical and operational standpoint.

13. AL SB 317, § 1(b)(1) ("Except as otherwise provided . . . a law enforcement agency may not use a drone to gather evidence or other information."); AK HB 159a, *amending* § 4. AS 1865, Art. 13, § 18.65.900(a) ("Except as provided . . . a government employee or agent, including a police officer, may not participate in an investigation in which an unmanned aerial vehicle is being used, or otherwise direct the use of an unmanned aerial vehicle . . ."); AZ HB

2574, *amending* § 1, tit. 13, Ch. 30 ARS, 13-3007, § A ("it is unlawful for a law enforcement agency or a state county or municipal agency to use a drone to gather, sort or collect evidence of any type . . ."); AR HB 1904, *amending* AR Code tit. 12, as 12-19-104(a) ("It is unlawful for a local law enforcement agency to operate an unmanned aerial vehicle or to disclose or receive information acquired through the operation of an unmanned aerial vehicle except . . ."); CA SB 15, tit. 14, § 14352(a) ("a law enforcement agency shall obtain a search warrant to use" a drone) and CA Assembly Bill 1327, § 1, tit. 14, 14350(a) ("a public agency shall not use an unmanned aircraft system, or contract for the use of an unmanned aircraft system, except as provided in this title."); FL SB 92, § 1(3) ("A law enforcement agency may not use a drone to gather evidence or other information . . ."); GA SB 200, § 5(b) ("An unmanned aircraft shall not be used to conduct a search and seizure except . . .") and GA HB 560, § 2(b)–(c) ("Any law enforcement agent of the United States/State of Georgia who utilizes an unmanned aerial vehicle for any purpose whatsoever within the airspace of the State of Georgia without first obtaining a warrant shall be guilty of a misdemeanor"); HI SB, 2563B-2(b) (". . . it is unlawful for an agent of the state or any political subdivision thereof, or an individual . . . to operate an unmanned aerial vehicle or to disclose or receive information acquired through the operation of an unmanned aerial vehicle . . ."); ID SB 1134, § 1., 21-213(2)(a) (". . . no person, entity or state agency shall use an unmanned aircraft system to intentionally conduct surveillance of, gather evidence or collect information about, or photographically or electronically record specifically targeted persons or specifically targeted private property . . ."); IL SB 1587, § 10 ("Except as provided . . . a law enforcement agency may not use a drone to gather information"); IN SB 20, *amending* IN Code, Ch. 10, § 4(a) ("A person may not make use of an unmanned aerial vehicle without the written consent. . . "); IA HF 410, § 1. ("A state agency . . . shall not utilize an unmanned aircraft system prior to Jul 1, 2015") and IA HF 427, § 1.2. ("a law enforcement agency shall not use a drone to gather evidence or other information"); KS HB 2394, § 1(a) ("No law enforcement agency shall use a drone to obtain evidence or other information"); KY HB 454, § 1 of KRS Ch. 500(2) ("Except as provided . . . no law enforcement agency shall use a drone to gather evidence or other information.") and KY 14 RS BR 1, Sec.1(3)(". . . no prohibited agency shall use a drone to gather evidence or other information"); ME SP 72, *amends* § 1, 25 MRSA Pt. 12, § 4502.2. ("A law enforcement agency may not operate an unmanned aerial vehicle or collect, disclose or receive information acquired through the operation of an unmanned aerial vehicle . . ."); MD HB 1233, 1-203-1(B)(1) ("Except as provided . . . a law enforcement agency may not use a drone to gather evidence or other information . . ."); MA SB 1664, § 1, *amending* Ch. 272 of GEN. LAWS as 99C(c) and MA HB 1357 ("It is unlawful for a government entity or official to operate an unmanned aerial vehicle except . . ."); MI HB 4455, § 3(3) ("Except as provided . . . a law enforcement agency of this state or political subdivision shall not disclose or receive information acquired through the operation of an unmanned aerial vehicle."); MN HF 1620/ 1706, § 3, Subd. 2 and SF 1506, § 1, Subd. 2. ("A law enforcement agency may not use a drone to gather evidence or other information on individuals) and MN HF 990, § 3, Subd. 2 ("no person may operate in MN airspace an unmanned aircraft that is equipped with a surveillance device"); MO HB 46, § 305.637.2. ("No person, entity or state agency shall use a drone or other unmanned aircraft to gather evidence or other information pertaining to criminal conduct in violation of a statute or regulation except . . ."); MT SB 196, § 1(1) ("In any prosecution or proceeding within the state of Montana, information from an unmanned aerial vehicle is not admissible unless . . ."); NE LB 412, § (3) ("A law enforcement agency shall not use a drone to gather evidence or other information."); NJ Assembly No. 3157, § 2.b. ("No law enforcement agency or officer shall utilize an unmanned aerial system unless . . .") and NJ AB 3929, 1.b. (". . . to conduct surveillance or to gather any evidence or engage in any other law enforcement activity . . ."); NM SB 556, § 3.A.–B. ("A person or state agency shall not use a drone or unmanned aircraft to gather evidence or other information pertaining to criminal conduct . . . except . . ."); NY AO 6370/ SO 4537, § 1, S 52-A.1. ("No law enforcement agency or a state, county or municipal agency shall use a drone or other unmanned aircraft to gather, store or collect evidence of any type, including audio or video recordings, or both, or other information pertaining to criminal conduct . . . except . . ."), NY AO 6244, § 1. S 700.16, ¶ 1 ("No person or entity acting under color of the authority of any state, county, municipal or local governmental entity or authority . . . shall use, operate, engage or employ an unmanned aerial vehicle a . . . to gather evidence or other information related to a criminal investigation . . . except . . .") and NY AO 6541, § 66-A.2 ("except as provided . . . unlawful for an agent of the state . . . to operate an unmanned aerial vehicle, or to disclose or receive information acquired through the operation of an unmanned aerial vehicle . . .); NC HB 312, § 15A-232.(b) ("Except . . . it shall be unlawful for any person or municipal, county, or State law enforcement agency to use a drone for the purpose of gathering evidence or other information or data pertaining to criminal conduct or conduct in violation of a statute or a rule") and NC SB 402, § 7.16(e) ("no State or local government entity . . . may . . . operate an unmanned aircraft system or disclose personal information about any person acquired unless . . .); ND HB 1373, § 2.1. ("Except . . . a law enforcement agency may not use an unmanned aircraft for surveillance of a person with in the state or for the surveillance of personal or business property located within the borders of the state to gather evidence or other information pertaining to criminal conduct . . ."); OH HB 207, § 4561.50(A) ("no law enforcement agency, or any person acting on behalf of . . . shall operate a drone in order to obtain evidence or any other information, except . . ."); OK HB 1556, § 3.A. ("Except . . . it shall be unlawful to operate an unmanned aircraft system for or in connection to surveillance within the state."); OR HB 2710, § 3.(1) and OR SB 524, § 1(2) ("A law enforcement agency may use a drone for the purpose surveillance of a person only if . . ."), OR SB 71 ("A person may not possess or control a drone unless . . ."), OR SB 853 § 2(1) ("Except as otherwise provided . . . a public body may not operate a drone, acquire information through the operation of a drone or disclose information acquired through the operation of a drone."); PA HB 961, *amending* Ch. 57 of tit. 18 of PA. CONS. STAT., Subch. E.1., § 5776(a) permits the Pa. Att'y Gen. to submit an application to the court to use a drone in criminal investigations, pursuant to Pennsylvania's "wiretap" provisions; RI Gen. Assembly Jan. 2013, *amending* tit. 12 of GEN. LAWS, Ch. 5.3, 12-5.3.-2. ("it shall be unlawful for a municipal law enforcement agency, or any individual or entity on such agency's behalf, to operate an unmanned aerial vehicle, or to disclose or receive information acquired through the operation of an unmanned aerial vehicle") and RI LC00564, § 1, § 12-5.3-2(a) ("a law enforcement agency . . . shall first obtain a warrant prior to utilizing a UAV"); SC H 3415, *amending* Ch. 13, tit. 17 of 1976 Code as 17-13-180(b) ("A law enforcement agency many not use a drone, or other substantially similar device, to gather evidence or other information in this State without a legally issued search warrant.") and SC GA Bill 395, § 1, Ch. 39, § 6-39-30(A) ("no law enforcement agency may conduct general surveillance or conduct surveillance of a targeted person or location utilizing an unmanned aerial vehicle"); TN HB 591, § 1(c) ("Notwithstanding any law to the contrary, no law enforcement agency shall use a drone to gather evidence or other information.") and TN SB 470, § 1(c)("Except as provided . . . no law enforcement agency shall use a drone to gather evidence or other information"); TX HB 912, Ch. 423, § 423.003(a) ("A person commits an offense if the person uses or authorizes the use of an unmanned vehicle or aircraft to capture an image without the express consent of the person who owns or occupies the real property captured in the image."); VT HB 540/SB 16, *amending* § 1 20 V.S.A. Ch. 205 as § 4622(a) ("Except . . . a law enforcement agency shall not use a drone for any purpose or disclose or receive information acquired through the operation of a drone."); WA HB 1771, § 3, and WA SB 5782, § 3 ("Except . . . it shall be unlawful to operate a public unmanned aircraft system or disclose personal information about any person acquired through the operation of a public unmanned aircraft system."); WV HB 2732 and WV HB 2948, Art. 7, § 1-7-3 ("A law enforcement agency may not use a drone to gather evidence or other information.") and WV HB 2997, Art. 7, § 1-7-2(a) ("Except as otherwise provided . . . a law enforcement agency may not use an unmanned aircraft for surveillance of a person within the state . . .); WI SB 196/AB 203, § 2, 175.55(2) ("No Wisconsin law enforcement agency may use a drone to gather evidence or other information in a criminal investigation without first obtaining a search warrant."); WY HB 0242, 7-3-1003 ("Except . . . a law enforcement agency shall not use a drone to gather evidence or other information pertaining to criminal conduct . . ."). Two states specifically allow drone use if not for an intelligence or law enforcement purpose: MI HB 4455 § 5, ¶ (e) ("if no evidence derived from the operation is admitted into evidence . . . or [used] for any intelligence purpose") and NC HB 312, § 2(b) ("A person or municipal, county, or State law enforcement agency may use a drone for purposes other than gathering evidence"). Three others, Iowa, Pennsylvania, and Virginia, prohibit drone use, with limited exceptions, prior to July 1, 2015. *See* IA SF 276, 80C.1., PA SB 875, § 3 and VA HB 2012, 1. § 1.

14.   Besides Iowa, Pennsylvania, and Virginia, which prohibit drone use until 2015, only Indiana, Nebraska, and one of the New Jersey and West Virginia bills fail to include a warrant exception. The crux of the Indiana bill is obtaining consent. IN SB 20, § 4(a). The Nebraska bill prohibits law enforcement from using a drone to gather evidence and does not contain a warrant exception. It does, however, include a "terrorist attack" exception. NE LB 412, § 4. Although neither NJ AB 3929 nor WV HB 2948 contains a warrant exception, they both permit drone use for terrorist attacks. NJ also permits use during disasters or emergencies.

15.   *See* AL SB 317, § 1(b)(2)(a); FL SB 92, § 1(4)(a); IA HF 427, § 1.3(a); IL SB 1587, § 15(1); KS HB 2394, § 1(c); KY HB 454, § 1 of KRS Ch. 500, § 1(1)(3)(a); MD HB 1233, 1-203-1(B)(2)(I); MN SF 1506, § 1, Sub. 3(1) and MN HF 990, § 3, Subd. 4(4); NE LB 412, § (4); NJ AB 3929, ¶ 1.c.; NY AO 6370/ SO 4537, § 1, § 52-A.3.A.(4); OH HB 207, § 4561.50(A)(1); SC HB 3415, *amending* Ch. 13, tit. 17 of 1976 Code as 17-13-180.(B)(1); TN HB 591, § 1(d)(1); WV HB 2732, Art. 7, § 1-7-4, WV HB 2948, § 1-7-4; and WY HB 0242, 7-3-1004(a)(ii). ME SP 72, § 4503.1.A.(1)-(2) contains an emergency enforcement exception for threats to national, state, or local security. KS HB 2394, § 1(c) and WV HB 2732, § 1-7-4 require a warrant to use a drone in terrorist attack scenarios.

16.   The DHS electronic publication, *Definition of Terms*, does not contain a definition of "terror," "terrorism," "domestic terrorism" or "attack;" nor does the *DHS Risk Lexicon—2010 Edition. See* http://www.dhs.gov/definition-terms#top and http://www.dhs.gov/xlibrary/assets/dhs-risk-lexicon-2010.pdf, respectively. However, the latter contains examples of domestic terror attacks in its discussion of "attack method" and "attack path." These include weaponization of an aircraft and a car bombing involving dozens of individuals moving money, arms,and operatives from the terrorist safe haven to the target area. DHS RISK LEXICON, p.8. However, JP 1-02 defines "terrorism" as "[t]unlawful use of violence or threat of violence to instill fear and coerce governments or societies. Terrorism is often motivated by religious, political, or other ideological beliefs and committed in the pursuit of goals that are usually political." JP 1-02, p.80.

17.   All the "conspiratorial activities" threatening a national security interest also include "conspiratorial activities characteristic of organized crime": AR HB 1904 § 12-19-104, ¶ (a)(2)(i)(a); HI SB 783 § 1, ¶ 263B-4(1); ME SP 72 § 4504, ¶ 1(A); and MI HB 4455 § 9, ¶ (1)(a).

18.   Joint doctrine defines "national security interest" as "the foundation for the development of valid national objectives that define United States goals or purposes." JP 1-02, p.191. The *U.S. National Security Strategy (NSS)* describes the full range of threats and hazards to the homeland

as including terrorism, natural disasters, large-scale cyber-attacks, and pandemics. NSS, May 2010, http://www.whitehouse.gov/sites/default/files/rss_viewer/national_security_strategy.pdf.

19. Bills that do not contain an imminent danger to life exception include: AK HB 159a; AZ HB 2574; GA HB 560, IN SB 20; KS HB 2394; MT SB 196; NE LB 412; NJ AB 3157; OR SB 71; PA HB 961; RI LC00564; SC GA Bill 395; WV HB 2732; and WV HB 2948. A West Virginia bill and the Kansas bill would allow drones to be used for purposes of an "imminent terrorist attack," but only after obtaining a warrant. KS HB 2394, § 1(c) and WV HB 2732, § 1-7-4.

20. For "danger to life" exceptions, *see* AL SB 317, § 1(b)(2)(c) ("prevent imminent danger to life"); AR HB1904, amending AR Code tit. 12, as 12-19-104(a)(2)(A)(i)(a)(1) ("immediate danger of death or serious physical injury to a person"); CA Assembly Bill 1327, § 1, tit. 14, 14350(c)(1) ("imminent threat to life . . .") and CA Senate Bill No. 15, § 5, *amending* 14352 of Penal Code, ¶ (b) ("exigent circumstances"—undefined) ; FL SB 92, § 1(4)(c) ("swift action is needed to prevent imminent danger to life . . ."); GA SB 200, § 5(e)(1) ("imminent danger to life or bodily harm . . ."); HI SB, 2563B-4(1)(A) (". . . immediate danger of death or serious physical injury to any person . . ."); ID SB 1134, § 1.21-213(2)(a) (". . . emergency response for safety. . ."); IL SB 1587, § 15(3) (to prevent imminent harm to life . . ."); IA SF 276 ("necessary to protect life, health . . ."), IA HF 410, § 2.c. ("during search and rescue operation if . . . necessary to protect life, health"), and IA HF 427, § 3.c. ("to save a person"); KY HB 454, § 1 of KRS Ch. 500(3)(c) (". . . swift action is needed to prevent imminent danger to life . . ."); ME SP 72, *amends* § 1, 25 MRSA Pt. 12, § 4503.1(A)(3) ("threatens life or safety of one or more persons"); MD HB 1233, 1-203-1(B)(2)(II) ("respond to an emergency . . ."); MA SB 1664 and MA HB 1357§ 1, *amending* Ch. 272 of GEN. LAWS as 99C(c)(3) ("reasonable cause to believe that a threat to the life or safety of a person is imminent . . ."); MI HB 4455, § 5(b) (". . . reasonable to believe that there is imminent threat to the life or safety of a person." All MI exceptions apply only to public property. All imaging of private property requires a warrant); MN HF 1620/1706, § 4, Subd. 3(3), MN SF 1506, § 1, Sub 3. ("prevent imminent danger to life"), and MN HF 990, § 1, Subd. 4(5) ("by a public safety agency to prevent imminent serious bodily harm or loss of life"); MO HB 46, § 305.639.1. ("swift action to prevent imminent danger to life is necessary"); NJ AB 3157, ¶ 1.d. ("emergency . . . that endangers the public health, safety, or wellbeing of the citizens and residents of this State"); NM SB 556, § 4. ("reasonable suspicion that, under particular circumstances, swift action is necessary to prevent imminent danger to life"); NY AO 6370/ SO 4537, § 1, S 52-A.1. ("reasonable suspicion that swift action is necessary to prevent imminent danger to life") and NY AO 6541, § 66-A.3.(B) ("imminent threat to the life or safety or a person"); NC HB 312, § 15A-232.(c)(3)(i) ("imminent danger to life"); ND HB 1373, § 3.2. ("reasonable suspicion that absent swift preventative action, there is an imminent danger to life or bodily harm . . ."); OH HB 207, § 4561.50(A)(3) ("to prevent imminent harm to life"); OK HB 1556, § 3.B.3. ("when conducting a search for a mission person, provided it is reasonable to believe that there is an imminent threat to the life or safety of the person"); OR HB 2710, § 1.(2)(b) ("risk of serious physical harm to an individual . . ."), OR SB 524, § 1(2)(b) ("emergency situation in which there is risk of serious physical harm to the individual"), and OR SB 853, § 6(1) ("imminent threat to life or safety of the individual"); PA SB 875, § 4 ("during a search and rescue operation if the deployment is necessary to protect life, health"); RI Gen. Assembly Jan. 2013, *amending* tit. 12 of GEN. LAWS, Ch. 5.3, 12-5.3.-2.(f)(1) ("imminent threat to the life or safety of that person"); SC H 3415, *amending* Ch. 13, tit. 17 of 1976 Code as 17-13-180(B)(3) ("prevent imminent danger to life"); TN HB 591 and TN SB 796, § 1(d)(3) ("necessary to prevent imminent danger to life"); TX HB 912, Ch. 423, § 423.002(a)(12) (". . . rescuing a person whose life is in imminent danger"); VT HB 540/SB 16, *amending* § 1 20 V.S.A. Ch. 205 as

§ 4622(b)(2) ("emergency circumstances . . ."); and WA HB 1771, § 9.(1)(a) and WA SB 5782, § 8(1) (". . . immediate danger of death or (serious) physical injury to any person"; however, requires grounds upon which a warrant could be entered to authorize the operation); WV HB 2997, § 1-7-3(a) ("imminent danger to life or bodily harm") and WI SB 196/AB 203, § 2, 175.55(2) ("to prevent imminent danger to an individual"); NH HB 619 does not contain an explicit "danger to life" exception but its bill was written so as not to be "construed to impair or limit any otherwise lawful activities of law enforcement personnel." *See* § 2.V. Even though the following do not contain an explicit "danger to life" exception, other provisions would fairly embrace it: AR SB 1109 (permits law enforcement to use drones for any purpose) and NY AO 6244 (permits lawful exceptions to the warrant requirement).

21.   Danger to property provisions include: CA AB 1327 § 14350, ¶ (d)(2) ("court order shall not apply in circumstances involving an imminent threat to persons or property"); FL SB 92 § 1, ¶ (4)(c) (drone use not prohibited if reasonable suspicion exists that "swift action is needed to prevent . . . serious damage to property"); GA SB 200 § 5(e)(2) (protection of property is an "exigent circumstance" granting law enforcement use of drones); IL SB 1587, § 15, ¶ (3) ("to prevent . . . serious damage to property"); IA SB 276 § 11, ¶ (b) ("to protect life, health, or property"), IA HF 410, § 1.2.c. (protection of property as part of SAR) and IA HF 427, § 1.2.c. ("prevent serious damage to property"); KY HB 454 § 1, ¶ 3(c) ("needed to prevent . . . serious damage to property"); MD HB 1233 § 1-203, ¶ (B)(II) ("Respond to an emergency"); MN HF 1620 § 3, Sub. 4, ¶ (3) and MN HF 990, § 3, Subd. 4(5) ("prevent . . . serious damage to property"); NC HB 312 § 2(c)(3) ("immediate action is needed to prevent . . . serious damage to property"); ND HB 1373 § 3.3. (". . . to . . . protect property"); OH HB 207, § 4561.50(A)(3) ("prevent serious damage to property"); SC H3415 § 2, ¶ (B)(3) ("prevent . . . serious damage to property"); OR HB 853, § 8(1) (to protect property during declared emergency); PA SB 875, § 4 (protect property); and TX HB 912 § 423.002 (contains numerous "non-applicability" paragraphs aimed at protecting property including utilities, oil wells, vegetation, etc.).

22.   Public land exception bills include: AK HB 159 § 2, ¶ (b)(3) ("to monitor public land"); AZ HB 2574 § 1, ¶ D(2) (law enforcement actively engaged in enforcement on public lands); IL SB 1587 § 15, ¶ (5) ("on lands, highways, roadways, or areas belonging to this State"); MI HB 4455 § 9(1) ("shall only . . . target public property"), MT SB 196 § 2, ¶ (2)(B) ("to monitor public lands"); OK HB 1556 § 3(B)(6) ("when conducting exclusively on public land"); and TX HB 912, Ch. 423, § 423.002(a)(15)–(16) ("without magnification or other enhancement from no more than six feet above ground level in a public place of public real property or a person on that property"). OK allows drones to transit public land (overflight), including for military aircraft carrying weapons. OK HB 1556, § 4.A. AK and TX, which permit drone use over public lands, also allow their use to monitor borders. AK HB 159 § 2, ¶ (b)(3) and TX HB 912, Ch. 423, § 423.002(a)(14). Other states that allow drone border monitoring include NYS 4537 § 1, ¶ 3.A(3), and ND HB 1373 § 3, ¶ 1.

23.   Sixteen bills include a "fleeing felon" exception, which would allow law enforcement officers to pursue suspects or escaped prisoners: AL SB 317 § 1, ¶ (a)2(c) ("to forestall the imminent escape of a suspect"); CA AB 1327, § 1, tit. 14, § 14350(c) ("hot pursuit" where there is "imminent threat to life") and CA HB No. 15, amending PENAL CODE § 14352(b) ("exigent circumstances"); FL SB 92 § 1, ¶ (4)(c) ("to forestall the imminent escape of a suspect"); IL SB 1587 § 15 (3) ("to forestall the imminent escape of a suspect"); KY HB 454 § 1, ¶ 3(c) ("to forestall the imminent escape of a suspect"); IA HF 427, § 1.3.c. ("prevent the imminent escape of a suspect"); MN HB 1620 § 1, Sub. 3 ("to forestall the imminent escape of a suspect") and MN HF 990, § 3, Subd. 4(5)(iii) ("prevent imminent . . . escape of a suspect"); NC HB 312 § 2, ¶ (c)(3)(iii) (prevent the "imminent escape of a suspect"); OH HB 207, § 4561.50(A)(3)

("forestall the imminent escape of a suspect"); SC H 3415, § 2, ¶ (B)(3) ("to forestall the imminent escape of a suspect"); TN SB 796, § 1(d)(4) ("searching for a fugitive or escapee"); TX HB 912, Ch. 423, § 423.002(8)(A) ("in immediate pursuit of a person law enforcement officers have probable cause to suspect has committed a felony"); WI SB 196/AB 203, § 2, 175.55(2) ("to locate an escaped prisoner"); WY HB 242 § 1, ¶ 7-3-1004(a)(iv) ("in immediate pursuit of a person law enforcement officers have reasonable suspicion or probable cause to suspect has committed an offense, not including misdemeanors . . ."). Depending on interpretation, the following additional state bills may apply to fleeing suspects: CA AB 1327 § 14350, ¶ (c) ("emergency situations"); ID SB 1134 § 1, ¶ 21-213(2) (". . . emergency response to for safety"); MD HB 1233 § 1-203.1(B)(2)(II) (emergency exception likely to encompass fleeing suspect); and ND HB 1373 § 3, ¶ 3 ("exigent circumstances"). Eleven bills provide a carve-out to prevent the destruction of evidence and all use the same language, "to forestall (or prevent) . . . the destruction of evidence." *See* FL SB 92, § 1(3)(c); IL SB 1587, § 15(3); IA HF 427, § 1.3.c.; KY HB 454, § 1(3)(c); MN HF 1620/ 1706, § 3, Sub. 4(3) and MN HF 990, § 3, Subd. 4(5)(iv); ND HB 1373, § 2(c)(3)(iv) (adds the qualifier "imminent"); OH HB 207, § 4561.50(A)(3); SC H 3415, § 2.(B)(3), and WI SB 196/AB 203, § 2, 175.55(2). Only Alaska, California, Illinois, Montana, New York, and Tennessee contain explicit provisos to permit drone use where any judicially recognized exceptions to the warrant requirement would apply. AK HB 159a, *amending* § 2(b)(2) ("in accordance with judicially recognized exception to the warrant requirement"); CA SB No. 15, § 5, *amending* 14352 of Penal Code, ¶ (b)("where there is an exception to the search warrant requirement"); IL SB 1587, § 30 (State may overcome presumption of inadmissibility by proving judicially recognized exception to the exclusionary rule of the Fourth Amendment . . .); MT SB 196, § 1(1)(b)("in accordance with judicially recognized exceptions to the warrant requirement . . ."); NY AO 6244, § 1.1 ("or justified by lawful exception to the warrant requirement"); and TN SB 796, § 1(g)(2) ("absent exigent circumstances or another authorized exception to the warrant requirement" evidence obtained in violation inadmissible).

24. Bills with consent provisions include: AK HB 159a, *amending* § 2(b)(4) ("to monitor private land with the consent of the landowner"); AZ HB 2574, *amending* § 1, tit. 13, Ch. 30 ARS, 13-3007, § D.2. (". . . enforcement . . . on public lands . . . or on private land with the written permission from the landowner"); AR HB1904, *amending* AR Code tit. 12, as 12-19-104(a)(1) ("operating lawfully and a person about whom information was acquired by the unmanned aerial vehicle consents to the disclosure of the information . . ."); HI SB, 263B-2(c)(1) (". . . Consent. It shall not be unlawful under this chapter to disclose or receive information about any person acquired through the operation of an unmanned aerial vehicle if such person has given written consent to such disclosure."); ID SB 1134, § 1.21-213(2)(a)(i)–(ii) (". . . an individual or a dwelling owned by an individual and such dwelling's curtilage, without such individual's written consent; A farm, dairy, ranch or other agricultural industry without the written consent of the owner of such farm, dairy, ranch or other agricultural industry. . ."); IL SB 1586, § 15(5)("lawful consent to search" on private property); IN SB 20, § 4(a) ("A person may not make use of an unmanned aerial vehicle without the written consent of: the person or the owner of the property or thing that is the subject of the use."); ME SP 72, *amends* § 1, 25 MRSA Pt. 12, § 4502.2(B) ("To collect, disclose or receive information about a person or the person's property or area if that person has given written consent"); MA SB 1664, § 1(e) (relating to incidentally acquired information, "data collected on an individual, home, or area other than the target that justified deployment shall not be used, stored, copied, transmitted or disclosed for any purpose, except with the written consent of the data subject . . ."); MI HB 4455, § 5(a) (". . . shall not be disclosed or received unless . . . the person has given written consent to the disclosure"); MN HF 1620/ 1706, § 2, Sub 2. (applying to private use of drones—"felony . . . if . . . without the permission of

the individual and the owner of the private property or appropriate public authority." Consent is not mentioned regarding "agency" use of drones.); MO HB 46, § 305.637.2. (". . . to conduct surveillance of any individual, property owned by an individual, farm or agricultural industry without the consent of that individual, property owner, farm or agricultural industry "); NM SB 556, § 3.A. (". . . to conduct surveillance of any individual, property owned by an individual, farm or agricultural industry without the consent of that individual, property owner, farm or agricultural industry"); OK HB 1556, § 3.B.5 ("Any agency, person, organization, when acting on the informed and freely given consent of the person or organization whose person or property are the subject of the surveillance, provided the consent is made in writing prior to the commencement of surveillance"); OR HB 2710, § 4 and SB 853, § 5 (written consent); and TX HB 912, Ch. 423, § 423.002(6) ("consent of the individual who owns or lawfully occupies the real property captured in the image"). Consent would presumably be implied for state bills containing a proviso allowing drone use in accordance with judicially recognized exceptions to the warrant requirement. Massachusetts and New York bills contain provisions that permit dissemination or receipt of information only with the individual's consent. MA SB 1664/BH 1357, § 99-C(e) (relating to incidental information collected) and NYAO 6541, § 66-A.3.(A) (relating to any person targeted).

25.   Disaster response clauses can be found at: CA Assembly Bill 1327, § 14350(c)(1) and (e)(1)–(2) (law enforcement/ CAL-FIRE/other agencies can use for fires; other agencies can use for detecting oil spills); GA SB 200 § 5, ¶ (e)(2) ("to preserve public safety, protect property or conduct surveillance for the assessment and evaluation of environmental or weather related damage, erosion, flooding, or contamination during a lawfully declared state of emergency"); IA SF 276, ("during the occurrence of a disaster . . ."); ME SP 72, § 4503.2.(A), (B), (D) (natural disasters, monitor dams and flood-control systems and weather forecasting); MN HF 1620 § 3, Sub. 4, ¶ (4) (first responder may use in emergency situation) and MN HF 440, § 3, Subd.4 (6) ("during a declared state of emergency"); NJ Assembly No. 3157, ¶ 4 ("to survey or monitor the extent of a forest fire") and NJ AB 3929, § 1.d. ("during any declared disaster or emergency to monitor, observe, photograph or record . . ."); OR HB 2710, § 5(3) and OR SB 853, § 8(1) (during a declared state of emergency to assess environmental, weather damage, erosion or contamination); TX HB 912, § 423.001(c)(3) ("fire suppression"); PA SB 85, § 5(3) and VA HB 2012, 1. § 1 (National Guard drone exception for "purposes other than law enforcement including damage assessment . . . flood stages, and wildfire assessment"); and WV HB 2997, § 1-7-3(b) (survey environmental damage to determine if state of emergency should be declared or assess environmental, weather damage, erosion, or contamination). For SAR clauses, *see* CA AB 1327 § 14350, ¶ (c)(1); FL SB 92 § 1, ¶ (4)(c); ID SB 1134, § 21-213, ¶ (2); IL SB 1587, § 15(4); IA SB 276 § 12 and IA HF 410, § 2.c.; ME SP 72, § 4503.2.E.; OK HB 1556 § 3.3; OR HB 2710, § 5(1); PA SB 875, § 4; TN SB 796, § 1(d)(5); TX HB 912 § 423.002(8)(D); VA H 2012 § 1, ¶ (iv) and WI SB 196/AB 203, § 2(2). Of these, some require an imminent danger to life before a drone can be used for SAR. *See, e.g.*, CA AB 1327 § 14350, ¶ (c)(1) ("imminent threat to life or of great bodily harm, including, but not limited to . . . search and rescue operations on land and water"); IA HF 410, § 2.c. ("during search and rescue operation if . . . necessary to protect life, health"); OK HB 1556, § 3.B.3. ("when conducting a search for a mission person, provided it is reasonable to believe that there is an imminent threat to the life or safety of the person"), PA SB 875, § 4 ("during a search and rescue operation if the deployment is necessary to protect life, health"); VA H 2012 § 1, ¶ (iv) ("for the purpose of a search and rescue operation where use of an unmanned system is determined to be necessary to alleviate an immediate danger to any person").

26.   IL SB 1587, § 15(5) (crime scenes); OR HB 2710, § 6(1) and OR SB 853, § 7(1) (crime scene reconstruction) and TX HB 912, § 423.002(8)(B)-(C) (crime scene investigation and reconstruction).

27.   CA AB 1327 § 14350, ¶ (d)(2) ("maximum duration not to exceed two hours"); GA HB 560, § 2(a)(4) (warrant "shall expire within 24 hours after issuance"); HI SB 783 § 1, ¶ (3)(B) (can receive a judicial order to operate drone for "no period greater than 48 hours" and within 30 days of issuance); IL SB 1587, § 15(3) (emergency operations limited to 48 hours); ME SP 72, § 4502.2. D (court order . . . "may not allow operation for a period greater than 48 hours" . . . but not to exceed 30 days); MI HB 4455 § 5(d) (court orders valid for 48 hours, with possibility of extension up to 30 days); NC HB 312 § 2(3) ("no later than 48 hours" from the date drone was used); and WA HB 1771 § 6.(4) and SB 5782, § 8(1)(c) ("Warrants shall not be issued for a [surveillance] period greater than 48 hours . . . for no longer than 30 days.")

28.   For place restrictions, *see* AZ HB 2574, *amending* § 1, tit. 13, Ch. 30 ARS, 13-3007, § B ("unlawful for a person to use drones to monitor other persons inside their homes or places of worship or within the close confines of their property or other locations where a person would have an expectation of privacy"); CA SB No. 15, § 3(j) (drone shall not be used to view "the interior of a bedroom, bathroom, changing room, fitting room, dressing room or tanning booth, or the interior of any other area in which the occupant has a reasonable expectation of privacy, with the intent to invade the privacy"); HI SB, 2563B-2(c)(3)(A)–(B) (warrants required for "non-public" areas; public areas require court orders); ID SB 1134, § 1., 21-213(2)(A)(i)(ii) (requires warrant or consent for imaging a "dwelling owned by an individual . . . dwelling's curtilage" and "farm, dairy, ranch, or other agricultural industry"); NM SB 556, § 3.B. (no "surveillance of an individual, or of property owned by an individual, farm or other agricultural industry" without consent); NY AO 6370/ SO 4537, § 1, S 52-A.2. (No . . . drone . . . to conduct surveillance of or to monitor any individual inside his or her home or place of worship or within the closed confines of their property or other locations where a person would have an expectation of privacy"); and ND HB 1373, § 6.4. (no surveillance "within a home or place" unless in compliance with state intercept statutes).

29.   Manner restrictions with an emphasis on collecting data only on the target include: AR HB 1904, *amending* AR Code tit. 12, as 12-19-104(b)(1) ("in a manner to collect data only on the target and to avoid data collection on individuals, homes, or areas other than the target"); CA SB 15, tit. 14, § 14354(a) ("minimize the collection and retention of data"); HI SB, 263B-2(d) ("collect only on the target"); ME SP 72, *amends* § 1, 25 MRSA Pt. 12, § 4502.3 ("do not collect information on a person, residence, property or area not related to a permitted purpose . . ."); MA SB 1664, § 1, *amending* Ch. 272 of GEN. LAWS as 99C(d)(1) and (3) ("in a manner to collect data only on the warrant subject and to avoid data collection on individuals, homes, or areas other than the warrant subject"); MI HB 4455 § 5(e) ("avoid data collection on individuals, homes, or areas other than the target"); NC HB 312, § 15A-232.(d) ("in a manner to collect data only on the subject of the search and to avoid data collection on individuals, homes, or areas other than the subject of the search"); NY AO 6541, § 66-A.4. ("collect data only on the target and to avoid data collection in individuals, homes or areas other than the target"); OK HB 1556, § 3.F ("in a manner to collect data only on the target of the surveillance and to avoid data collection on individuals, homes, or areas other than the target"); OR HB 2710, § 1.(4) ("limited to collection of information about the target person . . . and must avoid collection . . . on other persons, residences or places") and OR SB 524, § 1(4) (limit collection to target); RI Gen. Assembly Jan. 2013, *amending* tit. 12 of GEN. LAWS, Ch. 5.3, 12-5.3.-2.(h) ("collect data only on the designated target and shall avoid data collection on individuals, homes or areas of than the target"); VT HB 540/SB 16, *amending* § 1 20 V.S.A. Ch. 205 as § 4622(c)(1) ("collect data only on the target of

the surveillance and to avoid data collection on any other person, home or area"); WA HB 1771, § 4 ("conducted in such a way as to minimize the collection and disclosure of personal information not authorized under this chapter"). Some states contain unique "one off" manner restrictions or constraints. For example, GA SB 200, § 5(c) allows drones to be used only in the investigation of a felony. IL SB 1587, § 15(5) allows drone use just for crime-scene photography over public highways.

30. MA SB 1664, § 1, *amending* Ch. 272 of GEN. LAWS as 99C(d)(3) ("under no circumstances used . . . to collect . . . about the political, religious or social views, associations or activities of any individual, group, association or organization," . . . etc., unless criminal investigation); ND HB 1373, § 4.3 and WV HB 2997, § 1-7-4(c) (may not use . . . "for surveillance of persons engaged in the lawful exercise of the constitutional right to freedom of speech and freedom of assembly").

31. Biometrics is addressed in: AR HB1904, *amending* AR Code tit. 12, as 12-19-104(b)(3); HI SB, 2563B-2(d) ("Neither facial recognition or other biometric matching technology may be used on non-target data collected."); MA SB 1664, § 1, *amending* Ch. 272 of GEN. LAWS as 99C(d)(2) ("facial recognition or other biometric matching technology shall not be used on data collected . . . except to identify the subject of a warrant"); MI HB 4455 § 5(e) ("Neither facial recognition or other biometric matching technology shall be used on non-target data collected"); NC HB 312, § 15A-232.(d) ("Neither facial recognition or other biometric matching technology may be used . . . on individuals, homes or areas other than the subject of the search"); NY AO 6541, § 66-A.4 ("neither facial recognition nor other biometric matching technology shall be used on non-target data"); OR SB 853, § 4.1 (no facial recognition or biometric matching technology on non-targets); RI Gen. Assembly Jan. 2013, *amending* tit. 12 of GEN. LAWS, Ch. 5.3, 12-5.3.-2.(h) ("Neither facial recognition or other biometric matching technology shall be used on non-target data."); VT HB 540/SB 16, *amending* § 1 20 V.S.A. Ch. 205 as § 4622(c)(3) ("Facial recognition or any other biometric matching technology shall not be used on . . . other than the target . . ."); and WA HB 1771, § 6(3) (warrants shall "not authorize the use of a biometric identification system").

32. ME SP 72, § 4502.3 ("may not . . . employ the use of facial recognition technology").

33. CA SB No. 15, § 5, *amending* PENAL CODE 14353(b) (prohibits law enforcement from receiving drone information from another agency unless they obtain warrant); CA AO 1327, § 14350(e)(3) ("no dissemination outside collecting agency"; no dissemination to LEA unless they obtain a warrant); IL SB 1587, § 25 (no disclosure except to another government agency if evidence of criminal activity or relevant to ongoing investigation or trial); MA HB 1357, § 99C(e) (no disclosure of non-target information for any purpose without written consent); WV HB 2997, § 1-7-6(c) (no distribution unless there is evidence of a crime and complies with evidentiary rules).

34. For notice to subject provisions, *see* HI SB, 2563B-5 (may request a delay on notification up to 90 days); ME SP 72 *amends* § 1, 25 MRSA Pt. 12, § 4504.3 (may request a delay on notification up to 10 days); MA SB 1664, § 1, *amending* Ch. 272 of GEN. LAWS as 99C(g) and HB 1357, § 99C(h) (delay not to exceed 90 days; otherwise, serve notice within 7 days); MI HB 4455 § 11(1) (delay not to exceed 90 days, with possibility of 90-day extensions and delivery upon termination); OR SB 853, § 9(1) and (3) (notice to subject 10 days post-collection, can delay up to 10 days); RI Gen. Assembly Jan. 2013, *amending* tit. 12 of GEN. LAWS, Ch. 5.3, 12-5.3.-7 (not later than 10 days after the termination of an order, the subject shall be served with information on data collected); WA HB 1771, § 6.(4) and WA SB 5782, § 6(5) (within 10 days of execution, serve a copy of warrant upon the person—may be delayed under § 7).

35. The requirement to delete information on non-targets is located in AR HB1904, *amending* AR Code tit. 12, as 12-19-105 (data on non-targets not to be used or disclosed and must be deleted within 24 hours after collection); HI SB, 263B-3(a) (data on non-targets not to be used or disclosed and must be deleted within 24 hours after collection); ME SP 72 *amends* § 1, 25 MRSA Pt. 12, § 4503 (noncompliant information must be deleted within 24 hours); MA SB 1664/MA HB 1357, § 1, *amending* Ch. 272 of GEN. LAWS as 99C(e) (data on non-targets not to be used or disclosed and deleted within 24 hours after collection); MI HB 4455 § 7(1) (data on non-targets not to be used or disclosed and deleted within 24 hours after collection); NY AO 6541, § 66-B (delete non-target data within 24 hours); NJ Assembly No. 3157, § 2.d. (information incidentally collected "shall be discarded"); NC HB 312, § 15A-232(g) (if collected in violation of Act, must be destroyed within 24 hours); ND HB 1373, § 6.2 (information in violation of Act "may not be preserved); OK HB 1556, § 3.F (data on non-targets not to be used or disclosed and deleted within one week after collection); RI Gen. Assembly Jan. 2013, *amending* tit. 12 of GEN. LAWS, Ch. 5.3, 12-5.3.-11 (data on non-targets not to be used or disclosed and deleted within 24 hours after collection); TN SB 796, § 1(f) (non-target data to be deleted "as soon as possible" but not later than 24 hours after collection); VT HB 540/SB 16, *amending* § 1 20 V.S.A. Ch. 205 as § 4622(c)(2)(A)–(B) (data on non-targets not to be used or disclosed and must be deleted within 24 hours after collection); WA HB 1771/WA SB 5782, § 11 (data on non-targets not to be used or disclosed and must be deleted within 24 hours after collection); WV HB 2997, § 1-7-6(b) (evidence in violation of bill "may not be preserved").

36. Retention limits on target information can be found in: CA Assembly Bill 1327, § 1, tit. 14, 14353(a) ("Images . . . shall be permanently destroyed within 10 days except . . . as evidence of a crime, as part of an ongoing investigation of a crime, for training purposes" or if collected pursuant to a warrant); CA SB No. 15, § 5, *amending* 14354 of PENAL CODE, ¶ (a) ("minimize . . . retention of data," destroy after one year unless needed for crime investigation, "training purposes" or pursuant to a court order); IL SB 1587, § 20 (destroy within 30 days unless contains evidence of a crime, as part of an ongoing investigation, or needed for pending criminal trial); ND HB 1373, § 6.3 (90-day limit unless meets agency guidelines for evidence preservation criminal cases); OR HB 2710, § 1.(4) and OR SB 524, § 1(5) ("any images . . . must be destroyed within 30 days" unless needed as evidence); TN SB 796, § 1(f) (delete target information within 24 hours); WA HB 1771/WA SB 5782, § 12 (target information, 30-day retention unless "evidence of criminal activity"); WV HB 2997, § 1-7-6(c) (90-day limitation unless there is evidence of a crime and meets evidentiary rules).

37. States with post-emergency documentation requirements include: AR HB1904, *amending* AR Code tit. 12, as 12-19-104(a)(2)(B) (file for warrant for emergency use of drones within 48 hours); HI SB, 263B-4(a)(4) (file for warrant or order for emergency use of drones within 48 hours); IL SB 1587, § 15(3) (law enforcement agency chief executive officer must report emergency use to state attorney within 24 hours); ME SP 72, § 4503.1.B ("not later than 48 hours after the emergency operation begins, a supervisory official for the law enforcement agency files a sworn statement setting forth the grounds for the emergency operation"); MA SB 1664, § 1, *amending* Ch. 272 of GEN. LAWS as 99C(c)(3) (operator must document factual basis and file an affidavit not later than 48 hours later); MI HB 4455, § 5(b)(i)–(ii) (supervisory official files sworn statement containing factual basis for emergency within 48 hours after operation); MN HF 990, § 3, Subd. 5 (file detailed record of operation exercising "exception" with AG within 48 hours); NC HB 312, § 15A-232(c)(3) (supervisory official files sworn statement with clerk of the court containing factual basis for emergency within 48 hours after operation); OK HB 1556, § 3.B.3. ("reasonable articulable basis for belief . . . in a written sworn statement shall be placed in a written, sworn statement within 24 hours and . . . maintained by LEA" and by

firefighting and emergency services); OR SB 853, § 6(2) (file sworn statement with circuit court within 48 hours of emergency operation); RI Gen. Assembly Jan. 2013, *amending* tit. 12 of GEN. LAWS, Ch. 5.3, 12-5.3.-2(f)(2) (supervisory official files written statement with approval of AG to court of competent jurisdiction no later than 24 hours after operation); VT HB 540/SB 16, *amending* § 1 20 V.S.A. Ch. 205 as § 4623(a)(2) (requires law enforcement agency to obtain warrant within 48 hours after emergency commenced); and WA HB 1771 § 6./WA HB 5782, § 8(c) (requires warrant within 48 hours after operation begins or has occurred). Oversight and reporting requirements can be found in AR HB1904, *amending* AR Code tit. 12, as 12-19-106 (law enforcement agency shall file yearly reports with Legislative Council with the number of crime investigations aided by the use of drones, description of how they were helpful, number other uses and how they were helpful, frequency and type of data collected on non-targeted individuals/areas, and total cost of the program); CA AB 1327, § 14351(a) (annual reports to governor on drone purchases and details of deployments); HI SB, 263B-7 (same as AR plus reporting for judges and court administrative directors on warrants and court orders issued and denied, convictions garnered, etc.); IL SB 1587, § 35 (law enforcement agency report to criminal justice information authority annually the number of drones it owns); ME SP 72, *amends* § 1, 25 MRSA Pt. 12, § 4507 (same as AR, also includes provisions for AG reporting); MA SB 1664, § 1, *amending* Ch. 272 of GEN. LAWS as 99C(i)/MA HB 1357(i) (judges report annually to court administrator on drone warrants issued or denied; court administer to transmit compiled report to legislature annually); MI HB 4455, § 15(1)–(3) (requires operators to report biannually to legislature on public website same information as AR plus specific flight parameters; also requires extensive judiciary and AG reporting, including affidavit that no existing data violates the Act); NY AO 6541, § 66-D (annual public website reports of times used, crimes aided, collection on non-targets, and cost); NC HB 312, § 15A-232(h) (annual reporting from judiciary to Administrative Office of Courts, and then to General Assembly—law enforcement agency to which warrant was issued, offense, and nature of facilities or property searched); OR SB 71 § 4(1) (requires drone registration with state police, presumed reportable), OR SB 853, § 10 and OR 2710, § 8 (both require drone registration with OR Dep't of Aviation and annual public reporting of use of drones by public bodies); (RI Gen. Assembly Jan. 2013, *amending* tit. 12 of GEN. LAWS, Ch. 5.3, 12-5.3.-12 (AG reports to General Assembly annually number of times drone used, justification, number of persons upon whom information was gathered, reasons used for other than criminal, number of times collections made on non-targets, orders granted and denied, and number of resultant convictions); TX HB 912, § 423.008 (reporting every other year by law enforcement agency to governor on times used, crimes aided, collection on non-targets, and cost); VT HB 540/SB 16, *amending* § 1 20 V.S.A. Ch. 205 as § 4625 (law enforcement agency reports annually to Dep't of Public Safety number of times drone used, rationale, number of investigations aided and arrests made, numbers of collections on non-targets, and cost of program; report to legislature; also administrative judge reports annually applications and issuance of warrants); WA HB 1771, § 15-18 and 21 and WA SB 5782, § 15-18 (extensive reporting requirements and annual "comprehensive audit" by governing body of locality; WA SB 5782 adds requirement to report on public website). For record-keeping requirements, *see* ME SP 72, *amends* § 1, 25 MRSA Pt. 12, § 4506.4 (law enforcement agency to keep records of each operation, including all information to be otherwise reported by the AG); ND HB 1373, § 7 (all persons shall document drone flights—duration, flight path, mission objectives, etc., and retain for 5 years); WA HB 1771, § 20 (requires ordinances for law enforcement agency to maintain records of each drone use); WV HB 2997, § 1-7-7 (document all surveillance flights as to duration, flight path, mission objectives, and authorizing officials; retain for 5 years).

38.   CA Assembly Bill 1327, § 1, tit. 14, 14352 ("shall provide reasonable notice to the public . . . minimum . . . a one-time announcement of . . . intent to deploy . . . and a description of technology's capabilities") and § 14352 ("images . . . shall be open to public inspection . . . unless expressly exempt by law") and CA SB No. 15, *amending* PENAL CODE 14354(c) ("reasonable notice to the public of acquisition" of drone); IL SB 1587, § 35 (public website listing law enforcement agencies that own drones and number they own); ME SP 72, *amends* § 1, 25 MRSA Pt. 12, § 4507.3 (AG annual posting to website number of applications for warrants/ court orders and delays of notice granted and denied); NJ Assembly No. 3157, § 3.a. (law enforcement agency must provide public notice of purchases of UAS, including price paid, size and supplier); NY AO 6541, § 66-D (annual public website reports); NC HB 312, § 15A-232.(h) (administrative office of courts will post drone reports on its website); OR SB 853, § 10 and OR 2710, § 8 (annual public reporting of use of drones by public bodies), and WA HB 1771, §§ 19–21 ("publically (sic) available written policies and procedures" for law enforcement agencies' use of drones; audits publicly available) and WA SB 5782, §§ 15–18 (post reports on public website). *See also* OR SB 524, § 1(7)(a) and SB 853, § 11 (1) (must establish written training for operators, criteria for when drones will be used, description of areas in which they may be used, and procedures for informing the public on policies); VA HB 2012, 1. § 1.1 (VA Dept. of Criminal Justice and Office of AG to develop "model protocols for use of UAS by LEA and report findings to the Governor and General Assembly" by Nov. 1, 2013).

39.   CA Senate Bill No. 15, § 5, *amending* 14356 of PENAL CODE ("painted and labeled in a way that provides high visibility of the unmanned aircraft system"); MI HB 4455, § 3(5) (requiring drones to have the name of the owning political entity clearly printed with visible lettering on it).

40.   The following bills create civil liability for drone users who violate state provisions: AZ HB 2574, *amending* § 1, tit. 13, Ch. 30 ARS, 13-3007, § E ("civil action against a law enforcement agency (LEA) to obtain all appropriate relief in order to prevent, restrain, or remedy a violation of this section"); CA Assembly Bill 1327, § 1, tit. 14, 14352 (personal liability) and CA SB 15, § 2, *amending* § 1708.8 of CIVIL CODE (creates several civil actions for actual or constructive invasion of privacy and imaging "familial activity"); FL SB 92, § 1(5) ("civil action against an LEA to obtain all appropriate relief in order to prevent, restrain or remedy a violation of this act"); ID SB 1134, § 1, 21-213(3)(a) ("civil cause of action against the person, entity or state agency"); IA HF 427, § 1.4 (civil action "to prevent or remedy"); KS HB 2394 § 1(d) ("civil cause of action" against LEA); KY HB 454, § 4 (civil action against "to obtain all appropriate relief in order to prevent or remedy"); ME SP 72, *amends* § 1, 25 MRSA Pt. 12, § 4505 (private civil action "for legal or equitable relief" against LEA); MD HB 1233, 1-203-1(C) (civil action against "to obtain all appropriate relief in order to prevent or remedy"); MN HF SF 1506, § 1, Sub. 4 ("civil action") and MN 1620/1706, § 3, Sub. 5 ("civil action" against an LEA "to obtain all appropriate relief in order to prevent or remedy") and MN HF 990, § 1, Subd. 6(b) (civil action against LEA or agency to recover damages, injunctive or appropriate relief); MO HB 46, § 305.641.1 and .3 ("to obtain all appropriate relief in order to prevent or remedy"; "sovereign immunity is waived"); NE LB 412, § 4 ("civil action against a LEA to obtain all appropriate relief in order to prevent or remedy"); NJ AO 3929, § 2 (civil action against LEA); NM SB 556, § 5.A. (civil action "to obtain all appropriate relief in order to prevent or remedy a violation"); NY AO 6370/SO 4537, § 1, S 52-A.4.C. ("civil action against a LEA to obtain all appropriate relief in order to prevent, restrain, or remedy") and NY AO 6244, § 1. S 700.16, ¶ 3 ("may seek civil and equitable relief for a violation"); NC HB 312, § 15A-232.(e) ("civil action"); ND HB 1373, § 4 ("civil action to obtain all appropriate relief to prevent or remedy"); OH HB 207, § 4561.50(C) (civil action for damages); OK HB 1556, § 3.D. ("civil action against responsible party"); OR

HB 2710, § 14–15 (liability for taking control of FAA-licensed or U.S. Armed Forces–operated drone; liability for flying less than 400 feet over private property), OR SB 71, §§ 5–6 (strict liability for injuries caused by drone operation; liability for gaining unauthorized control over a drone); RI Gen. Assembly Jan. 2013, *amending* tit. 12 of GEN. LAWS, Ch. 5.3, 12-5.3.-10. (civil cause of action); SC H 3415, § 2(C) (civil action to prevent or remedy); TN HB 591, § 1(e) (civil action "to obtain all appropriate relief in order to prevent or remedy a violation"); TX HB 912, Ch. 423, § 423.006(2)–(3) (civil action to recover civil penalties); WA HB 1771, § 13 ("legal action for damages"); WV HB 2732, Art. 7, § 1-7-5. ("civil action against LEA to obtain all appropriate relief in order to prevent or remedy a violation") and WV HB 2997, § 1-7-5 ("all appropriate relief to prevent or remedy").

41. Injunctive relief provisions include: AL SB 317, § 1(c) ("civil action . . . to prevent"); AZ HB 2574, *amending* § 1, tit. 13, Ch. 30 ARS, 13-3007, § E ("civil action against a law enforcement agency to obtain all appropriate relief in order to prevent"); CA Assembly Bill 1327, § 1, tit. 14, 14352 (personal liability . . . person imaged without consent may seek "injunction prohibiting use of images . . .") and CA SB No. 15, § 2(h) ("an injunction and restraining order"); FL SB 92, § 1(5) ("civil action against a LEA to obtain all appropriate relief in order to prevent, restrain or remedy a violation of this act"); IA HF 427, § 1.4 (civil action "to prevent or remedy"); KS HB 2394 § 1(d) (equitable relief); KY HB 454, § 4 (civil action against "to obtain all appropriate relief in order to prevent or remedy"); ME SP 72, *amends* § 1, 25 MRSA Pt. 12, § 4506 (private or AG-initiated civil action "for legal or equitable relief"); MD HB 1233, 1-203-1(C) (civil action against "to obtain all appropriate relief in order to prevent or remedy"); MN 1620/ 1706, § 3, Sub. 5 ("civil action" against an LEA "to obtain all appropriate relief in order to prevent or remedy"); MO HB 46, § 305.641.1 ("to obtain all appropriate relief in order to prevent or remedy"); NM SB 556, § 5.A. (civil action "to obtain all appropriate relief in order to prevent or remedy a violation"); NJ AO 3929, § 2 (includes equitable or injunctive relief); NY AO 6370/ SO 4537, § 1, S 52-A.4.C. ("civil action against a LEA to obtain all appropriate relief in order to prevent, restrain, or remedy") and NY AO 6244, § 1. S 700.16, ¶ 3 ("may seek civil and equitable relief for a violation"); ND HB 1373, § 4 ("civil action to obtain all appropriate relief in order to prevent or remedy"); SC H 3415, § 2(C) (civil action to prevent or remedy); TX HB 912, Ch. 423, § TX HB 912, Ch. 423, § 423.006(1) (civil action to enjoin violation or imminent violation"); WA HB 1771, § 13 ("legal action for damages"); WV HB 2732, Art. 7, § 1-7-5 ("civil action against LEA to obtain all appropriate relief in order to prevent or remedy a violation") and WV HB 2997, § 1-7-5 ("all appropriate relief to prevent or remedy").

42. A few examples of civil damages provisions include: CA Assembly Bill 1327, § 1, tit. 14, 14352(b) (personal liability . . . liquidated damages of $5000 for each day of surveillance and any actual damages in excess of that amount") and CA SB No. 15, § 2(c) ("liable up to three times the amount of any general or special damages proximately caused," punitive damages, and a fine between $5,000 and $50,000); ID SB 1134, § 1., 21-213(3)(b) ("damages in the amount of the greater of $1,000 or actual and general damages, plus reasonable attorney's fees and other litigation costs reasonably incurred"); KS HB 2394 § 1(d) (actual damages, punitive damages, equitable relief and reasonable attorney fees); ME SP 72, *amends* § 1, 25 MRSA Pt. 12, § 4506 ("no more than $5,000 plus reasonable attorney's fees and court costs"); OK HB 1556, § 3.D. ("shall be liable for treble actual damages" and for willful or wanton conduct or deliberate efforts to conceal violations, "punitive damages not to exceed $50,000"); RI Gen. Assembly Jan. 2013, *amending* tit. 12 of GEN. LAWS, Ch. 5.3, 12-5.3.-10 (actual damages but not less than liquidated damages of $100 per day of violation or $1,000, whichever is higher; punitive damages and reasonable attorney's fees; good-faith reliance on order is a defense); TX HB 912, Ch. 423, § 423.005(b)–(d) ($1,000 for each image—subject to adjustment of the amount—court costs and

reasonable attorney's fees); WA HB 1771, § 13 (actual damages, mental pain and suffering, or liquidated damages at $1,000 per day for each day of violation not to exceed $10,000, reasonable attorney's fees, and costs of litigation). *See* provisions outlined in note 91 for further details.

43. Criminal liability is found in: AK HB 159a, § 2(d) ("unlawful use of an unmanned aerial vehicle is a class A misdemeanor"); AZ HB 2574, *amending* § 1, tit. 13, Ch. 30 ARS, 13-3007, § F. ("Class 6 felony"); CA SB No. 15, § 3(j) (disorderly conduct misdemeanor for using unmanned aircraft system to view "the interior of a bedroom, bathroom, changing room, fitting room, dressing room or tanning both, or the interior of any other area in which the occupant has a reasonable expectation of privacy, with the intent to invade the privacy; view identifiable person under or through their clothing for the purpose of viewing the body or undergarments of . . . ; or viewing anyone in a state of full or partial undress," § 5(b) criminalizes use of a weaponized drone); GA HB 560, § 2(b)–(d) (any LEA of the U.S. or Georgia who uses a drone without a warrant, or assists them, "shall be guilty of a misdemeanor"); IN SB 20, § 4(b) (knowing or intentional use of drone in violation is "Class D felony"); MI HB 4455, § 17 (flying an armed drone is a felony punishable by no more than 10 years imprisonment or a fine between $1,000 to $10,000 or both; other violations are a misdemeanor of not more than a year imprisonment and fine between $500 and $5,000; also criminalizes intentional disclosure and "significant reporting errors" as separate misdemeanors); MN 1620/1706, § 3, Subd.2 (felony if private person uses a drone to capture images on public or private property without permission . . .), MN HF 990, § 1, Subd. 6(a) (gross misdemeanor for violating documentation requirements); MT SB 196, § 1(1)(c) (UAV collection offense—fined not more than $500, incarcerated not longer than 6 months, or both); NH HB 619, IV.-a. (Class A misdemeanor for knowingly creating or assisting in creating an image of the exterior of any residential dwelling by or with the assistance of a drone . . . but not applicable to LEA); NJ Assembly No. 3157, § 5 (criminalizes private purchase, ownership or possession of a drone as a "disorderly persons offense" and a fine of up to $10,000, up to 18 months imprisonment, or both—not applicable to LEA, Forest Service, or U.S. military member on duty traveling to or from an authorized place of duty); NM SB 556, § 5.C. (petty misdemeanor); NY AO 6370/SO 4537, § 1, S 52-A.4.A. (Class B misdemeanor unless used in the commission of a felony, then Class C felony); NC HB 312, § 15A-232.(e) (if used for gathering evidence, Class 1 misdemeanor; if violates data retention rules, Class 3 misdemeanor); OK HB 1556, § 4.D. and 5.B. (willful disclosure . . . misdemeanor not to exceed 6 months in the county jail and a fine between $250 and $2,500 per violation; felony to operate weaponized drone—10 years and between $1,000 and $10,000 for each violation—not applicable to military "over public land for purposes of testing or training"); OR HB 2710, § 13(1) (Class A felony to intentionally fire a bullet/projectile, direct a laser or crash into an aircraft in the air, or gain authorized control over an FAA-licensed or U.S. Armed Forces–operated drone) and OR SB 71, §§ 2–3 (contains laundry list of misdemeanors and felonies, similar to OR HB 2710 and adds "to hunt or stalk game"); TX HB 912, Ch. 423, § 423.004 (illegal use, possession, disclosure, display, distribution, or use of image all Class C misdemeanors; each image is a separate offense); WA SB 5782, § 13 (Class C felony to disclose personal information without court authorization); WI SB 196/AB 203, § 3, *amending* § 941.292 of the statutes (Class H felony to sell transport, manufacture, possess, or operate weaponized drone; collection on person with "reasonable expectation of privacy" is a Class A misdemeanor).

44. Administrative disciplinary provisions can be found in HI SB, 263B-3(c) and 263B-6 ("administrative discipline" for willful disclosure or use of information beyond that permitted); MI HB 4455, § 13(1) (willful or intentional violations require determination, and notification to AG, as to whether or not "disciplinary action" will occur; in cases of negligence, AG may have to

approve operator/agency's use of drone per § 13(2)); NY AO 6541, § 66-C.1. (for willful violations).

45.   *See* Appendix B for the list of federal drone bills. Several of these federal bills discuss use of drones for targeted killings overseas, focus on "civil unmanned aircraft systems" in the United States, or discuss the requirement for drones for border patrol in the context of immigration. *See* HR 2438, *Designating Requirement on Notification of Executive-Ordered Strikes Act of 2013(DRONES Act)* (R. Darrell Issa, R-CA), http://www.gpo.gov/fdsys/pkg/BILLS-113hr2438ih/pdf/BILLS-113hr2438ih.pdf and HR 2183, *Drones Accountability Act* (R. Barbara Lee, D-CA), http://www.gpo.gov/fdsys/pkg/BILLS-113hr2183ih/pdf/BILLS-113hr2183ih.pdf; The latter forbids the military to execute strikes for the Central Intelligence Agency. S 1057, the *Safeguarding Privacy and Fostering Aerospace Innovation Act of 2013* focuses on private users. It prohibits private drone users from "willfully" conducting surveillance on another person, unless given prior written consent, in an emergency situation or in a public location "where surveillance would not be highly offensive to a reasonable person." The remedies for violation include a civil action and fines. It also requires marking of civil drones with the name, address, and telephone number of the owner. Use of drones for border security is included in HR 830, *Secure America through Verification and Enforcement Act of 2013 (SAVE Act)*, and HR 2124, *Keeping the Promise of ICRA Act*, http://www.gpo.gov/fdsys/pkg/BILLS-113hr830ih/pdf/BILLS-113hr830ih.pdf.

46.   HR 972, *Preserving Freedom from Unwarranted Surveillance Act of 2013*, or *PAPA*.

47.   *Id.* § 2, warrant exception; § 3(2) for a danger to life, property, and fleeing-felon exception found in many states. Also, like most states, HR 972, § 3(3) defines the terrorist attack exception as "use of a drone to counter a high risk of a terrorist attack by a specific individual or organization, when the Secretary of Homeland Security determines credible intelligence indicates there is such a risk."

48.   *Id.* § 4.

49.   HR 1262, *Drone Aircraft Privacy and Transparency Act of 2013*; HR 2868, *Drone Aircraft Privacy and Transparency Act of 2013*. The only difference between these two bills is that HR 1262 contains a "Findings" section that HR 2868 does not.

50.   HR 1262, § 341; HR 2868, § 3(a)(1).

51.   HR 1262 and HR 2868, § 341(a)–(b).

52.   *Id.* § 341(b)(3)–(4).

53.   *Id.* §§ 337–339. The data minimization statement would include certification that non-target data and target data that is no longer relevant to investigation of a crime under a warrant or to an ongoing criminal proceeding will be redacted. *See id.* § 339(c)(1)(B).

54.   *Id.* § 340.

55.   HR 1262, § 4(c); HR 2868, § 3(c)(1). For private causes of action, remedies include injunction, damages up to $1,000 a day for each violation or both, and for intentional violations, treble damages. Recovery of attorney's fees and court costs is also possible.

56.   HR 1262 and HR 2868, § 341(b)(6).

57.   HR 1262, § 4(a)–(b); HR 2868, § 3(B)(1).

58.   HR 1262, § 4(f); HR 2868, § 3(f).

59.   H.R. 637, *Preserving American Privacy Act of 2013 (PAPA)*. As do some states, the PAPA also addresses private, or nongovernmental, use of drones. Like CA SB No. 15, it makes it unlawful to intentionally collect, "in a manner highly offensive to a reasonable person," images of individuals "engaging in a personal or familial activity under circumstances in which the individual had a reasonable expectation of privacy. Unlike the California bill, the PAPA fails to describe the remedy for such a violation." *Id.* § 3119f.; CA SB No. 15.

60.   *Id.* § 3119a(2)(A)–(B).

61. *Id.* Ch. 205A, § 3119c(c)(b)(1)–(5).
62. *Id.* § 3119c(5)(B).
63. *Id.* § 3119c(2)(B)–(D).
64. *Id.* § 3119c(1)(B).
65. *Id.* § 3119e.
66. *Id.* § 3119b(b) and (c). The data collection statement would include the purpose of the operation, whether the drone is capable of collecting covered information, data retention time, a point of contact for citizen feedback, the responsible unit, the rank and title of the person authorizing the operation, data minimization policies, as well as oversight procedures. Like the *DAPTAs*, information relevant to the investigation of a crime may be retained. HR 637, § 3119b(c)(1)(A)–(H). This is similar to information required in a DoD Proper Use Memorandum (PUM). *See, e.g.*, AFI 14-104, Attachment 4.
67. *Id.* § 3119d(a)
68. *Id.* § 3119i.
69. 18 U.S.C. § 1385. The PCA does not apply to National Guard forces in title 32, U.S. Code, or state active duty status, and they are thus able to more readily assist law enforcement. Joint Pub. 3-28, *Defense Support of Civil Authorities*, July 31, 2013, p.1-6, http://www.dtic.mil/doctrine/new_pubs/jp3_28.pdf.
70. DoDD 3025.18, *Defense Support to Civil Authorities (DSCA)*, Dec. 29, 2010, incorporating Change 1, Sept. 21, 2012, Glossary, Part II, Definitions, http://www.dtic.mil/whs/directives/corres/pdf/302518p.pdf. Note that upon approval of the governor, state National Guard forces may support state LEAs within their respective states and within the limits prescribed by state law. State NG forces from another state in title 32, U.S. Code, or state active-duty status, operating an agreement between the states, may only support civilian LEA as specified in a memorandum approved by both governors. JP 3-28, p. III-1.
71. DepSecDef Memo, *Interim Guidance for the Domestic Use of Unmanned Aircraft Systems*, September 28, 2006. The DepSecDef Memo also requires notification to the Chairman of the Joint Chiefs of Staff (CJCS) for any drone training to be conducted outside of DoD controlled airspace. *See also* Joint Pub. 3-28, CIVIL SUPPORT, Sept. 14, 2007, http://www.dtic.mil/doctrine/new_pubs/jp3_28.pdf. The SecDef has delegated his approval authority for DSCA to the Assistant Secretary of Defense for Homeland Defense and America's Security Affairs, but not for assistance to law enforcement or responding with assets "with the potential for lethality." Air Force Instr. (AFI) 10-801, DEFENSE SUPPORT TO CIVIL AUTHORITIES (DSCA), Sept. 19, 2012, ¶ 2.1, http://static.e-publishing.af.mil/production/1/af_a3_5/publication/afi10-801/afi10-801.pdf.
72. DoDI 3025.21, Encl. 3, § 5(a)–(b). *See also* DoDD 3025.18, ¶ 4o; DepSecDef Memo, Sept. 28, 2006; DoDI 3025.22, *The Use of the National Guard for Defense Support of Civil Authorities*, July 26, 2013, http://www.dtic.mil/whs/directives/corres/pdf/302522p.pdf. DoD Instructions implement DoD Directives. Requests for SecDef approval for domestic use of drones are forwarded to the CJCS through the military chain of command. The approval package includes sufficient information on the activity or event to allow deciding officials to make an informed judgment on its propriety, a Proper Use Memorandum (PUM), and an FAA Certificate of Authorization (CoA) or license. PUMs are required by regulation and signed by an officer in a position of authority, normally after legal review, who certifies the legitimacy of proposed domestic imagery requirements and the appropriateness of use parameters as well as legal and policy compliance. AFI 14-104, ¶ 9.5, Attachment 1 Terms and Attachment 4. For a detailed review of approval authorities for DoD domestic imagery missions, *see* Dawn M.K. Zoldi, Colonel, USAF, *Protecting Security and Privacy: An Analytical Framework for Airborne Domestic Imagery*, pending publication in AIR FORCE L. REV., Vol. 70, 2013 Ed.

73. 2013 Chairman Joint Chiefs of Staff Defense Support of Civil Authorities Execute Order (CJCS DSCA EXORD), 071415z Jun 13, ¶ 3.C.4.J.1. An EXORD is "[a]n order issued by the Chairman of the Joint Chiefs of Staff, at the direction of the Secretary of Defense, to implement a decision by the President to initiate military operations." JP 1-02, p.97.

74. *Id.* at ¶ 1.J.

75. The term "Incident Awareness and Assessment" (IAA) is defined as "The Secretary of Defense approved use of Department of Defense intelligence, surveillance, reconnaissance, and other intelligence capabilities for domestic non-intelligence support for defense support of civil authorities." JP 1-02, p.131.

76. CJCS DSCA EXORD 2013, ¶ 3.C.4.J.1. If a drone or other intelligence capability is used for these DSCA missions, they must be conducted in accordance with the intelligence oversight (IO) requirements, discussed below.

77. DoDI 3025.21, *Defense Support of Civilian Law Enforcement Agencies*, Feb. 27, 2013, http://www.dtic.mil/whs/directives/corres/pdf/302521p.pdf. 10 U.S.C. § 371 requires that the needs of civilian law enforcement agencies be taken into account in the planning and execution of military training or operations. 10 U.S.C. § 371, *Use of information collected during military operations*, http://www.law.cornell.edu/uscode/text/10/371; *see also* DoDI 1322.28, *Realistic Military Training (RMT) Off Federal Real Property*, March 18, 2013, which incorporates 10 U.S.C. § 371 requirements, http://www.dtic.mil/whs/directives/corres/pdf/132228p.pdf.

78. DoDI 3025.21, Enc. 3, ¶ 1c(1)(a)–(g).

79. DoDI 3025.21, Enc. 6.

80. *Id.*, Enc. 3; *see also* 10 U.S.C. § 374, Maintenance and operation of equipment, *available at* http://us-code.vlex.com/vid/maintenance-and-operation-equipment-19222062.

81. 10 U.S.C. § 374(b)(1)(C) and (b)(2)(C).

82. JP 1-02, DEPARTMENT OF DEFENSE DICTIONARY OF MILITARY AND ASSOCIATED TERMS, p. 231.

83. Drones are an intelligence, surveillance, and reconnaissance (ISR) platform and, as such, are considered an intelligence capability. ISR refers "to an activity that synchronizes and integrates the planning and operation of sensors, assets and processing, exploitation and dissemination systems in direct support of current and future operations. This is an integrated intelligence and operations function." DoD Directive 5143.01, *Under Secretary of Defense for Intelligence (USD(I))*, Nov. 23, 2005, ¶ E2.1.7 (citing to JP 1-02). That said, there is no doctrinal document that authoritatively states that drones should, in all circumstances, be considered an "intelligence capability." Some have suggested the RPA's categorization depends on the activity or mission it is conducting at any given moment. Dawn M.K. Zoldi, Colonel, USAF, *Protecting Security and Privacy: An Analytical Framework for Airborne Domestic Imagery*, pending publication in THE AIR FORCE L. REV., Vol. 70, 2013. However, the SecDef routinely directs that during DSCA missions, Intelligence Oversight (IO) rules will apply. *See also* 2013 CJCS DSCA EXORD.

84. Exec. Order 12,333, *United States Intelligence Activities* (as amended by Exec. Orders 13,284 (2003), 13,355 (2004), and 13,470 (2008)), http://www.archives.gov/federal-register/codification/executive-order/12333.html. The EO defines intelligence activities narrowly as countering foreign threats. However, implementing DoD and Service directives broaden this definition to "intelligence-related activities." DoD 5240.01-R broadens application of IO to non-intelligence organizations, staffs, or offices being used for counterintelligence and foreign intelligence. DoD 5240.01-R, *Procedures Governing the Activities of DoD Intel Components that Affect U.S. Persons,* December 1982, www.dtic.mil/whs/directives/corres/pdf/524001r.pdf. For example, AFI 14-104 applies IO to "non-intelligence organizations that perform intelligence-related activities that could collect, analyze, process, retain or disseminate information on U.S.

persons," including commanders of such units. Air Force Instr. 14-104, *Oversight of Intelligence Activities,* April 23, 2012, ¶ 3.1, http://static.e-publishing.af.mil/production/1/af_a2/publication/afi14-104/afi_14-104.pdf. Note that DoDD 5200.27, *Acquisition of Information Concerning Persons and Organizations Not Affiliated with the Department of Defense,* applies to non-intelligence capability (IC) collection of information on persons and organizations that are not affiliated with the DoD. The National Guard has adopted a similar application of the IO rules to personnel conducting intelligence activities. Chief National Guard Bureau Manual 2000.01, NATIONAL GUARD INTELLIGENCE ACTIVITIES, November 26, 2012, http://www.ngbpdc.ngb.army.mil/pubs/CNGBI/CNGBM2000_01_20121126.pdf; Chief National Guard Bureau Instruction 2000.01, NATIONAL GUARD INTELLIGENCE ACTIVITIES, Sept. 17, 2012, http://www.ngbpdc.ngb.army.mil/pubs/CNGBI/CNGBI.htm; ANGI 14-101, NATIONAL GUARD INSPECTOR GENERAL INTELLIGENCE OVERSIGHT PROCEDURES, June 13, 2011, http://www.ngbpdc.ngb.army.mil/pubs/14/angi14_101.pdf.

85. DoD 5240.1-R defines counterintelligence as "[i]nformation gathered and activities conducted to protect against espionage, other intelligence activities, sabotage, or assassinations conducted for or on behalf of foreign powers, organizations, or persons or international terrorist activities, including personnel, physical, document or communications security programs." *Id.* at DL1.1.5. Foreign intelligence is defined as "[i]nformation relating to the capabilities, intentions and activities of foreign powers, organizations or persons, but not including counterintelligence except for information on intentional terrorist activities." *Id.* at DL1.1.11.

86. E.O. 12,333, ¶ 2.3; DoD 5240.1-R, ¶ C2.3. Again, drones do not actually collect. Their sensor operators do.

87. DoD 5240.1-R, ¶ C2.4.2. Collection rules are contained in Procedure 2 of DoD 5240.1-R. DoD 5240-1R defines a USPER at DL1.1.25 as a U.S. citizen; an alien known to be a permanent resident alien; an unincorporated association substantially composed of U.S. citizens or permanent resident aliens; a corporation incorporated in the U.S. exception for those directed and controlled by a foreign government. A person located in the U.S. is presumed to be a USPER.

88. *Id.* ¶ C2.4.1

89. *Id.* ¶¶ C2.4.2.–2.4.2.4.

90. For example, in non-emergent situations, electronic surveillance, referred to as a Procedure 5, may only be conducted pursuant to a warrant under the Foreign Intelligence Surveillance Act (FISA) of 1978, 50 U.S.C. § 36. Only the SecDef, DepSecDef, the Secretary of the Air Force (SecAF), or the Director of the National Security Agency (NSA) can submit a request for a FISA warrant for this purpose. DoD 5240.1-R, ¶ C5.1.2. *See also*: Procedure 6—Concealed Monitoring, ¶ C.6.3.3.; Procedure 7—Non-Consensual Physical Searches, ¶ 7.3.2; Procedure 8—Mail Searches and Examination, ¶ 8.3; Procedure 9—Physical Surveillance, ¶ 9.3.3; Procedure 10—Undisclosed Participation in Organizations, ¶ 10.3.2.

91. DoD 5240.1-R, C.12.2.2.3, and 12.2.2.3.4.

92. DoDI 3025.21, Encl. 3.

93. DoD 5240.1-R, Procedure 9.

94. CJCS DSCA EXORD, ¶ 3.C.4.J.1.; 10 U.S.C. 374, ¶ (b)(2)(C).

95. DoD 5240-1.R, ¶ C3.3.4.

96. *Id.* ¶ C3.3.2.4. Other exceptions for retaining USPER data are outlined in Procedure 3.

97. *Id.* ¶ C4.2., also called "Procedure 4."

98. *Id.* ¶ C4.3.

99. JP 6-30, pp.II-29–30.

100.   The following drone bills contain weapons restrictions: AR HB 1904 § 12-19-104, ¶ (d) ("An unmanned aerial vehicle shall not be equipped with weapons."); CA SB No. 15, § 5, *amending* tit. 14, § 14350 of the PENAL CODE, § 14351(a) ("may not be equipped with a weapon") and CA AB 1327, § 14354.5 (not equip or arm an unmanned aircraft system with a weapon or other device that may be carried or launched . . .); GA SB 200 § 3, ¶ (1) (prohibits equipping an unmanned aircraft with weaponry); HI SB 783 § 1, ¶ (e) ("unmanned aerial vehicles may not be equipped with weapons"); IA SB 276 § 14 ("under no circumstances shall a weaponized unmanned aircraft system be deployed"), IA HF 410, § 1.3. ("under no circumstances shall a weaponized unmanned aircraft system be deployed . . . by the state . . .); KS HB 2394 § 1, ¶ (b) ("no drone shall be operated in this state while carrying a lethal payload"); KY 14 RS BR 1, § 1(2) ("no prohibited agency shall use a drone carrying a lethal payload"); ME SP 72 § 4502.3 ("An unmanned aerial vehicle may not be equipped with a weapon."); MA SB 1664 § 1, ¶ (b) and MA HB 1357, § 99-C(b) ("Unmanned aerial vehicles may not be equipped with weapons."); MI HB 4455 § 3, ¶ (4) ("shall not operate UAV that contains, mounts, or carries a lethal or nonlethal weapon or weapon system of any type"); MN HF 990, § 3, Subd. 3 (no drones equipped with dangerous weapons or nonlethal devices); ND HB 1373 § 4, ¶ 1 ("A state agency may not authorize the use, including grant a permit to use, of an unmanned aircraft while armed with any lethal or nonlethal weapons."); NY AO 6541 § 66-A.5. (no lethal or nonlethal weapons); OK HB 1556, § 5.A ("contains, mounts, or possesses any lethal or nonlethal weapon"); OR HB 2710, § 10 ("A public body may not operate a drone that is capable of firing a bullet or other projectile, directing a laser or otherwise being used as a weapon") and OR SB 524, § 1(6)("may not use a drone that is capable of firing a bullet or other projectile"); PA SB 875, § 5 ("a weaponized unmanned aircraft system may not be deployed or its use facilitated by a State or local agency or member of the public." Exempts National Guard); SC GA Bill 395, Ch. 39, § 6-39-20 ("may not own, use, contract for or otherwise obtain services from a drone containing 'an antipersonnel device'"); VT H 540, § 4622, ¶ (e) ("Drones shall not be equipped with weapons."); VA HB 2012 § 1, ¶ 1 ("In no case may a weaponized unmanned aircraft system be deployed."); WV HB 2732 § 1-7-3, ¶ (b) ("No drone operated within the State of West Virginia may carry a lethal payload.") and WV HB 2997, § 1-7-4(b) (may not authorize use of unmanned aircraft while "armed with any lethal or non-lethal weapons, including firearms, pepper spray, bean bag guns, mace and sound-based weapons"); and WI SB 196/AB 203, § 3 ("sale, transport, manufacture, possession or operation of weaponized drone is Class C felony").

101.   CA AB 1327, § 14354.5 ("may not equip or arm an unmanned aircraft system with . . . device that may be carried or launched . . ."); MI HB 4455 § 3, ¶ (4) ("shall not operate UAV that contains, mounts, or carries a . . . nonlethal weapon or weapon system of any type"); MN HF 990, § 3, Subd. 3 (no drones equipped with . . . non-lethal devices); ND HB 1373 § 4, ¶ 1 ("A state agency may not authorize the use, including grant a permit to use, of an unmanned aircraft while armed with any . . . nonlethal weapons."); NY AO 6541 § 66-A.5 (no nonlethal weapons); OK HB 1556, § 5.A ("contains, mounts or possesses any . . . nonlethal weapon"); OR HB 2710, § 10 ("A public body may not operate a drone that is capable of firing a . . . projectile, directing a laser or otherwise being used as a weapon") and OR SB 524, § 1(6) ("may not use a drone that is capable of firing . . . projectile"); WV HB 2997, § 1-7-4(b) (may not authorize use of unmanned aircraft while "armed with any . . . . non-lethal weapons, including firearms, pepper spray, bean bag guns, mace and sound-based weapons").

102.   WV HB 2997, § 1-7-4(b).

103.   OR HB 2710, § 10.

104.   States with criminal exclusionary rules include AL SB 317, § 1(d) ("criminal prosecution"); AK HB 159a, § 3(a) ("criminal action or proceeding"); AZ HB 2574, *amending*

§ 1, tit. 13, Ch. 30 ARS, 13-3007, § C ("collected or obtained in violation . . . not admissible in any . . . criminal proceeding"); AR HB1904, *amending* AR CODE tit. 12, as 12-19-105(b) (limited to non-targets; "information acquired and evidence derived from its use shall not be received in evidence in any trial, hearing or other proceeding"); FL SB 92, § 1(5) ("not admissible as evidence in a criminal prosecution in any court of law in this state"); GA HB 560, § 2(e) ("inadmissible in any . . . criminal proceeding"); HI SB, 2563B-3(b) ("in any trial"); IL SB 1587, § 30 (compliance a prerequisite for admissibility "but nothing in this Act shall prevent a court from independently reviewing the admissibility of evidence for compliance with the Fourth Amendment to the U.S. Constitution or with Article I, Section 6 of the Illinois Constitution"); IN SB 20, § (5) ("not admissible as evidence in an administrative or judicial proceeding"); IA HF 427, § 1.5 ("not admissible in criminal trial"); KS HB 2394 § 1(e) ("in any trial, hearing or other proceeding"); KY HB 454, § 5 (in any criminal proceeding . . . for the purpose of enforcing state or local laws") and KY 14 RS BR 1, § 1(5) ("not admissible as evidence in any civil, criminal or administrative proceeding . . . to enforce state or local law"); ME SP 72, *amends* § 1, 25 MRSA Pt. 12, § 4503 (compliance required for admissibility in "trial, hearing or other proceeding"); ME SP 72, *amends* § 1, 25 MRSA Pt. 12, § 4506.3. ("a court . . . shall grant a motion to suppress as evidence"); MD HB 1233, 1-203-1(D) ("not admissible as evidence in a criminal prosecution"); MA SB 1664, § 1, *amending* Ch. 272 of GEN. LAWS as 99C(f) and MA HB 1357, § 99-C(f) ("any judicial, regulatory or other government proceeding"); MI HB 4455 § 7(2) ("information acquired will not be admitted into evidence in a trial, hearing or other proceeding"); MN HF SF 1506, § 1, Sub. 5 (criminal prosecution), MN 1620/1706, § 3, Sub. 5 ("not admissible as evidence in a criminal prosecution"), MN HF 990, § 1, Subd. 7 ("in a civil action or criminal prosecution in this state"); MO HB 46, § 305.641.2 ("as evidence in a criminal proceeding . . ."); MT SB 196, § 1(1)(b) ("not admissible in any proceeding . . . may not be used for any purpose"); NE LB 412, § 6 ("not admissible as evidence in a criminal prosecution"); NJ Assembly No. 3157, § 2.d (incidentally collected information shall not "be used as evidence in court for a crime" unrelated to an investigation of the target) and NJ AB 3929, ¶ 3 ("as evidence in a criminal prosecution"); NM SB 556, § 5.B. ("evidence in criminal proceeding in any court"); NY AO 6370/SO 4537, § 1, S 52-A.4.B. (criminal proceeding in any court), NY AO 6244, § 1. S 700.16, ¶ 3 ("inadmissible in any criminal action"), NY AO 6541, § 66-B.2 ("in any trial, hearing or other proceeding"); NC HB 312, § 15A-232.(f) ("criminal, civil or administrative proceeding"); ND HB 1373, § 6.1 ("criminal prosecution or administrative hearing"—but exclusion does not apply to incidentally acquired information); OH HB 207, § 4561.50(B) ("trial, hearing or other proceeding"); OK HB 1556, § 3.E. and § 4.E. ("No information, data, media . . . shall be received in evidence in any trial, hearing or other proceeding."); OR HF 2710, § 11 (if drone has not been approved by FAA, evidence inadmissible in judicial and administrative proceedings), OR SB 71, § 4(3) (obtained in violation of act, not admissible in any judicial or administrative proceeding), and OR SB 853, § 4(2)(a) and 8(2)(a) (non-target data inadmissible in any judicial or administrative proceeding; surveillance during state of emergency not admissible); RI Gen. Assembly Jan. 2013, *amending* tit. 12 of GEN. LAWS, Ch. 5.3, 12-5.3.-8, .9, and 11. (exclusion of evidence and derivative evidence if person not served notice of information collected not 10 days prior to proceeding and very detailed parameters for suppression of evidence based on unlawfully obtaining information, facial insufficiency of order, drone use not in conformity with the order or notice/service not made pursuant to the Act; also exclusion for violating retention rules) and RI LC00564, § 12-5.3.2 (information gathered without a warrant, or derived therefrom, not admissible in any civil or criminal court); SC H 3415, § 2(D) ("not admissible as evidence in a criminal prosecution"); TN HB 591, § 1(f) ("shall not be admissible as evidence in a criminal prosecution") and TN SB 796, § 1(g)(2) (evidence obtained in violation not admissible as evidence in criminal prosecution); TX HB 912, Ch. 423, § 423.005(1) ("may not be used as evidence in any criminal or juvenile proceeding, civil action or administrative proceeding"—except to prove a violation of the Act); VT HB 540/SB 16, *amending* § 1 20 V.S.A. Ch. 205 as § 4622(d) ("inadmissible in any judicial or administrative proceeding"); WA HB 1771/WA SB 5782, § 10 (blanket exclusion on admissibility of any personal information acquired from a drone); WI SB 196/AB 203, § 5, *amending* § 972.113 (in violation, no admissible in criminal proceeding); WV HB 2732, Art. 7, § 1-7-6 ("not admissible as evidence in a criminal prosecution") and WV HB 2997, § 1-7-6(a) (in violation not admissible in criminal or administrative hearings); WY HB 0242, 7-3-1005 ("in any criminal proceeding"). Even if the state fails to include a specific criminal exclusionary provision in its drone bill, it is safe to assume that the courts in those states that require a warrant would still exclude the evidence consistent with their constitution or other law if law enforcement did not obtain a warrant, unless a judicial exception to the warrant requirement applied.

105. For civil or administrative exclusionary rules *see*: AK HB 159a, § 1(a) ("civil action or proceeding"); AZ HB 2574, *amending* § 1, tit. 13, Ch. 30 ARS, 13-3007, § C ("collected or obtained in violation . . . not admissible in any . . . civil proceeding"); AR HB1904, *amending* AR CODE tit. 12 as 12-19-105(b) (limited to non-targets only—"information acquired and evidence derived from its use shall not be received in evidence in any trial, hearing or other proceeding"); GA HB 560, § 2(e) (inadmissible in any civil . . . proceeding"); HI SB, 2563B-3(b) ("in any trial"); IL SB 1587, § 30 (compliance a prerequisite for admissibility, "but nothing in this Act shall prevent a court from independently reviewing the admissibility of evidence for compliance with the Fourth Amendment to the U.S. Constitution or with Article I, Section 6 of the Illinois Constitution"); IN SB 20, §(5) ("not admissible as evidence in an administrative or judicial proceeding"); KS HB 2394 § 1(e) ("in any trial, hearing or other proceeding"); KY HB 454, § 5 (in any civil . . . or administrative proceeding . . . "for the purpose of enforcing state or local laws") and KY 14 RS BR 1, § 1(5) ("not admissible as evidence in any civil, criminal or administrative proceeding . . . to enforce state or local law"); ME SP 72, *amends* § 1, 25 MRSA Pt. 12, § 4503 (compliance required for admissibility in "trial, hearing or other proceeding"); ME SP 72, *amends* § 1, 25 MRSA Pt. 12, § 4506.3. ("a court . . . shall grant a motion to suppress as evidence"); MA SB 1664, § 1, *amending* Ch. 272 of GEN. LAWS as 99C(f) ("any judicial, regulatory or other government proceeding") and MA HB 1357, § 99-C(f) ("any judicial, regulatory or other government proceeding"); MI HB 4455 § 7(2) ("information acquired will not be admitted into evidence in a trial, hearing or other proceeding"); MN HF 990, § 1, Subd. 7 ("in a civil action or criminal prosecution in this state"); MO HB 46, § 305.641.2 ("as evidence in . . . an administrative hearing"); MT SB 196, § 1(1)(b) ("not admissible in any proceeding . . . may not be used for any purpose"); MT SB 196, § 2(3) ("not admissible as evidence in any prosecution or proceeding"); NM SB 556, § 5.B ("evidence in administrative hearing"); NY AO 6370/SO 4537, § 1, S 52-A.4.B ("civil proceeding in any court . . . or in an administrative hearing") and NY AO 6541, § 66-B.2 ("in any trial, hearing or other proceeding"); NC HB 312, § 15A-232(f) ("criminal, civil or administrative proceeding"); OH HB 207, § 4561.50(B) ("trial, hearing or other proceeding"); OK HB 1556, § 3.E & 4.E ("No information, data, media . . . shall be received in evidence in any trial, hearing or other proceeding . . . except for that introduced in any proceeding brought against a violator of this act."); OR HF 2710, § 11 (if drone has not been approved by FAA, evidence inadmissible in judicial and administrative proceedings), OR SB 71, § 4(3) (obtained in violation of act, not admissible in any judicial or administrative proceeding), and OR SB 853, §§ 2(1), 4(2)(a) 8(2)(a) (collected in violation/derived therefrom not admissible; non-target data inadmissible in any judicial or administrative proceeding; surveillance during state of emergency not admissible); RI LC000564, § 12-5.3-2 (without a warrant, inadmissible in any

civil or criminal court); TX HB 912, Ch. 423, § 423.004 ("may not be used as evidence in any criminal or juvenile proceeding, civil action or administrative proceeding"—except to prove a violation of the Act); VT HB 540/SB 16, *amending* § 1 20 V.S.A. Ch. 205 as § 4622(d) ("inadmissible in any judicial or administrative proceeding"); WA HB 1771/WA SB 5782 § 10 (blanket exclusion on admissibility of any personal information acquired from a drone) and WV HB 2997, § 1-7-6(a) (in violation not admissible in criminal or administrative hearings).

106.   Derivative evidence exclusions include AR HB1904, *amending* AR CODE tit. 12 as 12-19-105(b) (limited to non-targets; "information acquired and evidence derived from its use shall not be received in evidence in any trial, hearing or other proceeding"); GA HB 560, § 2(e) (information "gathered as a result . . . of drone use without a warrant is inadmissible"); HI SB, 2563B-3(b) ("no evidence derived therefrom"); IN SB 20, § (5) ("evidence derived from a communication or image"); KS HB 2394 § 1(e) ("evidence derived therefrom"); MA SB 1664, § 1, amending Ch. 272 of GEN. LAWS as 99C(f) ("and information derived therefrom"); MI HB 4455 § 7(2) ("and evidence derived from the operation"); NJ Assembly No. 3157, § 2.d (incidentally collected information shall not "be used as evidence in court for a crime" unrelated to an investigation of the target); NY AO 6370/SO 4537, § 1, S 52-A.4.B ("and all evidence derived from such evidence or information"); OH HB 207, § 4561.50(B) ("no information collected . . . and no evidence derived therefrom"); OK HB 1556, § 3.E & 4.E ("and no evidence derived therefrom"); OR HF 2710, § 11 (if drone has not been approved by FAA, no information collected or evidence derived from that image), OR SB 853, § 2(1) and 4(2)(a) (collected in violation/derived therefrom not admissible; non-target data and information derived therefrom inadmissible); RI LC000564, § 12-5.3-2 (without a warrant, evidence and information derived therefrom inadmissible in any civil or criminal court); WA HB 1771/WA SB 5782 § 10 (blanket exclusion on admissibility of any personal information acquired from a drone and "no evidence derived therefrom").

107.   MT SB 196, § 2(3, "Information obtained from the operation of an UAV . . . may not be used in an affidavit of probable cause in an effort to obtain a search warrant (unless obtained in compliance with the Act)."; OR HF 2710, § 11(2) (if drone has not been approved by FAA, no information collected or evidence derived from that image to be used to establish probable cause), OR SB 853, § 2(1)(b) (information in violation may not be used to establish probable cause).

108.   H.R. 1083, *The No Armed Drones Act of 2013 (NADA)*. Person is defined at 49 U.S.C. § 40102(a)(37) as including "a governmental authority and a trustee, receiver, assignee, and other similar representative." It is beyond the scope of this chapter to discuss whether the SecTrans can preclude the President of the United States (POTUS) from operating a weaponized drone under his Article II authority.

109.   H.R. 637, § 3119h.

110.   H.R. 1269, *Life, Liberty, and Justice for All Americans Act* (Rep. Trey Radel, R-FL), *available at* http://www.gpo.gov/fdsys/pkg/BILLS-113hr1269ih/pdf/BILLS-113hr1269ih.pdf. The bill defines "lethal military force" as meaning "a targeted killing or other lethal action . . . that is typically used against an enemy of the United States."

111.   S. 505, *Bill to prohibit use of drones to kill US citizens in U.S.* (Sen. Ted Cruz, R-TX), *available at* http://www.gpo.gov/fdsys/pkg/BILLS-113s505pcs/pdf/BILLS-113s505pcs.pdf. Again, whether or not Congress can limit POTUS's Article II powers is a matter beyond the scope of this chapter.

112.   H.R. 1242, *To prohibit the use of drones to kill citizens of the US within the U.S.* (Rep. Reid Ribble, R-WI), *available at* http://www.gpo.gov/fdsys/pkg/BILLS-113hr1242ih/pdf/BILLS-113hr1242ih.pdf.

113. Att'y Gen. Eric Holder, Letter to Sen. Rand Paul, March 7, 2013, *available at* http://big.assets.huffingtonpost.com/holderletter.pdf.

114. H.R. 1262, § 341(b)(6); H.R. 2868, § 341(b)(5).

115. H.R. 637, Ch. 205A, § 3119c(c)(a).

116. DoDD 3025.18, ¶ 4.o.

117. Att'y Gen. Holder, Letter to Senator Paul, March 7, 2013, note 113, *supra*. Note that in a previous memo to Sen. Paul dated March 4, Holder had stated it was "possible . . . to imagine an extraordinary circumstance in which it would be necessary and appropriate under the Constitution and applicable laws of the United States for the President to authorize the military to use lethal force within the territory of the United States." The example he gave for this was "to protect the homeland in circumstances of a catastrophic attack like the ones suffered on December 7, 1941, and September 11, 2001." *See* note 2, *supra*. Jack Goldsmith, of the Brookings Institute, wrote an excellent exposition of the many legal bases for a President to actually, under some circumstances, lawfully order lethal force against an American on American soil, including Article II of the Constitution and the Insurrection Act. *See* http://www.lawfareblog.com/2013/02/of-course-president-obama-has-authority-under-some-circumstances-to-order-lethal-force-against-a-u-s-citizen-on-u-s-soil-and-a-free-draft-resposne-to-senator-paul-for-john-brennan/.

118. State exclusionary provisions, however, could impact the use of DoD-collected information in state court. For example, in the Air Force, intelligence components must report to the appropriate civilian law enforcement agencies any incidentally acquired information reasonably believed to be a violation of law or relating to potential threats to life or property (whether DoD personnel, installations, or activities, or civilian lives or property). AFI 14-104, ¶¶ 11.12.1, 11.12.2.2, and 12; 10 U.S.C. § 371, *Use of information collected during military operations,* http://www.law.cornell.edu/uscode/text/10/371. However, some states, like Michigan, prohibit their local law enforcement agencies from receiving information or evidence acquired by a drone and if they do so, preclude its admissibility in court. MI HB 4455, § 3(3): "Except as provided in section 5, a law enforcement agency of this state or a political subdivision of this state shall not disclose or receive information acquired through the operation of an unmanned aerial vehicle." Section 5 of the bill contains exceptions based upon consent, imminent threat to life, search warrant, court order, or for non-evidentiary or non-intelligence purposes. It is difficult to imagine why a law enforcement agency would want to receive drone information that has no evidentiary or intelligence value.

119. *See* DoD 5240-1R and DepSecDef Directive-Type Memorandum (DTM) 08-052—*DoD Guidance for Reporting Questionable Intelligence Activities and Significant or Highly Sensitive Matters,* June 17, 2009, *available at* http://www.dtic.mil/whs/directives/corres/pdf/DTM-08-052.pdf. The DTM outlines the required information for such Questionable Intelligence Activity (QIA) reports.

120. FL SB 92, § 1(2)(b).

121. *Id.* § 4(a)–(c). It also allows drones to be used "to achieve purposes including, but not limited, facilitating the search for a missing person."

122. *Id.* § 6.

123. ID SB 1134, § 1 (designating a new section of the Idaho Code as Section 21-213 "Restrictions on Use of Unmanned Aircraft Systems").

124. *Id.* § 21-213(2)(a).

125. *Id.*

126. IL SB 1587, § 10.

127. *Id.*

128. *Id.* § 15.

129. *Id.* §§ 30, 20, and 25, respectively.

130. Unlike most bills surveyed, the Illinois law specifically acknowledges the applicability of "judicially recognized exception(s) to the exclusionary rule of the Fourth Amendment to the U.S. Constitution or Article I, Section 6 of the Illinois Constitution." It explicitly states that courts can independently review admissibility for compliance with these constitutions.

131. *Id.* § 20.

132. MT SB 0196, § 1(1). The Fourth Amendment requires the government to obtain a proper warrant, issued by a neutral and detached magistrate, unless a specifically established and well-delineated exception to the warrant requirement applies. These exceptions include, but are not limited to, exigent circumstances, consent searches, and plain view. For exigent circumstances, *see* Coolidge v. New Hampshire, 403 U.S. 443, 474–75 (1920) ("it is accepted, at least as a matter of principle, that a search or seizure carried out on a suspect's premises without a warrant is *per se* unreasonable, unless the police can show that it falls within one of a carefully defined set of exceptions based on the presence of 'exigent circumstances'"); Schmerber v. California, 384 U.S. 757 (1966); *consent,* Schneckloth v. Bustamonte, 412 U.S. 218 (1973); and for plain view as it relates to aerial surveillance, California v. Ciraolo, 476 U.S. 207, 213 (1986); Florida v. Riley, 488 U.S. 445, 448 (1989). The Supreme Court has determined that exigent circumstances exist in the case of imminent danger to life, where a felon or suspect is fleeing and where the destruction of evidence is imminent. Warden, Maryland Penitentiary v. Hayden, 387 U.S. 294, 298–99 (1967) ("The Fourth Amendment does not require police officers to delay in the course of an investigation if to do so would gravely endanger their lives or the lives of others."); Tennessee v. Garner, 471 U.S. 1 (1985) (law enforcement may use nonlethal force to deter a fleeing felon); Roaden v. Kentucky, 413 U.S. 496, 505 (1973) ("Where there are exigent circumstances in which police action literally must be 'now or never' to preserve the evidence of the crime, it is reasonable to permit action without prior judicial evaluation.").

133. MT SB 0196, § 1(2).

134. Some may argue that state drone laws are preempted by federal law. The topic of federal preemption of state drone laws merits its own article and is beyond the scope of this chapter. Even assuming preemption applies, as a practical matter, a federal officer would have to be summoned into court, request DoJ substitution or representation, and affirmatively assert preemption. The better course of action would be for states to exclude federal officers from their laws from the inception, especially the U.S. military . . . Apparently, numerous states believe they can legislate federal and military actors' drone use. However, a plausible argument for preemption would be that the Federal Aviation Act (FAA) of 1958 and its supplements, including the 2012 FAA Modernization and Reform Act, when combined with comprehensive FAA regulations found at 14 C.F.R., illustrate Congress's intent that the FAA occupy the entire field of aircraft safety. *See* Thomas J. McLaughlin, Mary P. Gaston & Jared D. Hager, *Navigating the Nation's Waterways and Airways: Maritime Lessons for Federal Preemption Airworthiness Standards,* AIR & SPACE LAWYER, Vol. 23, No. 2, Oct. 25, 2010, *available at* http://www.perkinscoie.com/files/upload/10_27_ABAArticle.pdf. *See also* City of Burbank v. Lockheed Air Terminal, 411 U.S. 624, 639, 93 S. Ct. 1854, 36 L. Ed. 2d 547 (1973) and Nw. Airlines v. Minnesota, 322 U.S. 292, 303, 64 S. Ct. 950, 88 L. Ed. 1283 (1944) (Jackson, J., concurring).

135. OR HB 2710, § 2(1).

136. *Id.* §§ 3–7.

137. *Id.* § 16 for non-applicability to U.S. Armed Forces.

138. *Id.* § 10. The Oregon statutes define "public body" as "state government bodies, local government bodies and special government," the latter of which is undefined. OR. STAT. § 174.109, http://www.oregonlaws.org/ors/174.109.

139. *Id.* § 2(2)(a)–(b).
140. *Id.* § 5.
141. TN SB 796, § 1(c) (amending TENN. CODE ANN., tit. 39, Ch. 13, pt. 6).
142. *Id.* § 1(d)(1)–(5).
143. *Id.* § 1(g)(1)–(2).
144. *Id.* § 1(f).
145. *Black's Law Dictionary* defines fugitive as "[o]ne who flees; used in criminal law with the implication of a flight, evasion or escape from arrest, prosecution or imprisonment." BLACK'S LAW DICTIONARY, 5th ed., West Publishing Co., 1979, p.604.
146. TX HB 912, § 423.002 (amending subtit. B, tit. 4, Gov't Code by adding Chapter 423, "Use of Unmanned Aircraft").
147. *Id.*
148. *Id.* § 423.003.
149. *Id.*
150. *Id.* § 423.005.
151. *Id.* § 423.006.
152. VA HB 2012, § 1.
153. *Id.* With respect to the National Guard, VA law states:

> The prohibitions in this section shall not apply to the (State) National Guard while utilizing unmanned aircraft systems during training required to maintain readiness for its federal mission, when facilitating training for other United States Department of Defense units, or when such systems are utilized for the Commonwealth for purposes other than law enforcement, including damage assessment, traffic assessment, flood stages, and wildfire assessment . . . .

See also PA SB 875, § 5(1)–(3), which contains identical language. "Title 32" status is usually a "training" status, where the federal government provides training funds to National Guard units.
154. HR 972, § 2.
155. *Id.*
156. *Id.* § 4.
157. HR 1262, § 341; HR 2868, § 3(a)(1).
158. HR 1262 & HR 2868, § 341(a)–(b).
159. *Id.* § 341(b)(3)–(4).
160. *Id.* § 341(b)(6).
161. H.R. 637—*Preserving American Privacy Act of 2013.* As do some states, the PAPA also addresses private, or nongovernmental, use of drones. Like CA Senate Bill No. 15, it makes it unlawful to intentionally collect, "in a manner highly offensive to a reasonable person," images of individuals "engaging in a personal or familial activity under circumstances in which the individual had a reasonable expectation of privacy." Unlike the California bill, the PAPA fails to describe the remedy for such a violation. *Id.* § 3119f; CA SB No. 15.
162. *Id.* § 3119i.
163. *Id.* § 3119h.
164. *Id.* § 3119c(c)(b)(1)–(5).
165. *Id.* § 3119b(b) and (c). The data collection statement would include the purpose of the operation, whether the drone is capable of collecting covered information, data retention time, a point of contact for citizen feedback, the responsible unit, the rank and title of the person authorizing the operation, and data minimization policies, as well as oversight procedures. HR

637, § 3119b(c) (1)(A)–(H). This is similar to information required in a DoD PUM. *See, e.g.,* AFI 14-104, Attachment 4.

166. *Id.* § 3119c(5)(B); § 3119c(1)(B).

167. *Id.* § 3119c(c)(a).

168. *Id.* § 3119a(2)(A)–(B).

169. H.R. 1083. Person is defined at 49 U.S.C. § 40102(a)(37) as including "a governmental authority and a trustee, receiver, assignee, and other similar representative."

170. HR 1242, *To prohibit the use of drones to kill citizens of the US within the U.S.* (Rep. Reid Ribble, R-WI), *available at* http://www.gpo.gov/fdsys/pkg/BILLS-113hr1242ih/pdf/BILLS-113hr1242ih.pdf; S. 505, *Bill to prohibit use of drones to kill U.S. citizens in U.S.* (Sen. Ted Cruz, R-TX), *available at* http://www.gpo.gov/fdsys/pkg/BILLS-113s505pcs/pdf/BILLS-113s505pcs.pdf.

171. Att'y Gen. Holder, Letter to Sen. Paul, March 7, 2013, note 113, *supra.*

172. DoDI 3025.21, Encl. 3, § 5(a)–(b) and Encl. 3, §§ 1, 1c(1)(a)–(g); DoDD 3025.18, ¶ 4o and DepSecDef Memo, Sept. 28, 2006.

173. CJCS DSCA EXORD 2013, ¶ 3.C.4.J.1.

174. DoDD 3025.18, ¶ 4.o.

175. Att'y Gen. Holder, Letter to Sen. Paul, March 7, 2013, note 113, *supra.*

176. *See* notes 7, 13–14, *supra.*

177. For a more thorough discussion of state and federal drone proposals, DoD drone policies, and existing constitutional and other principles, in relation to a framework that allows drones to be used to their full potential while protecting personal privacy across all operations, *see* DAWN M.K. ZOLDI, COL., USAF, DRONES AT HOME: DOMESTIC LEGISLATION—A SURVEY, ANALYSIS AND FRAMEWORK, pending publication and available upon request from the author.

178. *See* note 20, *supra.*

179. *Id.*; *see also* notes 51 and 56, *supra.*

180. *See* notes 19 and 132, *supra.*

181. Florida, Illinois, and the federal bill use the language, "to forestall the imminent escape of a suspect." Tennessee allows drones to be used in "searching for a fugitive or escapee" and Texas for "immediate pursuit of a suspect (who may have committed an offense greater than a misdemeanor)." *See* notes 121, 128, 155, 142, 147, in that order.

182. *See* note 23, *supra,* for fleeing felon citations.

183. WI SB 196/AB 203, § 2, 175.55(2).

184. *See* notes 121, 128, and 164, *supra.*

185. All the "conspiratorial activities threatening a national security interest also include "conspiratorial activities characteristic of organized crime": AR HB 1904, § 12-19-104, ¶ (a)(2)(i)(a); HI SB 783, § 1, ¶ 263B-4(1); ME SP 72, § 4504, ¶ 1(A); and MI HB 4455, § 9, ¶ (1)(a).

186. *See also* note 25, *supra.*

187. *See* note 150, *supra.*

188. *See* note 144, *supra.*

189. *See respectively* notes 131, 53, and 66, *supra.*

190. *See* notes 95–96, *supra.*

191. *See* note 31, *supra,* for facial recognition or other biometric matching technology citations.

192. *See* note 69, *supra.*

193. Youngstown Sheet & Tube Co. et al. v. Sawyer, 343 U.S. 579 (1952), Justice Jackson concurring ("When the President acts pursuant to an express or implied authorization of Congress, his authority is at its maximum.").

194. *See respectively* notes 75 and 81, *supra.*

195. *See* note 138, *supra.*

196. *See* notes 108–09, *supra.*

197. *See* notes 110–12, *supra.*

198. CA SB 15, § 14351.

199. *See* note 134, *supra*

200. Oregon House Bill 2710, § 16, explicitly exempts the United States Armed Forces, defined as including the Army, Navy, Air Force, Marine Corps, and Coast Guard of the United States; Reserve components of the Army, Navy, Air Force, Marine Corps, and Coast Guard of the United States; and the National Guard of the United States and the Oregon National Guard.

201. *See, e.g.,* 10 U.S.C. 8013(b) for Air Force OT&E authority, *available at* http://us-code.vlex.com/vid/sec-secretary-the-air-force-19219318.

202. *See* notes 104–06 *supra,* for exclusionary rule citations.

203. United States v. Janis, 428 U.S. 433, 96 S. Ct. 3021, 49 L. Ed. 2d 1046 (1976) (Held that a determination of whether the exclusionary rule should be applied in a civil proceeding involved weighing the deterrent effect of application of the rule against the societal costs of exclusion. Up to that point, the Court had never applied the exclusionary rule to exclude evidence from a civil proceeding, federal or state.)

204. *See* notes 40, 43–44, *supra.*

Appendix A
State Drone Legislation

Alabama (AL), SB 317—"*An Act relating to searches and seizures, to prohibit any government agency from using a drone to gather evidence or information . . .*" http://openStates.org/al/bills/2013rs/SB317/documents/ALD00014604/

Alaska (AK), HB 159a—"*An act relating to the admissibility of evidence through the use of an unmanned aerial vehicle . . .*" (Amending AS 09.25; 11.61; 12.45.038; and 18.65), http://www.legis.State.ak.us/PDF/28/Bills/HB0159A.PDF

AK Enrolled HCR 6—http://www.legis.state.ak.us/basis/get_fulltext.asp?session=28&bill=HCR6

Arizona (AZ), HB 2574—*"Citizens Protection from Unwarranted Surveillance Act"* (Amending ARS 13-3007), http://www.azleg.gov/FormatDocument.asp?inDoc=/legtext/51leg/1r/bills/hb2574p.htm&Session_ID=110

AZ HB 2269—*"House Interim Study Committee on Unmanned Aircraft,"* http://legiscan.com/AZ/text/HB2269/id/691575

Arkansas (AR), HB 1904—*"Unmanned Aerial Vehicle Act"* (Amending Arkansas Code 12-19), http://www.arkleg.State.ar.us/assembly/2013/2013R/Pages/BillInformation.aspx?measureno=HB190

AR SB1109—*"Prohibiting Use of an Unmanned Aerial Device that Is Equipped with a Video Recording Device Except When Used by a Law Enforcement Agency or Authorized Emergency Personnel,"* http://www.arkleg.state.ar.us/assembly/2013/2013R/Bills/SB1109.pdf

California (CA), Assembly Bill 1327—*"Unmanned Aircraft Systems"* (Amending Title 14, Section 14350), http://www.leginfo.ca.gov/pub/13-14/bill/asm/ab_1301-1350/ab_1327_bill_20130429_amended_asm_v96.pdf,

CA Senate Bill No. 15, http://www.leginfo.ca.gov/pub/13-14/bill/sen/sb_0001-0050/sb_15_bill_20130627_amended_asm_v94.pdf and

CA Assembly Joint Resolution 6, http://leginfo.legislature.ca.gov/faces/billNavClient.xhtml?bill_id=201320140AJR6&search_keywords=

Florida (FL), SB 92 (*passed)—*"Freedom from Unwarranted Surveillance Act,"* http://www.flsenate.gov/Session/Bill/2013/0092

Georgia (GA), SB 200 (Amending Georgia Code Ann. 16-11-60; 16-11-121; 16-11-124)—http://legiscan.com/GA/text/SB200/id/755795

GA HB 560 (Amending Ga. Code Ann. 4-17)—http://www.legis.ga.gov/legislation/en-US/Display/20132014/HB/560

Hawaii (HI), SB 783—*"Unmanned Aerial Vehicles; Ban on Surveillance by Drones"* (Amending HI Rev. Stat. Chapter 63B), http://www.capitol.hawaii.gov/session2013/bills/SB783_.pdf

Idaho (ID), SB 1134 (*passed)—*"Restrictions on Use of Unmanned Aircraft Systems"* (Amending Title 21 Sections 213 through 216), http://legislature.idaho.gov/legislation/2013/S1051.pdf#xml=http://http://legislature.search.ida

Illinois (IL), SB 1587 (*passed)—*"Freedom from Drone Surveillance Act,"* http://www.ilga.gov/legislation/fulltext.asp?DocName=&SessionId=85&GA=98&DocTypeId=SB&DocNum=1587&GAID=12&LegID=72407&SpecSess=&Session=

IL HB 1652 (Amending the Fish and Aquatic Life Code), http://www.ilga.gov/legislation/BillStatus.asp?DocNum=1652&GAID=12&DocTypeID=HB&LegID=72844&SessionID=85&GA=98&SpecSess=0

Indiana (IN), SB 20—(Amending IC 35-46-10), http://www.in.gov/legislative/bills/2013/IN/IN0020.1.html

IN Senate Resolution 27, http://www.in.gov/legislative/bills/2013/SRESP/SR0027.html

Iowa (IA), SF 276—*"An Act relating to the use of an Unmanned Aircraft System by a State or local law enforcement agency,"* http://coolice.legis.iowa.gov/Cool-ICE/default.asp?Category=billinfo&Service=Billbook&menu=false&hbill=SF276

IA H.F. 410—*"Use of unmanned aircraft system—prohibition,"* http://coolice.legis.iowa.gov/Cool-ICE/default.asp?Category=billinfo&Service=Billbook&menu=false&hbill=HF410&ga=85

IA H.F. 427—*"Use of drones by law enforcement agencies prohibited—exceptions—remedy,"* http://search.legis.state.ia.us/NXT/gateway.dll/cl/85th%20ga%20-%20session%201/03___introduced/001___bills/01___house/hf%20042700.html?f=templates$fn=document-frameset.htm$q=drone%20$x=server$3.0#LPHit1

Kansas (KS), HB 2394—*"An Act concerning criminal procedure; prohibiting the use of drones by law enforcement agencies,"* http://www.kslegislature.org/li/b2013_14/measures/hb2394/

Kentucky (KY), HB 454—*"Citizens Freedom from Unwarranted Surveillance Act"* (Amending KRS Chapter 500), http://www.lrc.ky.gov/record/13RS/HB454.htm

KY 14 RS BR 1—*"Citizen's Freedom from Unwarranted Surveillance Act,"* http://www.lrc.ky.gov/record/14RS/HB11.htm

Maine (ME), SP 72—*"An Act to protect the privacy of citizens from domestic unmanned aerial vehicle use"* (Leg. Doc 236) (Amending 25 MRSA Pt 12), http://www.mainelegislature.org/legis/bills/display_ps.asp?snum=126&paper=SP0072PID=0;

Maryland (MD), ME HB 1233—*"An Act concerning criminal procedure—law enforcement agencies—use of drones,"* http://mgaleg.maryland.gov/2013RS/bills/hb/hb1233F.pdf

Massachusetts (MA), SB 1664—*"An Act to regulate the use of unmanned aerial vehicles,"* http://www.malegislature.gov/Bills/188/Senate/S1664

Michigan (MI), HB 4455—*"A bill to authorize and regulate the use of unmanned aircraft vehicles . . . ,"* http://www.legislature.mi.gov/documents/2013-2014/billintroduced/House/pdf/2013-HIB-4455.pdf

MI HB 4456—http://www.legislature.mi.gov/documents/2013-2014/billintroduced/House/pdf/2013-HIB-4456.pdf

Minnesota (MN), HF 1620/ 1706 & SF 1506—*"An Act relating to public safety; prohibiting law enforcement agencies from using drones to gather evidence,"* https://www.revisor.mn.gov/bills/text.php?number=HF1620&version=0&session=ls88&session_year=2013&session_number=0

MN H.F. 990—"*A bill for an act . . . regulating unmanned aircraft . . .* ," http://wdoc.house.leg.state.mn.us/leg/LS88/HF0990.0.pdf

Missouri (MO), HB 46—"*Preserving Freedom from Unwarranted Surveillance Act*" (Amending Ch. 305 RSMo), http://legiscan.com/MO/text/HB46/id/749046

Montana (MT), SB 196 (*passed)—"*An Act limiting the use of unmanned aerial vehicles by law enforcement; and prohibiting the use of unlawfully obtained info as evidence in court,*" (Amending 46-1-202) http://data.opi.mt.gov/bills/2013/billhtml/SB0196.htm

Nebraska (NE), LB 412—"*Freedom from Unwarranted Surveillance Act,*" http://nebraskalegislature.gov/FloorDocs/Current/PDF/Intro/LB412.pdf

Nevada (NV), S.B 385 and Assembly Bill 507 (appropriations)—http://www.leg.state.nv.us/Session/77th2013/Bills/AB/AB507_EN.pdf and http://www.leg.state.nv.us/Session/77th2013/Reports/history.cfm?billname=SB385

New Hampshire (NH), HB 619—"*An act prohibiting images of a person's residence to be taken from the air,*" http://legiscan.com/NH/text/HB619/id/719399

New Jersey (NJ), No. 3157—"*An Act concerning police surveillance . . .*" (Supplementing Title 2A), http://www.njleg.State.nj.us/2012/Bills/A3500/3157_I1.PDF

NJ Assembly Bill 3929—"*An Act concerning the use of unmanned aerial vehicles by law enforcement,*" http://www.njleg.state.nj.us/2012/Bills/A4000/3929_I1.PDF

New Mexico (NM), SB 556—"*Freedom from Unwarranted Surveillance Act,*" http://www.nmlegis.gov/Sessions/13%20Regular/bills/senate/SB0556.pdf

New York (NY), AO 6370/ SO 4537 (same)—"*Empire State citizen's protection against Unwarranted Surveillance act,*" http://assembly.State.ny.us/leg/?sh=printbill&bn=S04537&term=2013

NY AO 6244—"*Protection against unwarranted surveillance,*" http://assembly.State.ny.us/leg/?sh=printbill&bn=A06244&term=2013

NY AO 8091—"*Unlawful surveillance by use of a drone,*" http://assembly.state.ny.us/leg/?sh=printbill&bn=A08091&term=2013

NY AO 6541—"*An Act to amend the civil rights law in relation to the use of unmanned aerial vehicles,*" http://assembly.state.ny.us/leg/?sh=printbill&bn=A06541&term=2013

North Carolina (NC), HB 312—"*Preserving Privacy Act of 2013,*" http://www.ncleg.net/Sessions/2013/Bills/House/PDF/H312v0.pdf

NC S.B. 402—"*An act to make base budget appropriations for current operations of state departments,*" http://ncleg.net/Sessions/2013/Bills/Senate/PDF/S402v7.pdf

North Dakota (ND), HB 1373 and (2)—"*A Bill for an Act to provide limitation on the use of UA for surveillance and to provide for a legislative management study,*" http://www.legis.nd.gov/assembly/63-2013/documents/13-0664-02000.pdf?20130520132201

ND SB 2018 (Appropriations Committee) (*passed)—http://www.legis.nd.gov/assembly/63-2013/documents/13-8168-05000.pdf? 20130806145059

Ohio (OH), H.B. 207—*"An act to limit the use of drones by law enforcement agencies and prohibit the defense of sovereign immunity,"* http://www.legislature.state.oh.us/bills.cfm?ID=130_HB_207

Oklahoma (OK), HB 1556—*"Oklahoma Unmanned Aerial Surveillance Act,"* http://webserver1.lsb.State.ok.us/cf_pdf/2013-14%20INT/hB/HB1556%20INT.PDF

OK H.B. 1795—*"Unmanned Aerial Vehicles and Drones Act,"* http://www.oklegislature.gov/BillInfo.aspx?Bill=HB179

Oregon (OR), HB 2710 (*passed)—*"A Bill for an Act relating to drones and declaring an emergency,"* www.leg.State.or.us/13reg/measures/hb2700.dir/hb2710.en.pdf

OR S.B. 524—*"Relating to drones and declaring an emergency,"* http://www.leg.state.or.us/13reg/measpdf/sb0500.dir/sb0524.intro.pdf

OR S.B. 71—*"Relating to drones and declaring an emergency,"* http://www.leg.state.or.us/13reg/measpdf/sb0001.dir/sb0071.intro.pdf

OR S.B. 853—"Relating to drones . . . and declaring an emergency," http://www. leg.state.or.us/13reg/measpdf/sb0800.dir/sb0853.intro.pdf

Pennsylvania (PA), HB 961—*"Unmanned Aerial Surveillance"* (18 PCS Chapter 57), http://www.legis.State.pa.us/CFDOCS/Legis/PN/Public/btCheck.cfm?txtType=PDF&sessYr=2013&sessInd=0&billBody=H&billTyp=B&billNbr=0961&pn=1102.

PA S.B. 875—*"Fourth Amendment Protection Act,"* http://www.legis.state.pa.us/CFDOCS/Legis/PN/Public/btCheck.cfm?txtType=PDF&sessYr=2013&sessInd=0&billBody=S&billTyp=B&billNbr=0875&pn=1028

Rhode Island (RI), GA—*"An Act relating to criminal procedure: unmanned aerial vehicles"* (Title 12 Chapter 5.3), http://webserver.rilin.State.ri.us/BillText/BillText13/HouseText13/H5780.pdf

RI LC00564—"Aerial Privacy Protection Act," http://webserver.rilin.state.ri.us/billtext13/senatetext13/s0411.pdf

South Carolina (SC), H3415—*"Freedom from Unwarranted Surveillance Act"* (17-13-180), http://www.scStatehouse.gov/query.php?search=DOC& searchtext=drones&category= LEGISLATION&session=120&conid= 7183564&result_pos=0&keyval =1203415&numrows=10

SC G.A. Bill 395—*"To prohibit . . . unmanned aerial vehicle containing an antipersonnel device,"* http://www.scstatehouse.gov/query.php?search=DOC& searchtext=surveillance&category=LEGISLATION&session=120&conid=7338399 &result_pos=0&keyval=1200395&numrows=10

Tennessee (TN), HB 591—"*Freedom from Unwarranted Surveillance Act*" (TCA 39, Ch. 13, Part 6), http://www.capitol.tn.gov/Bills/108/Bill/HB0591.pdf

TN S.B. 796,"*Freedom from Unwarranted Surveillance Act*," (*passed)—http://state.tn.us/sos/acts/108/pub/pc0470.pdf

Texas (TX), HB 912—"*Texas Privacy Act*," (Title 4, Chapter 423) (*passed), http://www.capitol.state.tx.us/tlodocs/83R/billtext/pdf/HB00912F.pdf #navpanes=0

Vermont (VT), HB 540/SB 169—"*An Act relating to regulating the use of drones*," http://www.leg.State.vt.us/docs/2014/bills/Intro/H-540.pdf

Virginia (VA), HB 2012— (*passed), http://leg1.State.va.us/cgi-bin/legp504.exe?131+ful+CHAP0755 VA S.B. No 954—"*Relating to willfully impeding hunting*," http://lis.virginia.gov/cgi-bin/legp604.exe?131+ful+SB954

Washington (WA), HB 1771—"*An Act relating to protecting Washington citizens from warrantless surveillance . . .* ," http://apps.leg.wa.gov/documents/billdocs/2013-14/Pdf/Bills/House%20Bills/1771-S.pdf

WA S.B. 5782—"*Relating to protecting WA citizens from warrantless surveillance*," http://apps.leg.wa.gov/documents/billdocs/2013-14/Pdf/Bills/Senate%20Bills/5782.pdf

West Virginia (WV), HB 2732—"*Freedom from Unwarranted Surveillance Act*," http://www.legis.State.wv.us/Bill_Text_HTML/2013_SESSIONS/RS/Bills/hb2732%20intr.htm

WV HB 2948—"*Freedom from Unwarranted Surveillance Act*," http://www.legis.state.wv.us/Bill_Text_HTML/2013_SESSIONS/RS/Bills/hb2948%20intr.htm

WV House Concurrent Resolution No. 101—http://www.legis.state.wv.us/Bill_Text_HTML/2013_SESSIONS/RS/Bills/hcr101%20intr.htm

WV H.B. 2997—"*Relating to prohibiting use of unmanned aircraft . . .* ," http://www.legis.state.wv.us/Bill_Text_HTML/2013_SESSIONS/RS/Bills/hb2997%20intr.htm

Wisconsin (WI), S.B. 196 and Assembly Bill 203—"*Relating to restricting the use of drones*" (same), https://docs.legis.wisconsin.gov/2013/related/proposals/ab203

Wyoming (WY), HB 0242—"*Unmanned Aerial Surveillance Act*" (WS 7-3010001 through 7-3-1005), http://legisweb.State.wy.us/2013/Introduced/HB0242.pdf

Appendix B
Federal Drone Legislation

H.R. 637—*"Preserving American Privacy Act of 2013"* (R. Ted Poe, R-TX) (Amends 18 USC 205), http://www.gpo.gov/fdsys/pkg/BILLS-113hr637ih/pdf/BILLS-113hr637ih.pdf

H.R. 830—*"Secure America Through Verification and Enforcement Act of 2013"* (SAVE Act), http://www.gpo.gov/fdsys/pkg/BILLS-112hr830rfs/pdf/BILLS-112hr830rfs.pdf

H.R. 972—*"Preserving Freedom from Unwarranted Surveillance Act of 2013"* (R. Austin Scott, R-GA), http://www.gpo.gov/fdsys/pkg/BILLS-113hr972ih/pdf/BILLS-113hr972ih.pdf

H.R. 1083—*"No Armed Drones Act or NADA Act of 2013"* (R. Michael Burgess, R-TX) (Amends FAA Mod and Reform Act 2012), http://www.gpo.gov/fdsys/pkg/BILLS-112hr5950ih/pdf/BILLS-112hr5950ih.pdf

H.R. 1242—*"To prohibit the use of drones to kill citizens of the U.S. within the U.S."* (R. Reid Ribble, R-WI), http://www.gpo.gov/fdsys/pkg/BILLS-113hr1242ih/pdf/BILLS-113hr1242ih.pdf

H.R. 1262—*"Drone Aircraft Privacy and Transparency Act"* (R. Ed Markey, D-MA) (Amends FAA Mod. And Reform Act 2012), http://www.gpo.gov/fdsys/pkg/BILLS-113hr1262ih/pdf/BILLS-113hr1262ih.pdf

H.R. 1269—*"Life, Liberty, and Justice for All Americans Act"* (R. Trey Radel, R-FL), http://www.gpo.gov/fdsys/pkg/BILLS-113hr1269ih/pdf/BILLS-113hr1269ih.pdf

H.R. 1960—NDAA for FY 2014 (R. Howard McKeon, R-CA); same as S 1197 (S. Carl Levin, D-MI), http://www.gpo.gov/fdsys/pkg/BILLS-113s1197pcs/pdf/BILLS-113s1197pcs.pdf

H.R. 2124—*"Keeping the Promise of ICRA Act,"* http://www.gpo.gov/fdsys/pkg/BILLS-113hr830ih/pdf/BILLS-113hr830ih.pdf

H.R. 2183—*"Drones Accountability Act"* (R. Barbara Lee, D-CA), http://www.gpo.gov/fdsys/pkg/BILLS-113hr2183ih/pdf/BILLS-113hr2183ih.pdf

H.R. 2438—*"Designating Requirement on Notification of Executive-ordered Strikes Act of 2013"* (DRONES Act) (R. Darrell Issa, R-CA) (DRONES Act), http://www.gpo.gov/fdsys/pkg/BILLS-113hr2438ih/pdf/BILLS-113hr2438ih.pdf

H.R. 2868—"*Drone Aircraft Privacy and Transparency Act of 2013*" (R. Peter Welch, D-VT), http://www.gpo.gov/fdsys/pkg/BILLS-113hr2868ih/pdf/BILLS-113hr2868ih.pdf

S. 505—"*Bill to prohibit use of drones to kill U.S. citizens in U.S.*" (S. Ted Cruz, R-TX), http://www.gpo.gov/fdsys/pkg/BILLS-113s505pcs/pdf/BILLS-113s505pcs.pdf

S, 1057—"*Safeguarding Privacy and Fostering Aerospace Innovation Act of 2013*" (S. Mark Udall, D-CO), http://www.gpo.gov/fdsys/pkg/BILLS-113s1057is/pdf/BILLS-113s1057is.pdf

Epilogue

The Laws of Counterterrorism: What Next?

W. George Jameson

"In enacting this legislation, it is the intent of Congress to provide a comprehensive program for the future security of the United States . . . ."
—National Security Act of 1947, Section 2 (50 U.S.C. § 401)

"Are we done yet?"

—Ice Cube, 2007

The evolution of U.S. policy and application of the laws in dealing with terrorism over the past 20-plus years—from a "criminal" focus to a "war and national security" focus to a "criminal and war and national security focus"—has left many confused about the sufficiency of U.S. laws, policies, and capabilities for addressing counterterrorism challenges. Twelve years after the catalytic events of 9/11, questions continue to arise over whether the United States is doing too little or too much to protect Americans; whether privacy and civil liberties are being violated, otherwise at risk, or neither; and whether organizational responsibilities and legal authorities are inadequate, overbroad, or both. Seemingly, the answer is "yes."

The public's continuing national and even international debates about U.S. counterterrorist efforts recently have been evidenced in the frenzied commentaries over the legality, propriety, and efficacy of intelligence-collection efforts epitomized by the National Security Agency's so-called PRISM and related programs. Both the Bush and the Obama administrations long resisted calls for greater transparency about the legal basis for operations, generally opposing public release of all the legal opinions interpreting the basis for interrogation and detention policies and the precise rationale for the use of drones to kill terrorists, respectively. Some—mostly, but not only, critics of U.S. policies—allege that there is confusion over the extent of and authorities for ongoing programs. They suggest a need for greater clarity as to both the laws and the principles that govern the U.S. approach to anticipating and dealing with terrorist threats and acts, from collection of information through disposition of those clearly involved in carrying out terrorist activities. In addition, critics and defenders alike assert that it is an open question whether U.S. laws are fully adequate to address the significant challenges the nation faces in countering terrorism and defending national security while protecting civil liberties and privacy interests.

The chapters in this book, like those in its predecessor, *The Law of Counterterrorism*, commendably make significant contributions to an understanding of the laws currently available to address terrorism challenges. The purpose of this epilogue is to highlight issues that warrant attention and to stimulate thinking about the current phase of the post-9/11 era. This period has been described by some as the "new normal"—less frenetic than the period immediately following 9/11, but nevertheless a period fraught with danger to Americans and others in the U.S. and abroad. In this author's view, future discussions about possible solutions, and any successors to this book, should strive to take advantage of this period of relative calm to contribute to enactment of measures that can ensure clear, transparent policies and laws that address terrorism and homeland security–related problems both comprehensively and, rather than in piecemeal and reactive fashion, proactively.

The Challenge: Balancing National Security and Civil Liberties Interests

Following the horrific destruction of the World Trade Center towers on September 11, 2001, Congress and the Executive were pressed to act by the urgent demands of a nation fearing that additional attacks on U.S. soil were imminent. The result, as we know, was enactment of several statutes authorizing swift, adaptable, and direct action to bring the perpetrators and their affiliates to justice. The Authorization for the Use of Military Force (AUMF), PATRIOT Act, Foreign Intelligence Surveillance Act (FISA), and other legislative amendments, along with the creation of the Department of Homeland Security and a new Director of National Intelligence, were measures designed to empower and energize U.S. counterterrorism efforts. They were intended to provide both an organizational framework and requisite legal authorities to meet the challenges and threats ahead. These measures have met with some considerable, although not complete, success. Today, questions still persist and new questions continue to arise over matters relating to the policies and legal authorities and responsibilities to conduct warrantless searches and intelligence gathering, to capture and detain terrorist suspects or target them for killing, and the appropriate measures for U.S. authorities to bring terrorists to U.S. or foreign tribunals for prosecution and justice.

Some commentators have noted that suggestions to amend the laws sometimes are not much more than reactive, ad hoc proposals to address the most recent specific terrorist acts or alleged government missteps. For example, following one attempted terrorist plot, some urged the U.S. to lower the threshold for inclusion of names of suspected terrorists on the "no-fly list"; ironically, this was not long after calls to limit the inclusion of names. Others have sought legislation to provide for summary loss of U.S. citizenship for terrorists. Also, controversy over whether suspected terrorists could evade justice by refusing to answer questions without having a lawyer present led to calls to modify the requirements for implementing *Miranda* in order to hold suspects for questioning. Law enforcement practices now implement policies that enable U.S. officials to consider the timing of such "you have the right to remain silent" warnings in questioning terrorist suspects. Concerns over the installation of cameras on city streets have raised privacy interests, but those concerns became somewhat muted following the attacks at the Boston Marathon after street cameras, admittedly private and not government-owned, led to the speedy identification of suspects.

The government has touted its successes in preventing terrorist acts by citing to its use of electronic surveillance capabilities under the Foreign Intelligence Surveillance Act (FISA) enacted in 1978. That act was amended after 9/11 to enable intelligence and law enforcement authorities to collaborate more effectively in gathering and sharing intelligence. Officials from both the executive and legislative branches note the value of these authorities, including the much-publicized sections 215 and 702, which provide authority for broad collection of data without need to identify specific targets. They further note that the measures are a statutory response to the pressures to do more to identify and locate terrorists. Others cite civil liberty concerns that such efforts have gone too far. At least one noted authority has argued that the measures are unconstitutional, even if they are legally authorized by statute.

Debates over the legality and propriety of national security operations should not be surprising. As this author has heard a former CIA director say to an ABA audience, "When Americans are afraid, they want CIA to do more; and when not afraid, they think we are doing too much." The government deals with such situations as they occur, typically justifying what it has or has not done under existing legal authorities while seeking ways to modify and improve its practices to deal with the next case that raises those same scenarios. Sometimes, when there is time for reflection, officials seek to anticipate needs and provide statutory bases that are not simply reactive. Often, the focus of such efforts is driven by ever-increasing technological advances that threaten U.S. security. Typically standing in the way of change are either secrecy, concerns with civil liberties or unintended consequences, or bureaucratic or other priorities.

As other authors in this book indicate, calls for creation of a new "terrorism court" suggest to some an alternative to the confusion that can result from having to choose whether to bring suspects before Article III courts or military commissions. Congress and the President agreed on a special court to deal with electronic and, later, physical surveillance, and military commissions have operated since long before the post-9/11 establishment of commissions for detainees. Accordingly, a special court to prosecute terrorists provides a new but not unprecedented option for handling such cases properly and securely. Yet, 35 years after its establishment pursuant to the FISA, the so-called FISA court, or FISC, has become embroiled in controversy for approving—in secret, but absent any actual proof of wrongdoing or illegal action—government collection and amalgamation of vast amounts of data that pertain to the activities of Americans. Some assert these actions have, even if legal, crossed the boundaries of what this nation should do—even in the hunt for foreign terrorists who would attack U.S. interests and kill citizens and others. Others note a need for greater transparency into the processes and legal rationale, and further claim that the non-adversarial nature of FISA proceedings violates due process and is in need of change.

Concerns about ensuring protection of national security, equal justice under the law, and other important principles were heightened when senior officials urged public trial in federal court and not before a military commission. One official publicly remarked without elaboration that the U.S. authorities might not release certain terrorists even if they are acquitted in an Article III court. To those familiar with the laws of war, the notion that prisoners can be held until war's end is not new. To those more comfortable with the criminal justice system's handling of violations of U.S. criminal law, the concept is disconcerting to say the least, particularly when there is no clear sense of when or if hostilities will end.

Similarly, many have expressed concern that the U.S. government could and would target an American citizen for a drone strike without a judicial or some other public due process proceeding. The lack of full transparency over the legal rationale and factual basis for doing so fuels those who believe these, if not all, drone activities are ill-considered, counterproductive, and illegal. This view persists despite the Administration's public presentations—from senior officials in the State, Justice, and Defense departments as well as the National Security Council staff—of legal rationales that articulate the U.S. position. In large measure, the continued secrecy surrounding these activities, including the continued classification of legal opinions and court rulings, hinders full acceptance of the government's rationale.

Secrecy can present conflicting concerns. Although some profess to disagree, it is clear at least to this author that leaks of classified information can be damaging. Debates persist, and have probably always existed, over whether disclosures of classified operations are treason, other perfidy, or honorable whistle-blowing. The government's episodic successes and failures to take steps to identify and punish those who have, for whatever motive, violated their sworn oaths of secrecy further erode confidence in the reliability of the government, its promises to agents and allies, and, when members of the press are investigated or questioned, the inviolability of a free press.

Reliance on statutes designed to punish foreign espionage as the primary means of prosecuting those who leak secrets to the media strikes some as only fitting, as President Truman noted that such leaks can be as damaging as espionage. In 2001, DCI Tenet urged the need for comprehensive leaks laws to facilitate identification and punishment of leakers. This could remove the espionage stigma from those who might be disloyal, but not spies for hostile foreign governments so much as enablers of a commercial press or other real or perceived legitimate cause. As a nation, we have not yet determined how to balance the need for a free press with the need for government secrecy to protect sensitive counterterrorism operations that have been disrupted and even discontinued by the revelation of their existence.

Secrecy that protects and enables an effective U.S. response to terrorism also can stymie redress efforts of innocent persons harmed by acts of terrorists, as well as others who allege they have been harmed by U.S. counterterrorist activities. "State secret" privilege claims fuel the outrage of those who question U.S. actions and values when courts decline to hear cases brought by claimants alleging they have been wrongfully accused of being terrorists and subjected to physical and mental abuse and, as a result, lawfully denied remedial action. Remedies normally available to U.S. citizens are not always available under the law to adjudicate civil liberties claims when national security interests are present. Rulings that deny a claimant's action to proceed because of government secrecy deny access to information that could, allegedly, show the harm caused. This can lead to further frustration with, if not distrust of, a government that they see as so uninterested in righting real or perceived wrongs that it would not even allow inquiry into the matter. Nevertheless, such is the state of the law, and so it has been from early in the history of our nation. And for those more concerned with equity than with law, the fact that redress might be available from private bills enacted by Congress offers little comfort.

A Way Ahead

Comprehensive Framework

The Congress recognized when it enacted the National Security Act in 1947 as a reaction to the surprise attack at Pearl Harbor that it is important to ensure that the U.S. approach to dealing with national security interests is appropriately comprehensive. U.S. laws should provide a broad framework to anticipate, detect, prevent, and counter terrorist threats and attacks against the United States and other U.S. national security interests. Transparent policies and legal approach would enable appropriately integrated U.S. actions to identify and bring terrorists, their sponsors, and their surrogates to justice in the U.S. or abroad and, perhaps, deter terrorist acts and their underlying causes. Understandably, perhaps, the U.S. solutions to terrorism concerns since 2001 have been largely reactive, as was the reaction to Pearl Harbor. It is time for an assessment of the adequacy of U.S. laws and policies to deal with terrorism both comprehensively and, to the extent possible, in an anticipatory fashion. As others have noted, this is best done by Congress and the Executive rather than left to the courts to address on an ad hoc basis.

In reviewing the adequacy of the laws relating to counterterrorism, several elements must be considered, including organizational structures, authorities, and relationships; tools for collection and analysis of information; and clear guiding principles. In addressing these matters, it might be useful to think in terms familiar to most junior high school students who have been told by their English teachers to be sure their school essays address "who, when, where, what, how, and why."

Who Should Do What: Form Versus Function

Much of the early debate regarding counterterrorism challenges has been directed at the "who"—which elements of the U.S. government should conduct particular operations. This is a typically bureaucratic approach, but one with operational implications if not imperatives. The Title 10 versus Title 50 discussions focus on whether the Department of Defense (DoD) and the military or, instead, the Central Intelligence Agency should have responsibility for paramilitary operations—for example, to conduct drone operations that target terrorists. Following proposals to consider transfer of paramilitary capabilities from CIA to DoD, the Bush Administration rejected that option after extensive interagency review. Moreover, as the successful UBL operation showed, a merger of the two can be highly effective. Yet questions persist. The answers, however, should depend less on bureaucratic organizational charts and more on which element has the capabilities to operate effectively in a particular situation to carry out the U.S. policies, goals, and objectives. In the sliding scale from covert (that is, non-attributable) action to open war, there is much gray area and room for debate over "who" should conduct an operation and why.

Similarly, renditions have long been a tool in the U.S. arsenal of options to bring criminals to justice. Whether they or other national security–related operations should be conducted solely by law enforcement or also by intelligence and military organizations precluded from having domestic law enforcement functions raises the question of the roles of law enforcement agencies in national security affairs. Amendments to FISA since 9/11 have been designed to improve collection capabilities against known or suspected terrorists, to detect unknown actors, and to enhance collaboration among intelligence and law enforcement agencies. This adjustment of authorities followed decades of enforcing varying degrees of separation between law enforcement and intelligence activities. This dynamic was driven by post–World War II fears that demanded that the new central intelligence organization, the CIA, not be a Gestapo-like entity that merged foreign and domestic responsibilities and, more dangerously, exercised authoritarian powers.

Even within any of the three intelligence and national security communities (that is, the national intelligence, law enforcement, and military communities), jurisdictional lines are sometimes unclear. For example, the demarcation lines for FBI and Department of Homeland Security responsibilities in the U.S. continue to lack precision as each element continues to refine its role for investigating and handling domestic homeland security–related threats and coordination with state and local authorities.

Some private efforts, like those of the Project on National Security Reform, have suggested consideration of an approach that ensures "unity of effort" as well as, in appropriate cases, "unity of command." This assumes as a basic premise that the U.S. as a whole has the capacity and authority to combat terrorism, but that dispersal of command and control reduces U.S. effectiveness and efficiency. A "unity" approach would revamp how operations are managed and redefine the role of the NSC as well as centralize oversight responsibilities of several congressional committees. Under this formulation, it shouldn't really matter who takes action so long as the full authorities of the U.S. are appropriately available and there is, as in the military model, someone in charge. Critics sometimes note that overseas the ambassador does not control the combatant commander nor, for that matter, the CIA's chief of station. On the other hand, it is not clear how a diplomat would effectively command troops in combat or coordinate the activities of spies.

This largely organizational issue involves legal, policy, and bureaucratic constraints that hamper effectiveness but also reflect a dynamic dictated by our national "DNA" that recognizes and values a separation of powers among the three distinct branches—legislative, executive, and judicial. A similar constitutional dynamic exists in how our nation distinguishes federal and state powers and responsibilities; not all power resides in one place. Tensions, therefore, are inherent in our system—a system designed in part to ensure that government conduct is constrained where necessary, even if this results in bureaucratic inertia, or worse.

Distinguishing military, intelligence, and law enforcement roles may appear to be unduly bureaucratic and inefficient, but also can provide necessary safeguards to protect the people from the risk of an overly powerful central organizational entity. The CIA is not authorized to perform law enforcement functions—a guard against another "Gestapo" that leaves to law enforcement experts the job of bringing criminals to trial; the Posse Comitatus Act precludes the military from exercising law enforcement authorities in light of experiences in post–Civil War politics; more recently, use of special collection authorities under FISA demands that do not envision adversarial, public proceedings are not permitted where the only interest is law enforcement. Also, some would recall the fears raised when the Department of Defense was established in 1947. Initially named the National Military Establishment, or NME, the name was changed upon realization that its pronunciation—"enemy" for NME—inappropriately suggested a powerful and sinister force. Today the FBI has both law enforcement and intelligence missions, and the military plays a lead role in countering terrorism. Any debate over "who" should do what to counter terrorism would be well-served by an examination of all these roles to guard against, or to ensure effective management of, any aggregation of power that could, left unchecked, run counter to the values and system upon which our nation is based.

Oversight

Another aspect of who should do what involves the important question of oversight responsibilities. Government agencies face multiple layers of oversight, both internal and external: agency counsel, inspectors general, the National Security Council, the President's Intelligence Advisory Board, House and Senate committees, the courts and, unofficially, the press. The President's Privacy and Civil Liberties Board has been recently constituted to help balance national security and civil liberties interests.

With respect to Congress, the intelligence committees have oversight responsibilities regarding covert action; the armed services committees for military operations; judiciary committees for law enforcement; foreign affairs committees for State; and for Homeland Security, it has been said that more than 100 committees and subcommittees of Congress have interests in overseeing DHS. Oversight typically hinges on which U.S. element conducts an activity. If operations merge, or if authorities for the conduct of operations are dispersed, oversight responsibilities become murky, with a potential for overlap as well as gaps. More important, perhaps, than which element is to be overseen will be the nature of the activity if the consequences—operational, diplomatic, military, or economic—are likely to be the same. The question of who—that is, which element of Congress, if any—has cognizance over the totality of U.S. counterterrorism efforts should be given careful consideration in any effort to establish a comprehensive counterterrorism approach.

When Should the U.S. Act?

Regardless of which agencies of government have particular authorities for counterterrorism activities, an important question asks "when" the U.S. should act. From the perspective of the United States (as opposed to that of our foreign allies whose citizens the U.S. might target), intelligence and other agencies should always collect information relating to the capabilities and intentions of foreign countries, their agents, and persons when the threat of terrorism is at stake. Nevertheless, some have pointed out a need to define "terrorism" in light of the distinctions between international terrorism and local terrorist acts that do not cross international borders but are strictly local matters. It should be clear when acts of terrorism should justify U.S. attention and response.

With respect to U.S. citizens or others within the United States, what is the "trigger" that should permit the collection of information to determine if a person is a terrorist? How long must the U.S. government, or, for that matter, the New York Police Department or other local authorities, wait before attempting to gather information through infiltration of social or religious groups? What are the limits on acting if a terrorist threat exists or could develop when the so-called triggering activity also can be seen as a legitimate exercise of First Amendment rights? How should the fears of rights violations or other harm affect law enforcement practices that could include data mining when the issue is not a matter of connecting the dots but requires finding the dots to begin with? What use should be made of drones over the United States, as the FBI recently acknowledged, or profiling to prevent action, as opposed to simply finding, in a more traditional law enforcement approach, the perpetrators of acts already committed? More direct targeting of specific individuals raises other concerns that warrant discussion and clarity, such as when the U.S. may target for lethal action an American or, for that matter, any other person who is involved in activities that pose a threat to U.S. persons or national security interests.

The laws of war and the criminal code each offer some answers for those who ask when the U.S. may act, depending on the context, and further exploration of these legal vehicles and the appropriateness of their use will be essential to help guide counterterrorism leadership in determining when to act in our nation's interests.

Where Can the U.S. Operate?

The distinctions between law enforcement and intelligence functions have carried with them the general rule, albeit not absolute, that typically delineated the roles of U.S. government agencies as domestic (the FBI's domain) versus foreign (a CIA focus). Whether and how an intelligence agency operated depended upon whether the persons or threats were domestic or foreign-based. Moreover, development of the law established legal parameters depending upon whether the target was an agent—usually but not always abroad—of a foreign power. This often reflected a determination whether the purpose of the collection was to advise policymakers who set policy or to take counterintelligence measures against foreign States or their agents, or whether the purpose was to take action against specific persons, such as to prosecute an individual in open U.S. court proceedings for violation of the criminal code. The former permitted use of more extraordinary authorities with fewer requirements for judicial review and carried less of a risk that collection of information would violate rights of U.S. persons. The latter, however, involved specific targets, often U.S. persons whose constitutional safeguards demanded observation of additional formalities and presentation of evidence in an adversarial open court proceeding. Espionage cases, to be sure, always presented elements of both categories.

In general, therefore, collection of intelligence has been described in terms of collection inside and collection outside the United States, at least following the establishment of Attorney General procedures governing each intelligence element pursuant to the series of executive orders governing their conduct. The resulting dotted or virtual line at the border, however, has less meaning today in light of technological advances whereby communications move back and forth across borders. This can make the inside-outside distinctions almost meaningless, especially when the war on terror, or perhaps more properly the war waged by terrorists, has made the battlefield global. If this is the case, then the historic questions of who acts and where become more difficult to address.

- The military fights wars abroad but has a domestic (NORTHCOM) presence to protect the homeland.
- The FBI, as both a law enforcement and intelligence agency, has a domestic focus, but its counterterrorism mission demands overseas insights and, as in the past, the capability to exercise its responsibilities in conjunction with foreign partners abroad.
- The NSA's collection activities target communications that may or may not implicate the rights of U.S. persons, and questions of whether the "ether" where its collection might occur increasingly pose challenges in

determining the adequacy and currency of laws designed to function based on technologies of the past.

- The CIA's role, as a foreign intelligence agency with covert action responsibilities, enables it to operate uniquely abroad without the role of the U.S. being acknowledged or apparent, and to operate in collaboration with its foreign partners in ways that other U.S. elements cannot. At the same time, although constrained in collection activities by directive, the CIA collection activities in the U.S. are not expressly precluded by statute. Nor is it suggested they should be, as the opposite might be true.
- As with the discussion of organizational roles and how functions within the government are assigned to handle a specific mission or challenge, the concept of unity of effort and unity of command warrant consideration of whether legal impediments exist that demand a "handoff" of activities once a threat moves across the U.S. border, regardless of direction.

What Can the U.S. Do and How?

These two categories—what and how—will be intertwined for purposes of this discussion. They strike at the heart of the debates about the legality and propriety of U.S. counterterrorism activities, such as:

- Analysis of social media to identify illicit or threatening activities.
- Acquisition of email and telephone records.
- Use of National Security Letters to obtain otherwise private financial records.
- Aggregating data to detect patterns to identify financial or weapons transactions and terrorists.
- Diplomatic or economic measures to counter terrorists or enlist support.
- Overt use of military elements to engage a ruthless and unrelenting adversary.
- Employment of covert capabilities to counter threats or influence potential allies.
- Strikes targeting specific terrorists or groups of persons presumed to be threats.

These activities, and more, must proceed on a sound legal basis. The AUMF will be of limited utility as the threat of Al-Qaeda and its affiliates diminishes and their threats are replaced by others. Developments in the case law, as seen in the Supreme Court's *Jones* decision rejecting the government's analysis about authorities to track vehicles, similarly suggest ambiguity regarding the extent of current authorities. Moreover, as noted, debates about FISA have included questions about whether activities are appropriate—and whether the gain is worth the pain—even if they are legal.

Unmentioned in this epilogue thus far, but by no means insignificant, the challenges of cyber threats also bring with them the need to ensure clarity both for the government and the state, local, and private-sector partners on whom the U.S. must rely so heavily. To date, there has been limited movement toward a statutory cyber framework that would be acceptable to Congress, the Executive, and the private sectors alike. Finding solutions to cyber threats will require weighing civil liberties, privacy, and, increasingly, financial and economic interests.

Unquestionably, the questions of legality have particular meaning for citizens and others who are the targets of U.S. counterterrorism operations. Another constituency eager to ensure clarity of authorities, however, is that comprising the government officials, contractors, and others who support the U.S. government's efforts. Those persons who act in good-faith service to their country expect they will be protected by laws, directives, and guidance that permit them to understand what they may do and how, and with the assurance that what they understood was lawful conduct would not subject them to years of second-guessing or lead them to bankruptcy in defending themselves during legal proceedings in the U.S. or abroad. It is for this reason that a necessary element of this discussion should address the need for a clear framework for appropriate, not *carte blanche*, grants of immunity.

Why Would the U.S. Act?

In its simplest terms, of course, the U.S. acts to protect itself and its citizens and interests. Whether a particular action is necessary will depend on the circumstances, but it would be useful to articulate basic principles and core authorities that are a little more specific than the language in the U.S. Constitution. Under executive order procedures for intelligence collection, agencies are required to utilize the least intrusive means necessary to gather information on U.S. persons. Debates over the effectiveness of PRISM and related programs ask whether collection of less data, or shorter retention periods, would better serve civil liberties interests. The AUMF authorizes military force as a response to the World Trade Center attacks in 2001, but as the Al-Qaeda threat either diminishes or morphs into something else, there will be a need to clarify the basis for future military actions. In the absence of clear statutory authority, it is likely that presidential authority will surface again as the default basis for action, with all the attendant debates about legality that this would entail.

Legal scholars might, *repeat might*, appreciate the basis for secret U.S. actions, but the global impact of terrorism and counterterrorist activities brings with it not just a clash of state and non-state actors but of different cultures, laws, and legal principles. For all that we might think the world is "flat," the respective laws and underlying principles that govern the U.S. and other nations differ, so it will be important to articulate basic principles for a foreign, not merely a U.S., audience.

- U.S. notions of privacy differ from those of many if not most European nations;
- State sovereignty as seen by China and Russia guide their actions with respect to, for example, Syria in ways that run counter to the U.S. view;
- The U.S. authority under the *Ker-Frisbie* doctrine to bring felons before a tribunal without a warrant so long as the government's conduct does not shock the conscience is considered unacceptable to some other nations;
- In contrast, trials in absentia, not favored in the U.S., seemed to raise no eyebrows in Italy's prosecution of U.S. officials on charges of abducting a terrorist from Italian soil; and
- Hearsay admissibility under the rules of the Yugoslav war crimes tribunal and International Criminal Court seem to go beyond what U.S. law would consider constitutionally acceptable.

Although treaties are the law of the land, commentators have noted the uproar over any actions by U.S. judges to cite to international law as appropriate legal authority for a judicial ruling. Nevertheless, as terrorism and cyber increasingly reflect their global reach, measures that cross national boundaries will have to be utilized or instituted, and international cooperation may be essential. Perhaps this will involve the use of the ICC as a means of detaining terrorists. Perhaps there is a need for new bilateral or international treaties. Perhaps legal principles will be established that treat international terrorists like, for example, pirates or criminal racketeers and that lead to a RICO-like structure to prevent, detect, and sanction terrorists.

Regardless, it seems likely there will be a need for the U.S policymakers to establish a legal rationale for what we do and why that will help assuage our foreign allies. Although this might not necessarily result in uniform acceptance, at the least our objectives and principles should be presented in terms so clear and unequivocal that there will be no doubt or confusion as to the reasons for our actions, their underlying legal basis, and, hopefully, the propriety of their adoption. It has been said that fanaticism is doubling one's efforts when one has forgotten one's goals. There can be no doubt about U.S. resolve in countering terrorism. It will be important to continue to identify and affirm those goals and to articulate them and their legal basis clearly, unequivocally, and comprehensively.

Conclusion

Experts from the law enforcement, military, intelligence, and domestic communities appear to understand and take comfort from the laws that enable them to address terrorism-related problems within their respective areas of responsibility and expertise. What is less obvious is whether either an overlap or a gap in laws and authorities exists to hamper more effective and collaborative U.S. efforts *across* these communities. One approach to ensuring a comprehensive approach to addressing counterterrorism interests is through a series of events or public discourses to address the adequacy of U.S. laws. These events could convene experts from across several relevant issue areas to discuss the intersection of or any gaps in their respective abilities to address terrorism-related matters and to ensure a comprehensive U.S. approach. Participation would include nonpartisan, expert professionals who currently or previously held government positions as well as others with no prior government experience. A similar effort has been undertaken by the American Bar Association's establishment of a cyber task force; that is a useful model to be considered.

Events could consist of panels of legal and policy experts from the law enforcement, military, intelligence, diplomatic, and civil government communities, as well as private-sector participants from the academic, civil liberties, media, and commercial communities. They would address, for example:

- Information collection and sharing in light of privacy, civil liberties, or other domestic considerations; authority of the government over the private sector.
- Considerations in targeting terrorists for apprehension, interrogation, and detention in light of the availability of Article III courts and military commissions; implications of criminal law and laws of war.
- Liability of federal officials and their agents in the United States and abroad.
- International collaboration and whether new arrangements are needed.
- Foreign aid and assistance policies and laws and any impact on root causes of terrorism as well as counterinsurgency implications.
- Immigration and other border laws and responsibilities and their impact on counterterrorism capabilities.
- Adequacy of U.S. laws and policies to provide remedies either to persons aggrieved by alleged U.S. improper conduct or to persons harmed by terrorist acts.

Actions taken as a result of these efforts would be part of the incremental process that has included measures such as the PATRIOT Act's provisions to facilitate collaboration between law enforcement and intelligence, amendments of the FISA, reorganization of the FBI, and, more recently, the review of communications privacy laws and cyber authorities in light of rapidly changing technologies.

The authors in Chapter 1 superbly indicate that there is a need to address political, social, and economic factors that contribute to the causes of terrorism and make countering terrorism so difficult. As subsequent chapters suggest, it also is important not to restrict the focus to military or counterinsurgency interests. For this reason, efforts to counter terrorism will also, as the drafters of the PATRIOT Act recognized, rely upon appropriate disposition of changes to immigration laws, air- and sea-port security, and increasing use of biometric capabilities that can detect hostiles seeking to enter this country but also can identify clandestine U.S. operatives seeking to penetrate hostile elements abroad.

A coherent, cohesive strategy will be essential in the years ahead, and a comprehensive legal regime will be essential. That said, it will be important to keep in mind that there will be no quick or simple solution. This author has no illusions about the enormity of the task, and we should expect that the question raised in the first chapter—"Why is countering terrorism so difficult?"—will continue to present itself well into the future. Nevertheless, this book and the fine work of its editor, Lynne Zusman, in highlighting issues and challenges of terrorism add valuable insights to the discussion and, perhaps, will help make the task a little less difficult.

About the Editor

Lynne Zusman has practiced law for many years and served federal government clients, private individual clients, and private corporate clients. A graduate of Bryn Mawr College *cum laude* with honors in political science and the Yale Law School, during the administration of former President Jimmy Carter she was tasked with screening cases brought against the U.S. government under the Freedom of Information Act and the Privacy Act of 1974 for recommendations aligning this defensive litigation, which she was responsible for, with President Carter's many initiatives for openness in government and privacy protection of individual citizens. *Fundamentals of Counterterrorism Law* is a direct outgrowth of this experience in legal accountability for national security objectives, as well as other important American governmental responsibilities. She has developed and edited two previous American Bar Association books: *The Law of Counterterrorism* (2011) and *Homeland Security: Legal and Policy Issues* (2009, coeditor).

About the Authors

Rod Azama is a vice president at Integrated Resource Technologies, Inc. and is a managing director of The Chancellor Group. He is a Certified Information Systems Security Professional (CISSP) and has also been a principal in Computer Science Corporation's Federal Consulting Practice. Prior to CSC, Rod was a consultant in the homeland/corporate security, international trade, and venture financing sectors, after serving from 1996 to 1998 as the U.S. Trade & Development Agency's Regional Director for Europe. Colonel Azama is a former career Army officer, serving in Special Forces, Foreign Area Officer, intelligence, and security assignments. He is a graduate of the U.S. Military Academy, taught in the academy's Department of Social Sciences, and has graduate degrees in business economics from the Wharton School of Business and in systems management from the University of Southern California.

Robert Barnsby is a lieutenant colonel in the U.S. Army and the chief of International and Operational Law with the XVIII Airborne Corps at Fort Bragg, North Carolina. A 1996 West Point graduate, Lieutenant Colonel Barnsby earned his JD at William & Mary School of Law, where he served as executive editor of the *William & Mary Law Review*. He previously served as the lead detention operations legal adviser for U.S. forces in Afghanistan, chief military prosecutor at Fort Drum, New York, and in various other key positions as a military practitioner. Most recently, he taught intelligence law, cyber law, and jus ad bellum as a professor of international and operational law at the Judge Advocate General's (JAG) School in Charlottesville, Virginia.

Lieutenant Colonel Barnsby has published several articles on armed conflict and security-related matters, including works on the State Secrets Privilege (*So Long, and Thanks for All the Secrets*, 63 ALA. L. REV. 667 (2012)), detention operations (*Yes We Can: The Authority to Detain as Customary International Law*, 202 MIL. L. REV. 53 (Winter 2009)) and customary international law (*The New Griffin of International Law: Hybrid Armed Conflicts*, HARV. INT'L REV. (Vol. XXXIV, Issue 3, Winter 2013), as co-author with Shane Reeves). He has spoken on international humanitarian law panels at a variety of law schools, including Harvard, Emory, Santa Clara, Syracuse, and the University of Texas.

Robert M. Blitzer was employed from 2006 to 2012 as a vice president and Homeland Security Senior Fellow at ICF International, a professional services company, in Fairfax, Virginia. In this position he was involved in business development and consulting engagements. Since 2010 he has served as a Senior Fellow at the George Washington University Homeland Security Policy Institute (HSPI). At the institute he participates in studies and writes on current topical subjects. Prior to joining ICF, Mr. Blitzer served from 2003 to 2006 as the Deputy Assistant Secretary in Charge of the Office of Emergency Operations and Security Programs, within the Office of Public Health Emergency Preparedness, at the U.S. Department of Health and Human Services (HHS). At HHS, he was responsible for developing and implementing plans, processes, and procedures that enabled the department to effectively respond to both natural and manmade disasters. Mr. Blitzer served as a key member of the HHS Secretary's National Security team and was relied upon for his analytical skills relating to classified intelligence issues and threat assessments. During his time with HHS, Mr. Blitzer was in a critical leadership role during responses to hurricanes, the SARs epidemic, major high profile interagency exercises, pandemic influenza planning, and planning for and managing HHS assets during National Special Security Events.

Jeff Breinholt serves as an attorney-advisor in the Department of Justice's Office of Law and Policy, National Security Division. He previously served as the deputy chief of the Counterterrorism Section and as a white-collar fraud prosecutor with the Tax Division. He also served briefly as senior fellow and director of national security law at the International Assessment and Strategy Center, a Washington, D.C.-based think tank. He is the author of two books and several dozen law review and legal practitioner articles, and his legal commentary has appeared in a variety of news outlets. He is a graduate of Yale (BA) and the UCLA School of Law(JD), and is a member of the State Bar of California.

Tania M. Chacho, PhD (lieutenant colonel, U.S. Army), is an academy professor directing the Comparative Politics Program in the Department of Social Sciences at the United States Military Academy, West Point. She teaches courses in comparative politics, international security strategy, and the government and politics of China. As a military intelligence officer, she has deployed to Bosnia-Herzegovina and Kosovo in support of international peacekeeping and stabilization operations. From 2004 to 2007, she served as a foreign area officer and special advisor to the Supreme Allied Commander, Europe, working for NATO. In 2008 she spent time in Iraq, conducting a study on the new Human Terrain Teams (HTTs).

Lt. Col. Chacho's publications include articles and book chapters on soldier motivation, military relations with non-governmental organizations, European defense initiatives, U.S. foreign policy toward Europe, and the People's Republic of China's involvement in humanitarian assistance/disaster relief (HA/DR) operations. She is a graduate of Johns Hopkins University and the Naval War College, and holds an MA and a PhD in international relations from the Johns Hopkins University School of Advanced International Studies (SAIS).

Michael J. Davidson served as a field artillery officer and as an Army judge advocate, retiring as a lieutenant colonel. He is currently an attorney with the federal government. Dr. Davidson earned his BS degree from the U.S. Military Academy, his JD from the College of William & Mary, an LLM in military law from the Army's Judge Advocate General's School, and both a second LLM and a Doctor of Juridical Science degree in government procurement law from George Washington University (GWU). He is the author of two books and more than 40 law review and legal practitioner articles. Any opinions are those of the author and do not reflect the position of any federal agency.

Thomas V. Fuentes is president of Fuentes International, L.L.C., a consulting firm based in Washington, D.C. He is a frequent on-air contributor for CNN regarding U.S. and international law enforcement and national security matters. He has been an executive consultant to Tate, Inc., Palantir Technologies, Inc., and Deloitte Consulting, Inc. He is also a member of the U.S. State Department's Overseas Security Advisory Council. In 2013 he joined Morris & McDaniel, Inc. as Vice President for International Development. He also received the Society of Asian Federal Officers' Lifetime Achievement Award in 2013.

Mr. Fuentes served as assistant director of the Federal Bureau of Investigation's Office of International Operations from 2004 until his retirement in November 2008. His 29-year career in the FBI included 11 years as a member of the U.S. government's Senior Executive Service. Mr. Fuentes directed the Office of International Operations, which included offices at FBI Headquarters in Washington, D.C., and 76 Legal Attaché offices in U.S. embassies and consulates worldwide. He also directed FBI personnel assigned to Interpol in Washington, D.C., the United Nations, and the General Secretariat office in Lyon, France, as well as Europol's Headquarters in The Hague, Netherlands.

Gregory M. Huckabee received his AB, MBA, and JD from Gonzaga University in Spokane, Washington. Commissioned in ROTC in 1974, he entered active duty in 1976. He received an LLM from the Judge Advocate General's School in Charlottesville, Virginia; an MS in education from Jacksonville State University in Jacksonville, Alabama; an MA in congressional studies from the Catholic University of America in Washington, D.C.; and an LLM from the George Washington University National Law Center in Washington, D.C. Selected in 2000 by the Council for the International Exchange of Scholars and the U.S.

Department of State to be a J. William Fulbright Scholar, Professor Huckabee served as a senior lecturer at the Jagiellonian University Center for American Studies in Krakow, Poland, while on active duty. He was only the second judge advocate in history to be selected for a Fulbright Scholarship.

Professor Huckabee previously held a variety of legal positions as a Regular Army judge advocate. While serving in the Pentagon, he was selected to represent the Army in performing a legislative drafting service revising the Soldiers' and Sailors' Civil Relief Act (50 U.S.C. App. 501) for the U.S. House of Representatives and subsequently was appointed chair of the Department of Defense Task Force. The completed draft became known as The Servicemembers Civil Relief Act, signed into law by President Bush on December 19, 2003 (50 U.S.C. App. 501–596). He also served for three years as an associate professor in the Department of Law at the U.S. Military Academy, West Point, New York. After serving 27 years as a judge advocate in the Regular Army, he became an associate professor of business law, joining the faculty at the University of South Dakota Beacom School of Business in August 2003. In 2006 he was honored with the Belbas-Larsen Award for Excellence in Teaching, the highest award for teaching bestowed by the University of South Dakota. Professor Huckabee served as a distinguished visiting professor at the U.S. Air Force Academy from 2012 to 2013.

W. George Jameson co-founded and heads the Council on Intelligence Issues, a nonprofit educational organization that educates the public about intelligence and national security issues and provides legal resources for intelligence officers who may need assistance. His firm, Jameson Consulting, advises on national security matters, operations, and governance. He also is an adjunct staff member at the RAND Corporation. George lectures on national security matters and contributed a chapter, *Intelligence and the Law,* to this book's predecessor publication, *The Law of Counterterrorism.*

George served more than 33 years in the Central Intelligence Agency and the U.S. intelligence community, most of his career as an attorney and manager in CIA's Office of General Counsel. He also managed legislative affairs at the CIA and the Office of the DNI, and was the director of the CIA's policy and coordination office. His responsibilities have included reviewing the legality and propriety of covert action, counterterrorism, and counterintelligence operations; war crimes matters; foreign relationships; information and privacy; security; and matters relating to formulation and implementation of intelligence community policies and reform. George serves on the Advisory Committee for the ABA's Standing Committee on Law and National Security; he is a member of the Steering Group for the Bar Association of D.C.'s Committee on National Security Law, Policy & Practice; and he is a member of the ABA's Section on Administrative Law and Regulatory

Practice. A graduate of Harvard College and William & Mary Law School, he a member of the D.C. and Virginia bars.

Christopher L. Kannady is Of Counsel to the Federal Practice Group in Washington, D.C. He continues to serve as counsel for Noor Muhammed, a Guantanamo Bay detainee. He is a major in the Air National Guard. He has a BA, an MBA, and a JD from the University of Oklahoma. He also holds an LLM from George Washington University in national security and foreign relations law.

Raymond W. Kelly was appointed Police Commissioner of the City of New York in January 2002 by Mayor Michael R. Bloomberg, making Commissioner Kelly the first person to hold the post for a second, separate tenure. He also served as police commissioner under Mayor David N. Dinkins from 1992 to 1994. In 2002, Commissioner Kelly created the first counterterrorism bureau of any municipal police department in the country. He also established a new global intelligence program and stationed New York City detectives in 11 foreign cities. Despite dedicating extensive resources to preventing another terrorist attack, the NYPD has driven crime down by 40 percent from 2001 levels. Commissioner Kelly also established a Real Time Crime Center, a state-of-the-art facility that uses data mining to search millions of computer records and put investigative leads into the hands of detectives in the field.

Commissioner Kelly was formerly senior managing director of global corporate security at Bear, Stearns & Co. Inc. Before that, he served as commissioner of the U.S. Customs Service, where he managed the agency's 20,000 employees and $20 billion in annual revenue. For his accomplishments at Customs, Commissioner Kelly was awarded the Alexander Hamilton Medal for Exceptional Service. From 1996 to 1998, Commissioner Kelly was under secretary for enforcement at the U.S. Treasury Department. There, he supervised the department's enforcement bureaus, including the U.S. Customs Service, the U.S. Secret Service, the Bureau of Alcohol, Tobacco, and Firearms, and the Federal Law Enforcement Training Center.

In addition, Mr. Kelly served on the executive committee and was elected vice president for the Americas of Interpol, the international police organization, from 1996 to 2000. In 1994, he was appointed to serve as director of the International Police Monitors in Haiti, a U.S.-led force responsible for ending human rights abuses and establishing an interim police force there. For this service, Commissioner Kelly was awarded the Exceptionally Meritorious Service Commendation by the President of the United States.

A 43-year veteran of the NYPD, Commissioner Kelly served in 25 different commands before being named police commissioner. He was appointed to the New York City Police Department in 1963. Shortly thereafter he accepted a commission to the U.S. Marine Corps Officer Program. He served on active military duty for three years, including a combat tour in Vietnam. He returned to the police department in 1966 and entered the New York City Police Academy, graduating with the highest combined average for academics, physical achievement, and marksmanship. He was also a member of the inaugural class of the New York City Police Cadet Corps for three years while a student at Manhattan College.

Commissioner Kelly holds a BBA from Manhattan College, a JD from St. John's University School of Law, an LL.M. from New York University Graduate School of Law, and an MPA from the Kennedy School of Government at Harvard University. He has been awarded honorary degrees from the Catholic University of America, Manhattan College, St. John's University, the State University of New York, the College of St. Rose, Iona College, Marist College, New York University, Pace University, Quinnipiac University, and St. Thomas Aquinas College. In September 2006, Commissioner Kelly was awarded France's highest decoration, the Legion D'Honneur, by then French Minister of the Interior Nicholas Sarkozy. Commissioner Kelly retired as a colonel from the Marine Corps Reserves after 30 years of service.

David Lai is a captain in the U.S. Army JAG Corps and an assistant professor and executive officer for the Department of Law at the United States Military Academy, West Point, where he teaches constitutional and military law to senior cadets. Prior to his military service, Captain Lai was an assistant district attorney in Ohio and worked for the Judicial Chamber at the United Nations International Criminal Tribunal for the former Yugoslavia at The Hague, Netherlands. He was also an intern to Judge John M. Manos and Chief Judge Loretta A. Preska. In the Army, Captain Lai was appointed Chief of Legal Assistance and administrative law attorney at Fort Hood, Texas. In 2009, he deployed in support of Operation Iraqi Freedom as the senior prosecutor to Multi-National Division-Baghdad, Iraq. Captain Lai was also the legal adviser to commanders as a trial counsel to the Division Special Troops Battalion, 2nd Brigade Combat Team, and Air Cavalry Brigade of the 1st Cavalry Division. Additionally, he served as a military magistrate at Fort Hood, Texas, and West Point, New York. Captain Lai holds a BA from the University of Michigan, Ann Arbor; a JD from Case Western Reserve University Law School; and an MBA from the Weatherhead School of Management. He is currently a National Security LLM candidate at Georgetown University School of Law.

Thomas A. Marks is head of Department, War and Conflict Studies at the College of International Security Affairs (CISA) of the National Defense University in Washington, D.C., and the* author of *Maoist People's War in Post-Vietnam Asia* (2007), considered the current standard on the subject of "people's war." A graduate of the United States Military Academy, his PhD work at the University of Hawaii focused on the relationship between popular upheaval and revolutionary crisis. He has authored hundreds of scholarly and media publications, as well as spoken prolifically as an invited speaker. A longtime cross-country and track coach, he returned to government service following 9/11. His last field service, in a contract capacity prior to joining CISA, was as the operations consultant for a newly raised Saudi-Arabian commando unit. It may be added in passing that during the heyday of *Soldier of Fortune*, Marks was the magazine's chief foreign correspondent.

Mark S. Martins is a brigadier general in the United States Army. He is currently assigned as the Chief Prosecutor of Military Commissions. His education includes: BS (U.S. Military Academy, West Point); Rhodes Scholar (Balliol College, University of Oxford); JD (Harvard Law School); LLM (Judge Advocate General's School, U.S. Army); MA (U.S. National War College); and MMAS (Command & General Staff College). Beginning his career in the infantry, Brigadier General Martins later became a judge advocate and has since served in a variety of legal and non-legal positions, including as a trial counsel, operational law adviser, staff judge advocate, chief of staff, and commander. He has been deployed to zones of armed conflict for more than five years, including as chief of staff of the U.S. Kosovo Force, staff judge advocate for First Armored Division and then Multi-National Force-Iraq, and most recently commanding Rule of Law Field Support Teams across eight provinces and 23 contested districts in Afghanistan. In 2011, Brigadier General Martins was awarded the Harvard Law School Medal of Freedom.

Peter Masciola is the founding partner of MillerMasciola, a Washington, D.C. law firm specializing in civil litigation. Mr. Masciola is a brigadier general and a judge advocate in the Air National Guard Reserve Component. He has also served on extended active-duty deployments in Guantanamo Bay, Cuba, and Afghanistan, where he was in charge of joint interagency legal operations at both high-profile U.S. and international detention facilities.

Michael J. Meese, PhD (Brigadier General, U.S. Army, retired), is the chief operating officer of AAFMAA—a nonprofit association that assists service members, their families, and their survivors with insurance and other benefits. He recently retired from his position as a professor, USMA, and head of the Department of Social Sciences at West Point, concluding a 32-year Army career, including over 19 years teaching at West Point. He also was a visiting professor at the Woodrow Wilson School at Princeton for 10 years. In addition to teaching, he served in a variety of strategic political-military positions, including deployments to Afghanistan, Iraq, and Bosnia for a total of 31 months, including one year as the assistant chief of staff for all U.S. and NATO forces in Afghanistan and four separate three-month tours as a senior policy adviser in Iraq. He has written extensively on national security and economics, including the book *American National Security* (2009) and the *Armed Forces Guide to Personal Financial Planning*. He is a graduate of the National War College, U.S. Military Academy, and holds a PhD, MPA, and an M.A. from Princeton University.

Michael Noone is a research professor at Columbus School of Law, The Catholic University of America, in Washington, D.C. Professor Noone served in the U.S. Air Force as a judge advocate for 20 years, retiring as colonel from Strategic Air Command Headquarters, where he was the first lawyer to review the SIOP (Single Integrated Operational Plan for nuclear war) for compliance with the law of war. He is a distinguished graduate of the Air Force Command and Staff College and holds a doctorate in juridical science from George Washington University, masters and bachelor of laws degrees from Georgetown University's Law Center, and a bachelor's degree from that university's School of Foreign Service. He served as a distinguished visiting professor at the U.S. Military Academy and co-authored the military law text then used in their basic course.

Michel Paradis is presently an attorney in the U.S. Department of Defense, Office of the Chief Defense Counsel, where he has argued cases on behalf of Guantanamo detainees in the military commissions and the federal courts of appeal. Dr. Paradis is also an adjunct professor of constitutional and international law at Georgetown Law School. He has a BA and JD from Fordham and a doctorate from Oxford.

Shane Reeves is a major (promotable) in the U.S. Army and an academy professor in the Department of Law at the United States Military Academy, West Point, New York. A 1996 West Point graduate, Major Reeves was commissioned as an Armor officer and served as a platoon leader, fire support officer, and troop executive officer with 1st Squadron, 11th Armored Cavalry Regiment. After attending law school, Major Reeves transitioned into the Judge Advocate General's Corps in 2003. Since becoming a judge advocate, Major Reeves has served in a number of legal positions, including Chief of Legal Assistance, Ft. Riley, Kansas; Brigade Judge Advocate for 3rd Brigade, 1st Armored Division in Taji, Iraq; senior trial counsel, 1st Infantry Division at Ft. Riley, Kansas; and professor of international and operational law at the Judge Advocate General's Legal Center and School in Charlottesville, Virginia. Major Reeves holds an LLM in military law from the Judge Advocate General's School and a JD from the College of William & Mary.

Major Reeves has published several articles on armed conflict and security related matters, most recently including "Are We Reaching a Tipping Point? How Contemporary Challenges Are Affecting the Military Necessity-Humanity Balance," in *Harvard National Security Journal Online Features* (June 2013); "The Law of Armed Conflict's 'Wicked Problem': Levee en Masse in Cyber Warfare," in the U.S. Naval War College's *International Law Studies,* Vol. 89 (June 2013); "Non-State Armed Groups and Technology: The Humanitarian Tragedy at Our Doorstep?" in *University of Miami National Security & Armed Conflict Law Review* (May 2013); and "The New Griffin of War: Hybrid International Armed Conflicts," in *Harvard International Review* (Winter 2013 edition). At West Point, Major Reeves teaches constitutional and military law, jurisprudence, and the Capstone course required of all cadets majoring in law and legal studies at the U.S. Military Academy.

Paul Rundquist (BA, Loyola University (Chicago), MA, PhD, University of Chicago) has been a guest professor in Germany since 2005 at the universities of Halle-Wittenberg, Leipzig, and Dresden. His teaching in Germany has been supported by grants from the DAAD, DFG, and Fulbright programs. From 2005 to 2008, he taught courses on U.S. public policy processes at the London School of Economics. From 1996 to 1998, he was also a Fulbright professor in Poland at the Warsaw University and the Jagiellonian University. He was a specialist in American government with the Congressional Research Service in Washington from 1974 to 2005. There, his primary professional focus was on the operations of Congress, in particular its rules and procedures. Among other special assignments, after 2001, he advised the Congress on matters relating to government institution continuity in the wake of catastrophic events. During his time in Washington, he also served as an adjunct professor at American University, Catholic University of America, and George Washington University. He also worked extensively as a democracy development consultant in numerous countries as a consultant to the UNDP, the World Bank, the East-West Parliamentary Practice Project (Netherlands), and American and German political party foundations. For his work promoting closer relations between Poland and the United States, the Polish government awarded him the Knight's Cross of the Order of Merit.

Maritza S. Ryan (Colonel, U.S. Army) is the professor and head of the Department of Law at the U.S. Military Academy at West Point. A 1982 graduate of West Point, she was commissioned as a Second Lieutenant in the Field Artillery. During her tour in the 1st Armored Division, Nuremberg, Germany, she was selected for the Army's legal education scholarship program and attended Vanderbilt University Law School, graduating Order of the Coif in 1988. Her tours as a Judge Advocate include Senior Trial Counsel (prosecutor); Brigade Legal Counsel, Operation Desert Shield/Desert Storm; Senior Defense Counsel; Chief of Military Justice (chief prosecutor); Deputy Staff Judge Advocate (Office of the General Counsel); and Deputy Head, Department of Law, USMA. In 2006, Colonel Ryan was selected to be the professor and head of the Department of Law. In 2008, the West Point

Center for the Rule of Law was established under her leadership. She is a cofounder and former co-chair of the Military Lawyers Committee, Litigation Division, American Bar Association, and a member of the board of the National Association of Women Lawyers (NAWL). Colonel Ryan is a graduate of the Judge Advocate General's Center & School (LL.M., military law) and the Naval War College (MA, National Security and Strategic Studies). She teaches constitutional and military law and has published and presented in military law, the Law of Armed Conflict, and law and leadership.

Mark L. Toole (Colonel, U.S. Army) is an academy professor and the program director for the Legal Studies Program at the United States Military Academy, West Point, New York. He has a BA in political science from Penn State University and a master's degree in national security and strategic studies from the Naval War College, Newport, Rhode Island. He earned his JD at Western New England University School of Law, Springfield, Massachusetts, and holds LLM degrees from the U.S. Army Judge Advocate's Legal Center and School, Charlottesville, Virginia, and Georgetown University Law Center (with concentration in constitutional law). He has been in the Army for over 25 years and his postings include Germany; Fort Drum, New York; Fort Lewis, Washington; and Washington, D.C. His military assignments include service as prosecutor, appellate defense counsel, chief of criminal law, deputy staff judge advocate, and military judge. He has taught a seminar in constitutional law at USMA and currently teaches and is the course director for the USMA core course in constitutional and military law. (Submitted 7-2-2013)

David Wallace is a colonel in the United States Army. He is currently assigned as professor and deputy head, Department of Law, United States Military Academy, West Point, New York. His education includes: BA (Carnegie-Mellon University); JD (Seattle University); M(S) BA (Boston University); LLM (Judge Advocate General's School of the U.S. Army); and MA (U.S. Naval War College). In addition to his assignment at West Point, he has also served as a deputy staff judge advocate (Fort Bliss, Texas); instructor at the Judge Advocate General's School of the Army (Charlottesville, Virginia); trial attorney, Contract Appeals Division, United States Army Legal Service Agency (Arlington, Virginia); trial counsel and legal assistance attorney, 3rd Infantry Division (Kitzingen, Germany); and Public/Civil Affairs officer, 81st Infantry Brigade (Seattle, Washington).

Edward S. White is a captain in the United States Navy. He is currently assigned as Deputy Chief Prosecutor (Motions & Appeals) in the Office of the Chief Prosecutor of Military Commissions. His education includes: BSFS (Georgetown University); J.D. (Georgetown University Law Center); LLM (Judge Advocate

General's School, U.S. Army); and MA (U.S. Naval War College). In addition to his current assignment, he has also served as an appellate military judge on the U.S. Navy-Marine Corps Court of Criminal Appeals, staff judge advocate for Commander, Navy Region Mid-Atlantic and Commander, Submarine Force, U.S. Atlantic Fleet; executive officer of Naval Legal Service Office Southwest; officer-in-charge of Naval Legal Service Office Detachment, Rota, Spain; litigation counsel in the General Litigation Division, Office of the Judge Advocate General; assistant command judge advocate in *USS Ranger* (CV 61); and as a trial counsel, defense counsel, and legal assistance attorney.

James W. Zirkle is an Adjunct Professor of Law at the Georgetown University Law Center and American University's Washington College of Law, serving in these capacities for the past 25 years. He retired in 2009 from the Central Intelligence Agency, where he also served for 25 years as an Associate General Counsel. He previously served as an Associate Dean of the Yale Law School and on the law faculties of the College of William & Mary and the University of Mississippi.

Col. Dawn M.K. Zoldi, United States Air Force (USAF), is assigned to the Office of the Staff Judge Advocate at Headquarters, Air Combat Command (ACC), Joint Base Langley-Eustis, Virginia, as the Chief of Operations Law. As such, she serves as chief counsel to the four-star Commander and his staff on all international, intelligence, and operations law issues affecting the Combat Air Forces and provides training for ACC's Judge Advocate General's Corps (JAGC) members—18 legal offices providing legal services to 128,000 personnel—to prepare them for worldwide expeditionary service. In 1989, Colonel Zoldi simultaneously attained her B.A. degrees in history and philosophy and M.A. degree in history from the University of Scranton. After attaining her J.D. from the Villanova University School of Law in 1992, she was admitted to the Bar of the Supreme Court of the Commonwealth of Pennsylvania and subsequently commissioned as a direct appointee in the Air Force. In 2010, the Colonel received her M.S. with Academic Distinction in Military Strategic Studies from the Air War College. In her more than 20 years as a member of the USAF JAGC, Colonel Zoldi has performed myriad duties at various echelons, including Wing, Headquarters Air Force/ Secretary of the Air Force, Combatant Command, and Major Command and has deployed forward in support of Operations Enduring Freedom, Iraqi Freedom, and other HQ U.S. Central Command requirements. Throughout her career, Colonel Zoldi has frequently lectured and published, including as an Assistant Professor of Law at the U.S. Air Force Academy and adjunct faculty to the Air Force Judge Advocate General's School. Her publications include several Air Force guides used worldwide: *ACC Flying Evaluation Board Guide, SAF/IGQ*

Command Directed Investigations Guide, JAG Guide to IG Investigations and Air Force Drug Testing Program guides. Her recent work, *Protecting Security and Privacy: An Analytical Framework for Airborne Domestic Imagery*, is forthcoming in Volume 70 of the Air Force Law Review. Colonel Zoldi is the recipient of numerous awards and decorations, including the Defense Superior Service Medal. In 2008, the American Bar Association recognized Colonel Zoldi as the Air Force's Outstanding Military Career Service Judge Advocate.

Index